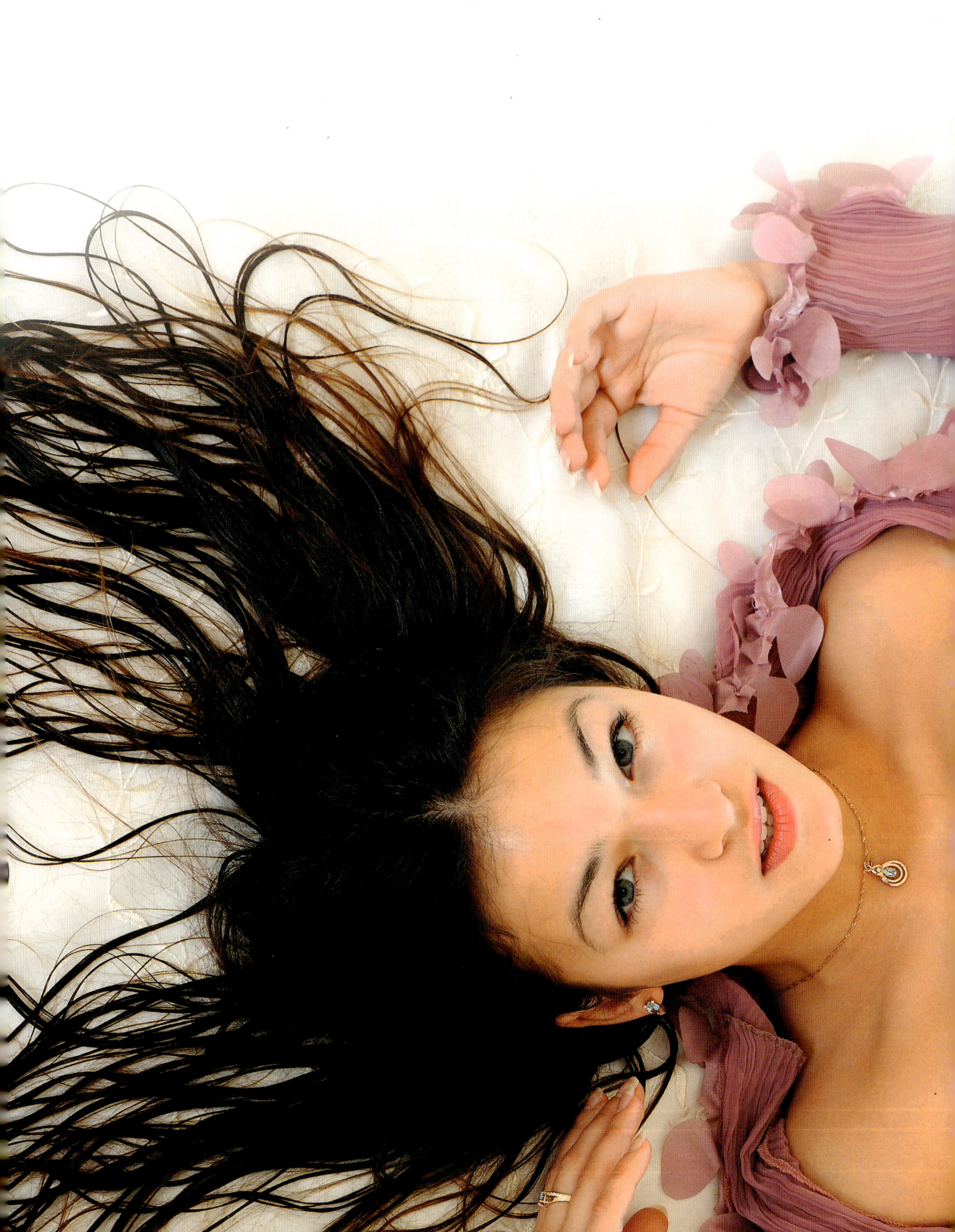

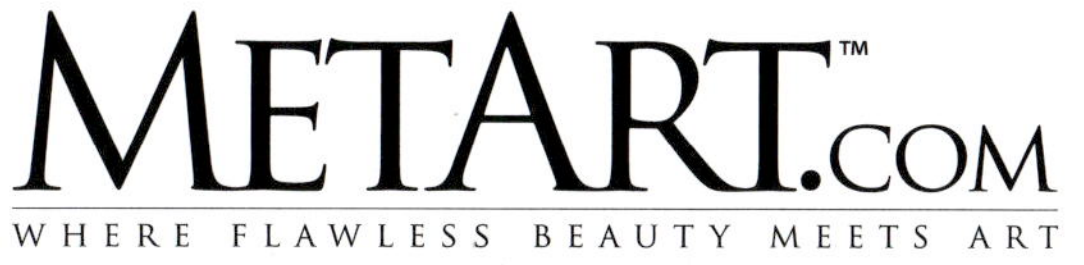


# 101
# WORLD'S TOP MODELS

Collected and edited by Alexandria Haig

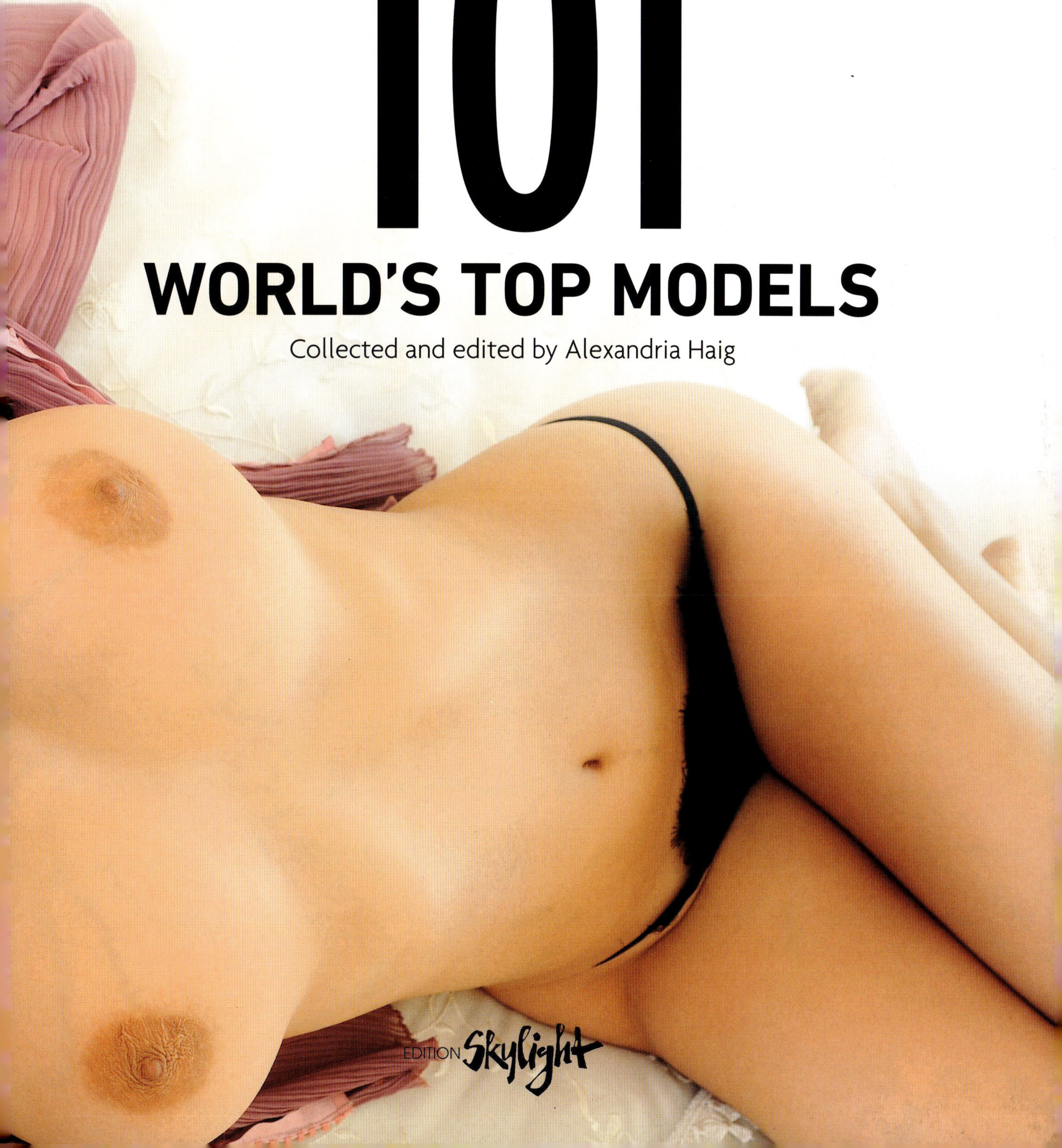

EDITION Skylight

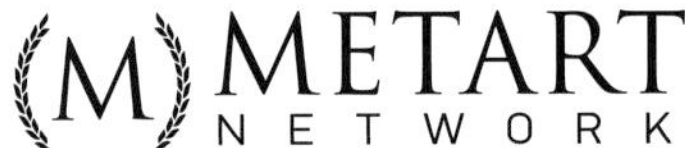



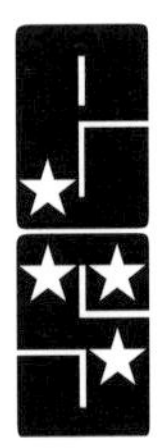

First edition 2019


EDITION SKYLIGHT
Willikonerstr. 10
CH-8618 Oetwil am See / Zürich
Switzerland
info@edition-skylight.com
www.edition-skylight.com

ISBN 978-3-03766-658-6



Bibliographic information published by Die Deutsche Bibliothek
Die Deutsche Bibliothek lists this publication in the Deutsche Nationalbibliografie; detailed bibliographic data are available in the Internet at http://dnb.ddb.de.

Printed in Germany

How do you define beauty? At MetArt, we've been pondering that question for the past twenty years.

A beautiful girl is pleasing to the eye, of course; but to indeed allure and arouse, she must be pleasing to the spirit also. She has that certain je ne sais quoi which comes from being comfortable in her skin; even – especially – when that skin is naked.

As a world leader in artistic nude photography and film, we've made it our mission to present the most enchanting girls to grace our planet, many of them undressing in front of the camera for the very first time. And as this collection of our World's Top 101 Models reveals, that means representing natural beauty in all its spellbinding diversity.

At the time of writing, we're proud to have featured over 3,500 gorgeous models on our ground-breaking website MetArt.com, in 20,000 photosets and over 3,000,000 images – united by the universal language of beauty but strikingly varied in their appeal. From the girl-next-door of your dreams to the unattainable goddess of your most intimate fantasies, you're sure to discover that unique woman who embodies your ideal of perfection.

Like rare and precious gemstones, no two women are the same, and our reaction to a naked photo of a gorgeous girl is immediate and natural. Who is she? What do her eyes convey? Posing nude is perhaps the ultimate form of self-expression; with no costume to conceal her, the model is liberated to share her naked truth, and these joyful, free-spirited women celebrate their sensuality and display their feminine power candidly.

We each have our proclivities of taste when it comes to what we find attractive. Maybe your thing is freckles and red hair. Amazonian babes with long legs; or petite cuties. Cool, classy blondes with green eyes. Sensual ebony skin. Voluptuous and sultry sexpots, or bubbly cheerleaders. Browsing this collection is like opening a door into a dazzling world filled with intriguing new possibilities. You can pick a different favorite every day if you wish, or follow the top erotic stars our members clamor to see time and time again. We love to give debutantes their first opportunity to shine, and it's this commitment to seeking out and encouraging fresh new talent that has resulted in some of our most provocative pictorials.

But all that natural beauty would go to waste without the core philosophy that guides everything we do. The "Art" in MetArt stands for something real. The lovely girls who choose to share their nakedness with us deserve the very best standard of presentation. That doesn't mean airbrushing them into cookie-cutter replicas – often a person's tiny imperfections are what makes them most attractive – but it does mean adhering to the highest standards of photography and production. Our hundreds of photographers excel in both adult and mainstream entertainment, garnering worldwide recognition and countless awards. Most importantly, they are skilled at cultivating an atmosphere that allows the model's authenticity to flourish, giving you, the viewer, a genuine connection.

Sometimes a connection between models is made too; we love photographing girls who organically fall for each other on set. The subtle eroticism of a gentle touch, a glance that hints at sexual chemistry, is thrilling to witness and can lead to all kinds of passionate imaginings.

Choosing 101 top models from a remarkable twenty-year archive was not easy. Our staff of content managers painstakingly went through thousands of images to present only a few of the best. Our guidelines were to find the few, only the exceptional models that can mesmerize you through eye contact, their smile, their body language – it's an invitation to look, to enjoy their natural grace and uninhibited poise.

That's the thing about beauty: it can inspire genuine admiration and subjective fervor simultaneously, stirring the senses and stimulating the wildest dreams, hopes, and fantasies. And like art, beauty does not exist to be hoarded, or hidden away; it needs to be seen, to live and breathe among us.

What better reason to share the pick of the crop – the most exquisite beauties who have made it into our World's Top 101 Models collection? Gathered together from the far-flung corners of the globe, the girls presented here represent the best of nature's bounty and humankind's artistry combined.

Join us on our erotic journey. Find your ideal woman. Appreciate the endless facets of natural female beauty and desirability in their dazzling variety. We hope it brings you many hours of pleasure.

*— Rose Eden*

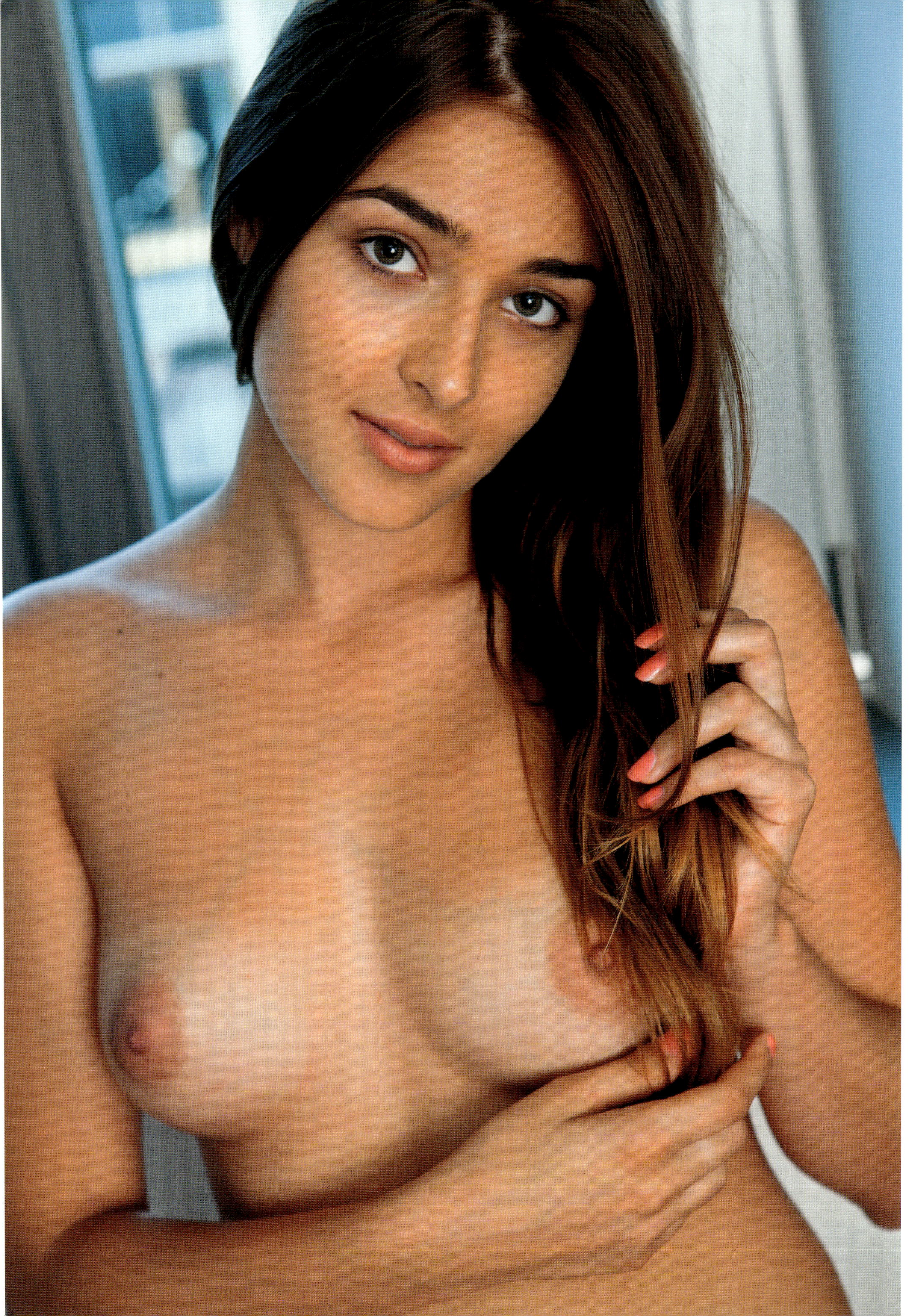

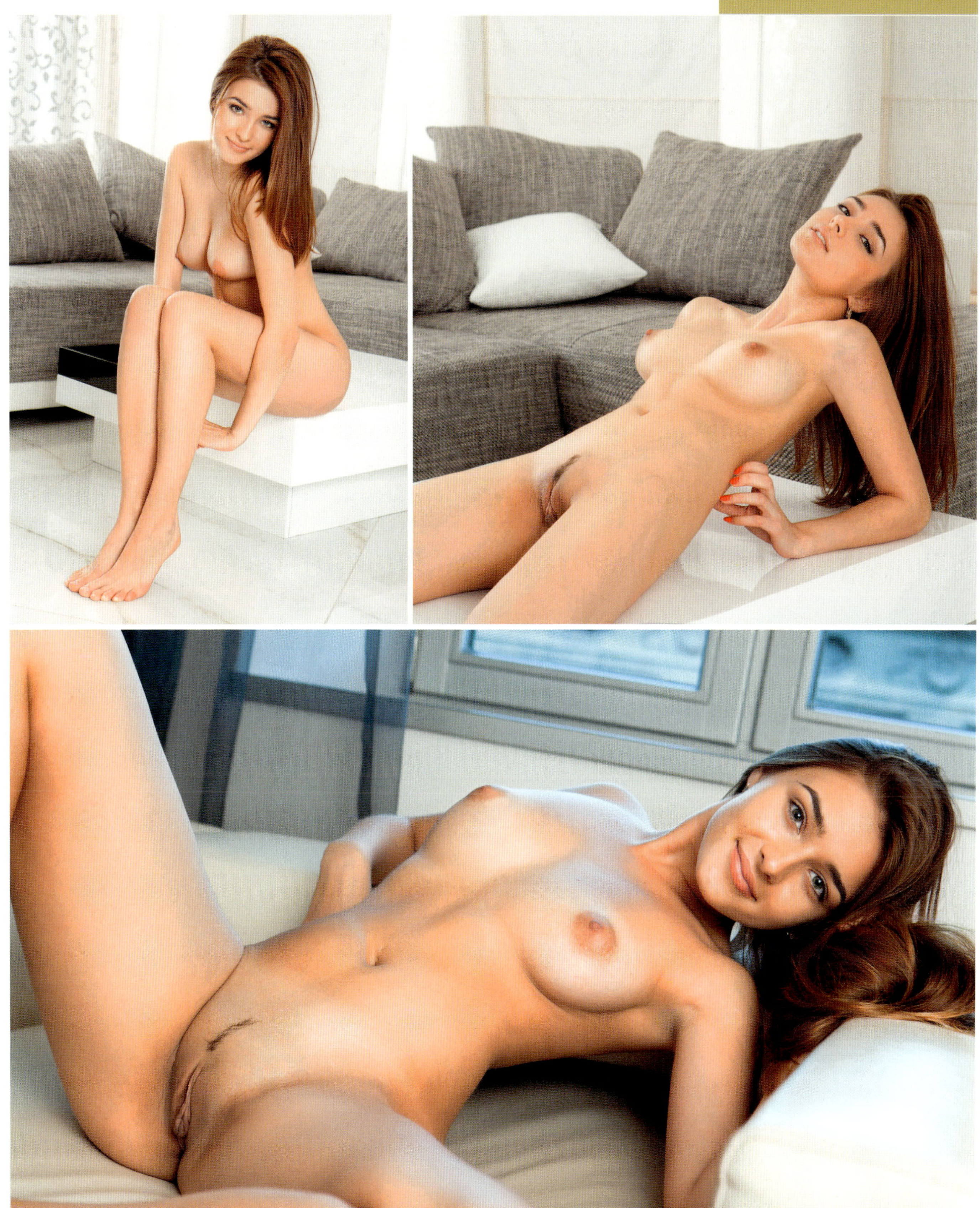

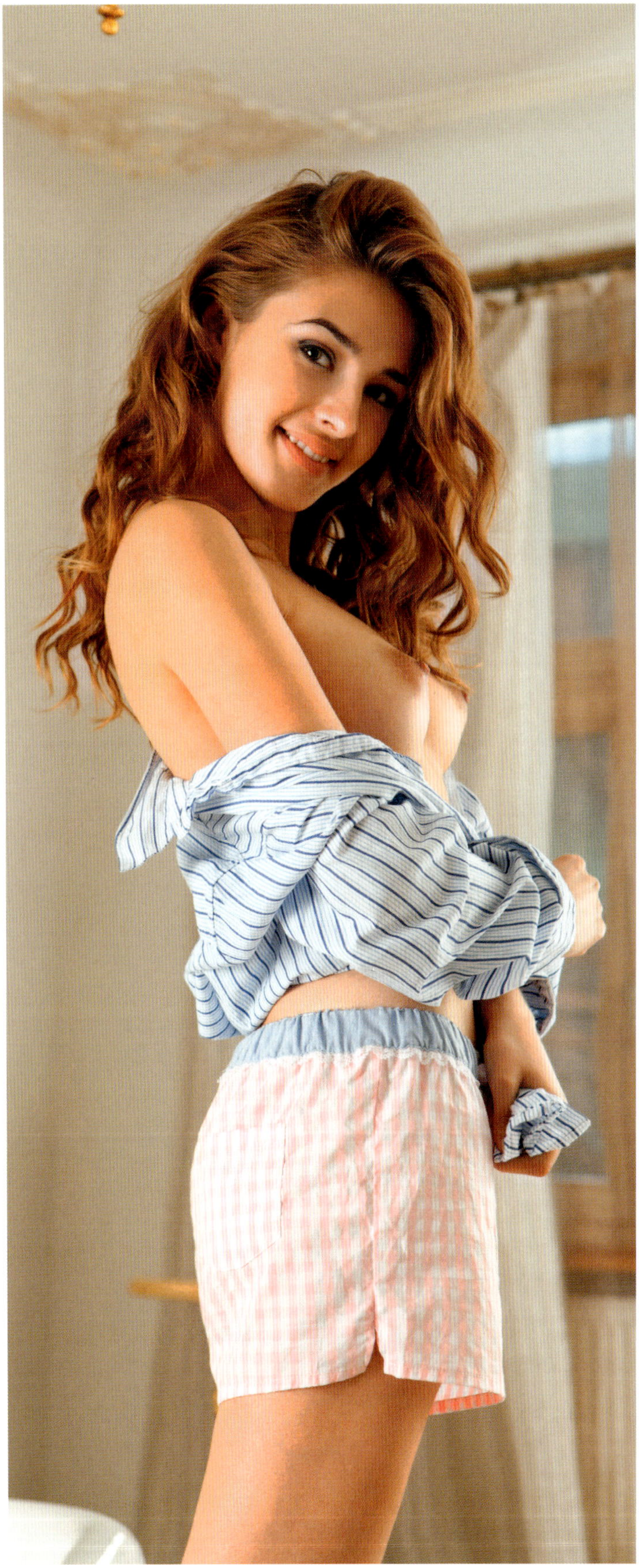

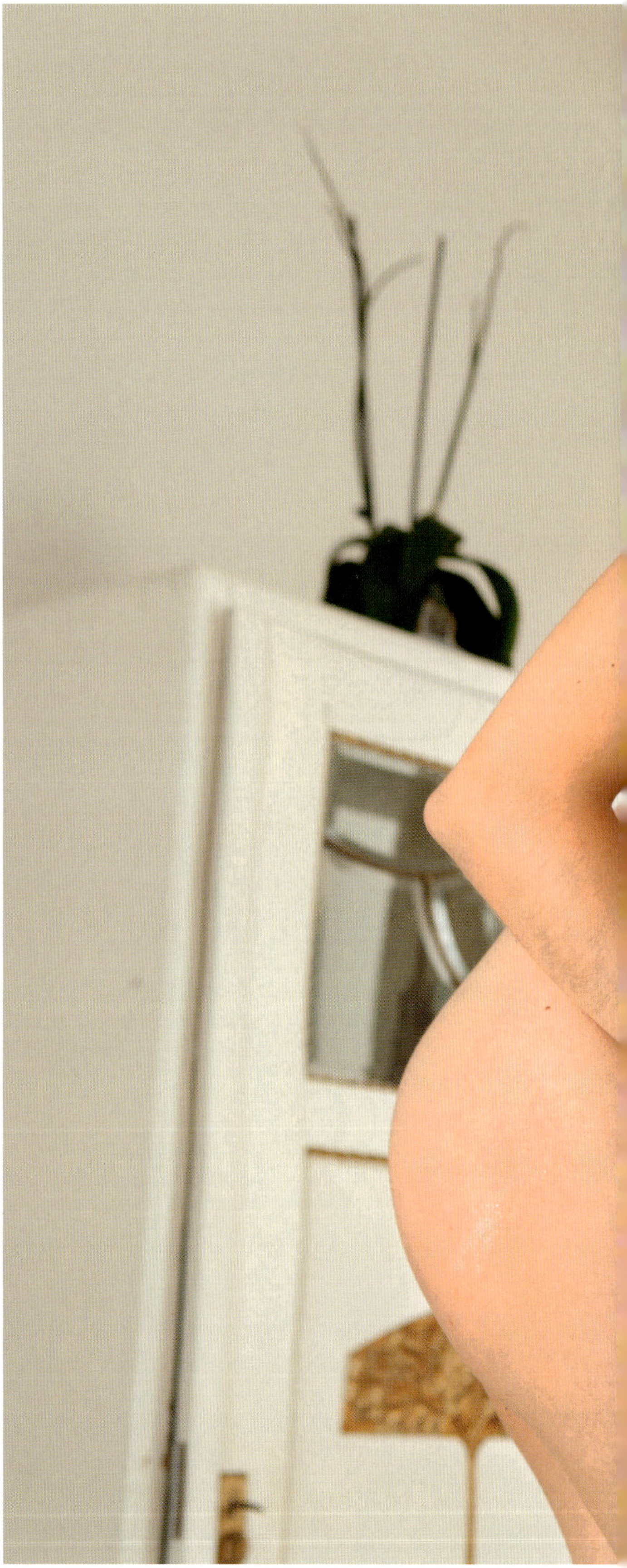

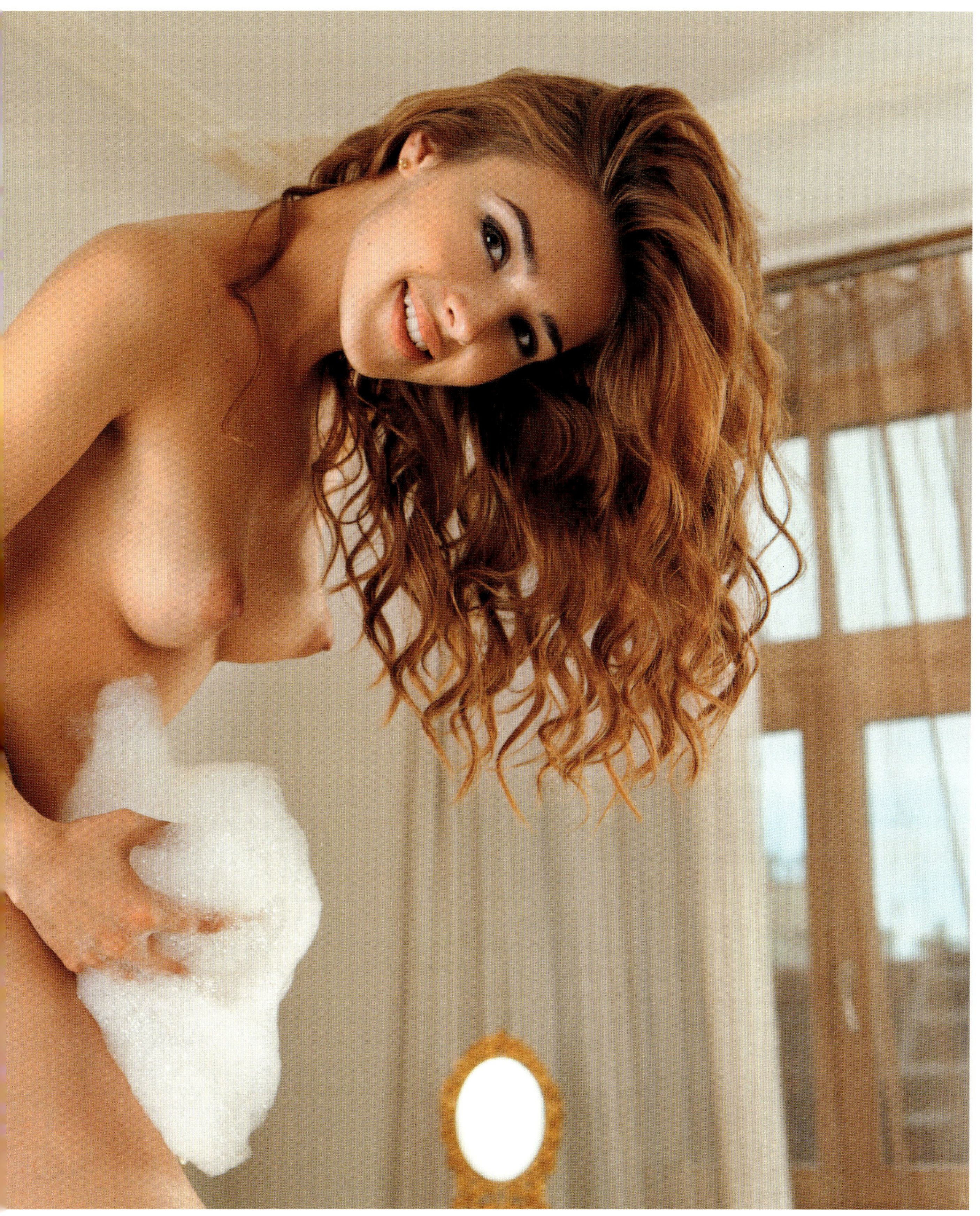

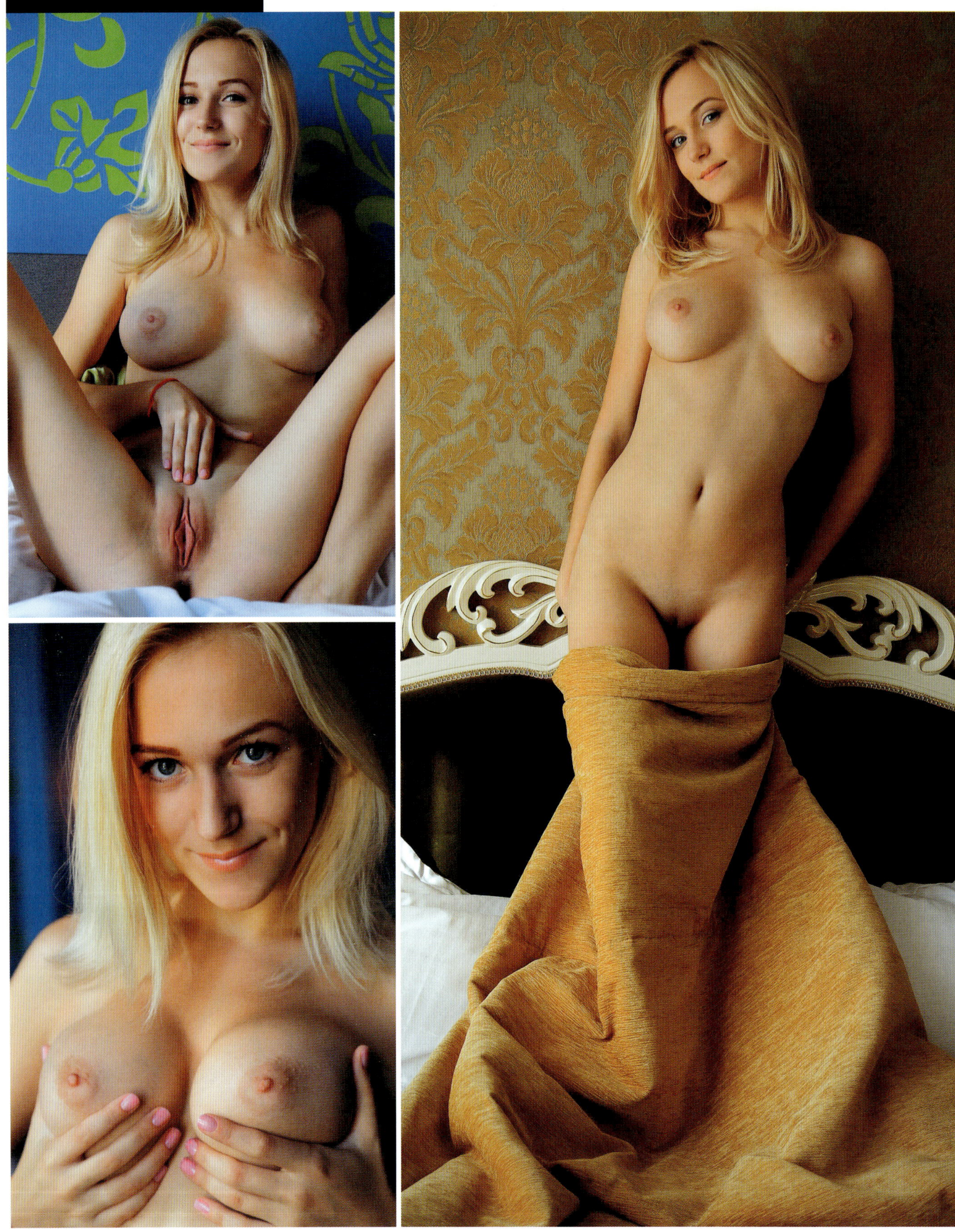

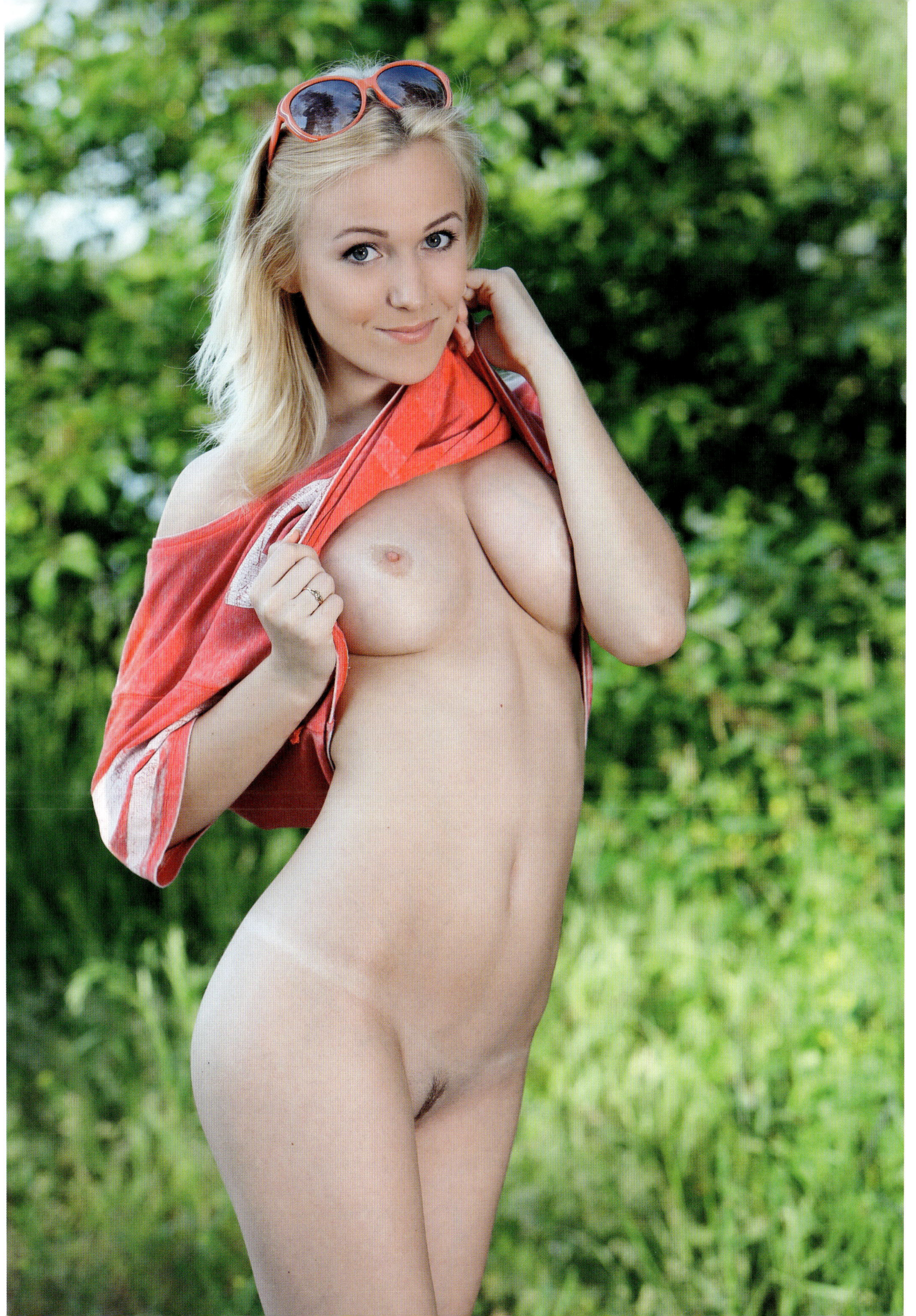

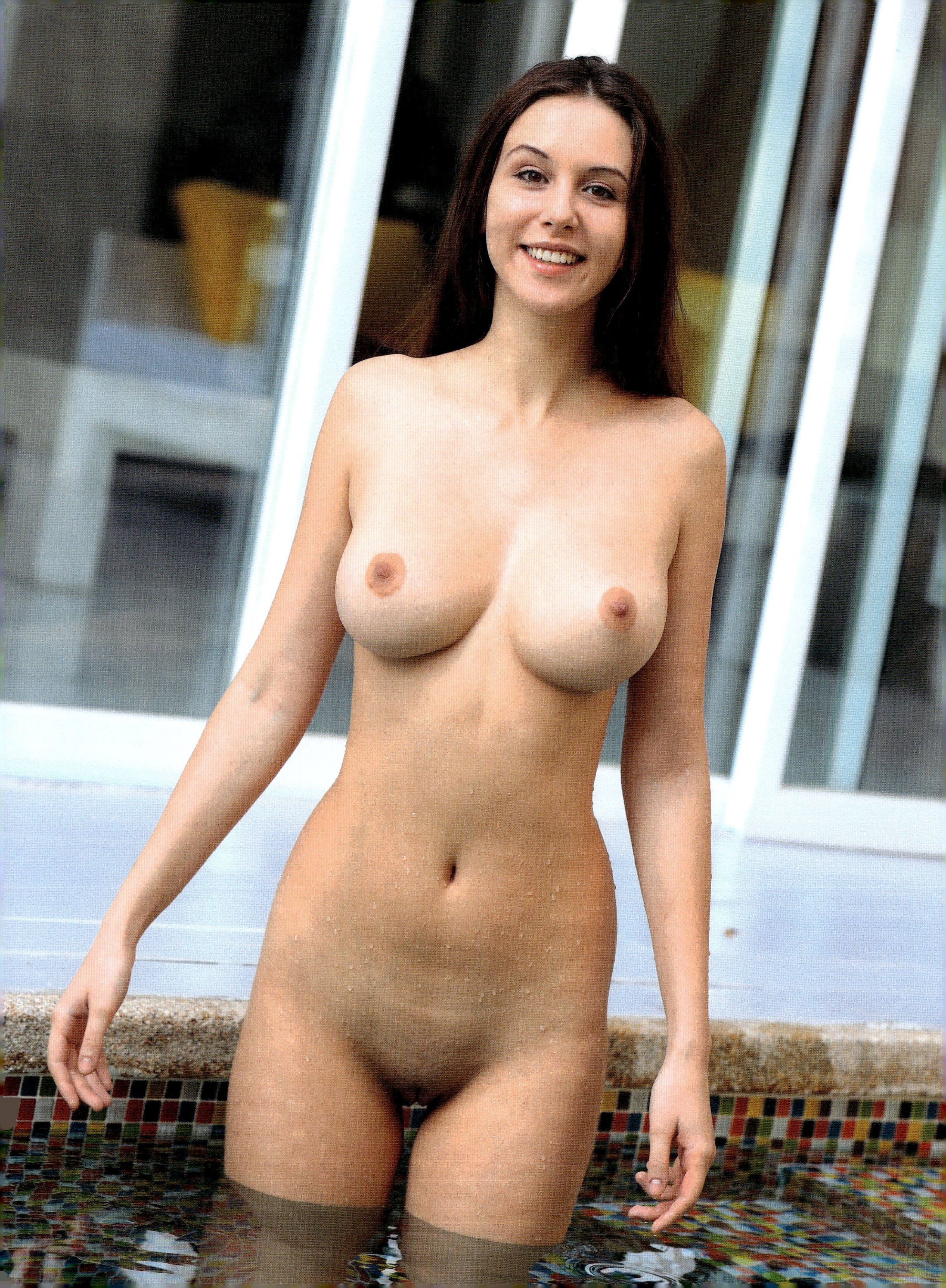

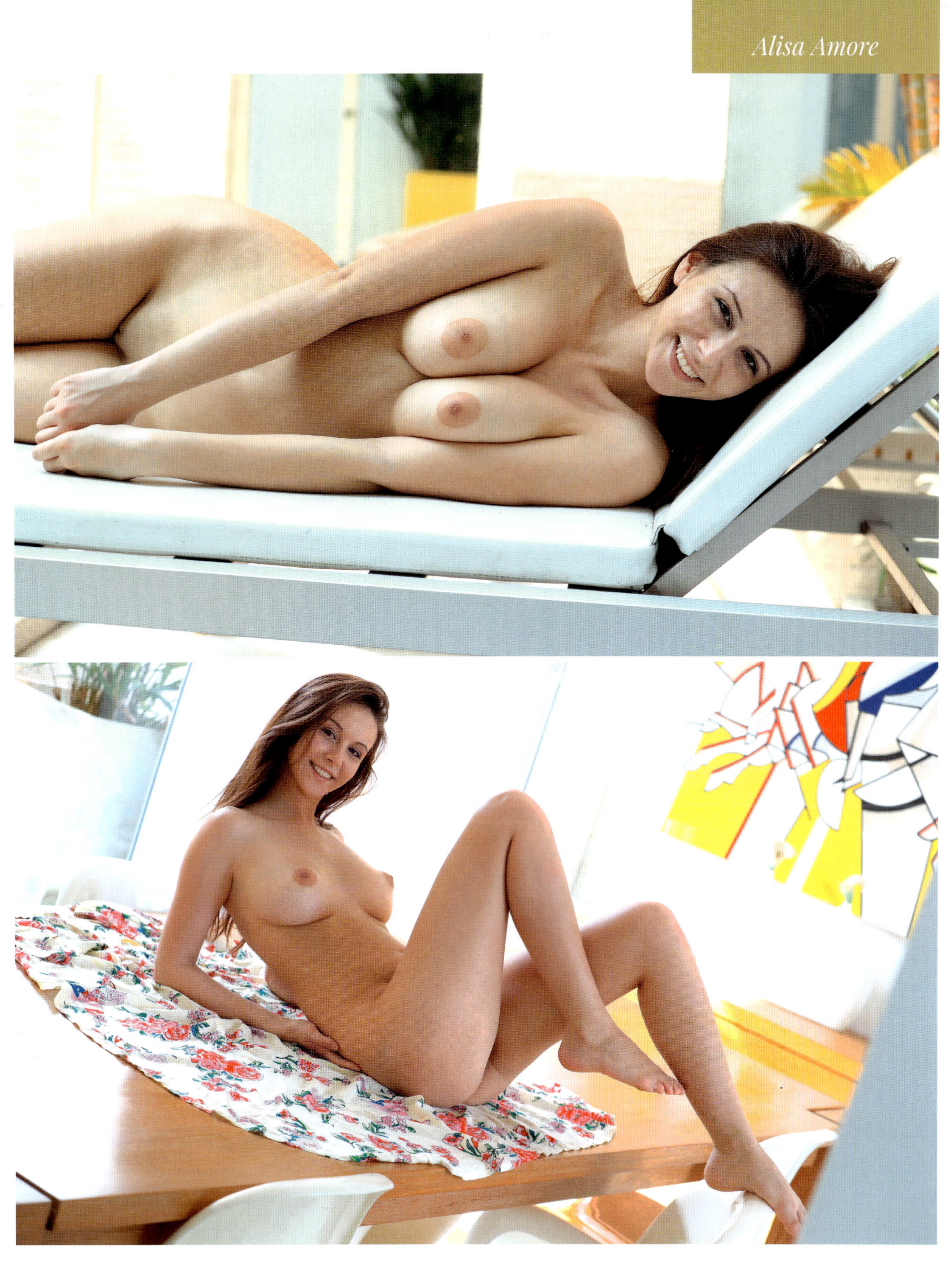

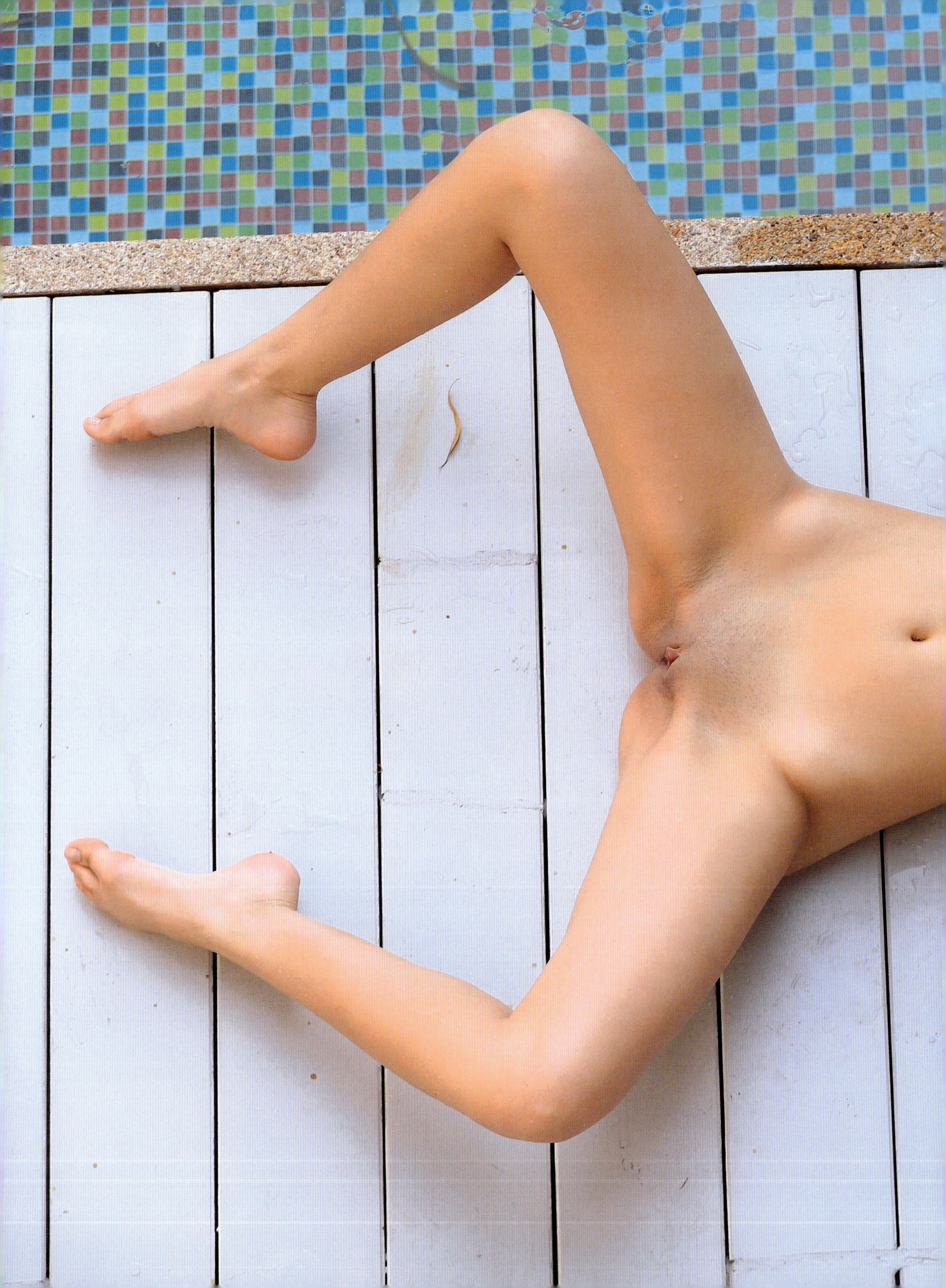

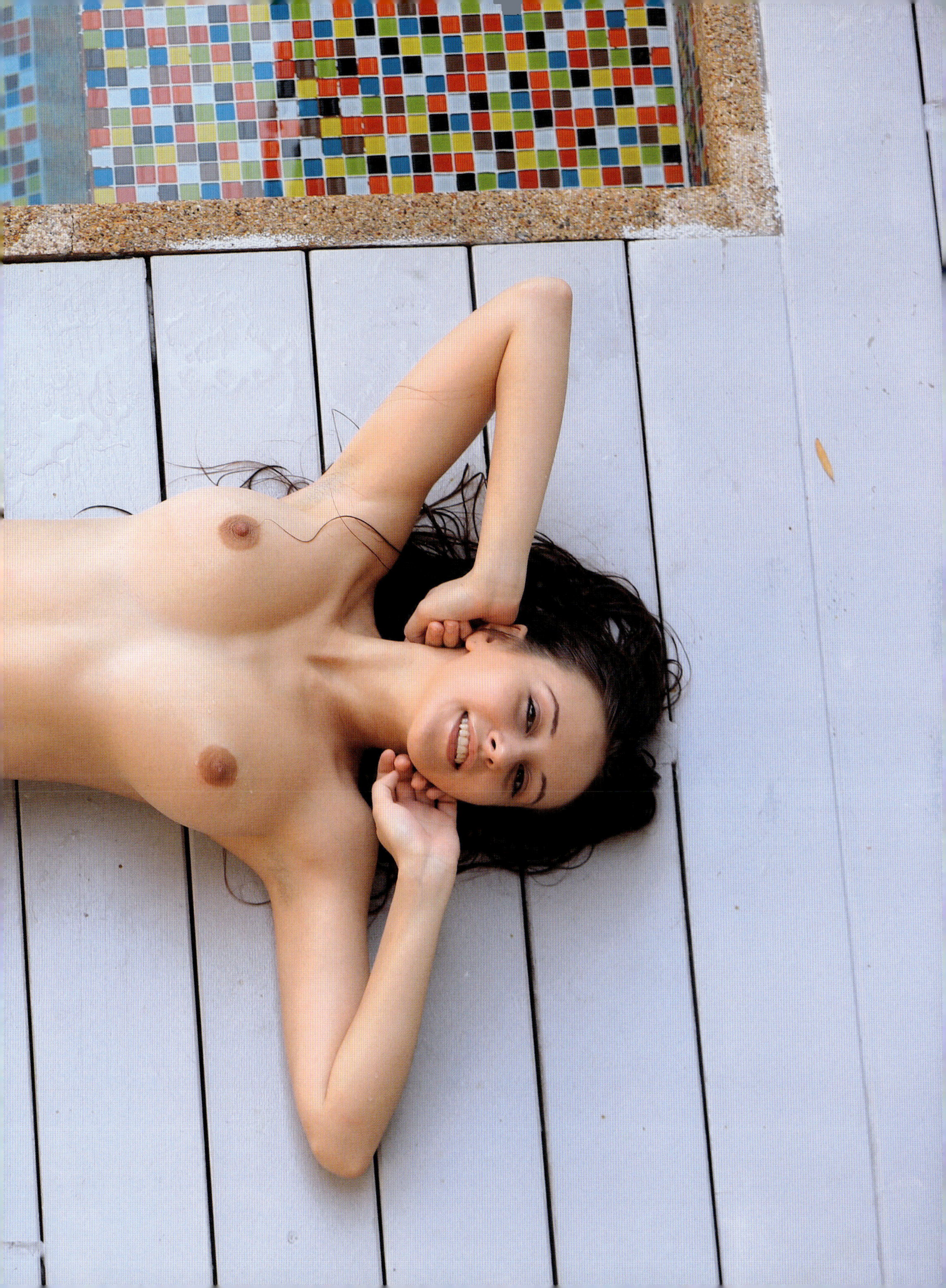

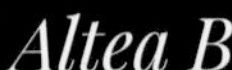
Altea B

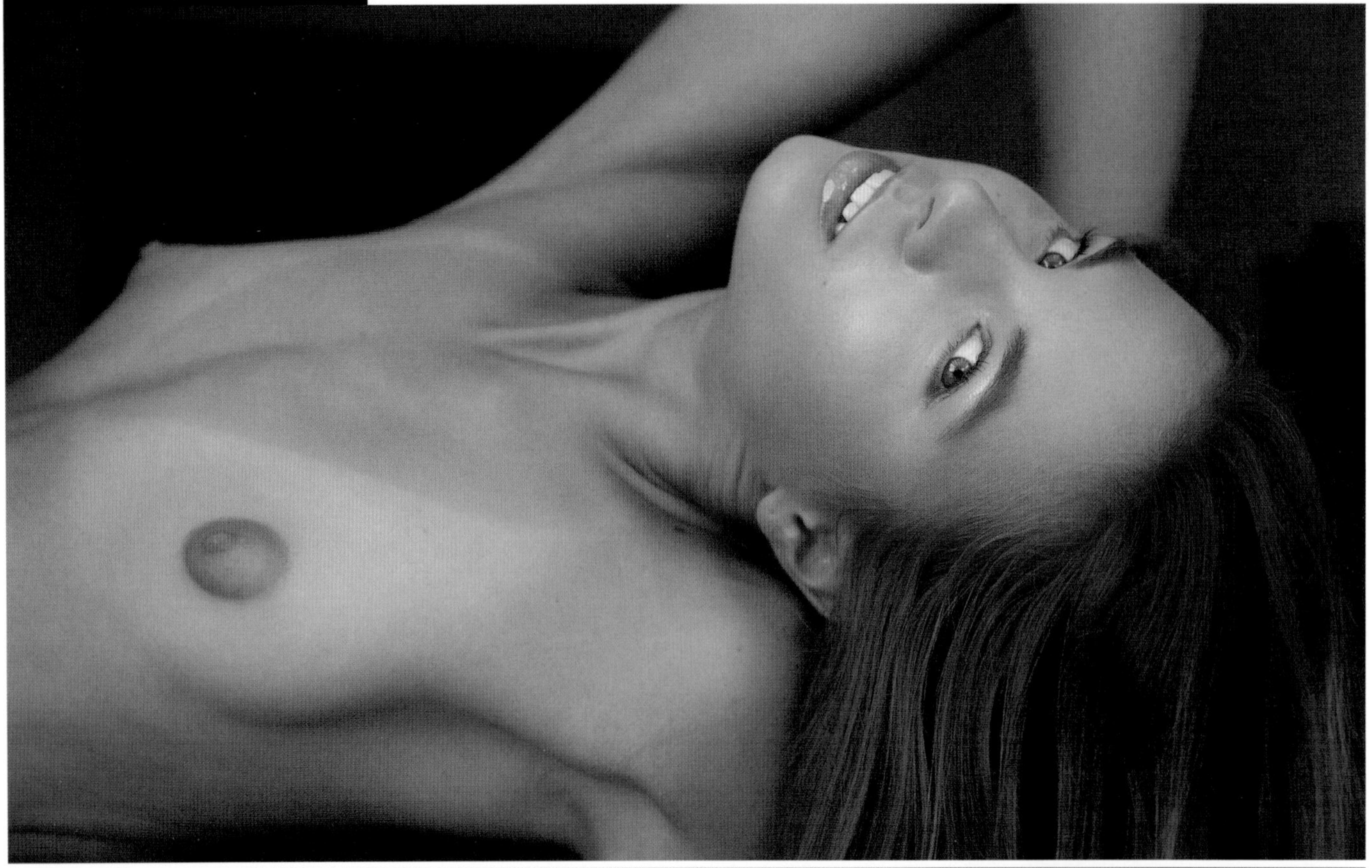

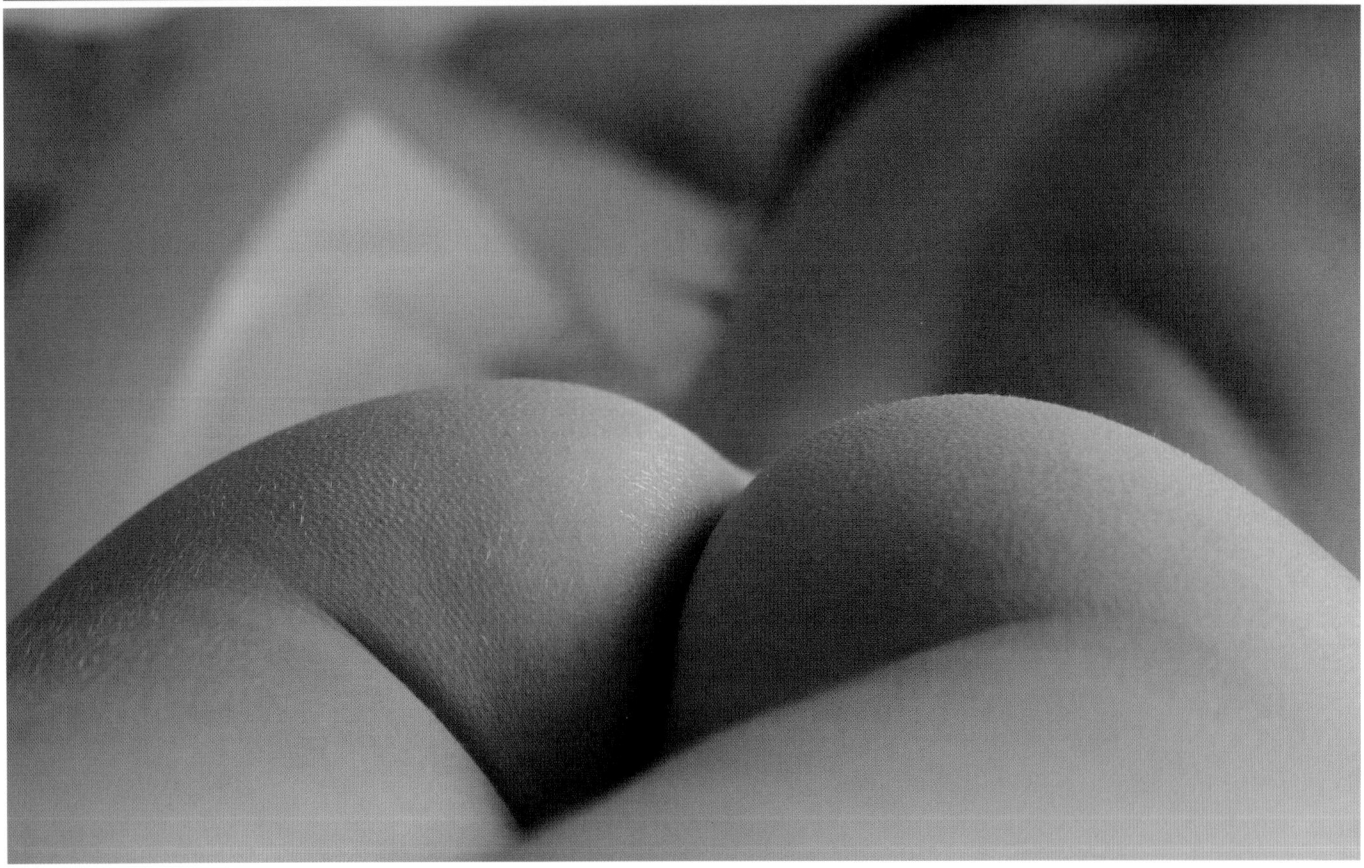

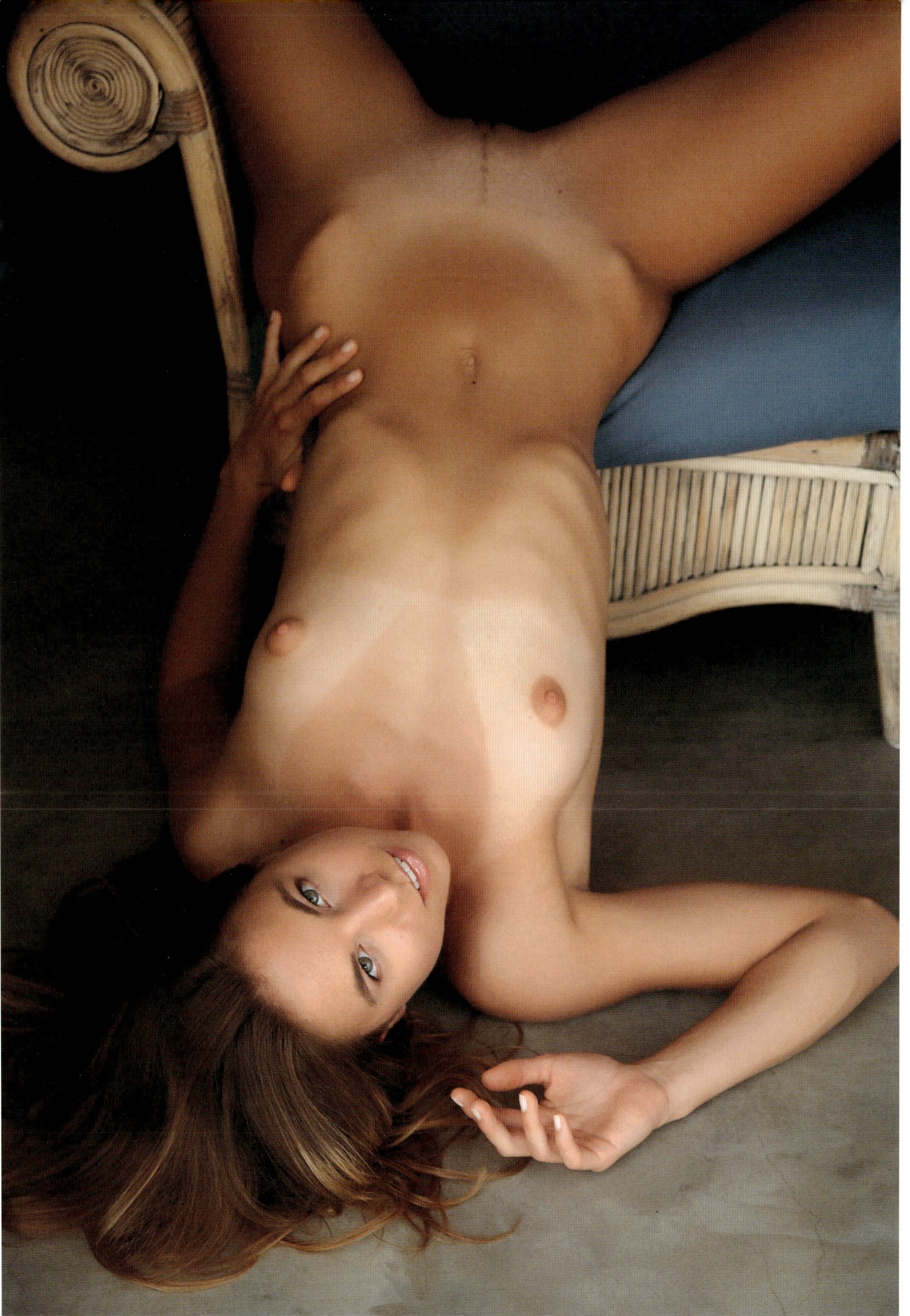

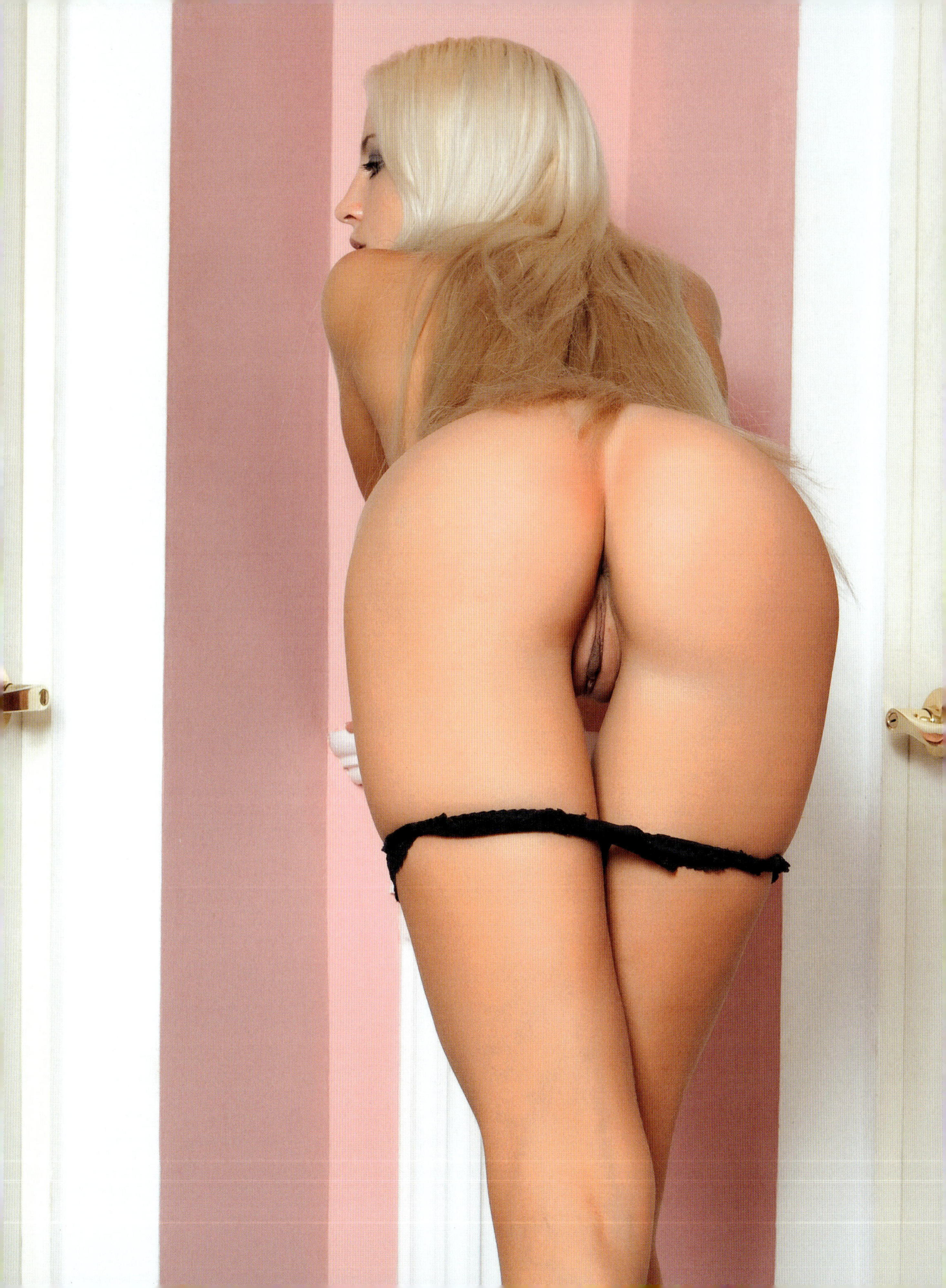

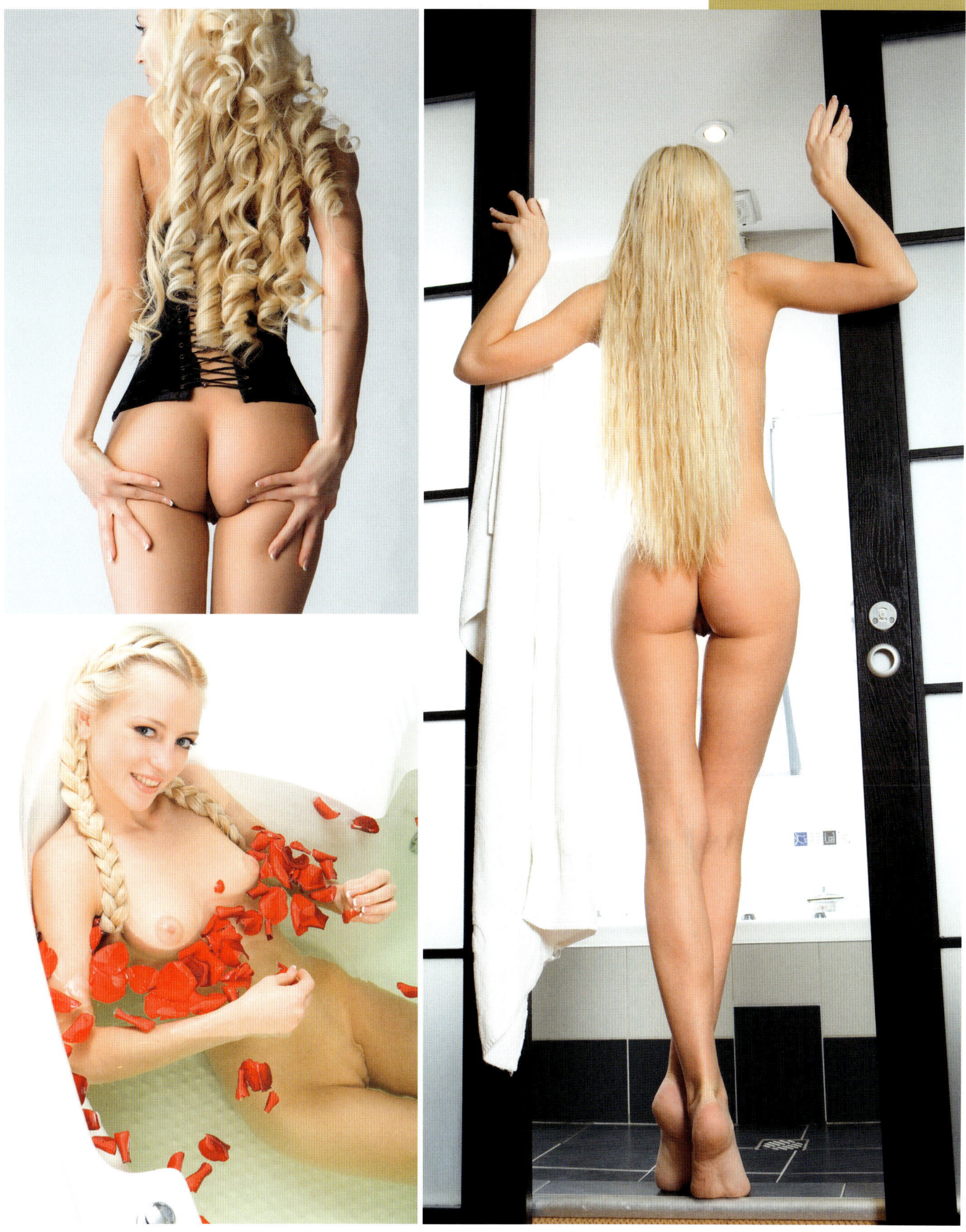

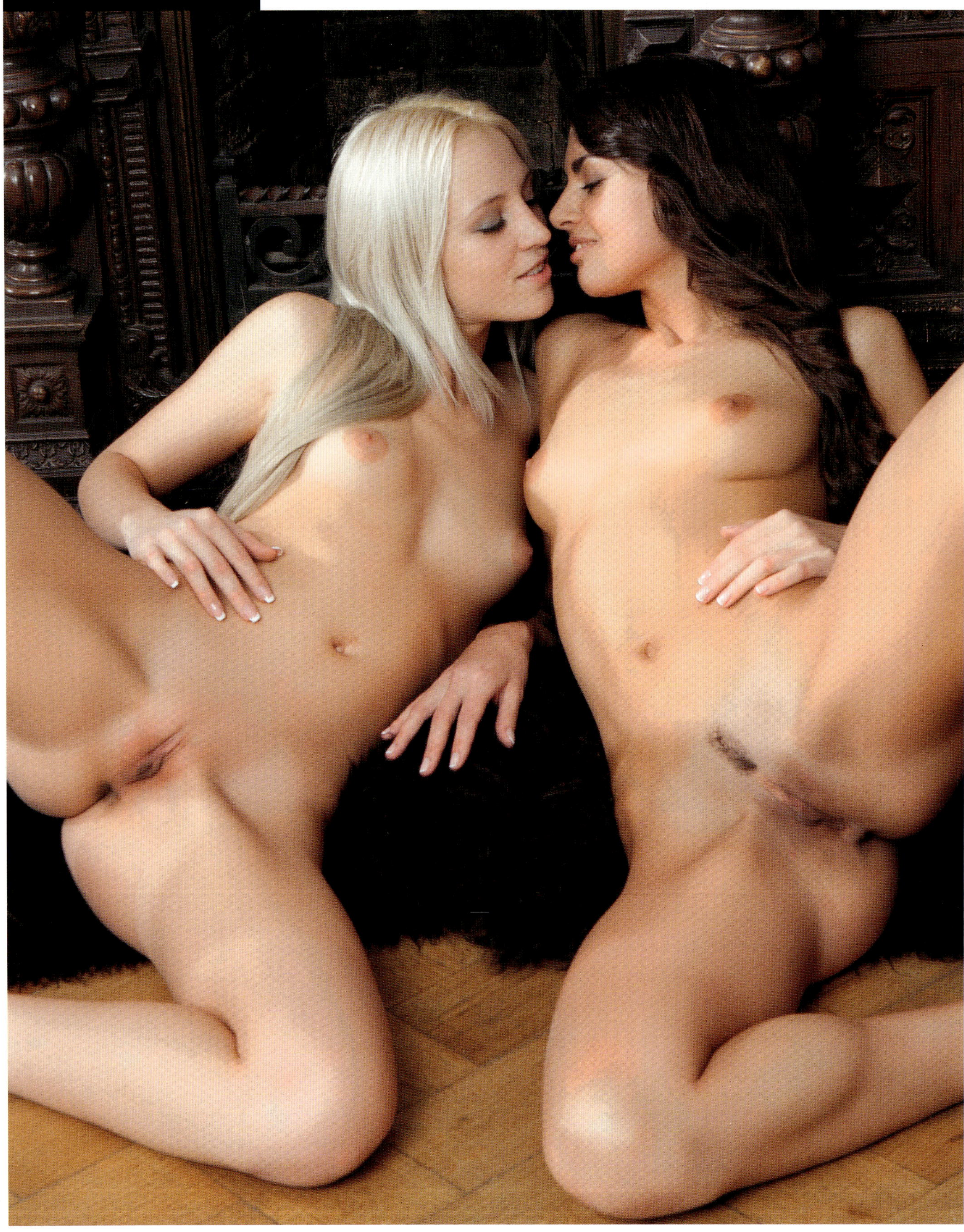

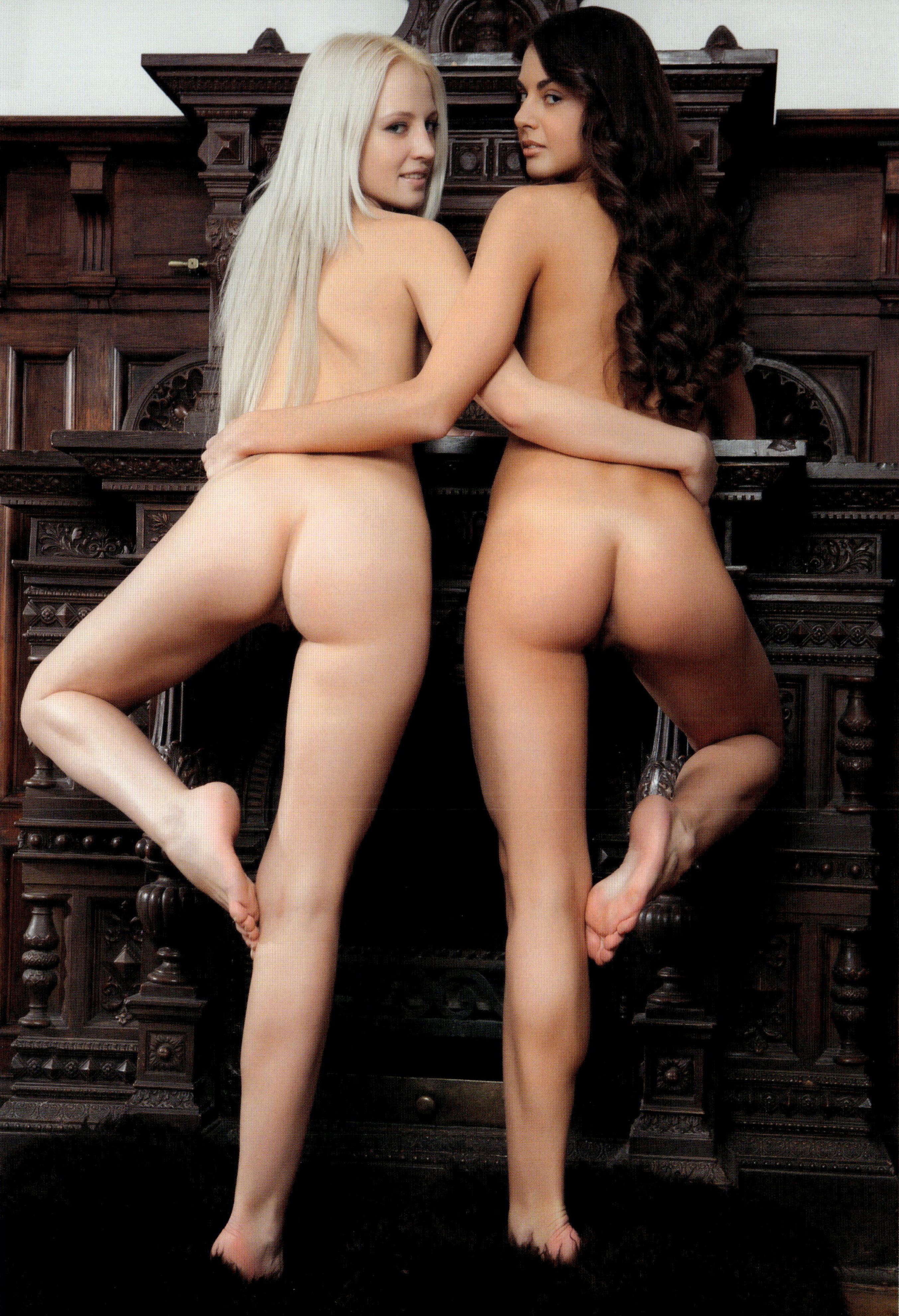

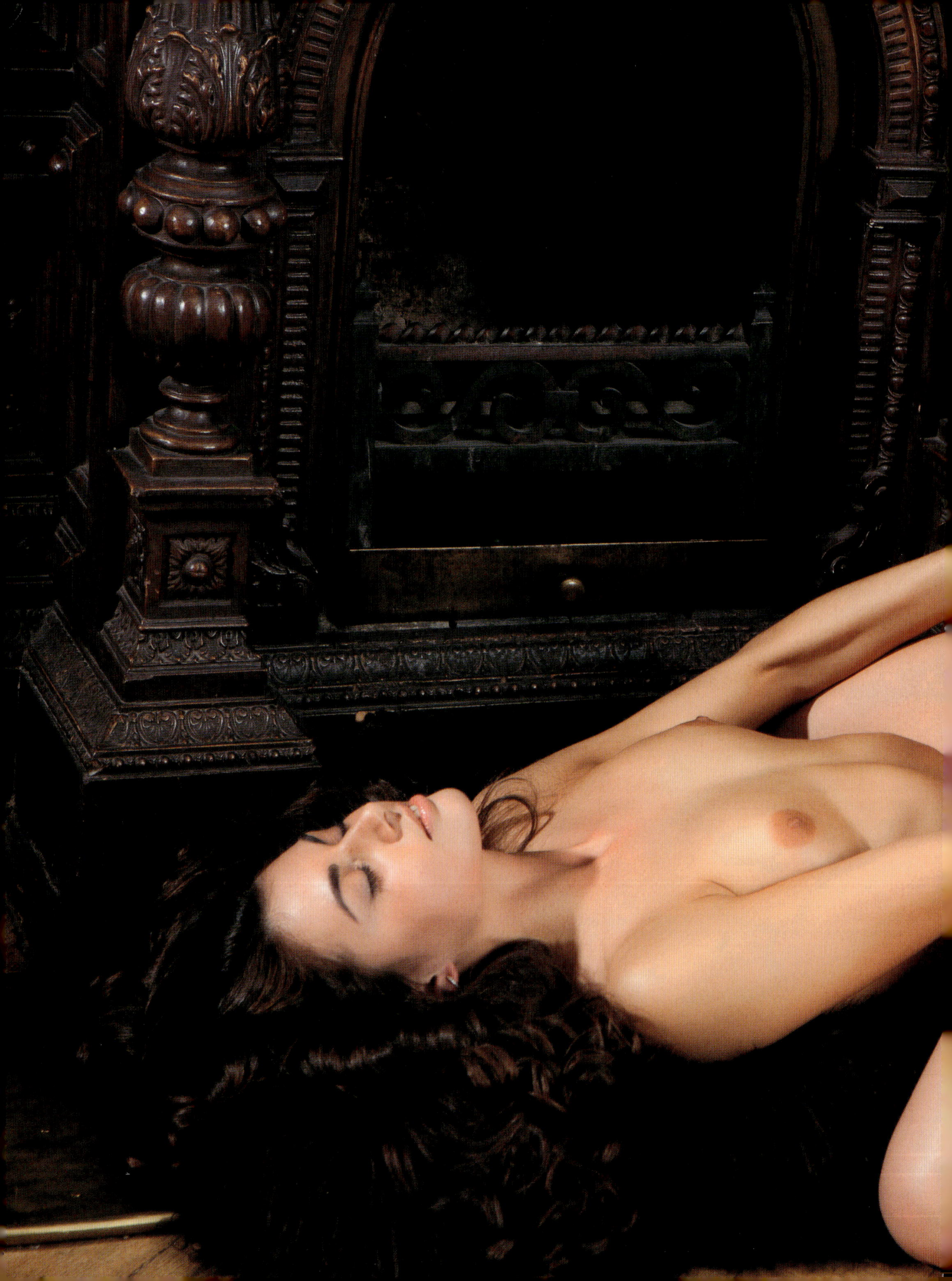

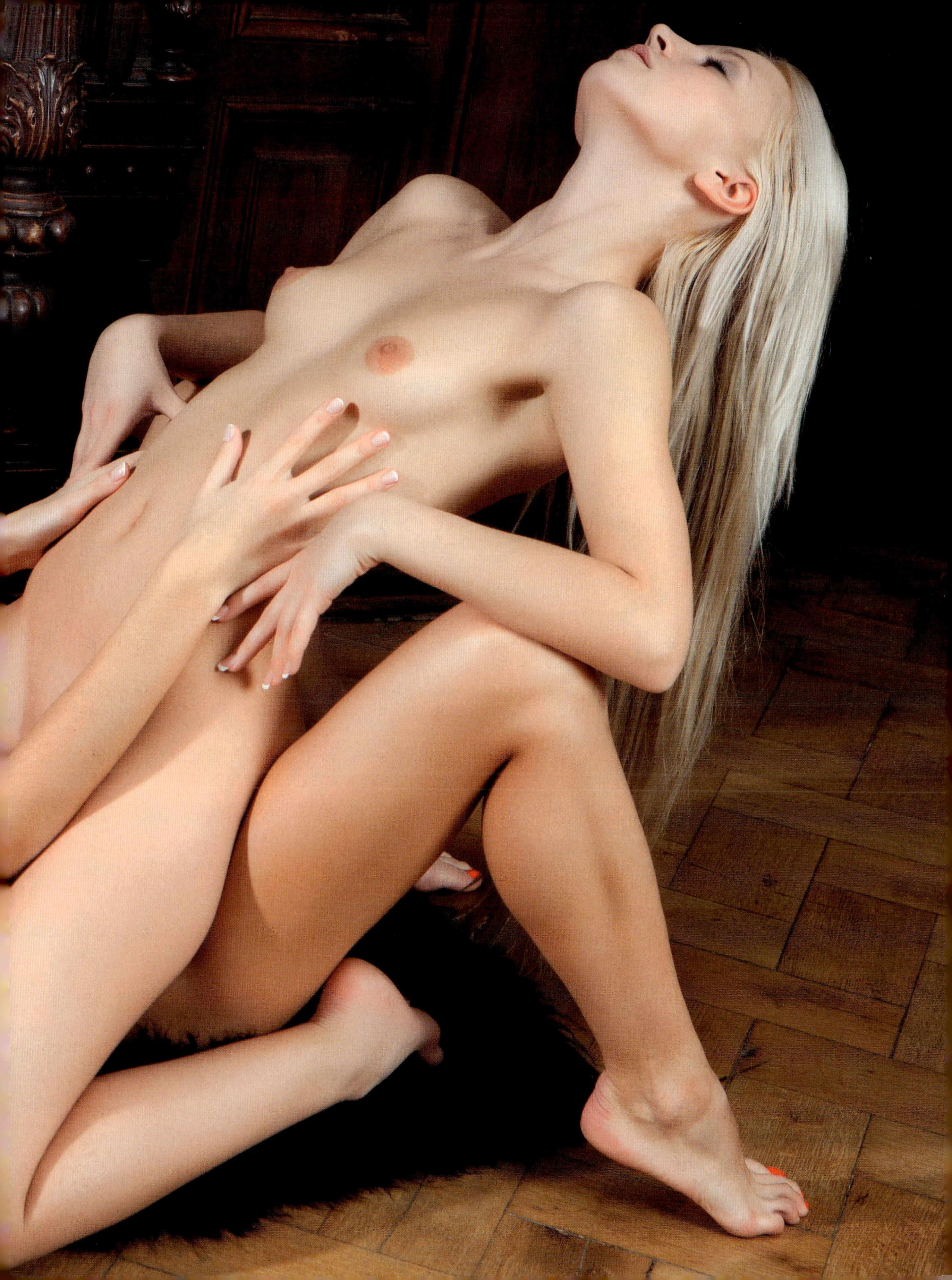

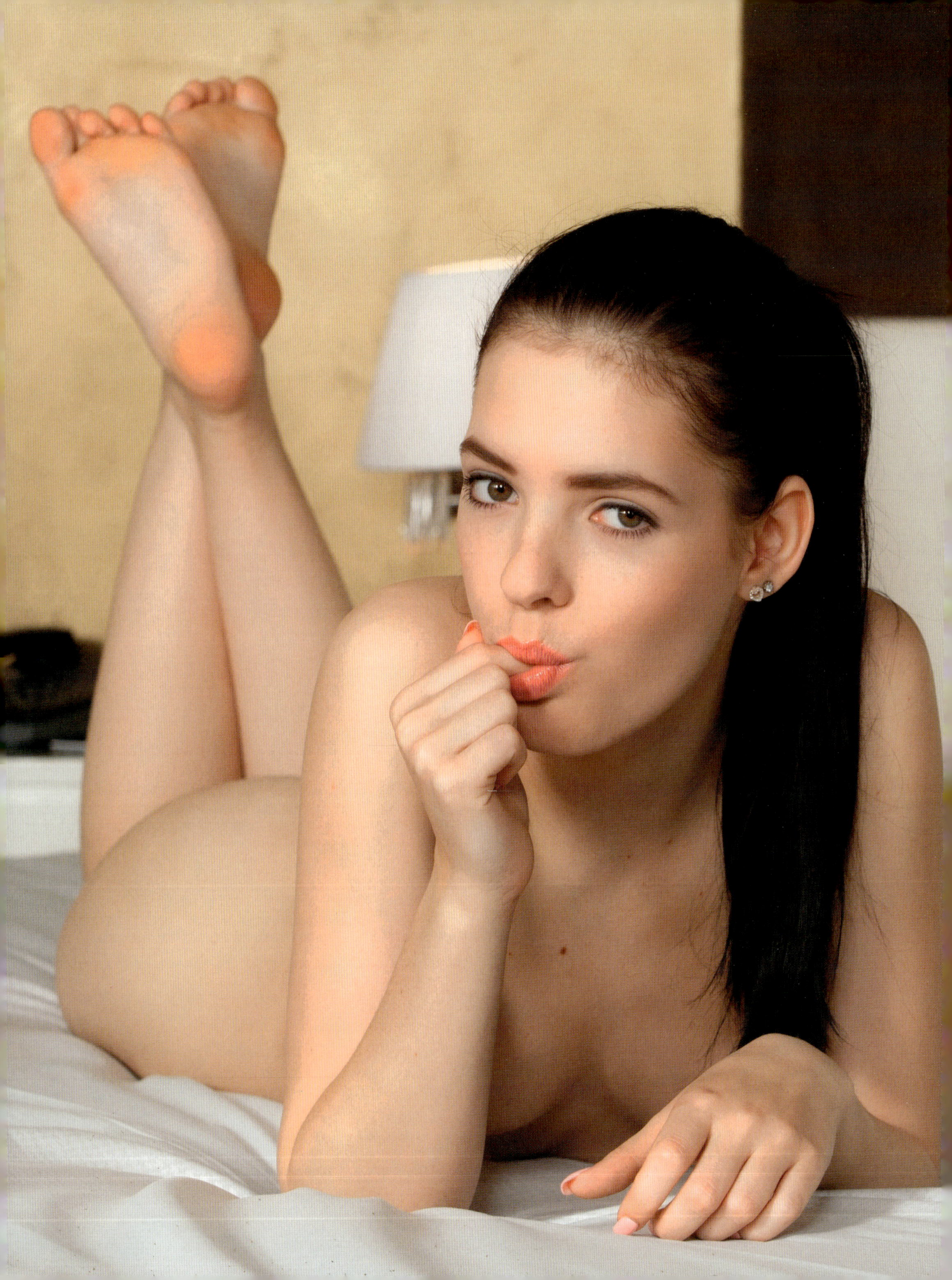

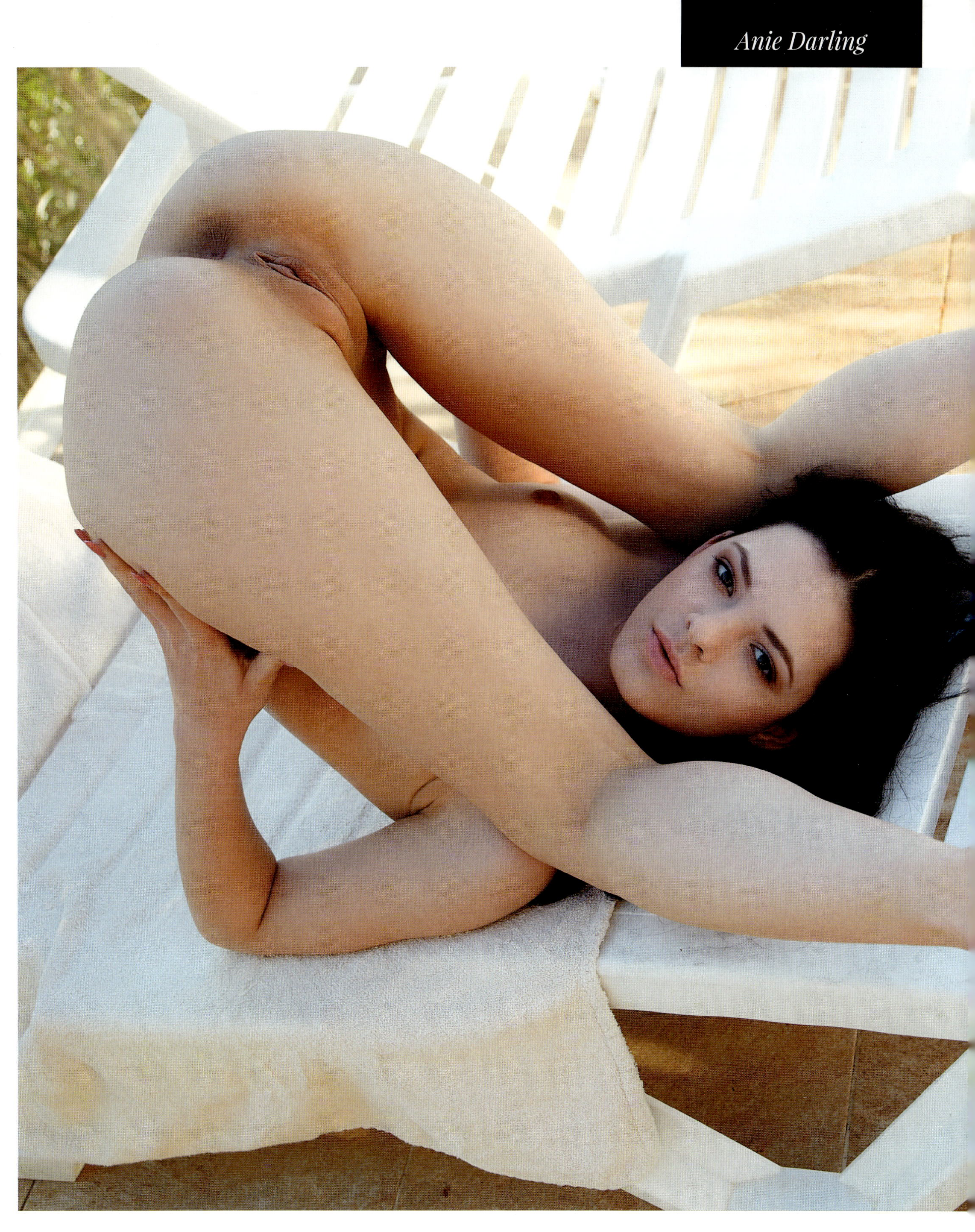

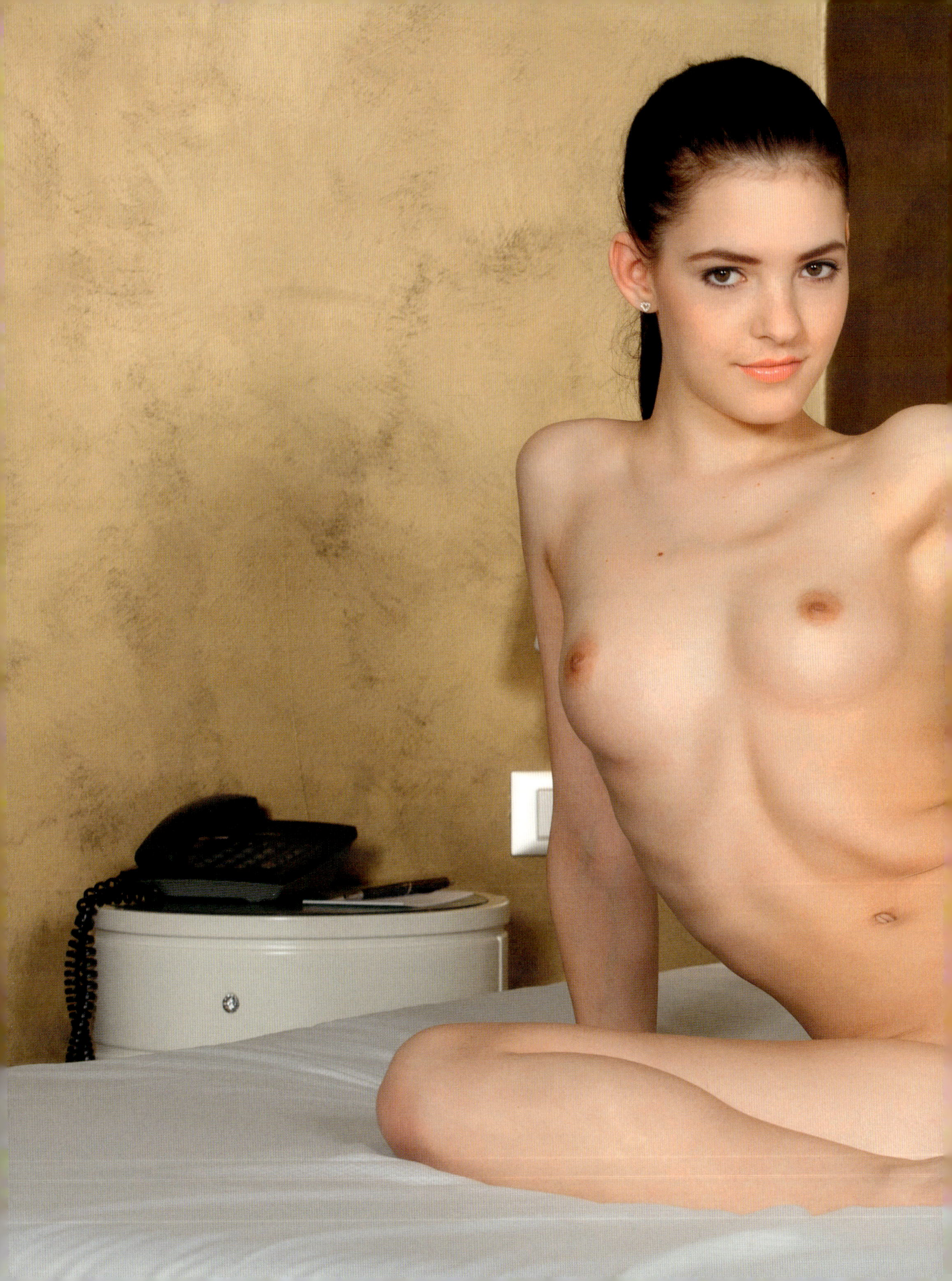

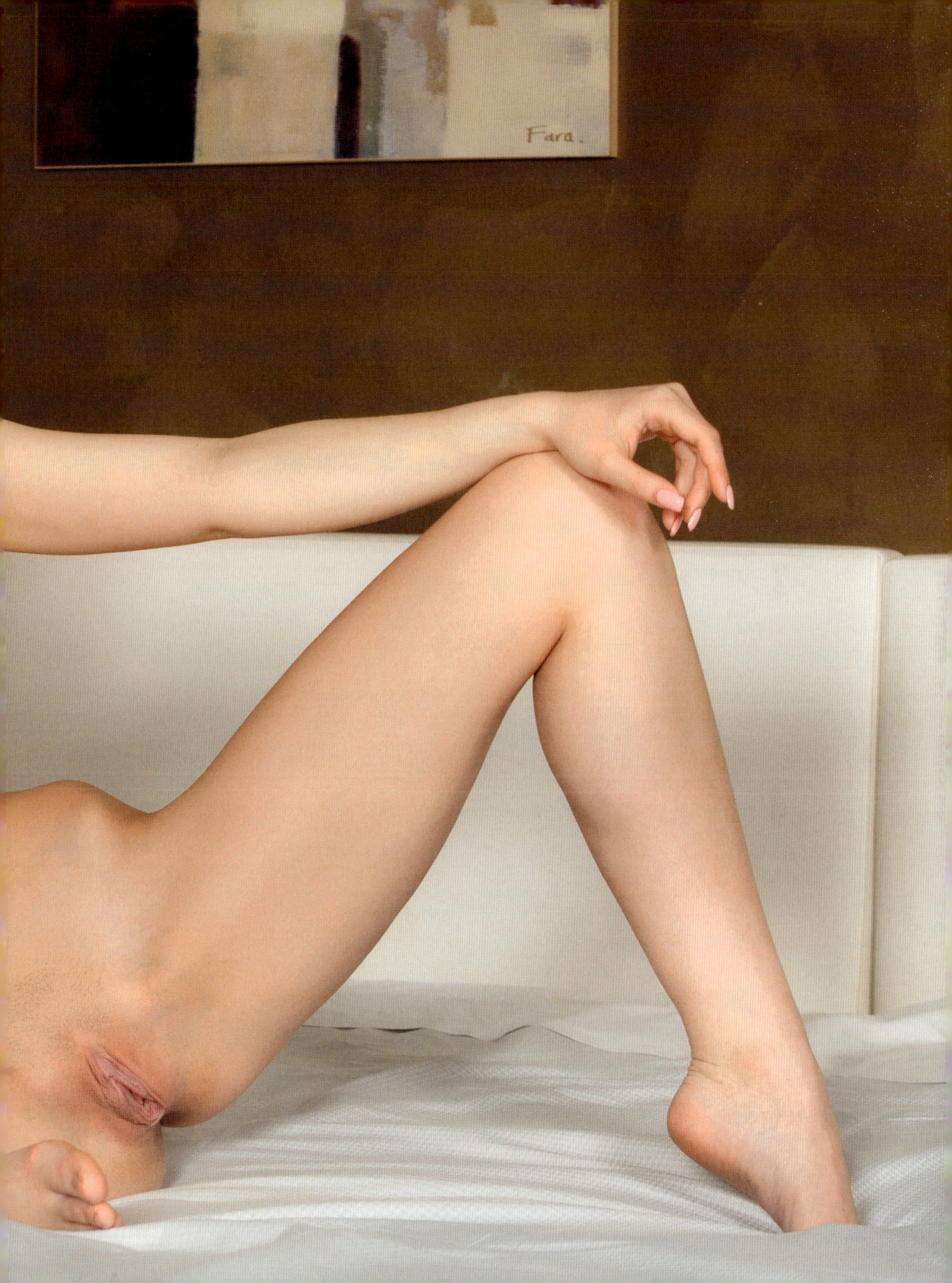
Fara.

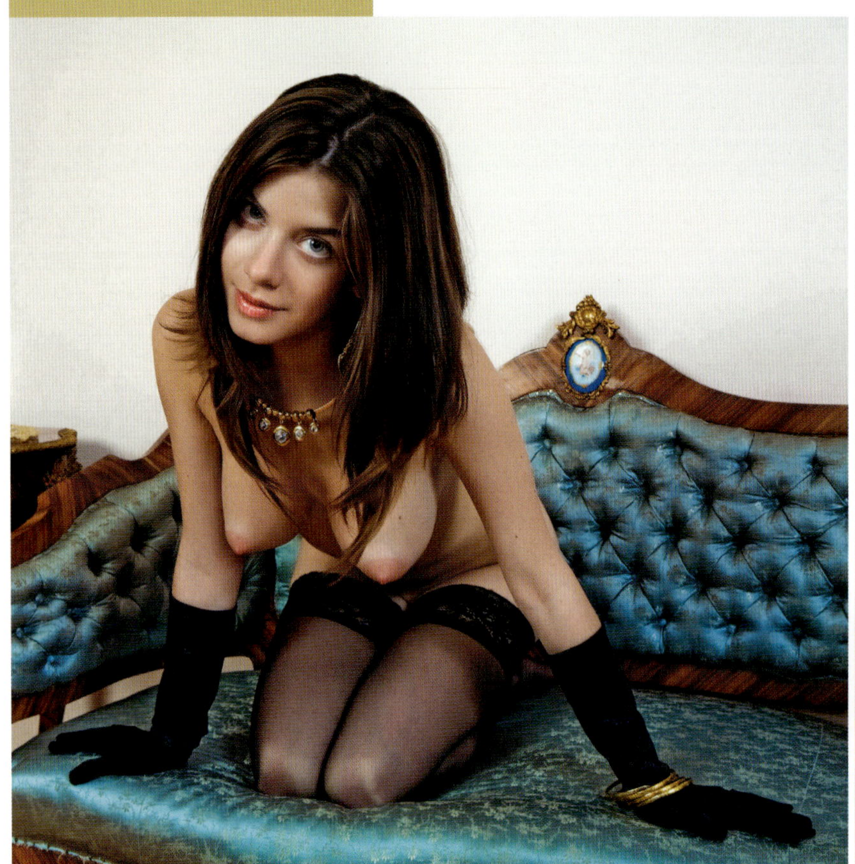

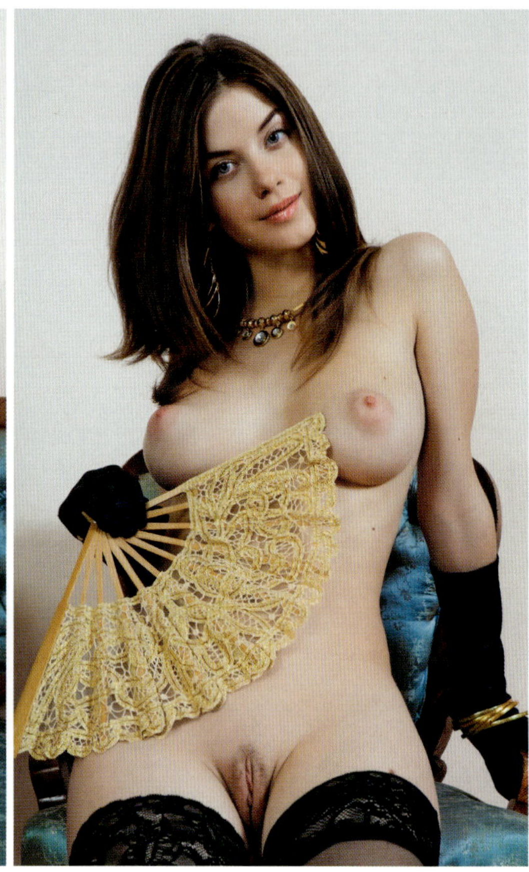

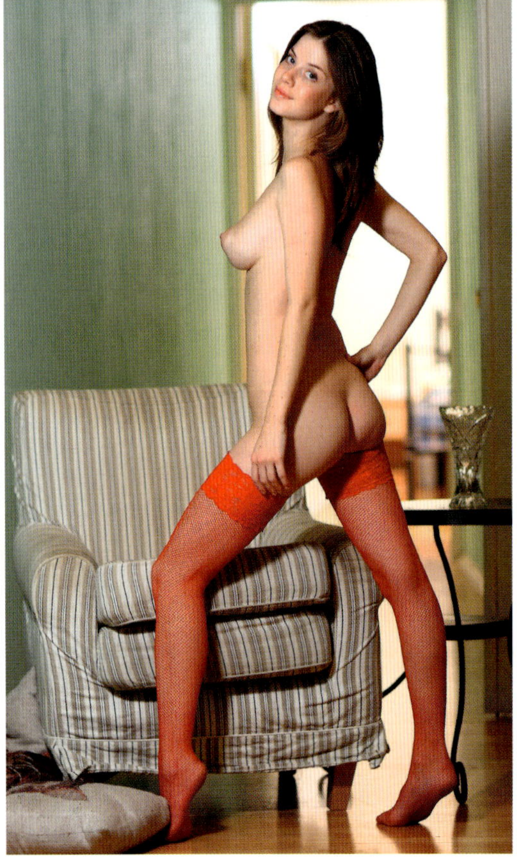

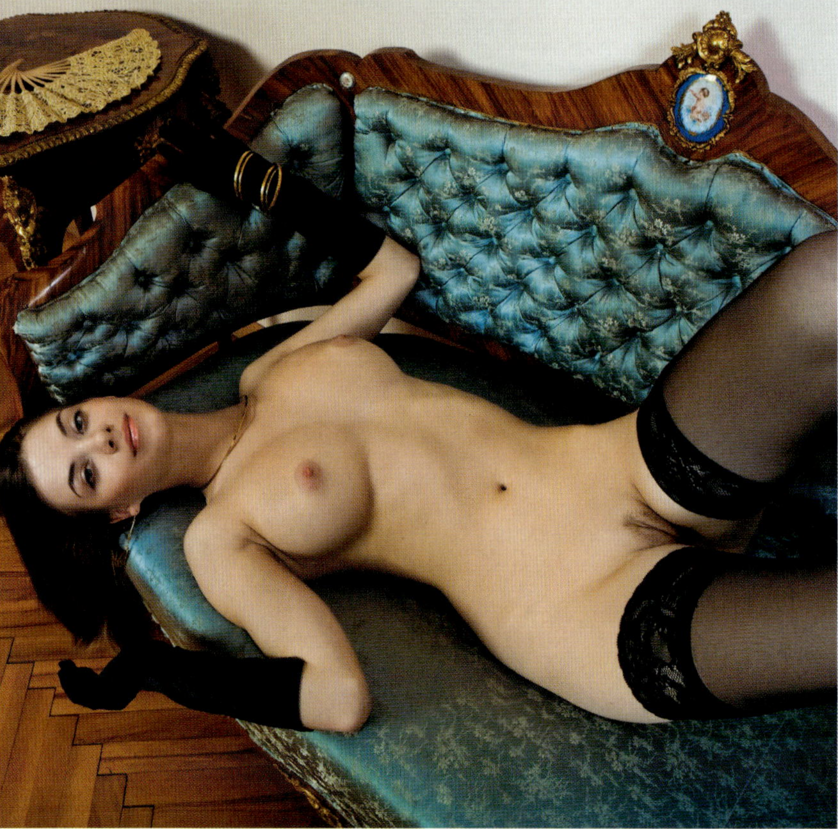

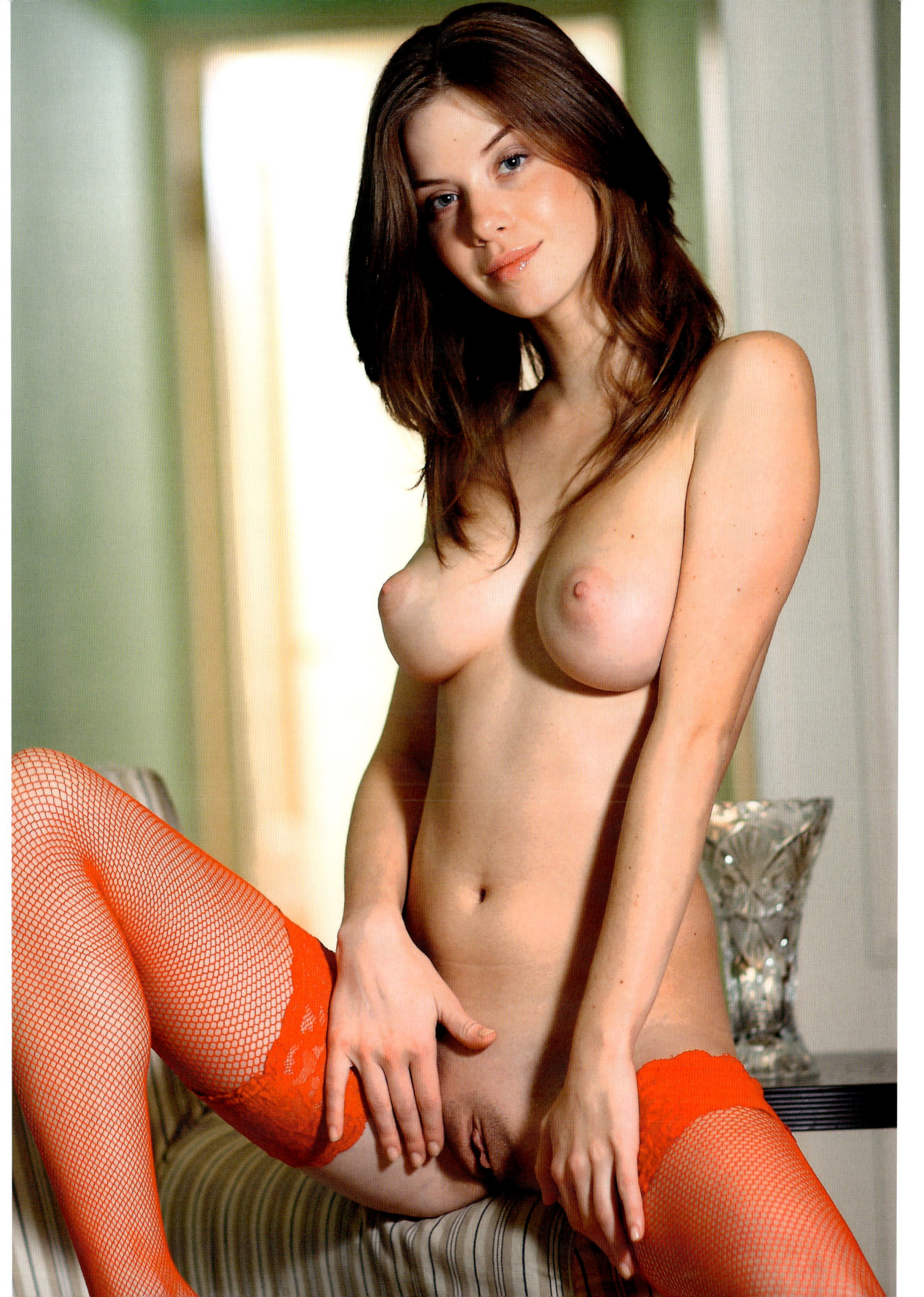

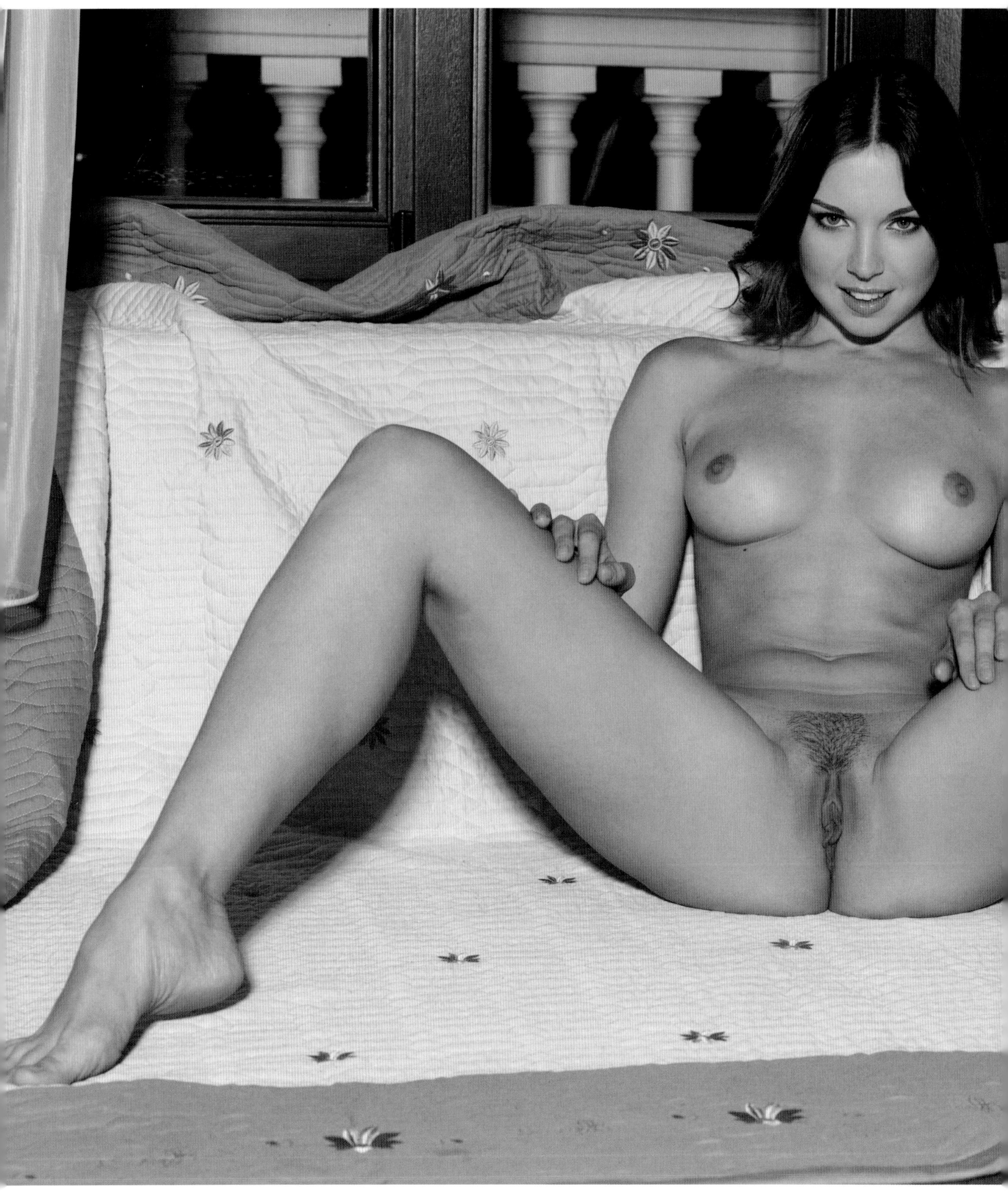

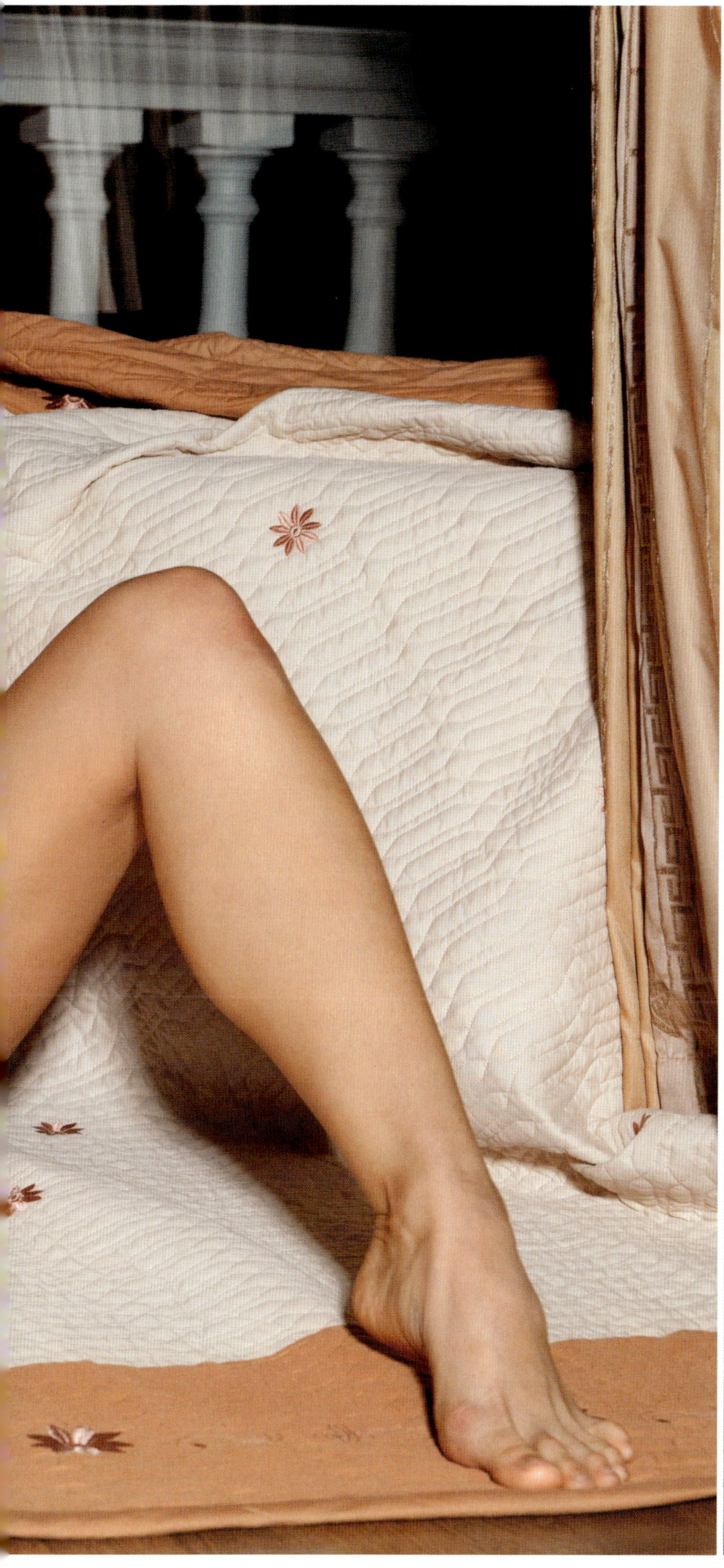

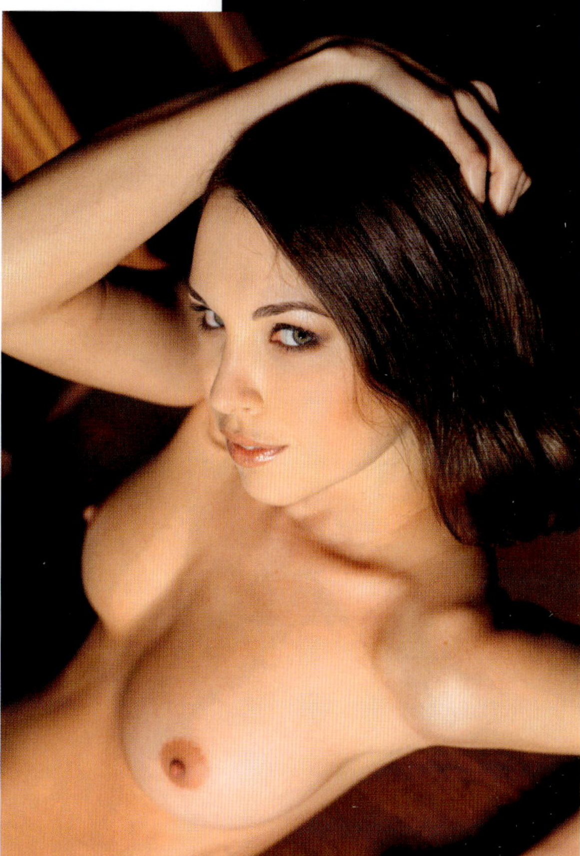

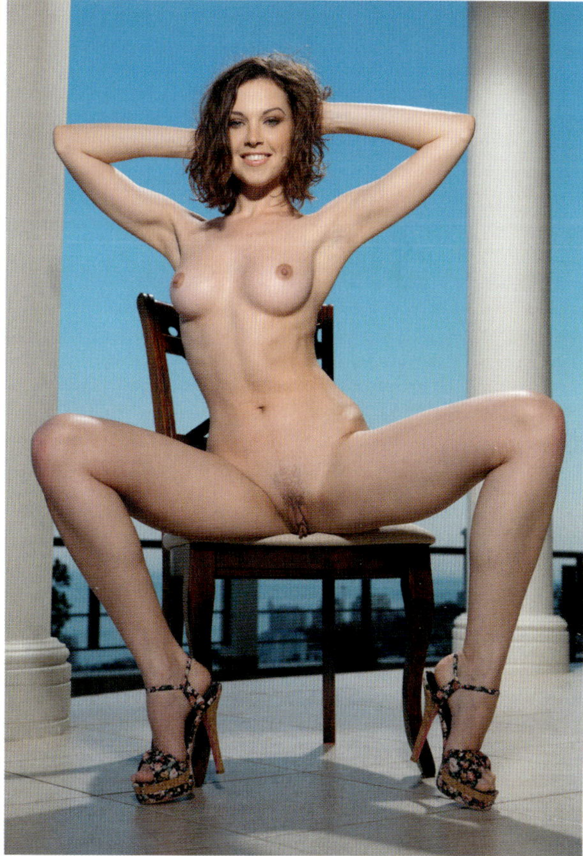

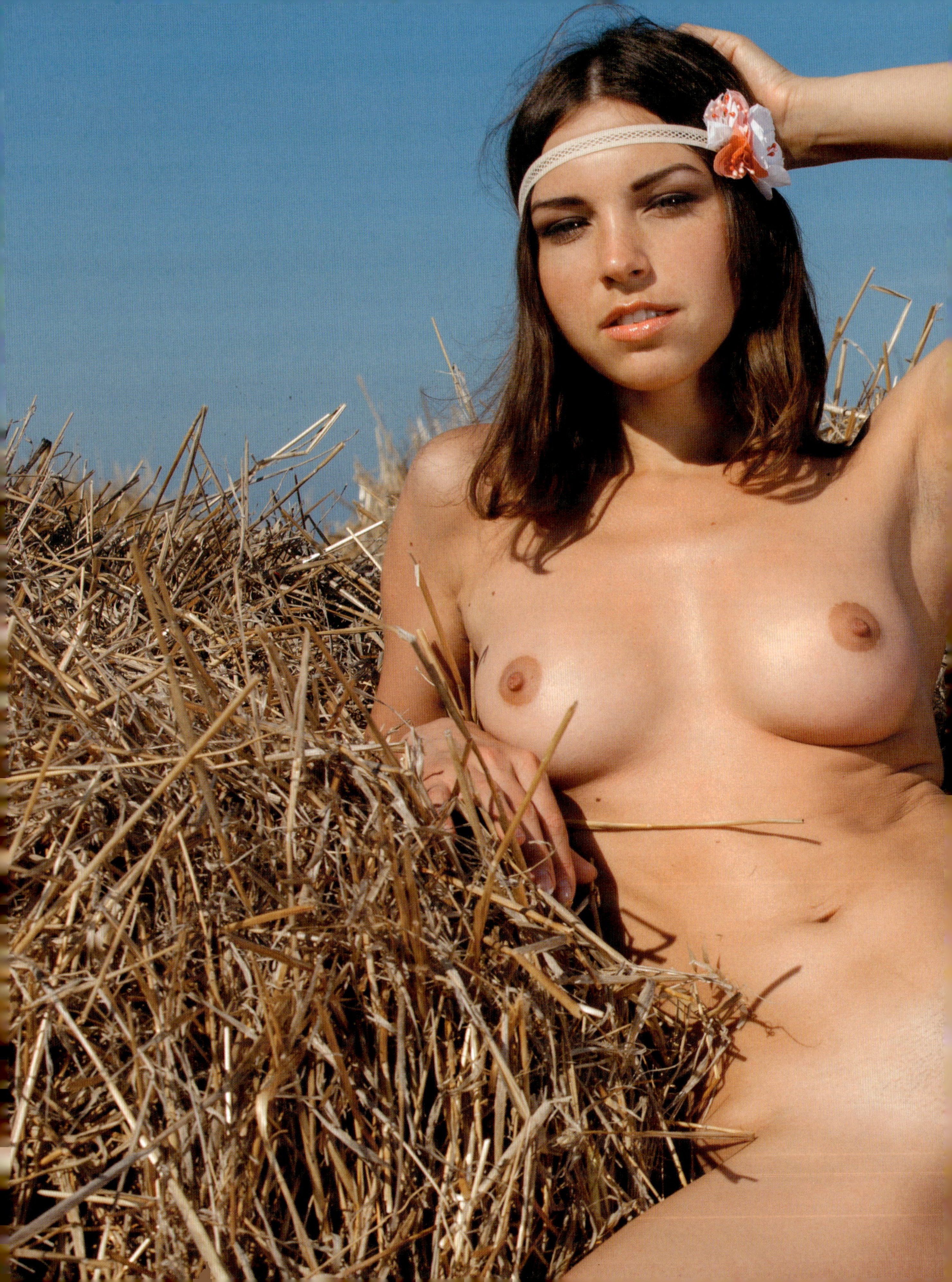

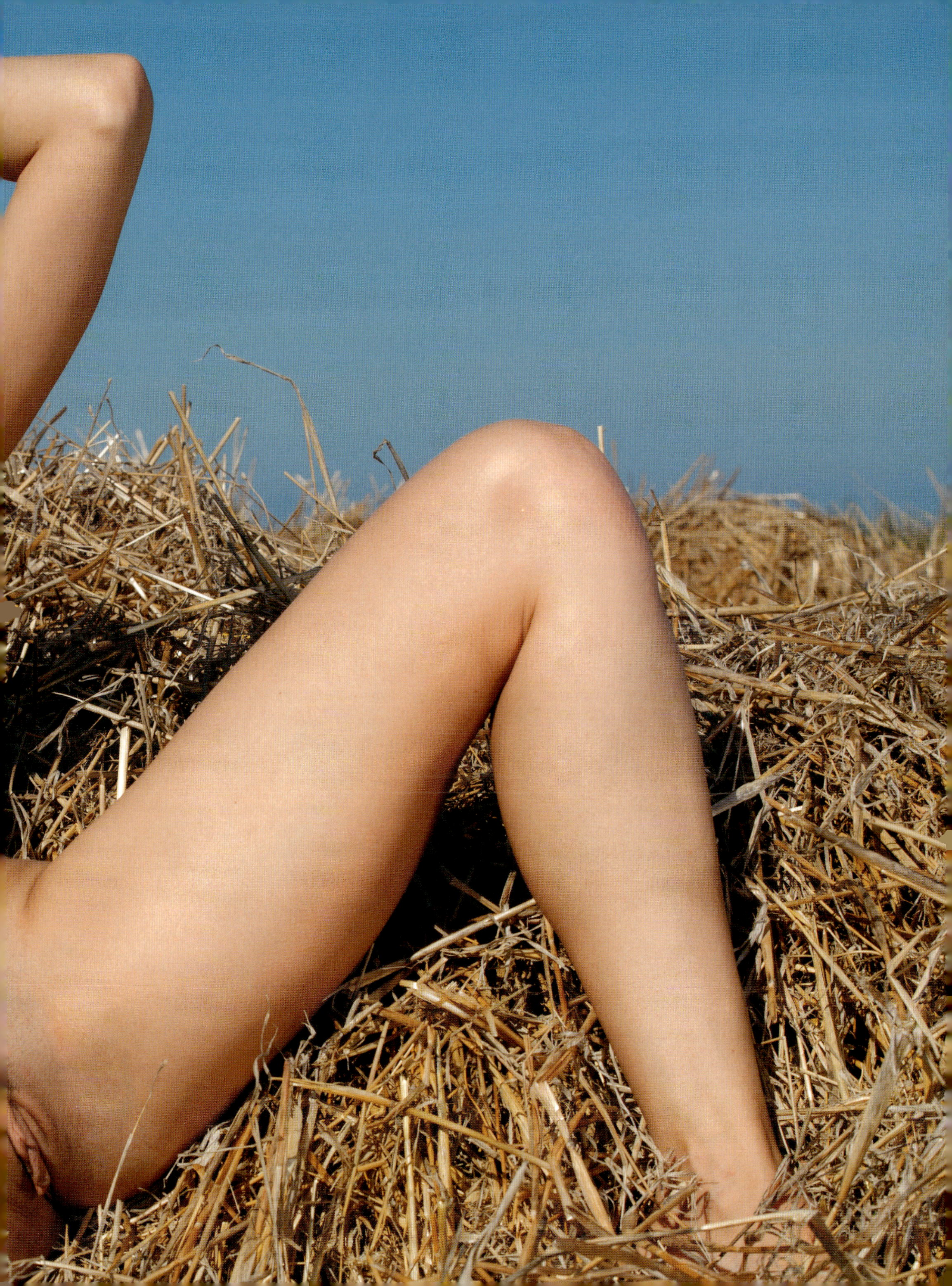

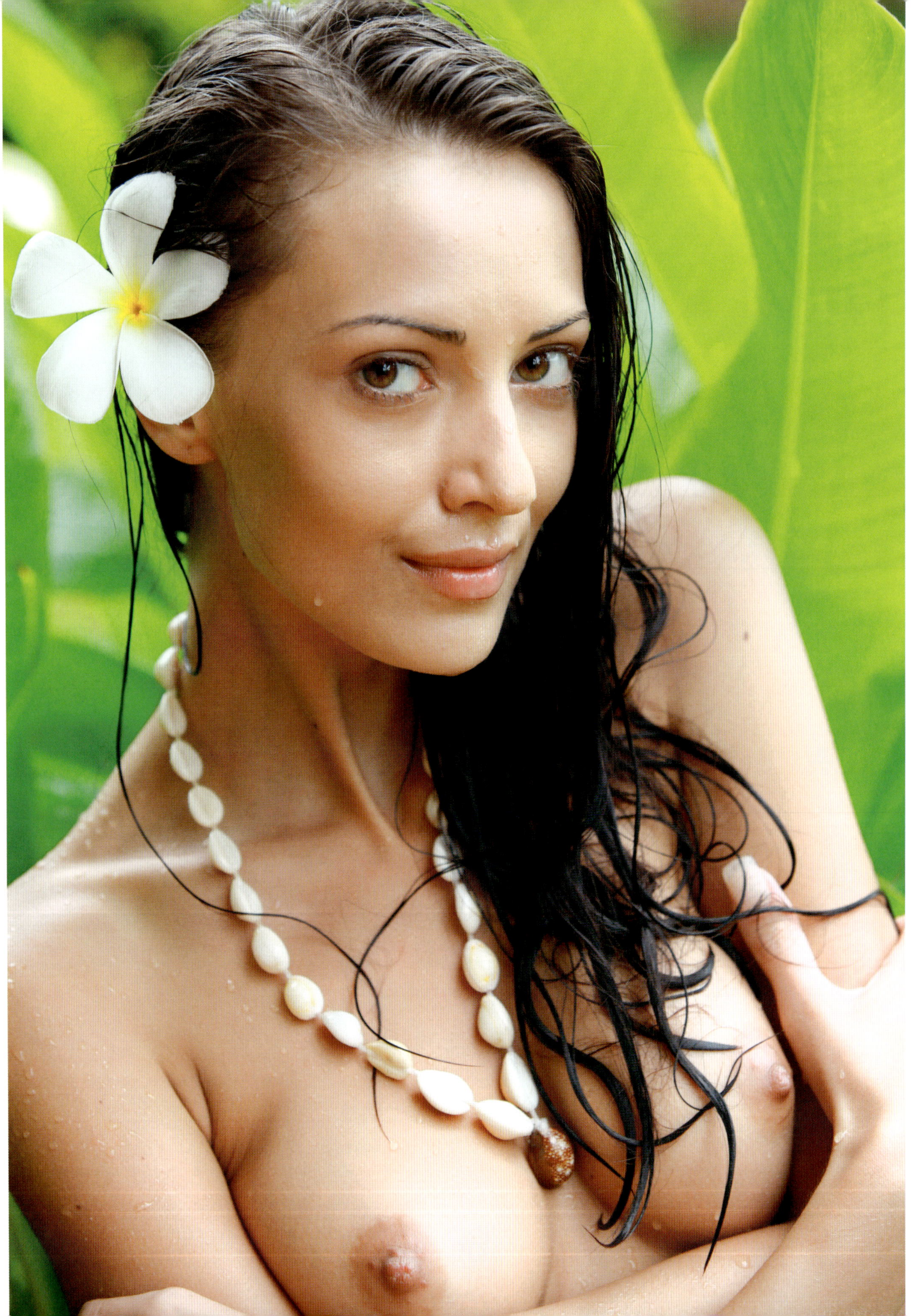

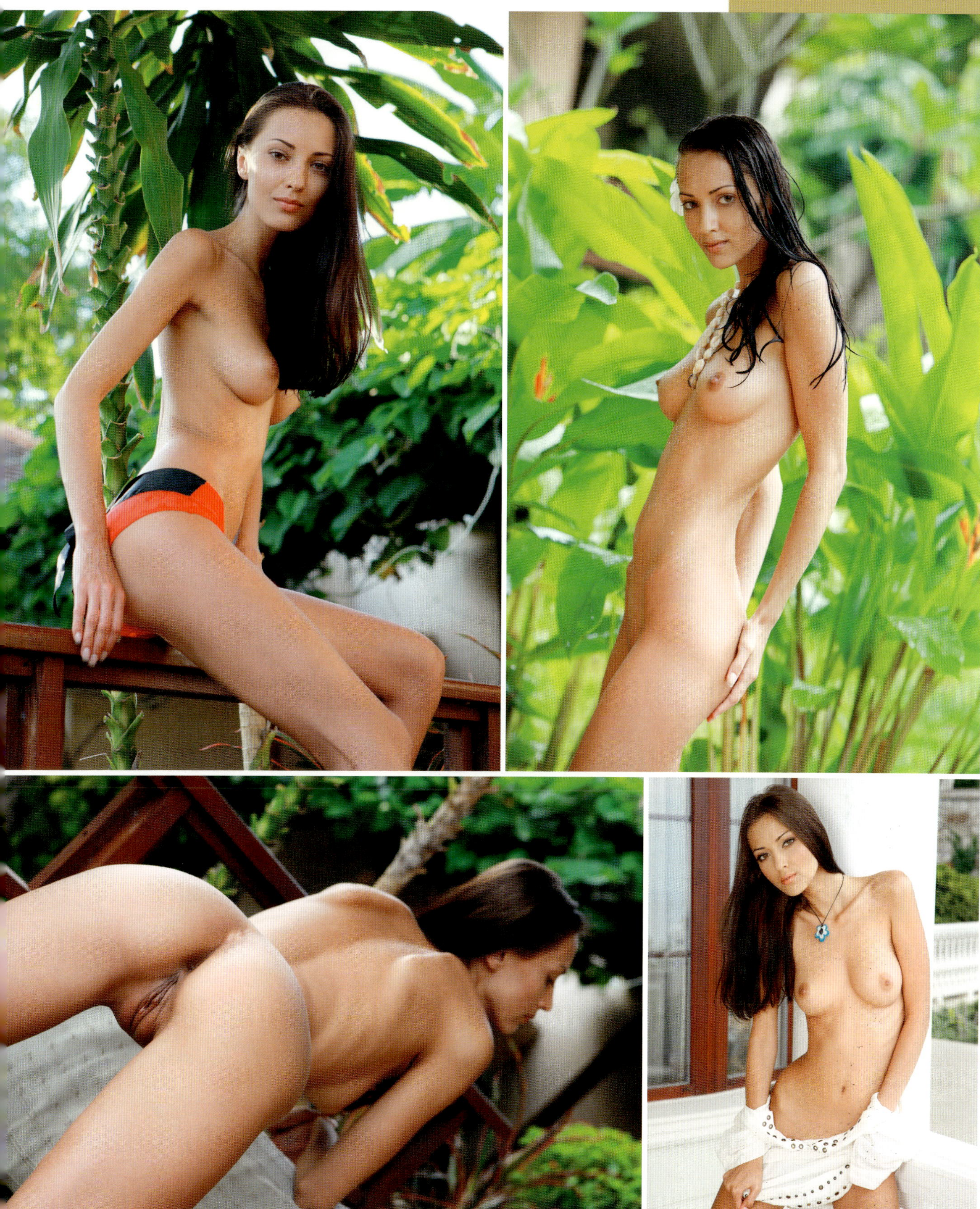

# *Ardelia A*

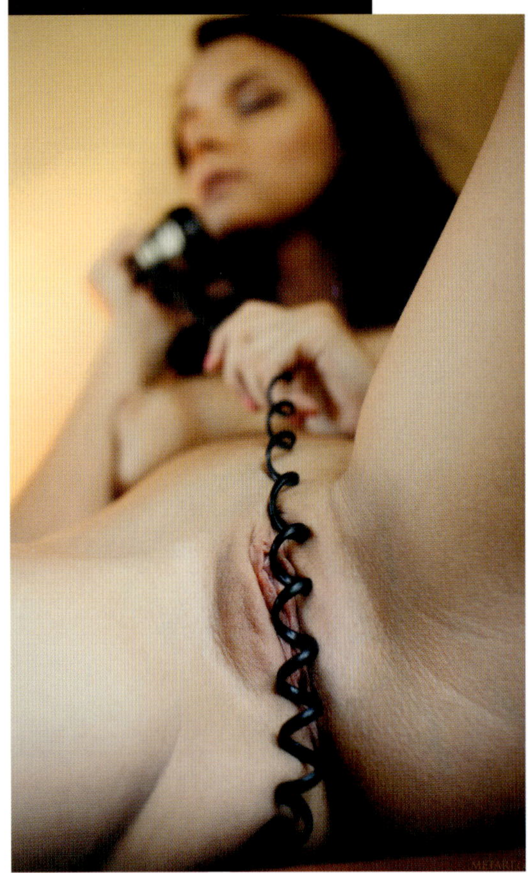

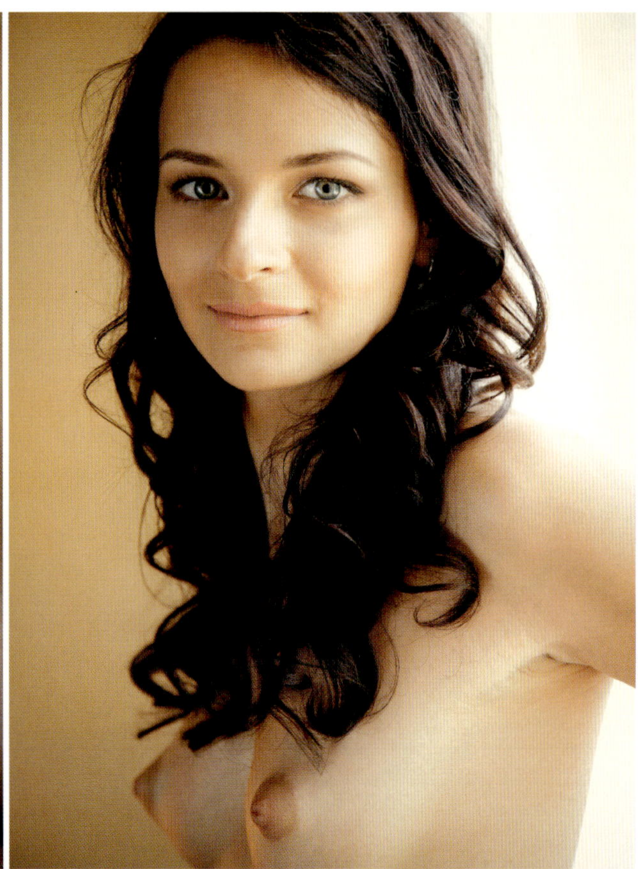

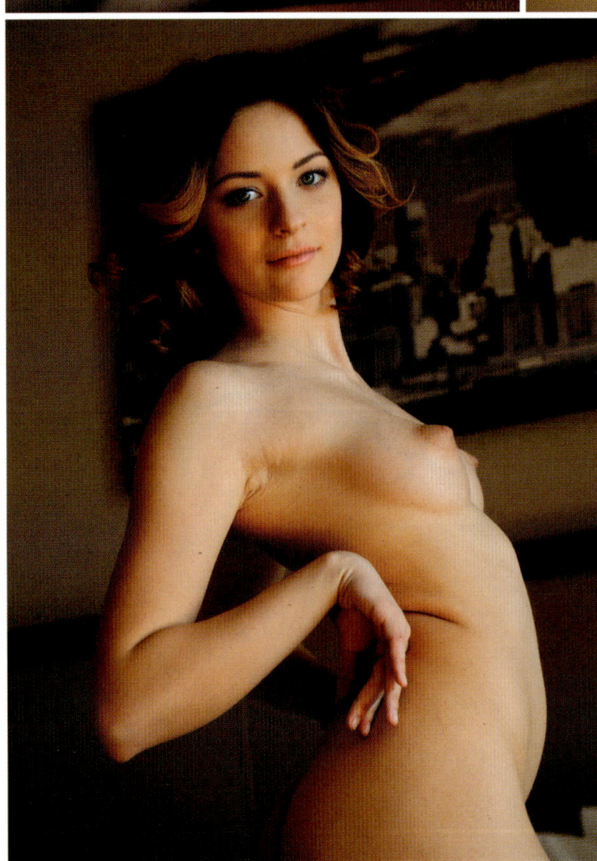

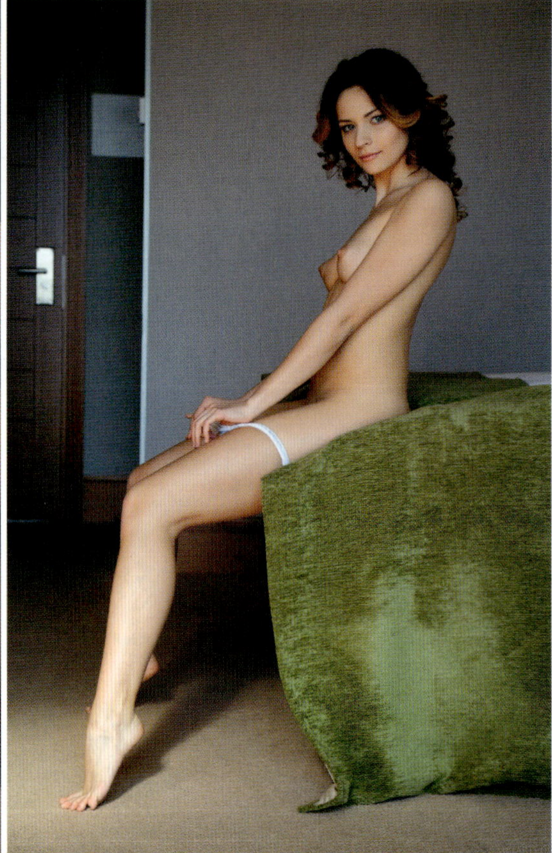

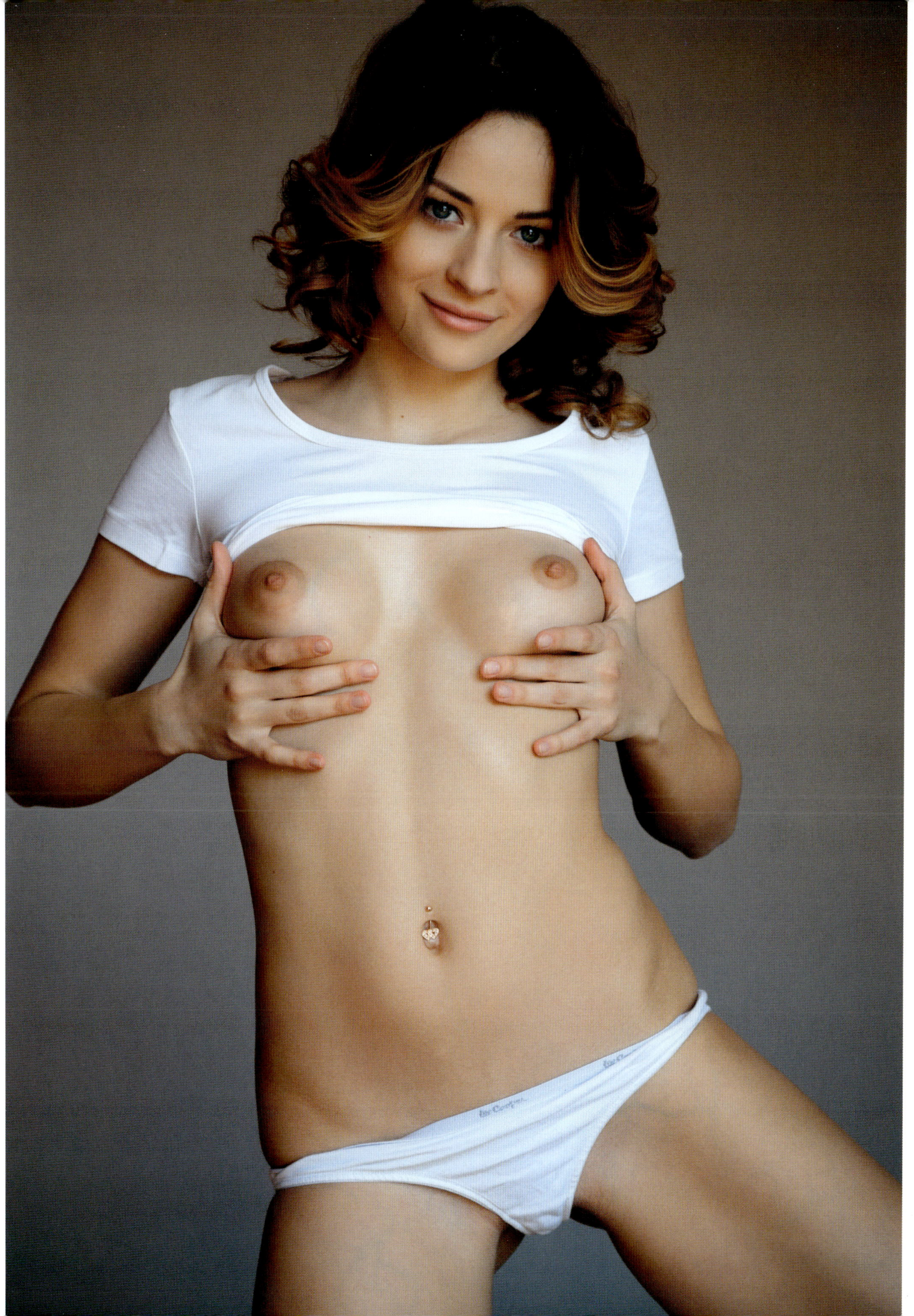

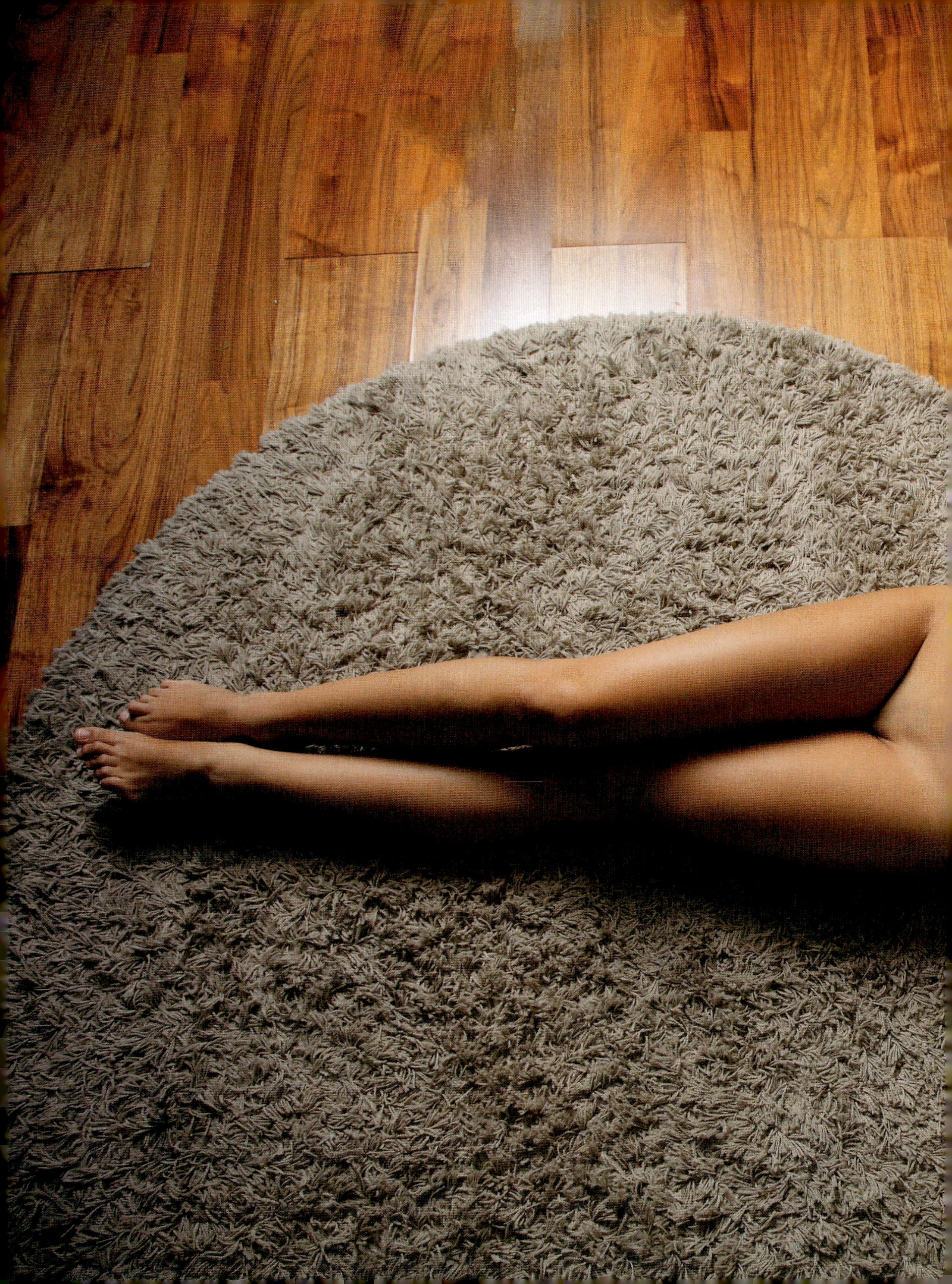

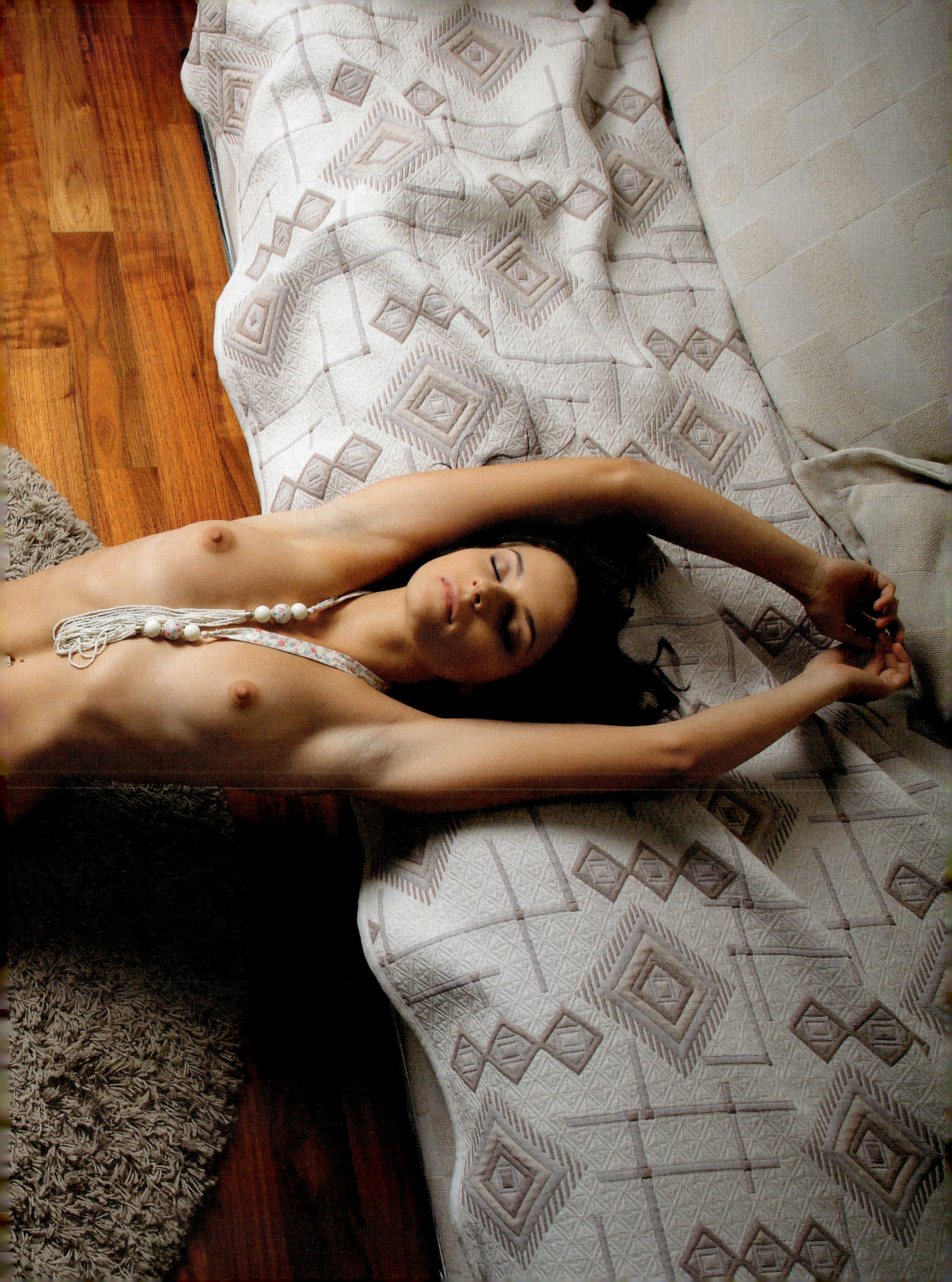

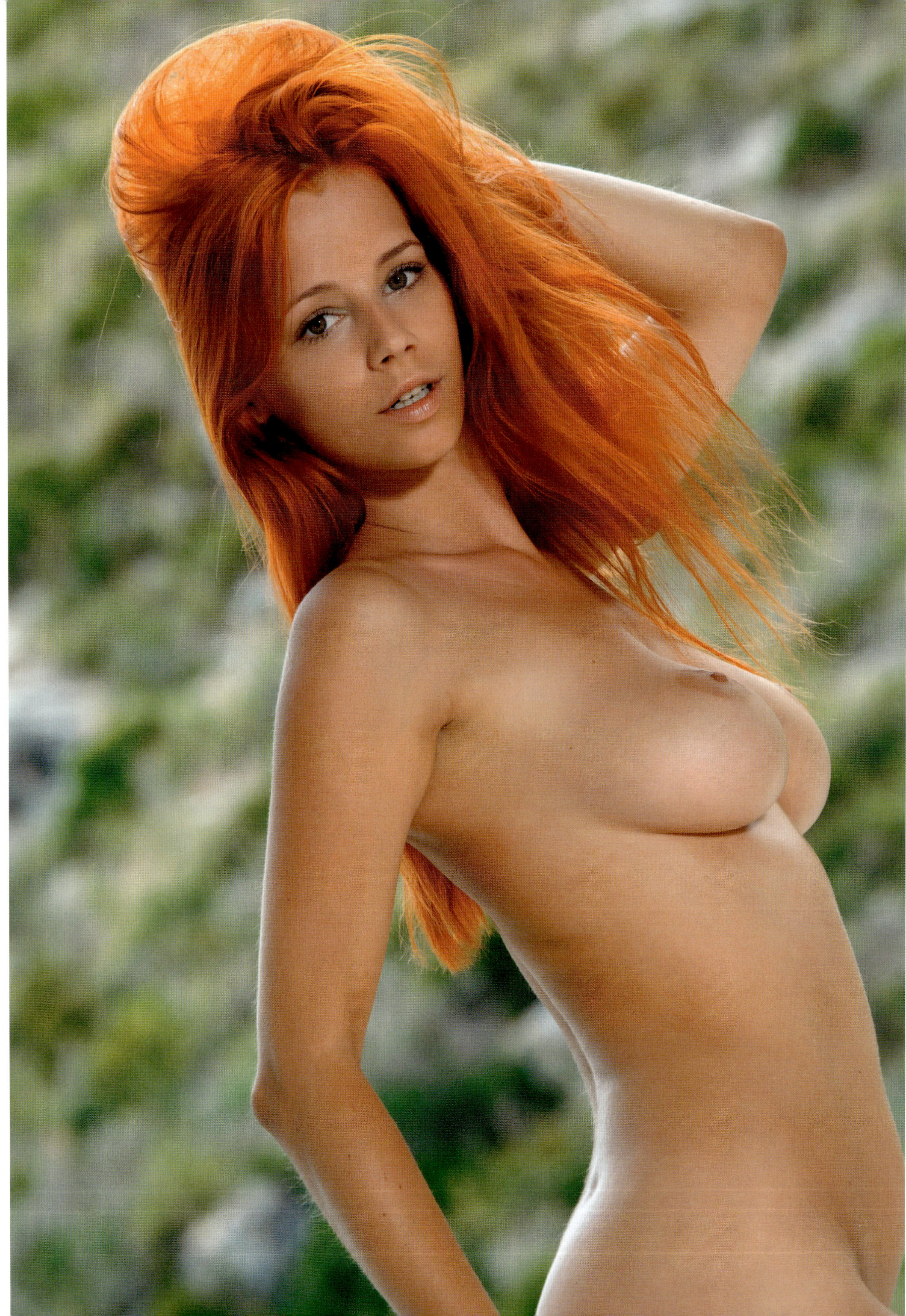

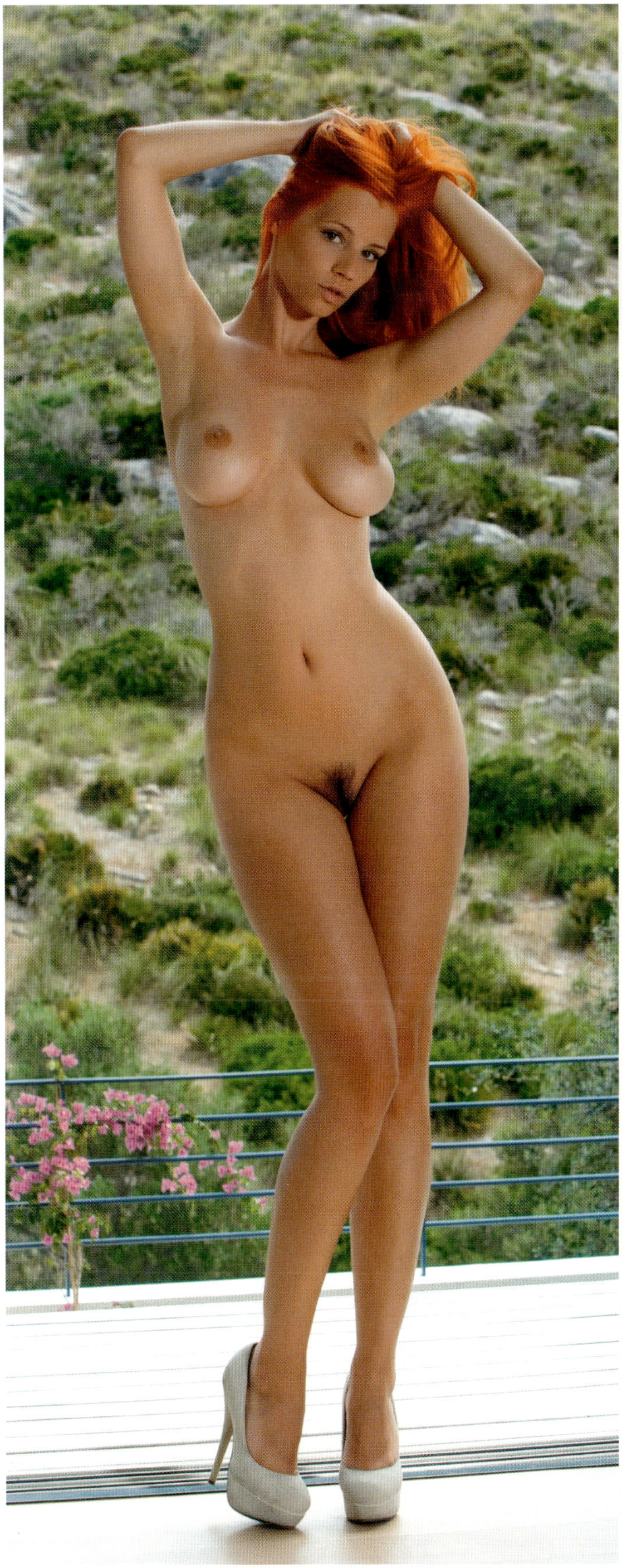

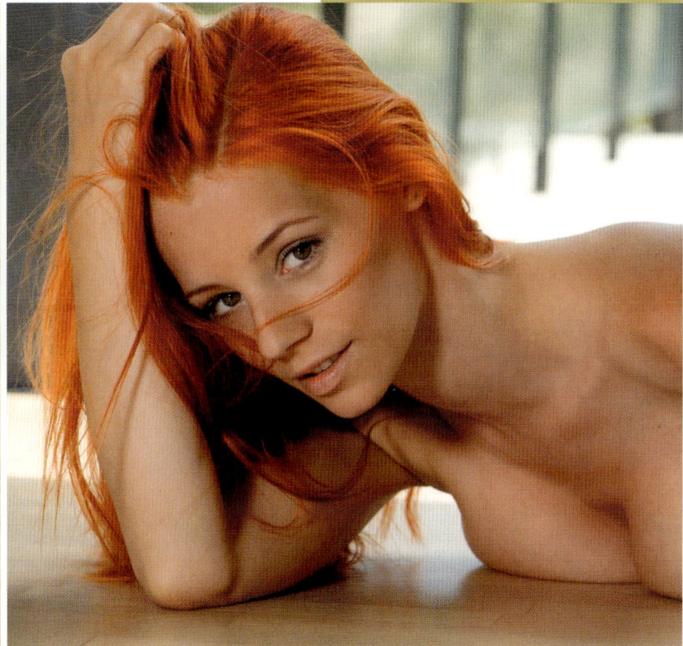

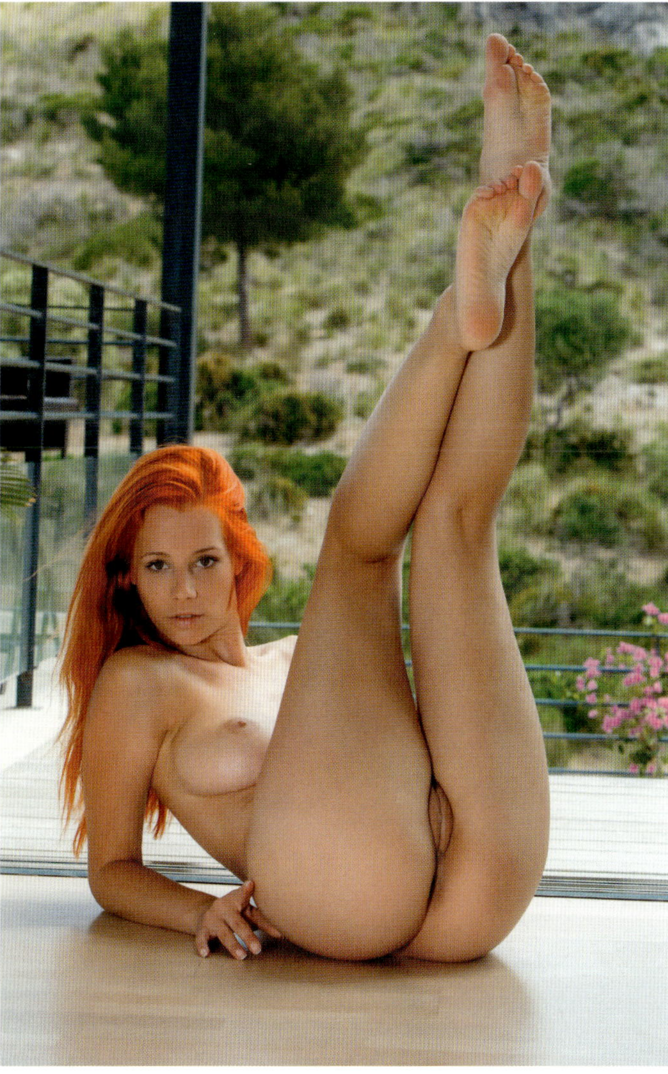

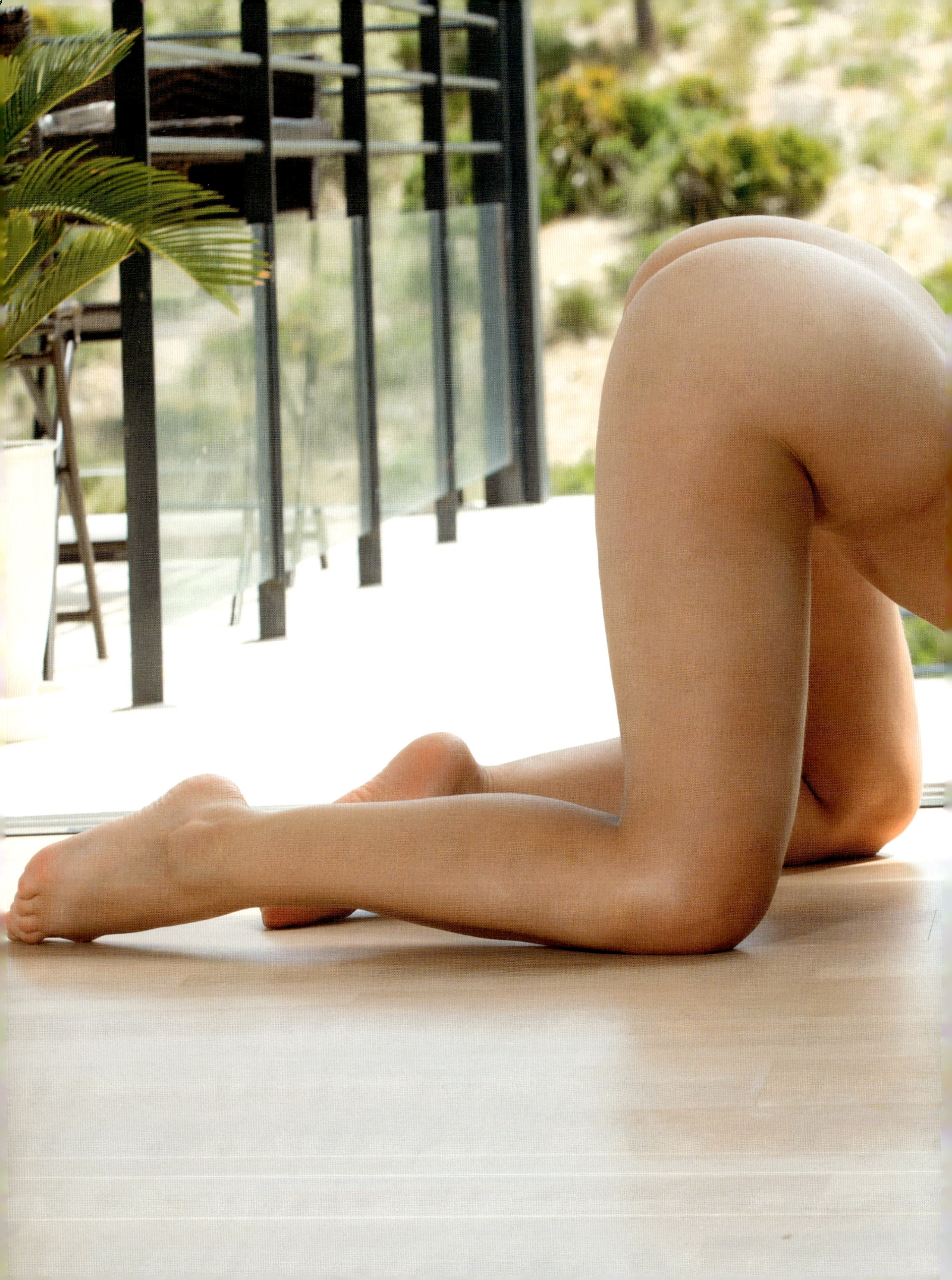

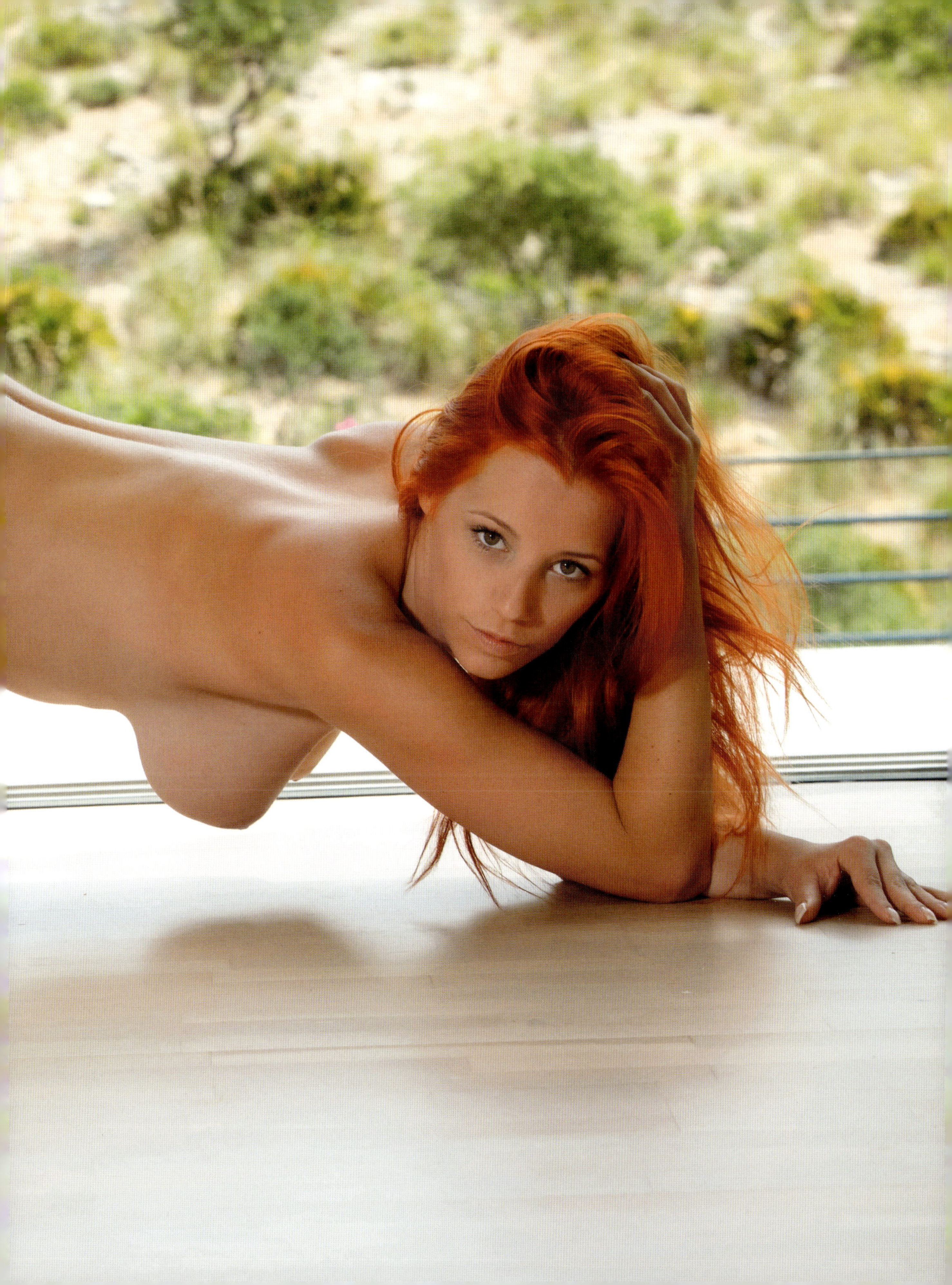

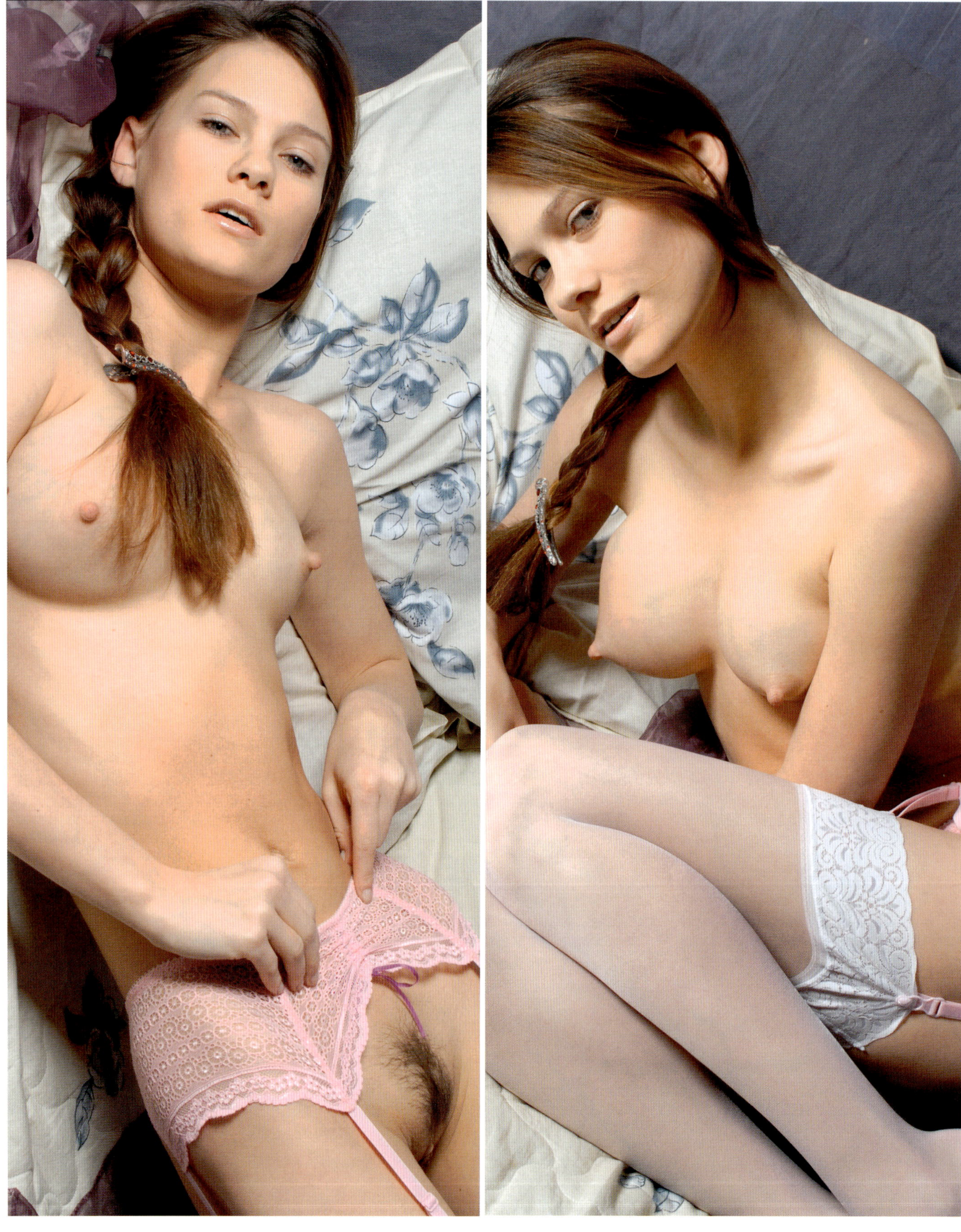

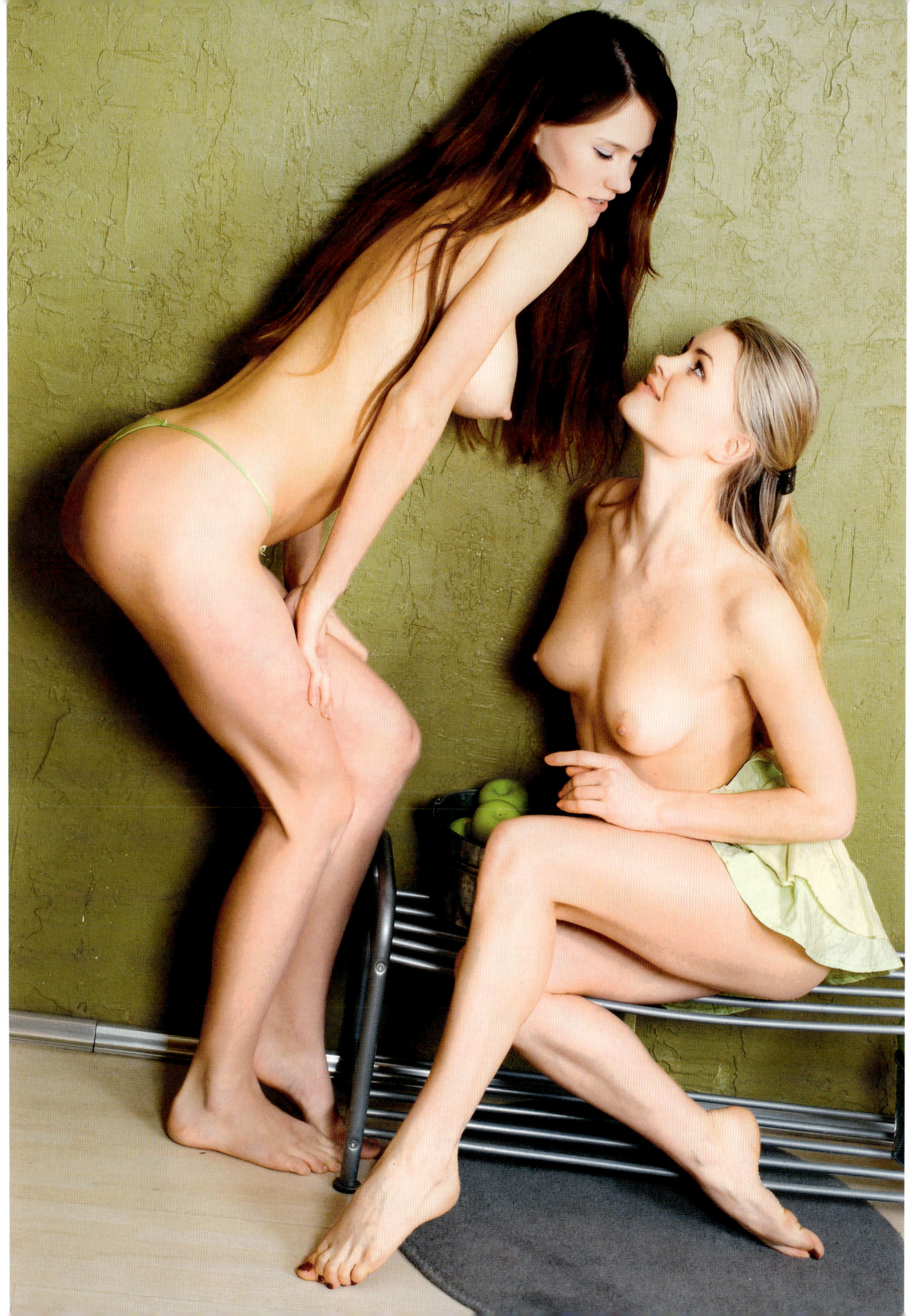

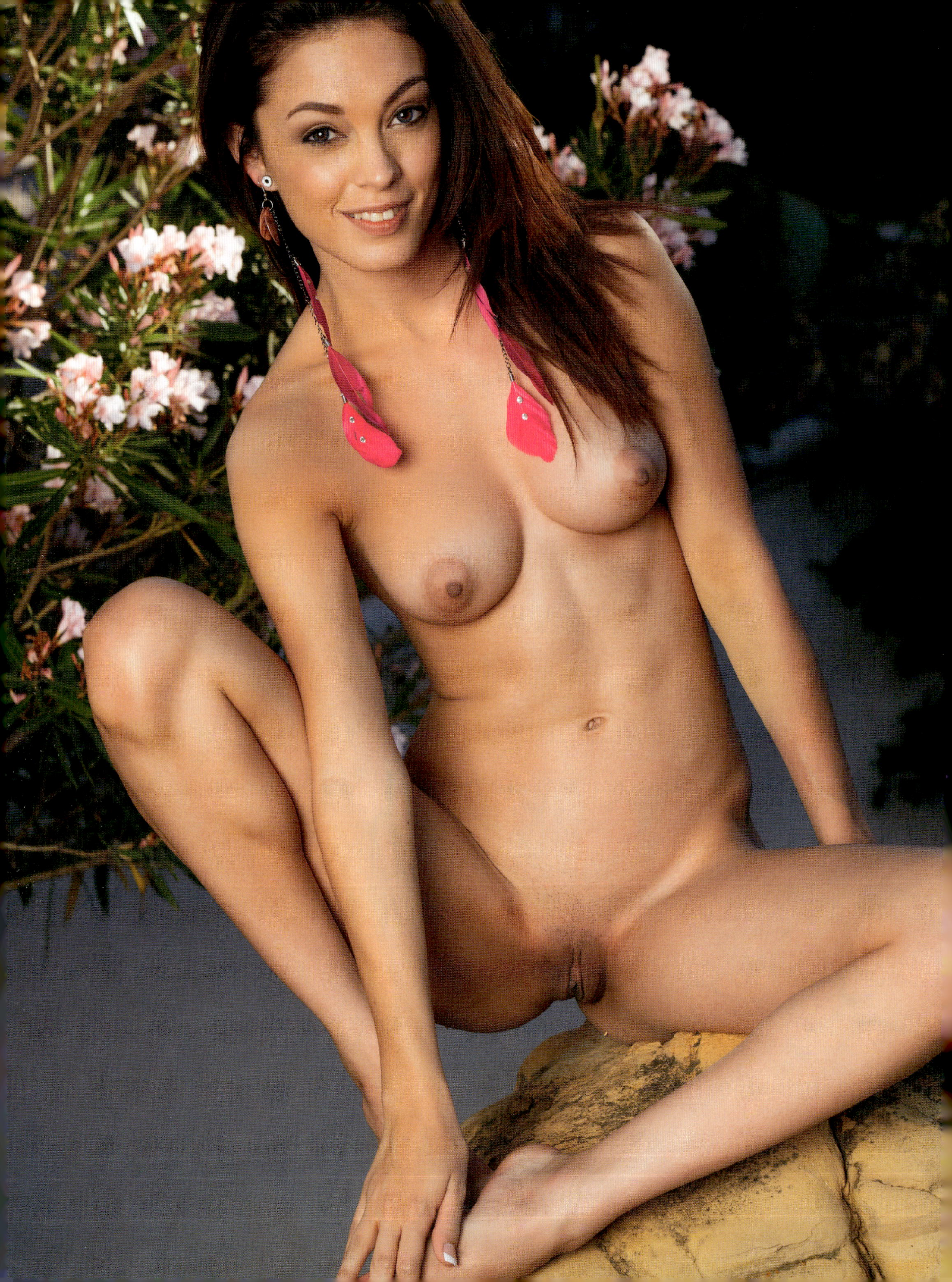

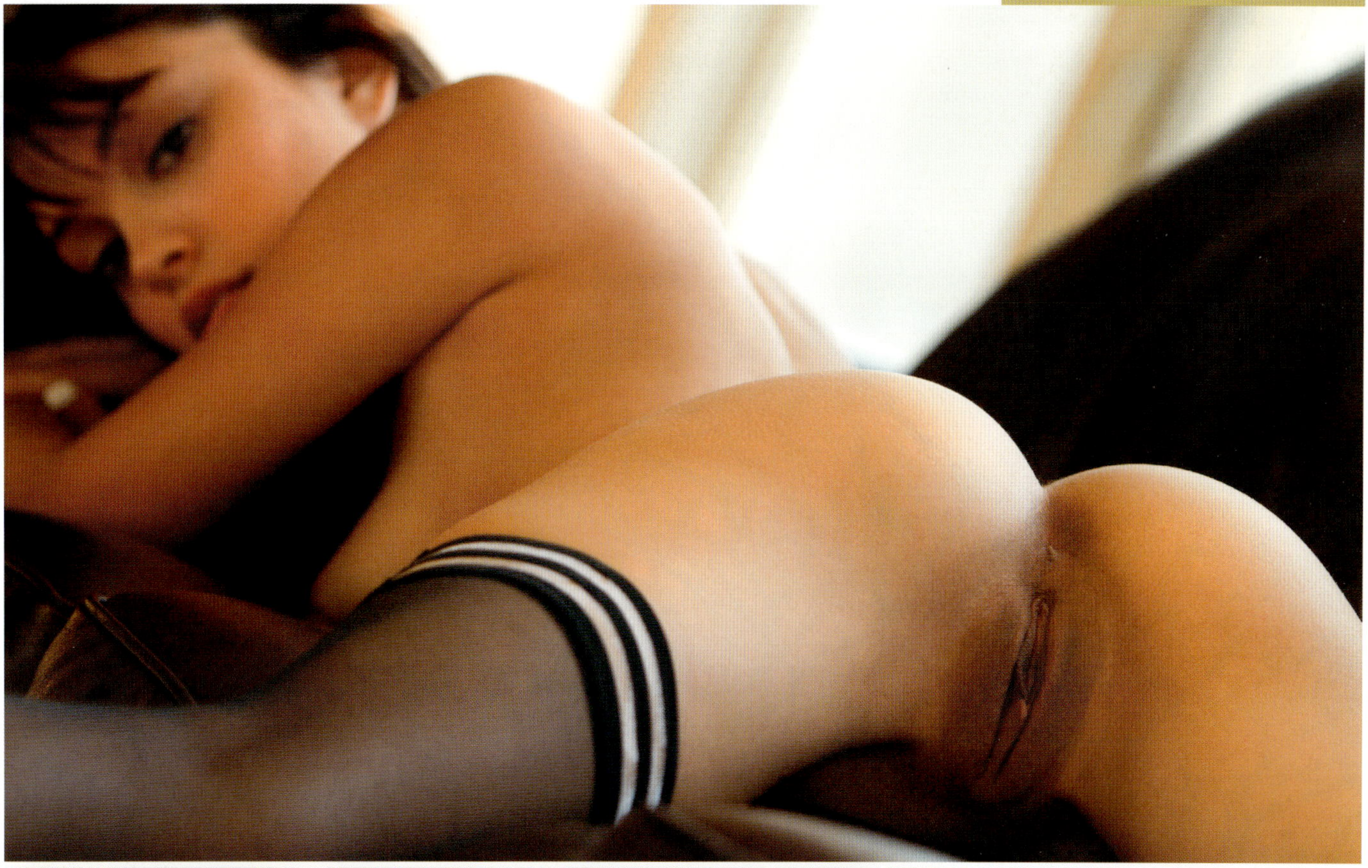

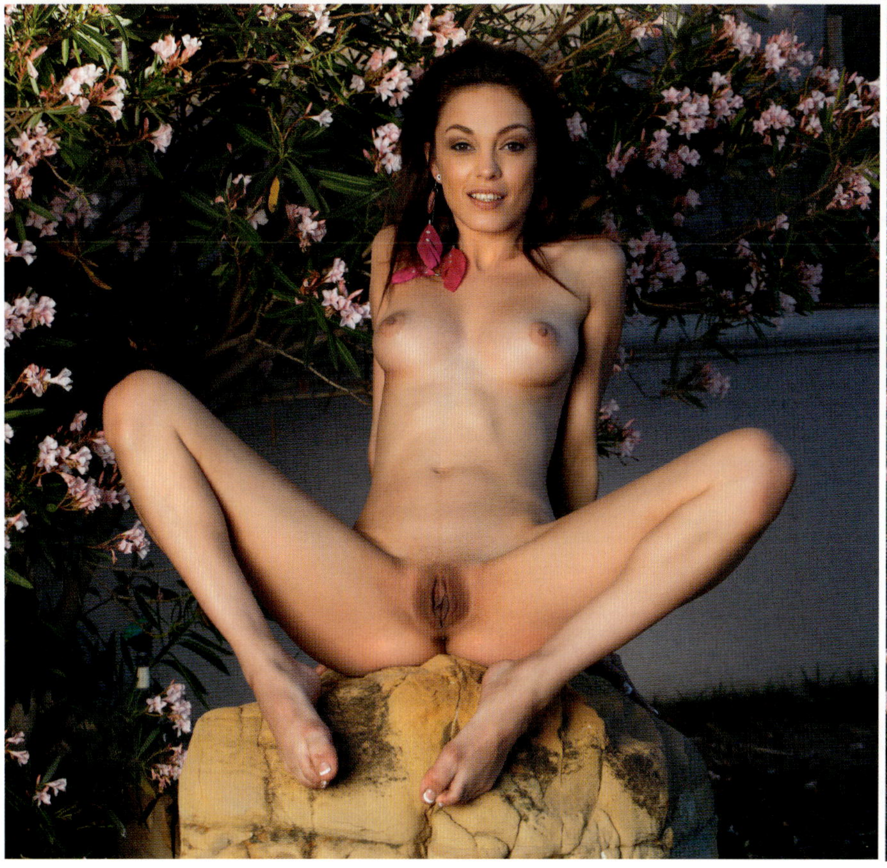

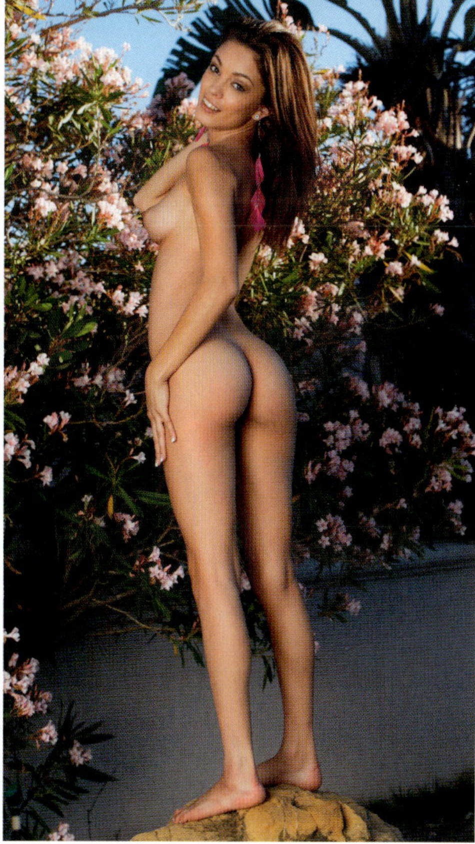

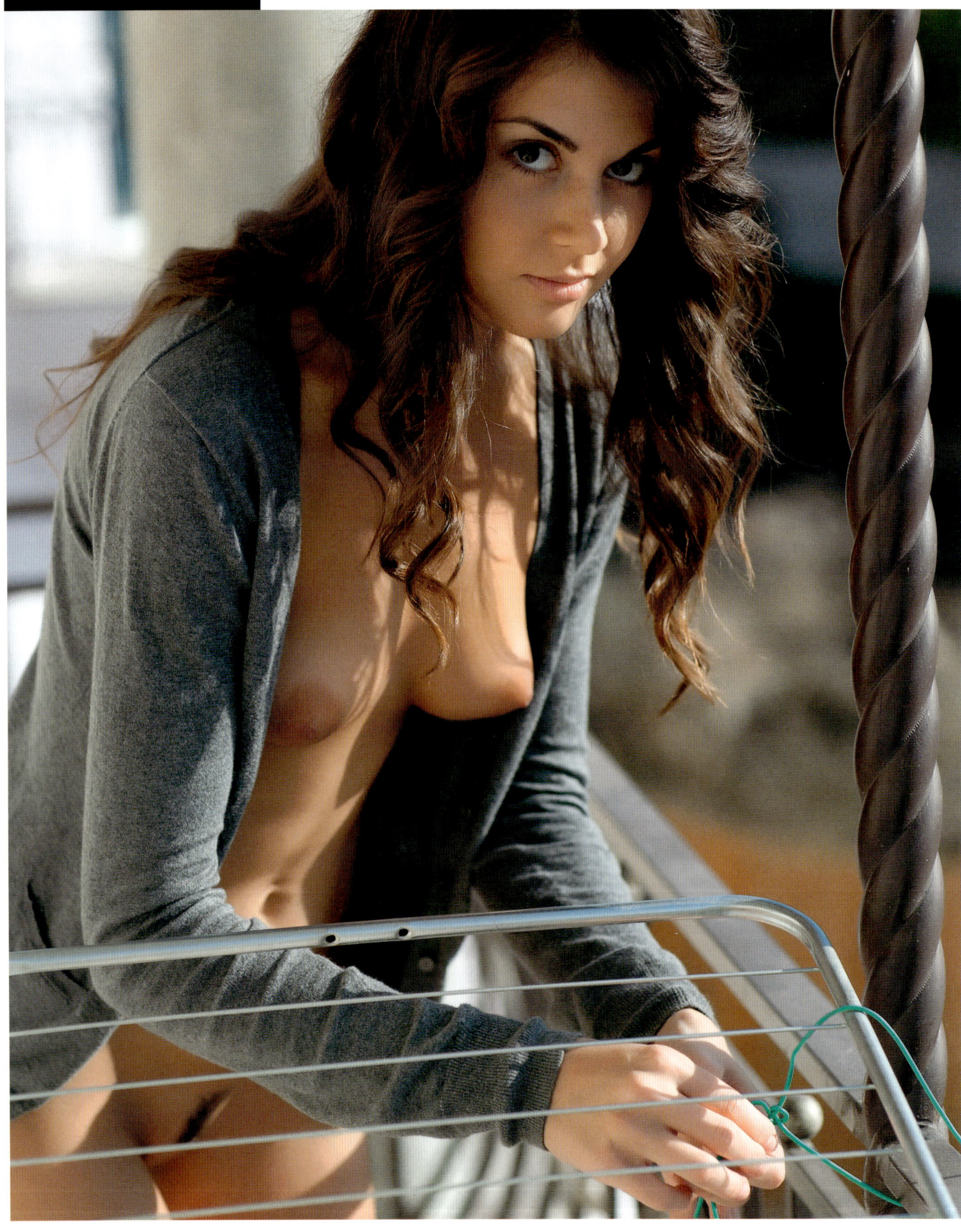

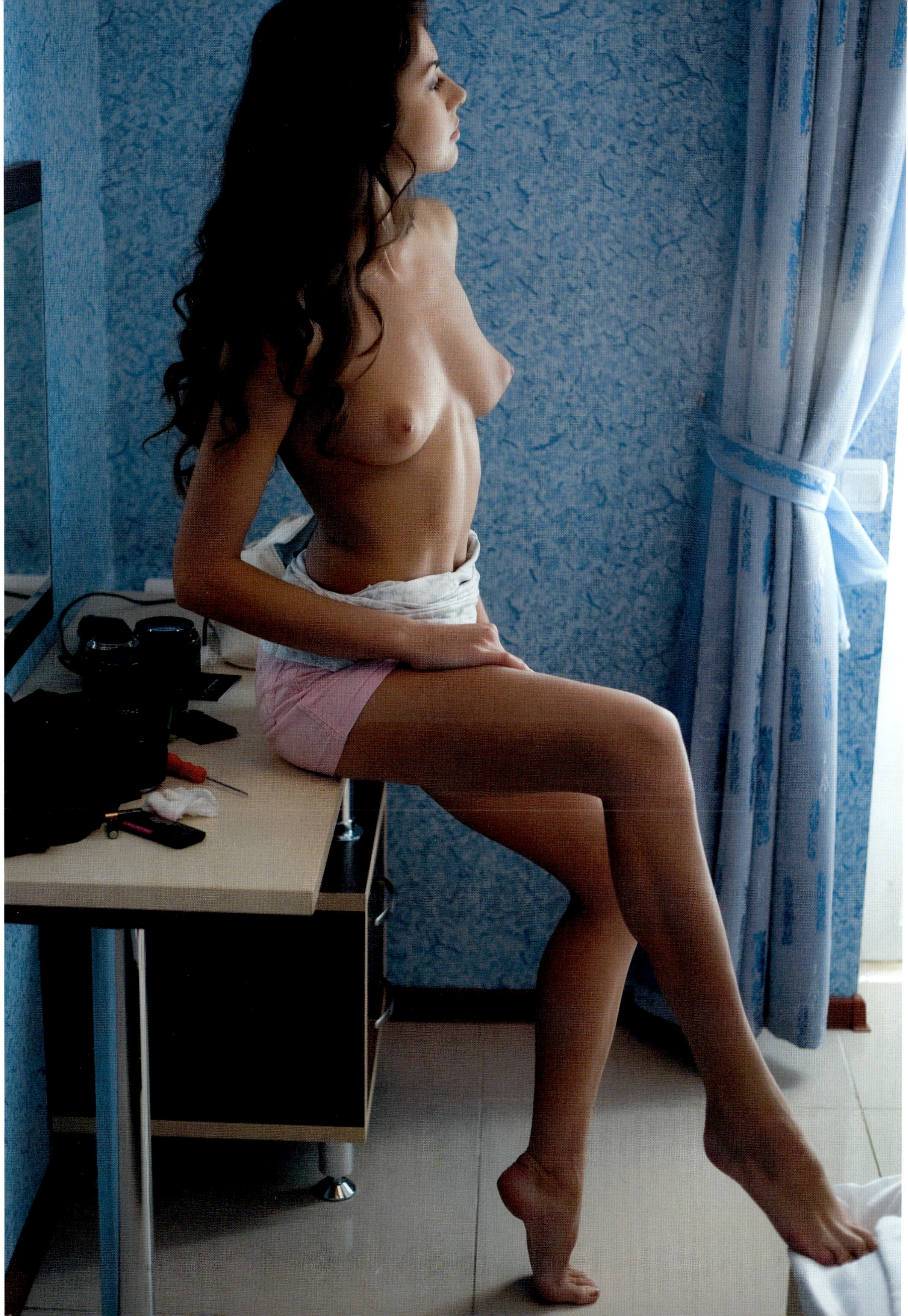

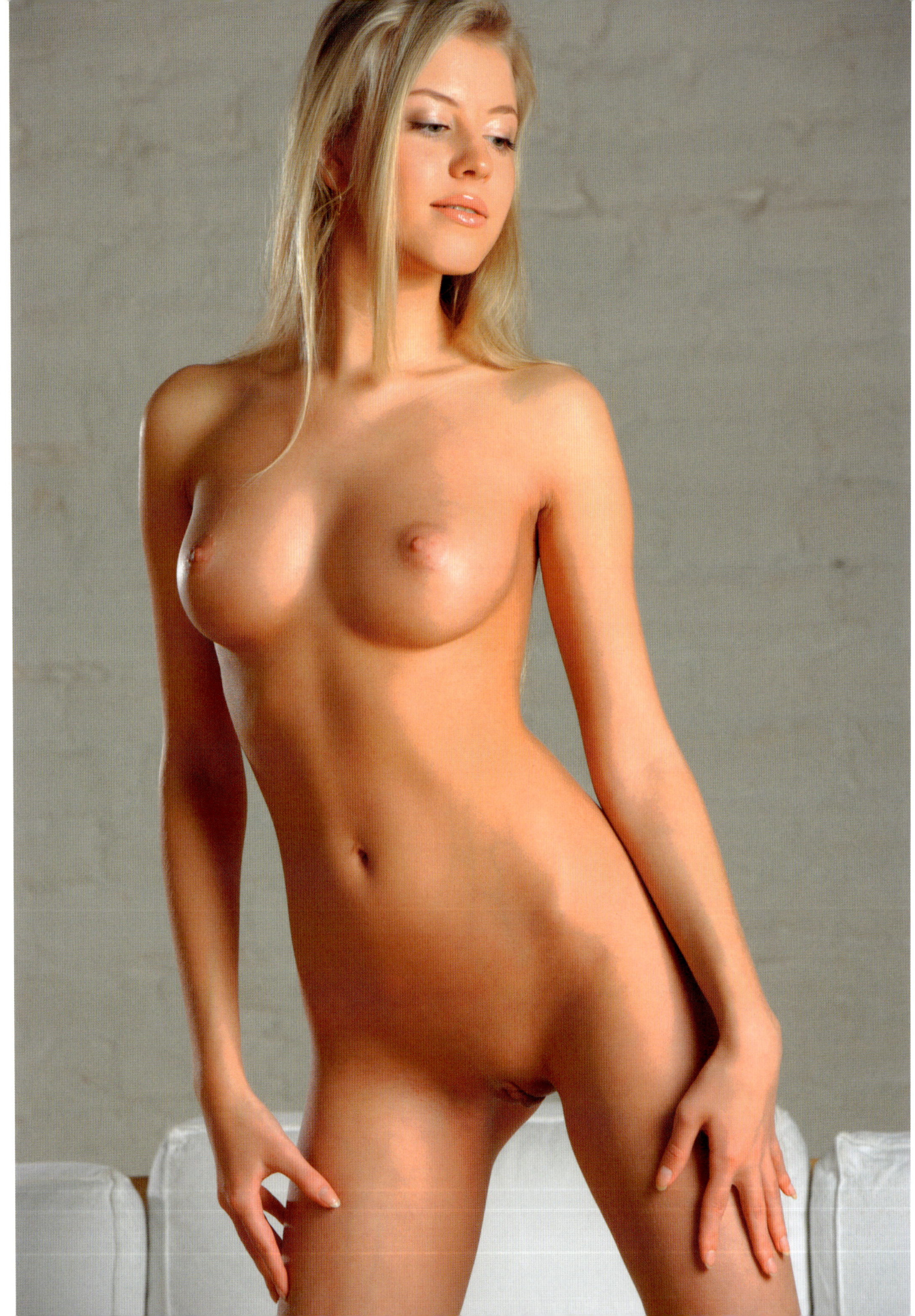

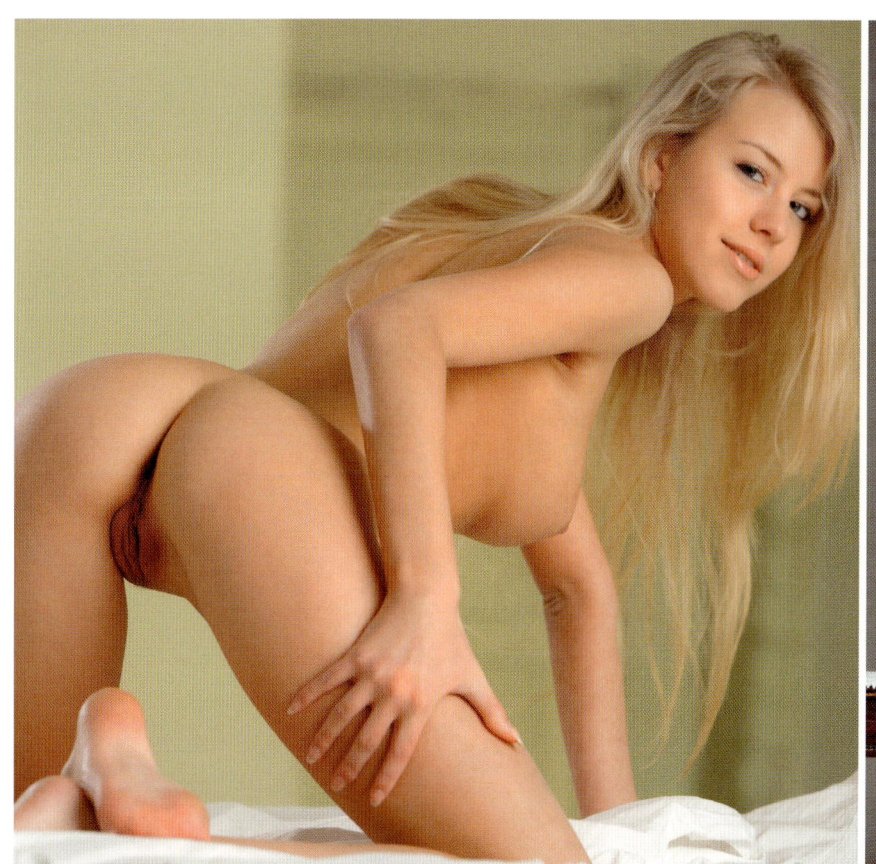

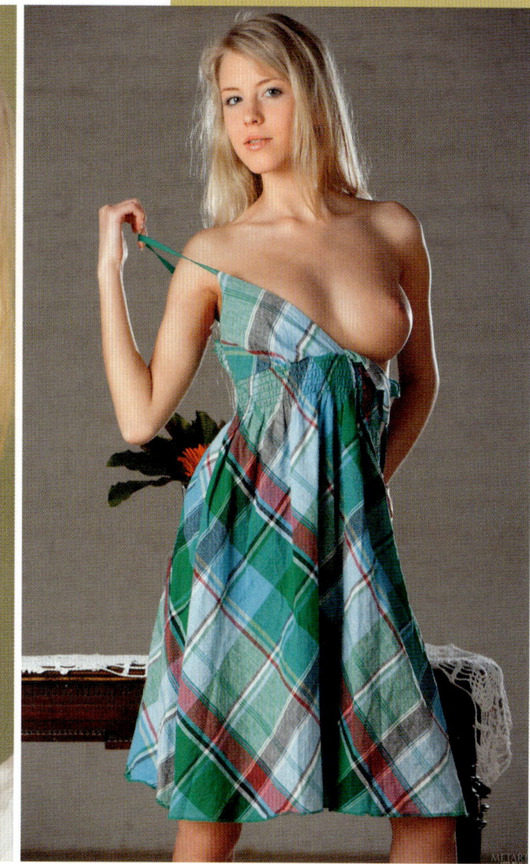

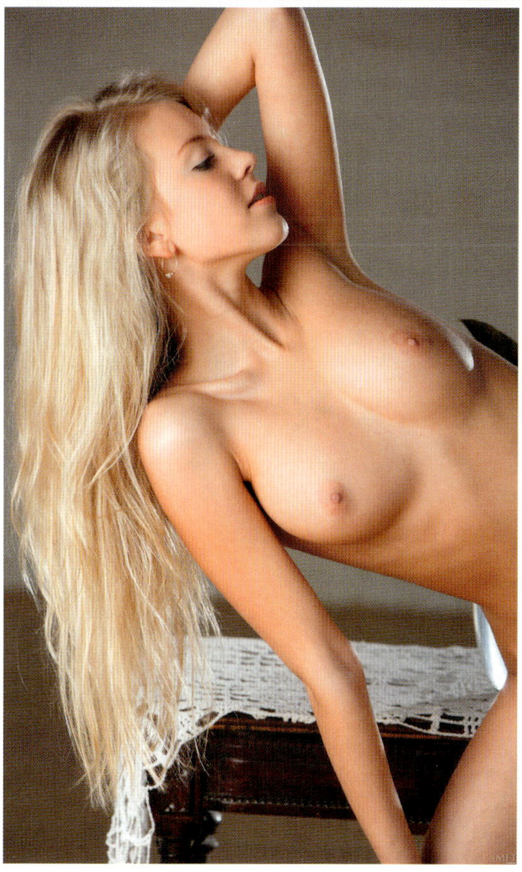

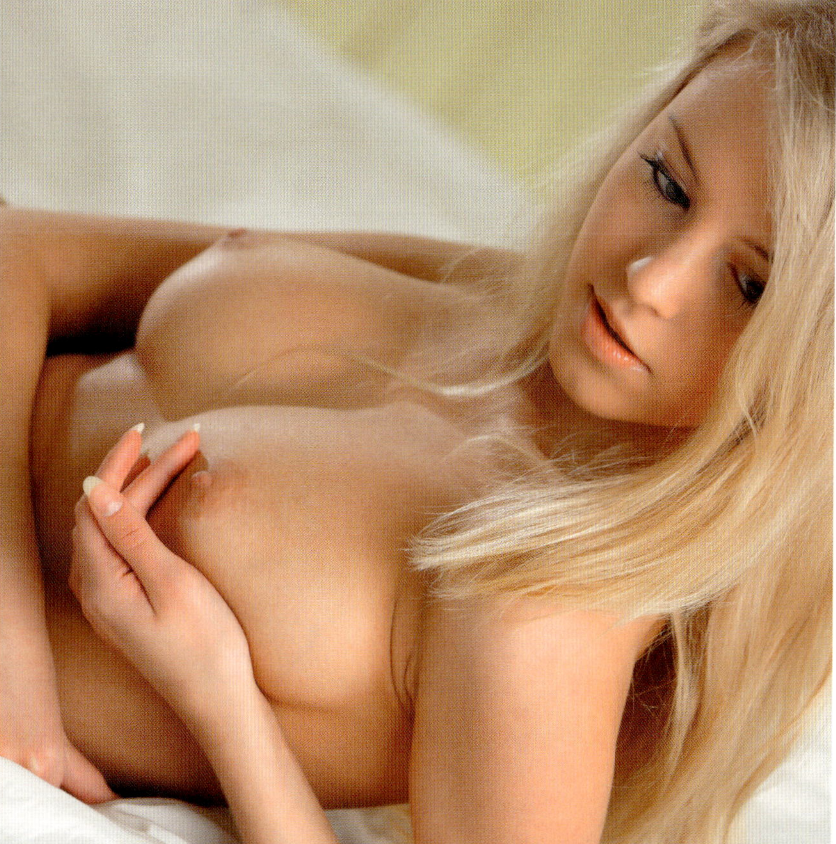

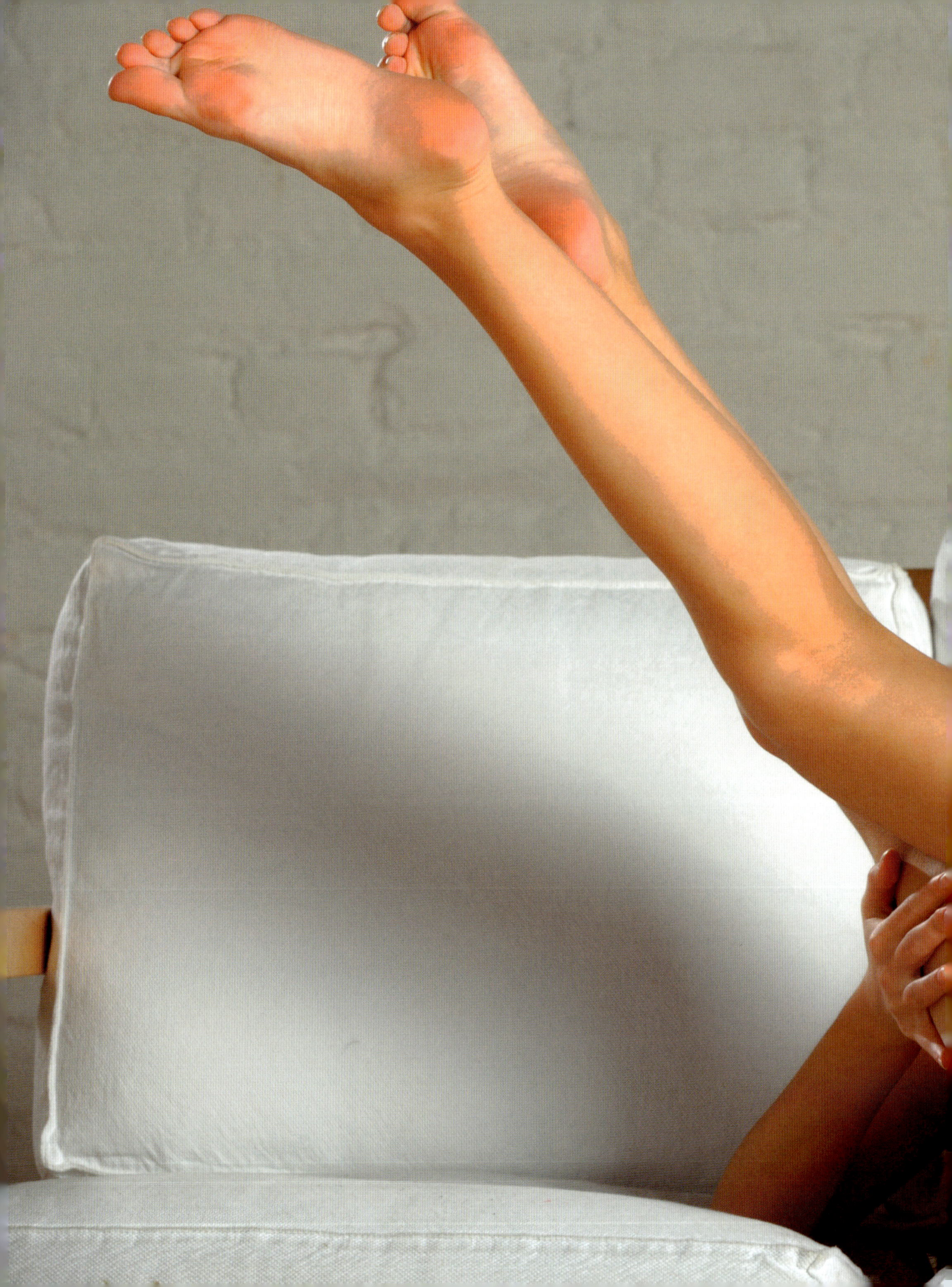

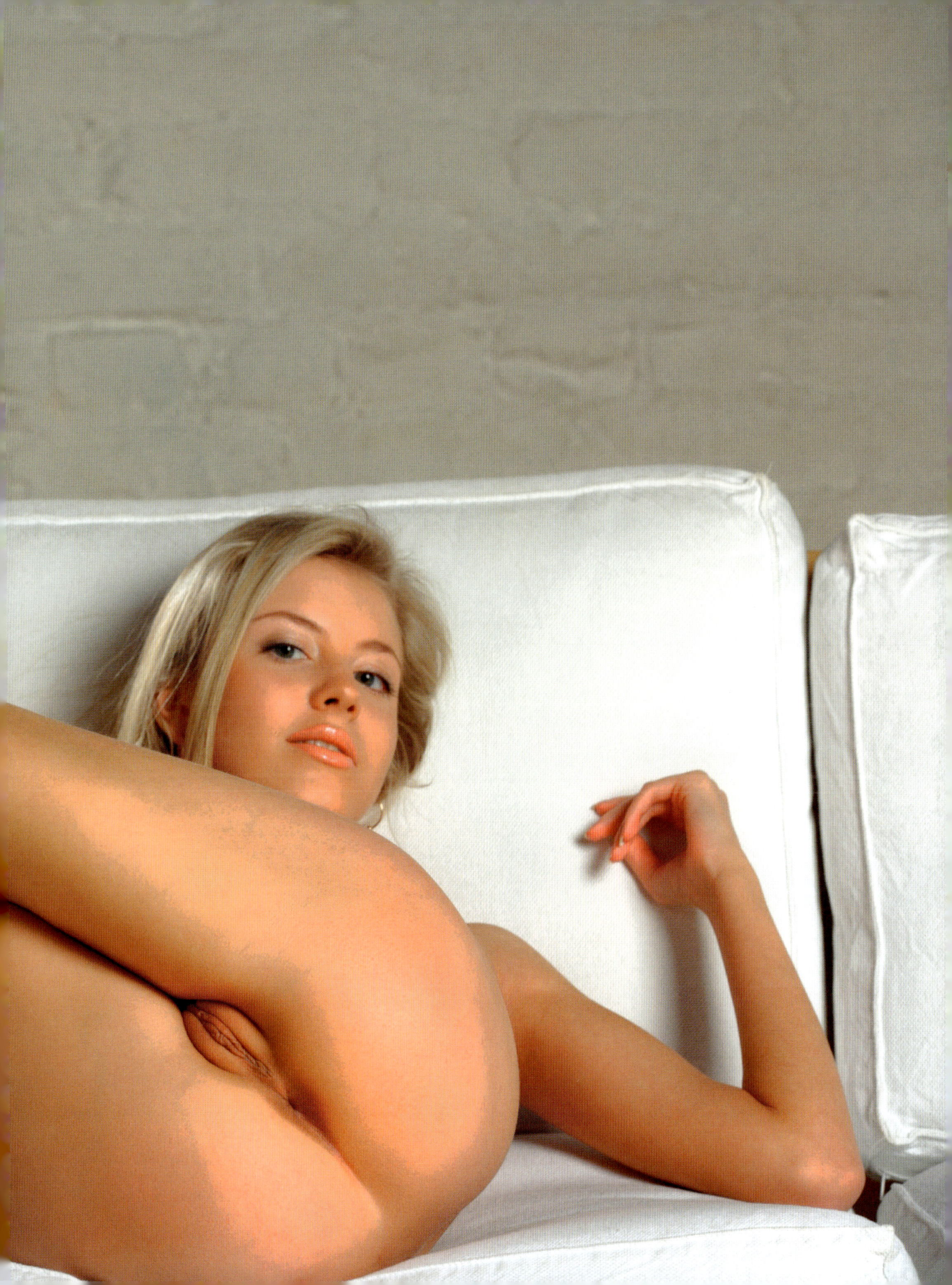

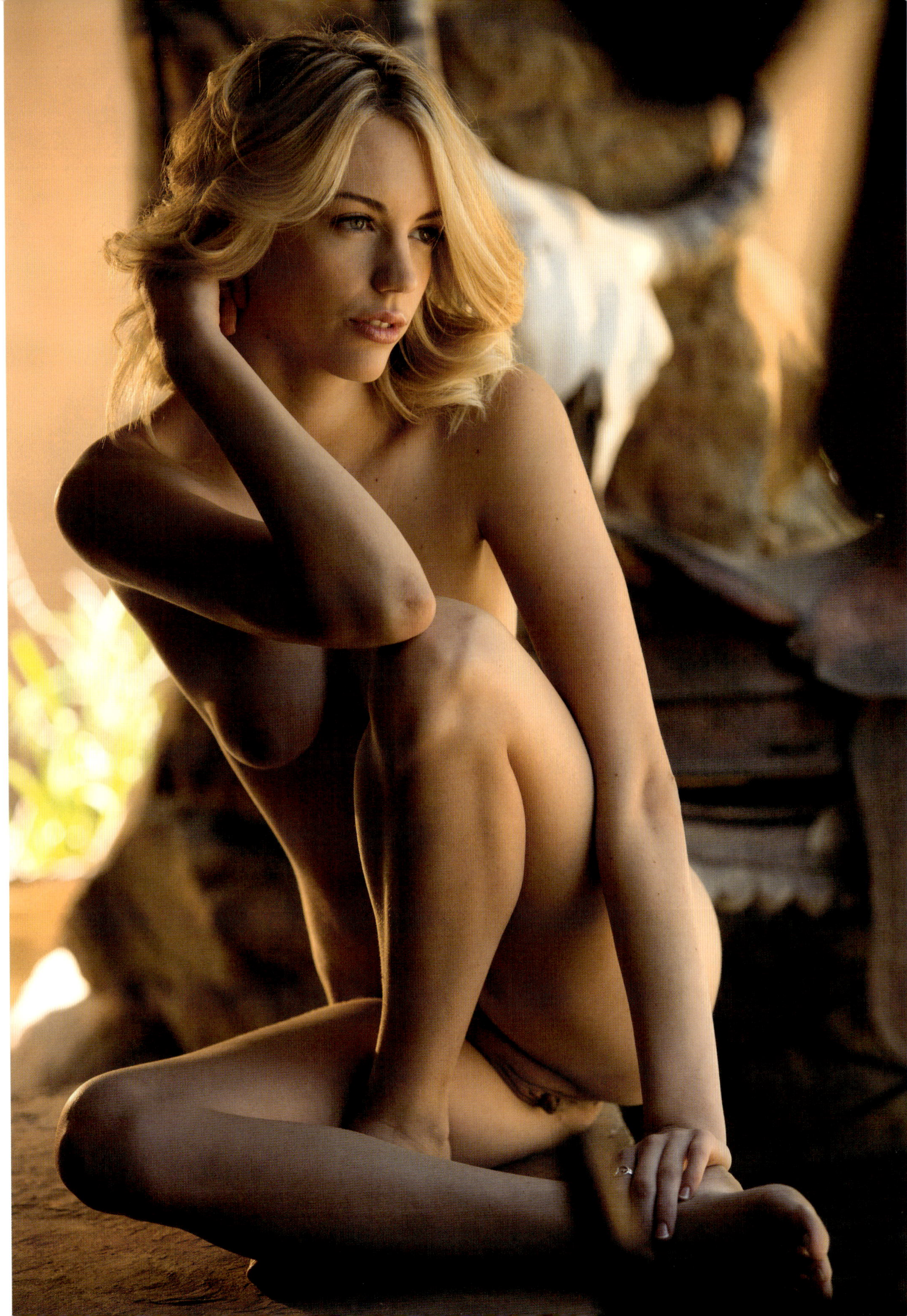

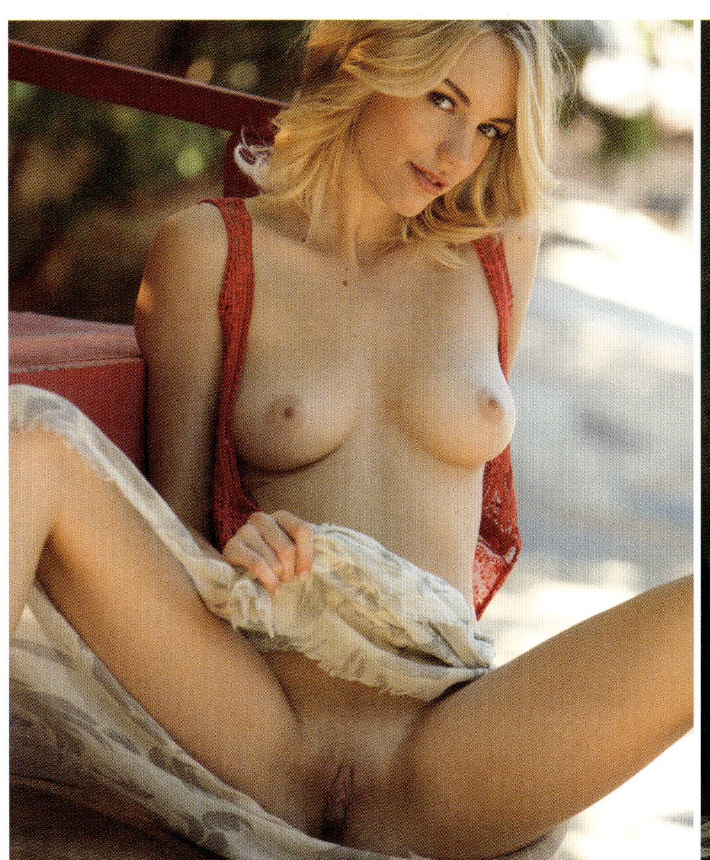

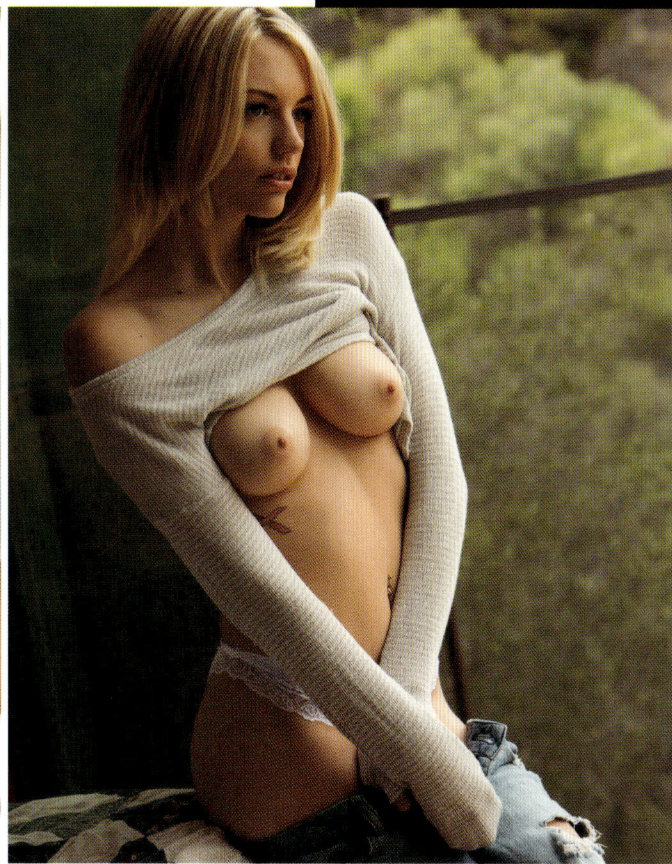

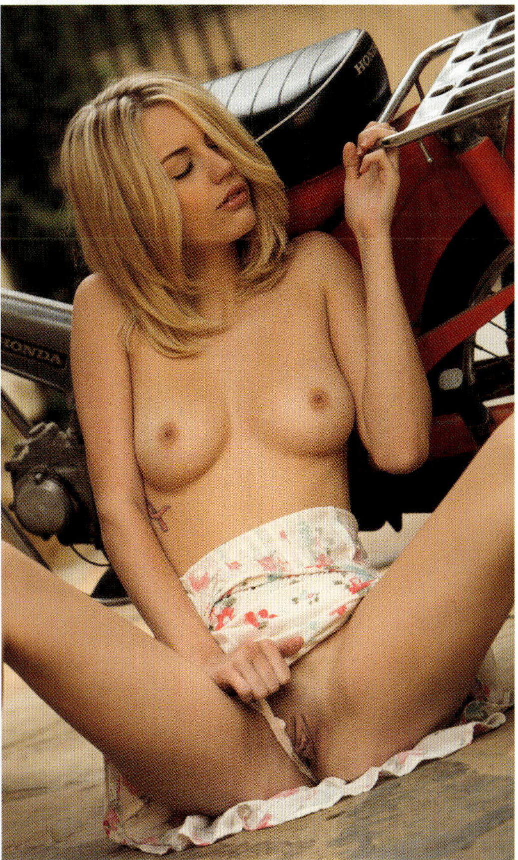
HONDA

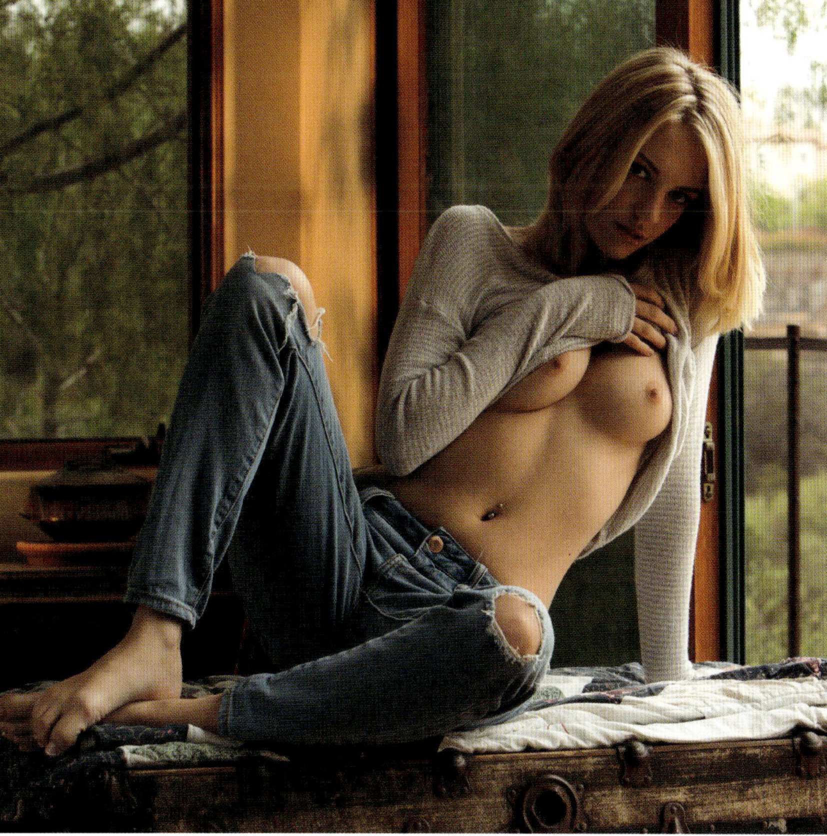

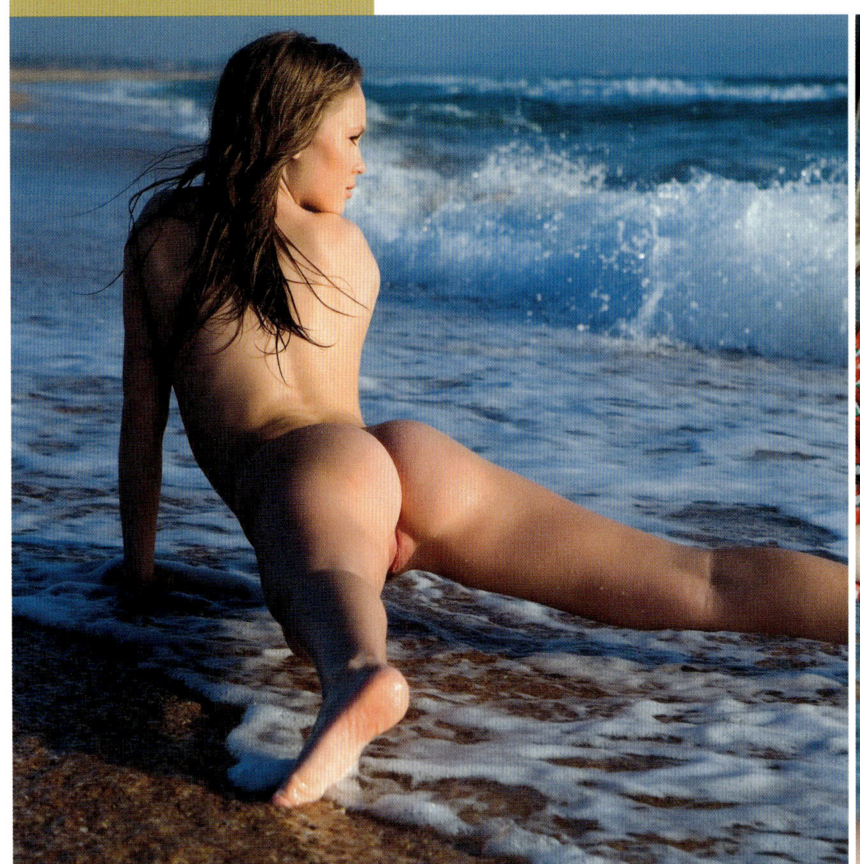

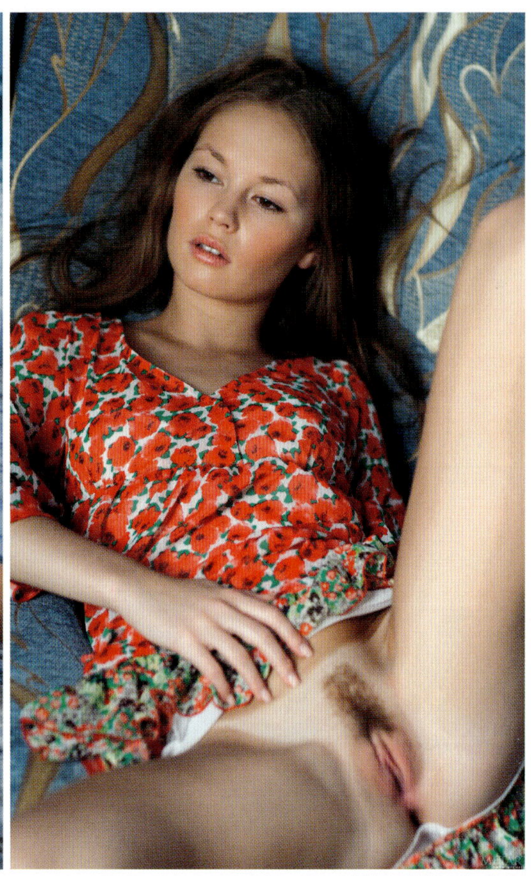

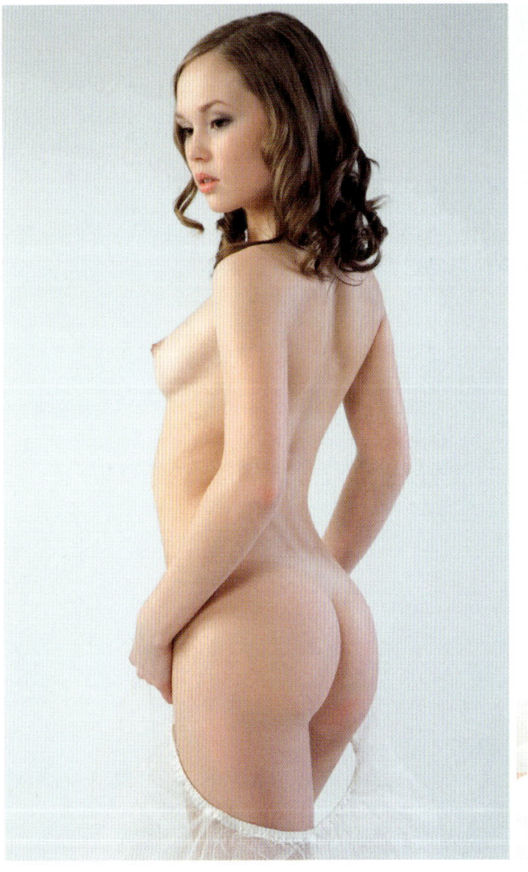

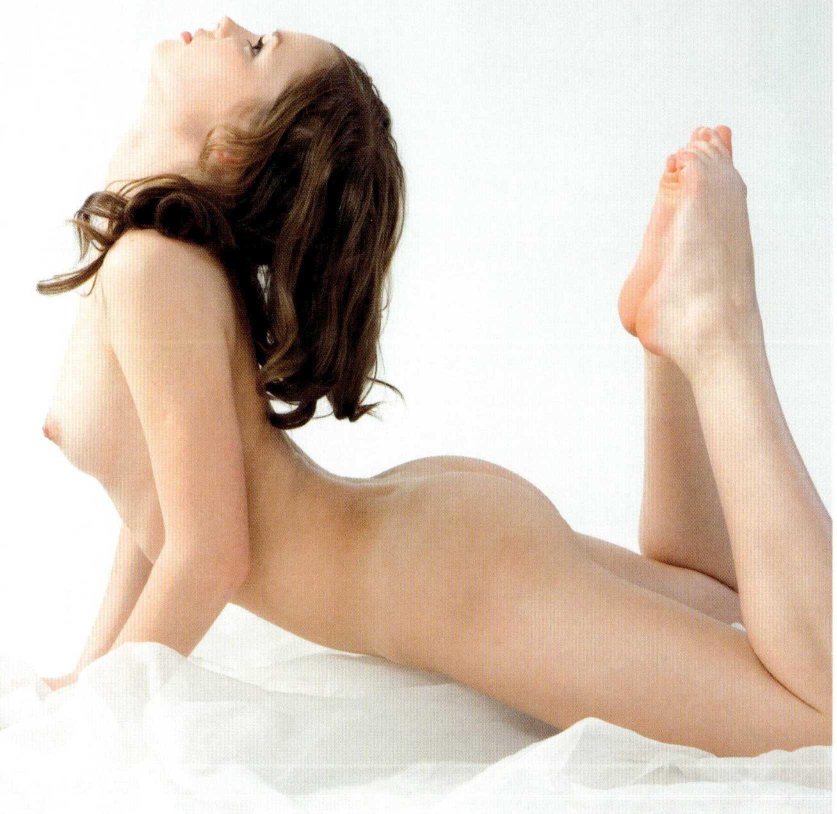

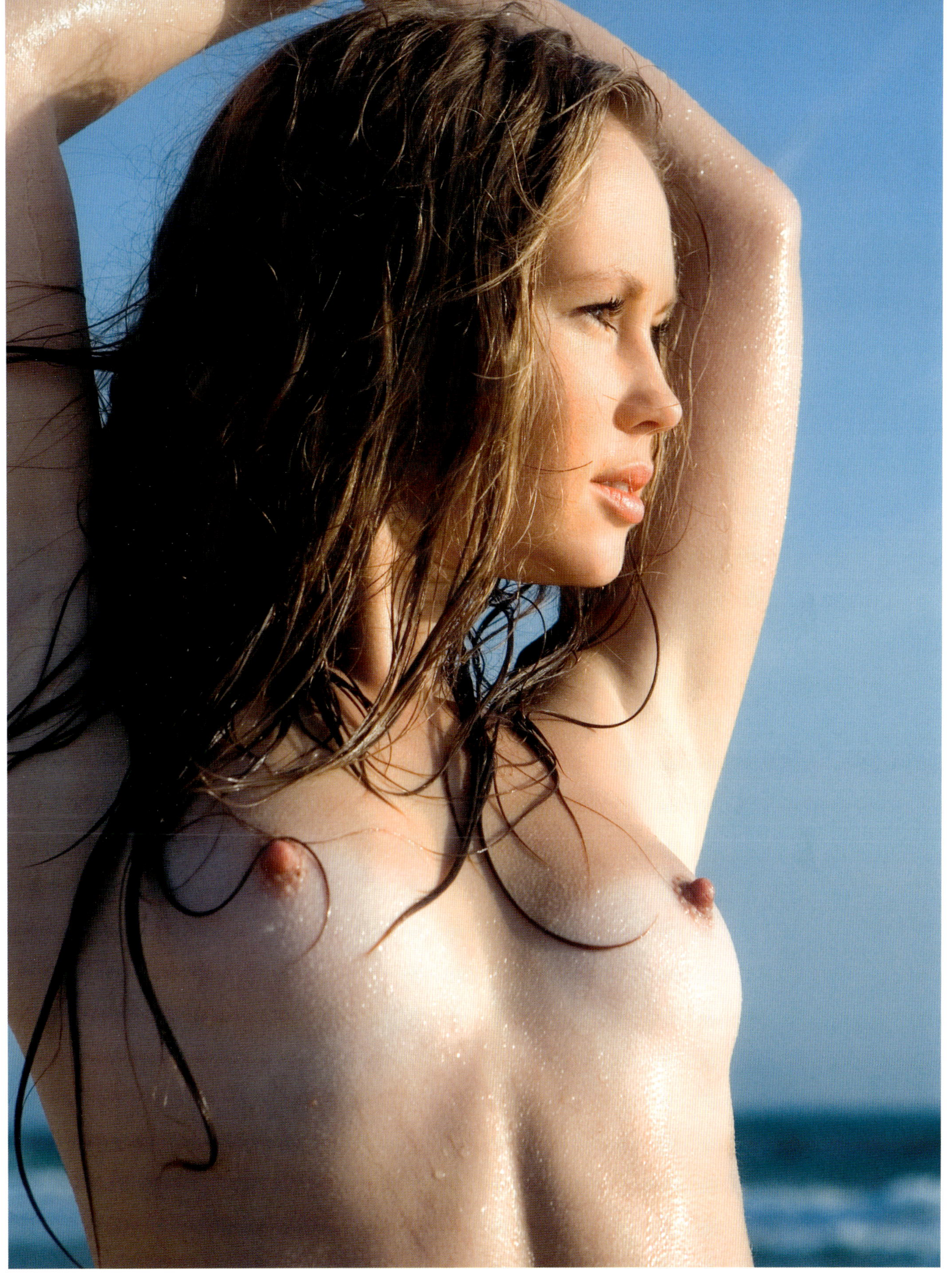

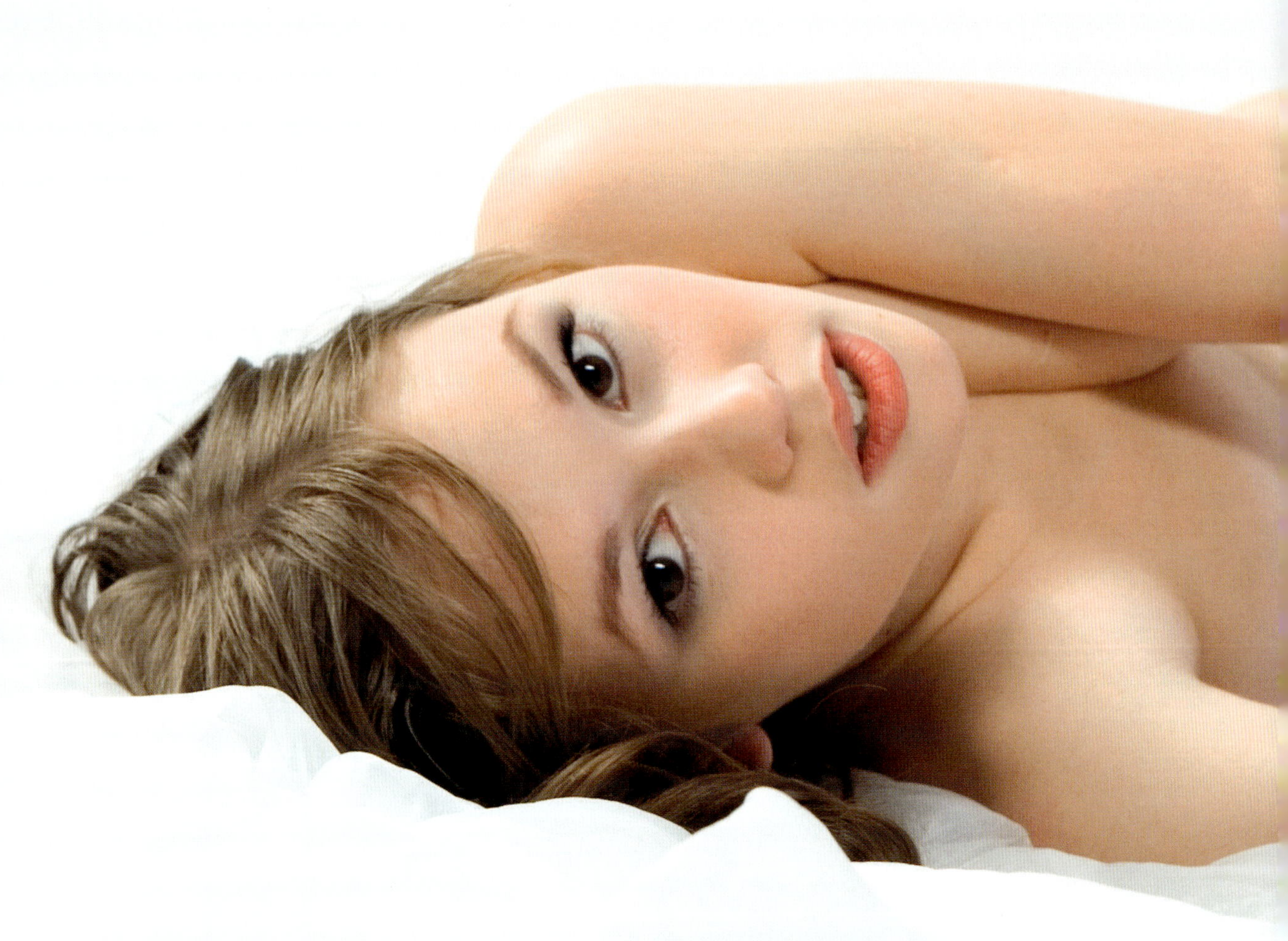

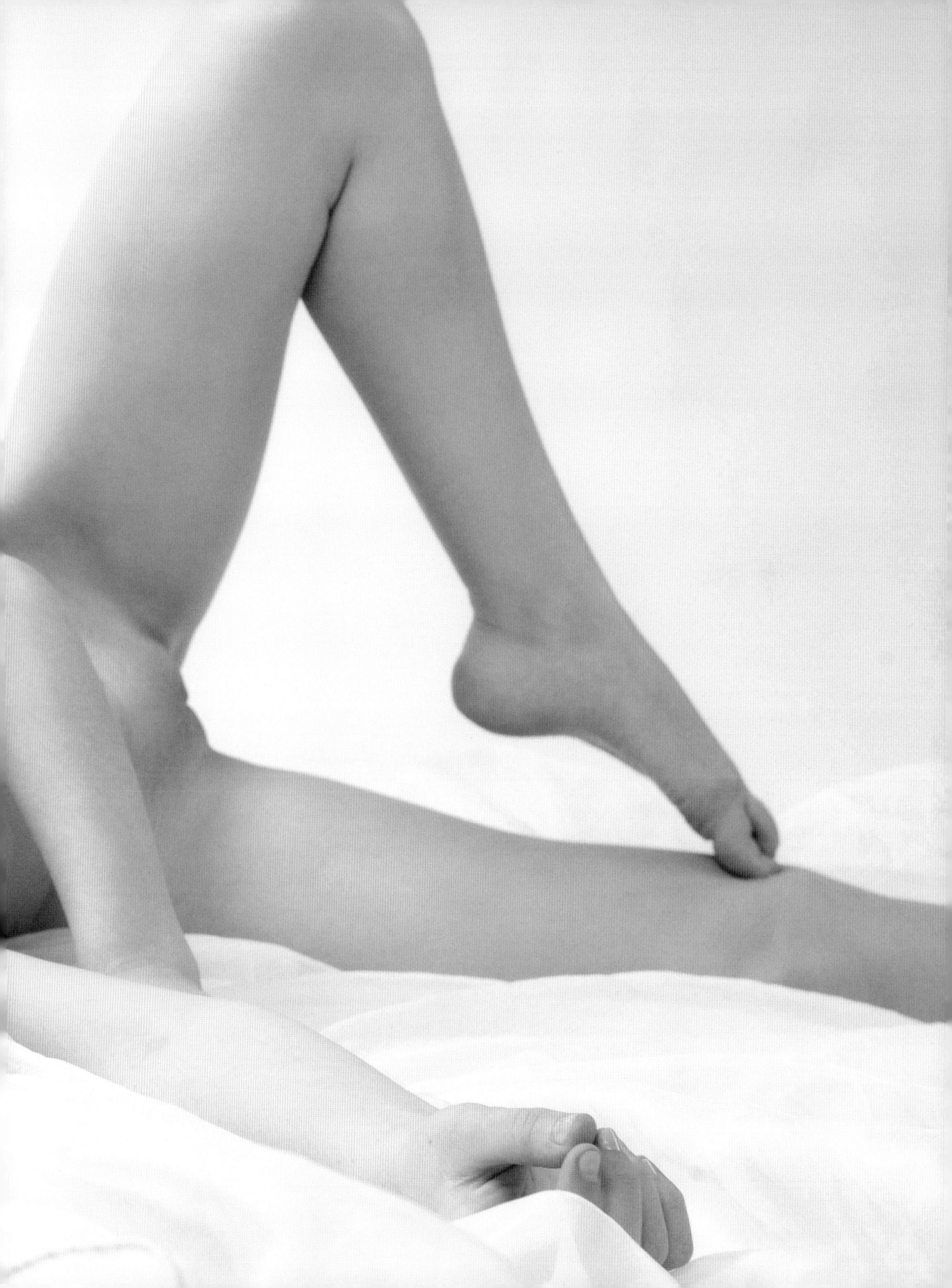

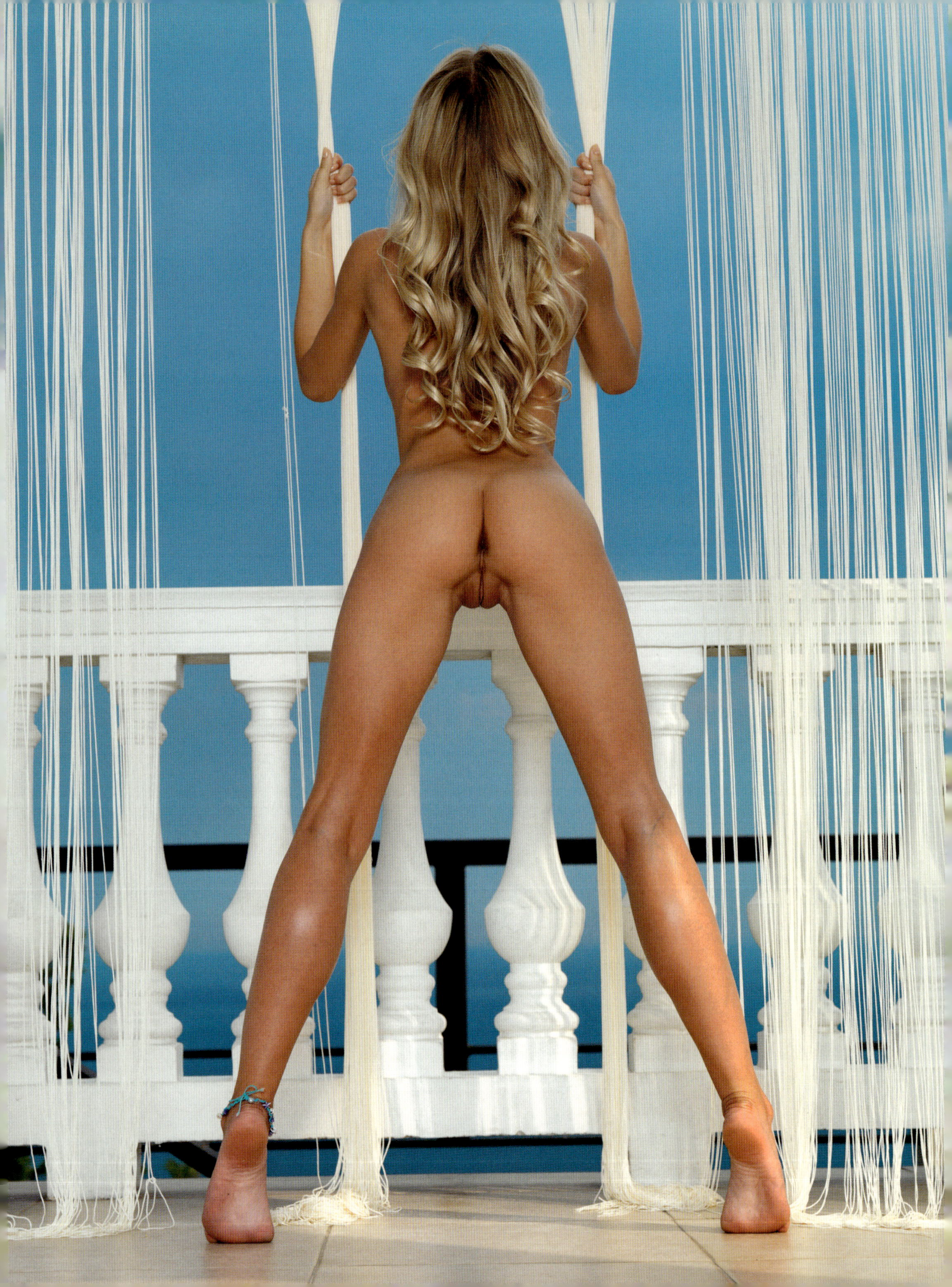

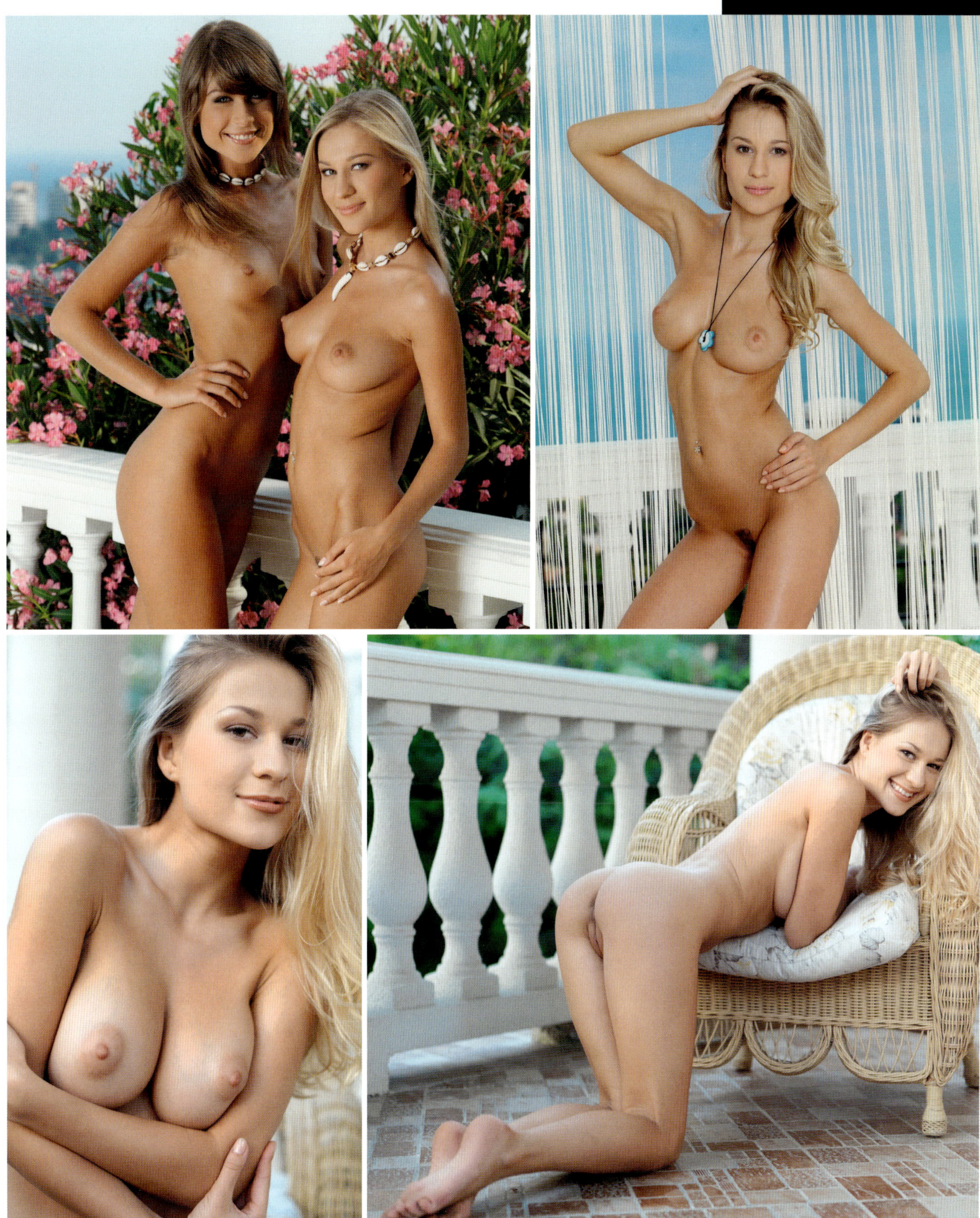

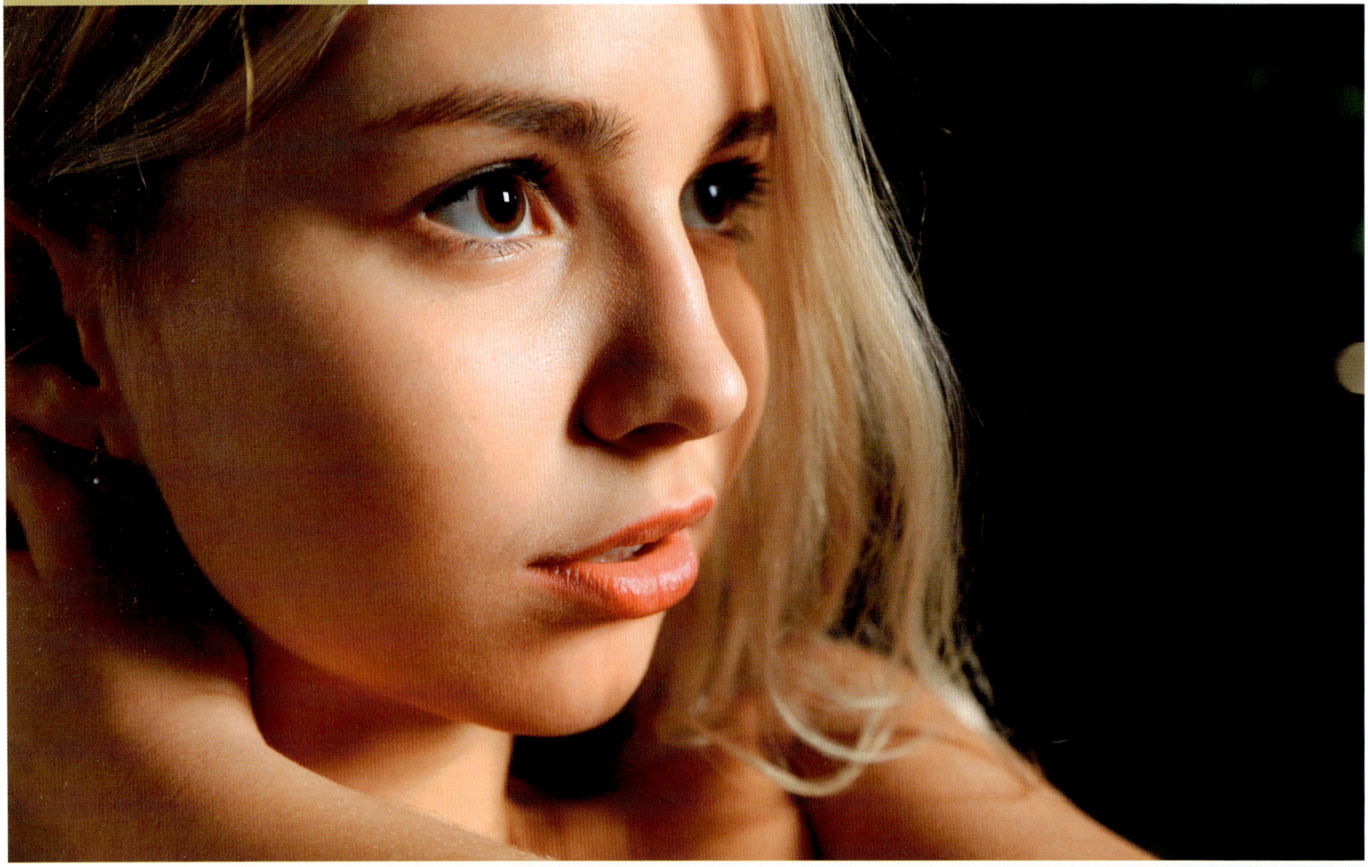

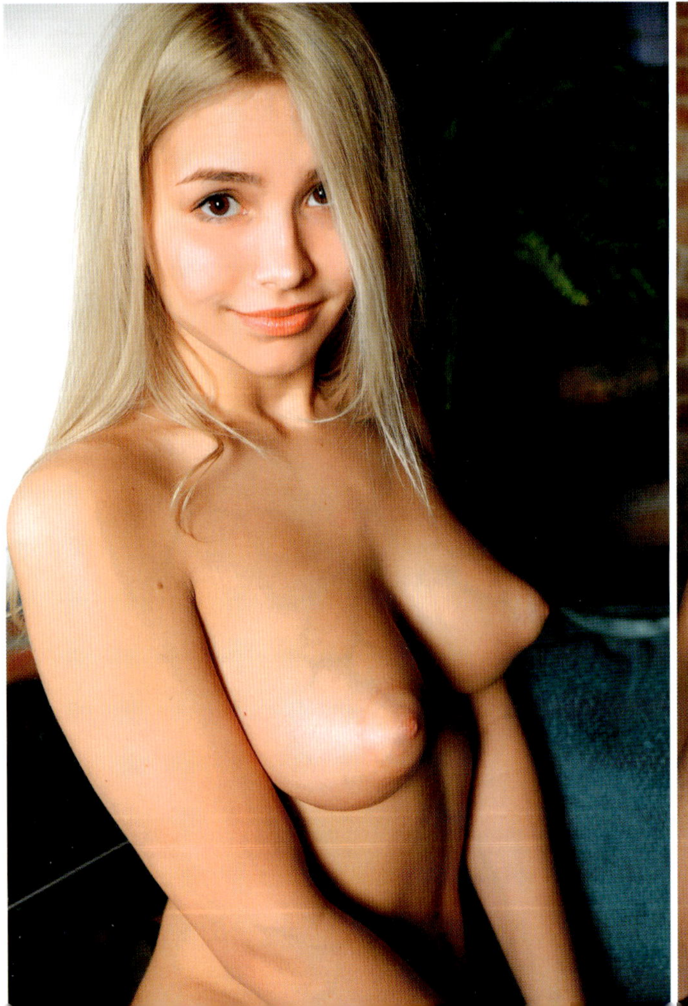

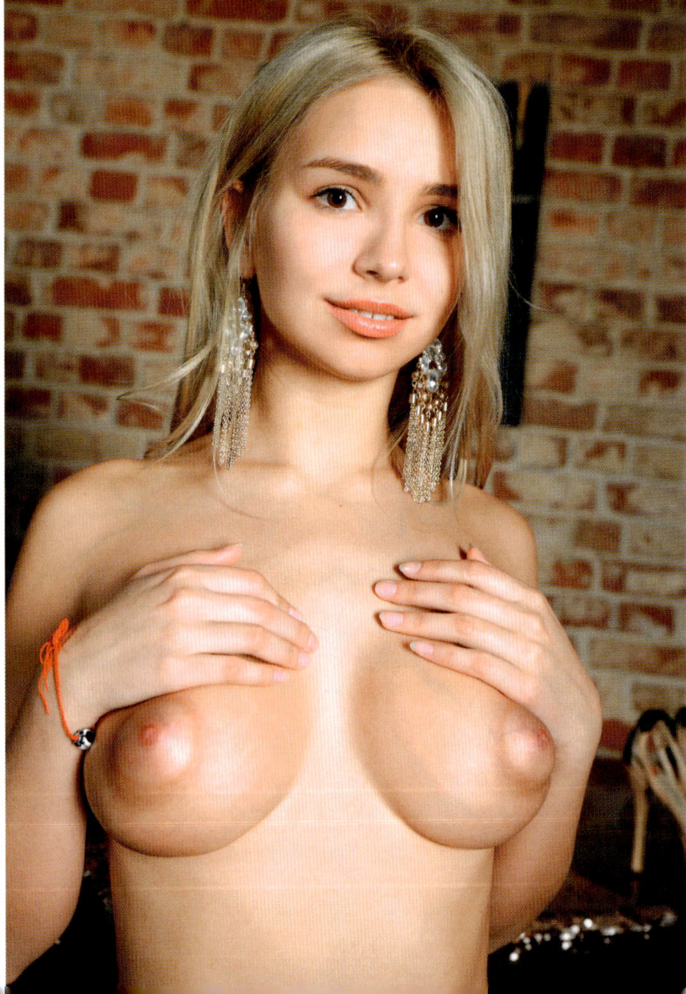

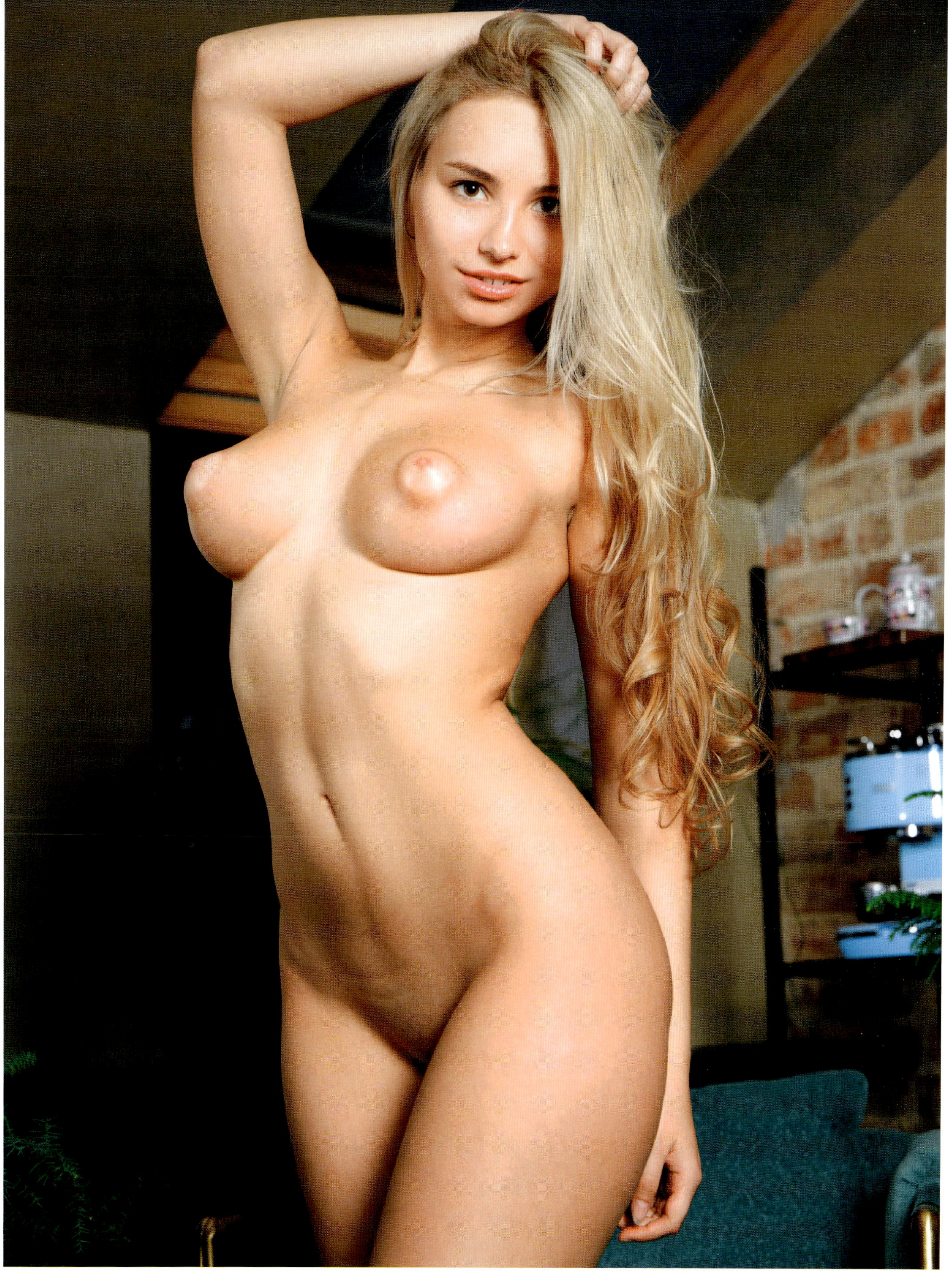

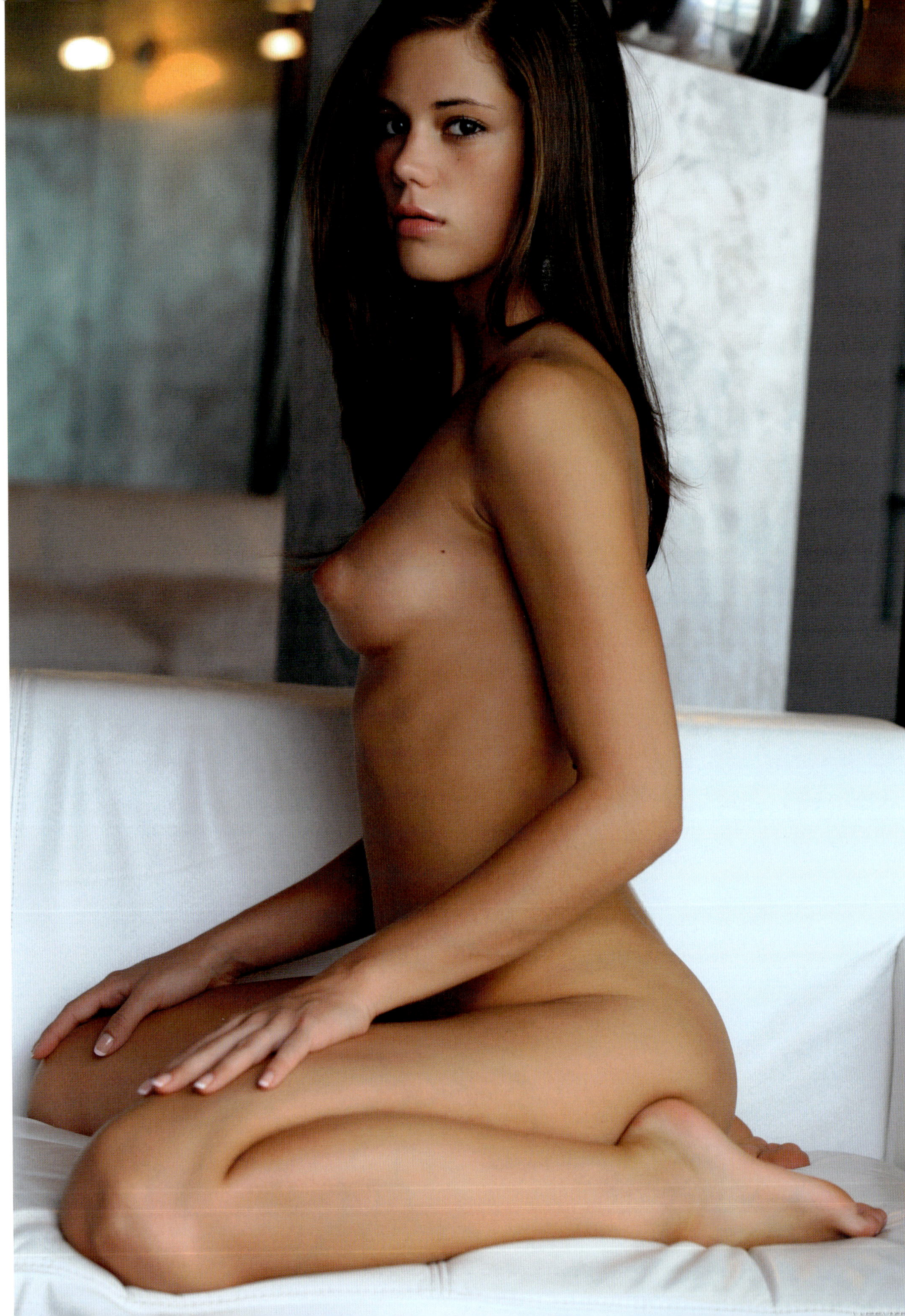

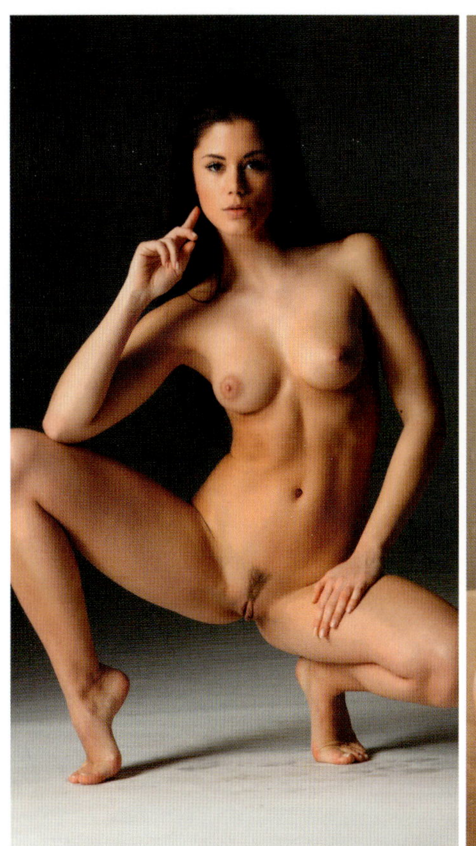

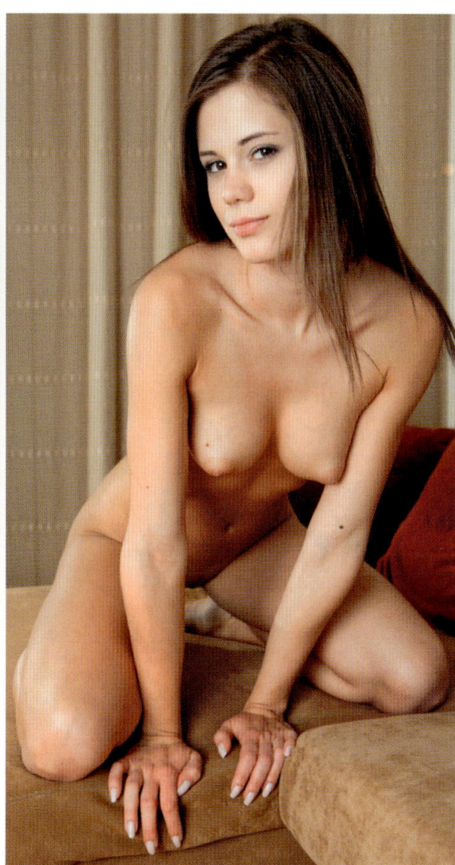

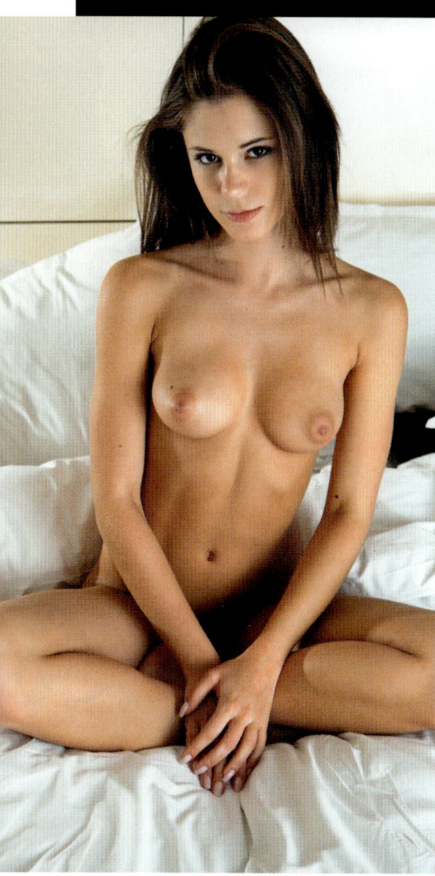

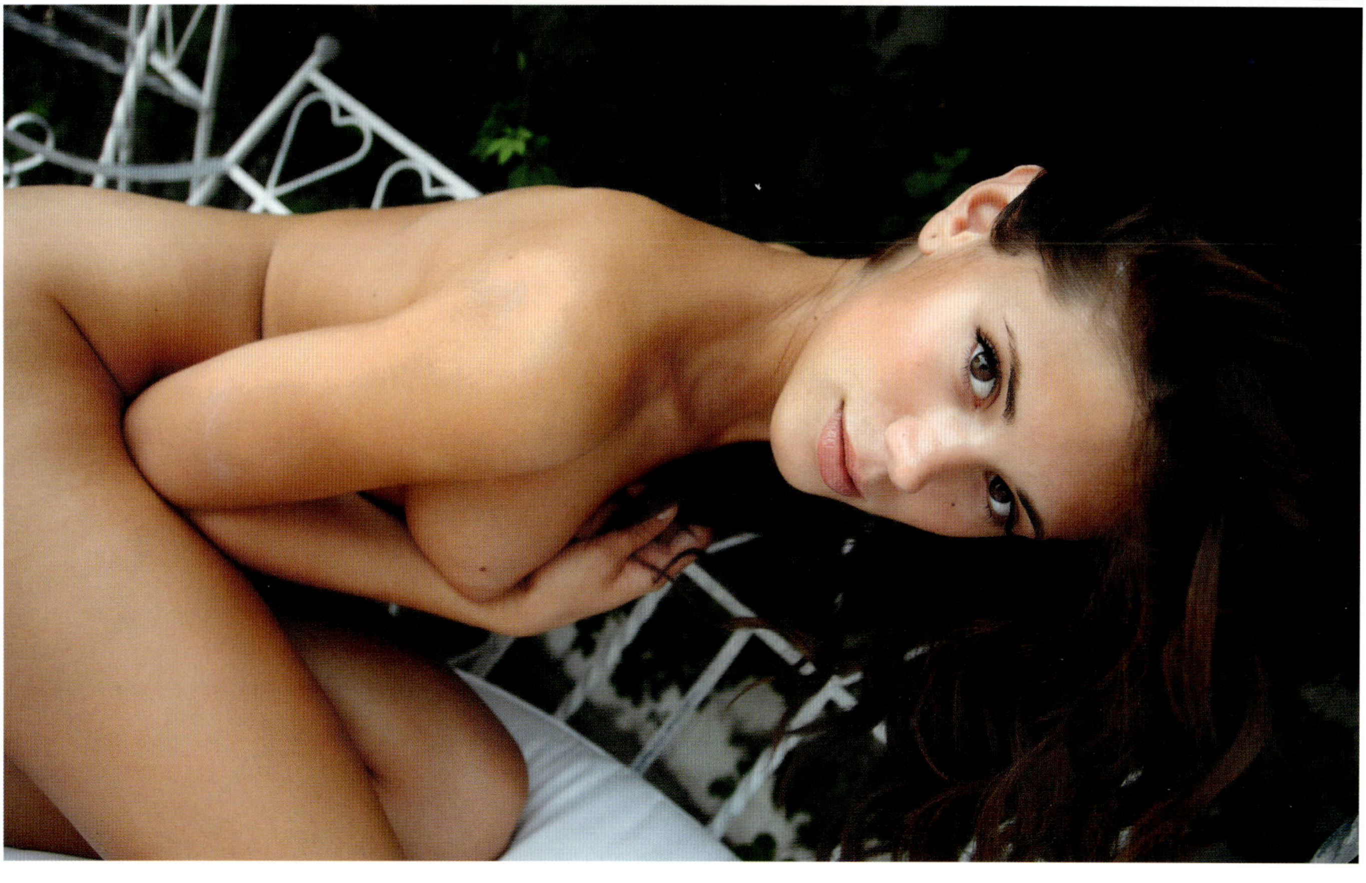

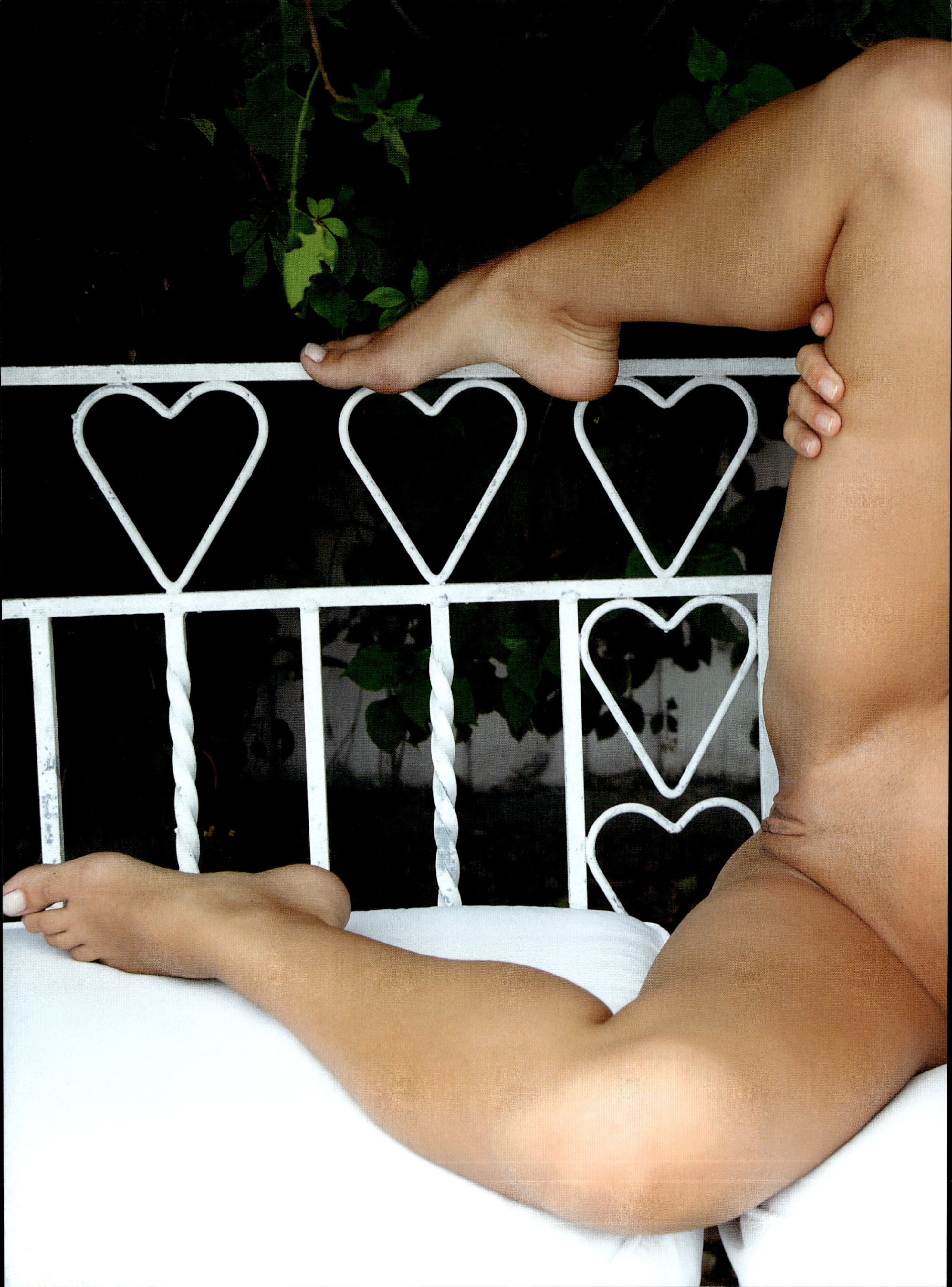

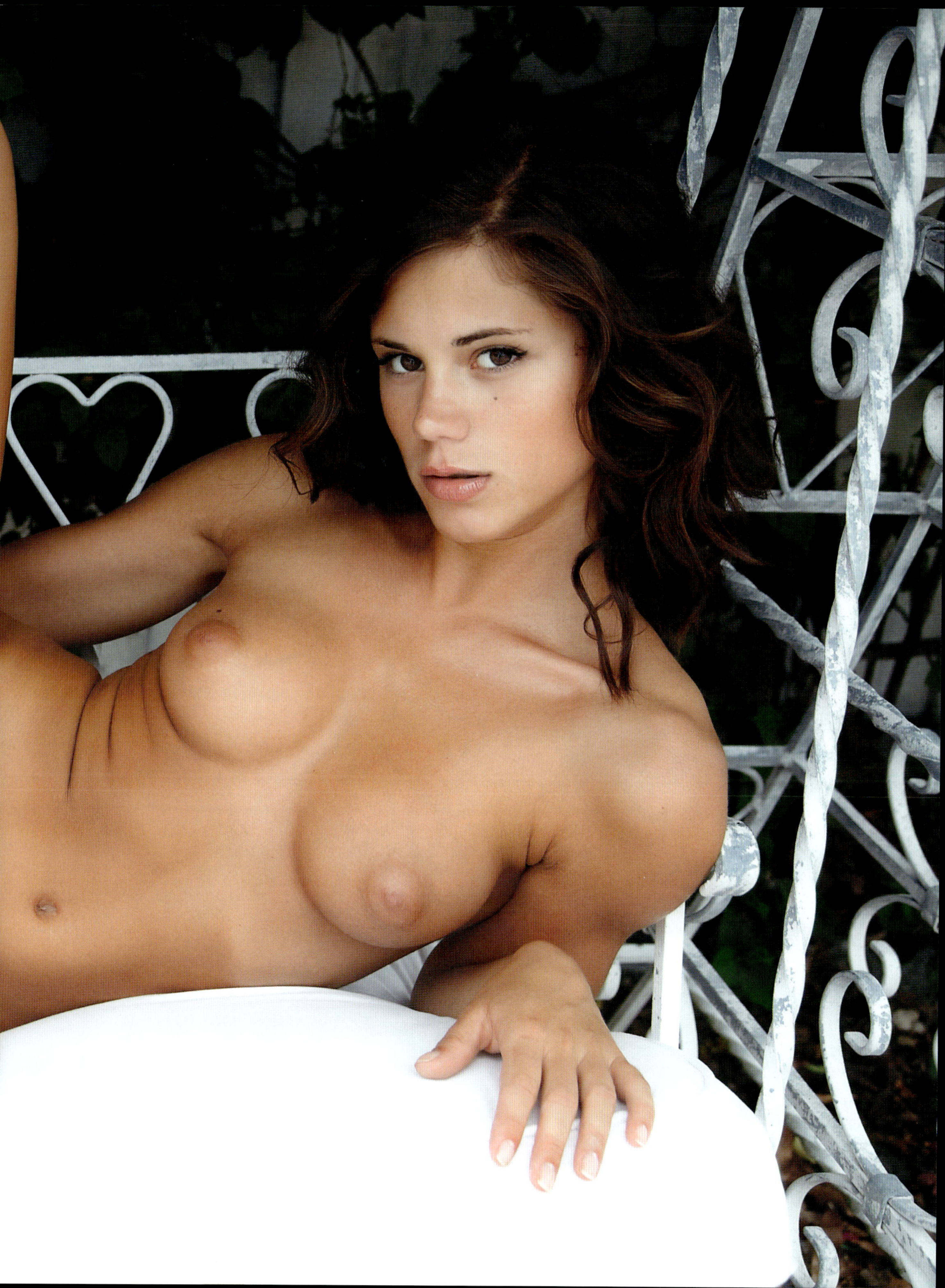

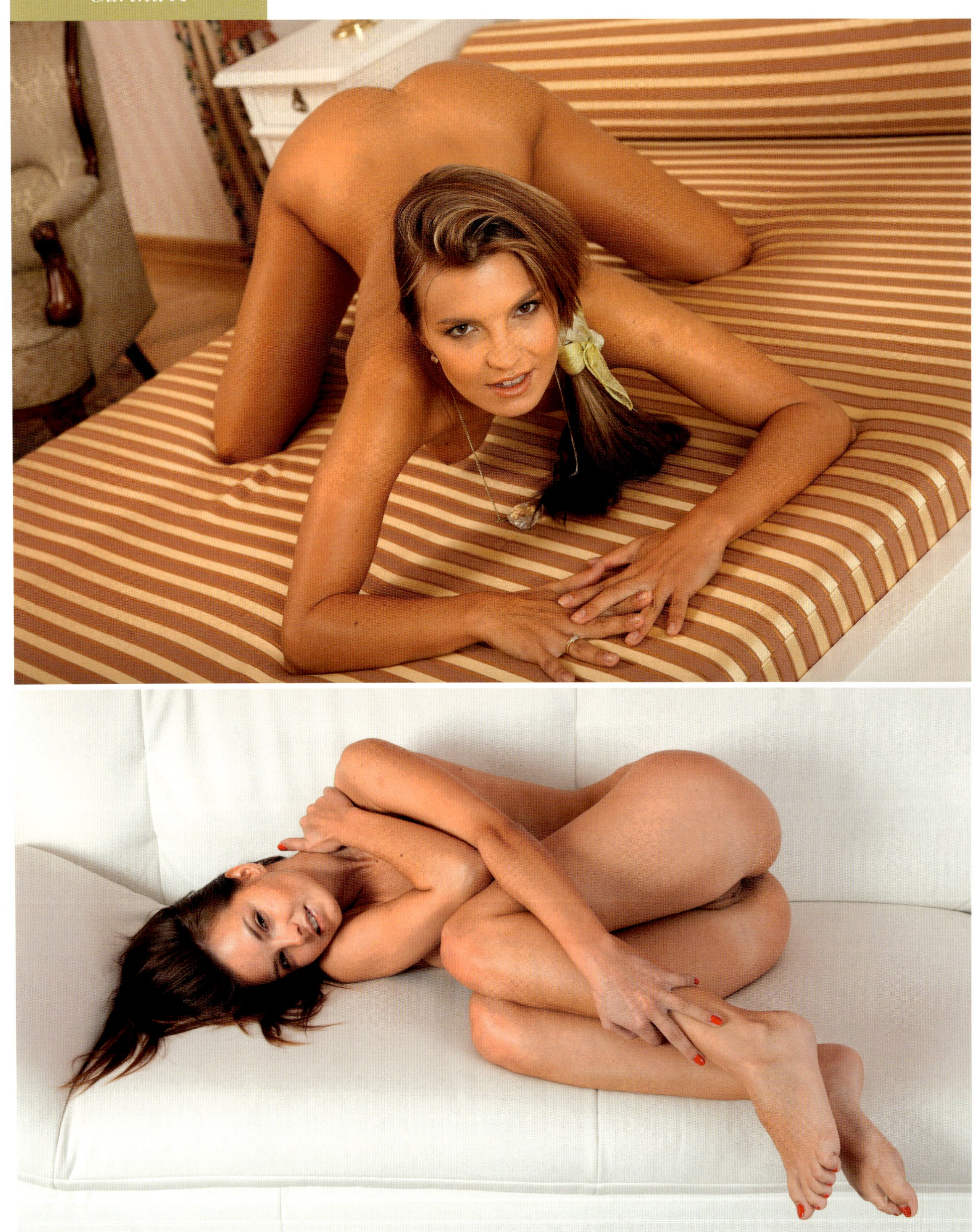

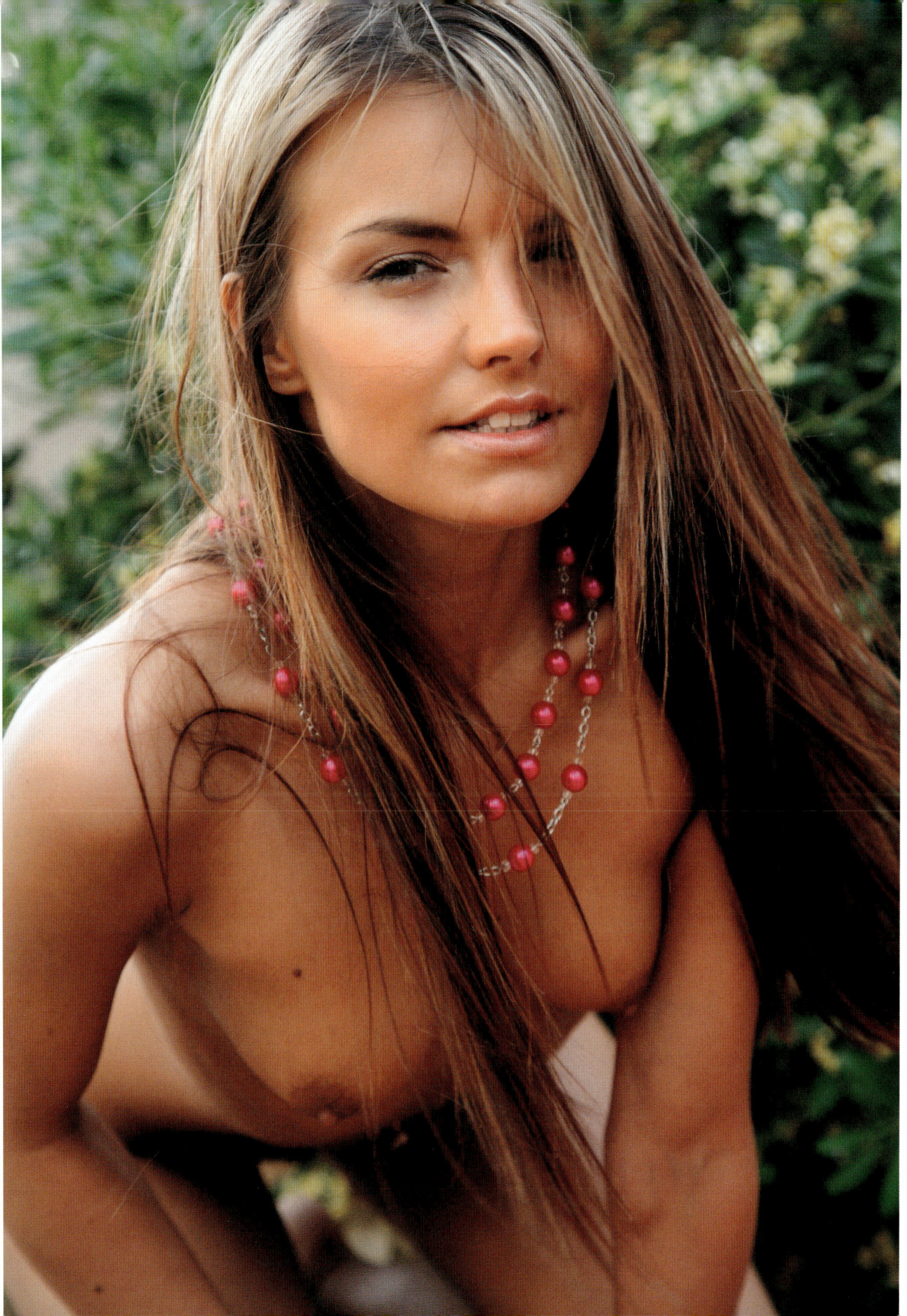

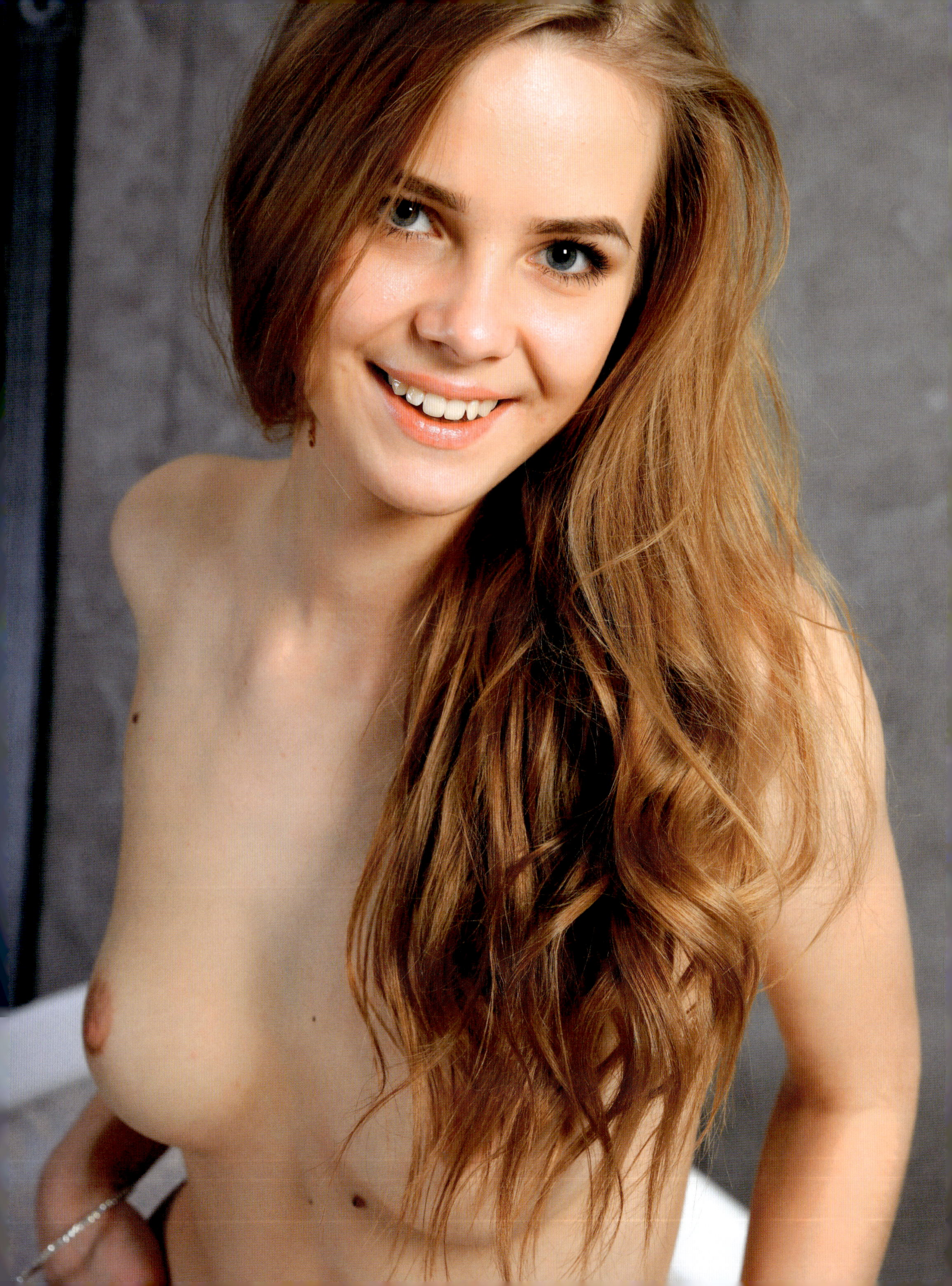

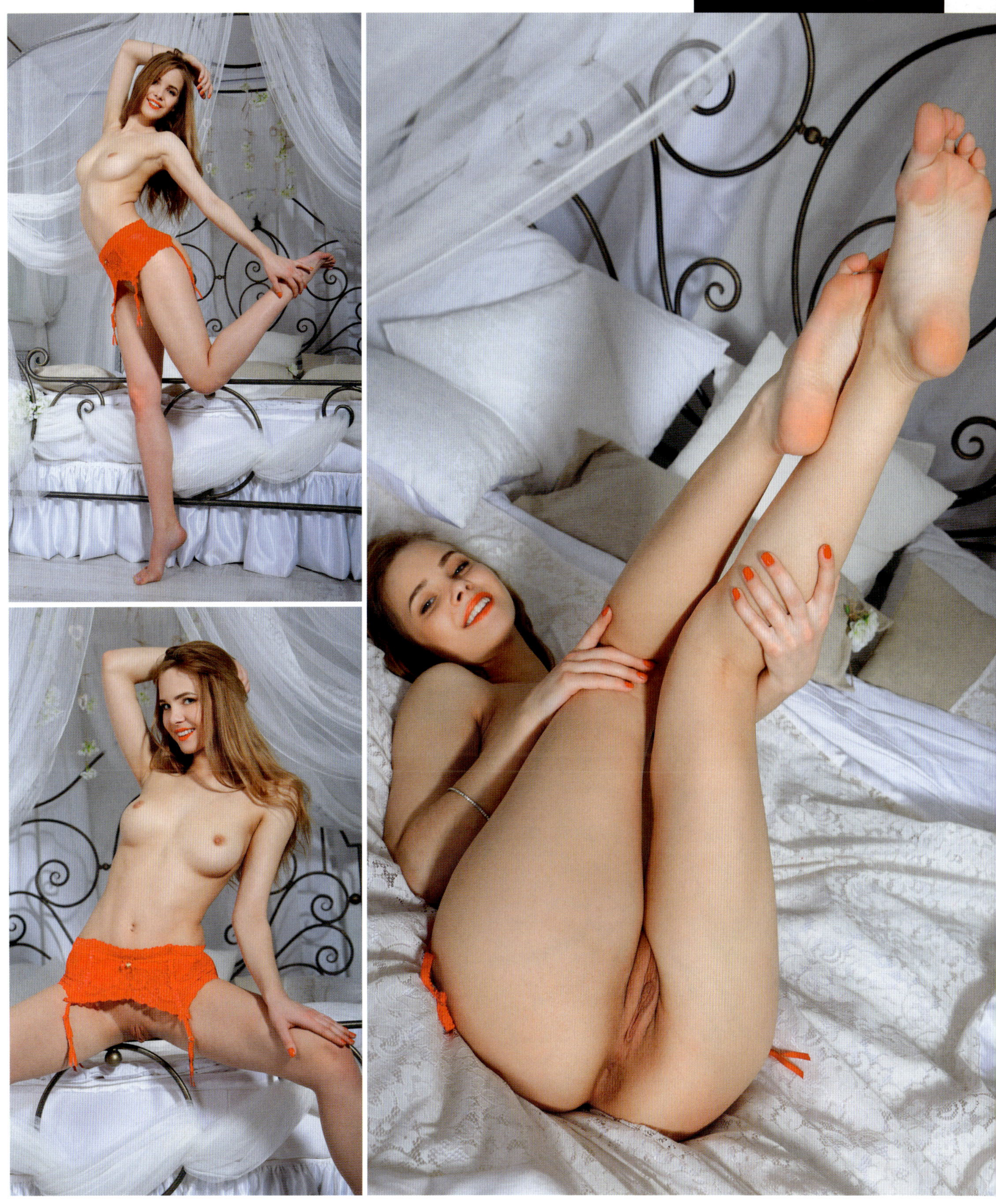

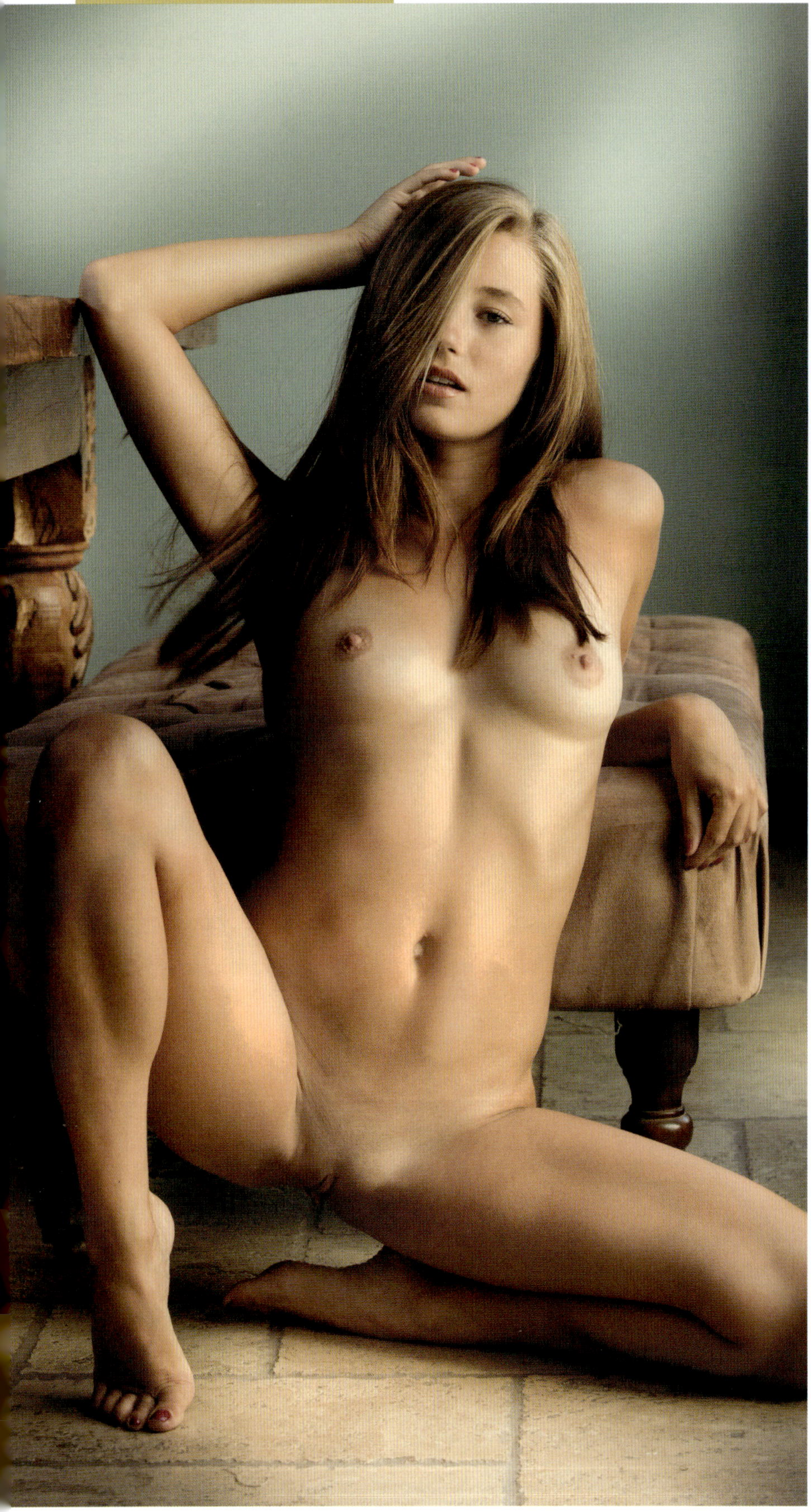

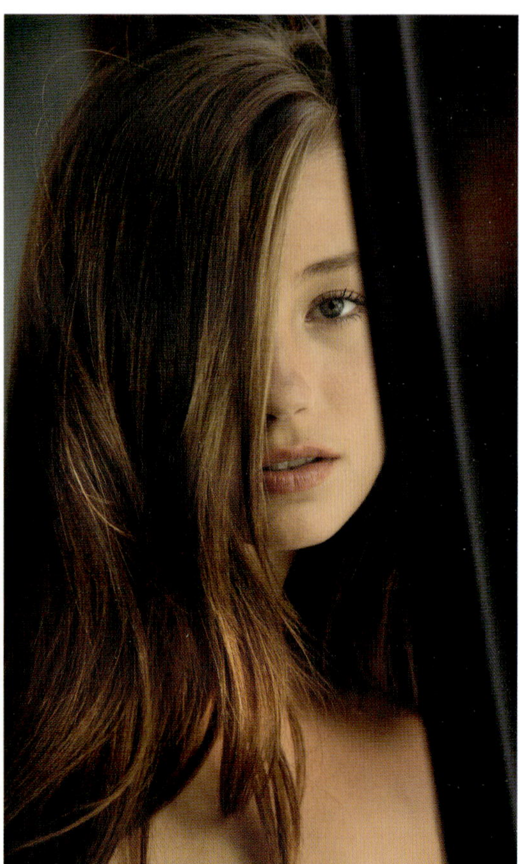

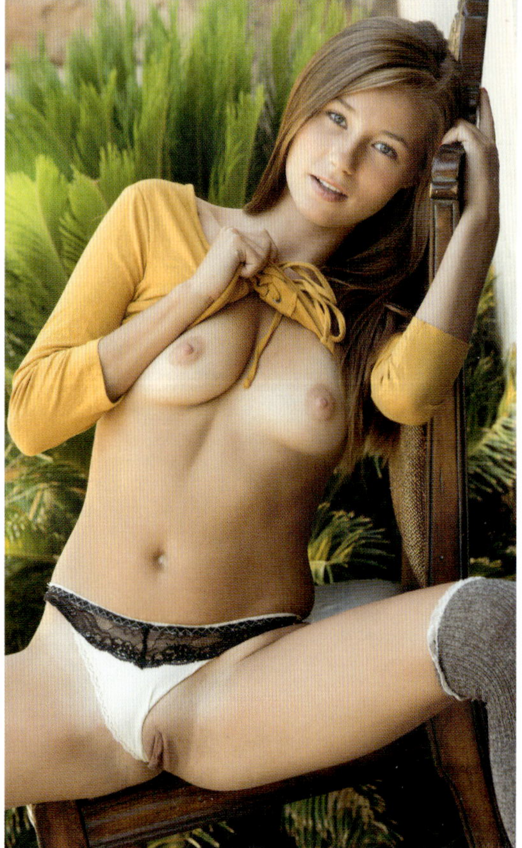

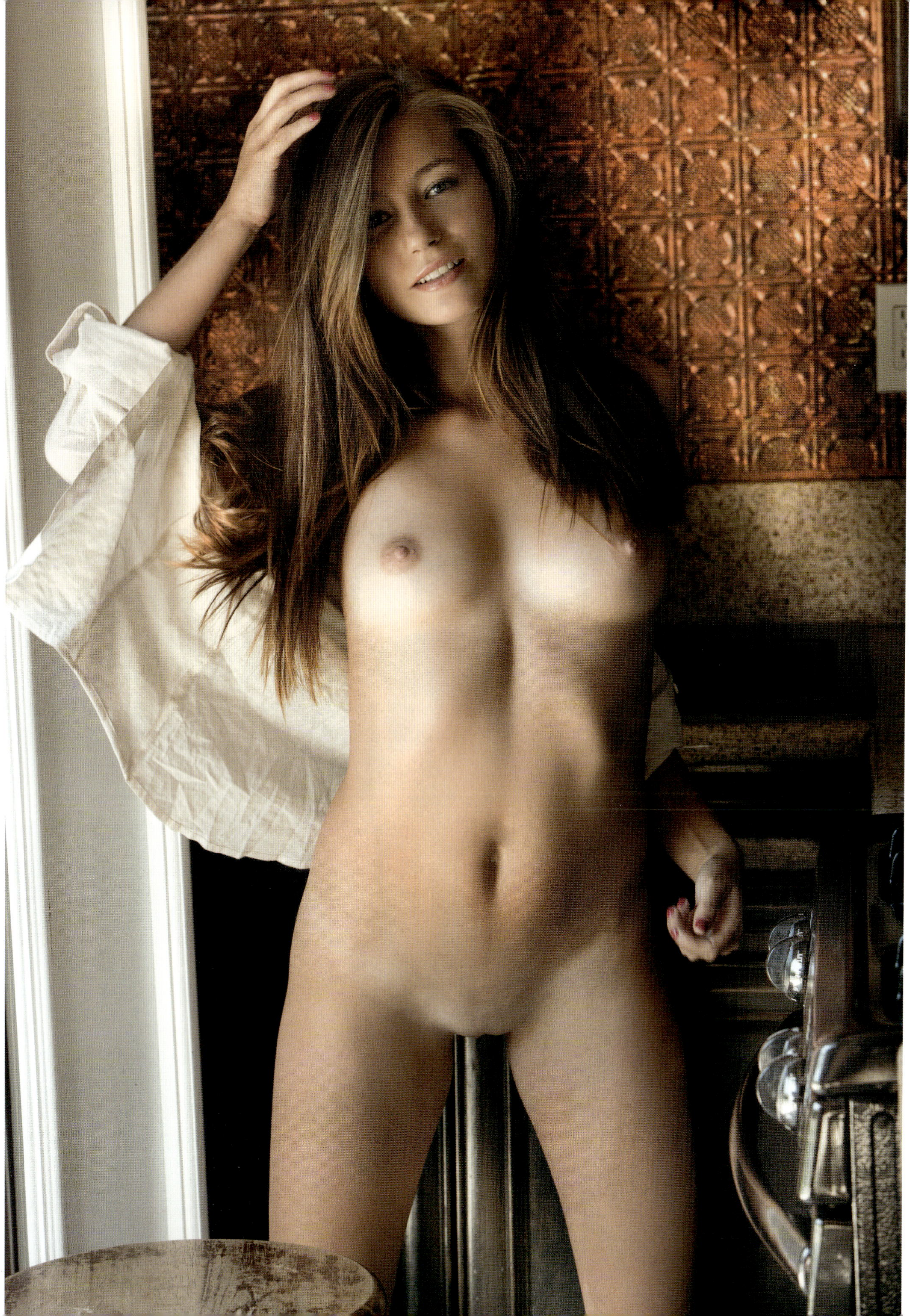

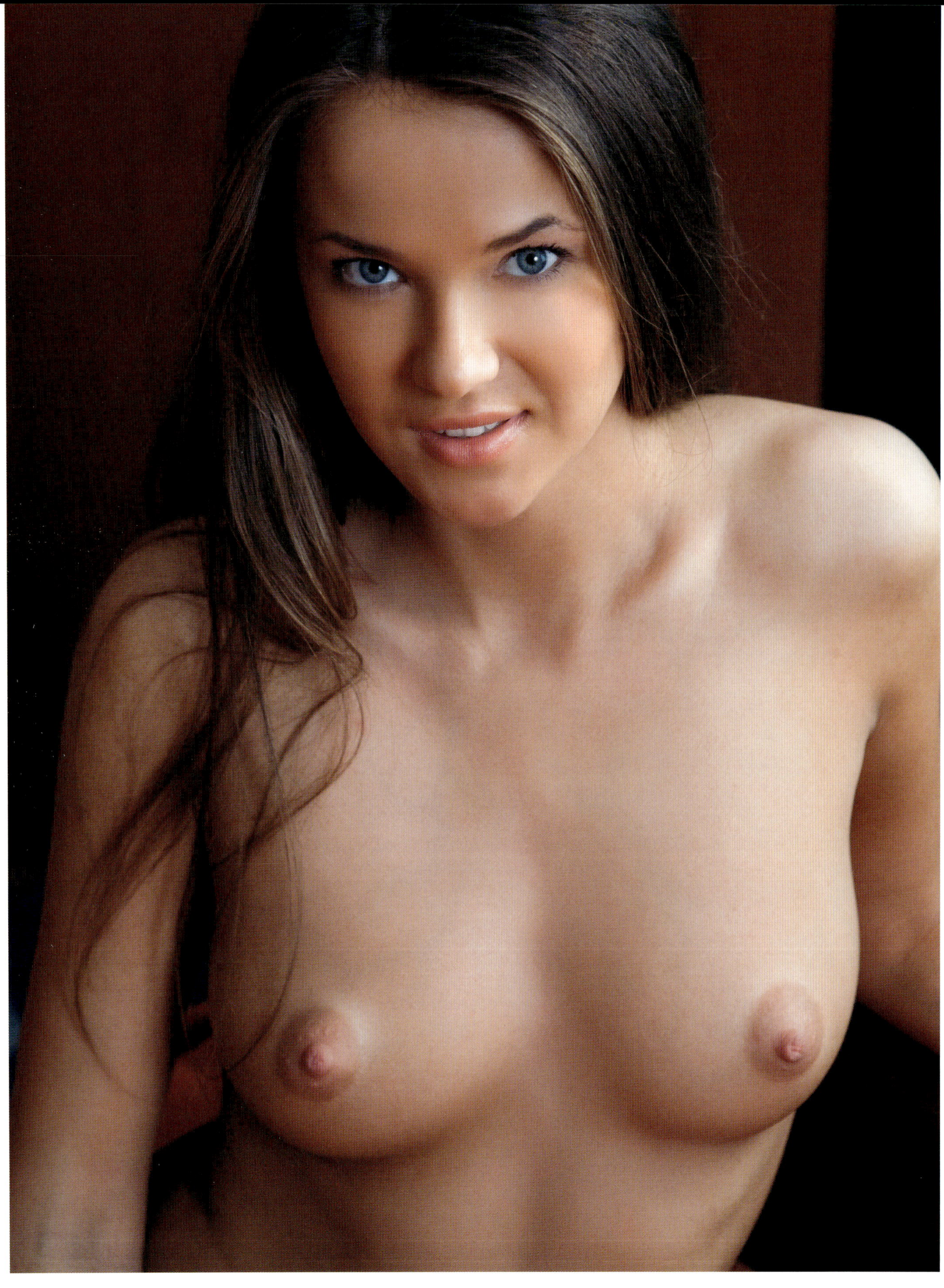

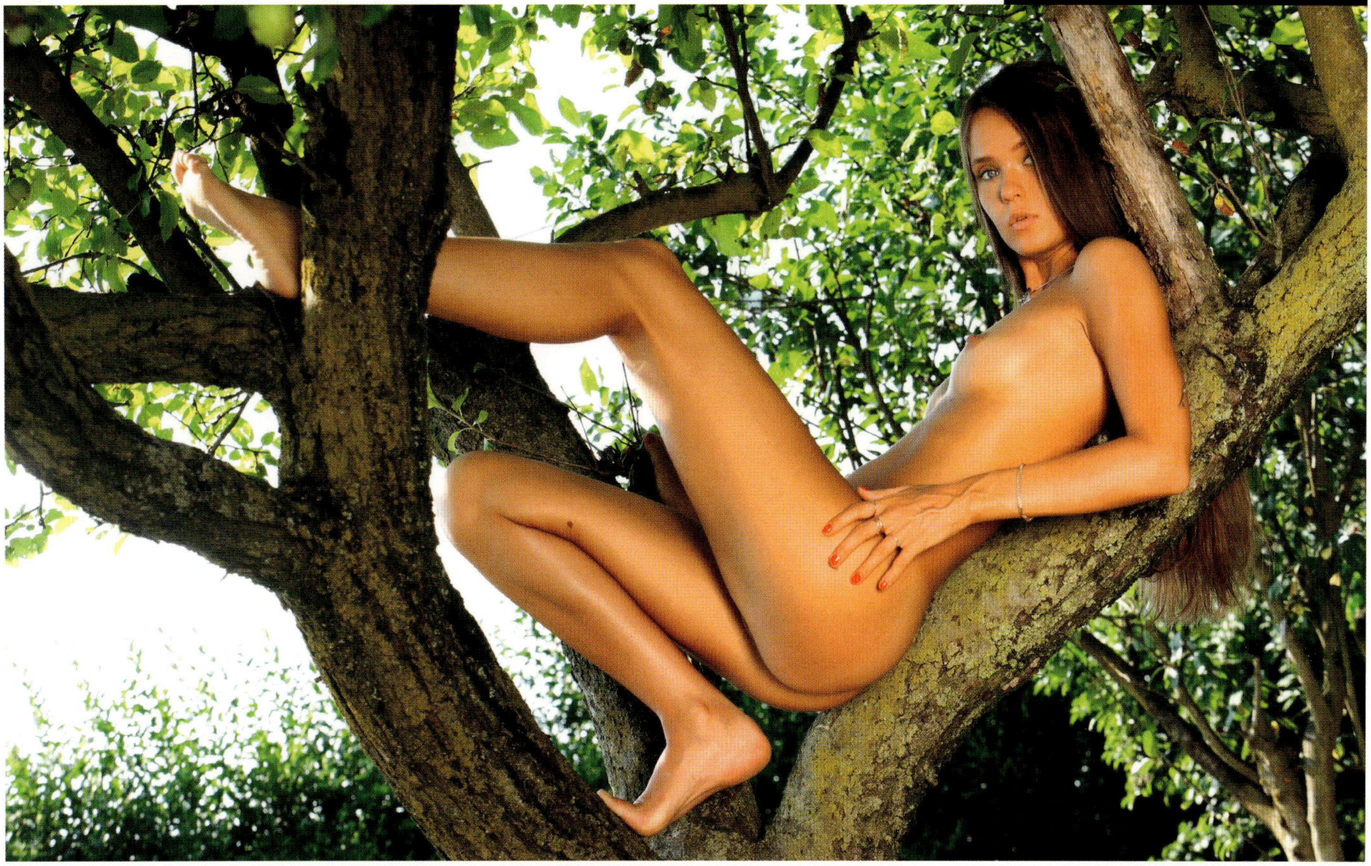

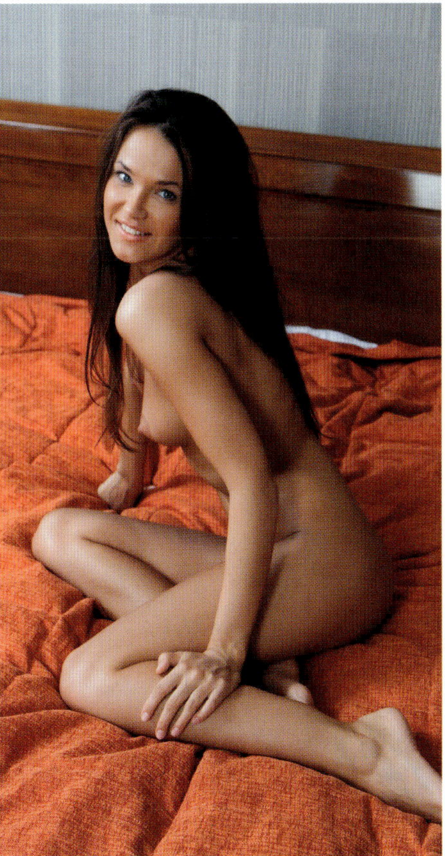

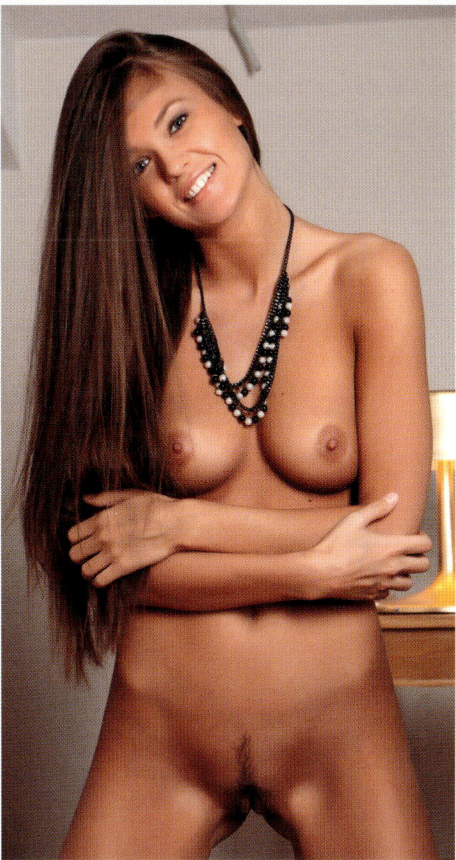

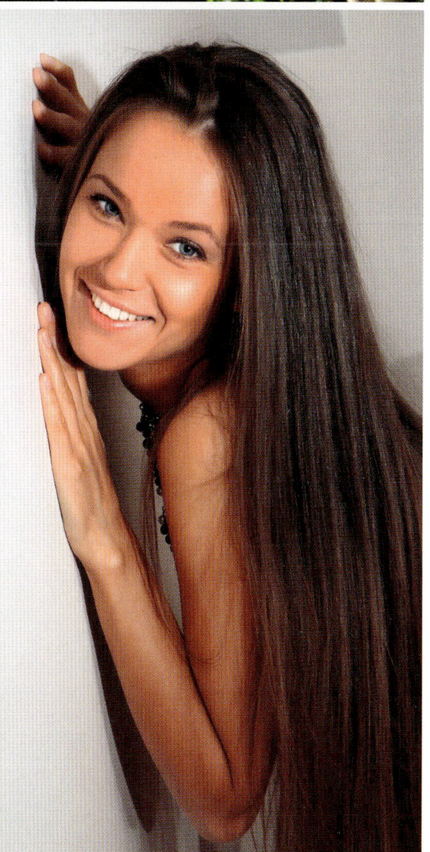

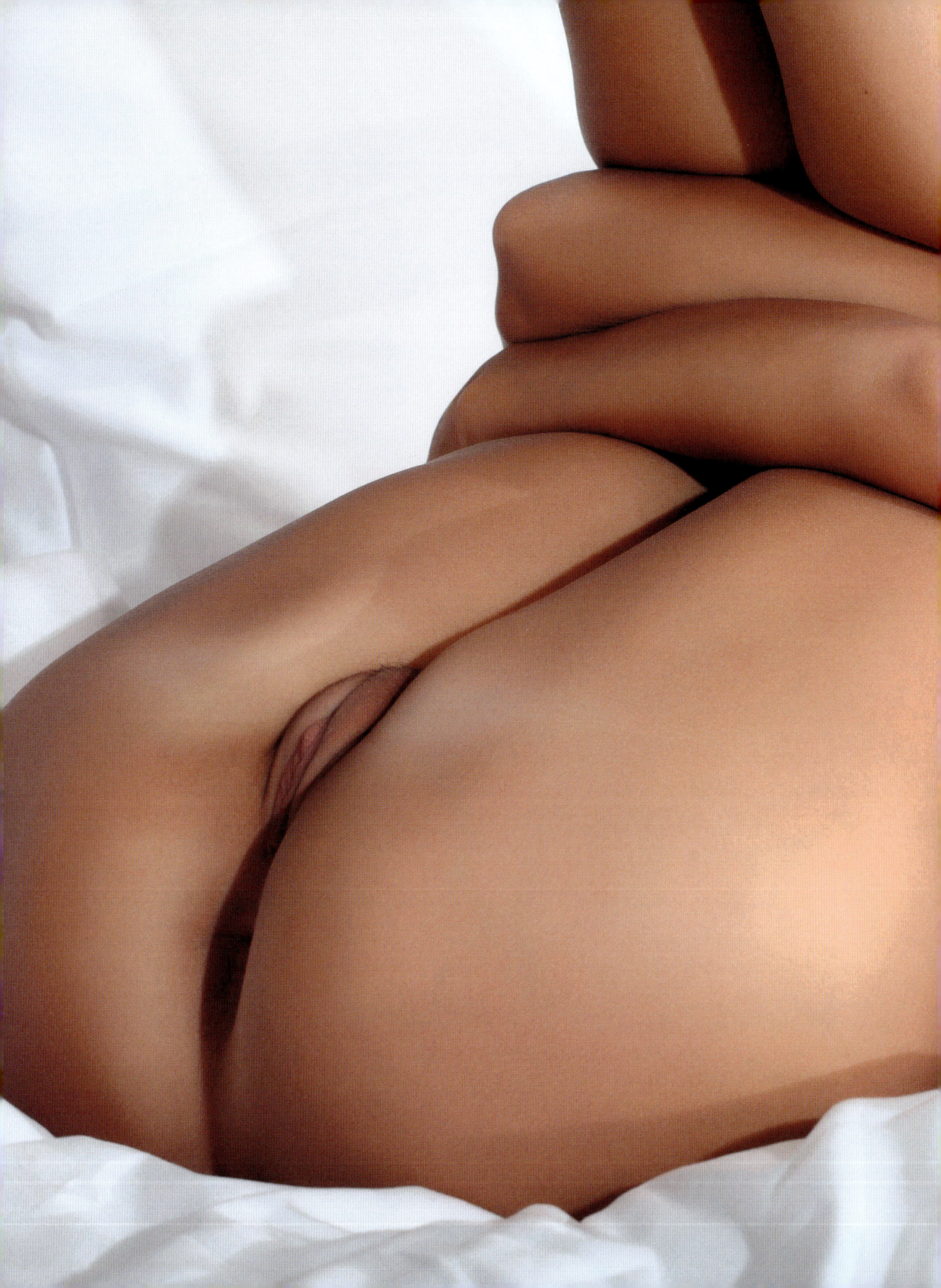

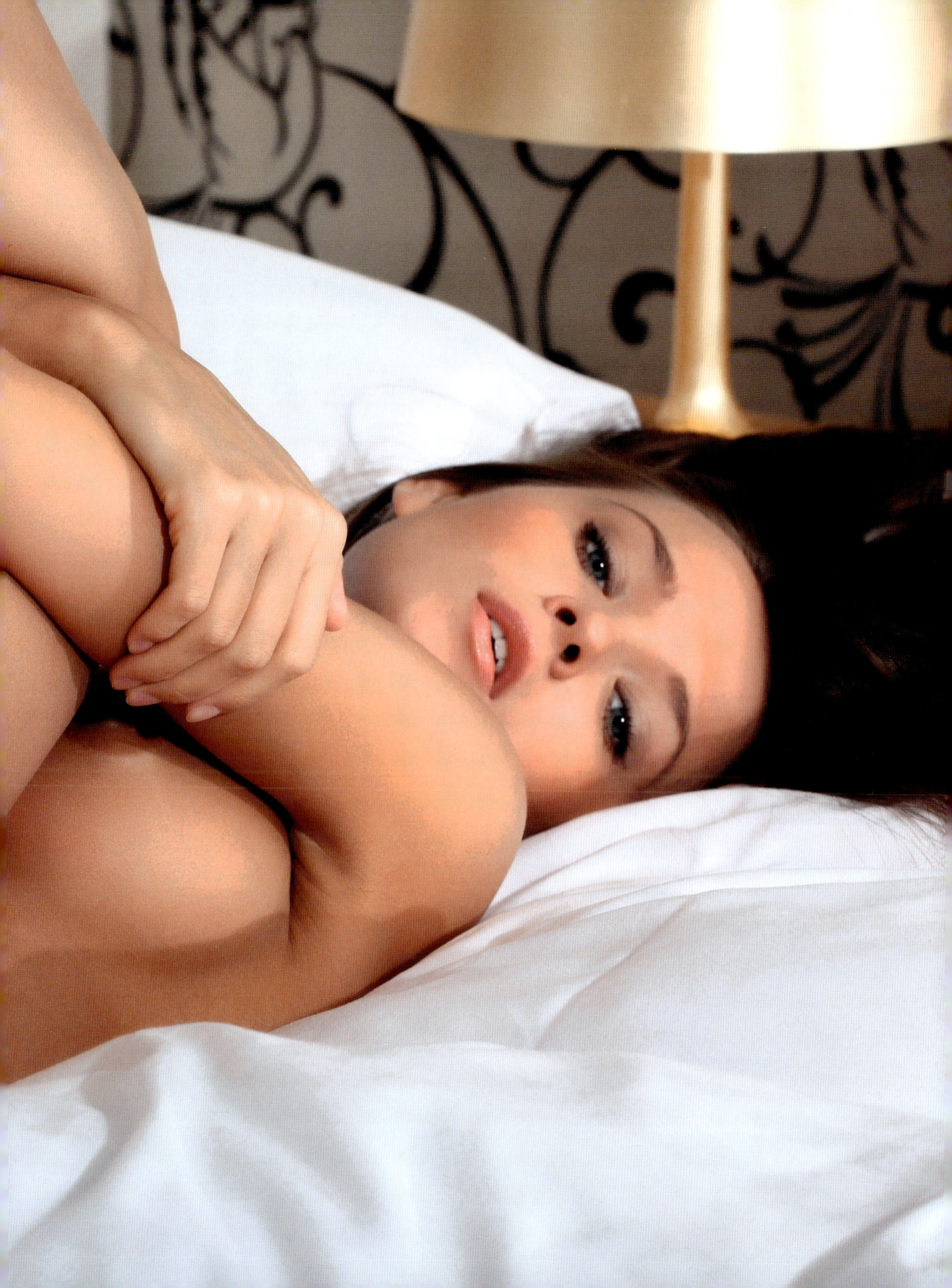

## *Chiara A*

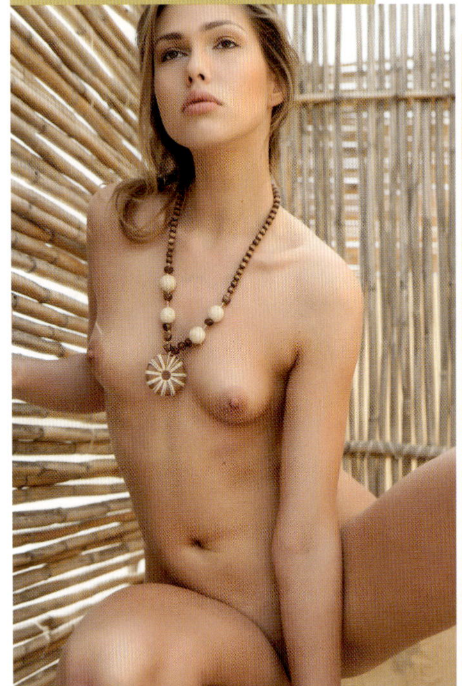

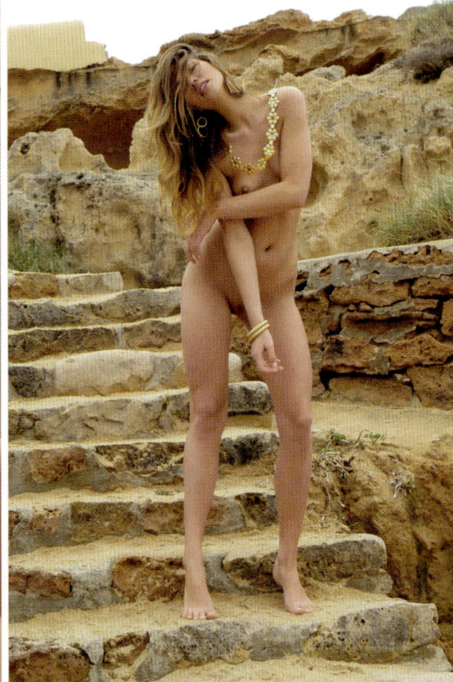

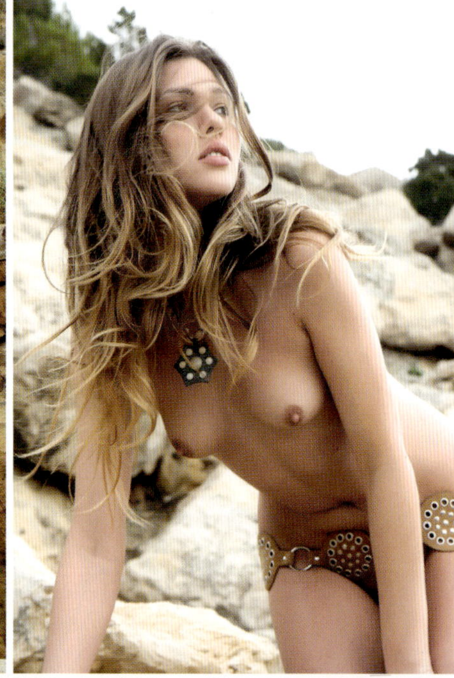

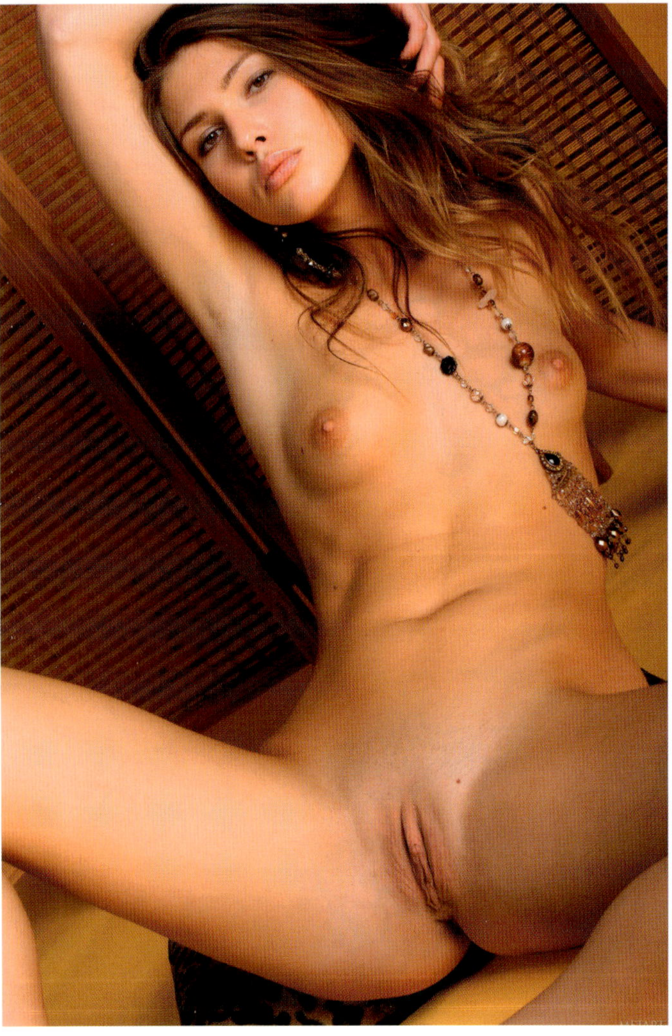

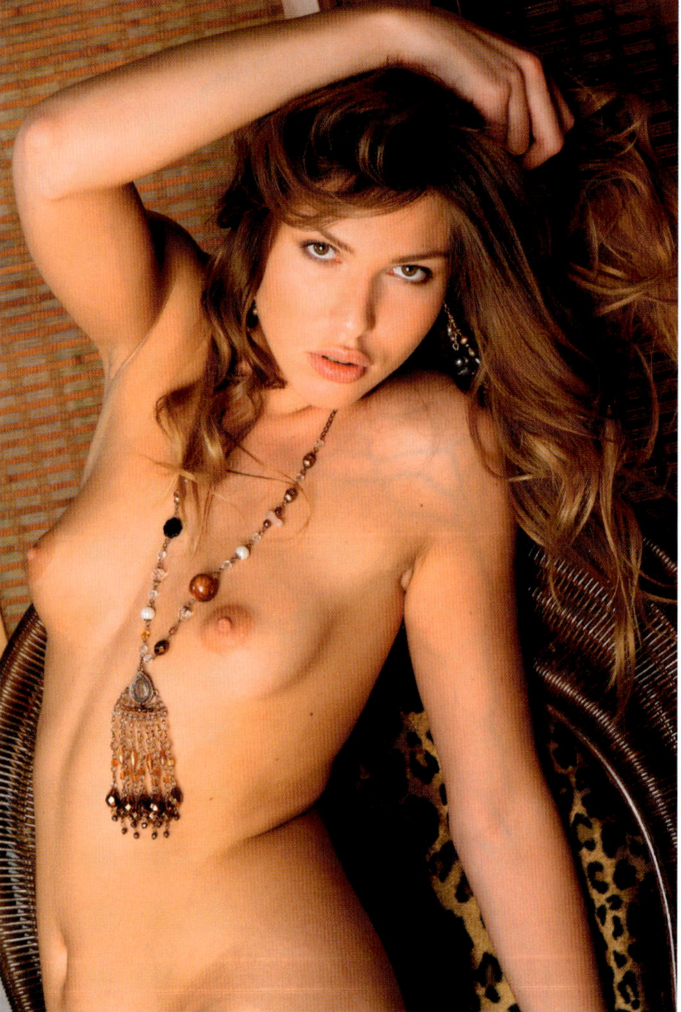

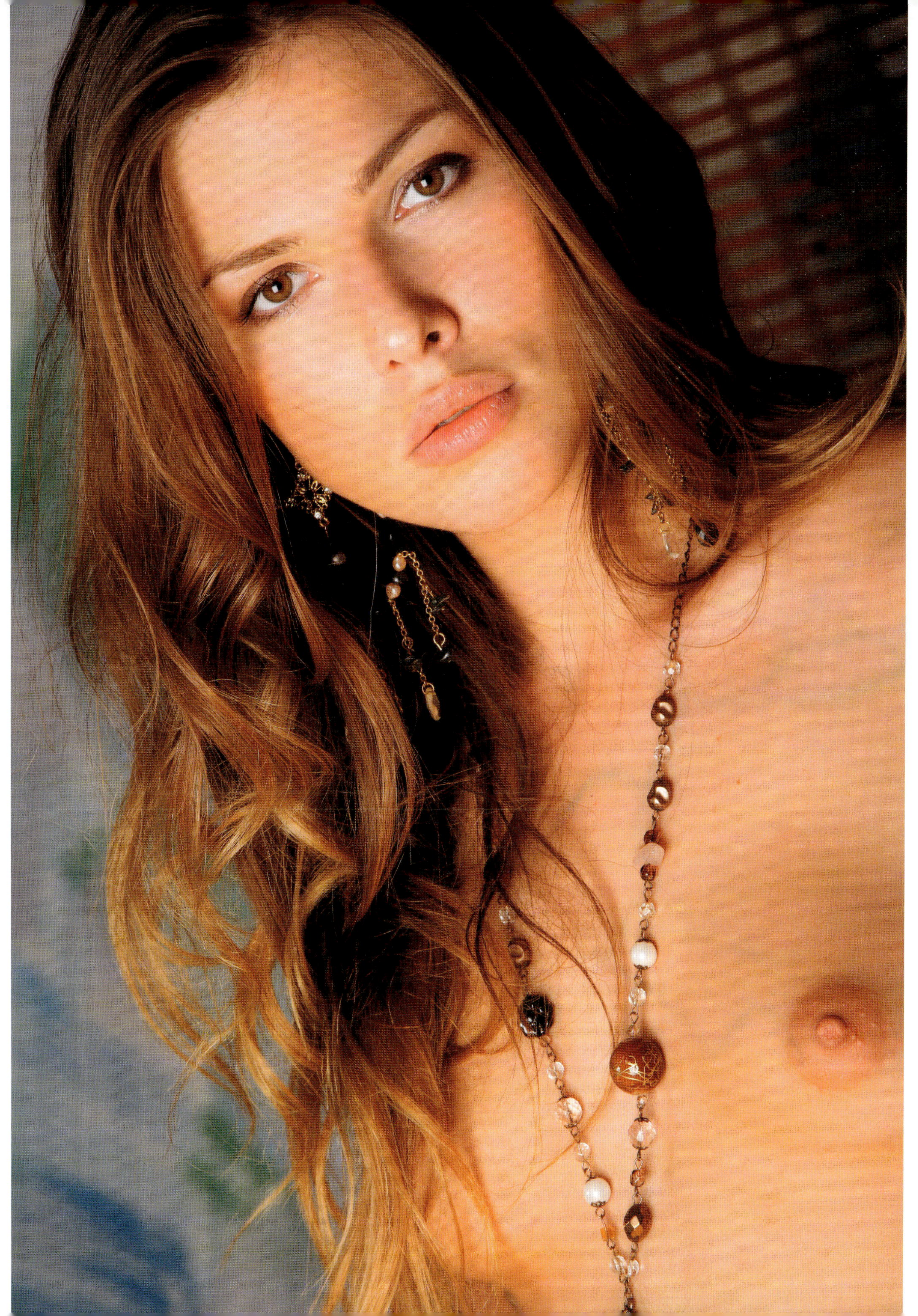

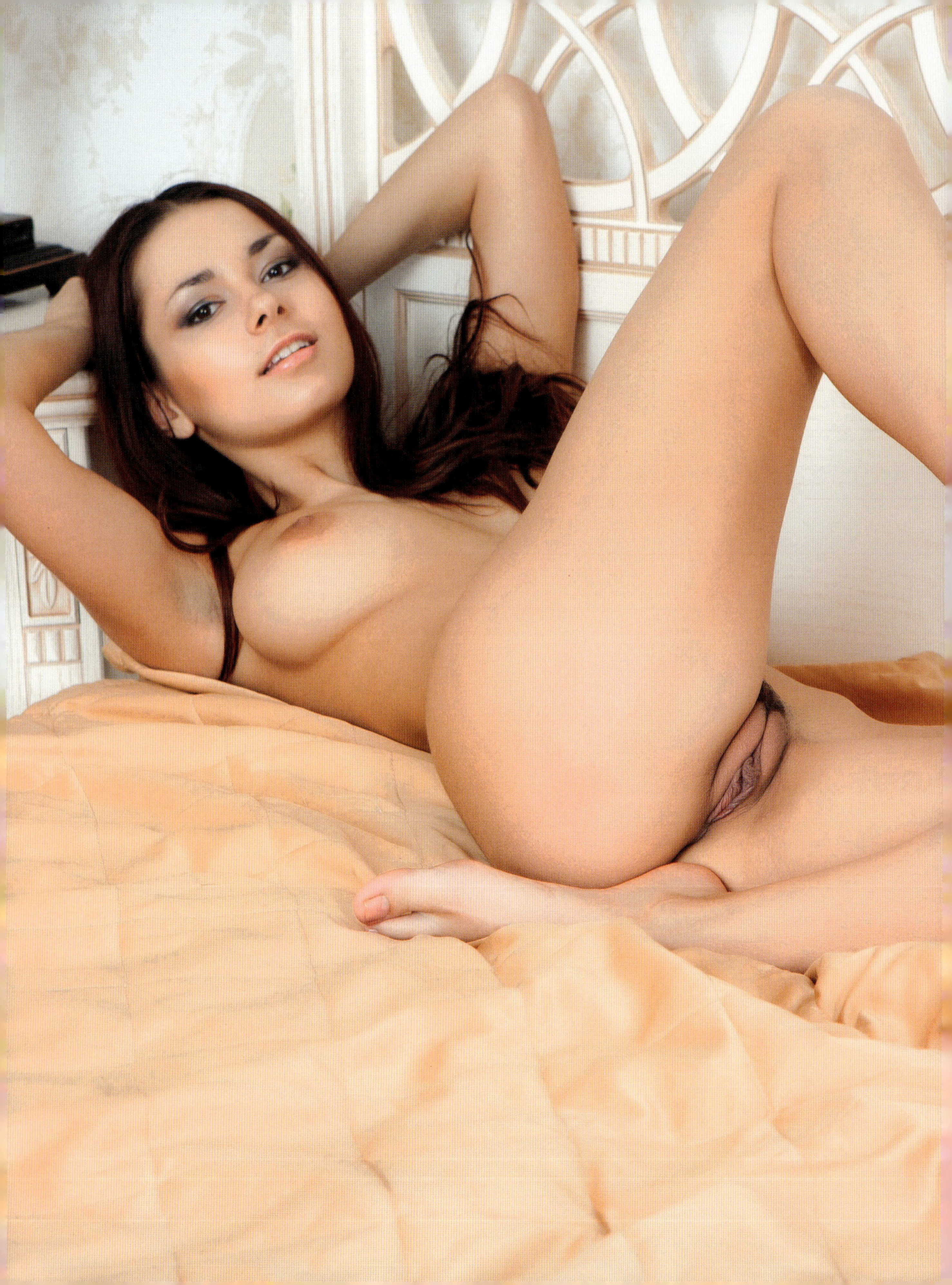

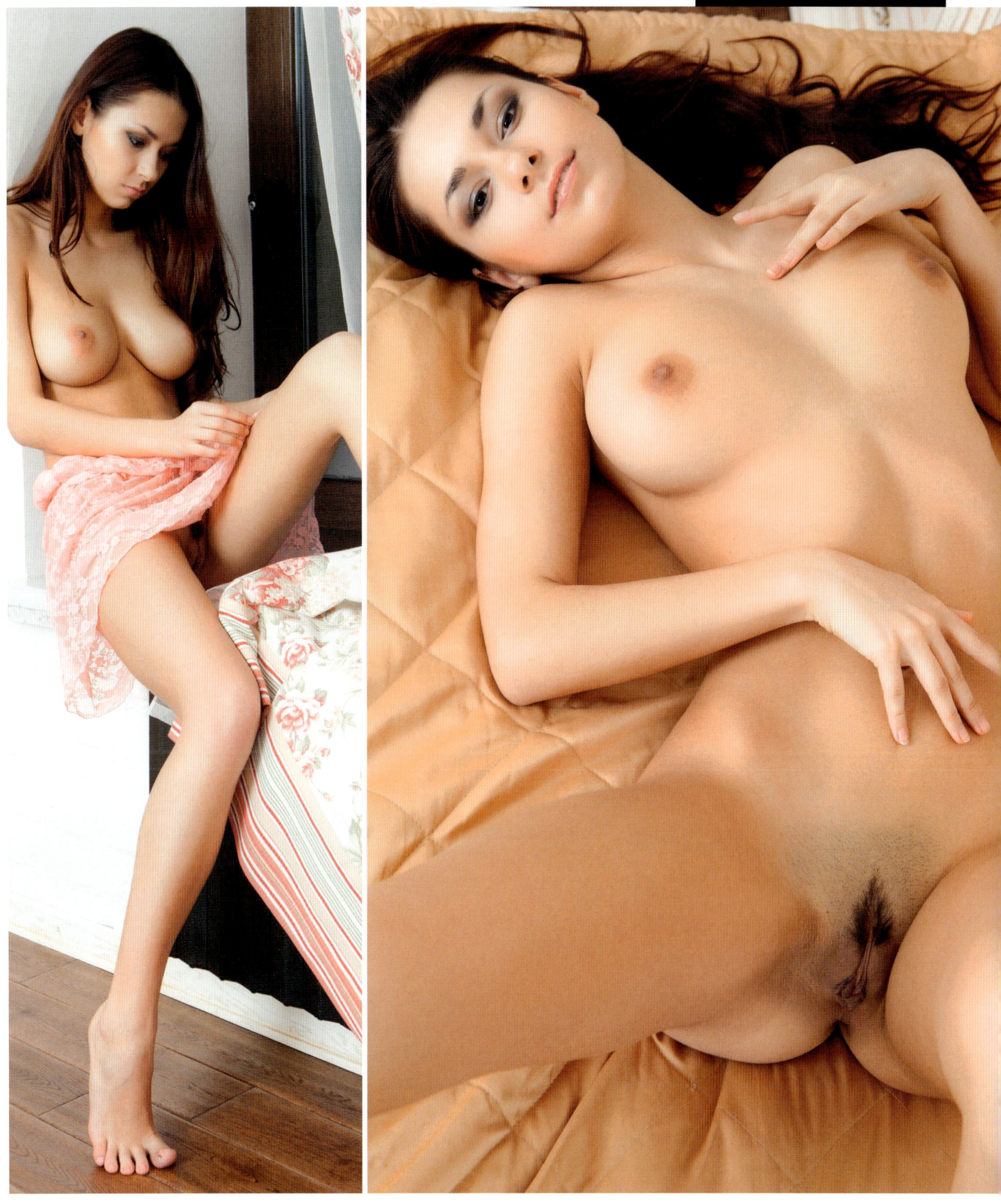

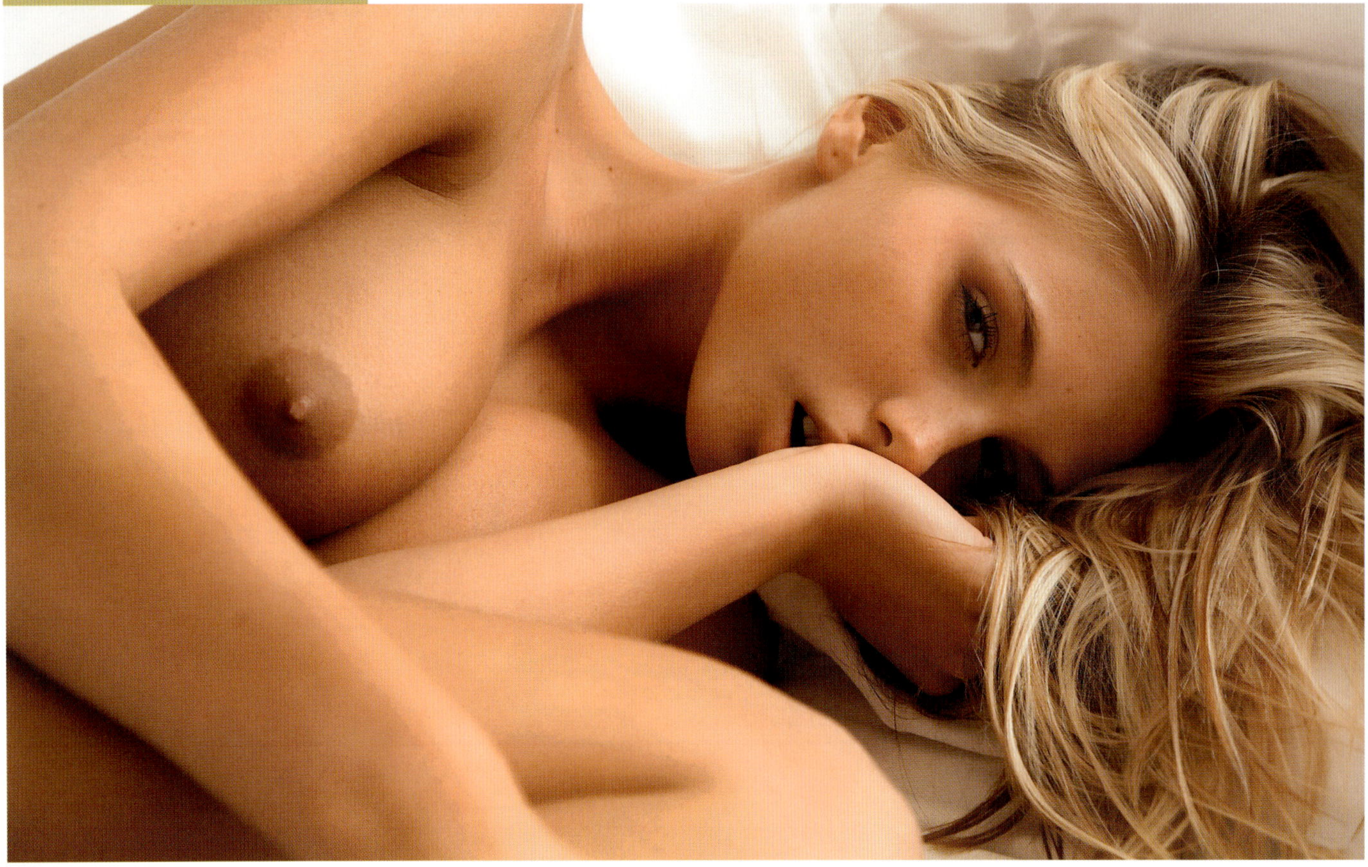

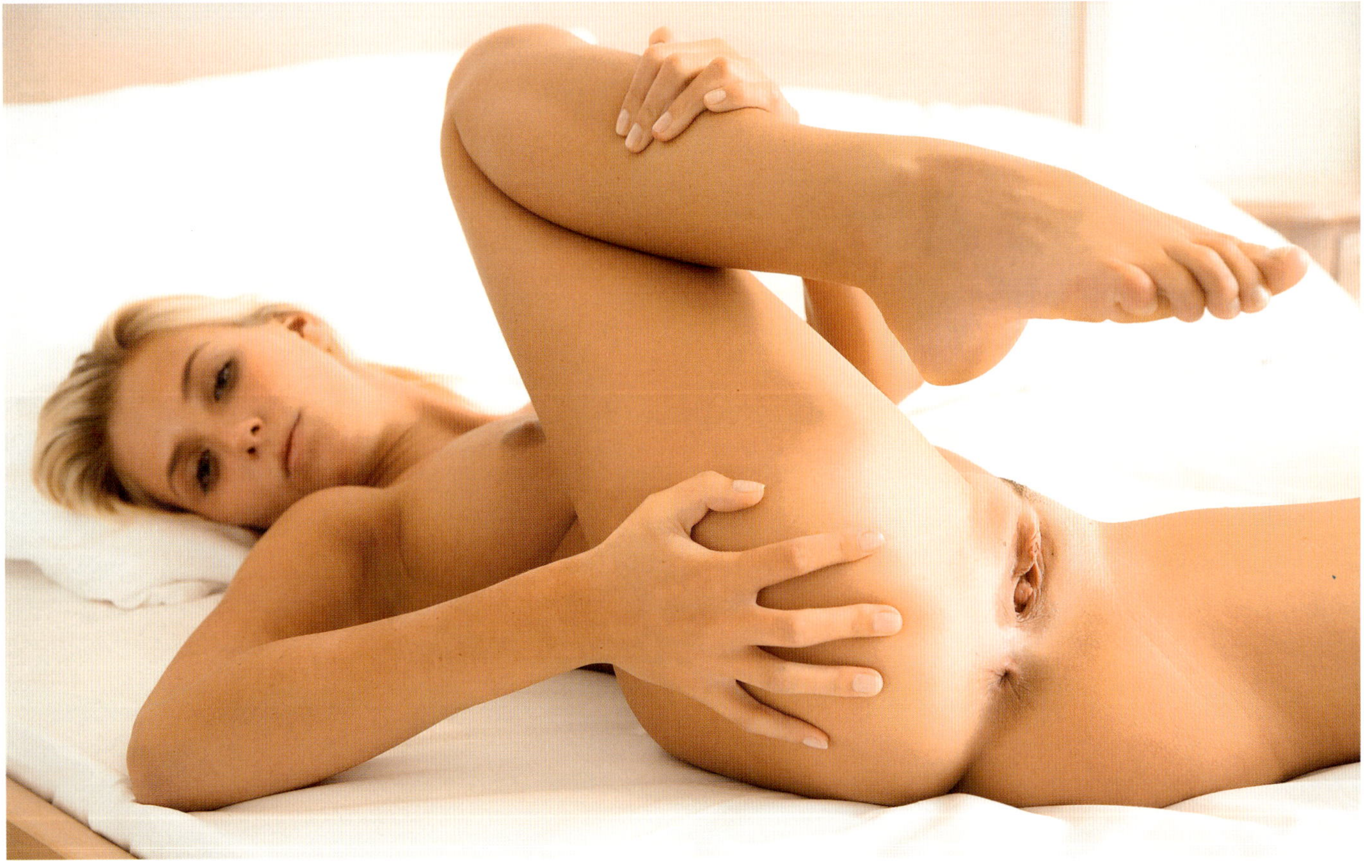

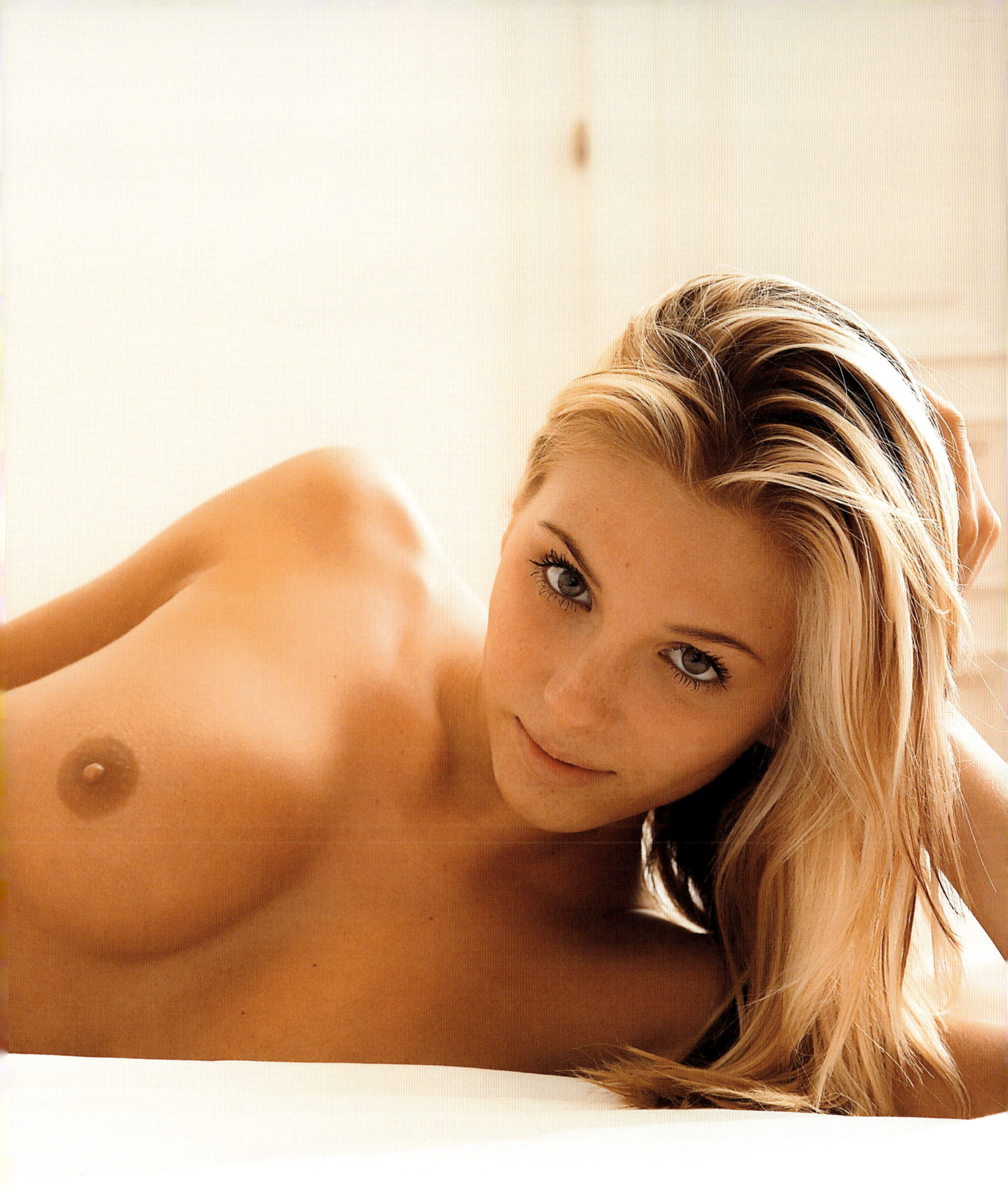

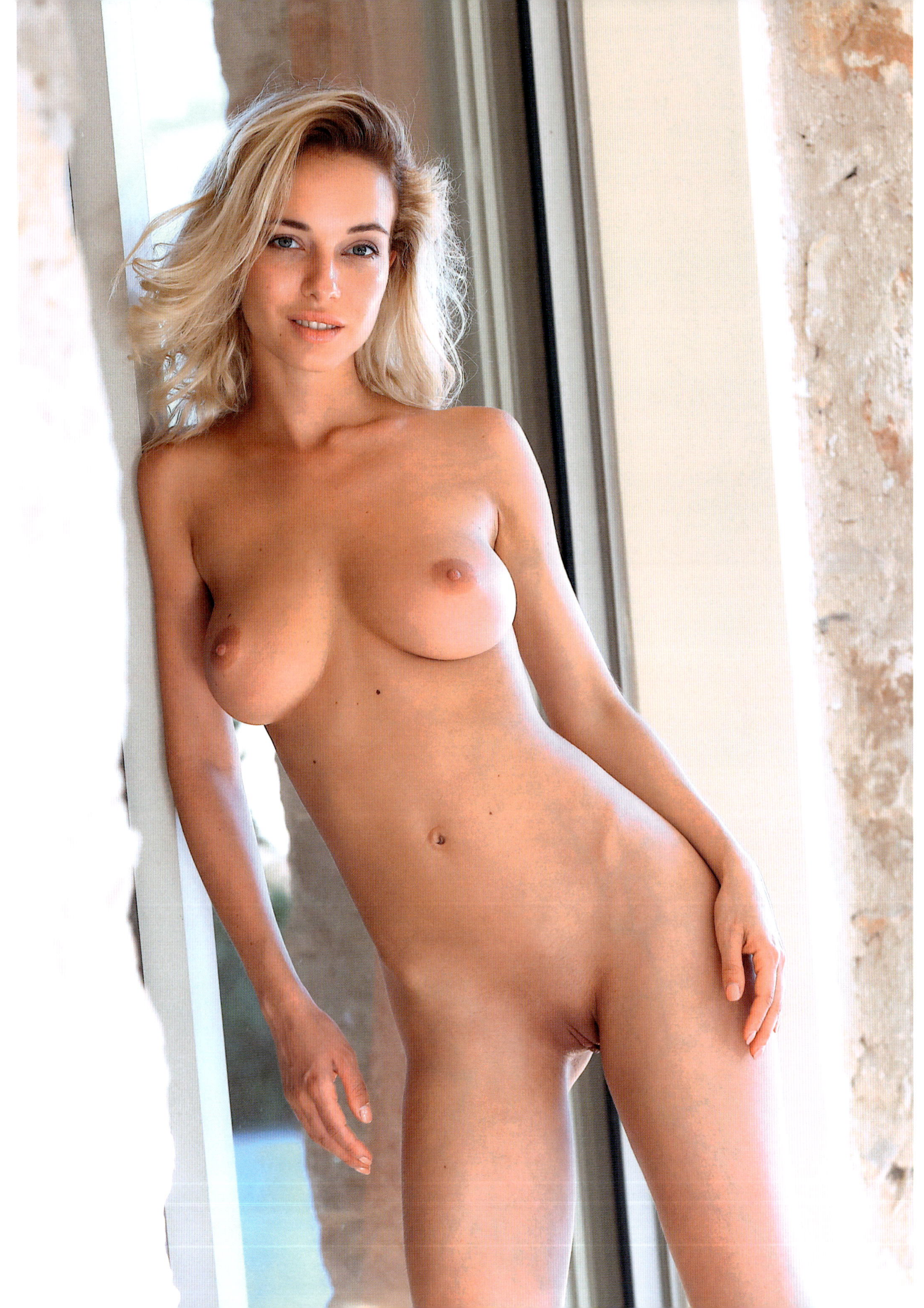

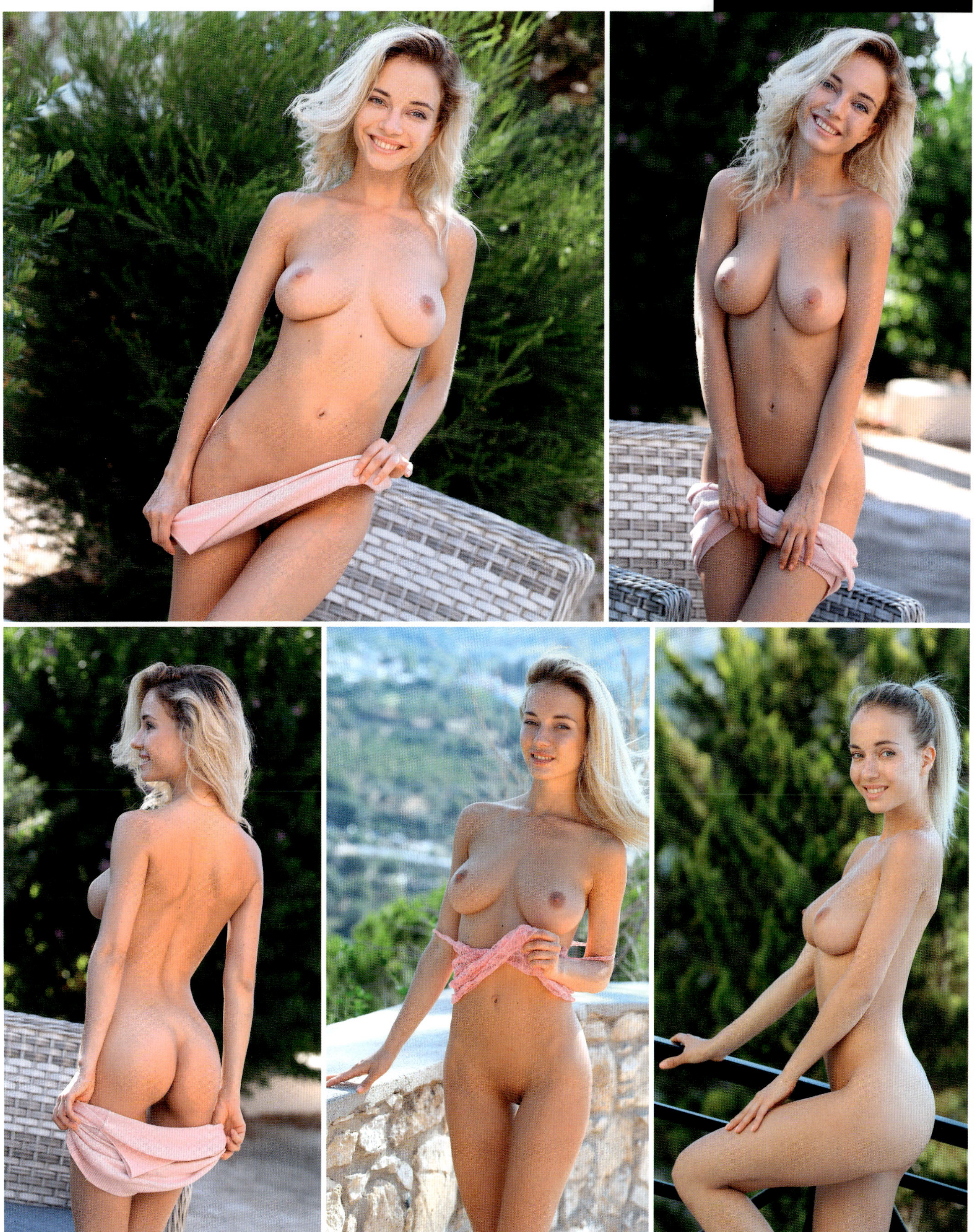

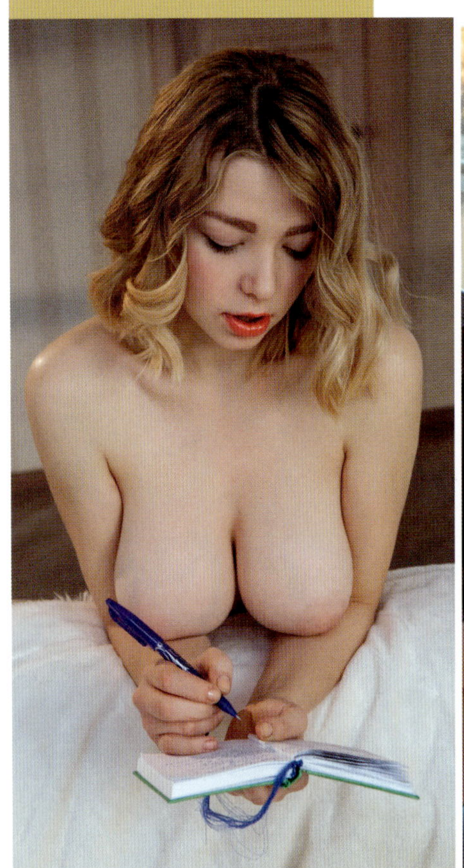

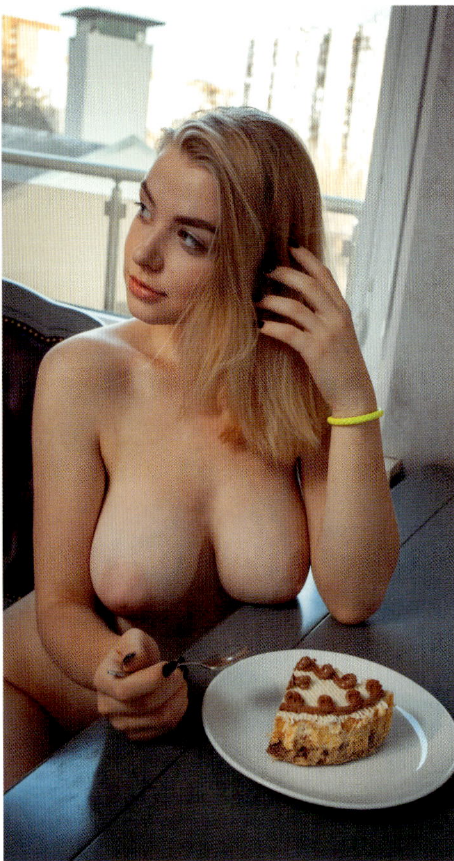

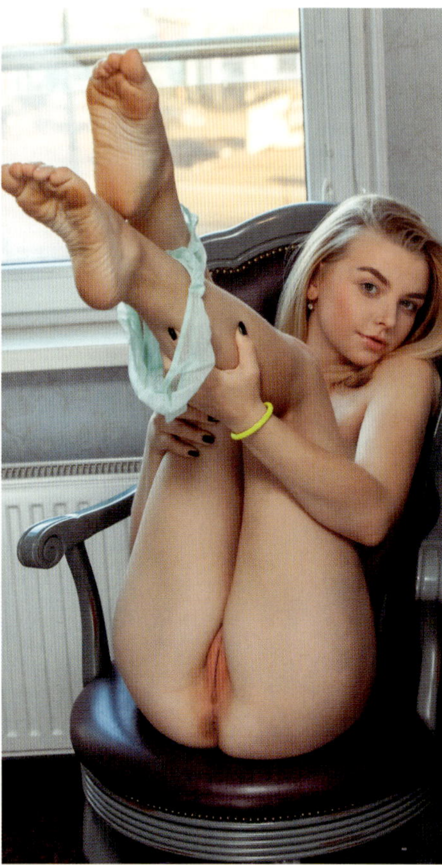

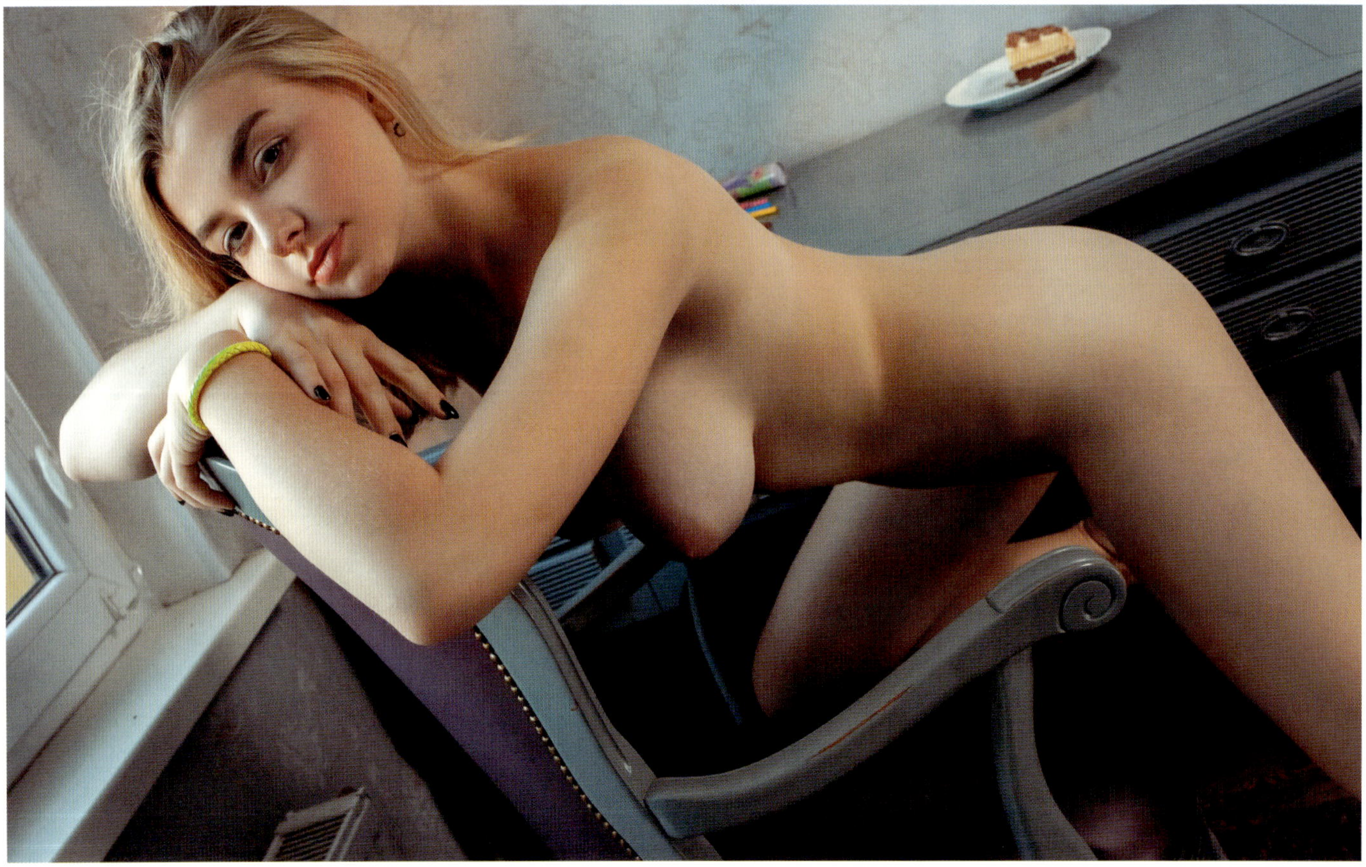

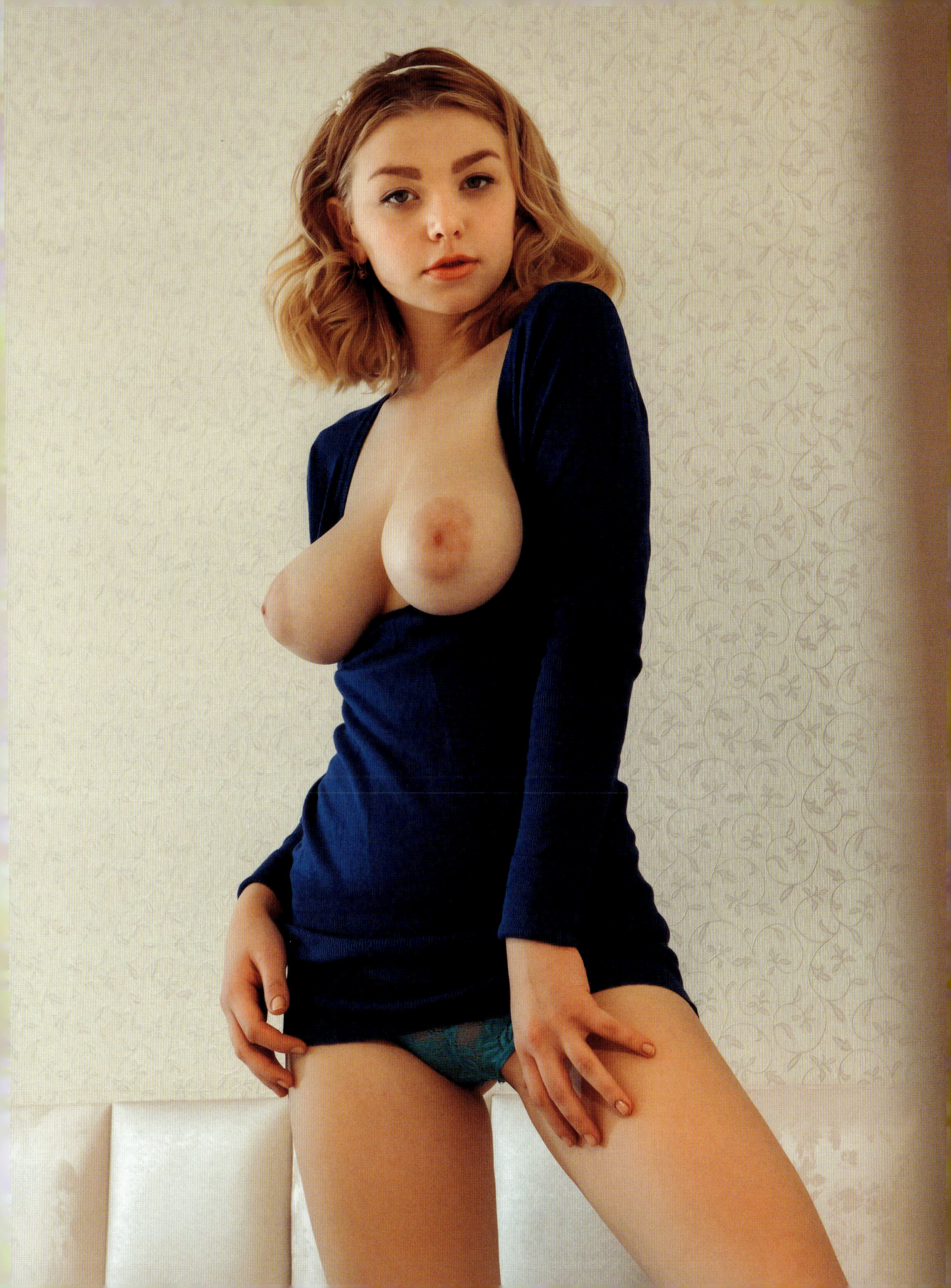

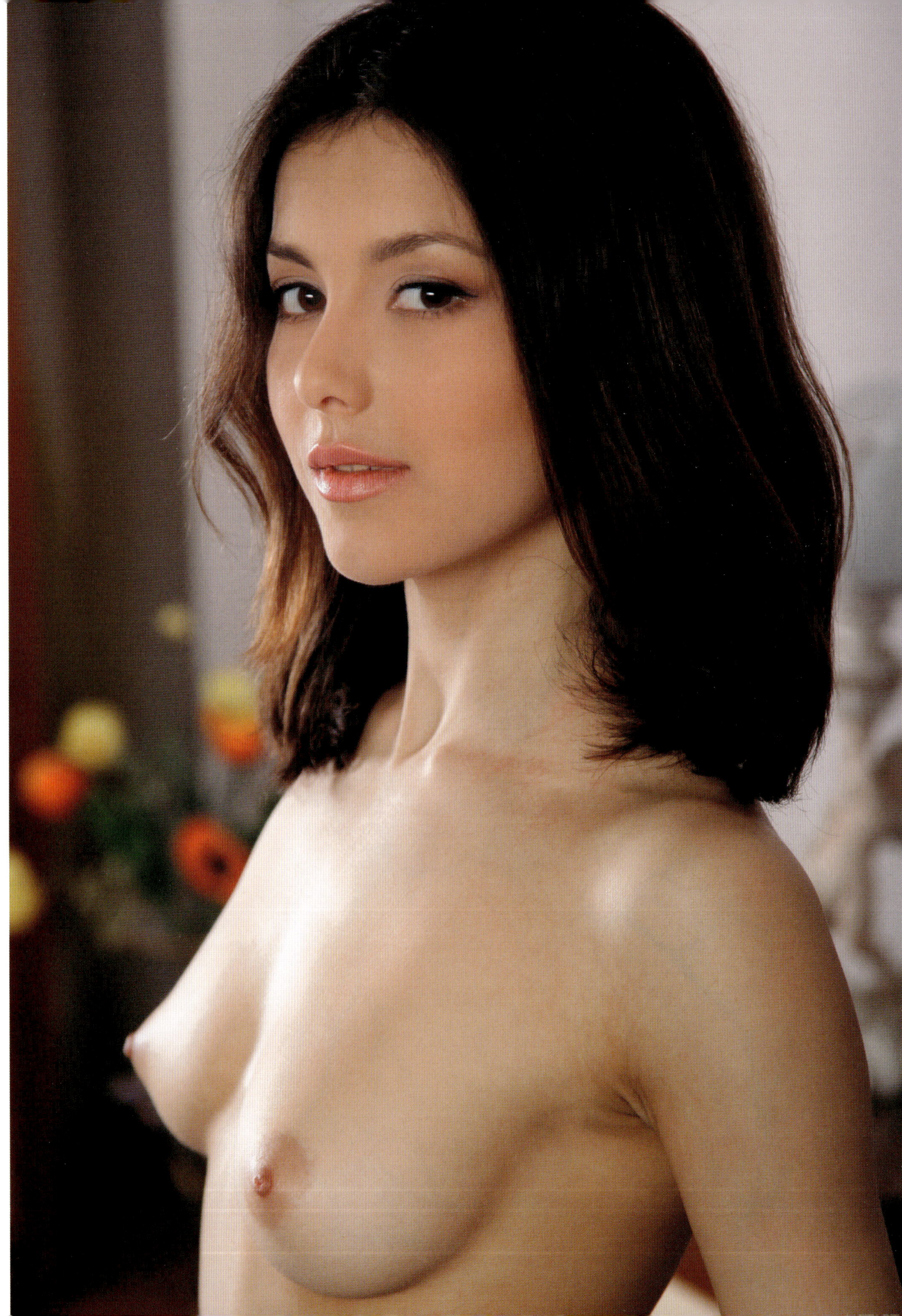

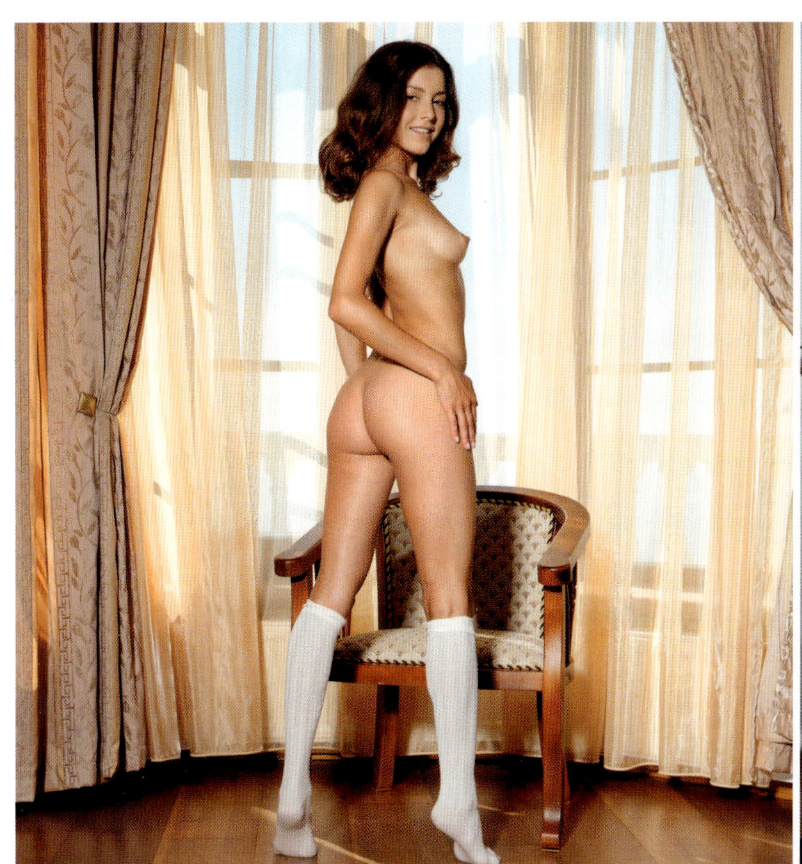

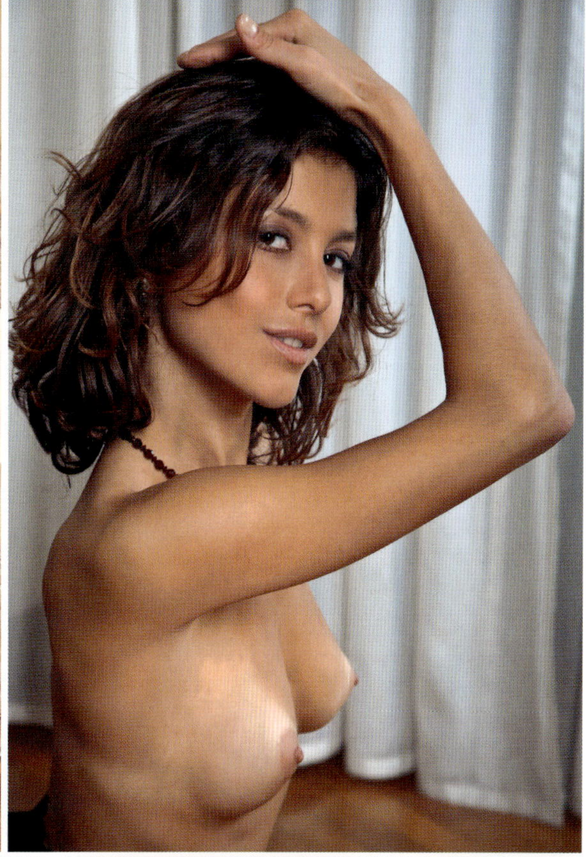

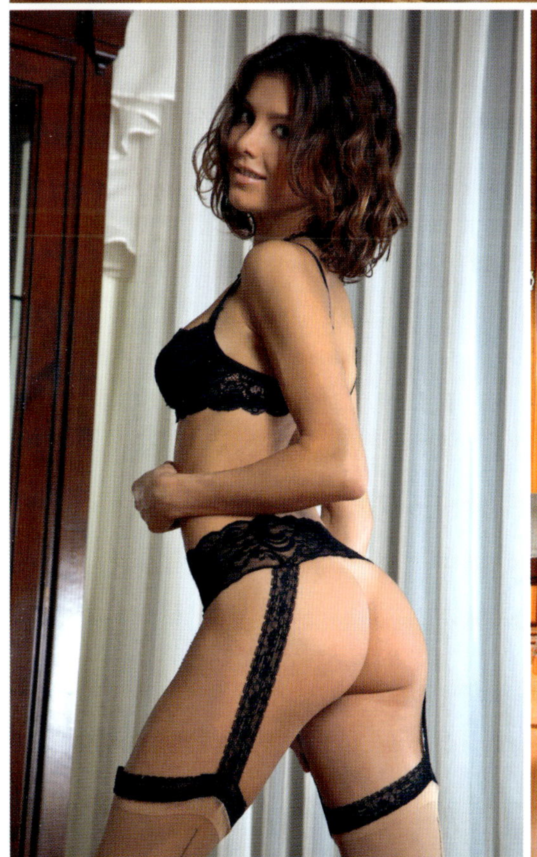

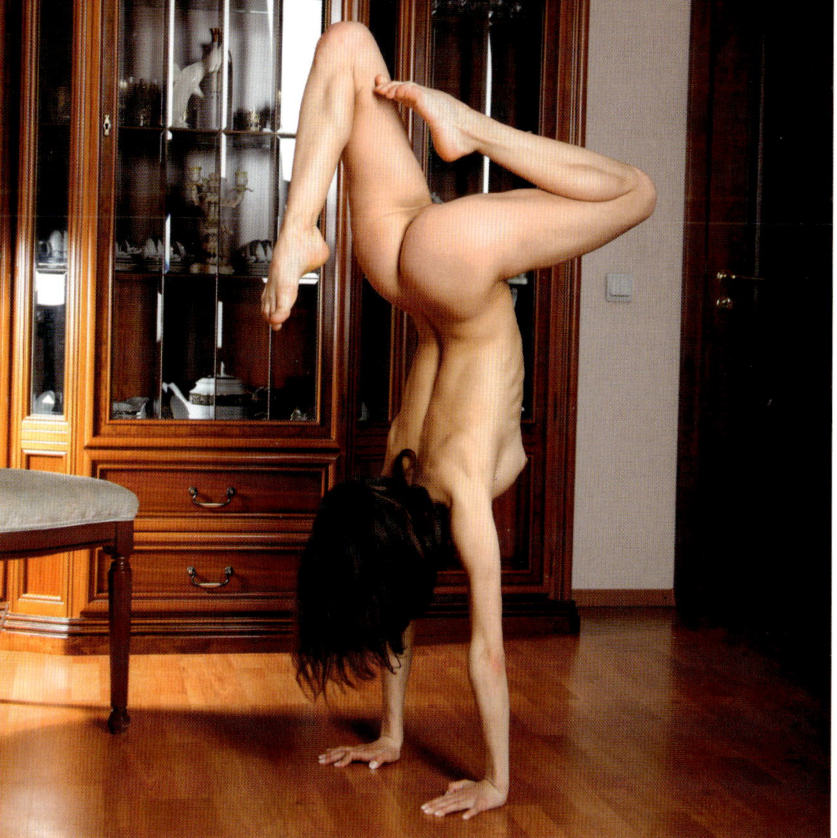

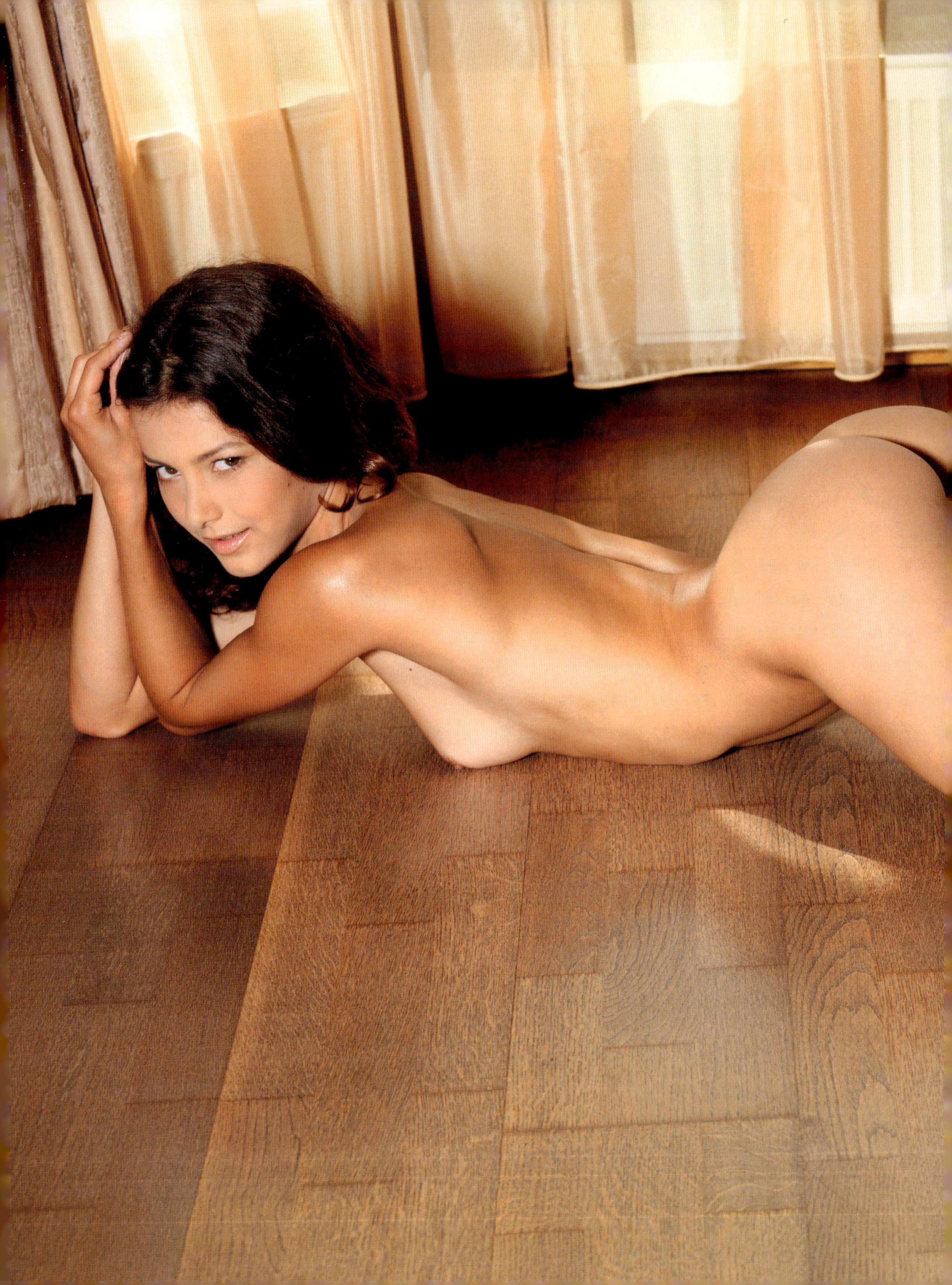

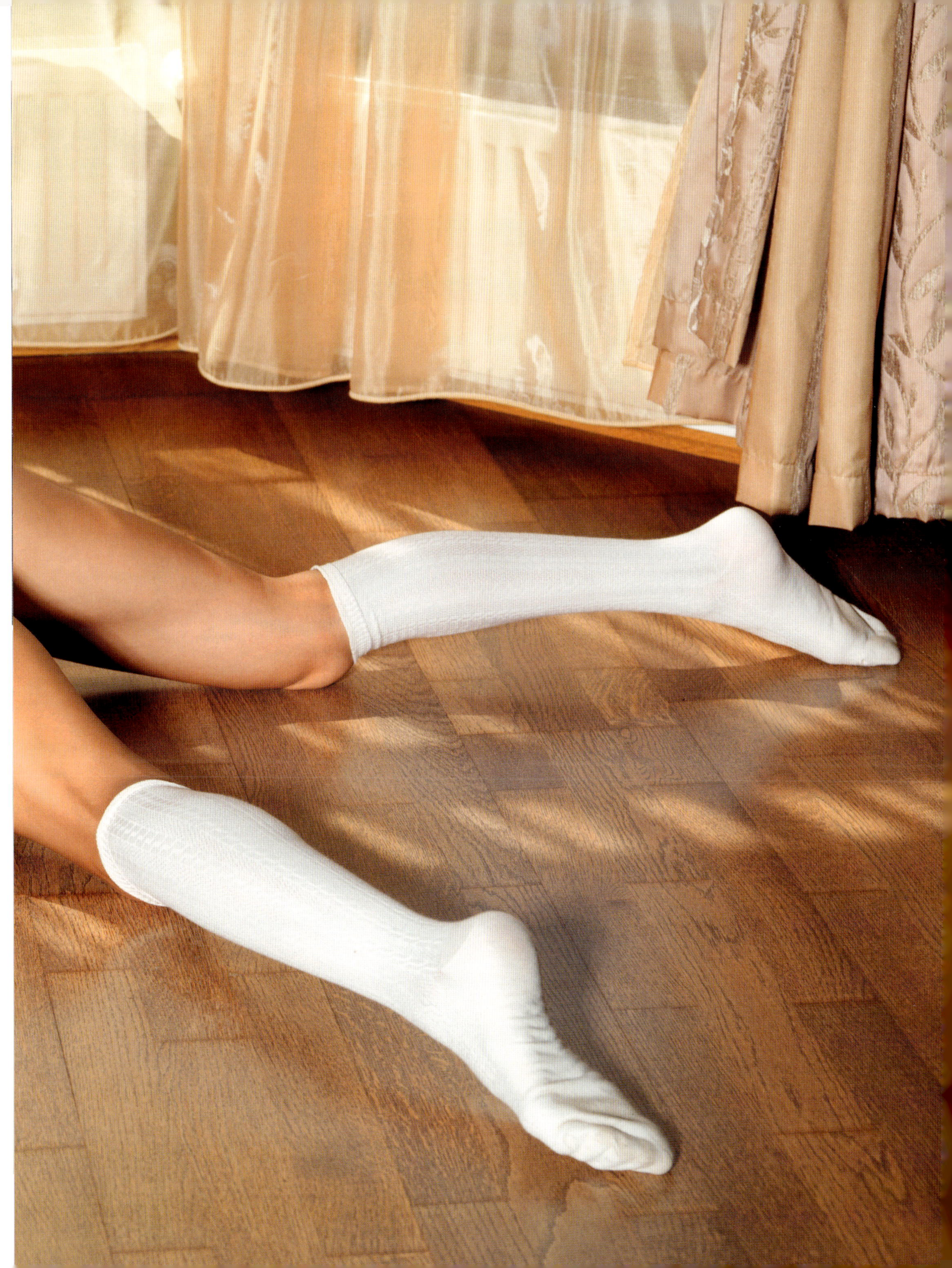

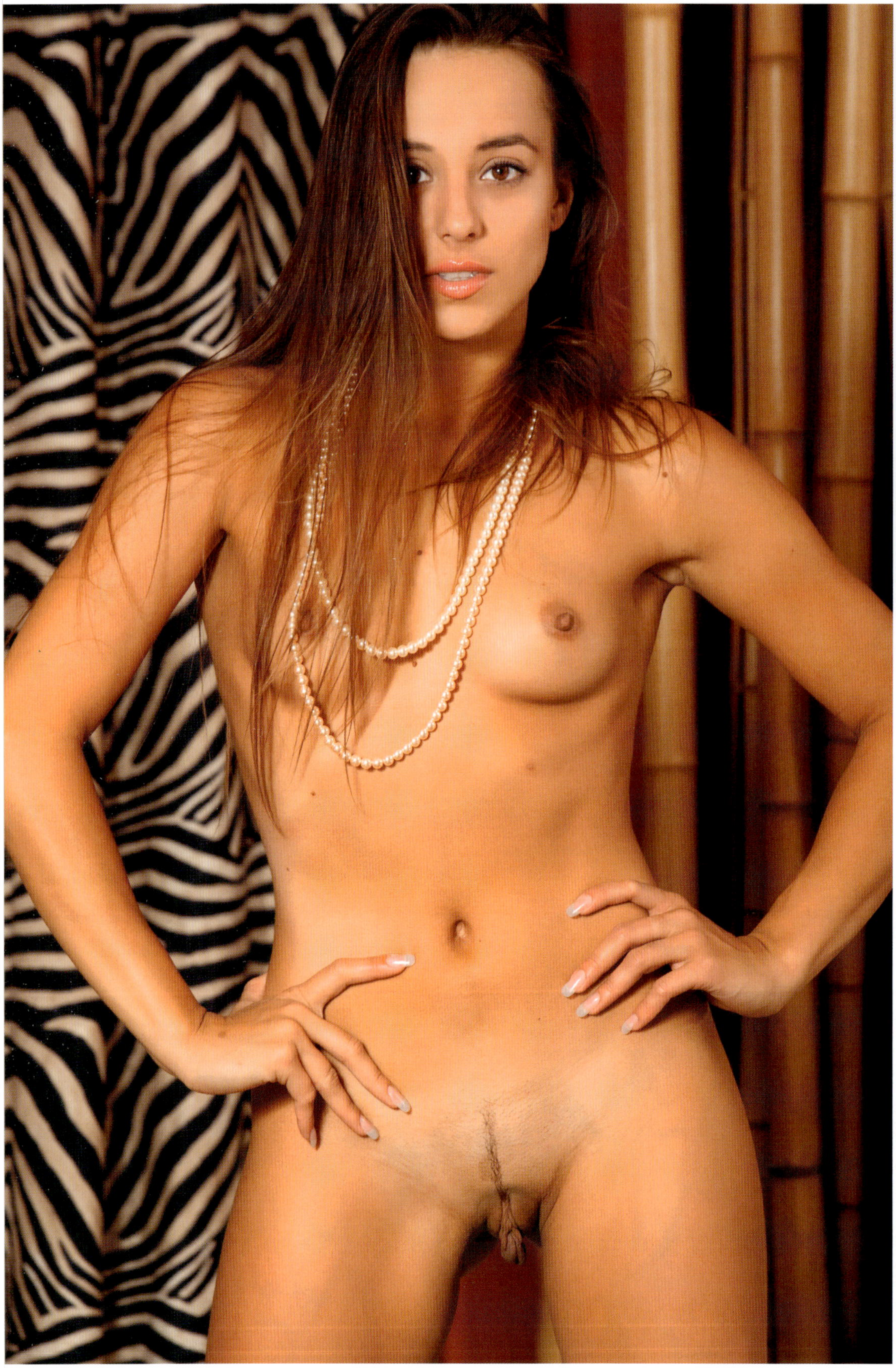

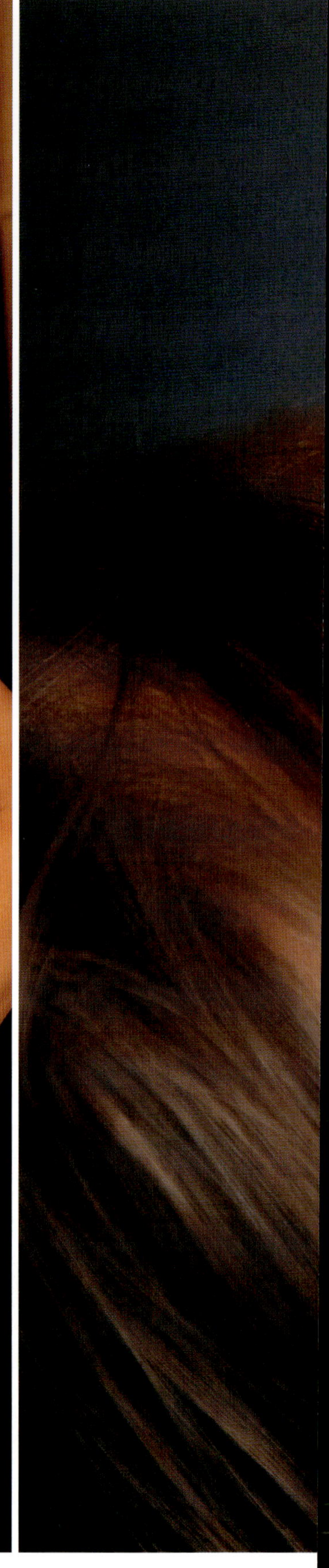

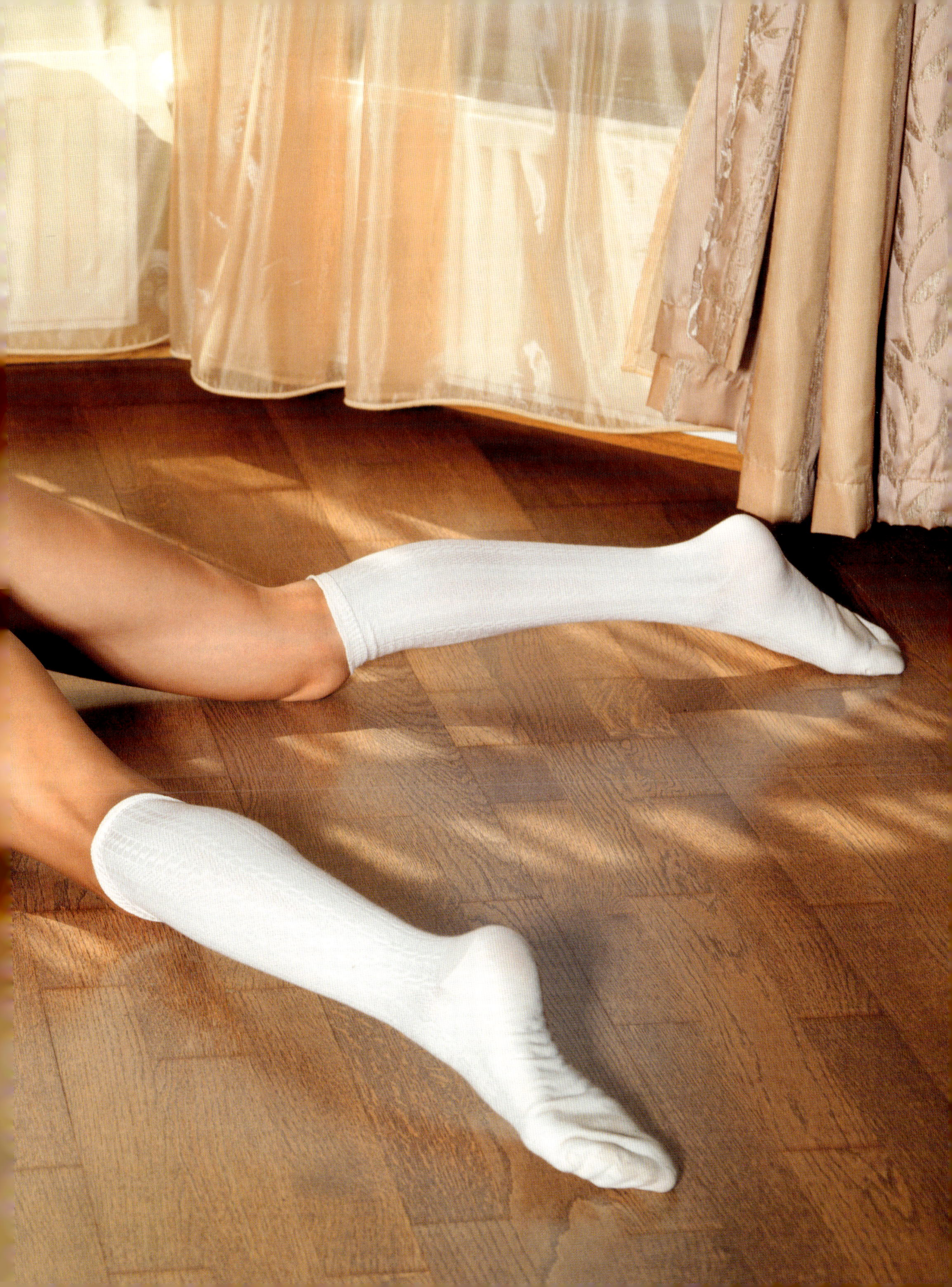

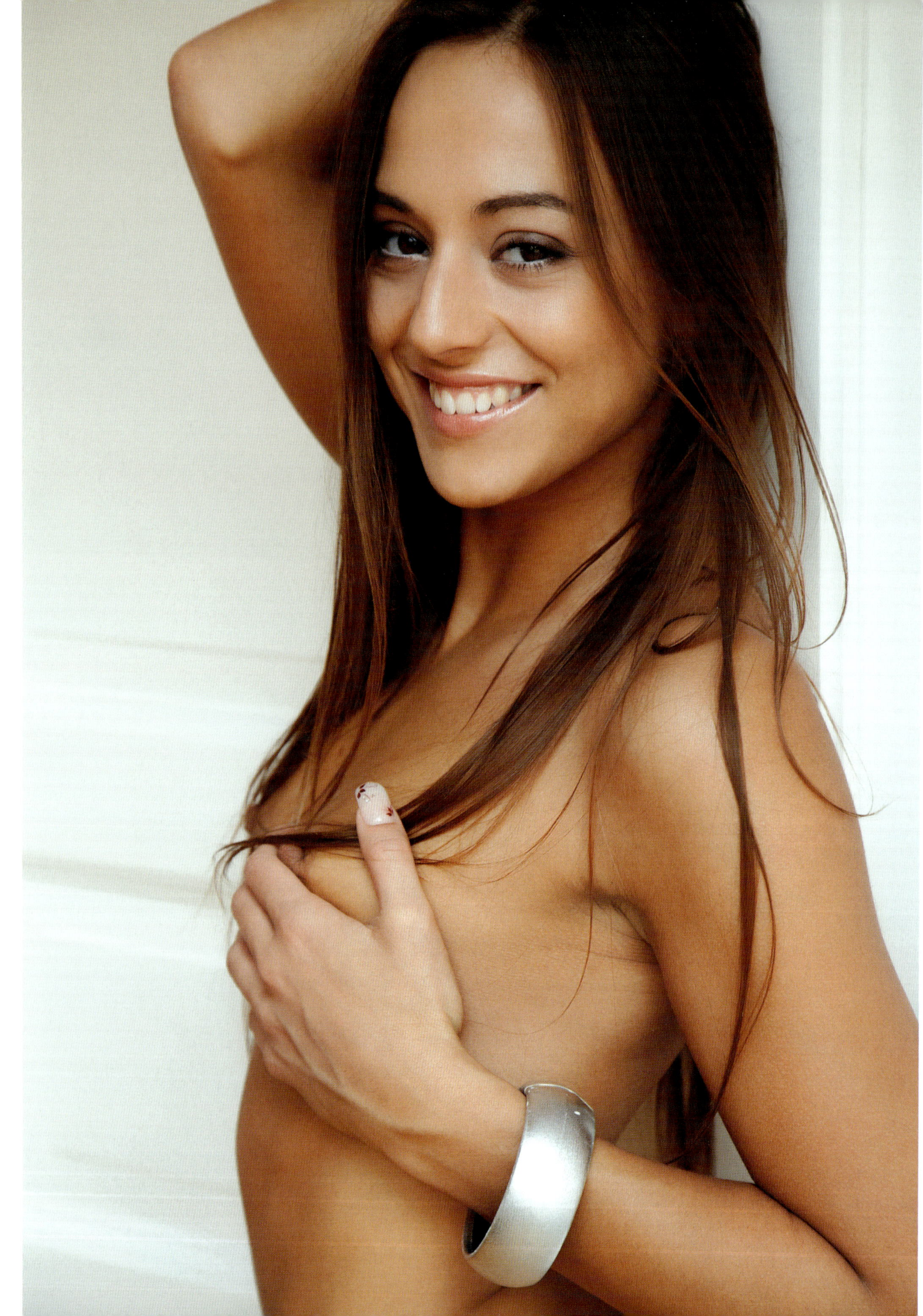

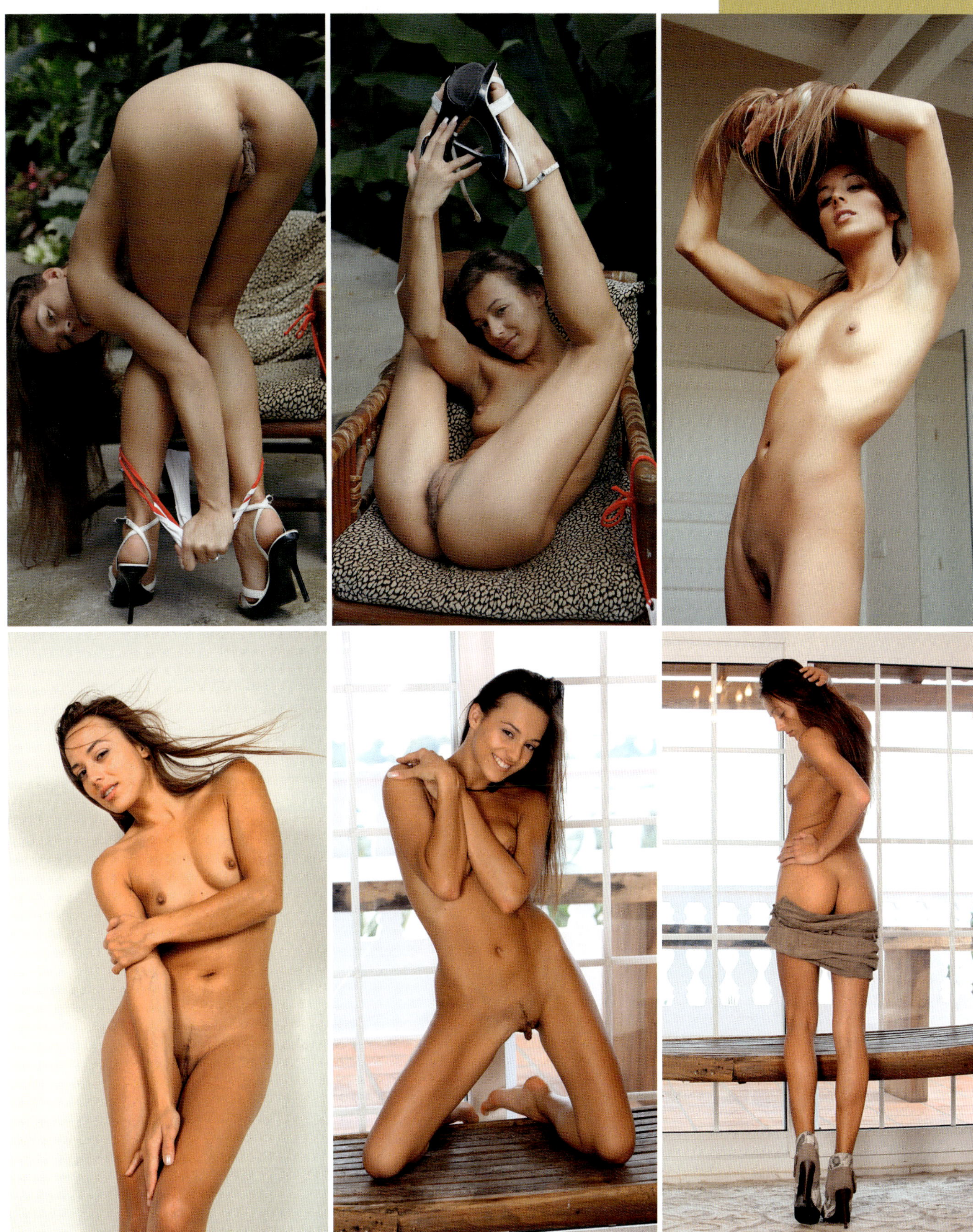

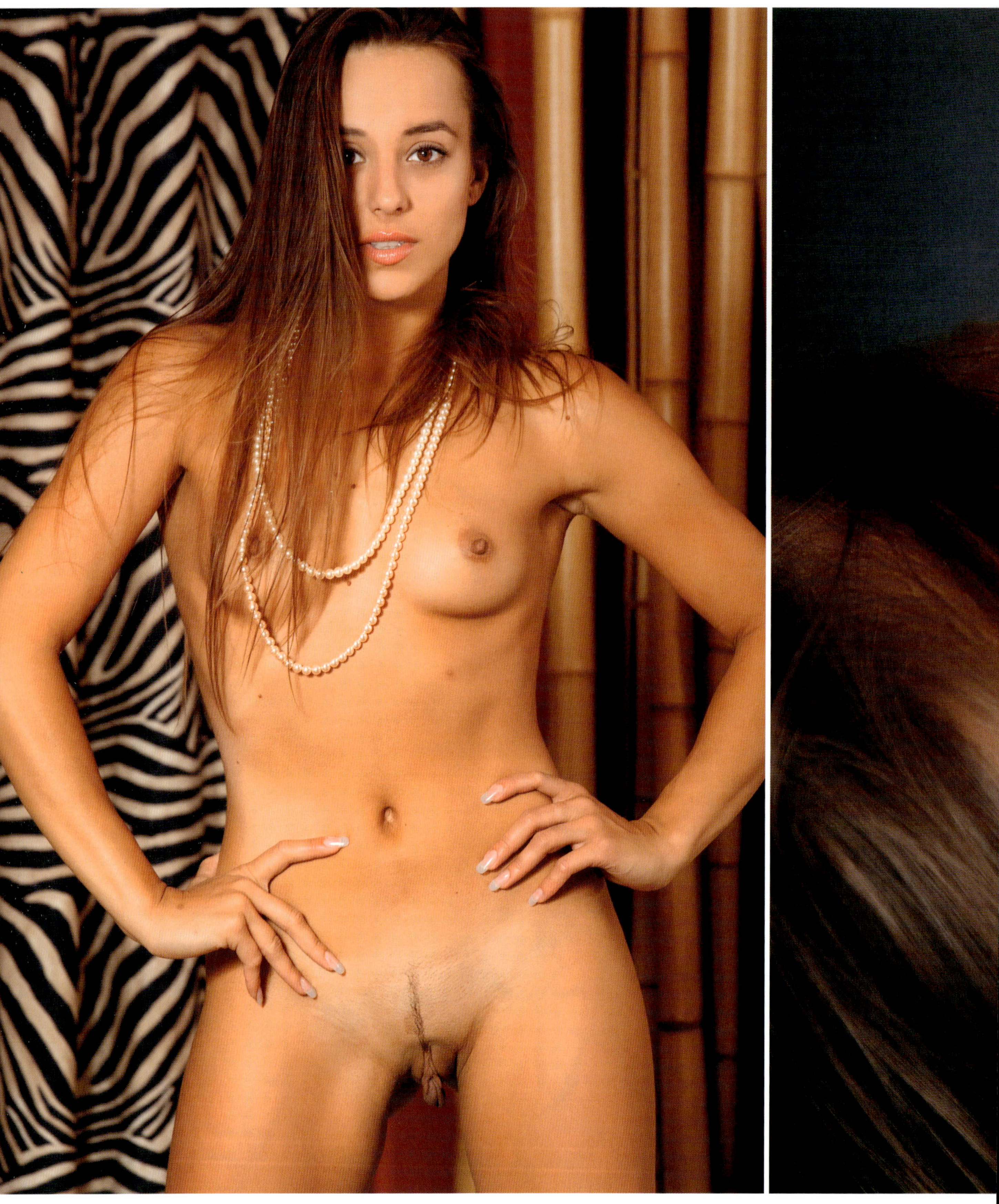

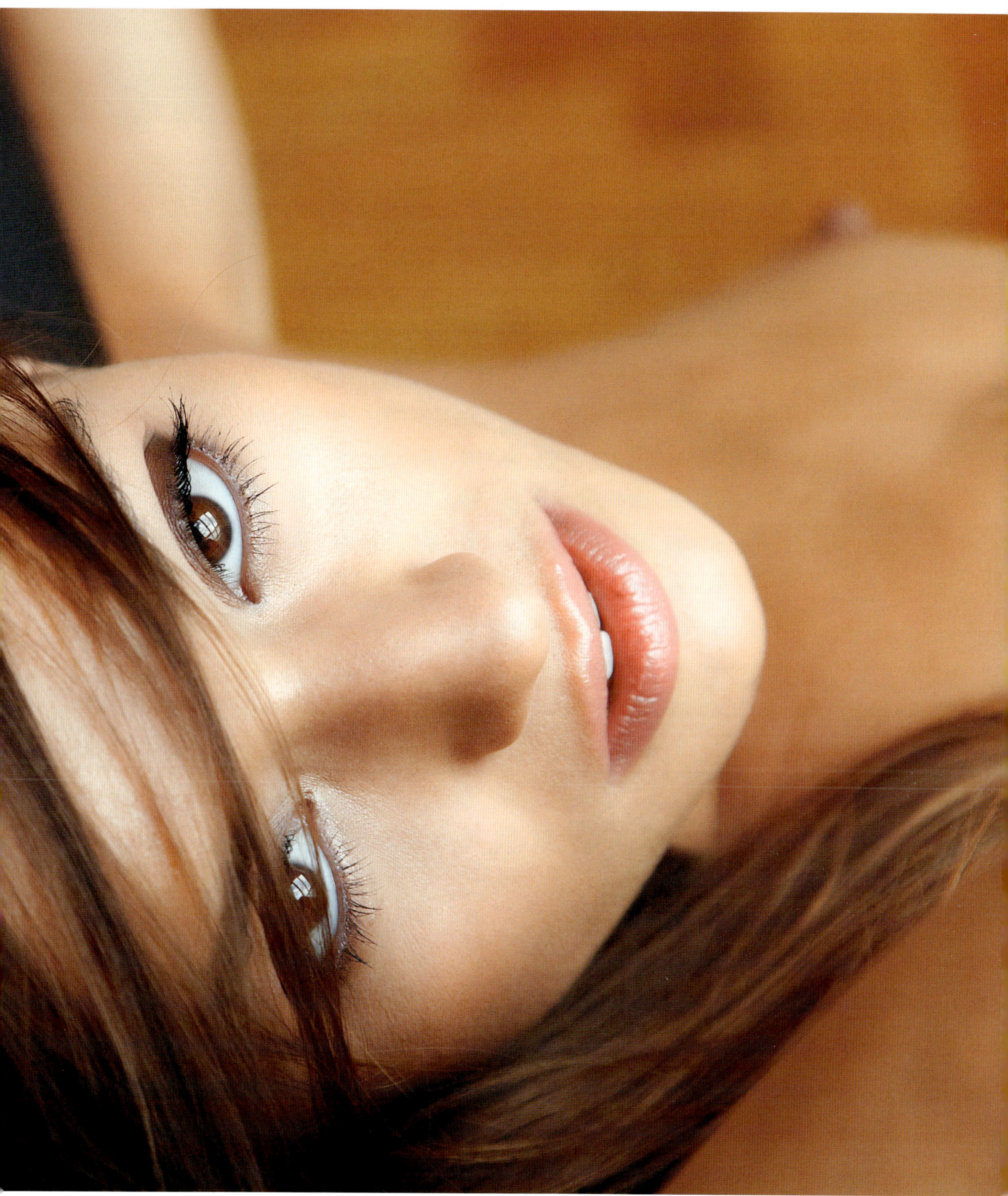

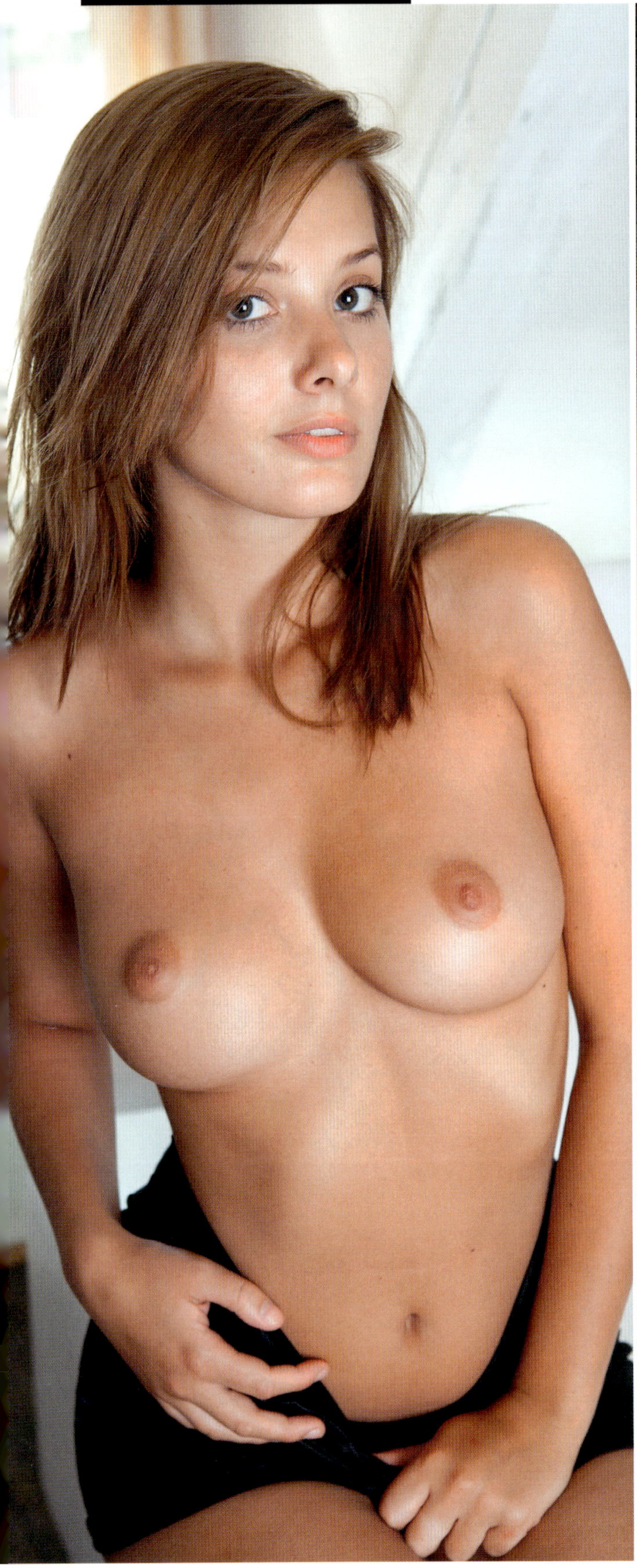

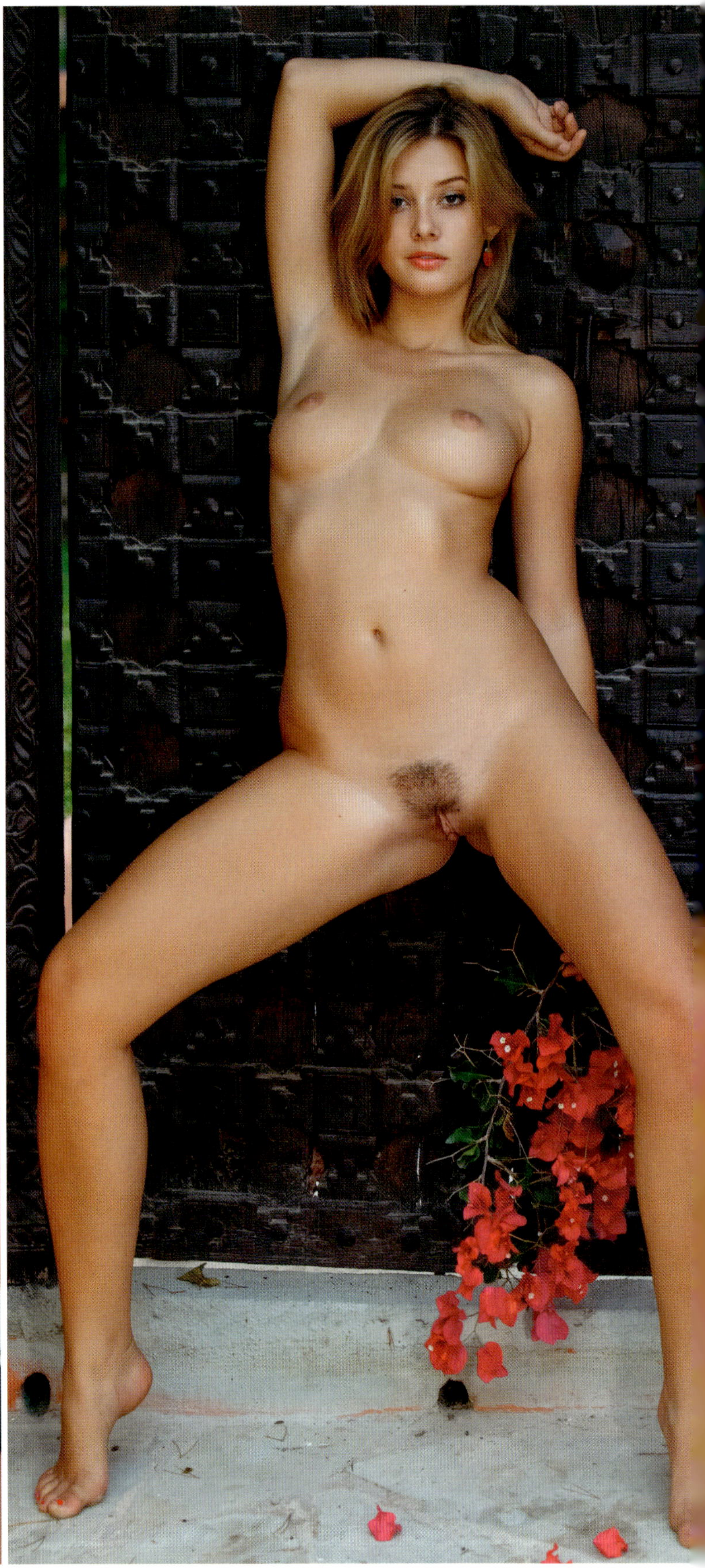

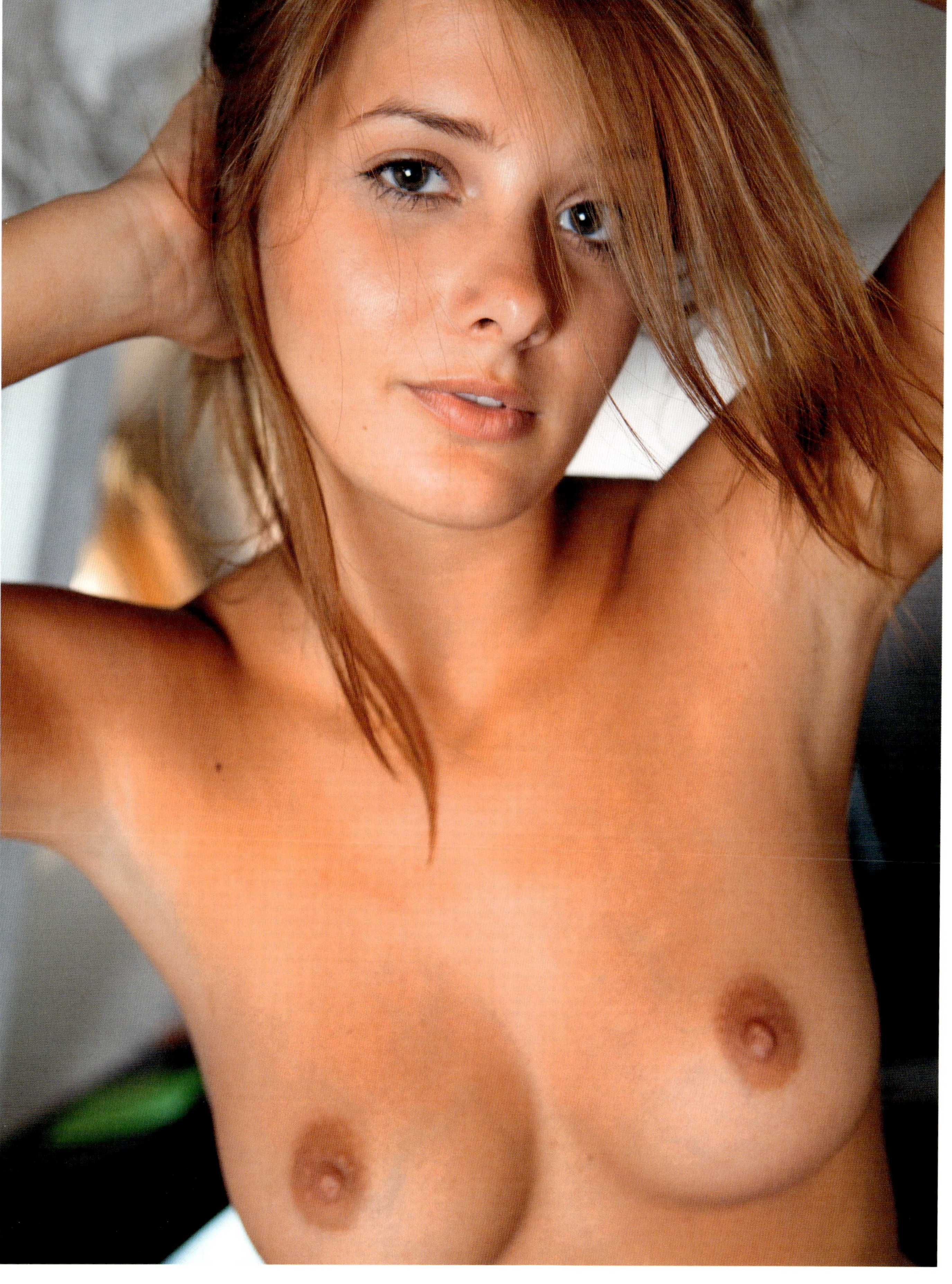

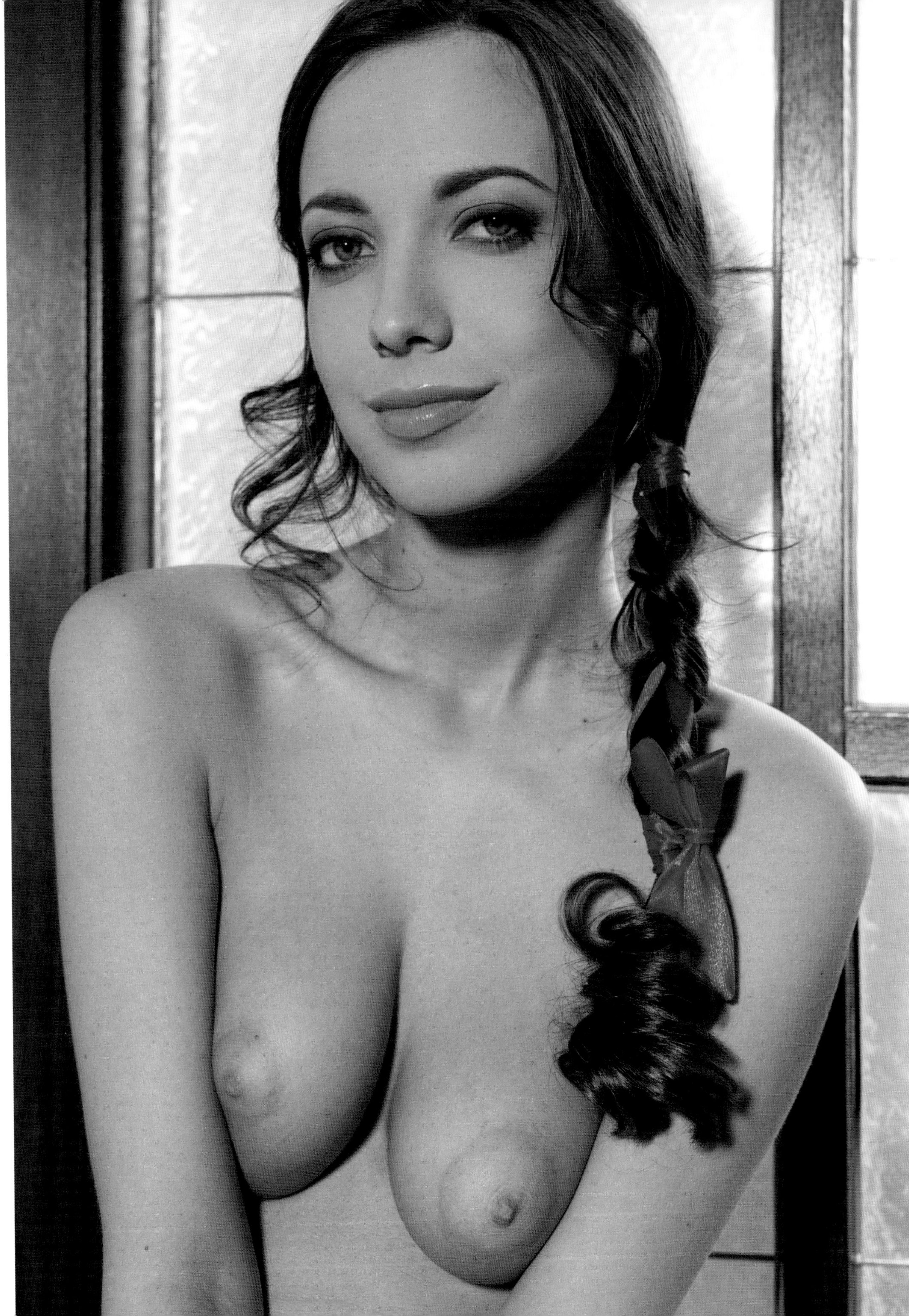

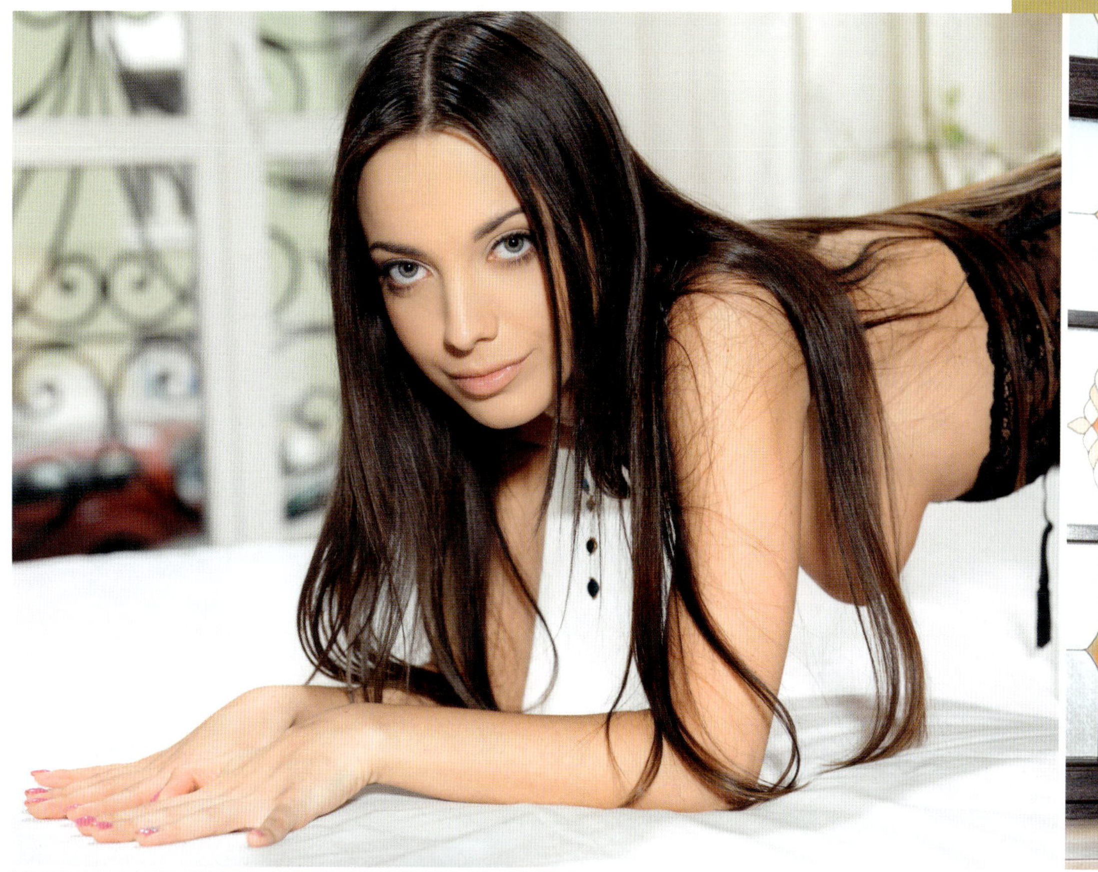

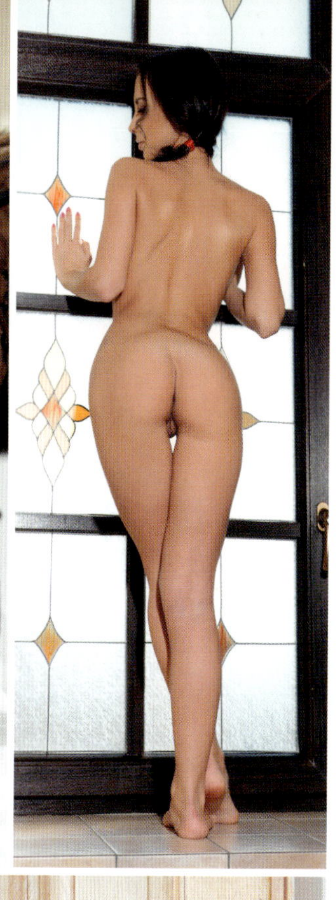

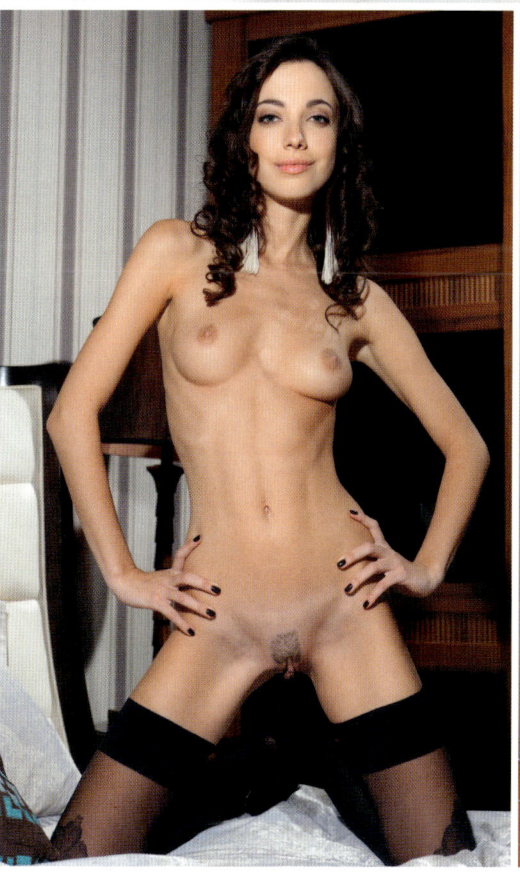

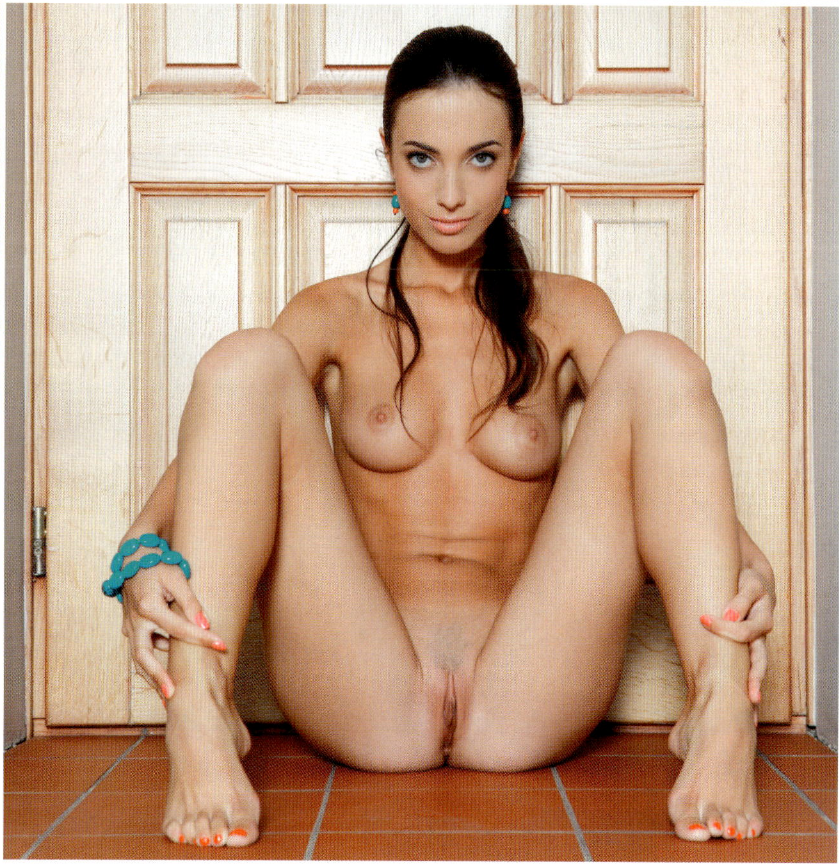

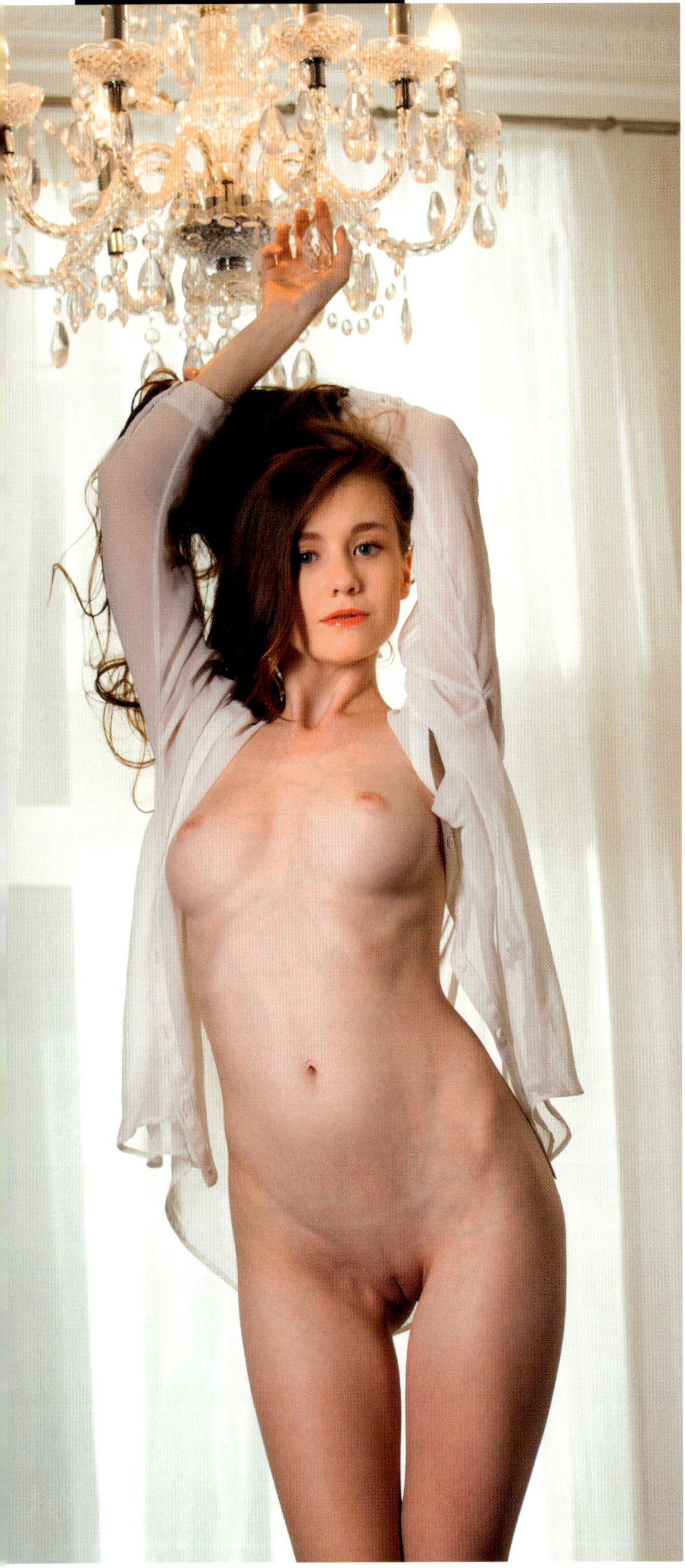

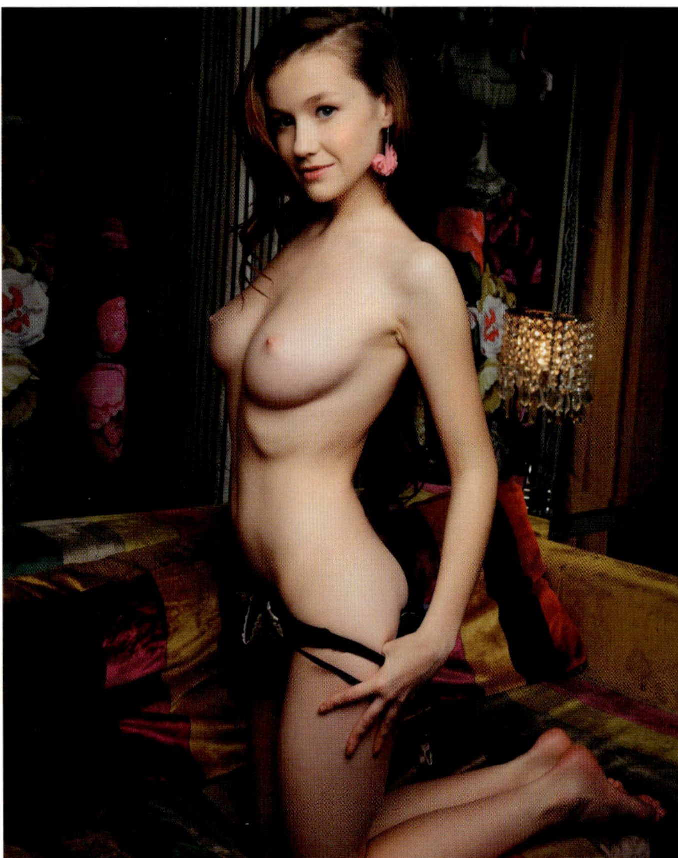

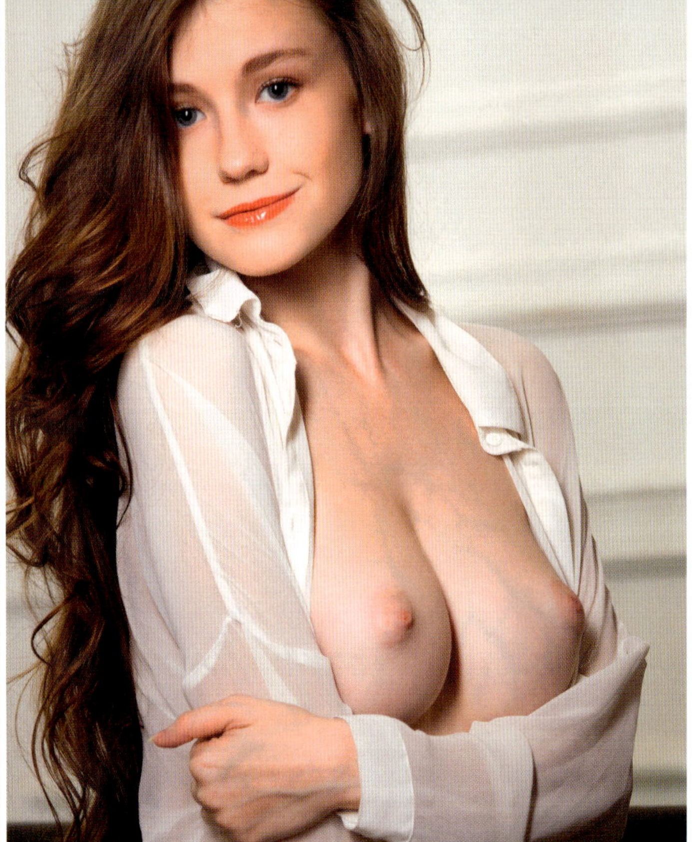

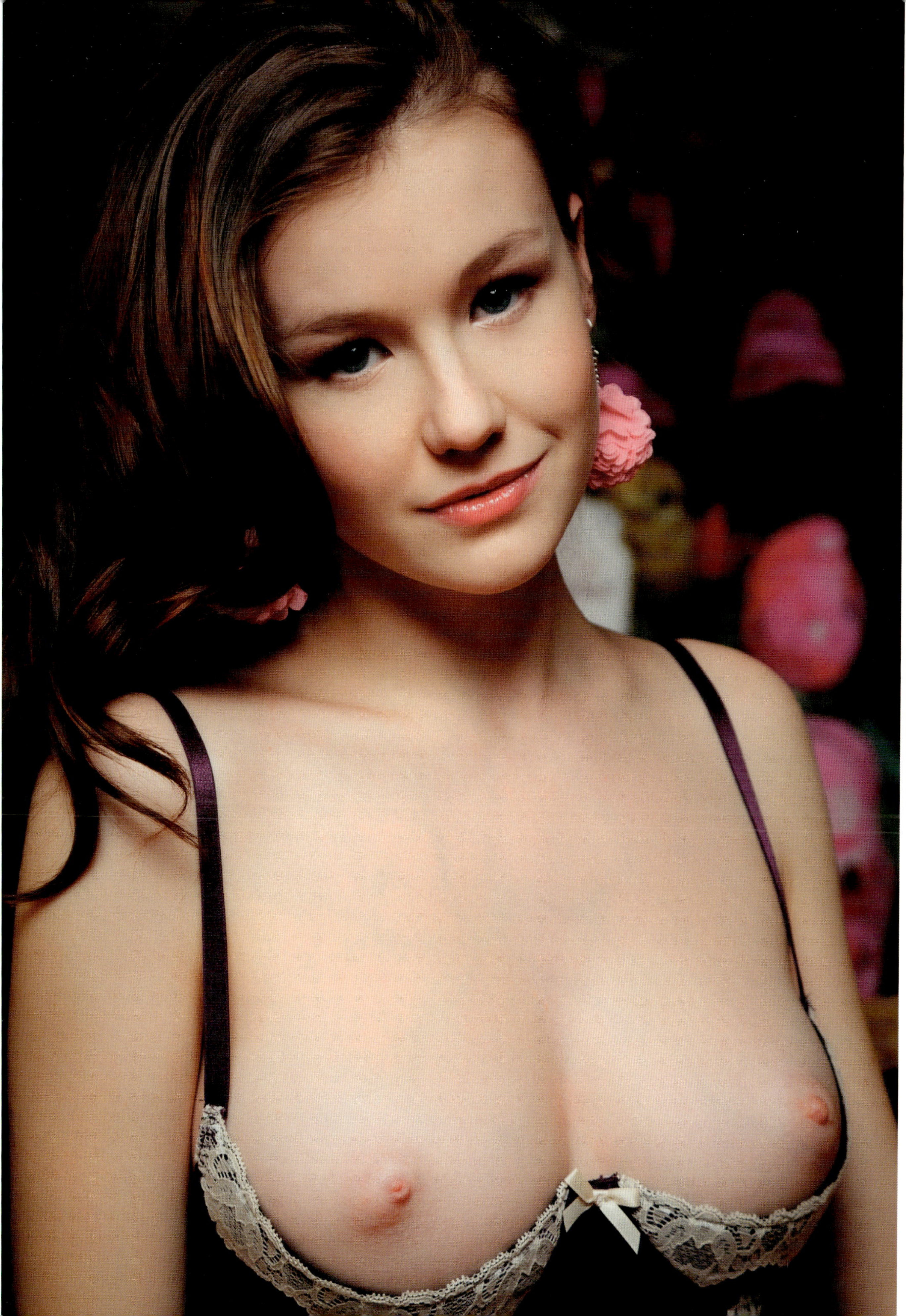

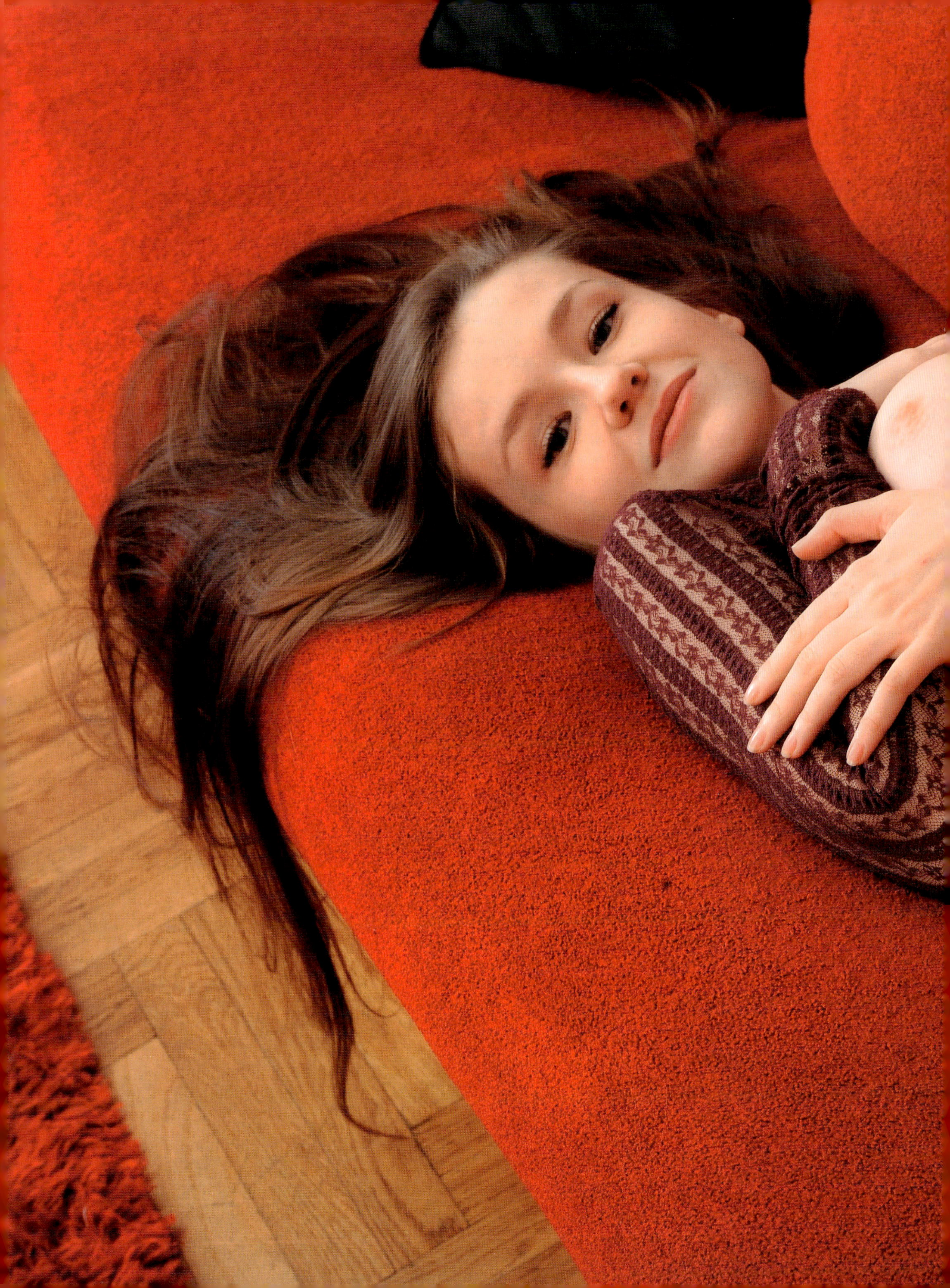

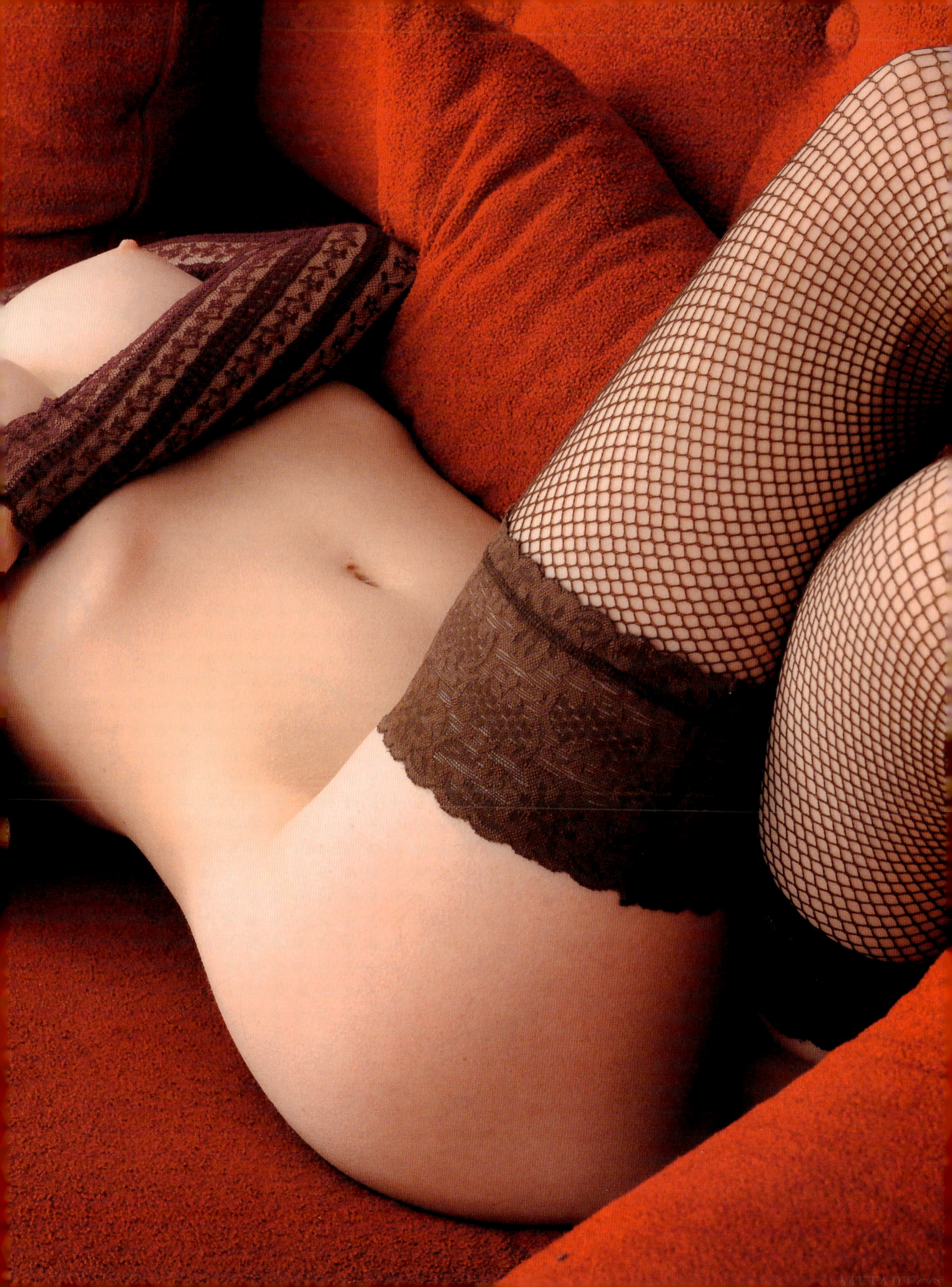

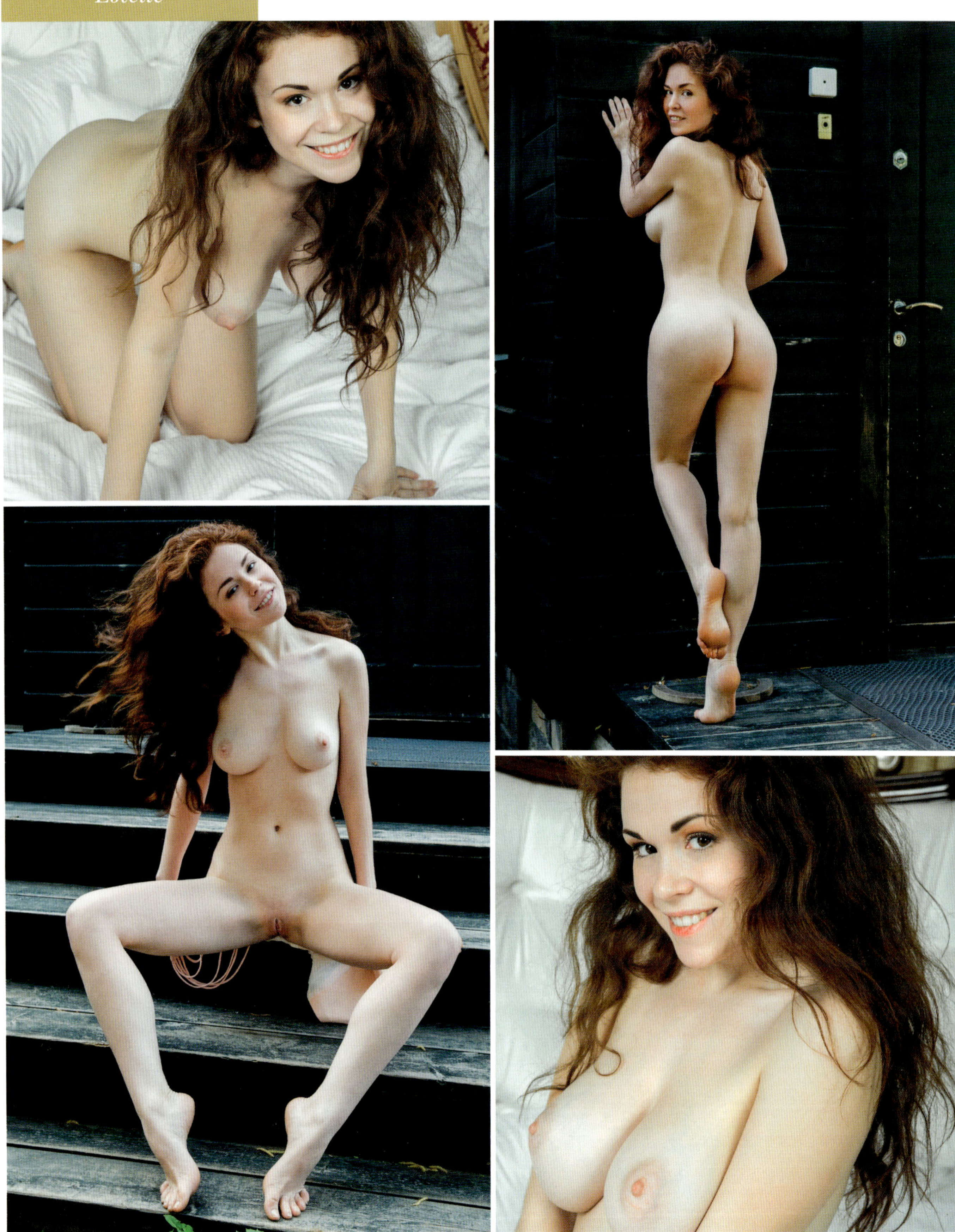

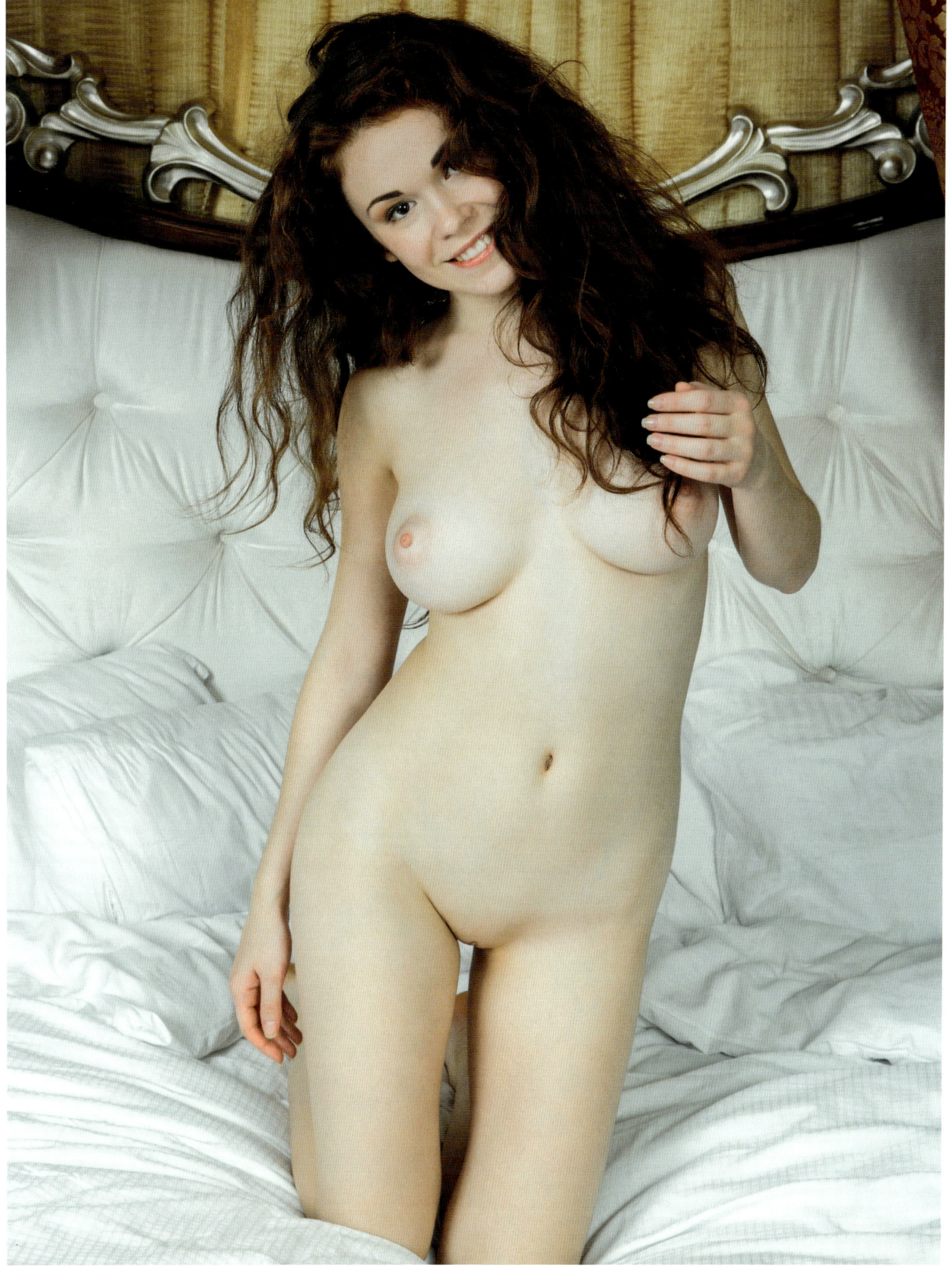

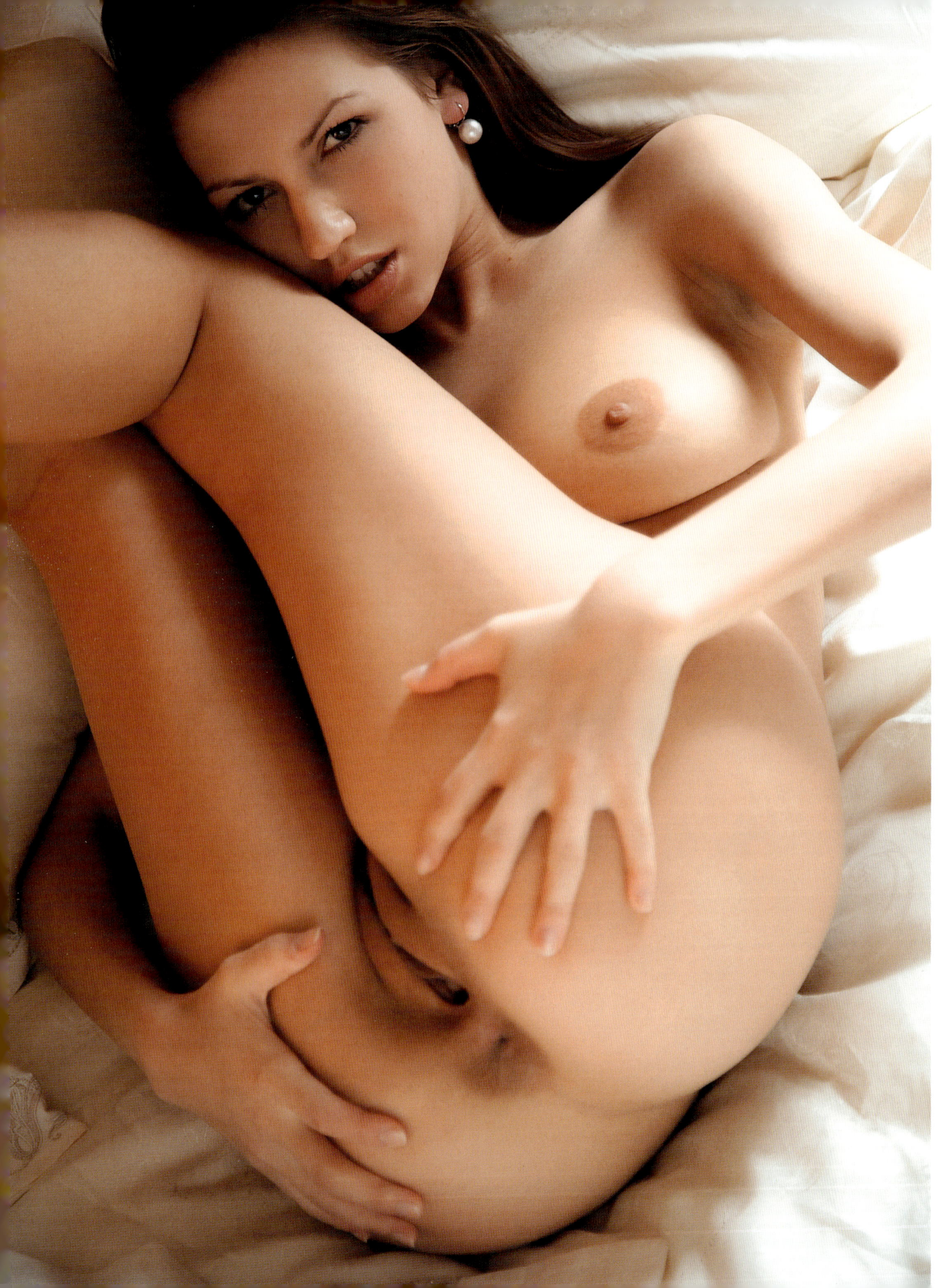

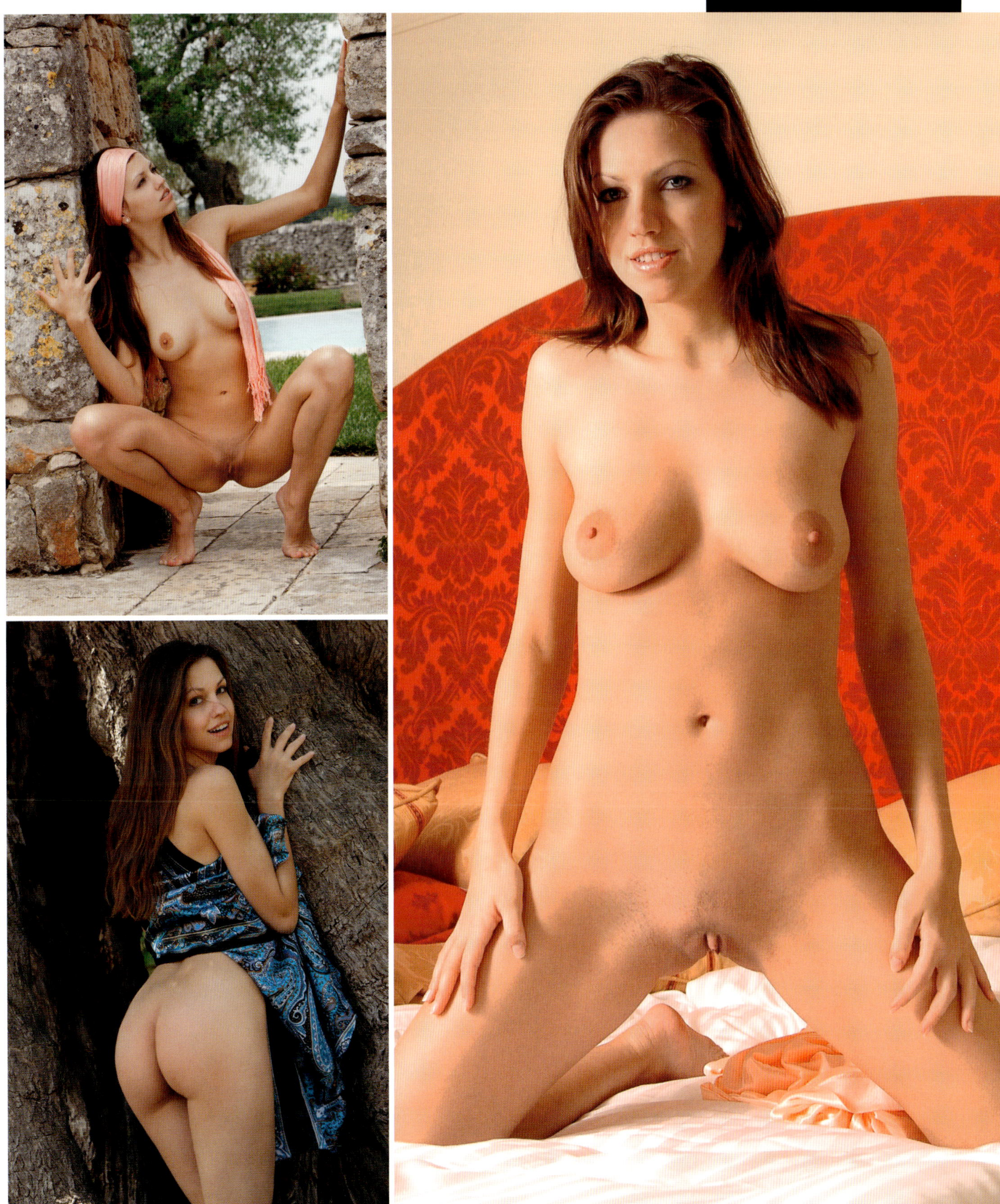

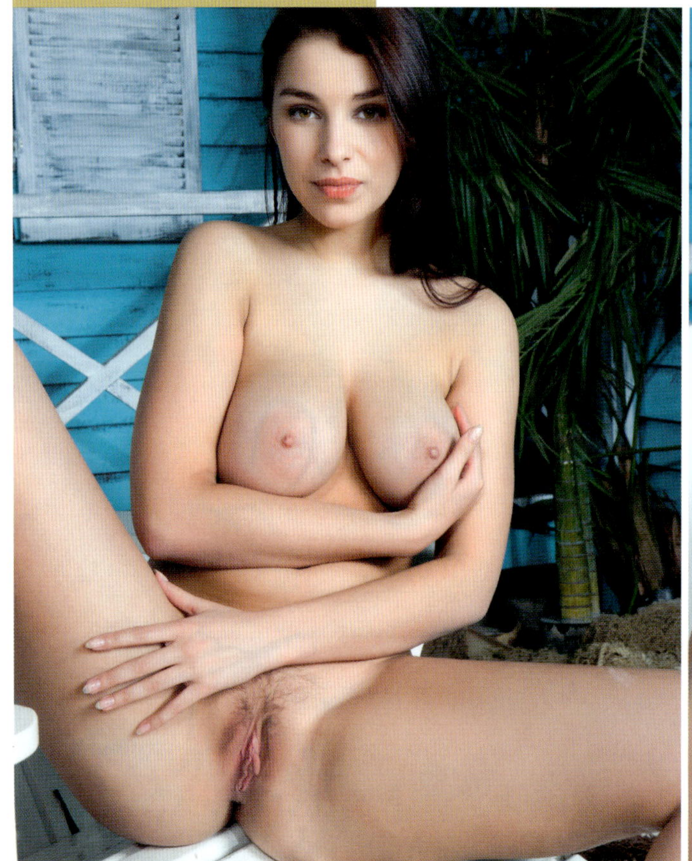

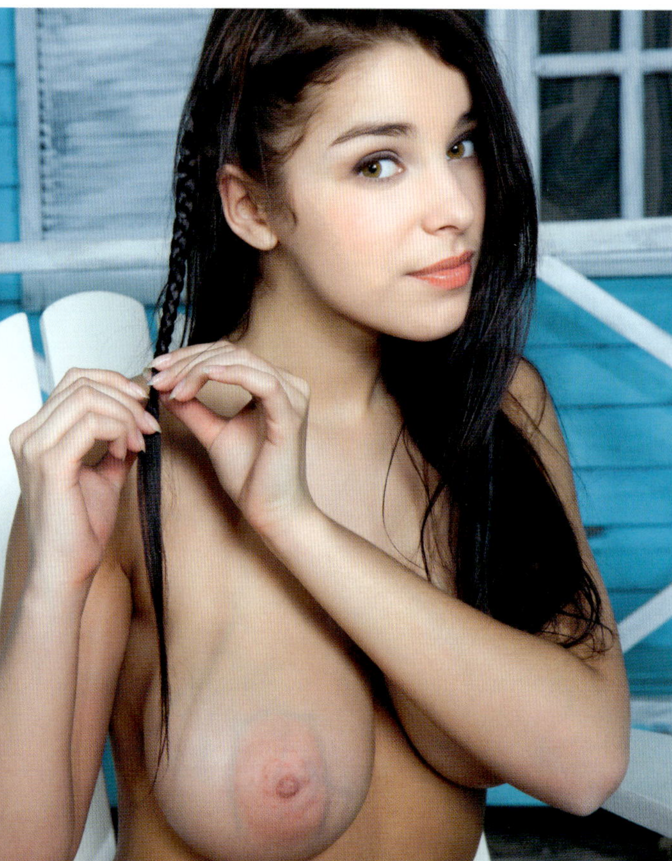

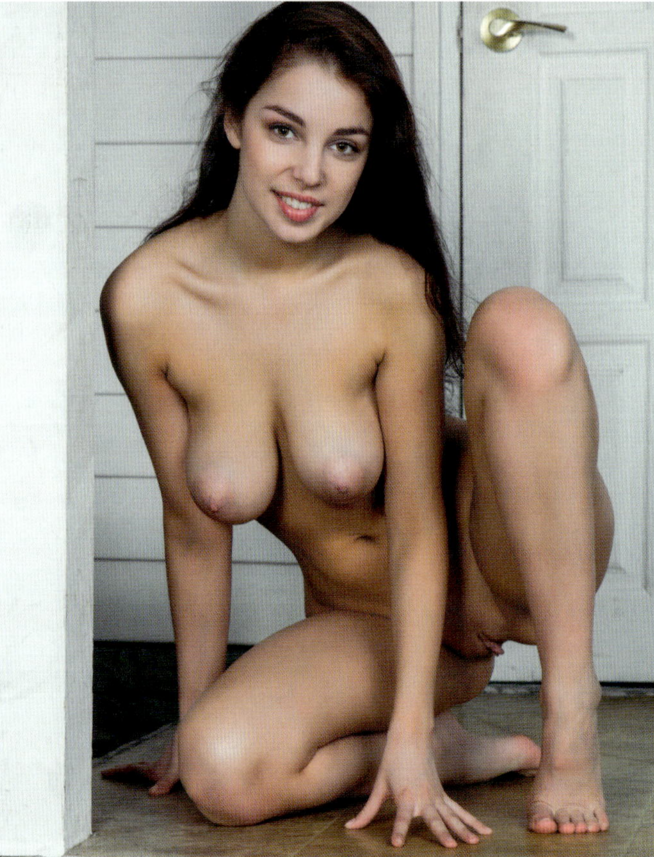

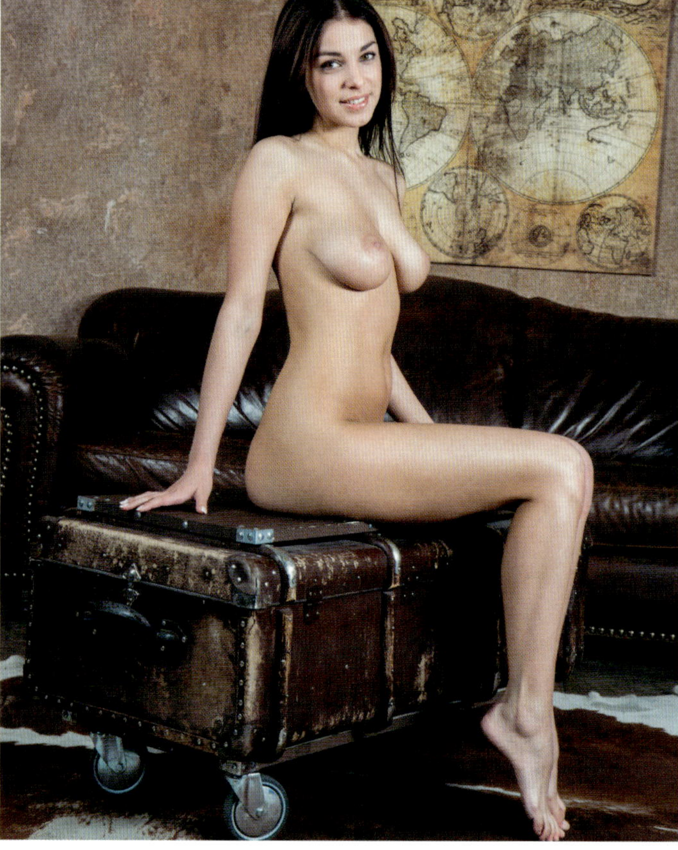

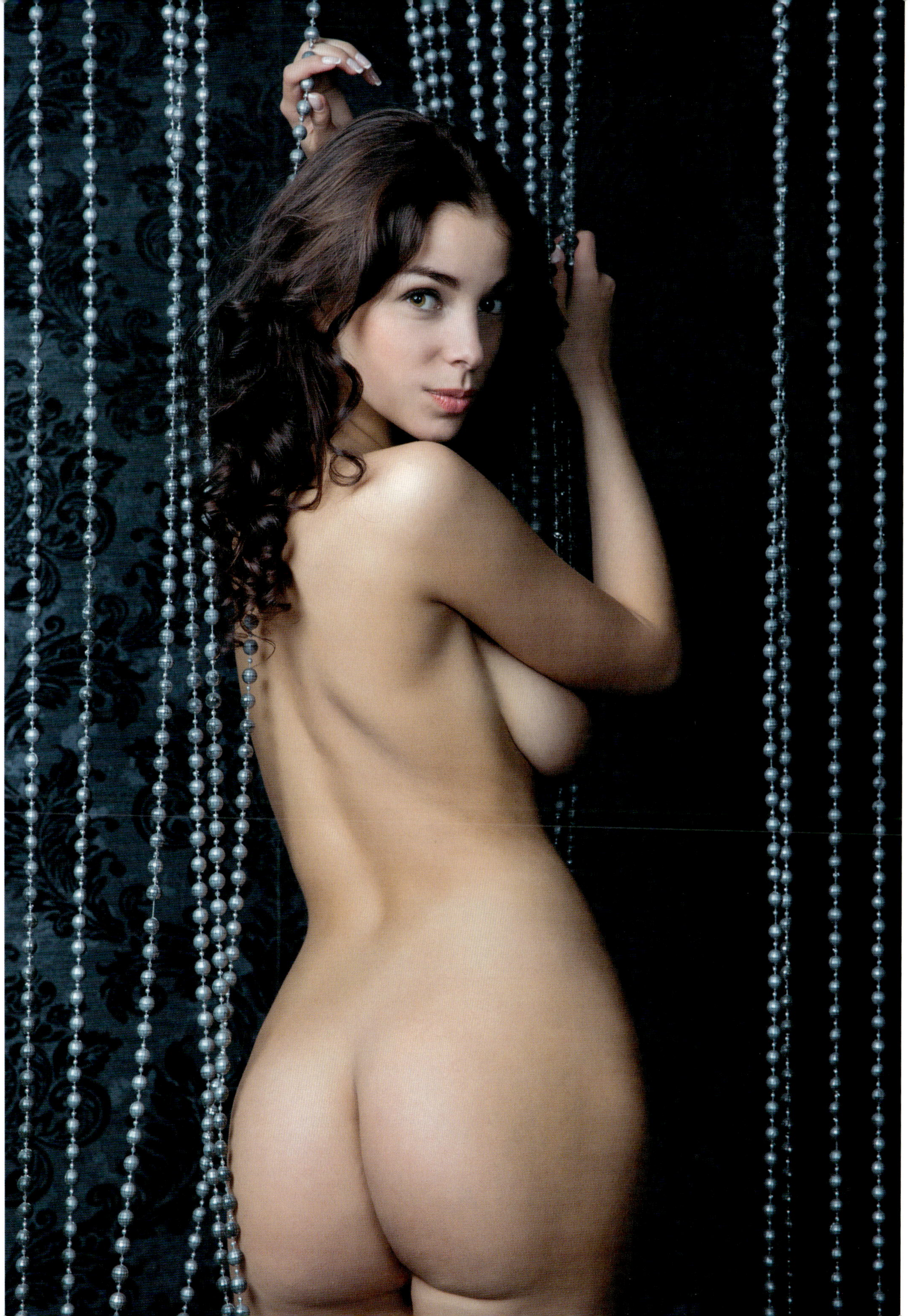

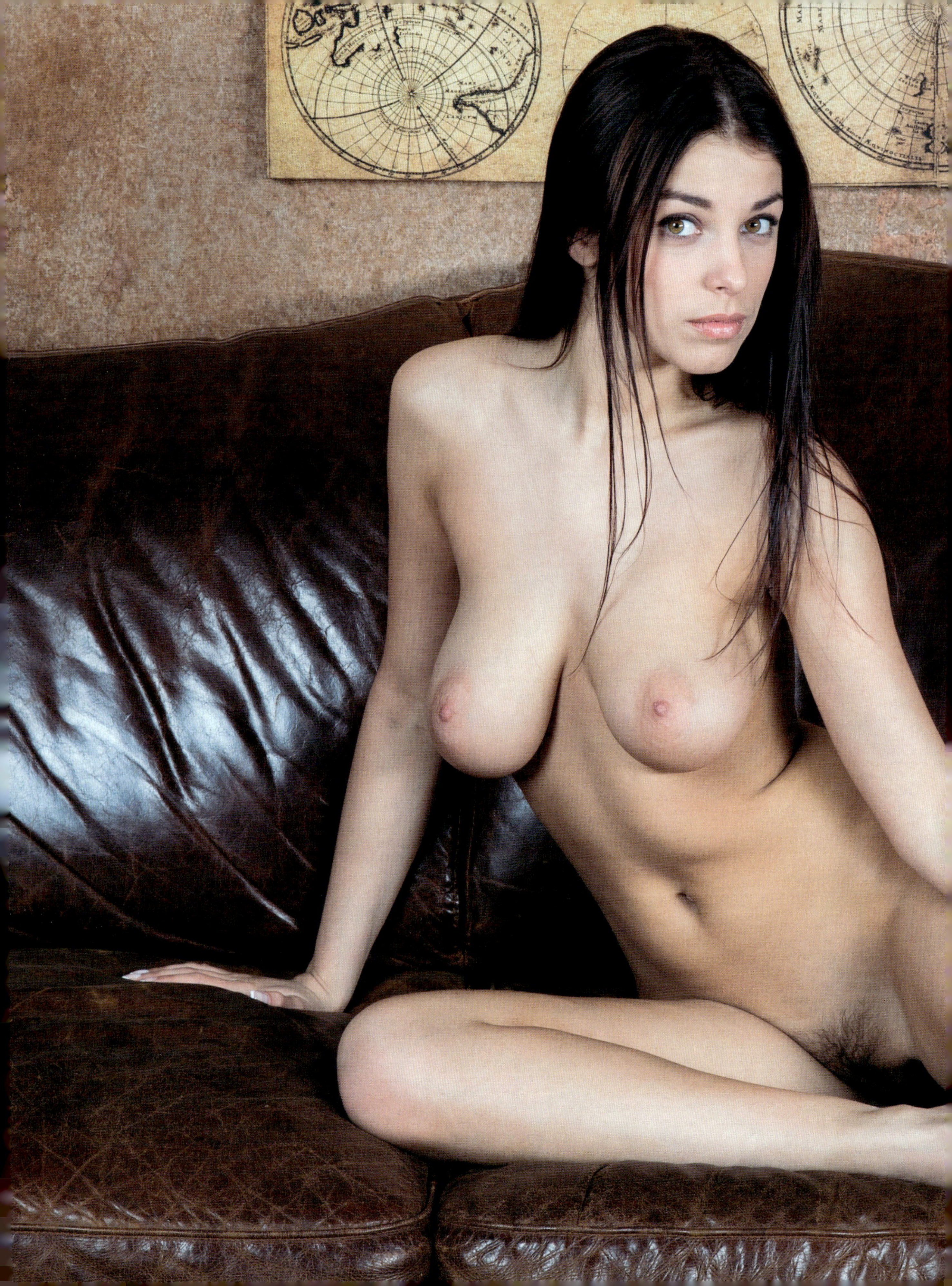

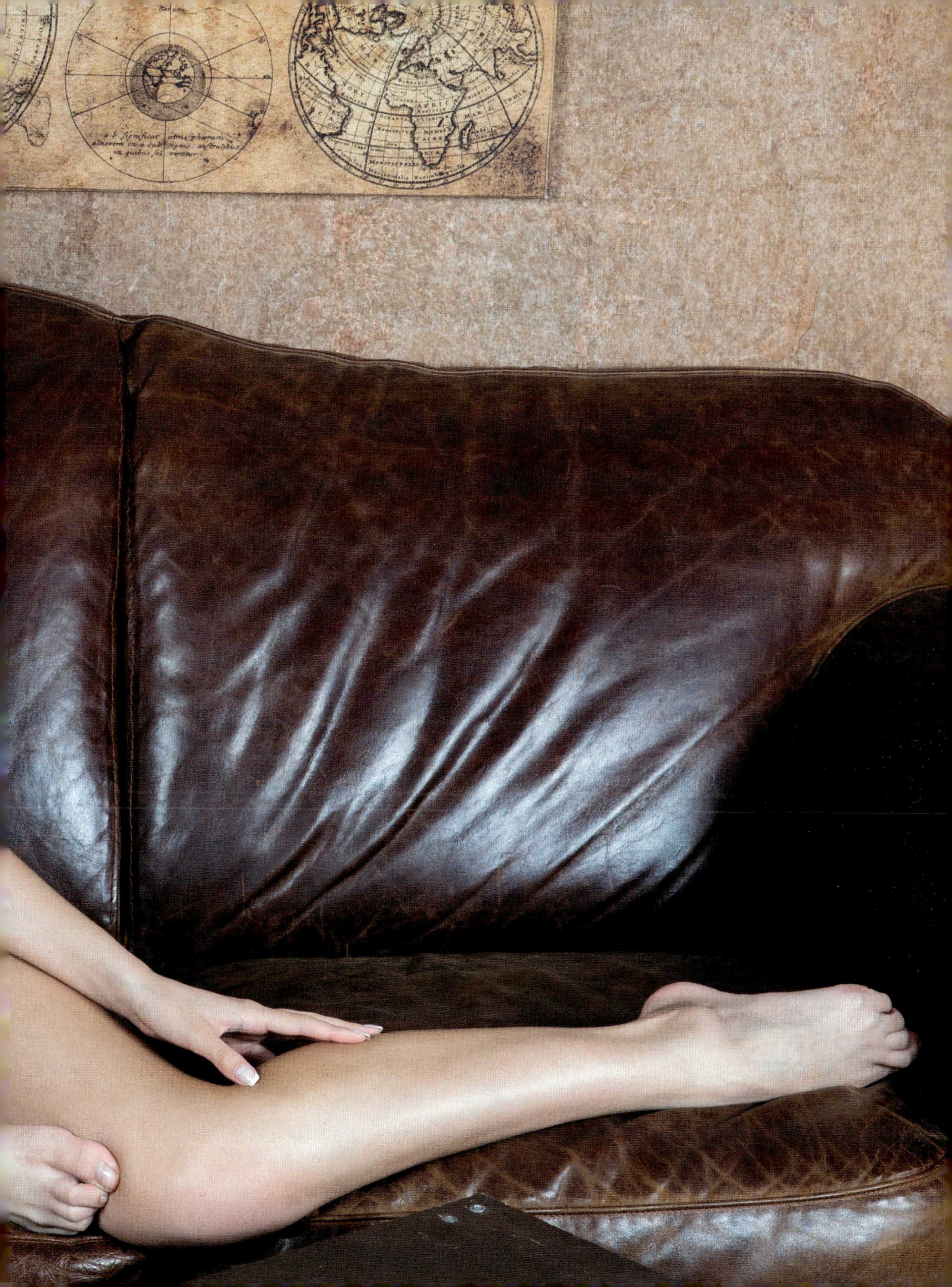

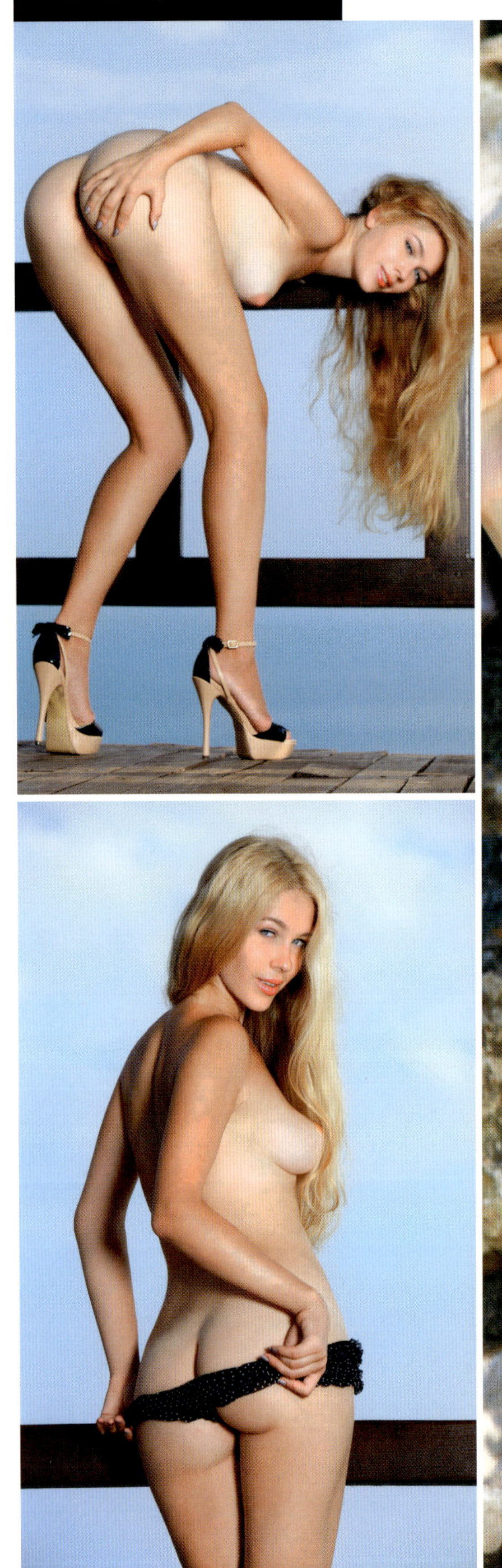

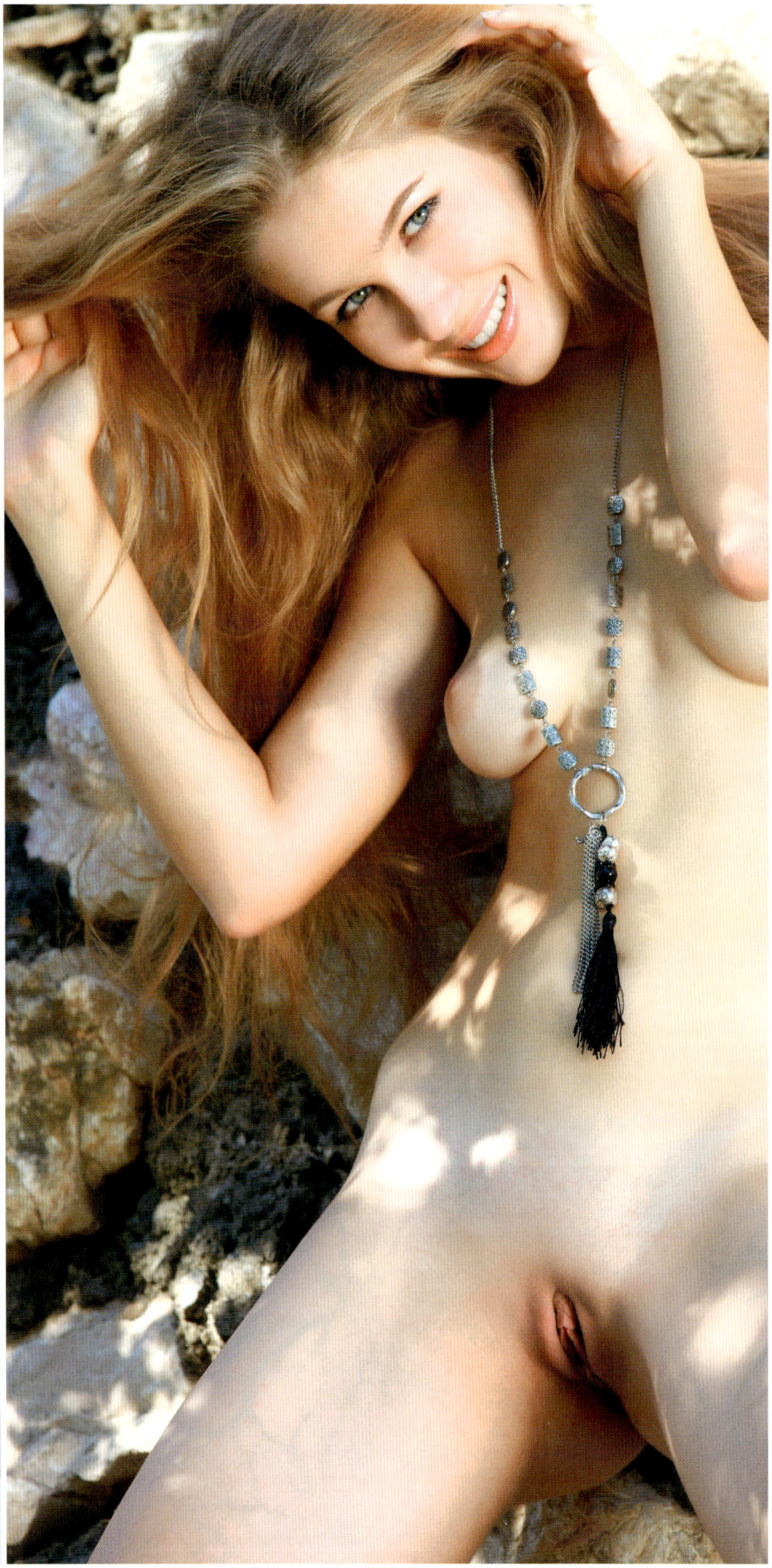

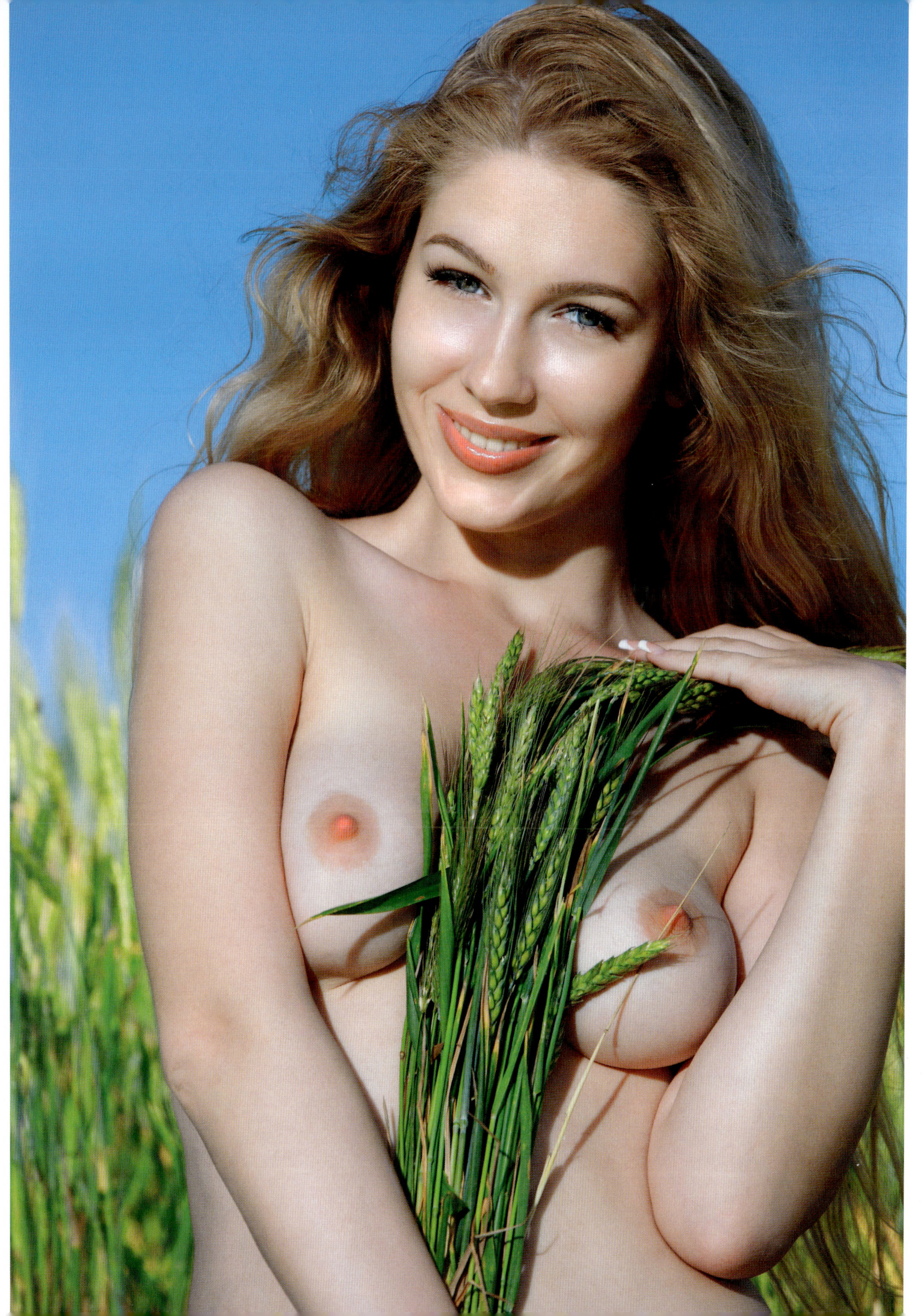

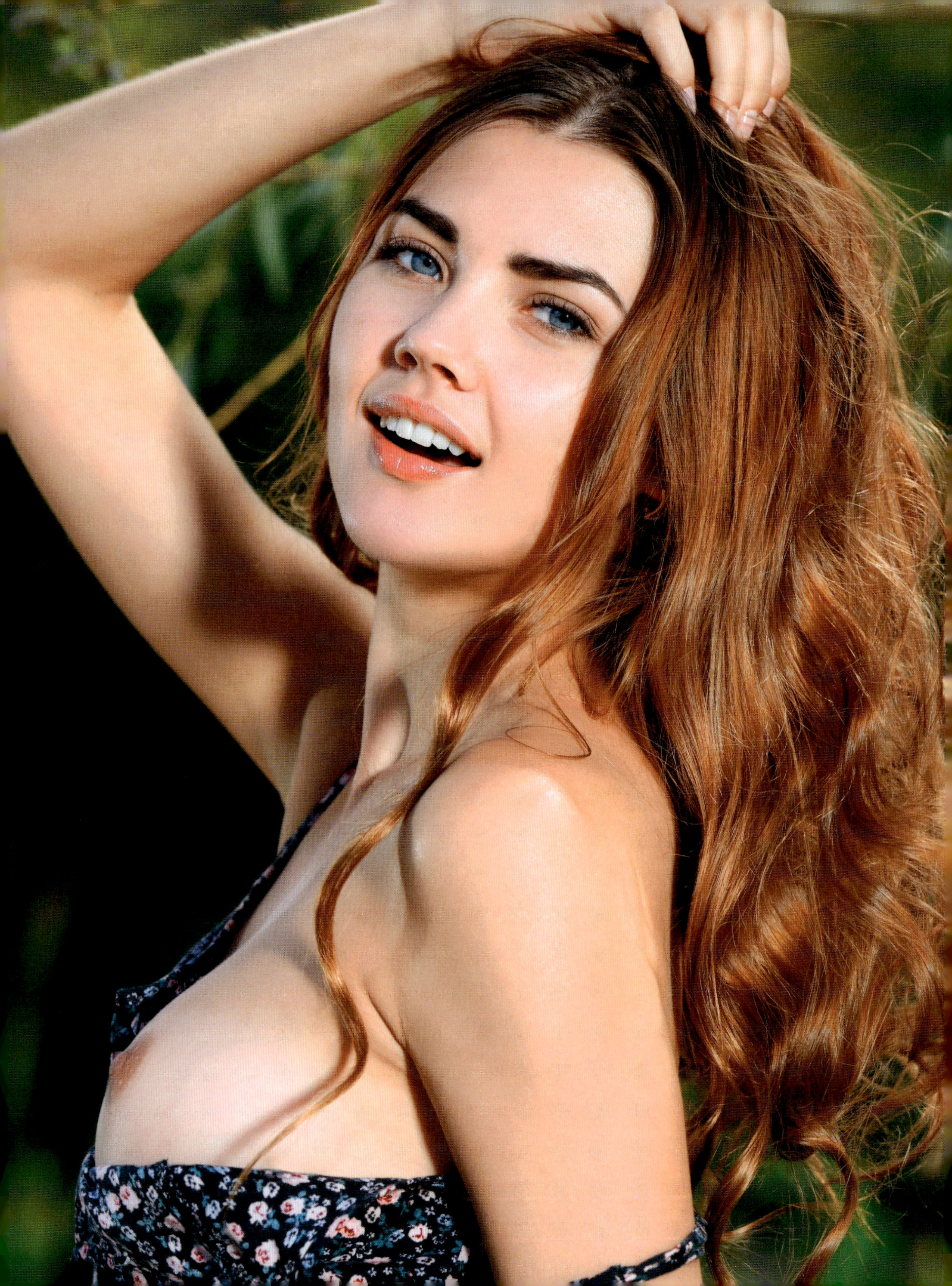

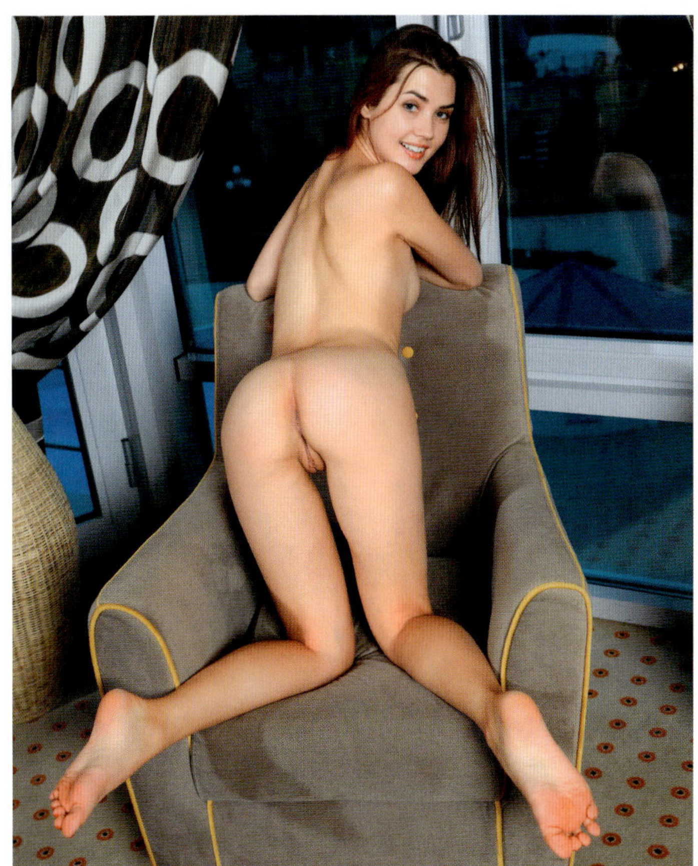

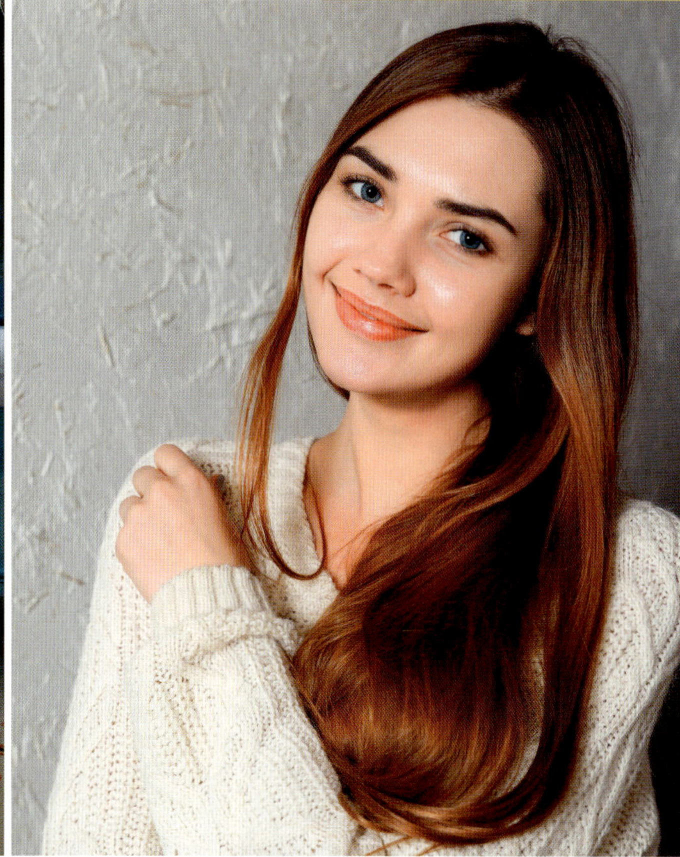

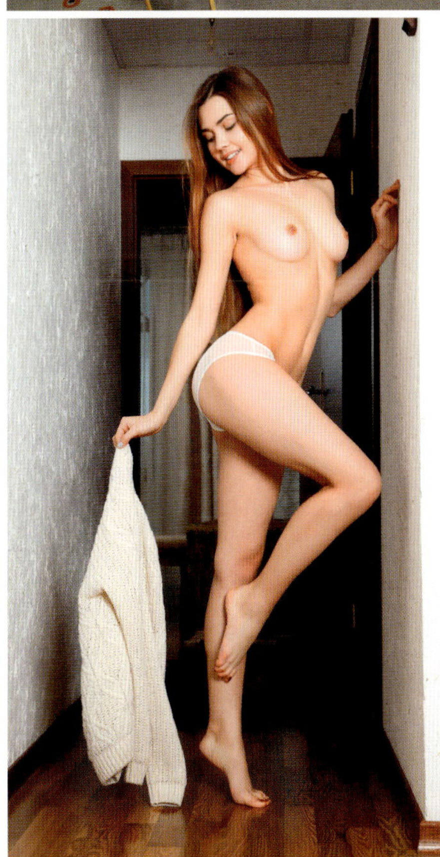

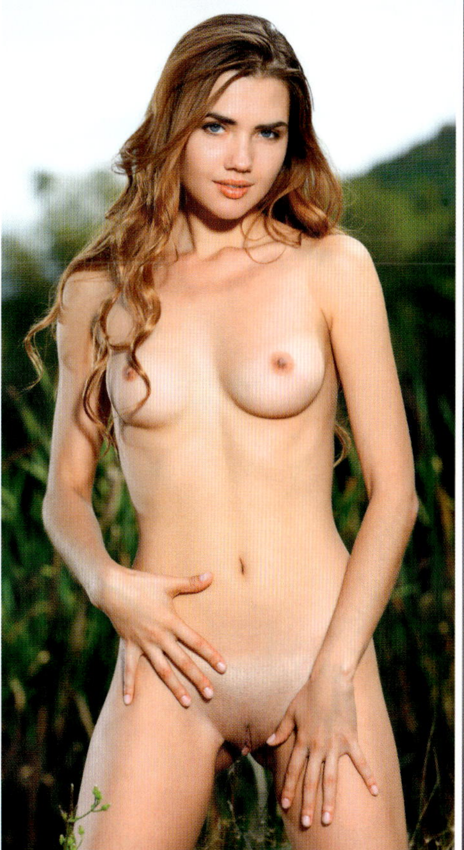

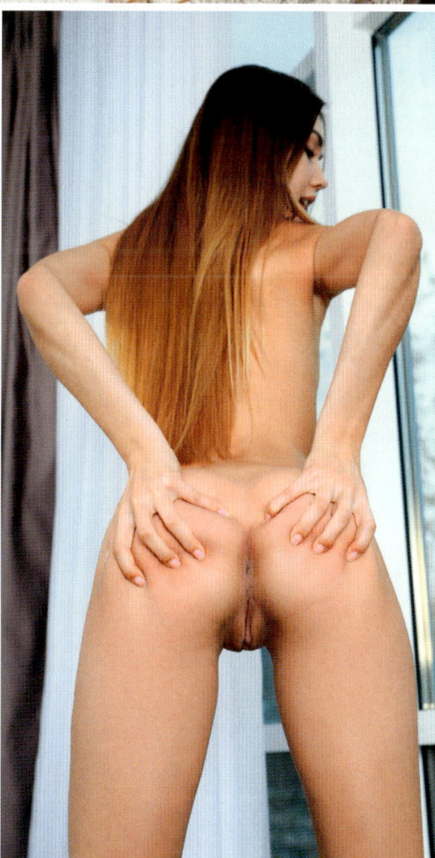

# Gloria Sol

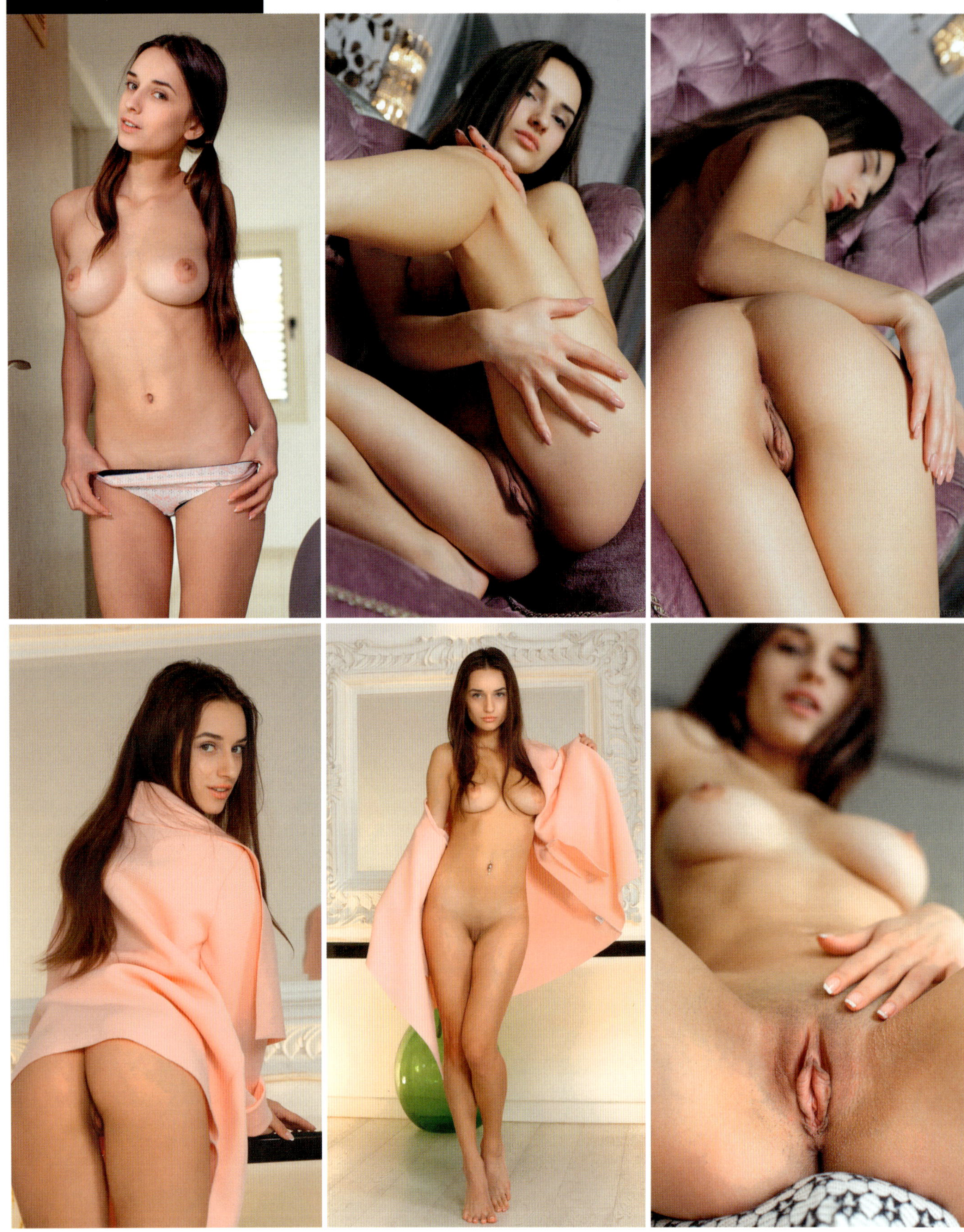

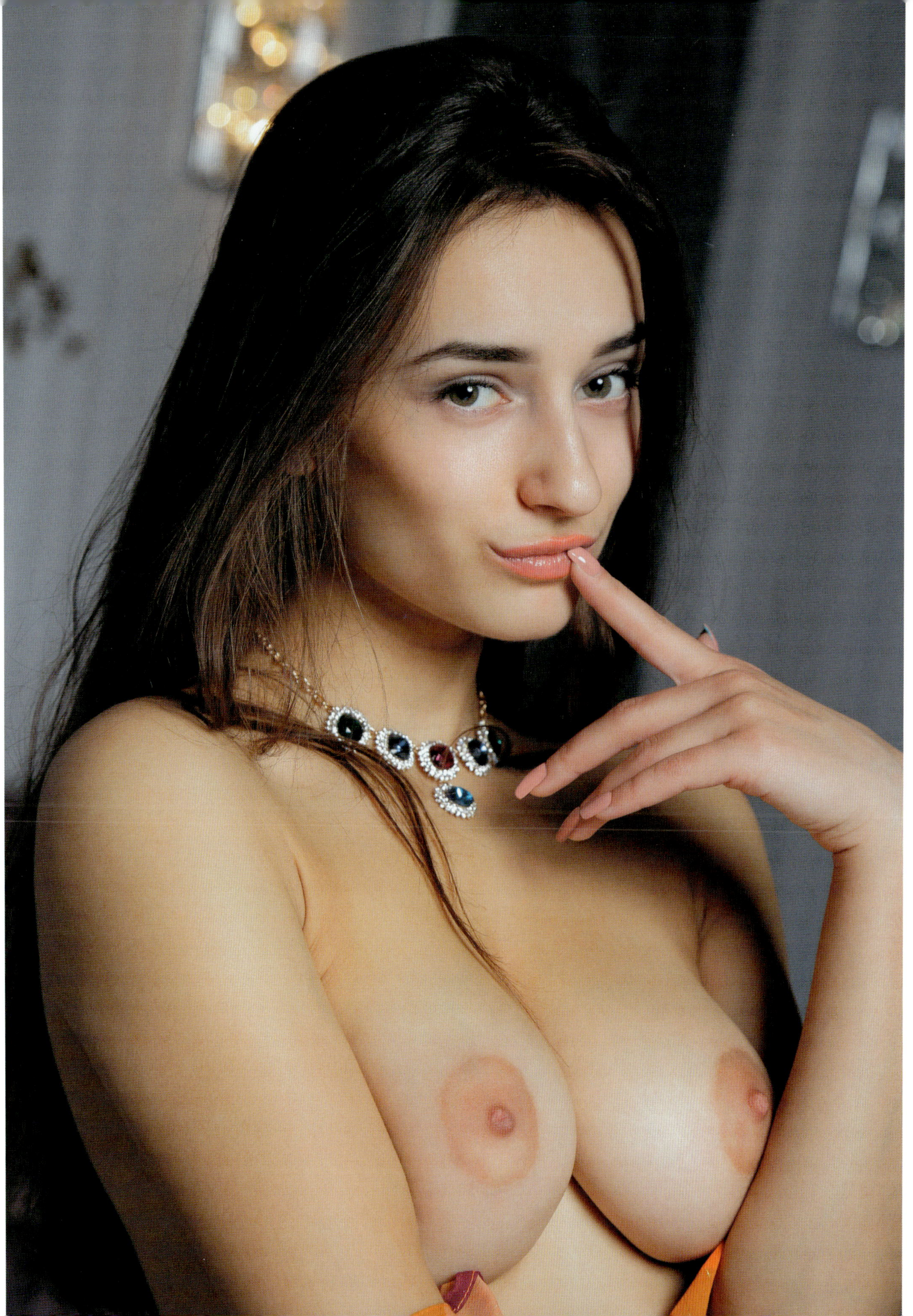

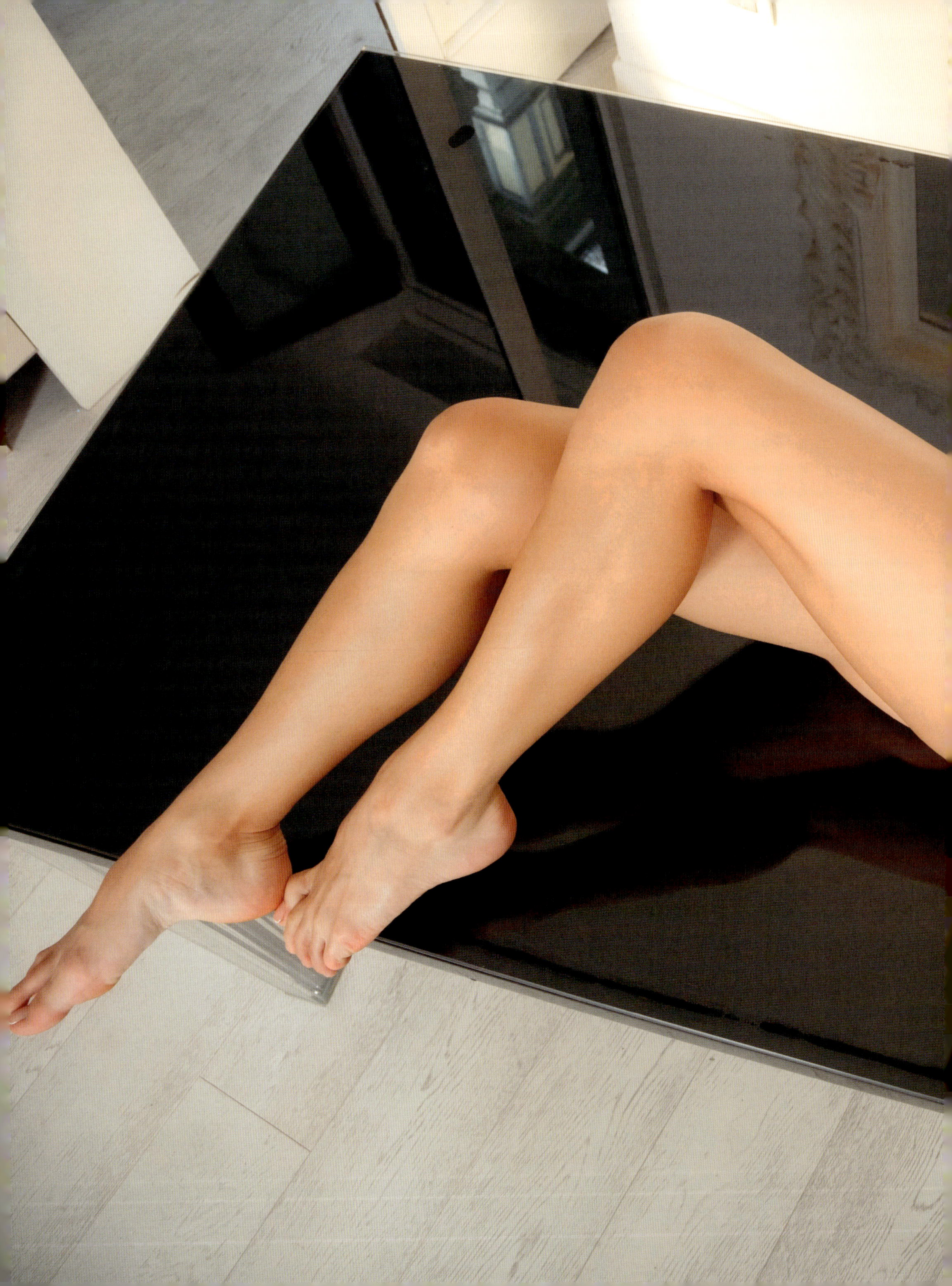

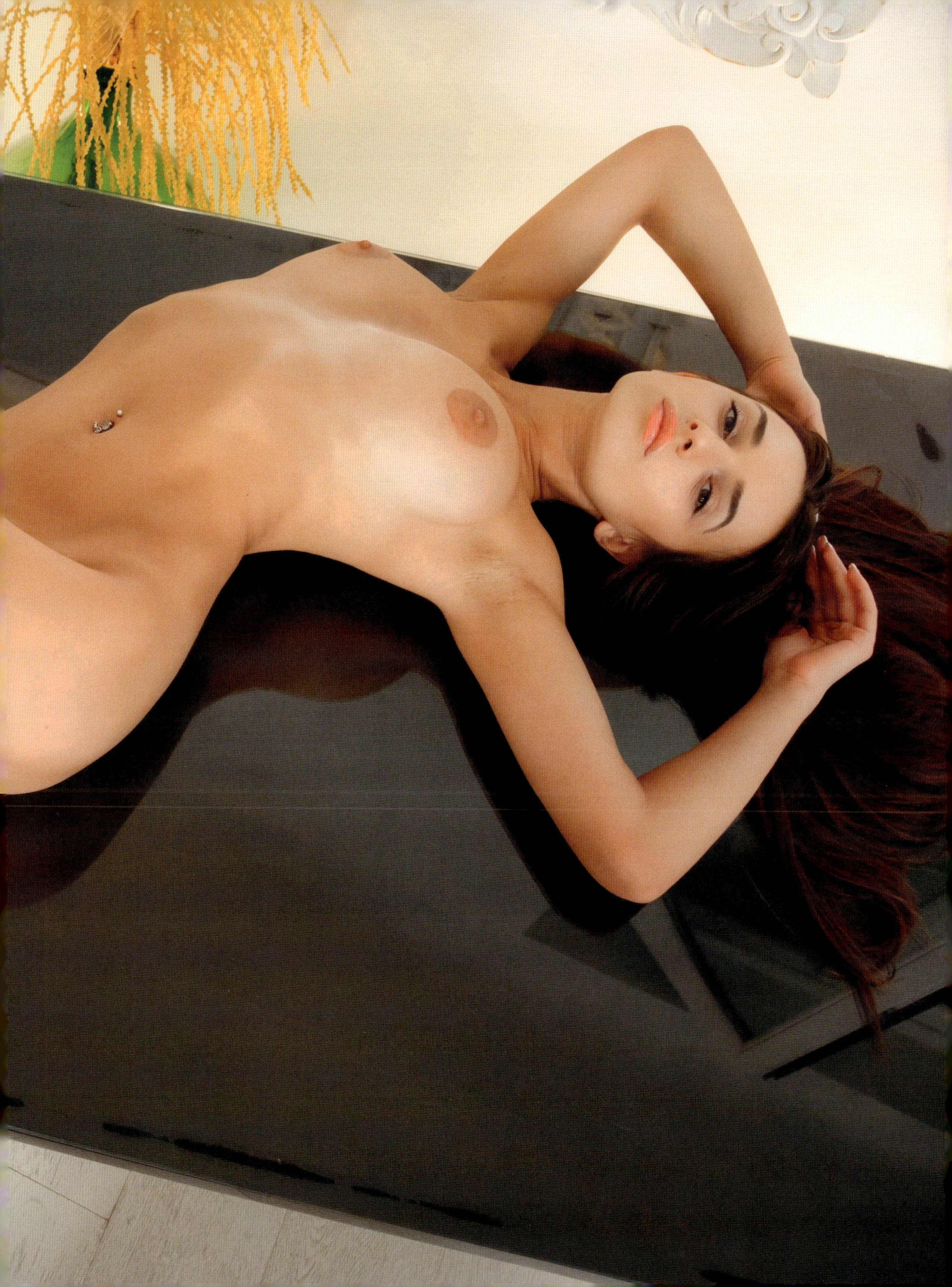

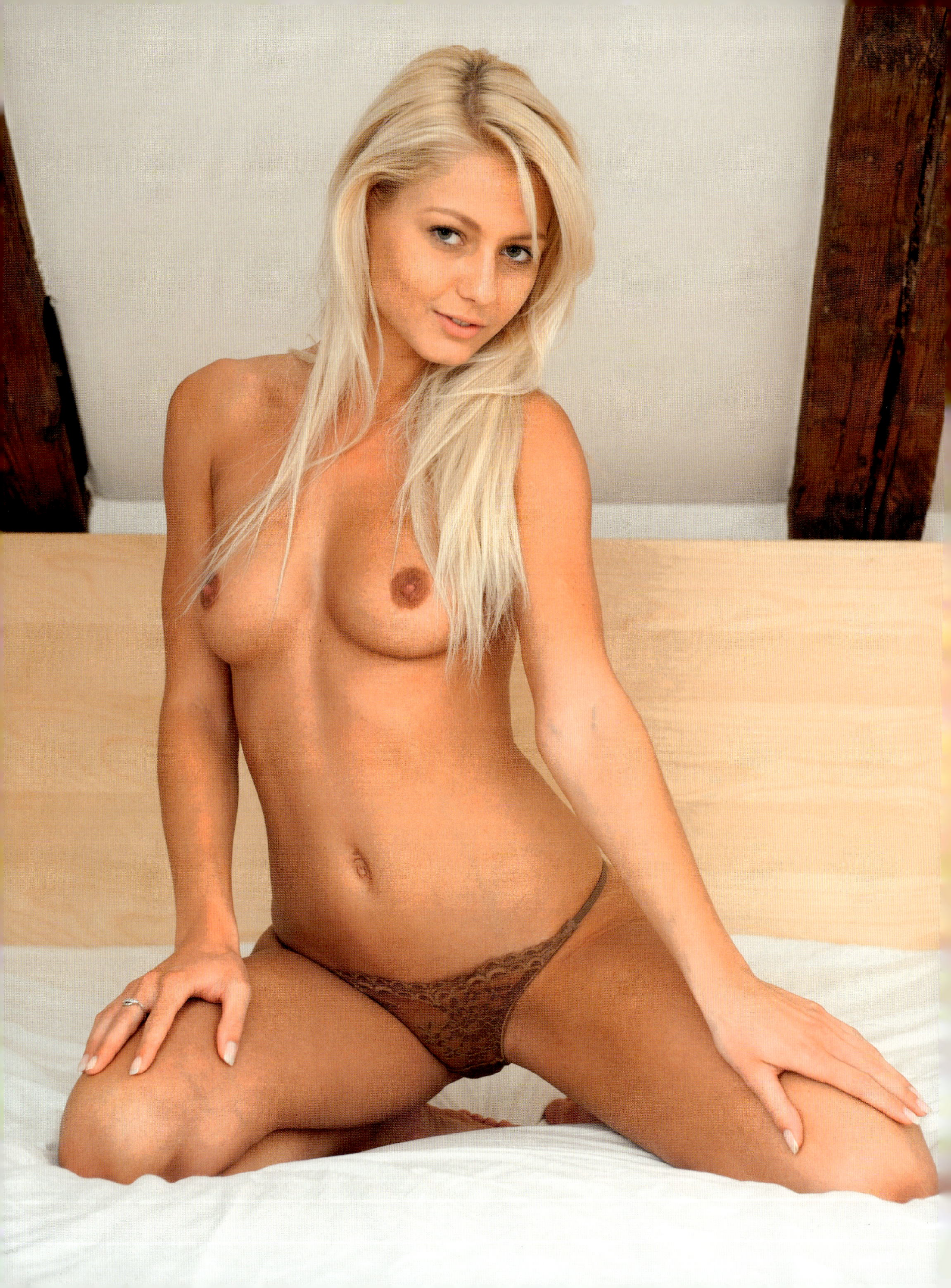

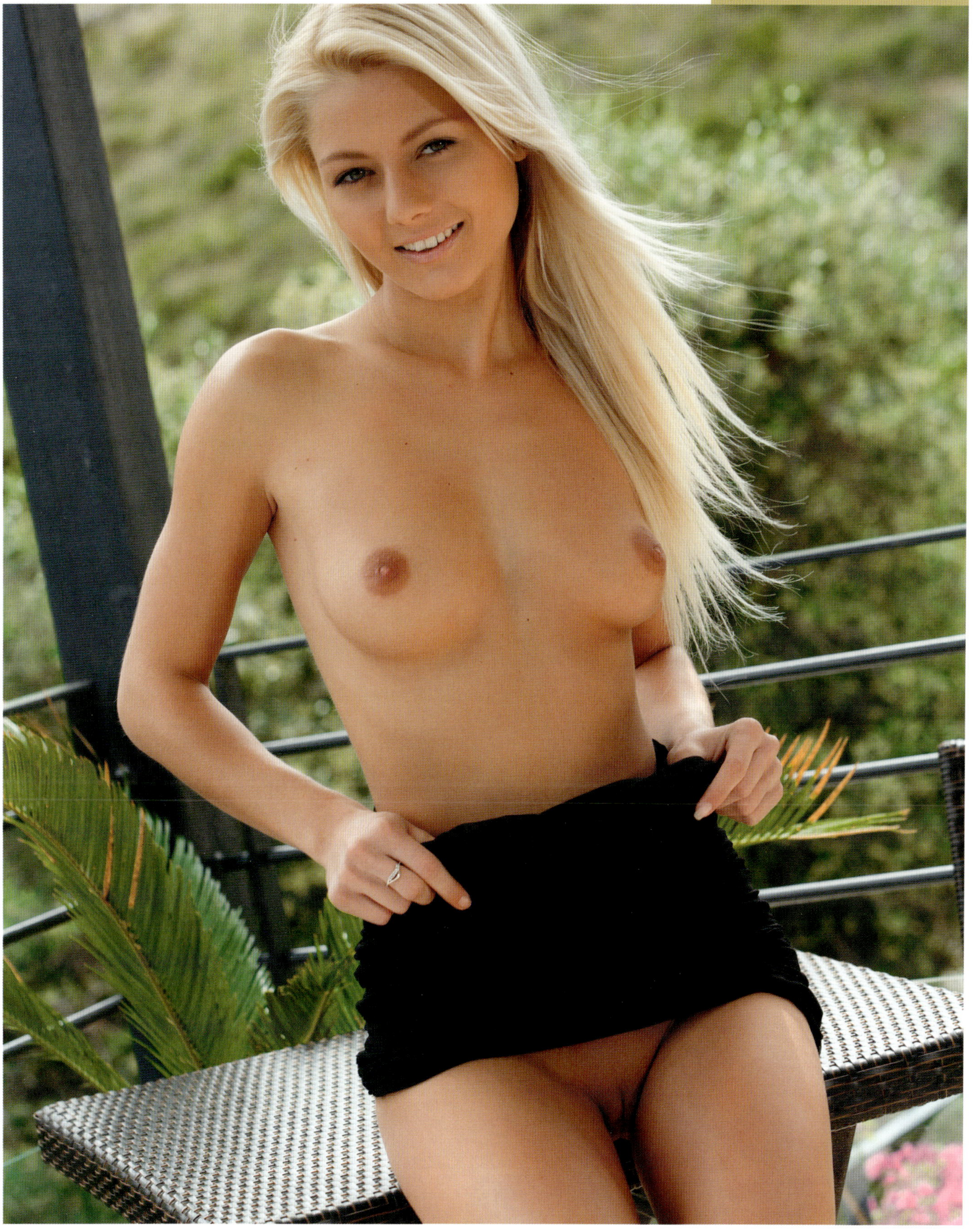

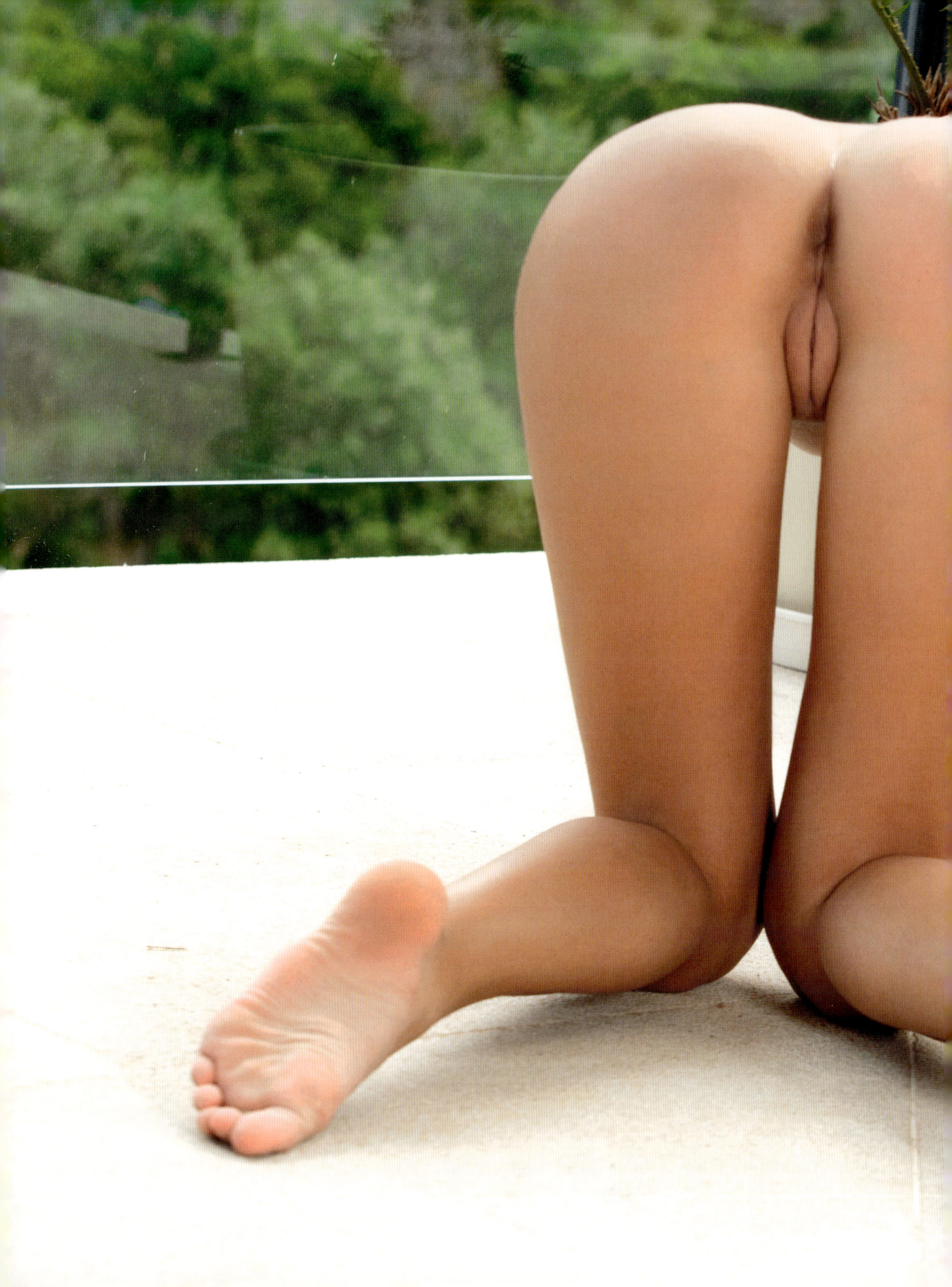

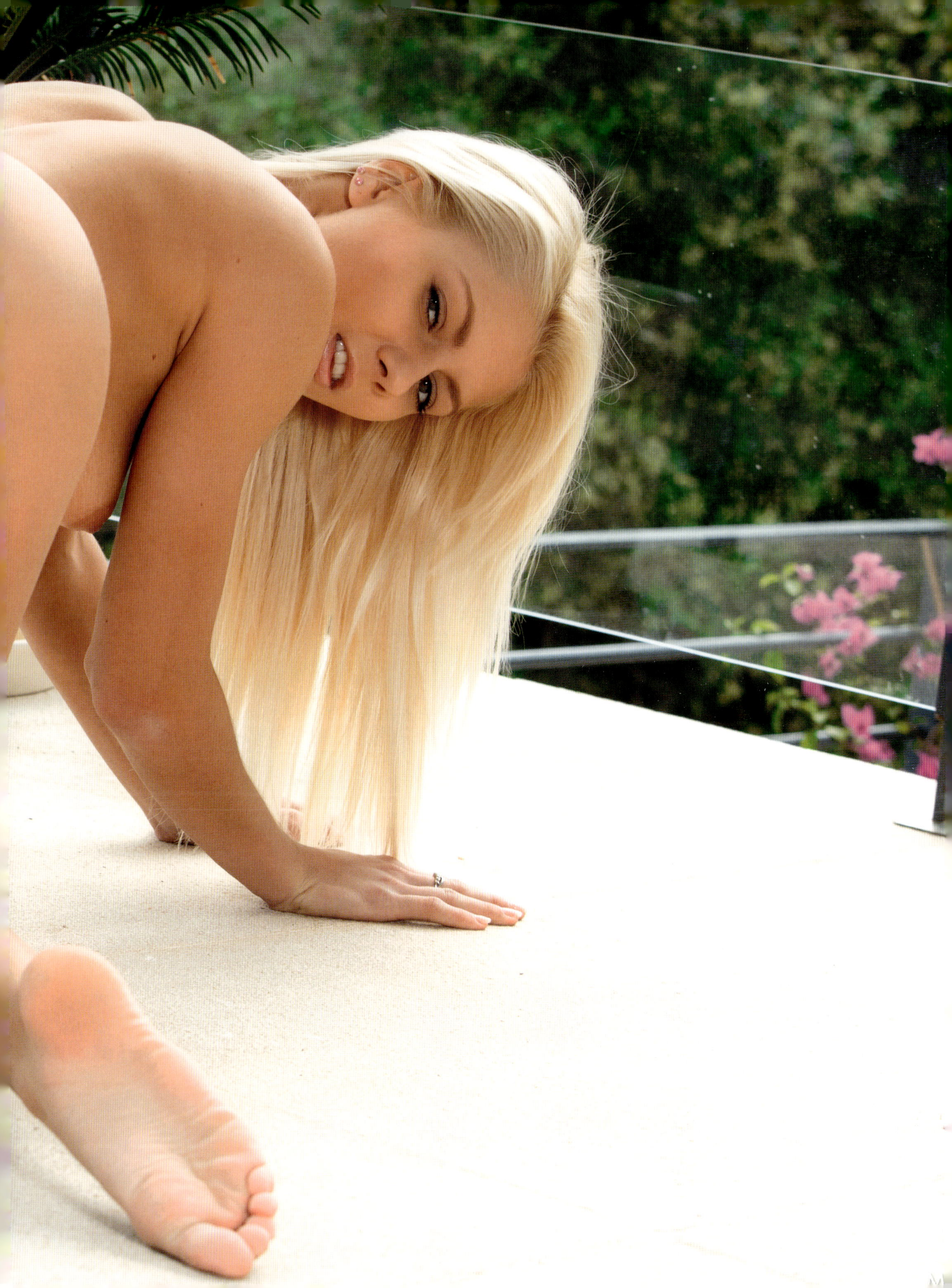

*Indiana A*

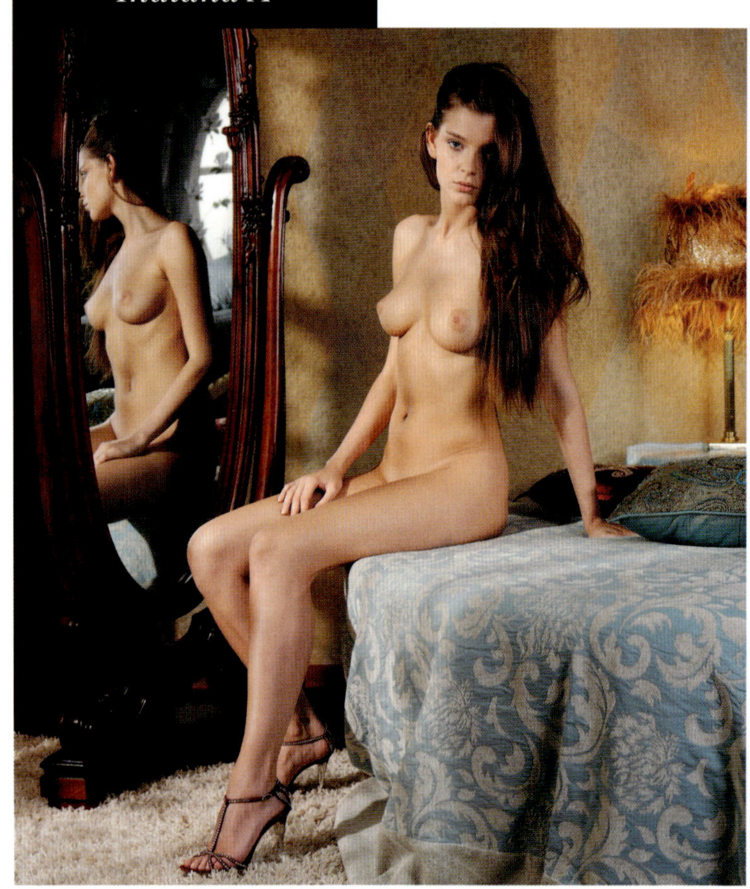

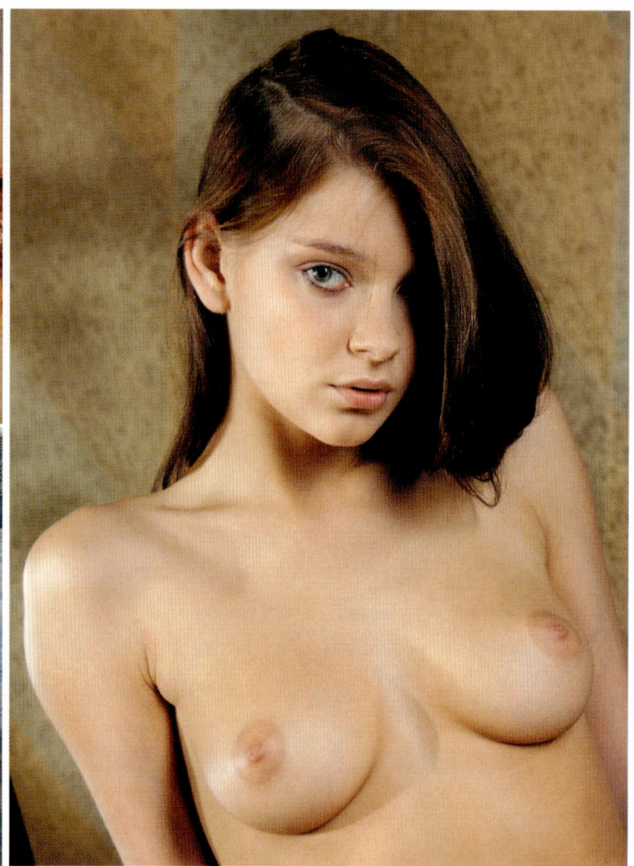

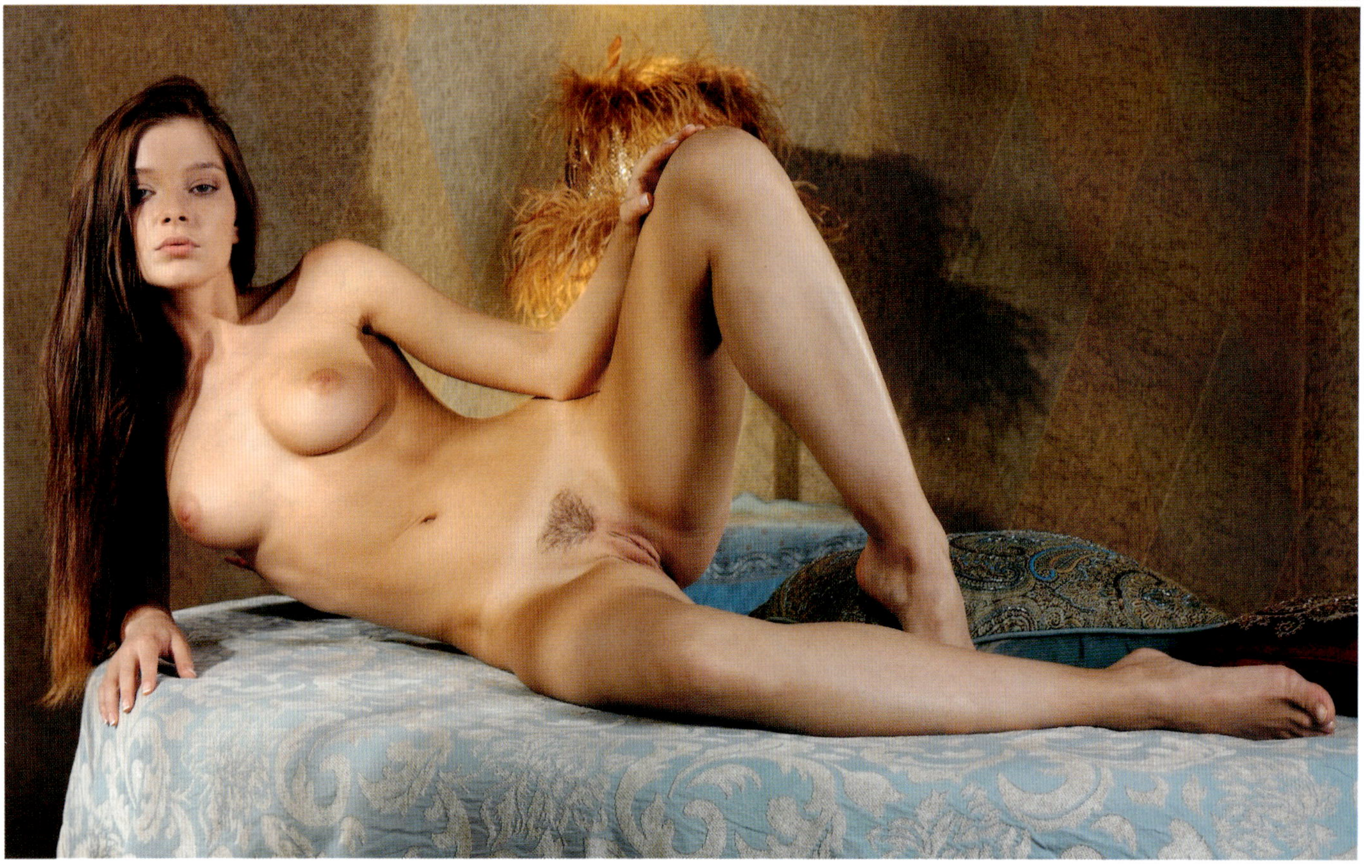

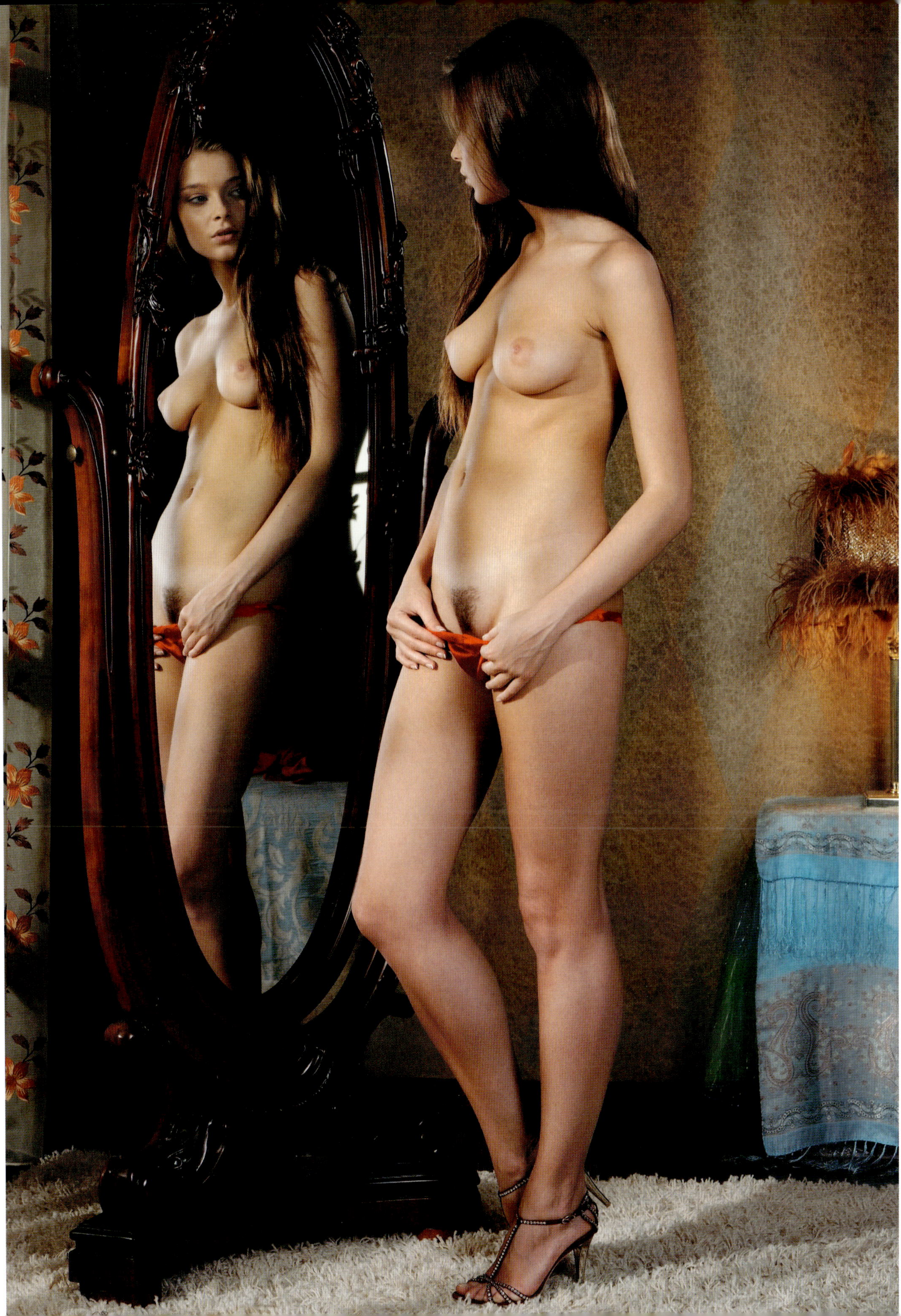

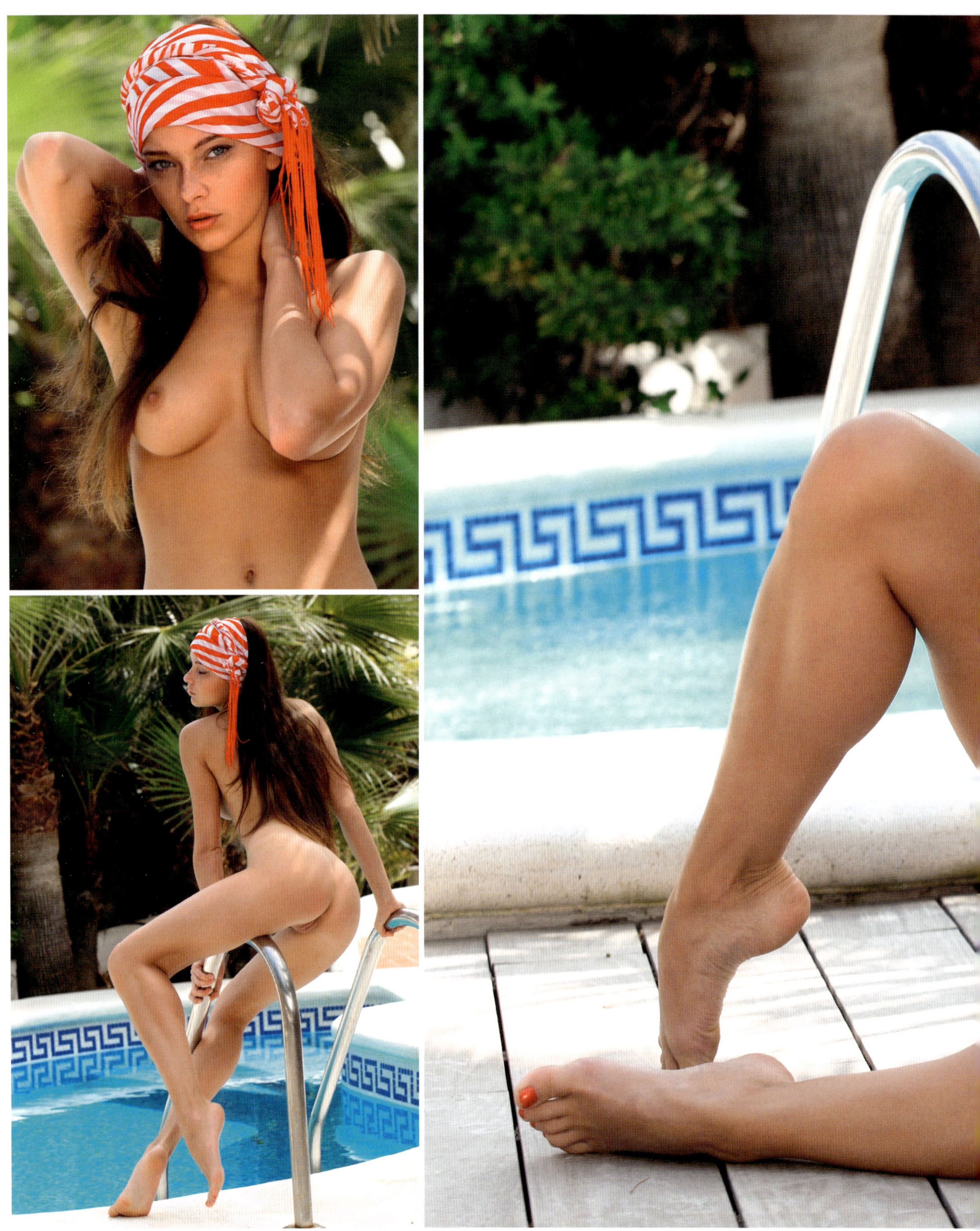

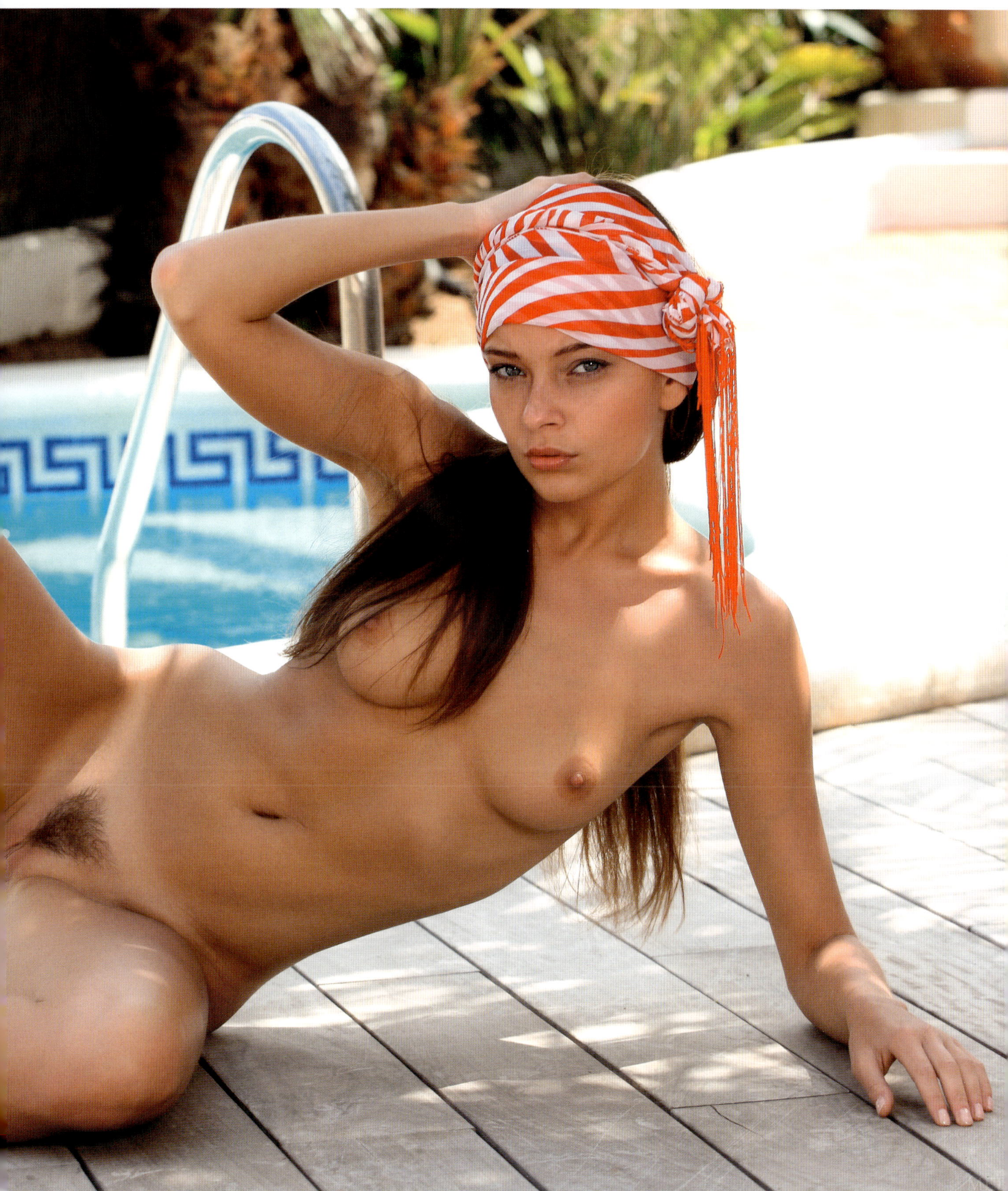

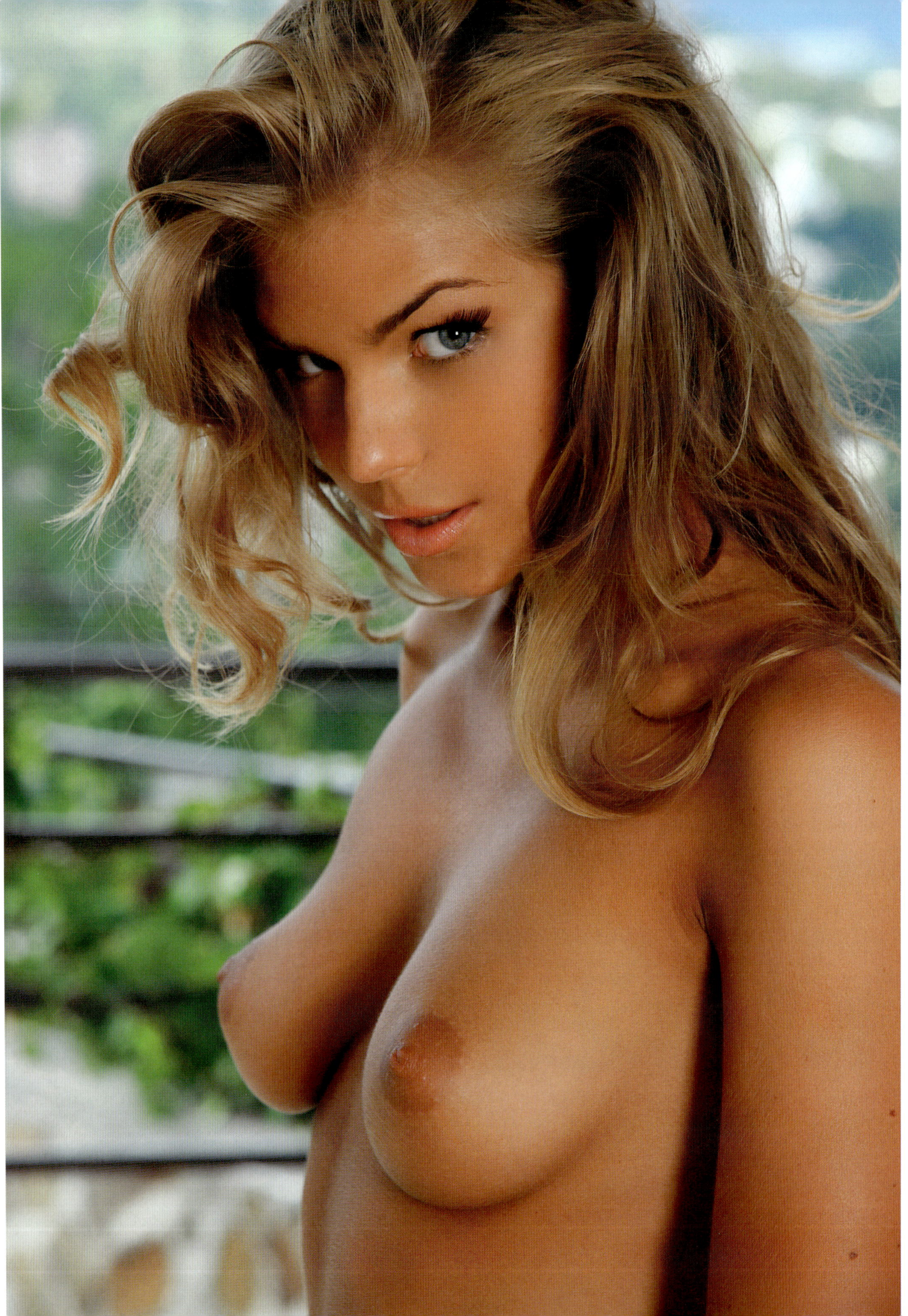

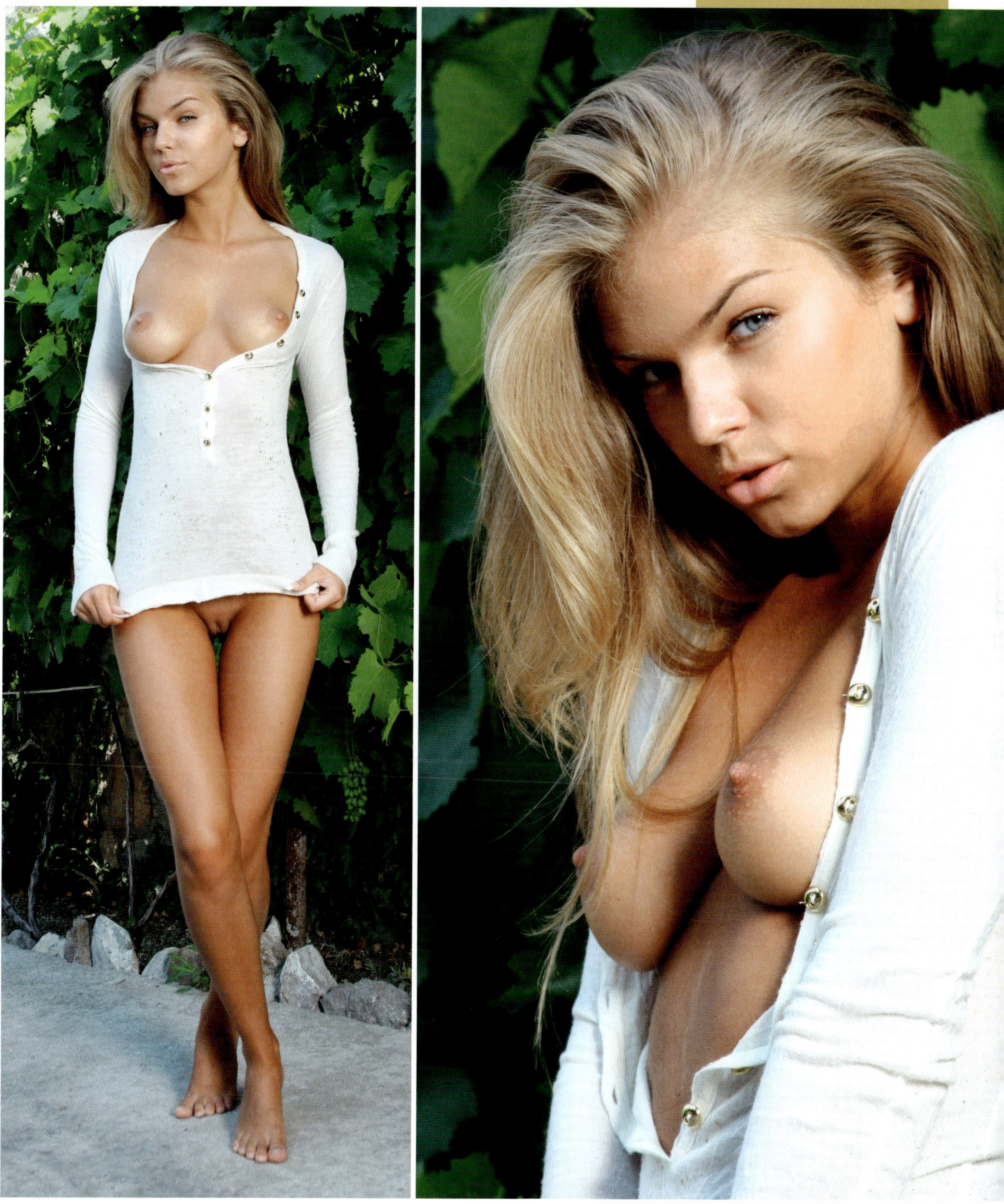

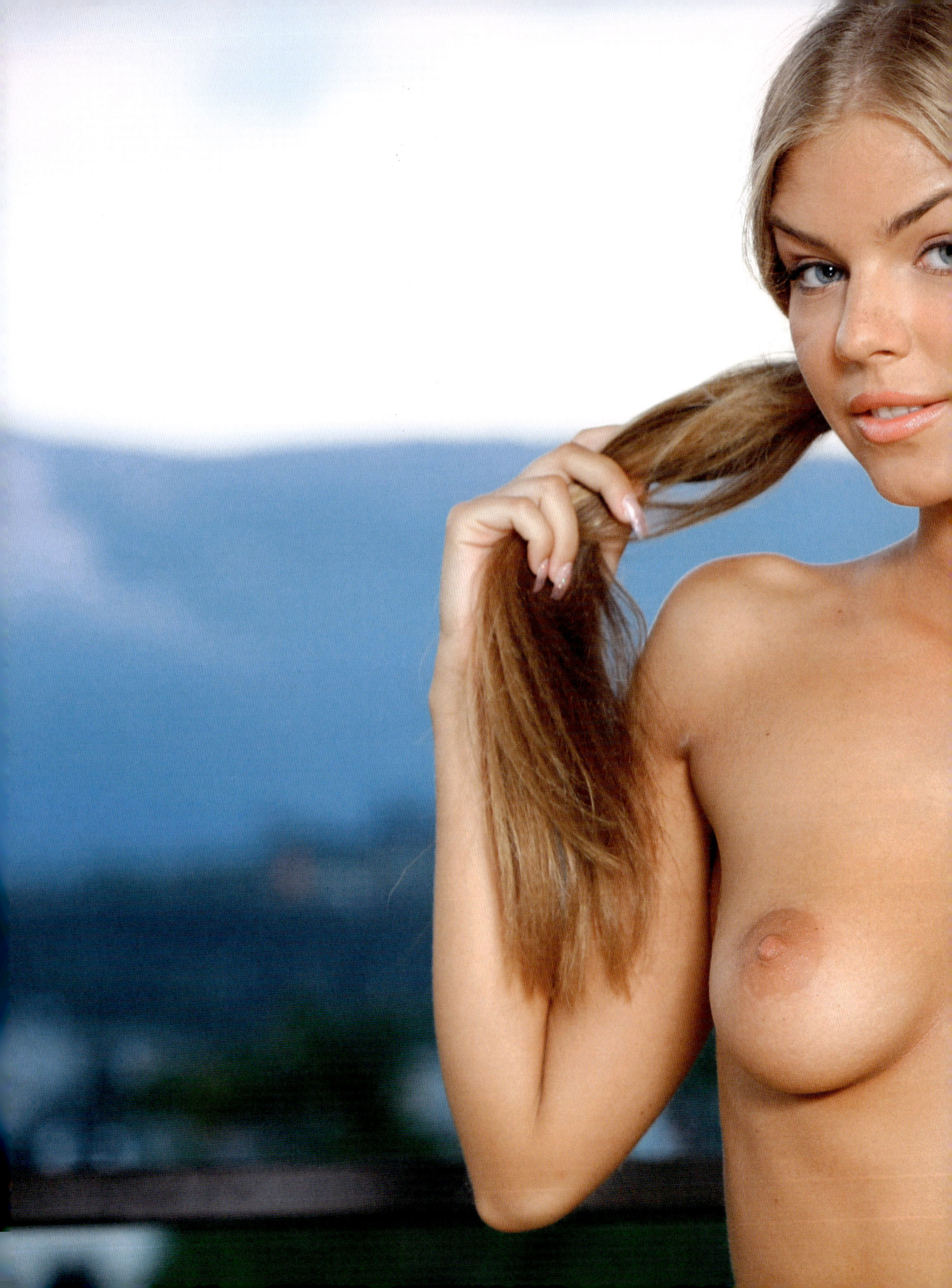

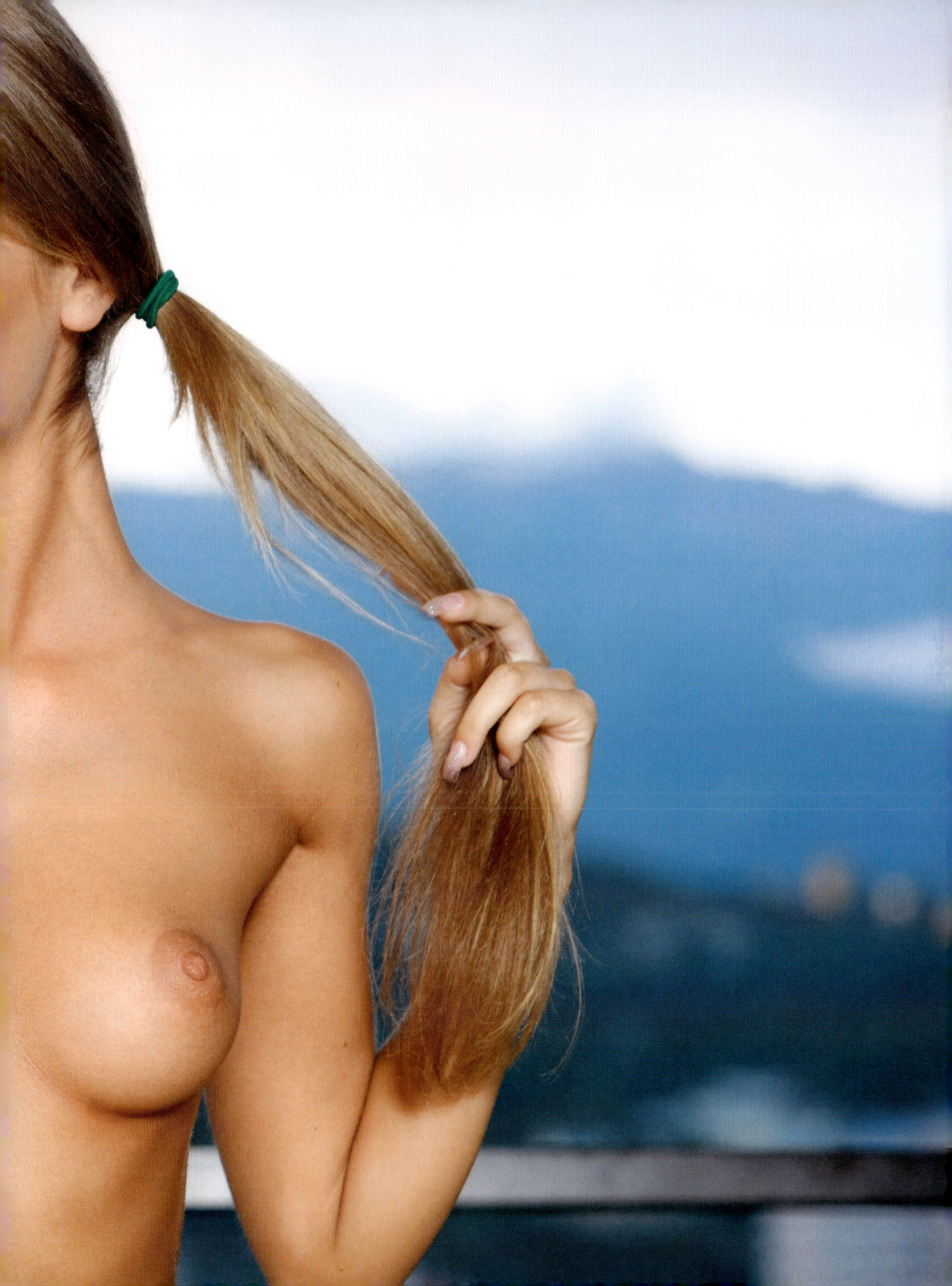

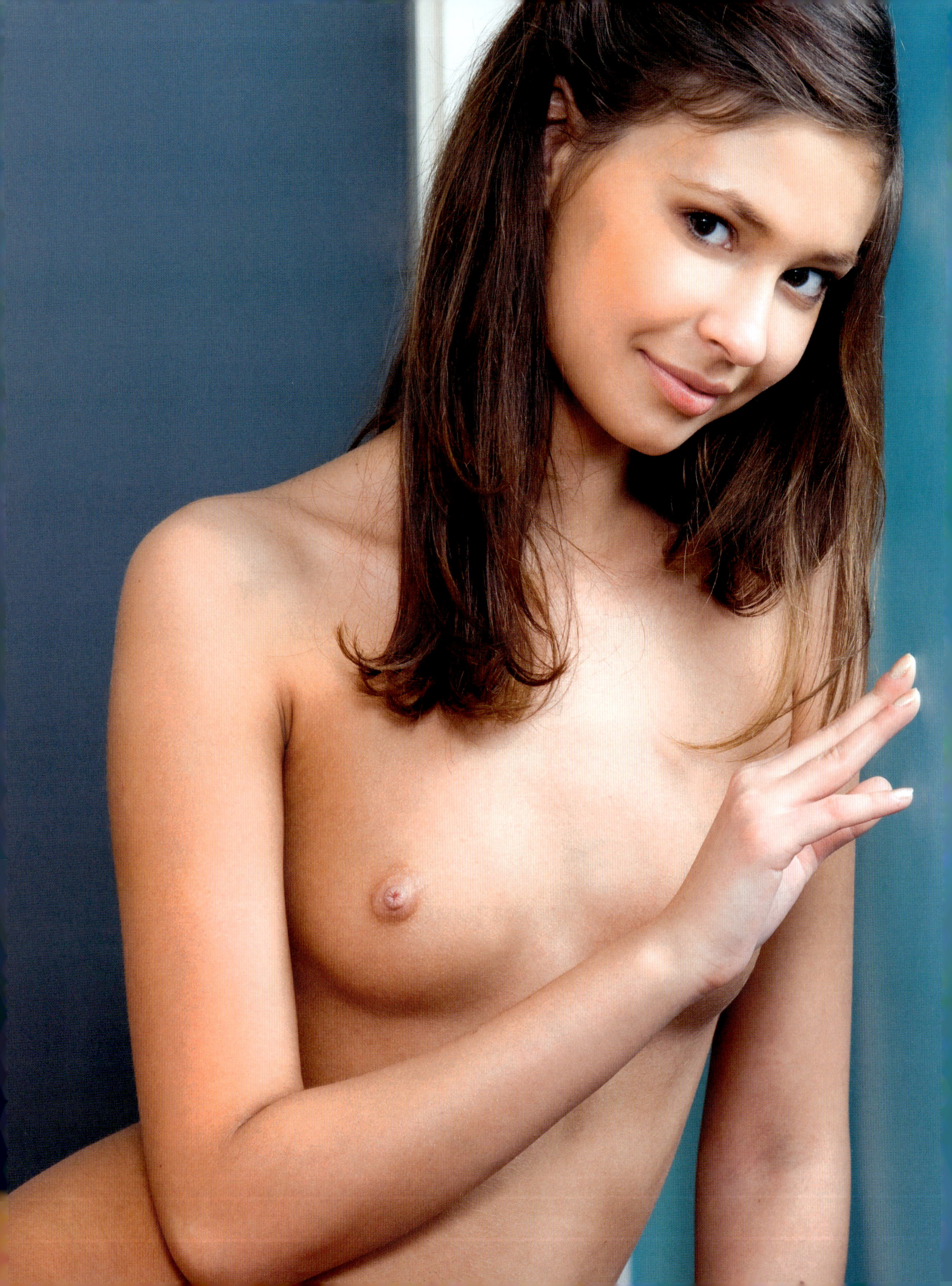

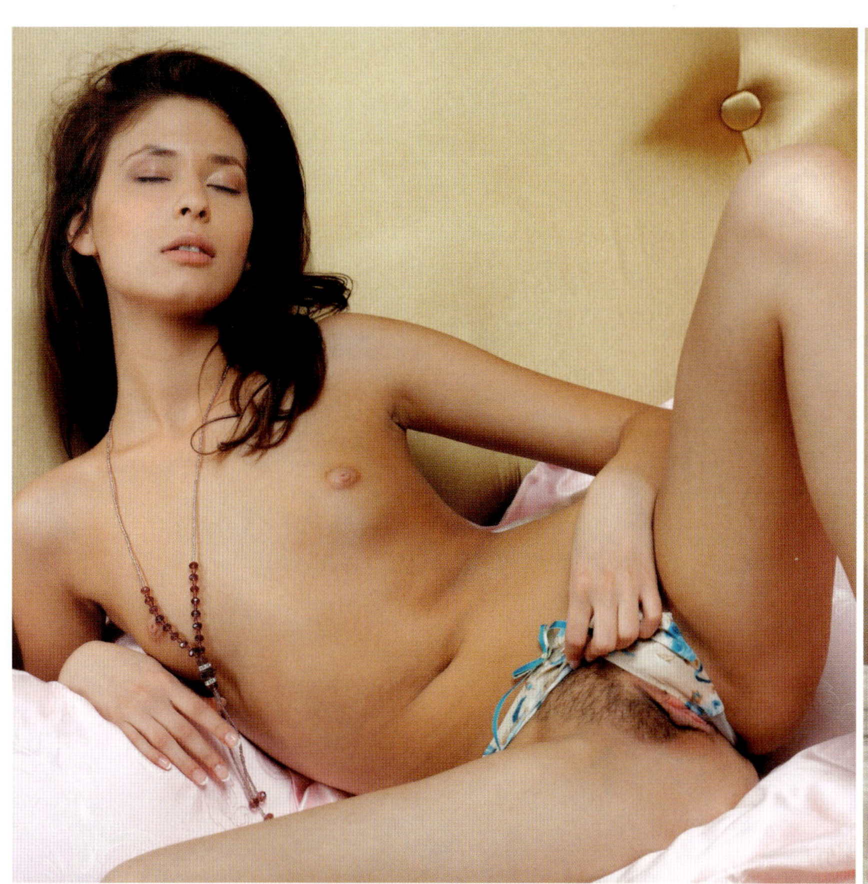

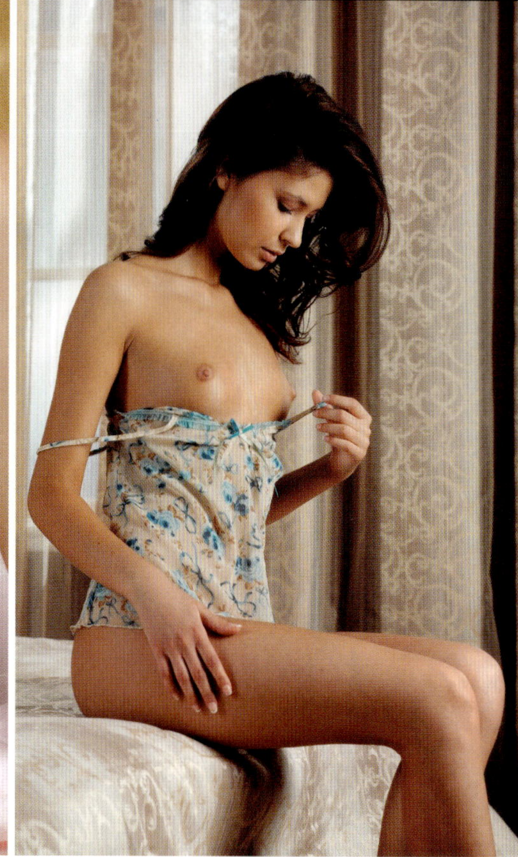

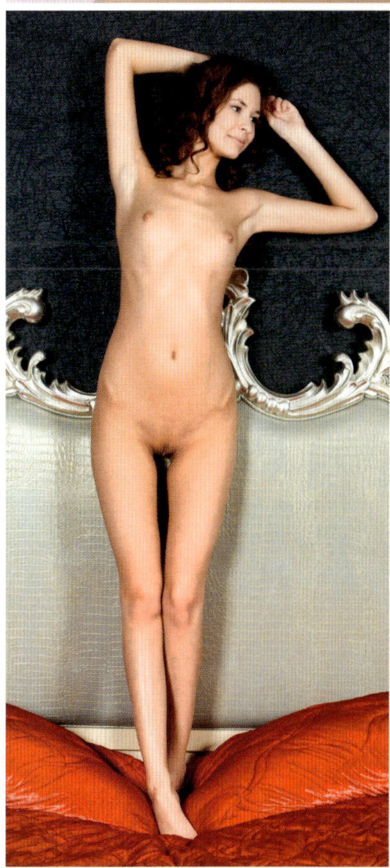

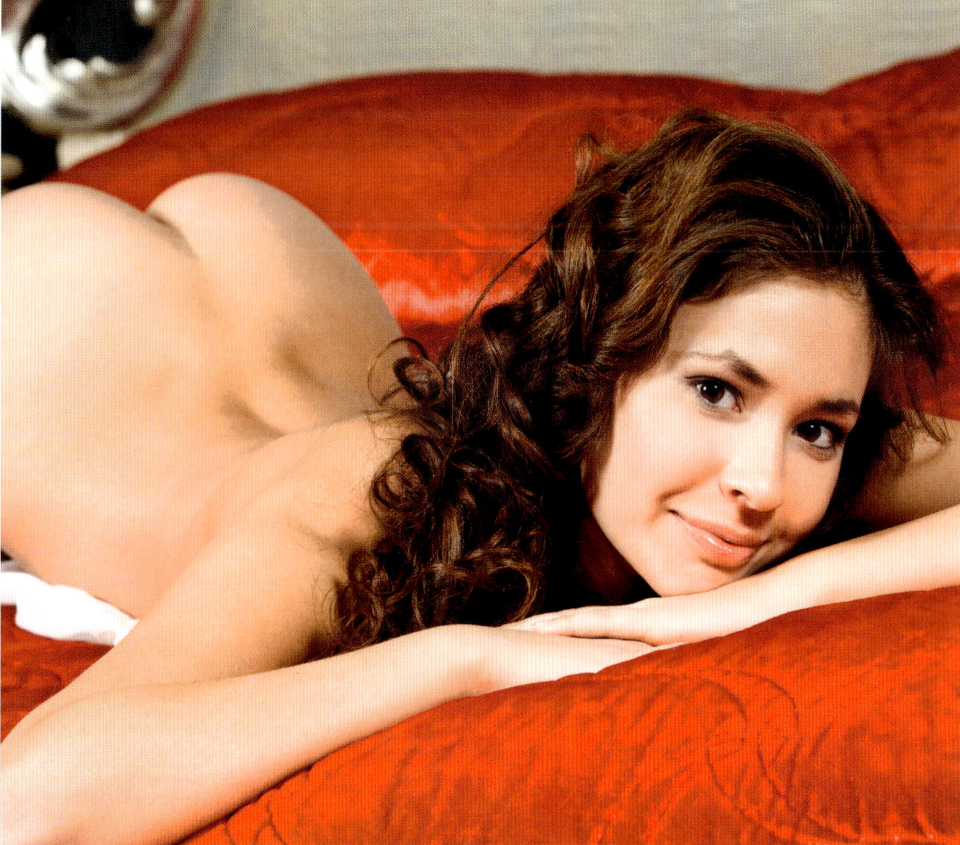

*Isabella D*

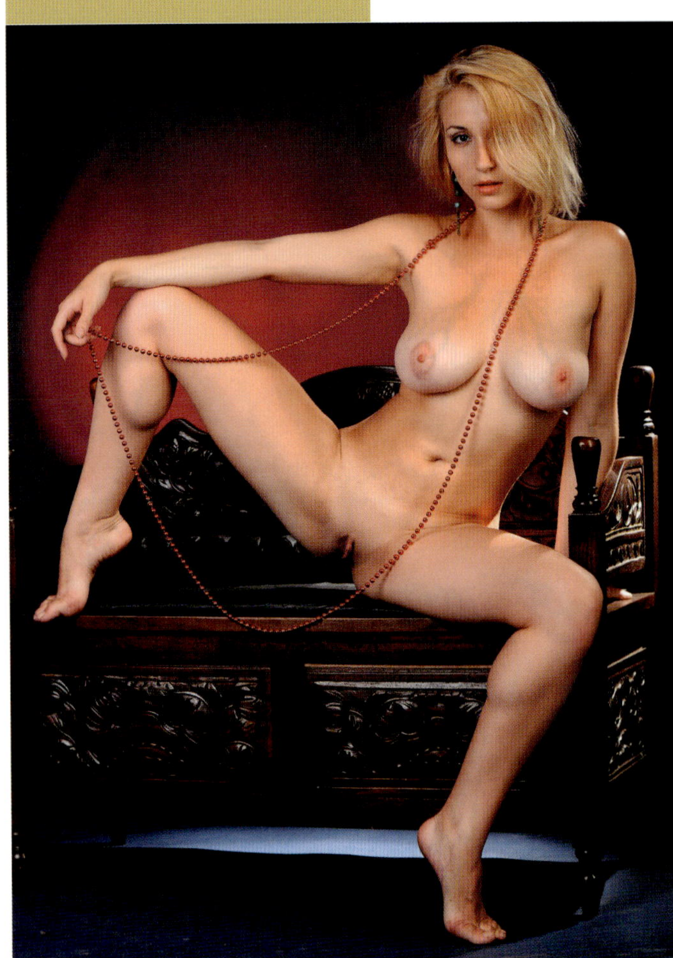

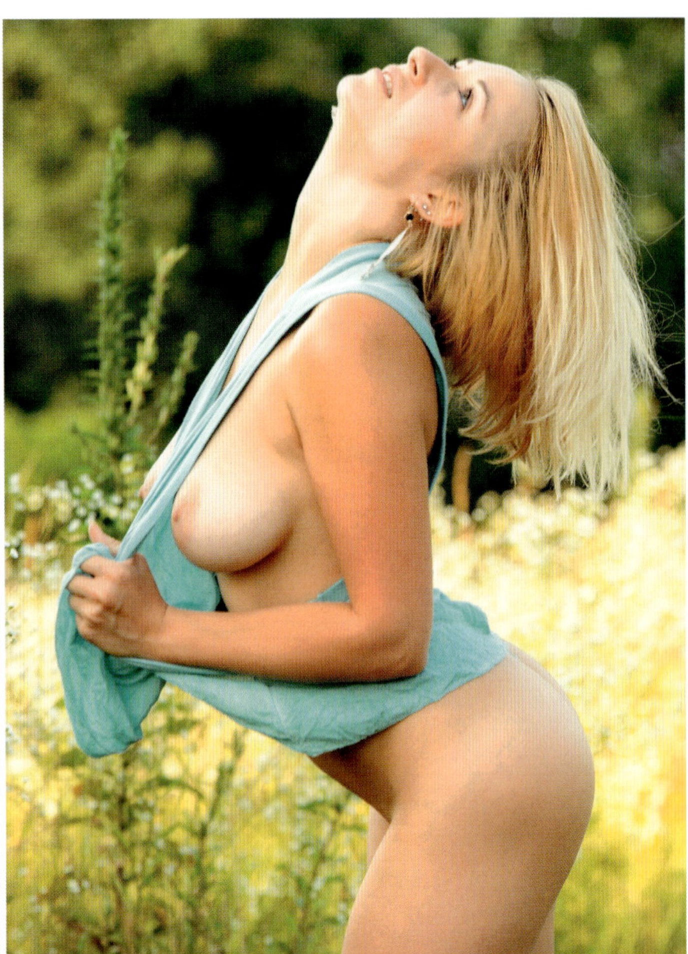

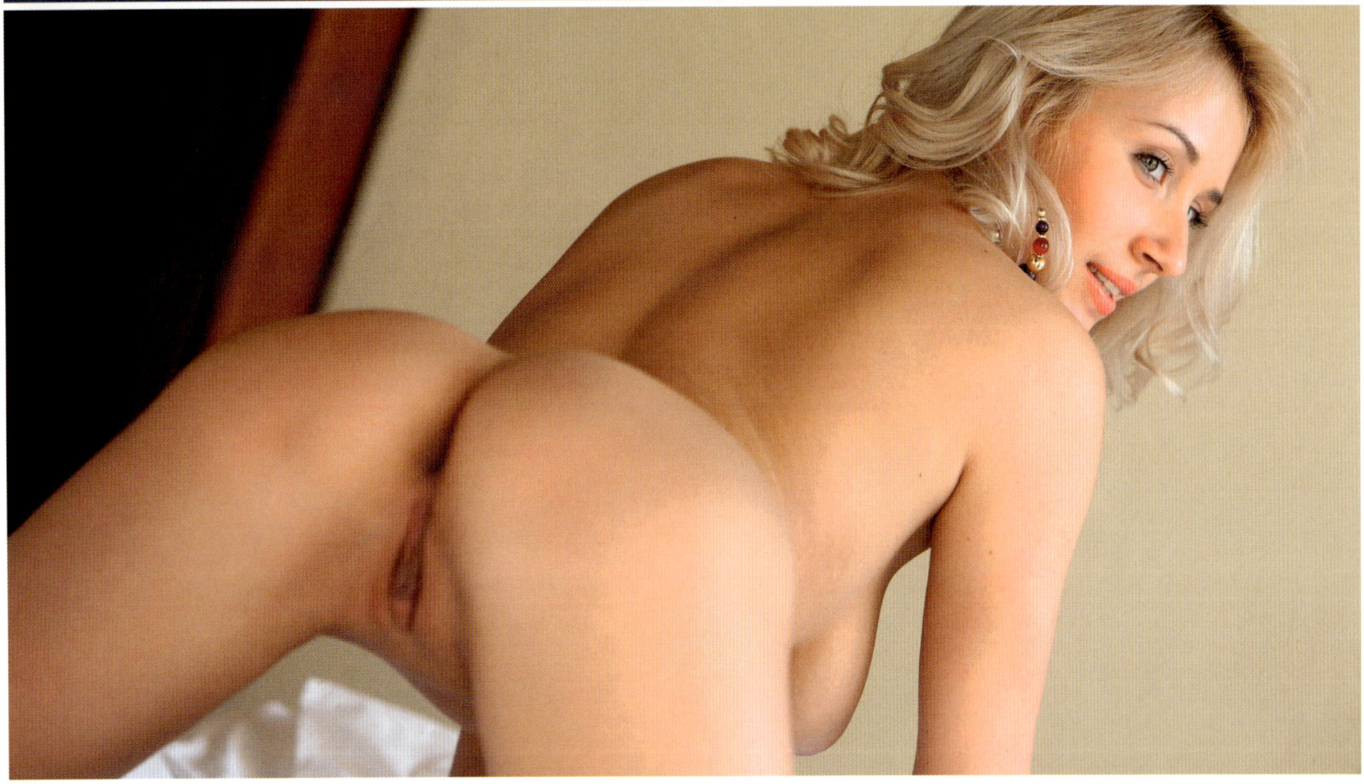

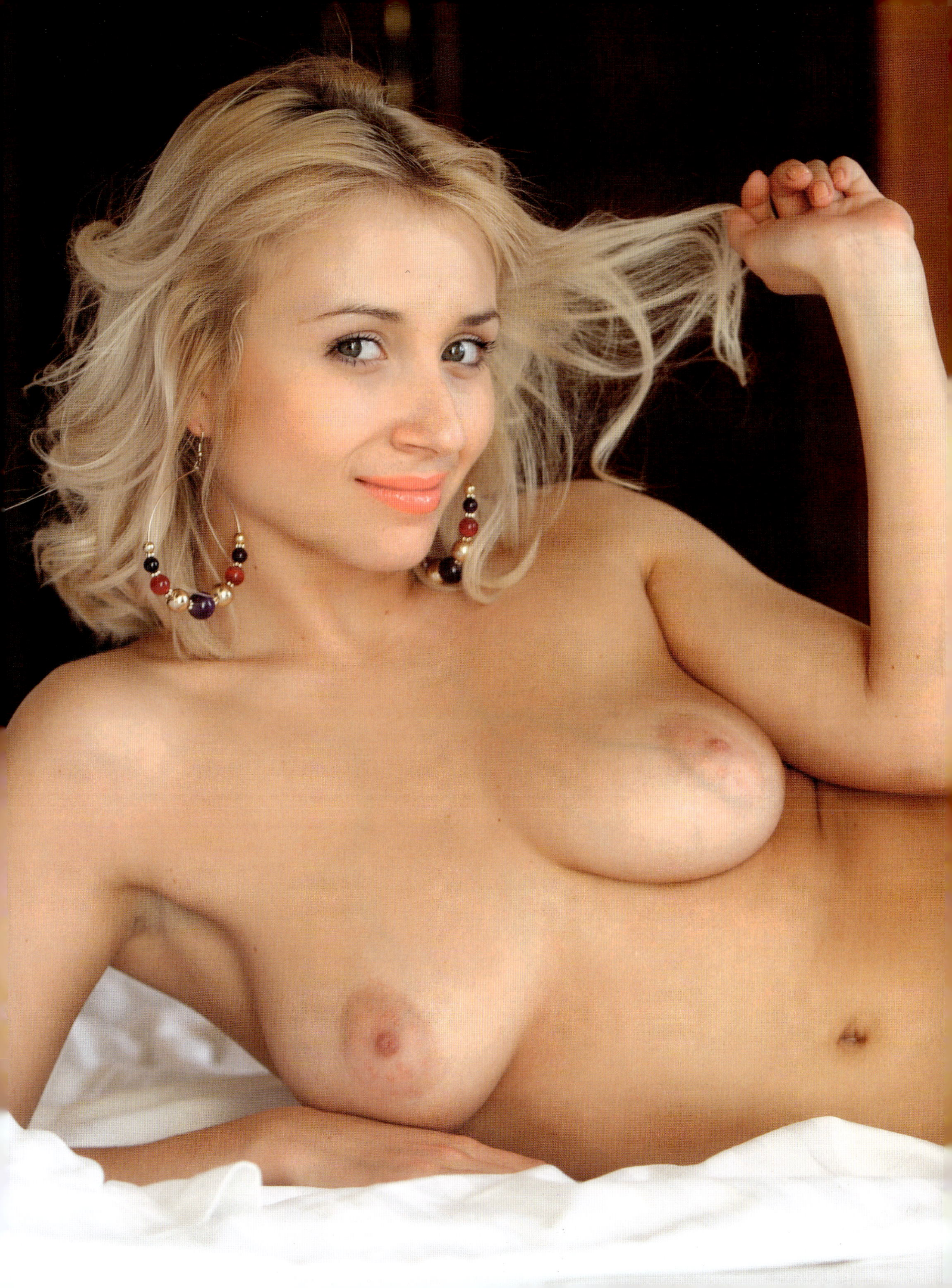

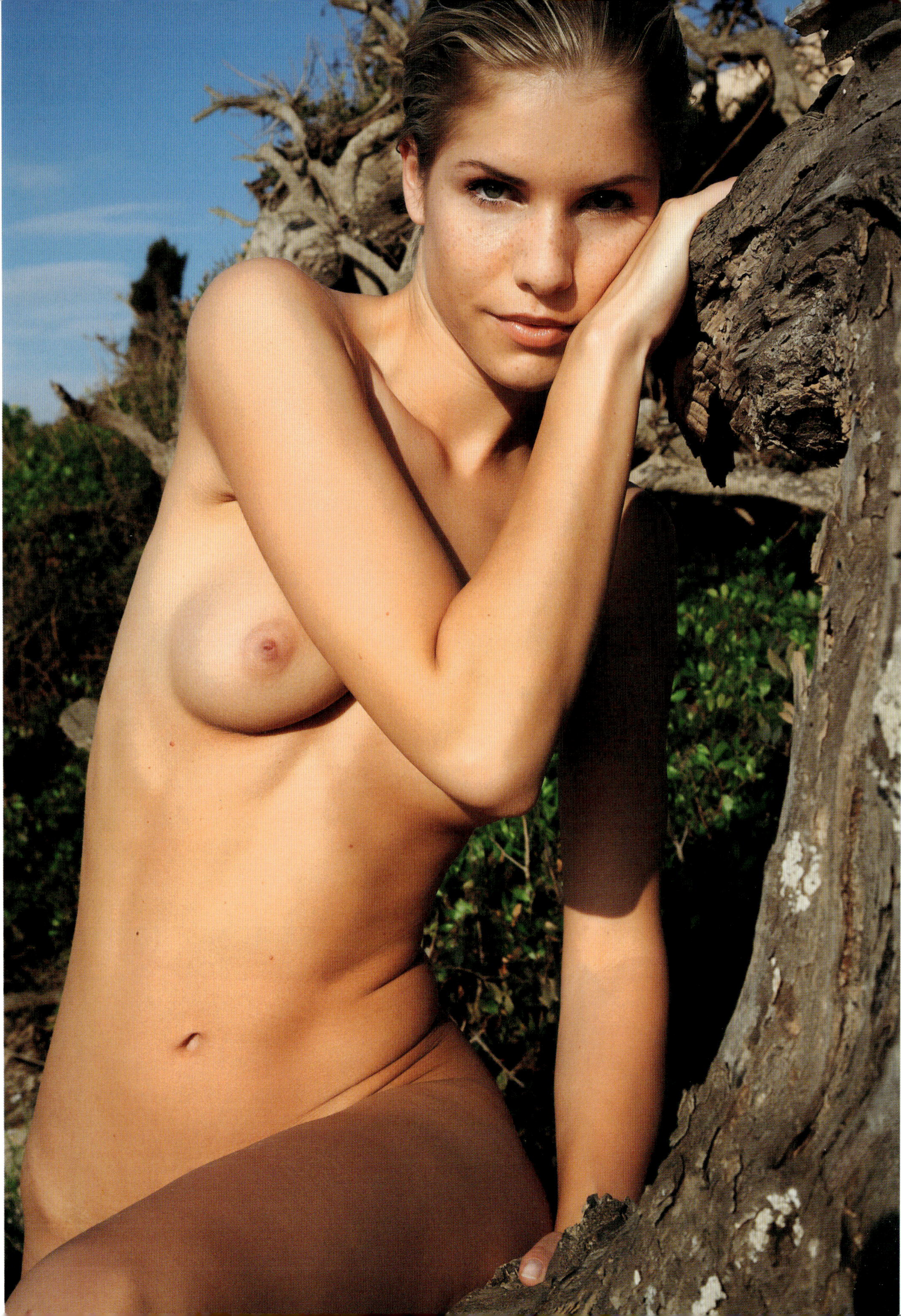

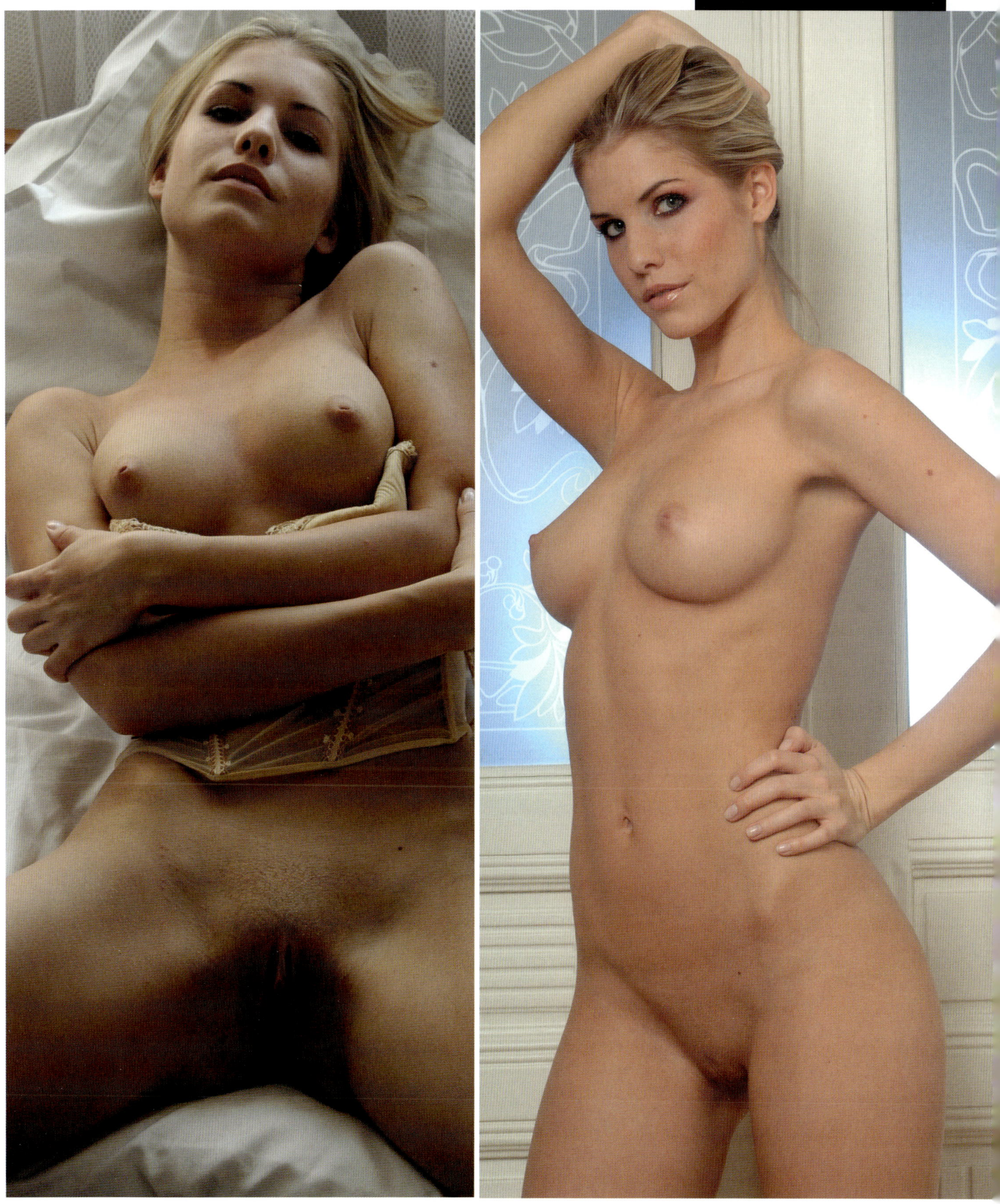

Janice A

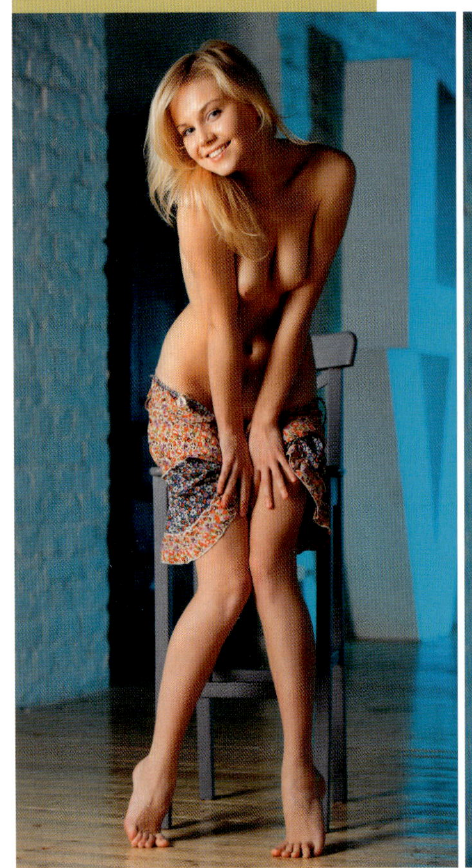

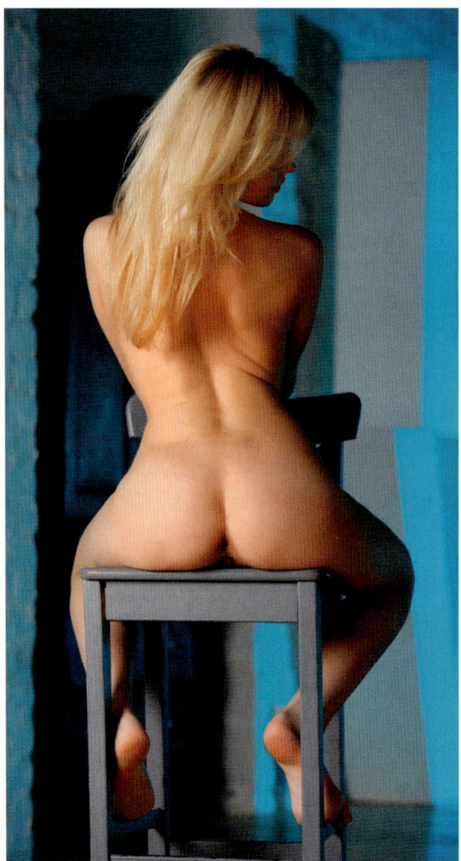

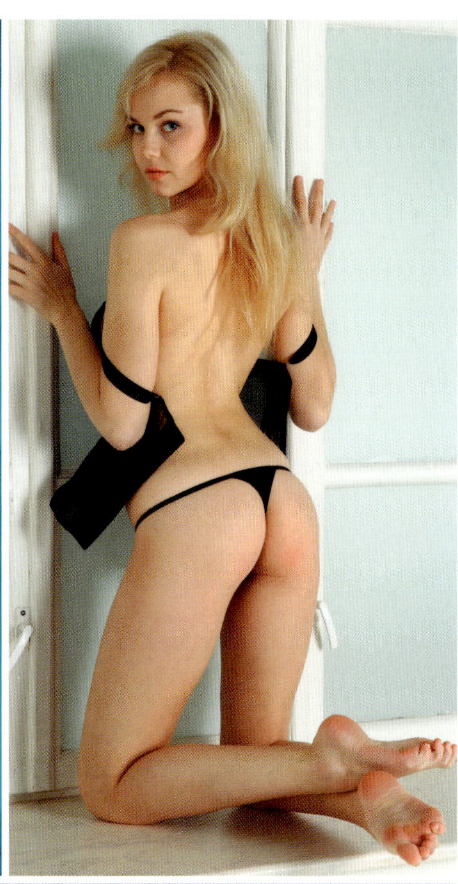

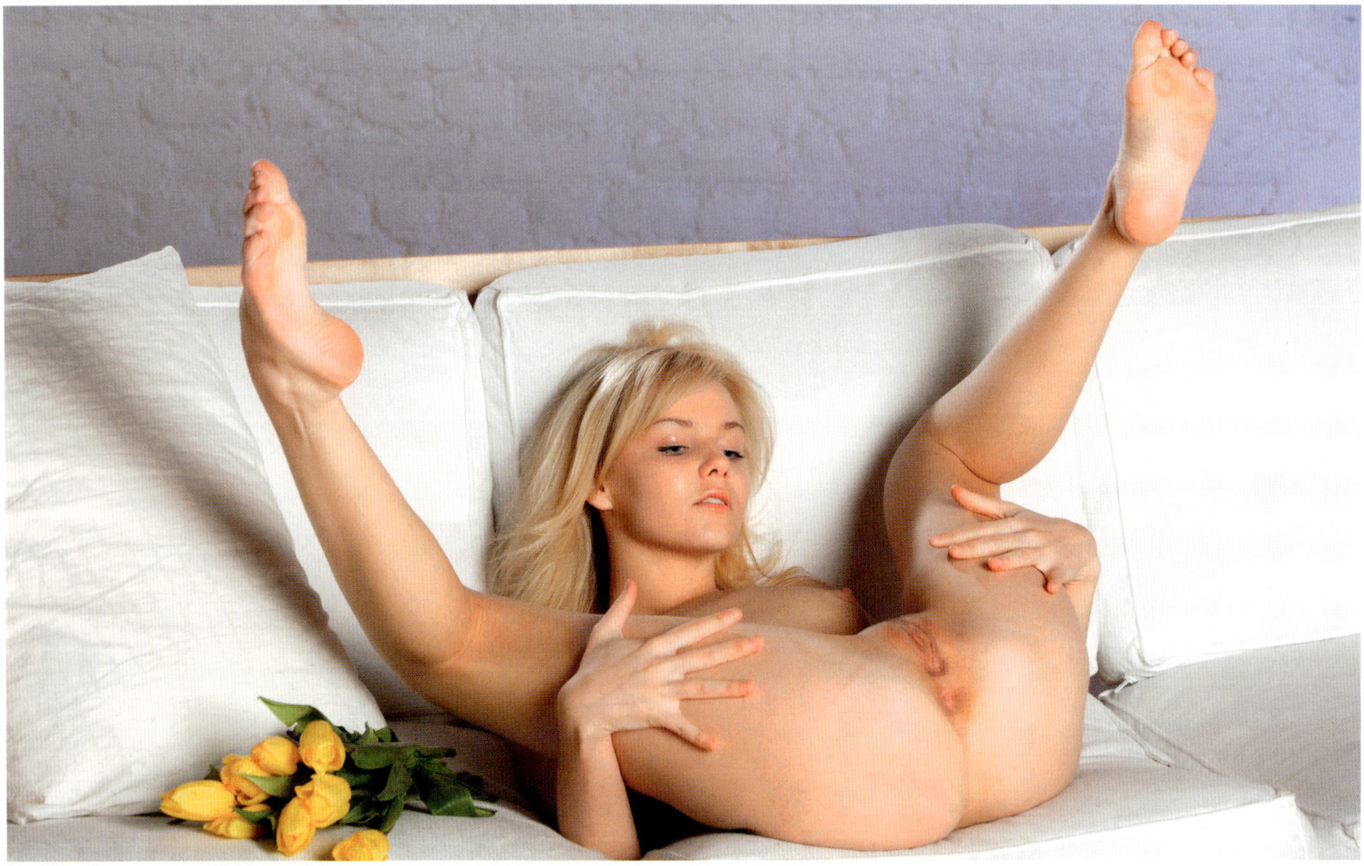

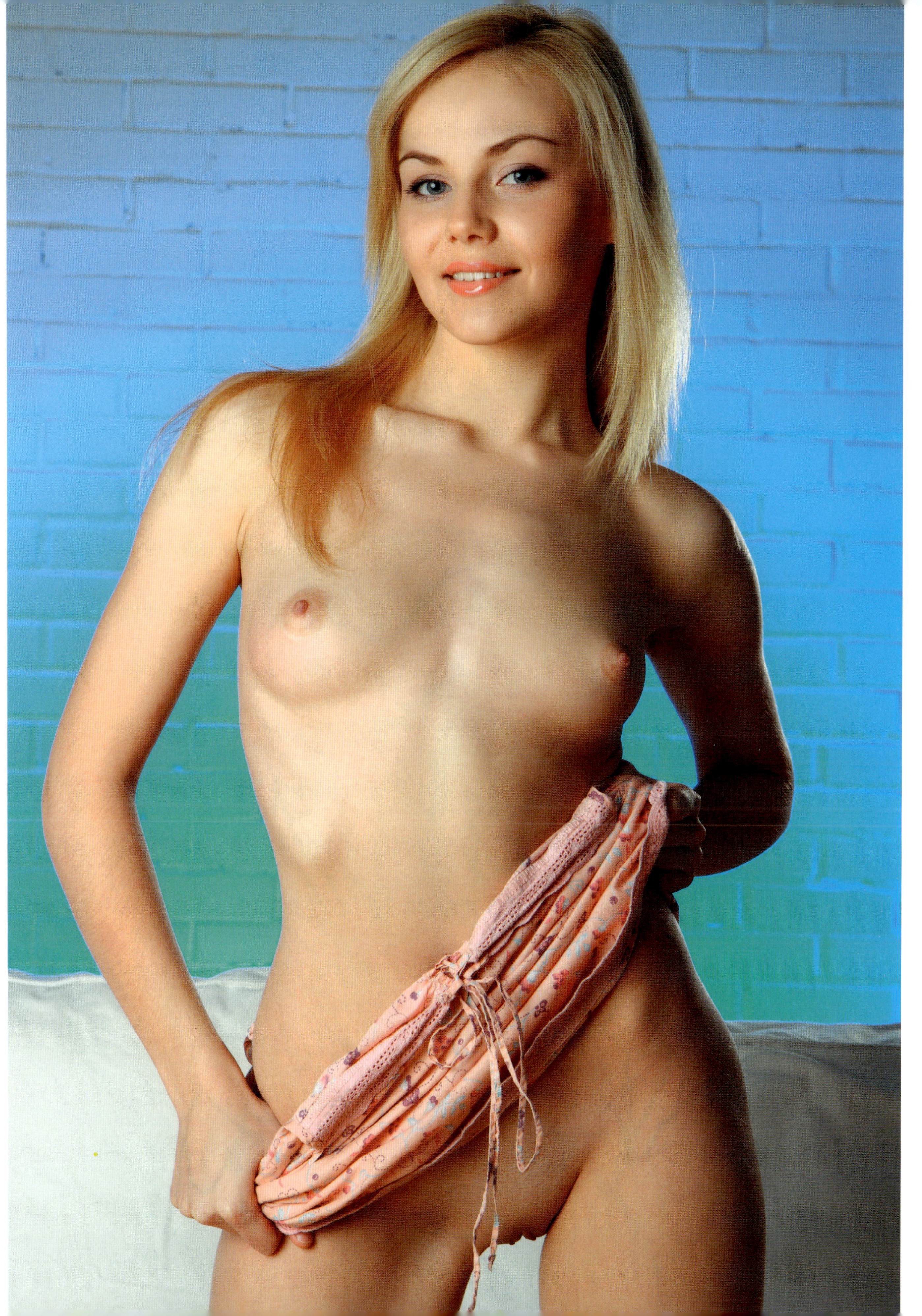

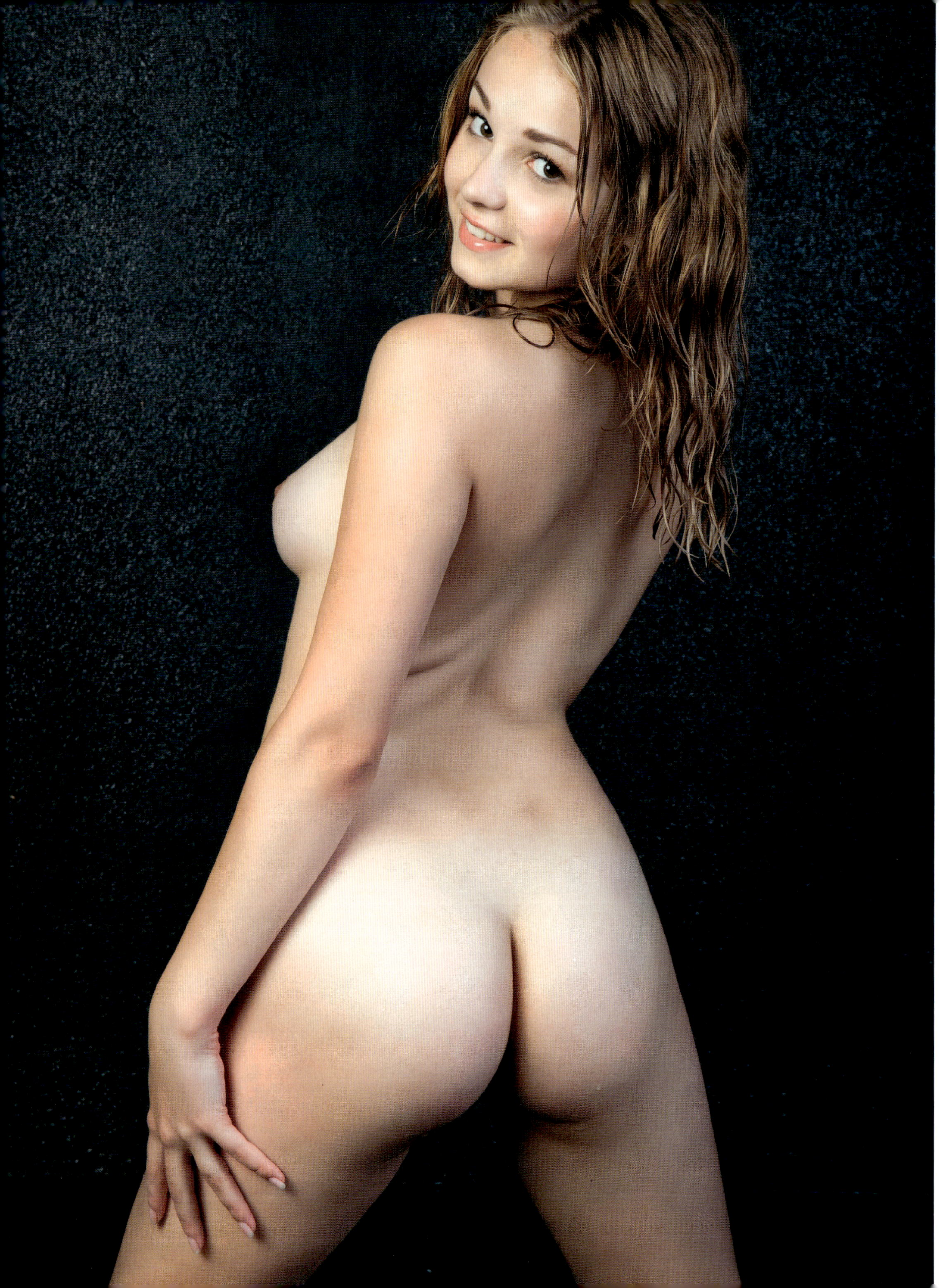

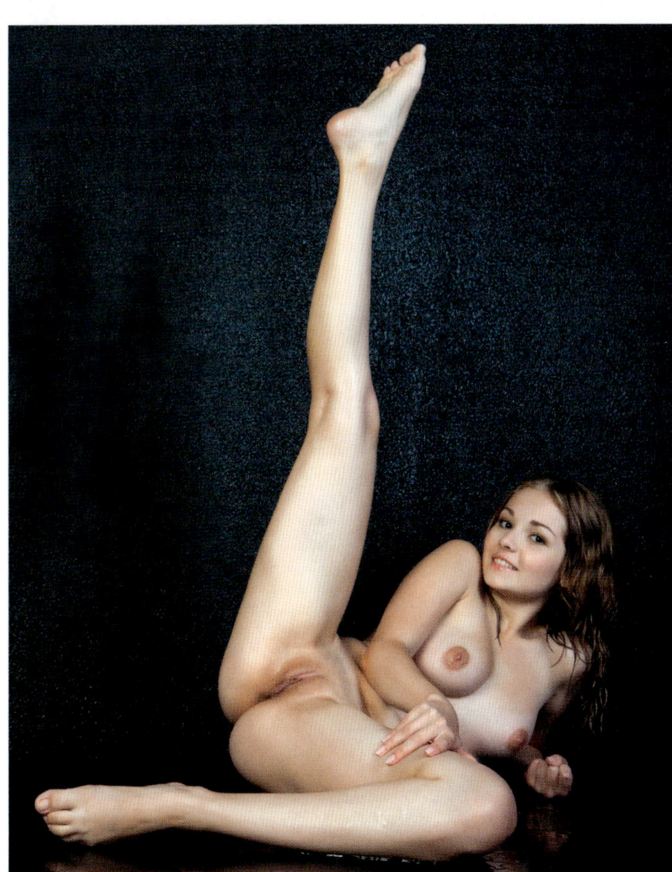

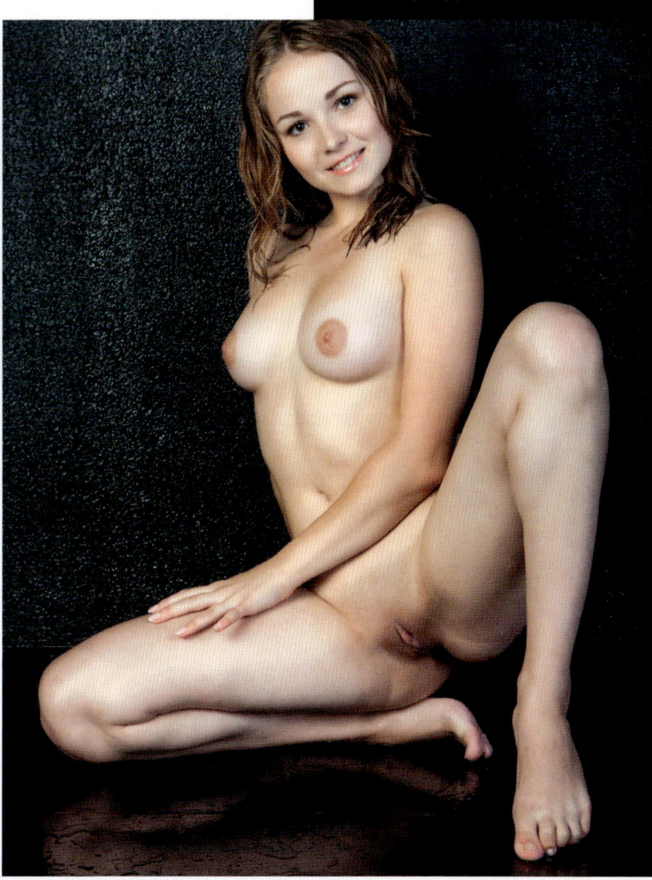

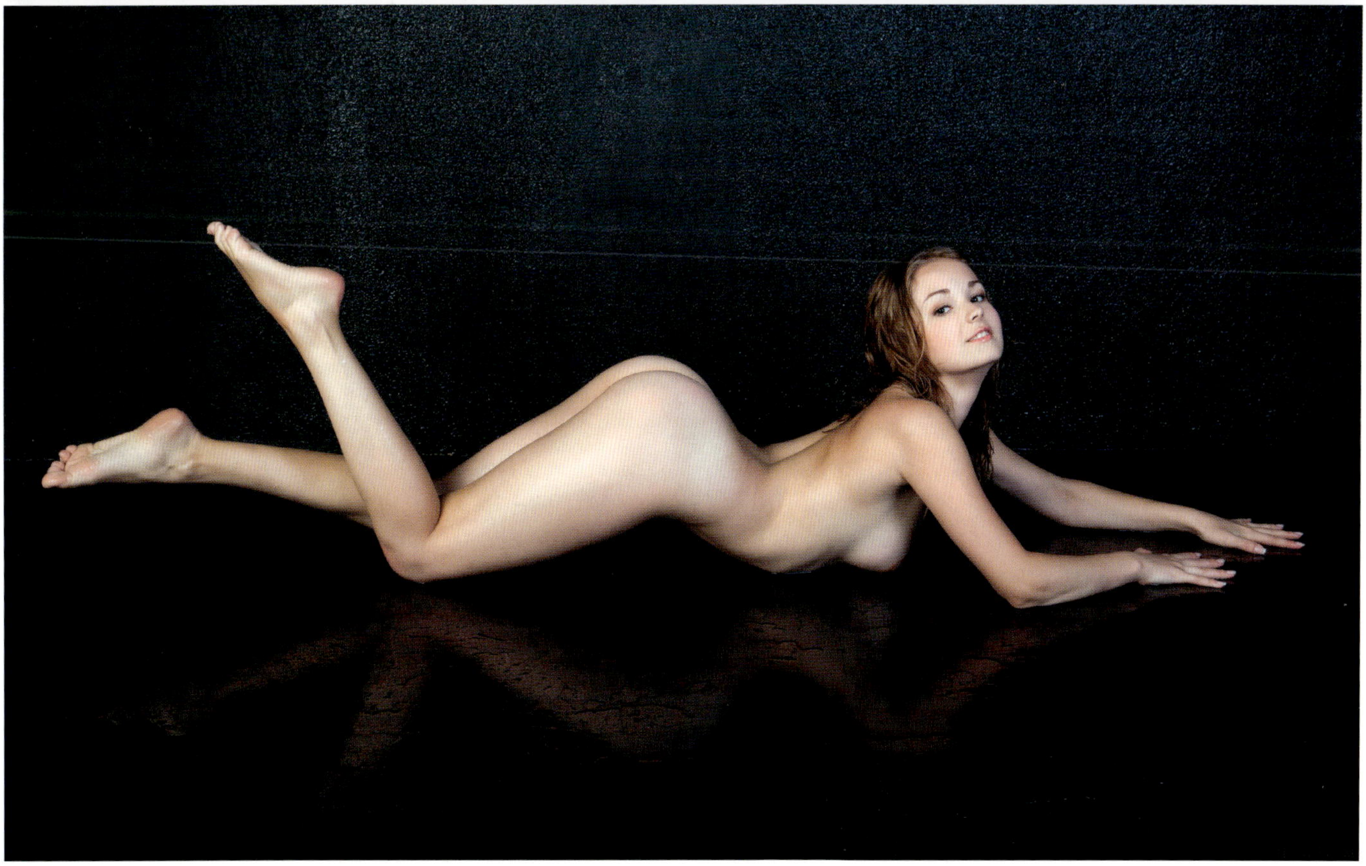

## Jenni A

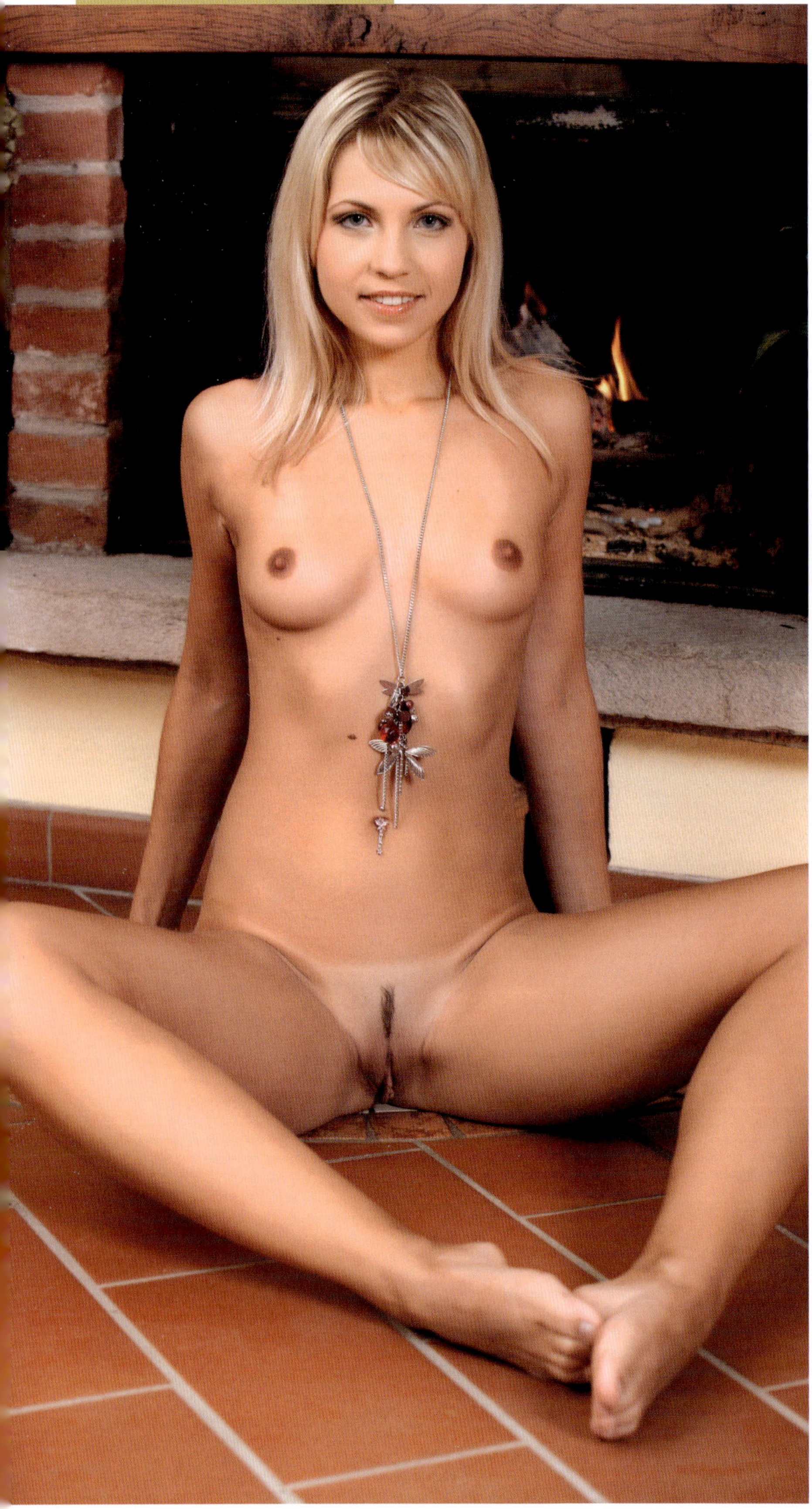

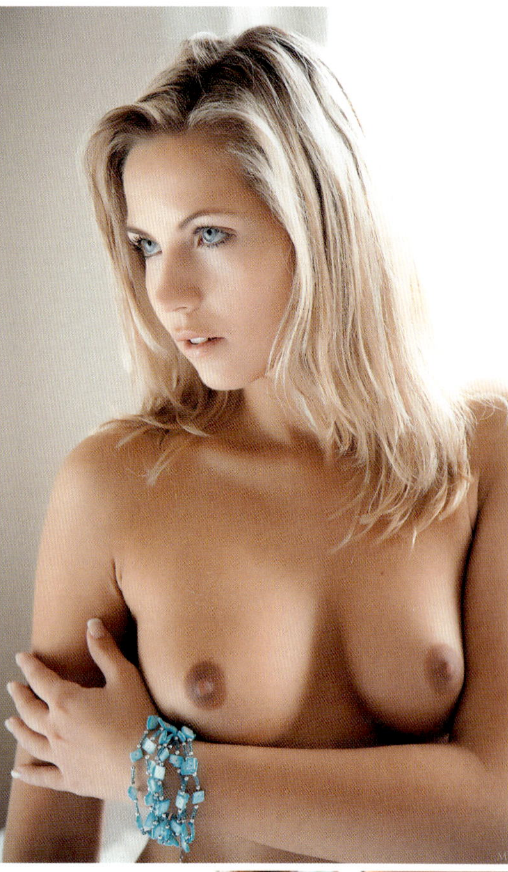

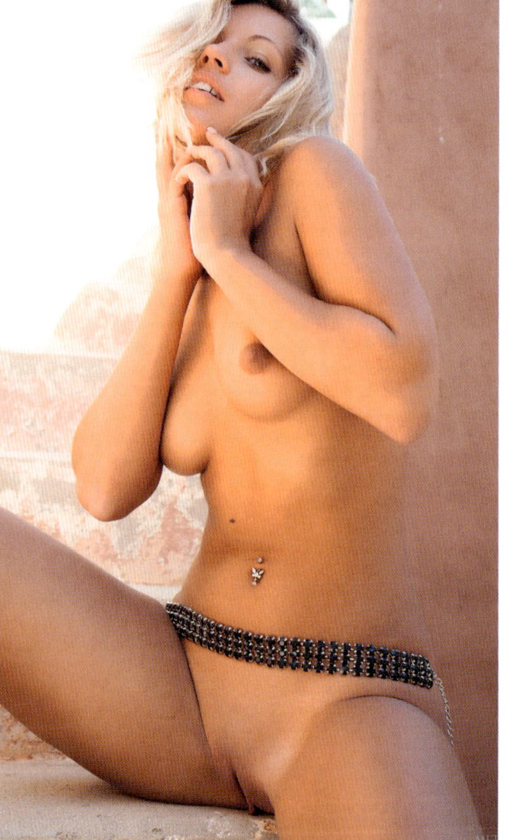

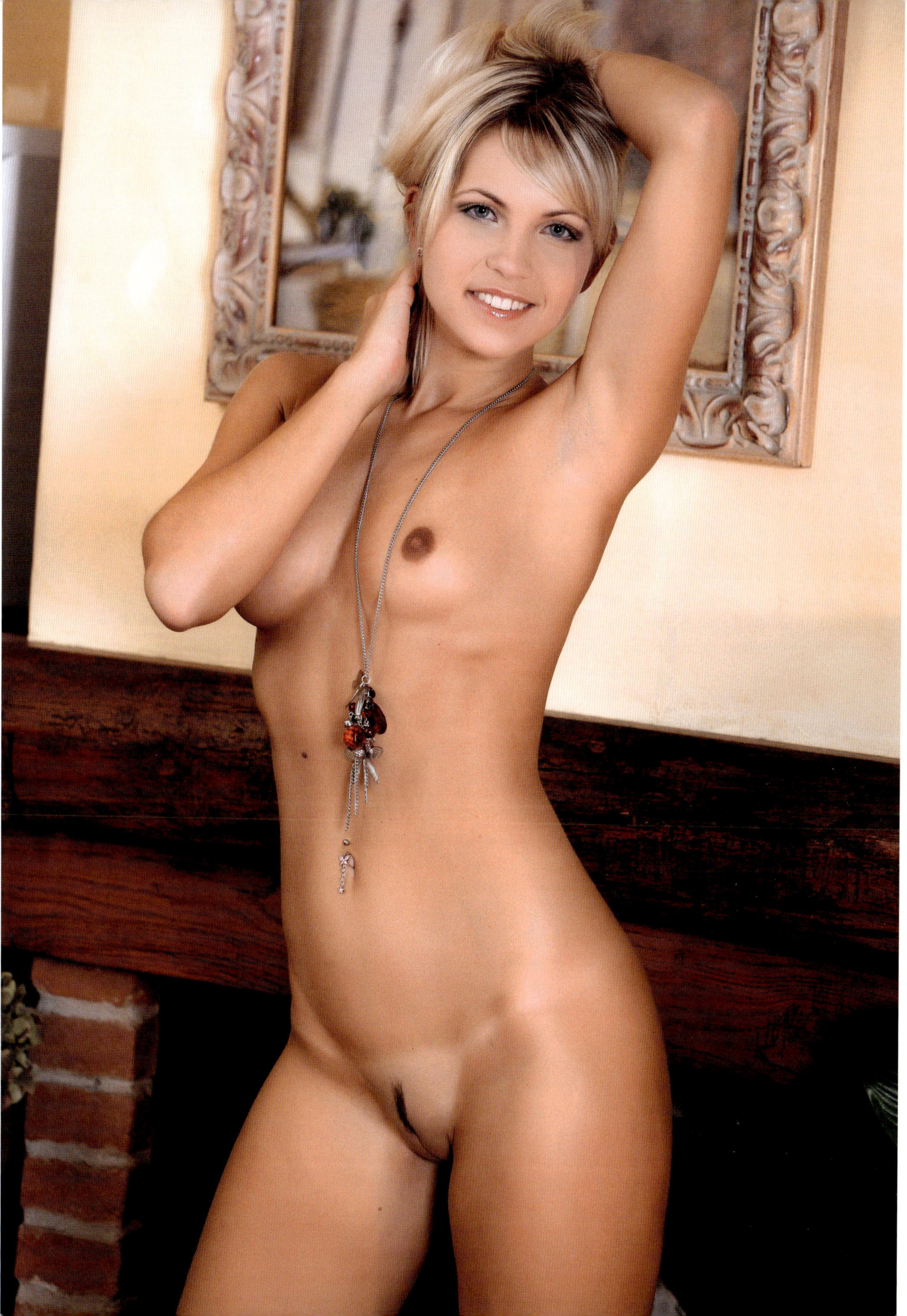

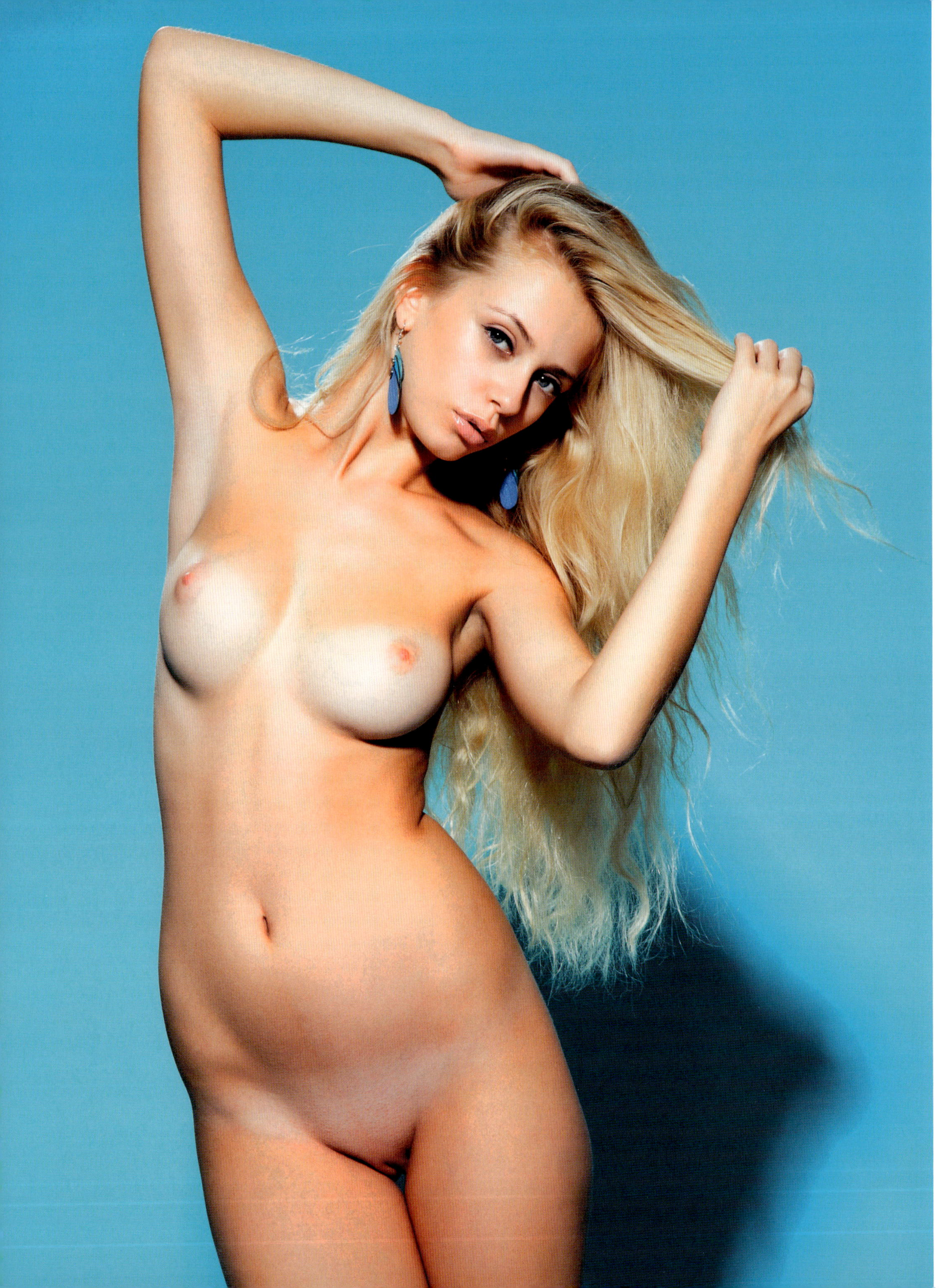

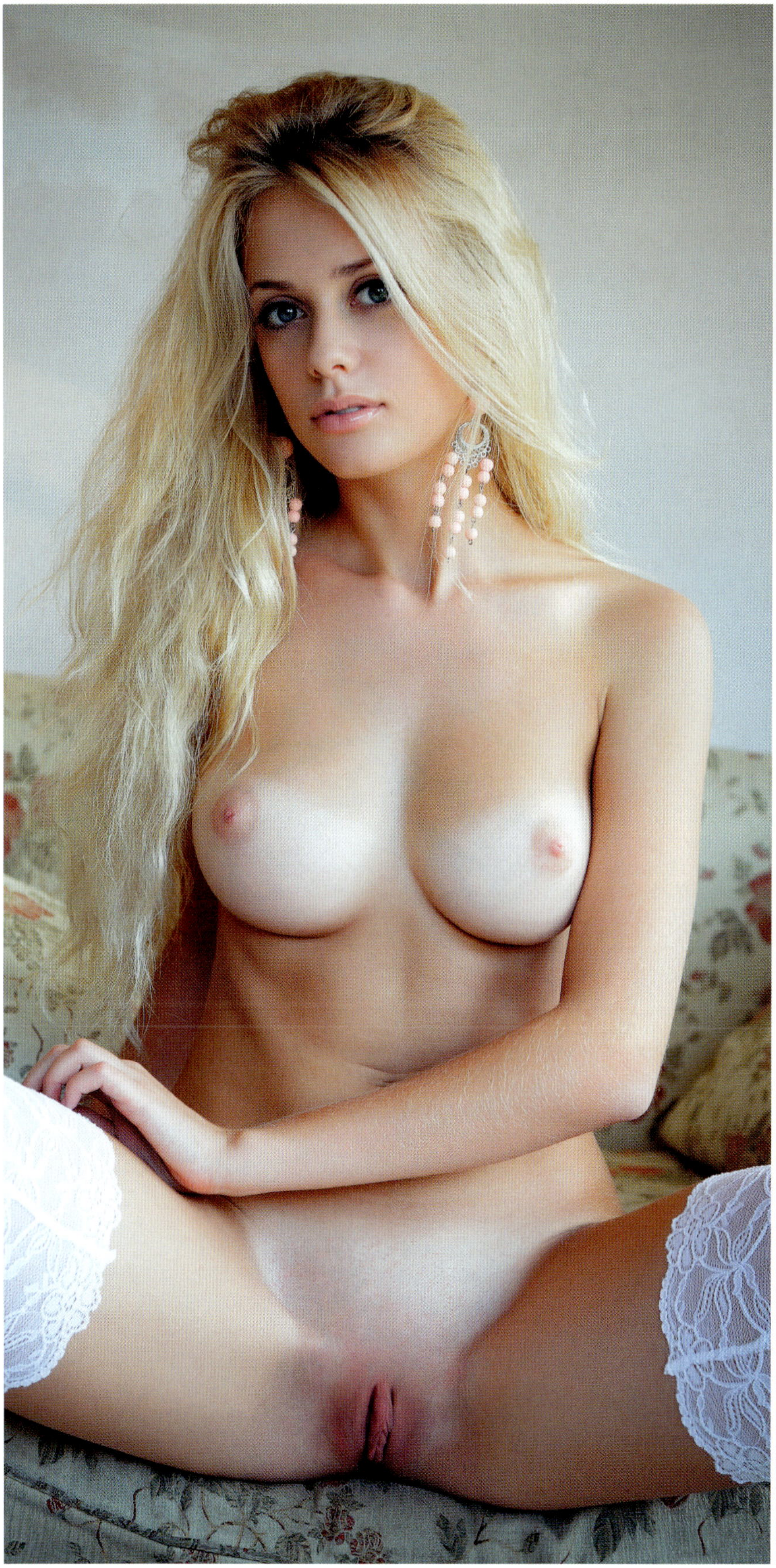

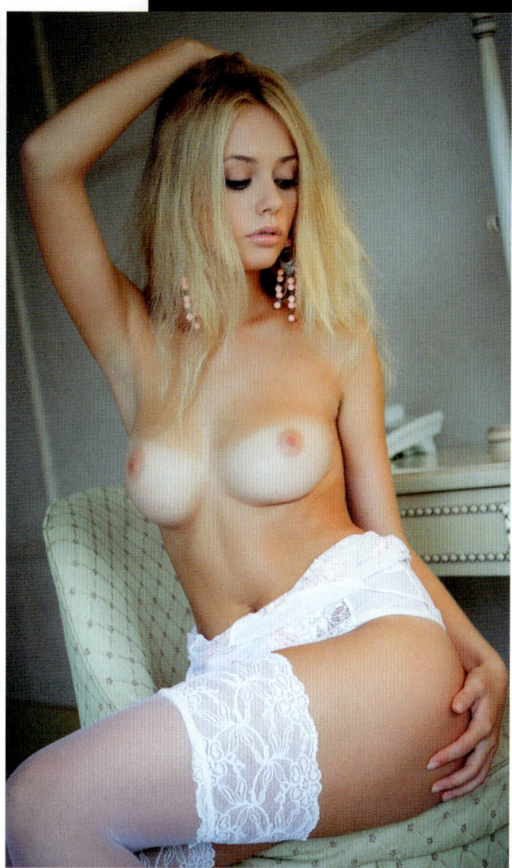

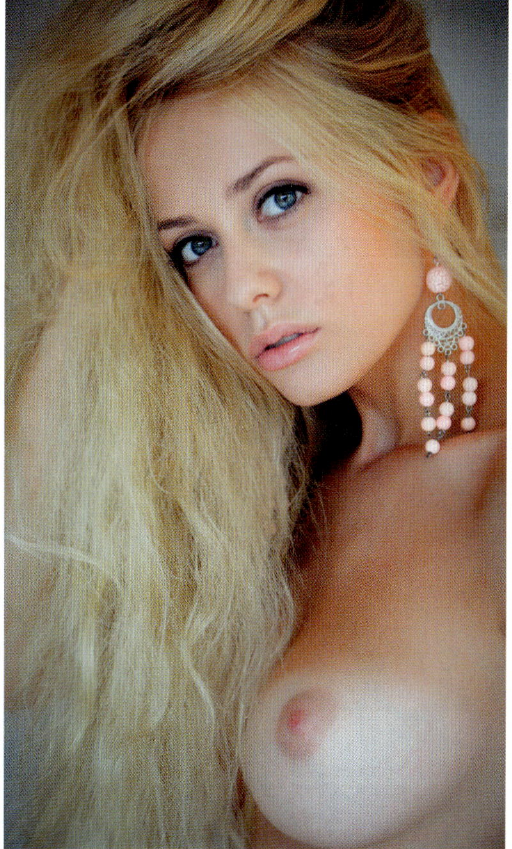

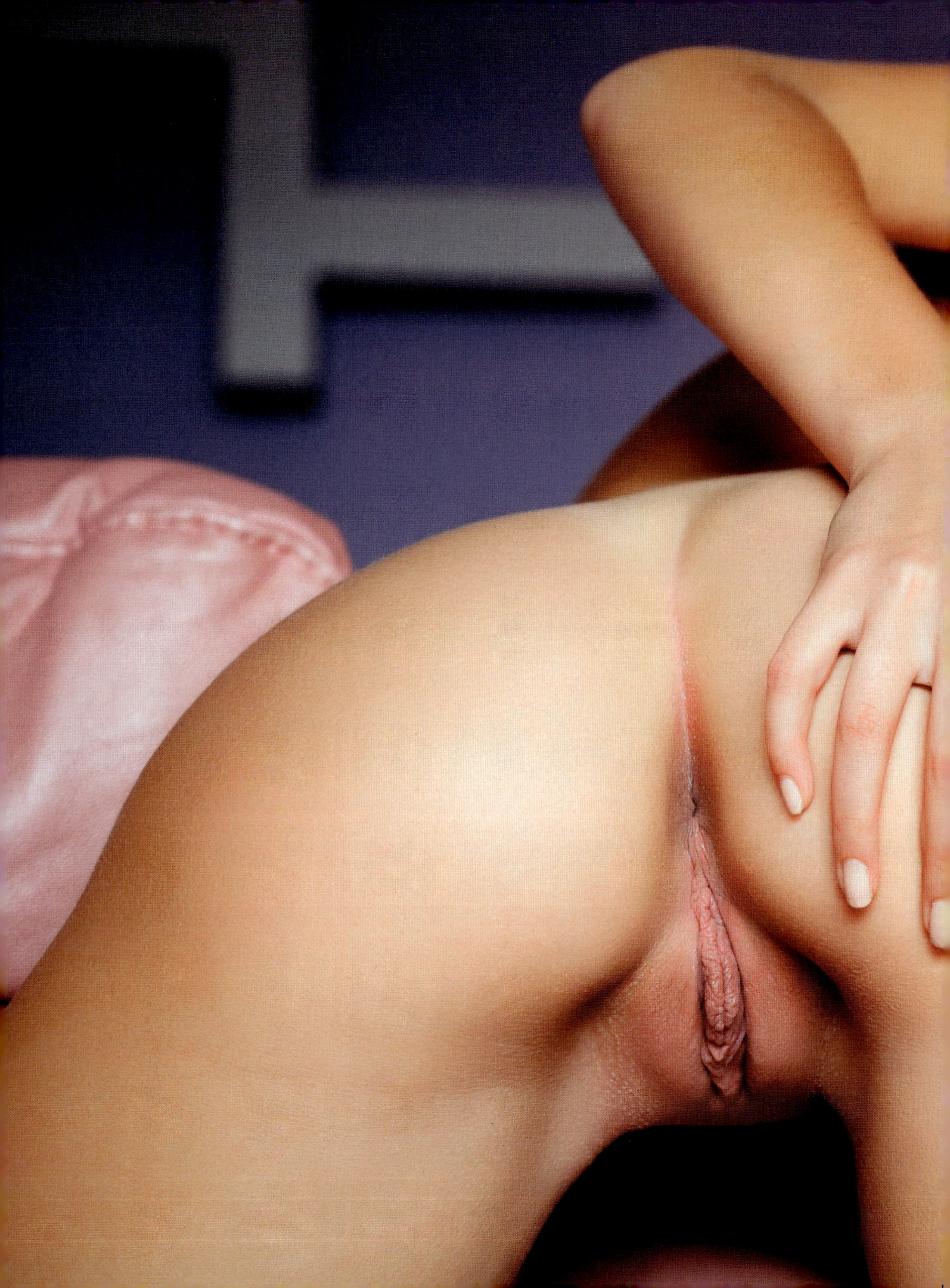

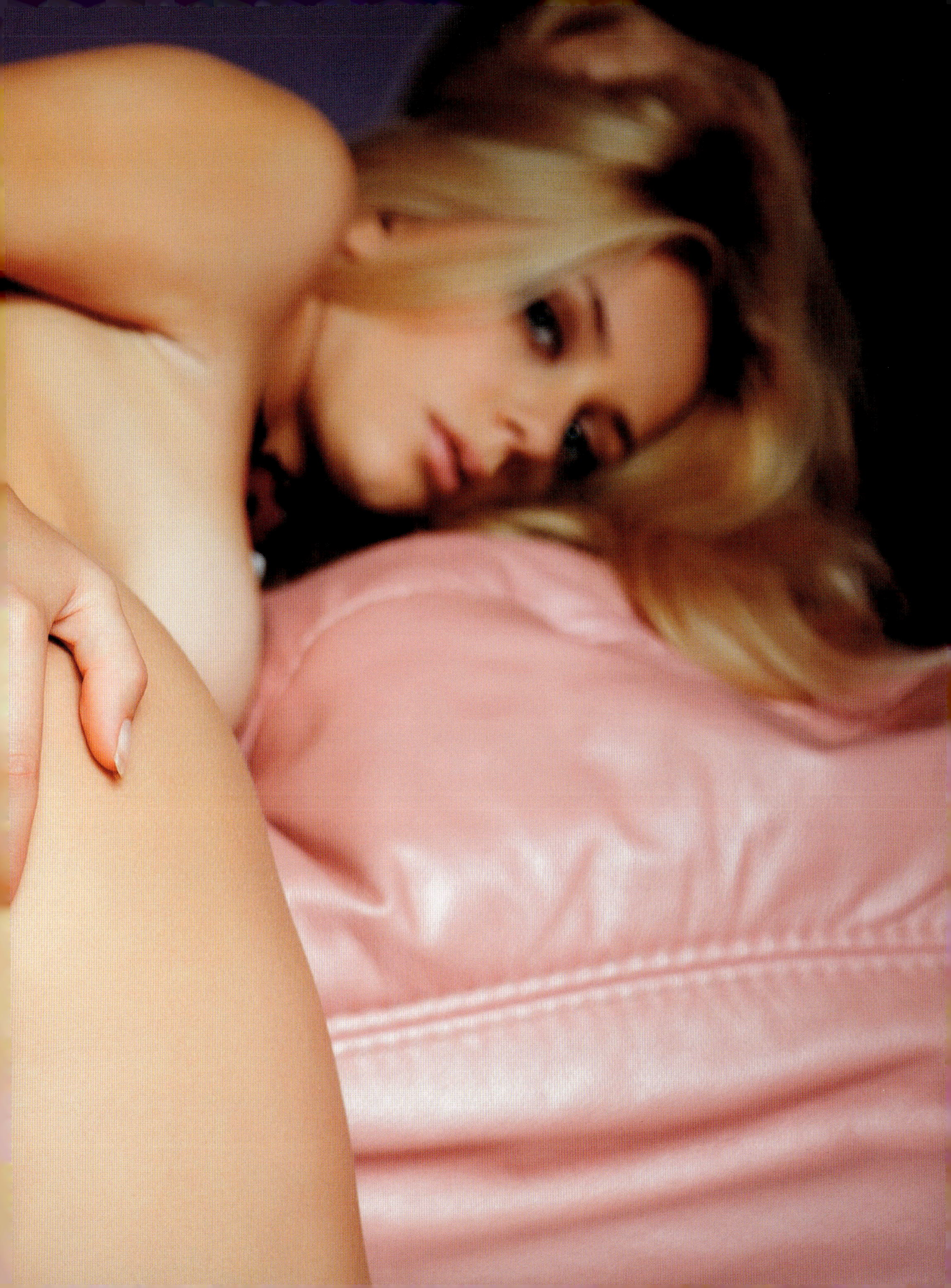

## Jenya D

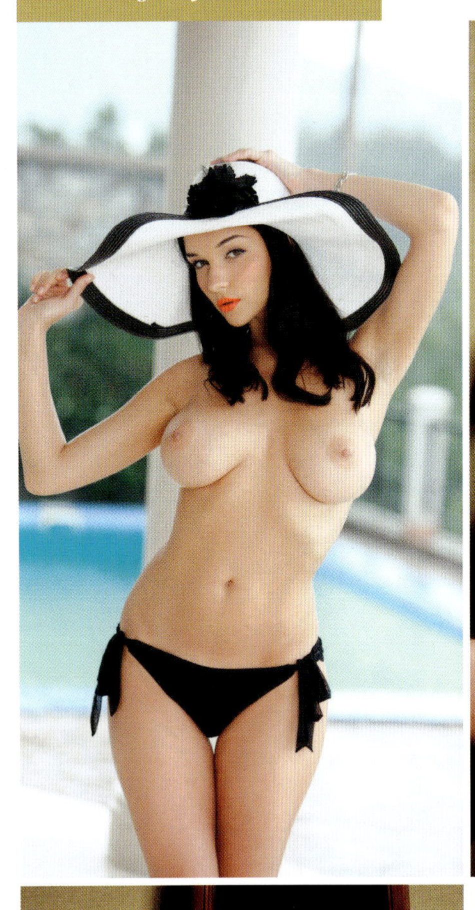

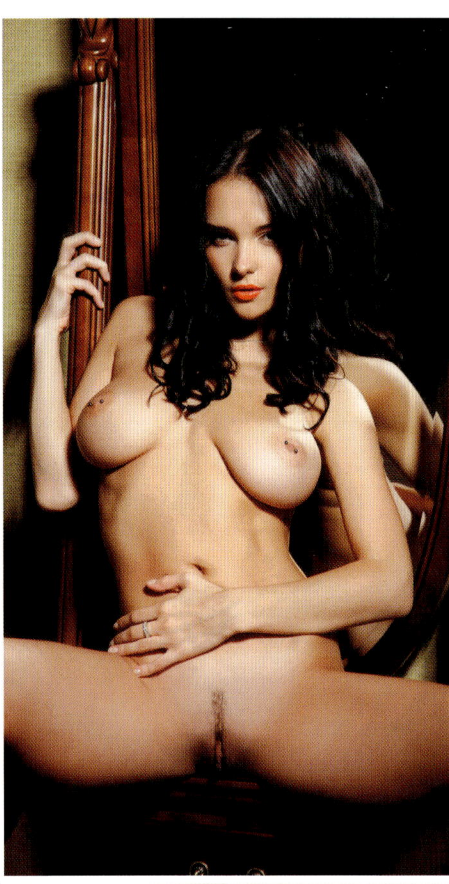

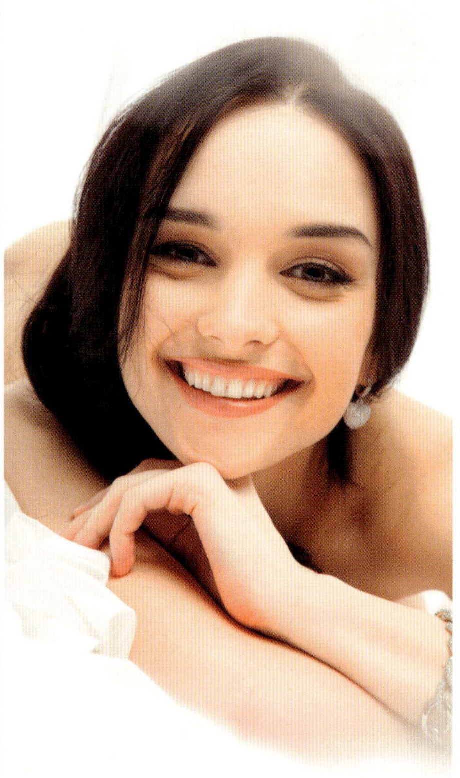

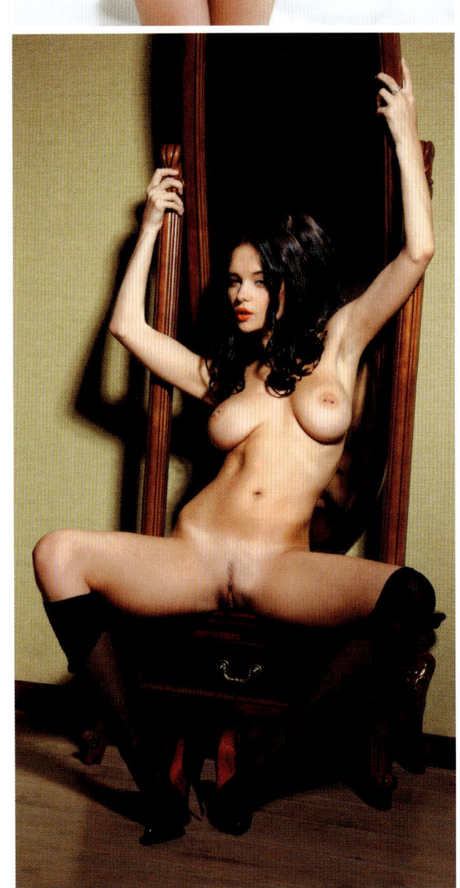

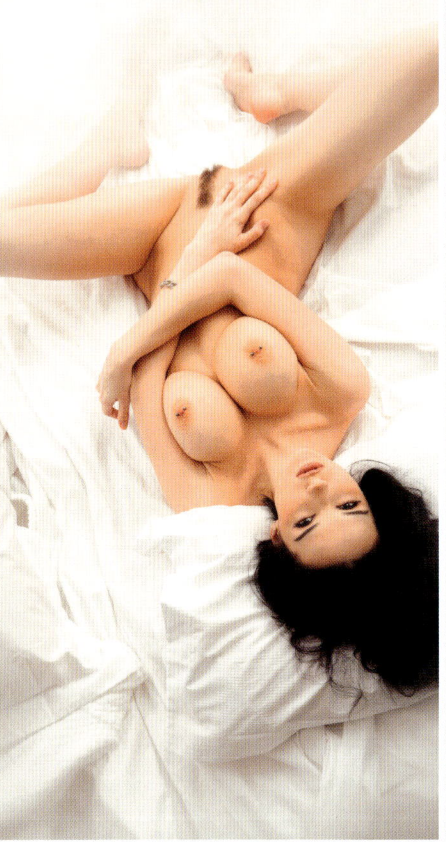

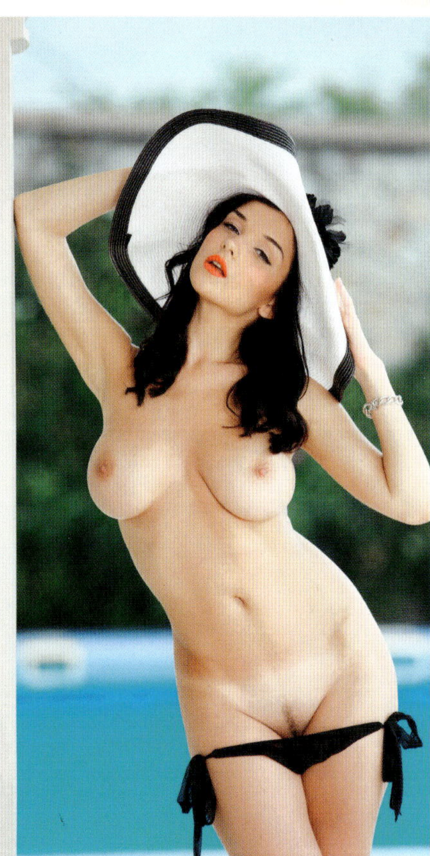

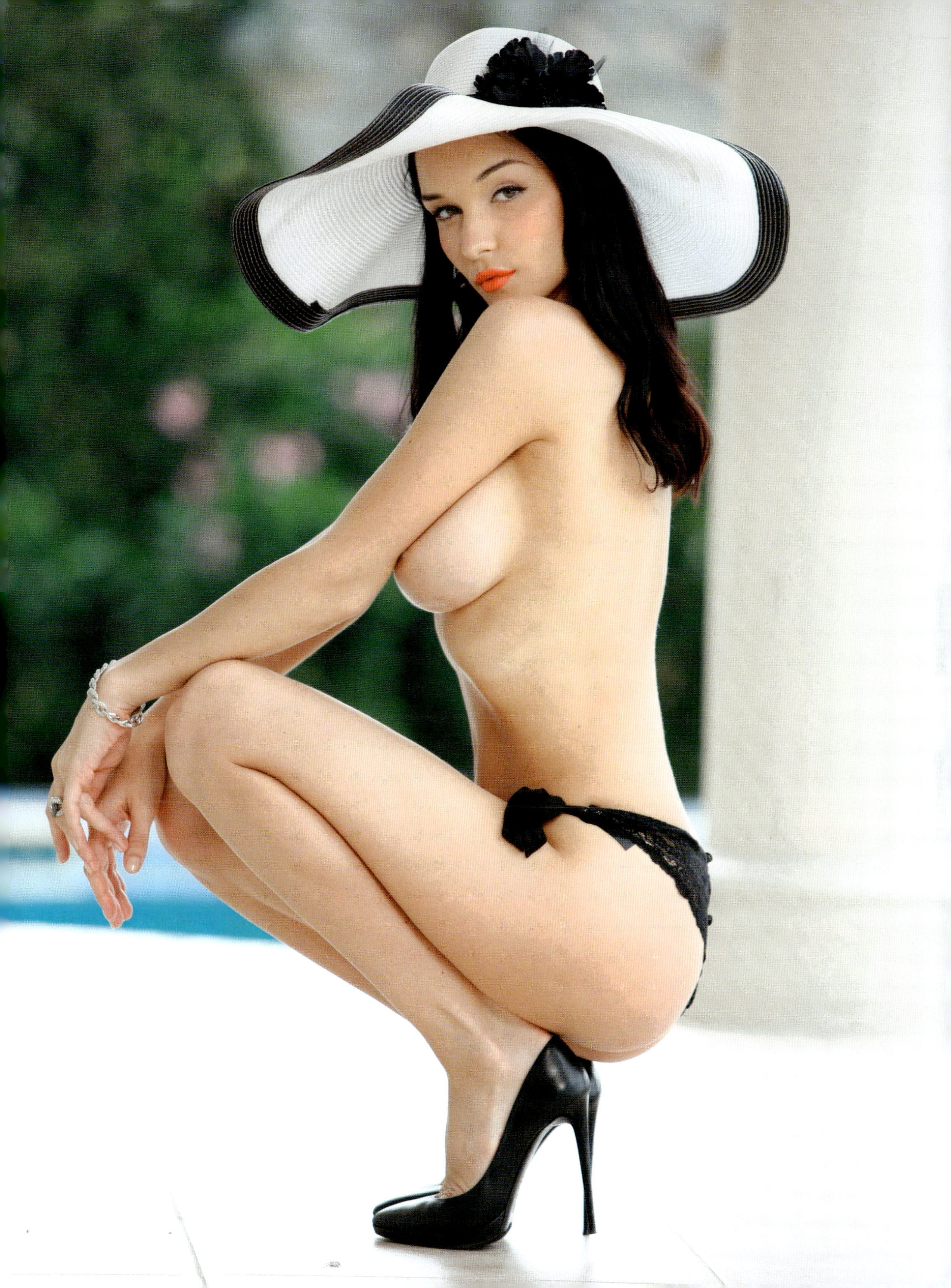

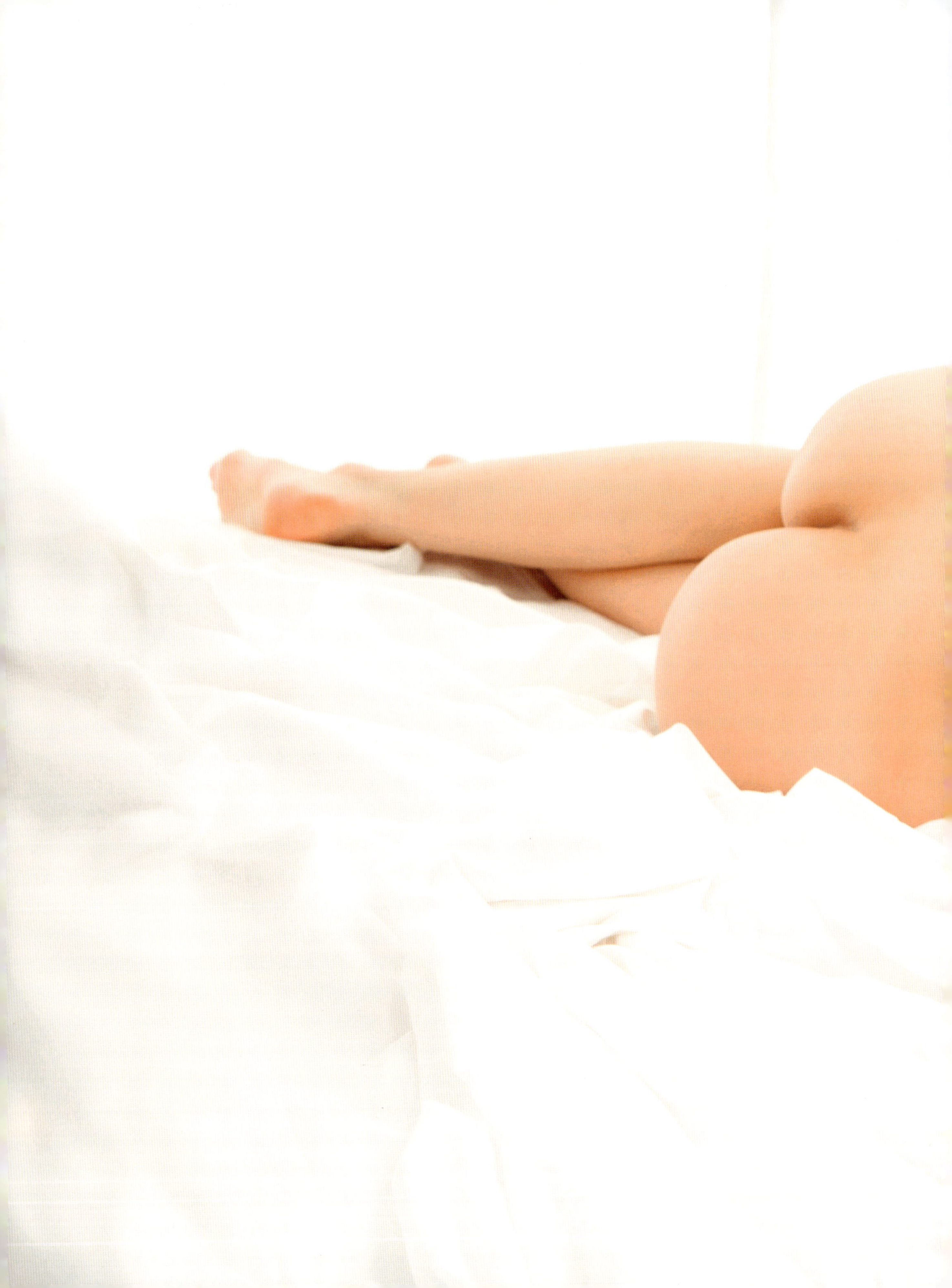

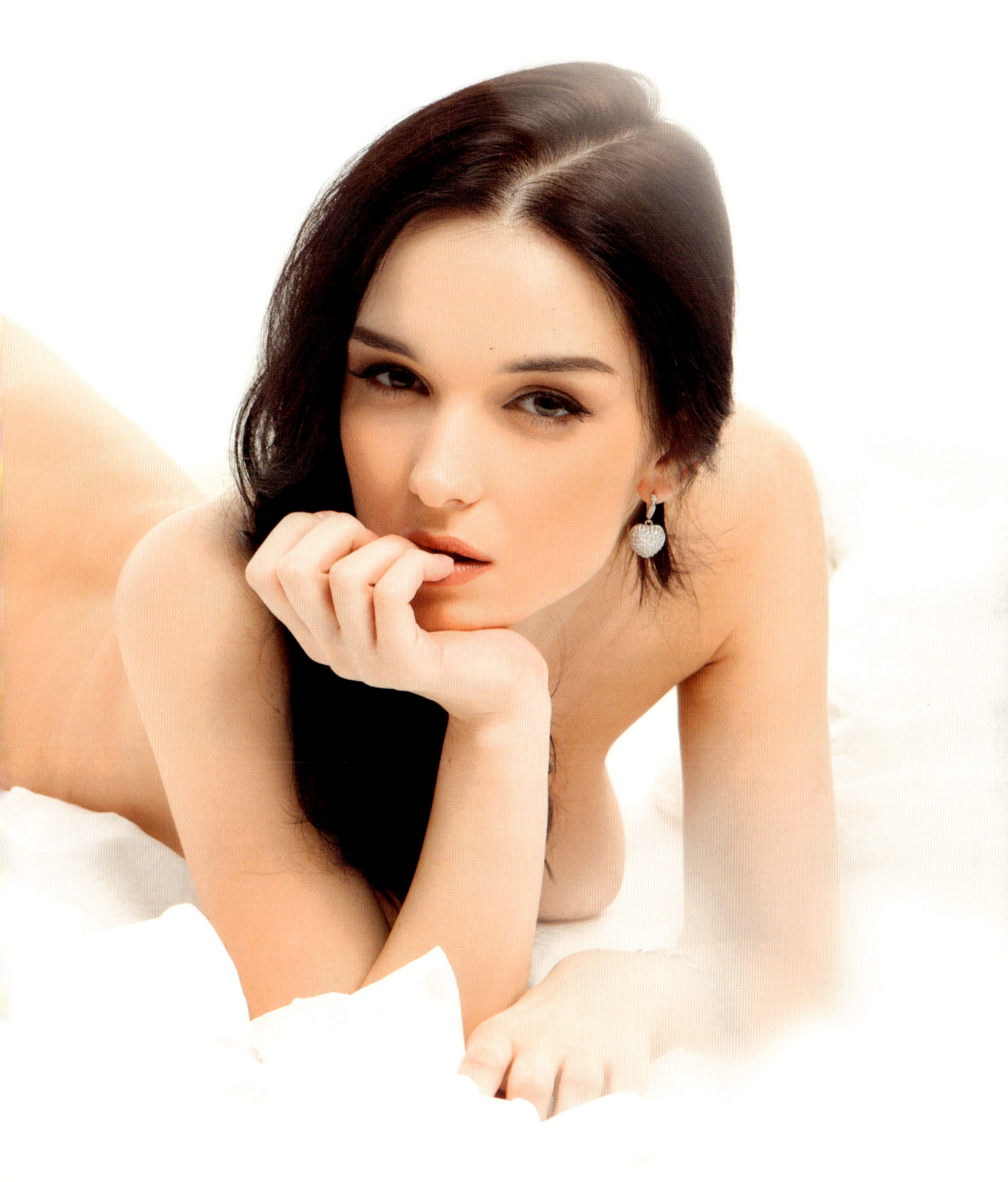

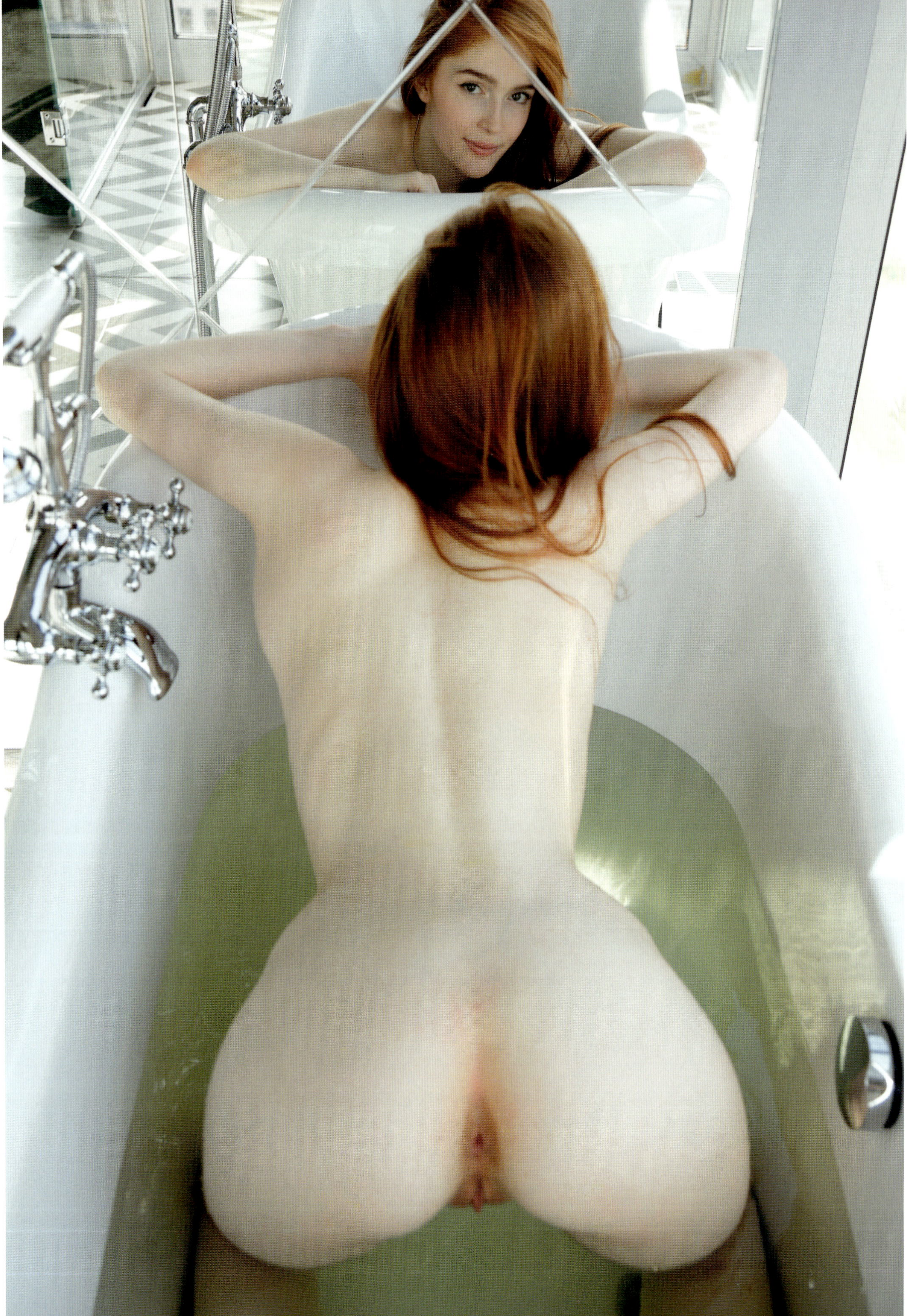

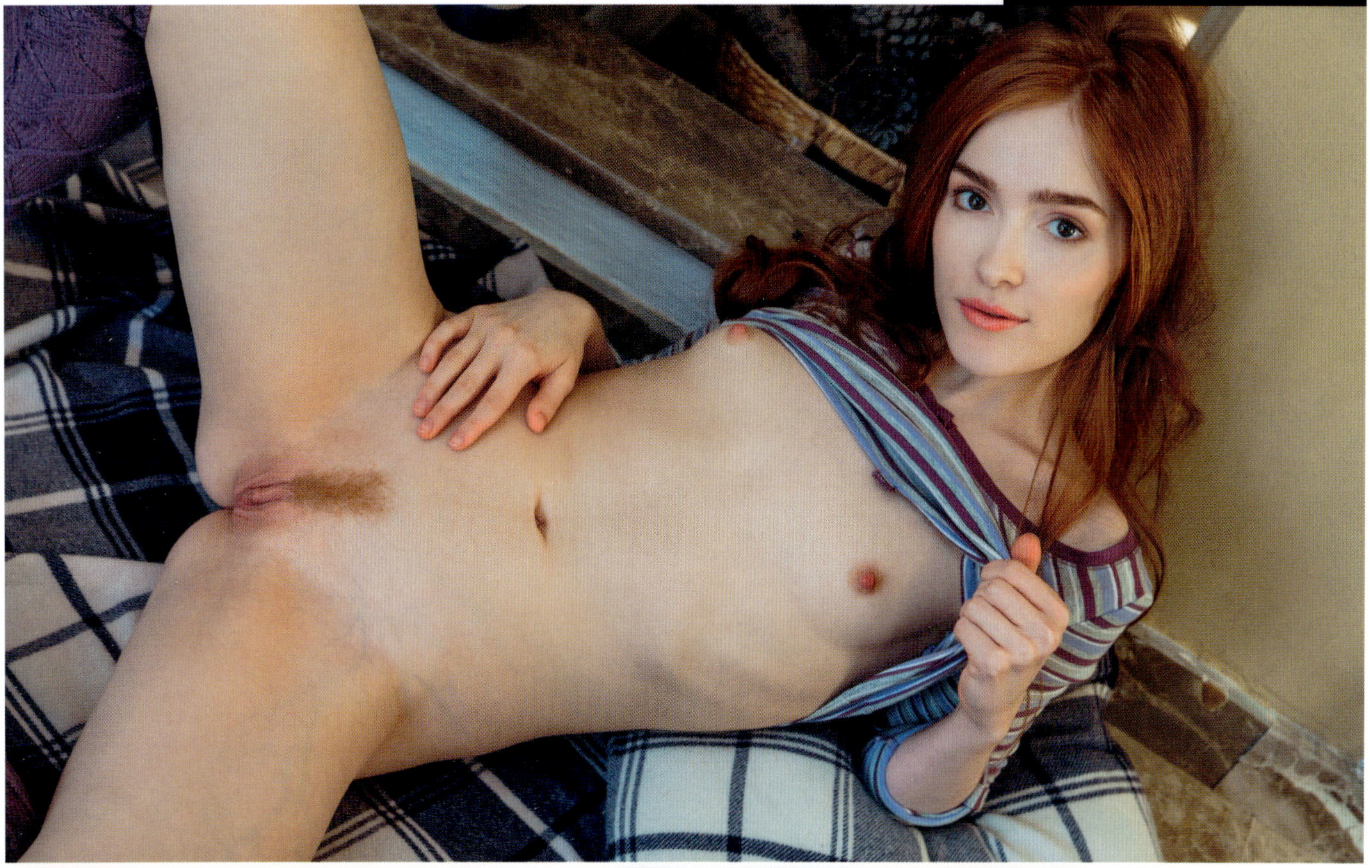

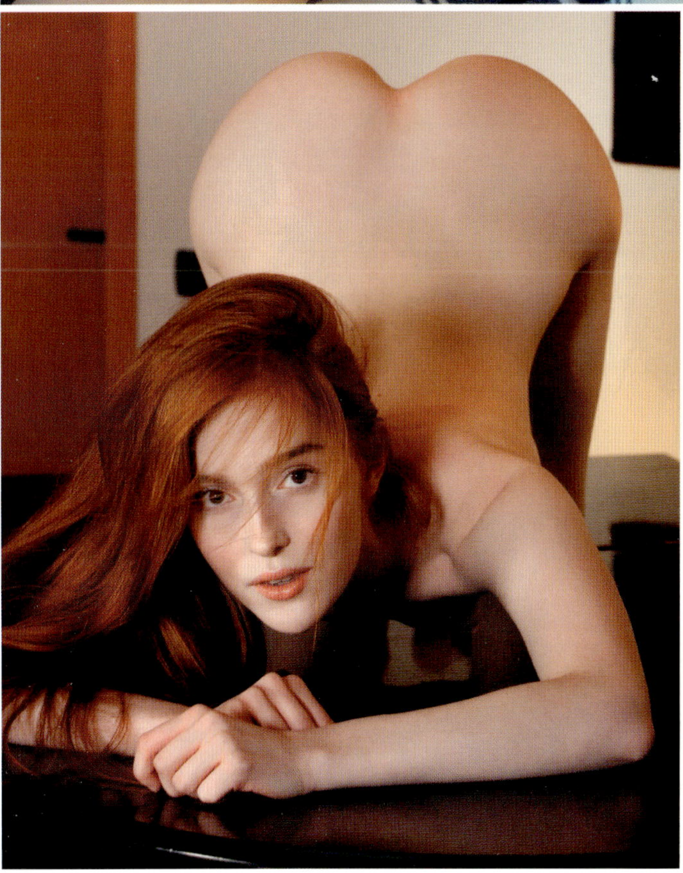

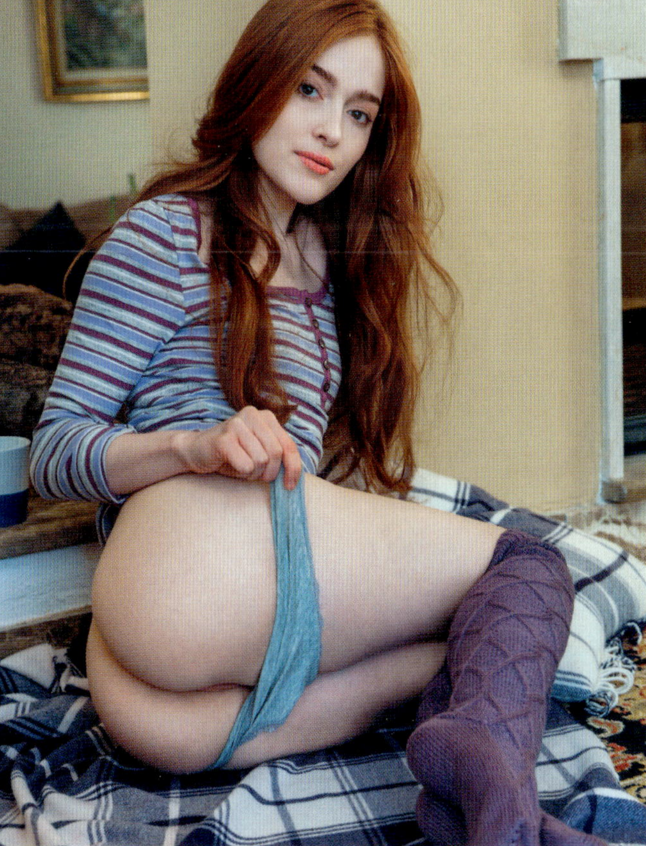

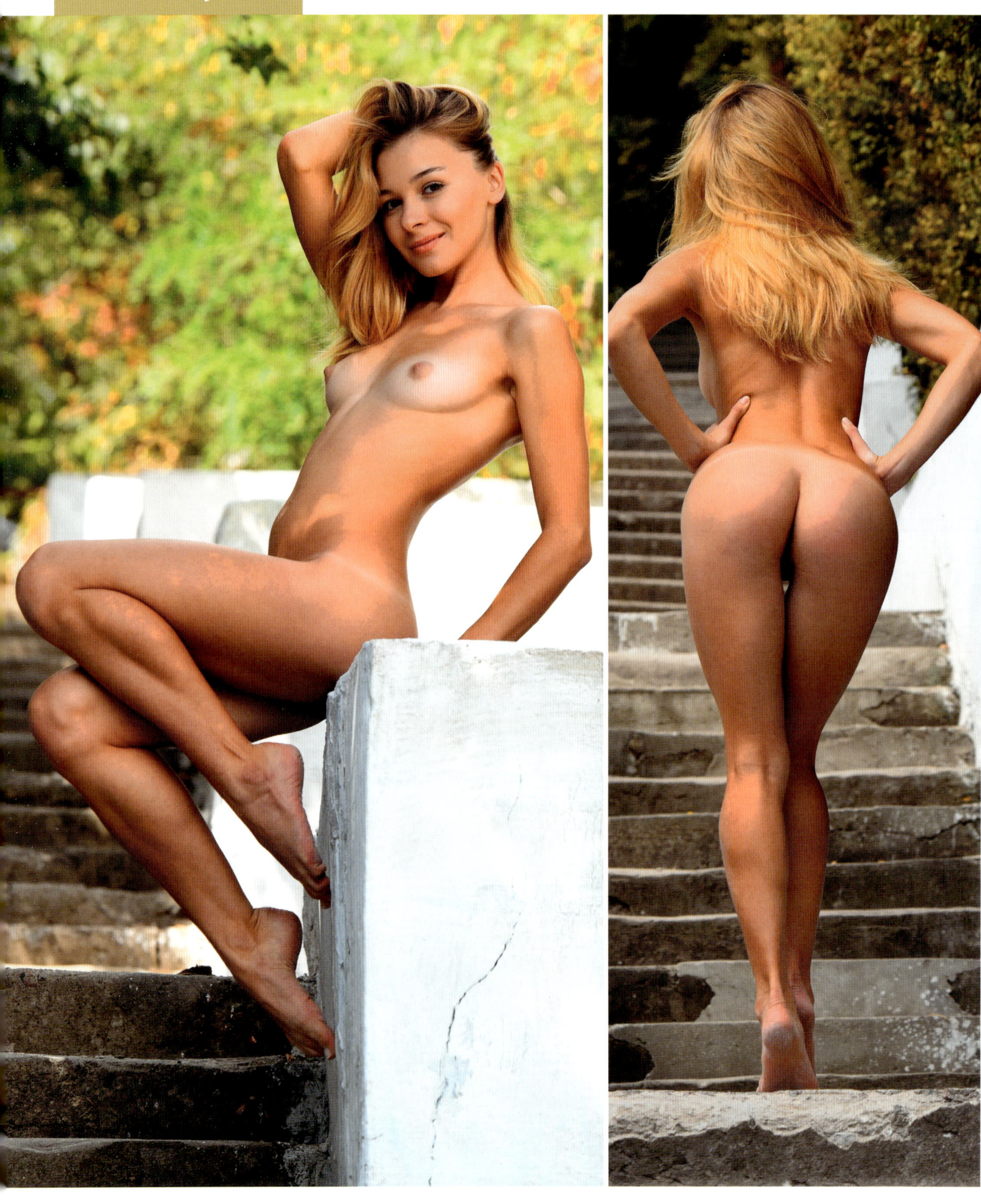

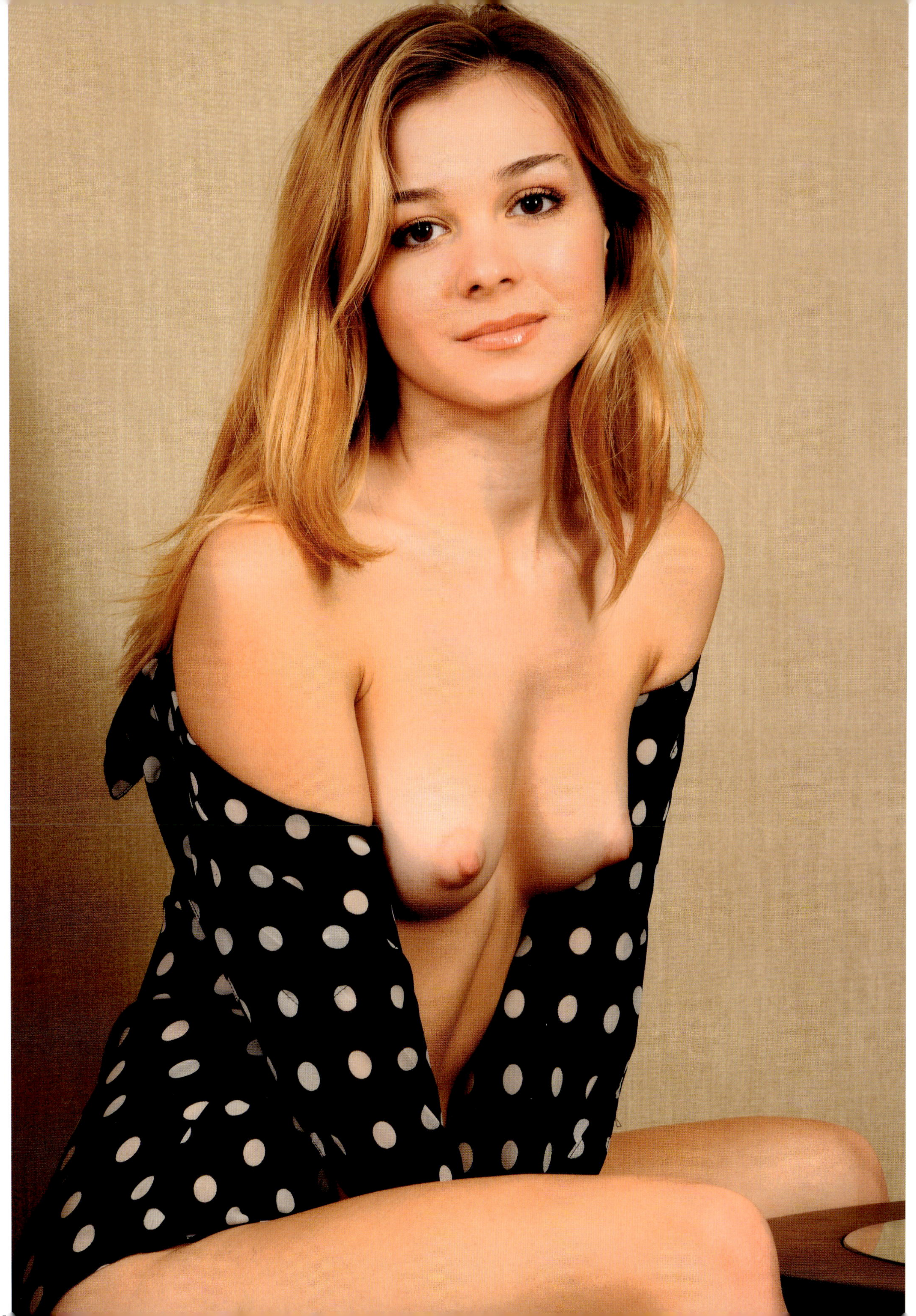

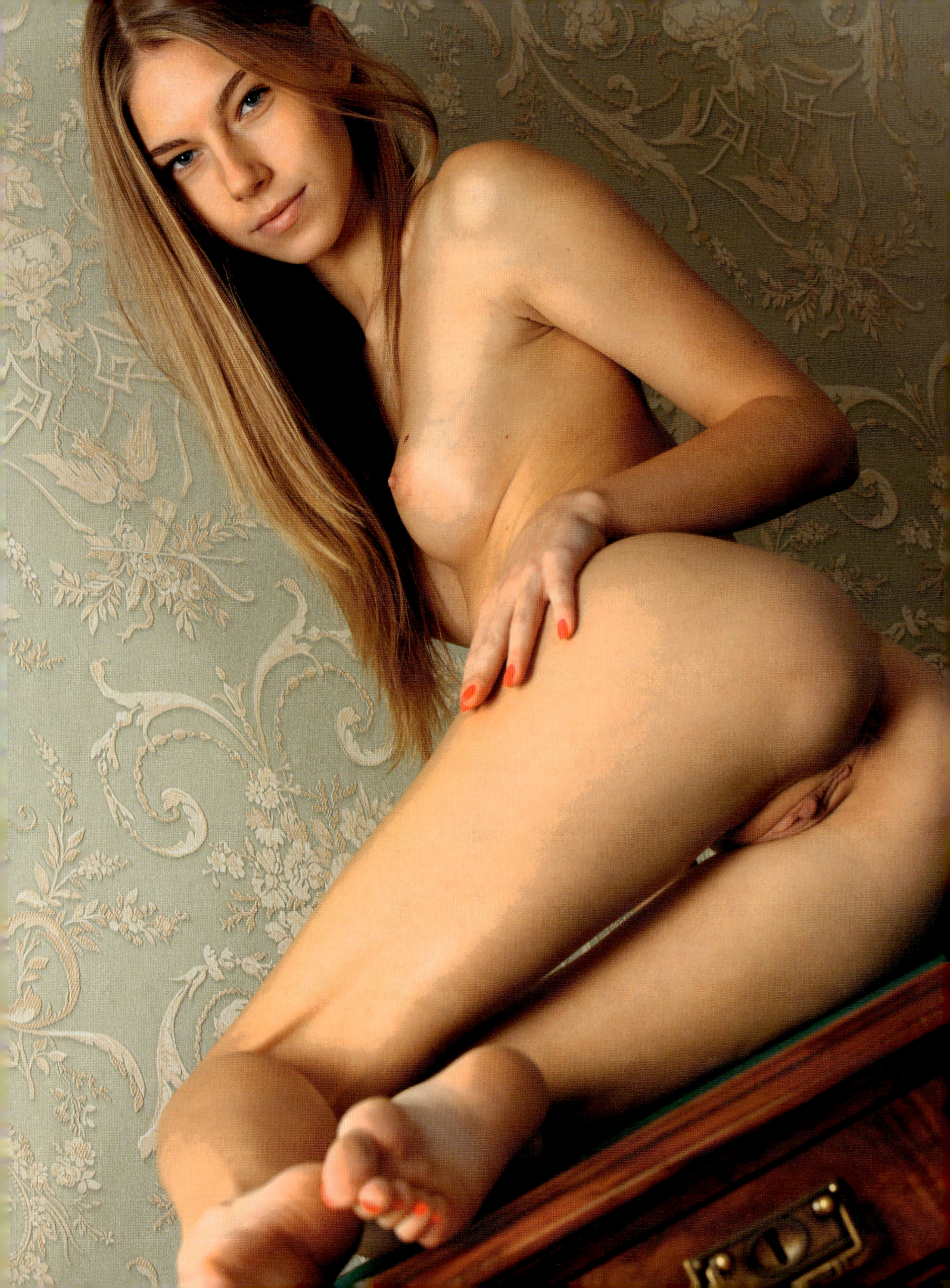

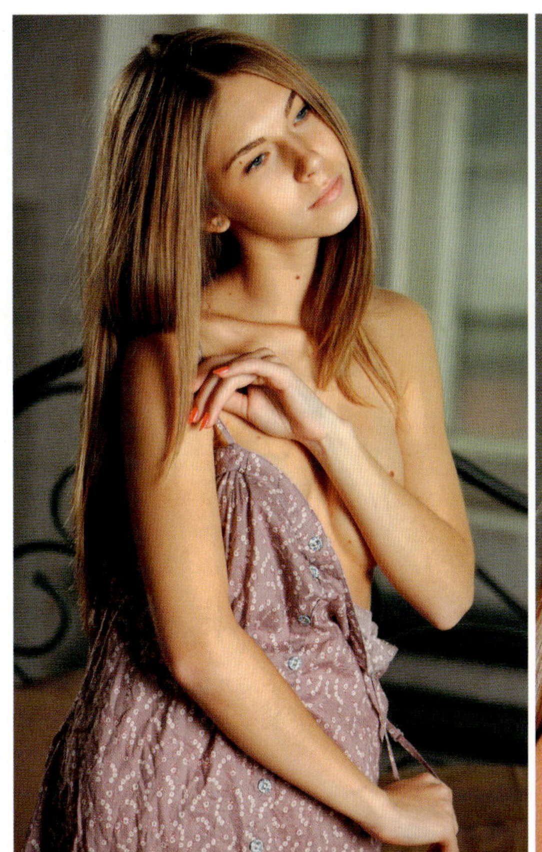
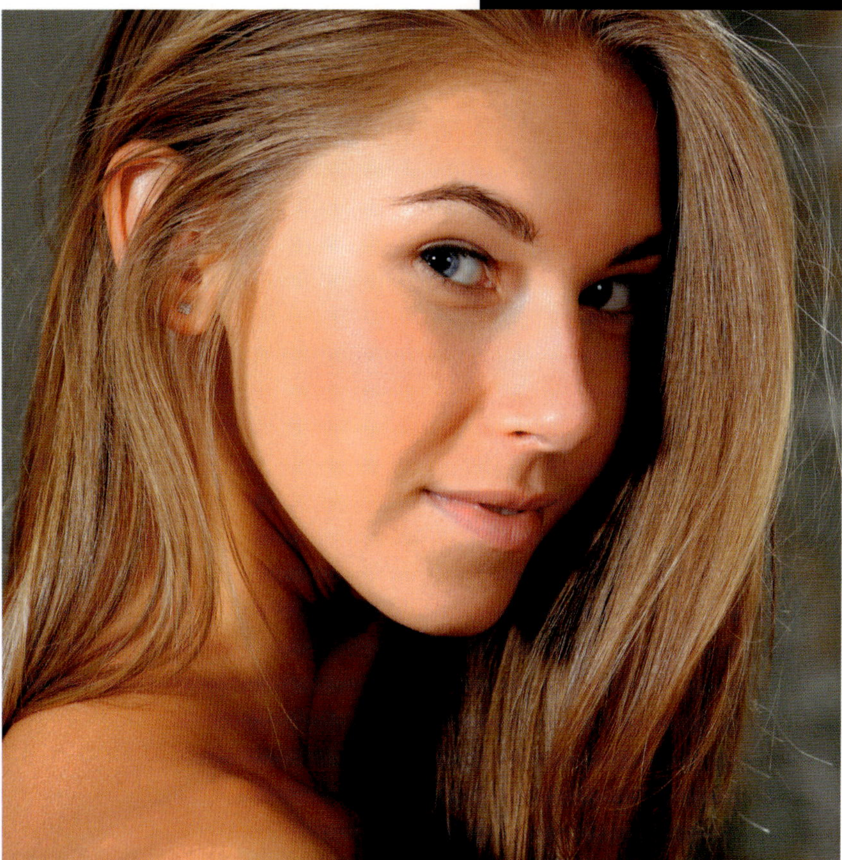
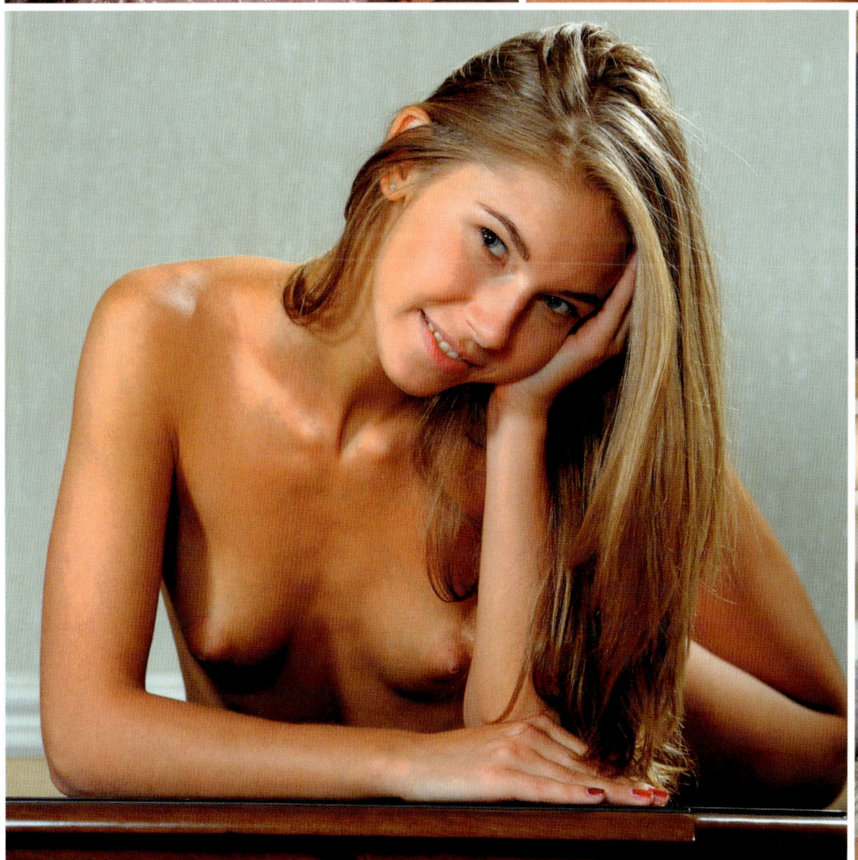
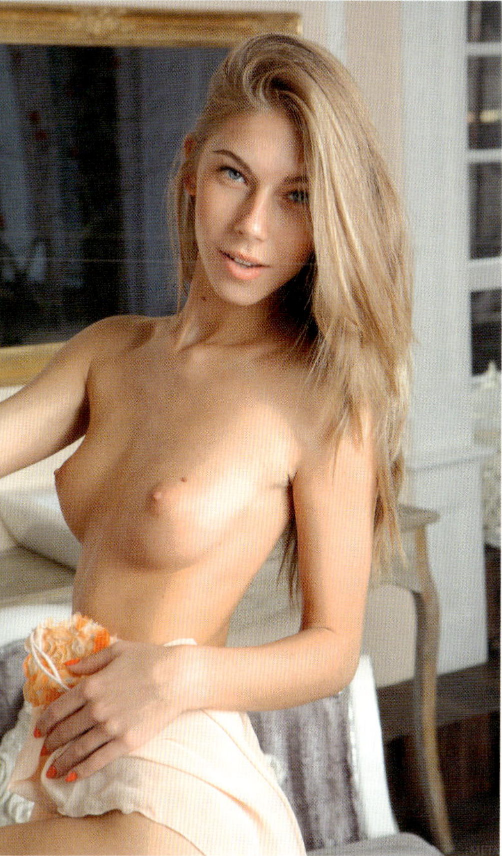

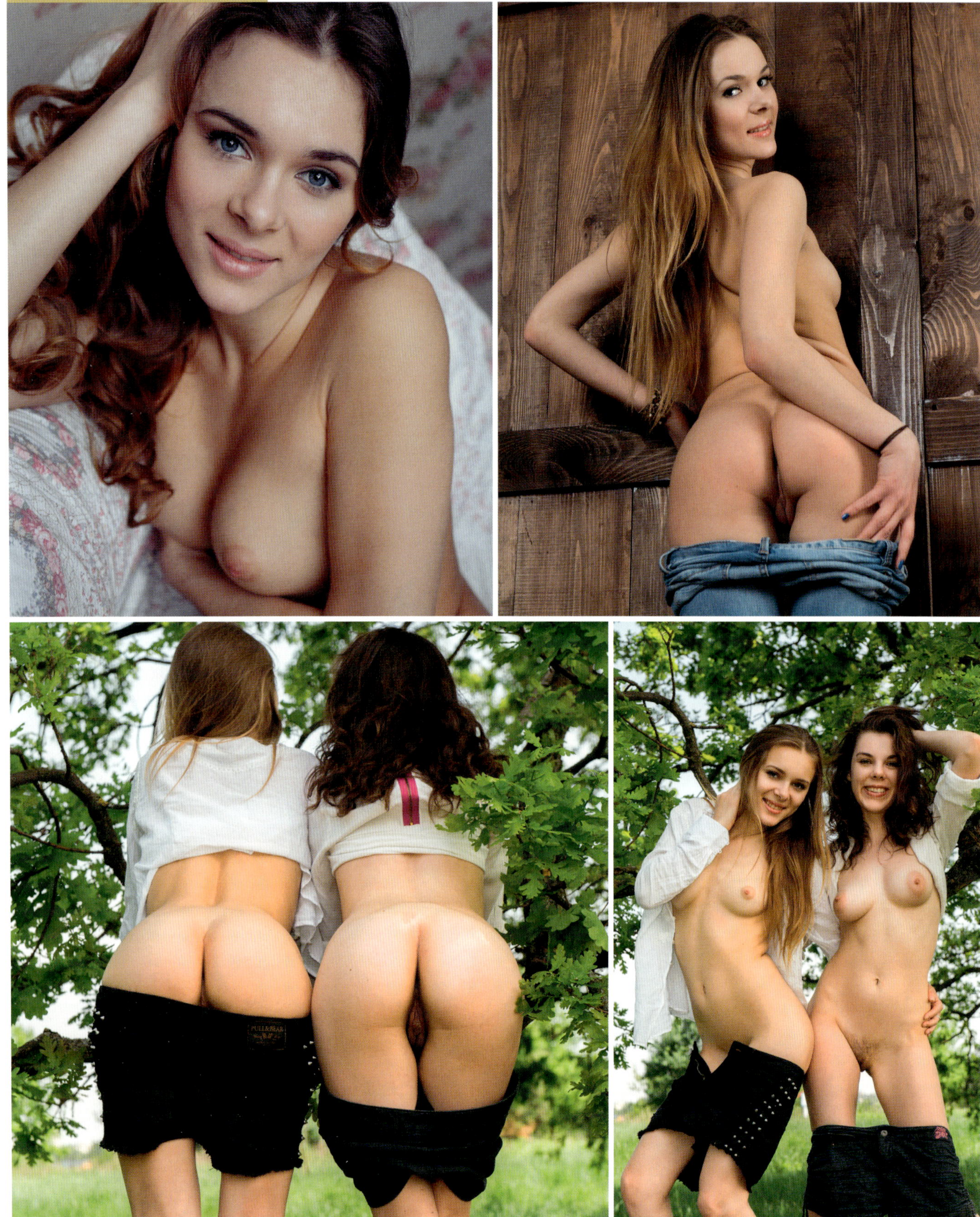

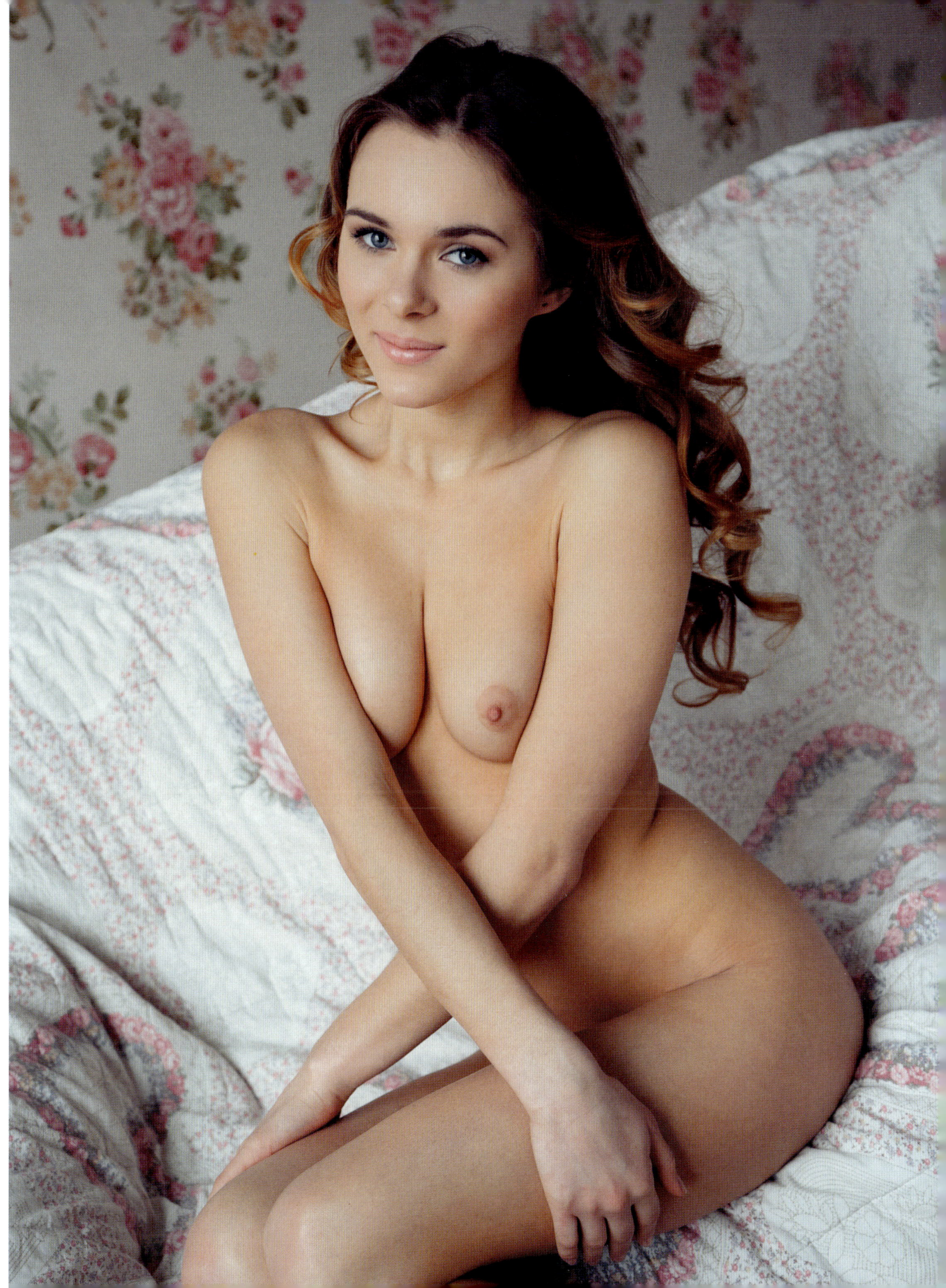

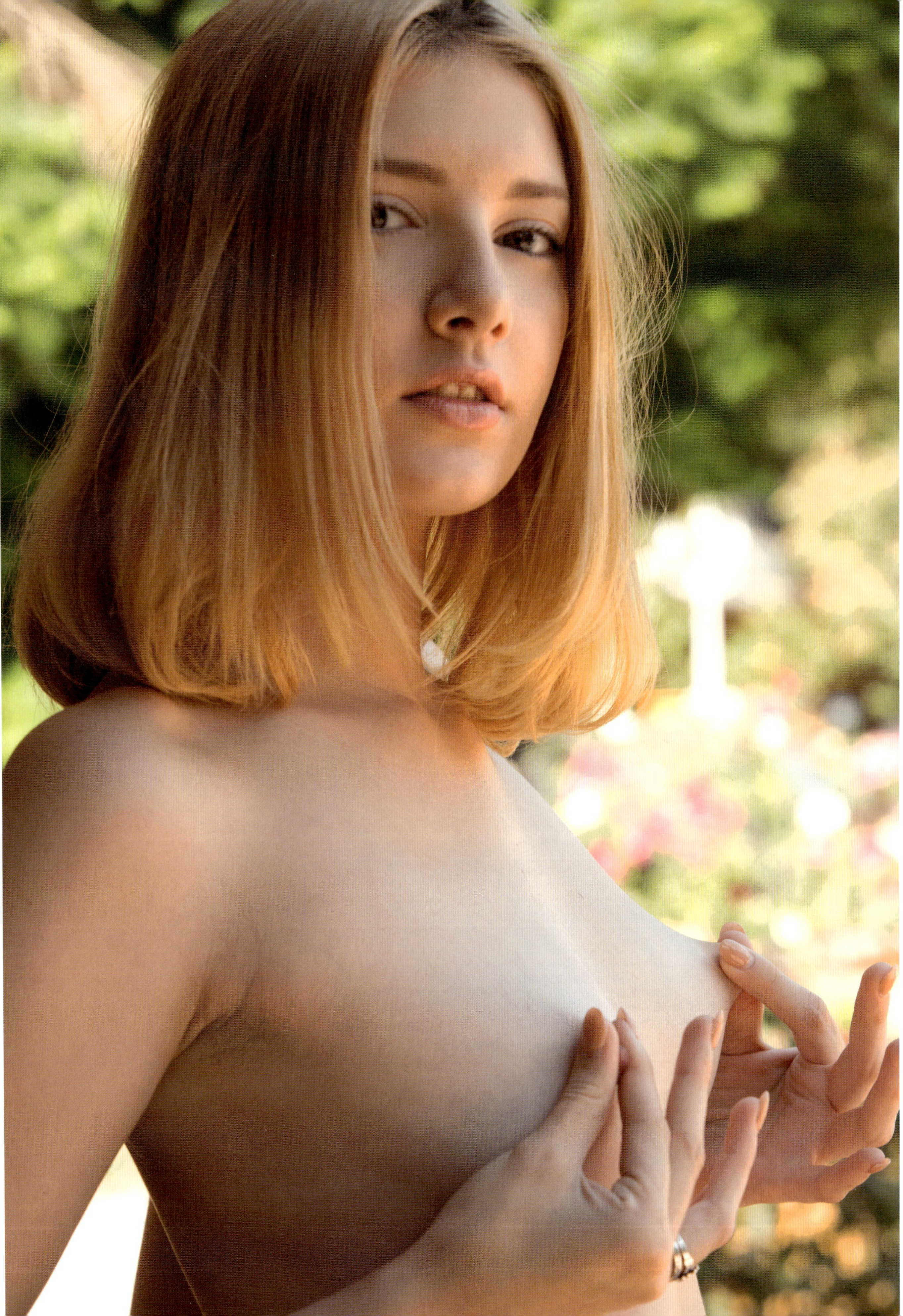

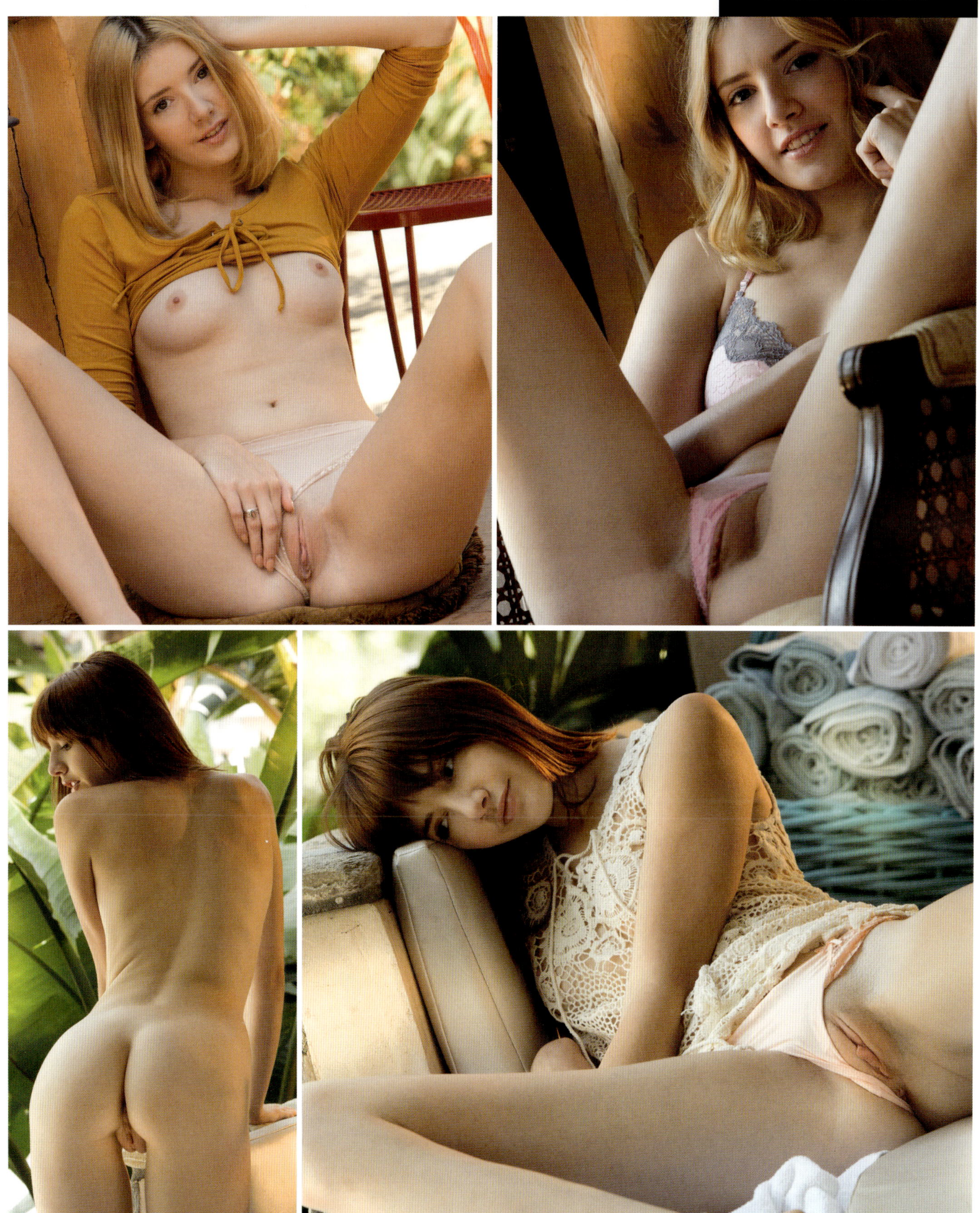

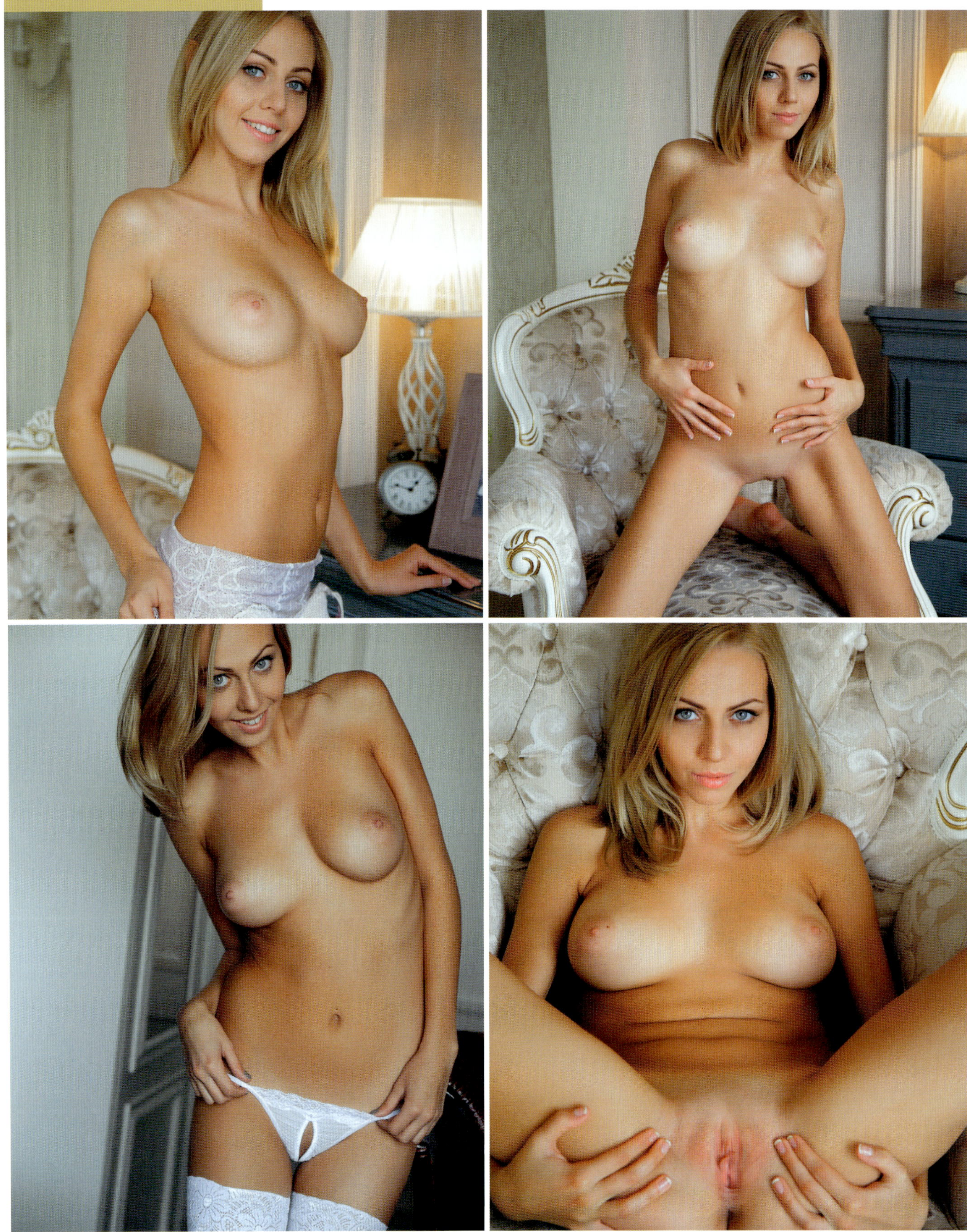

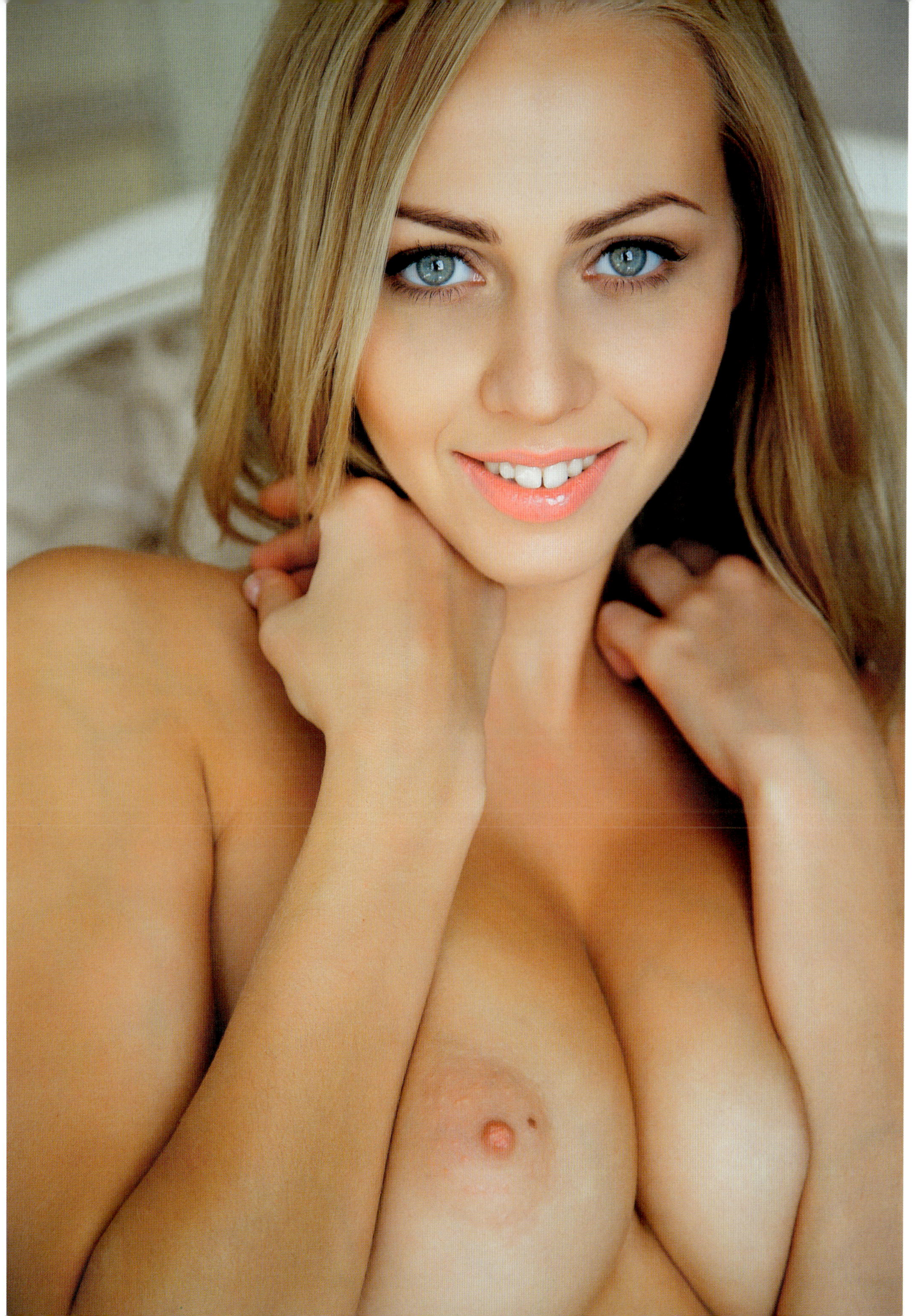

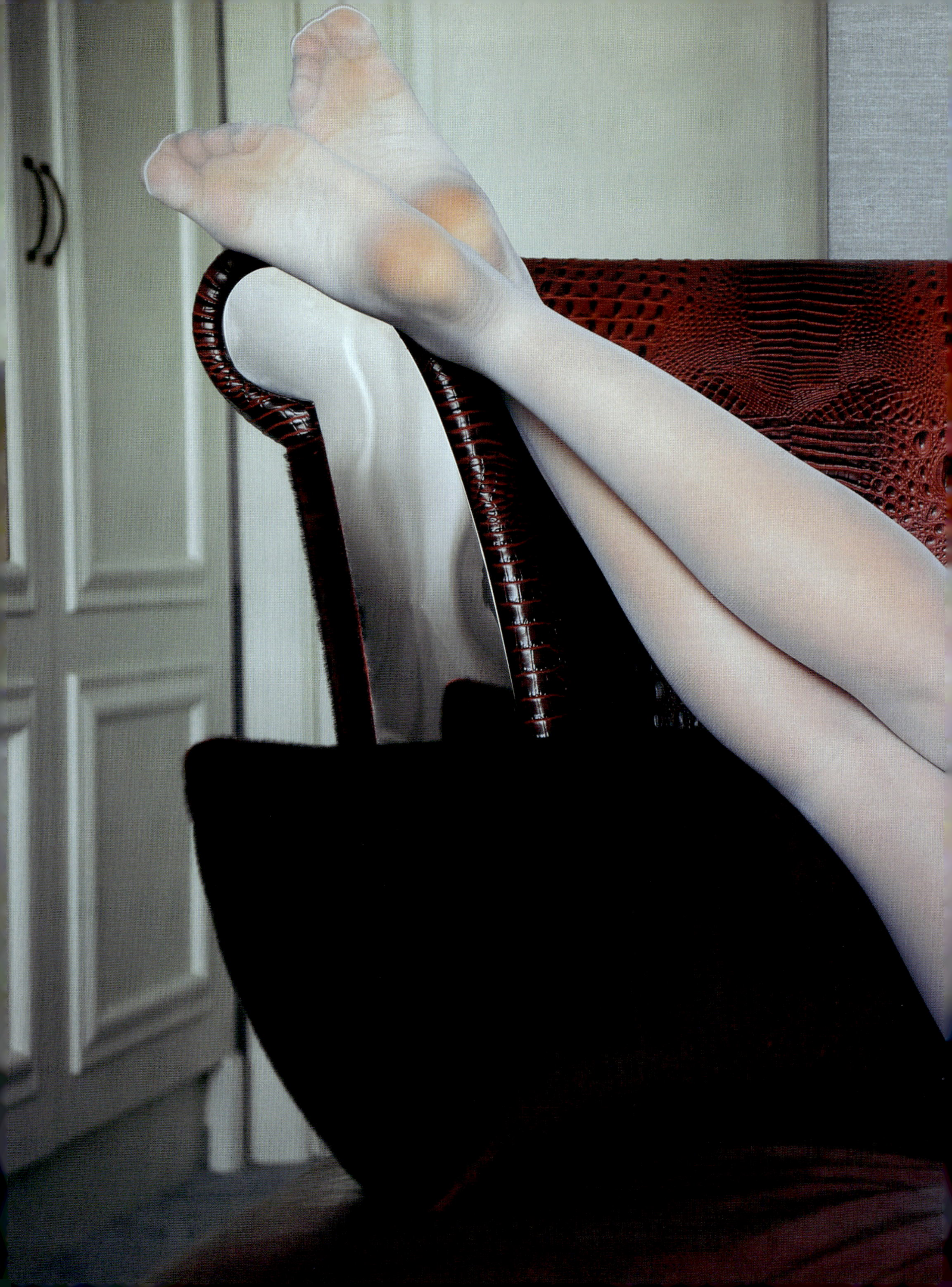

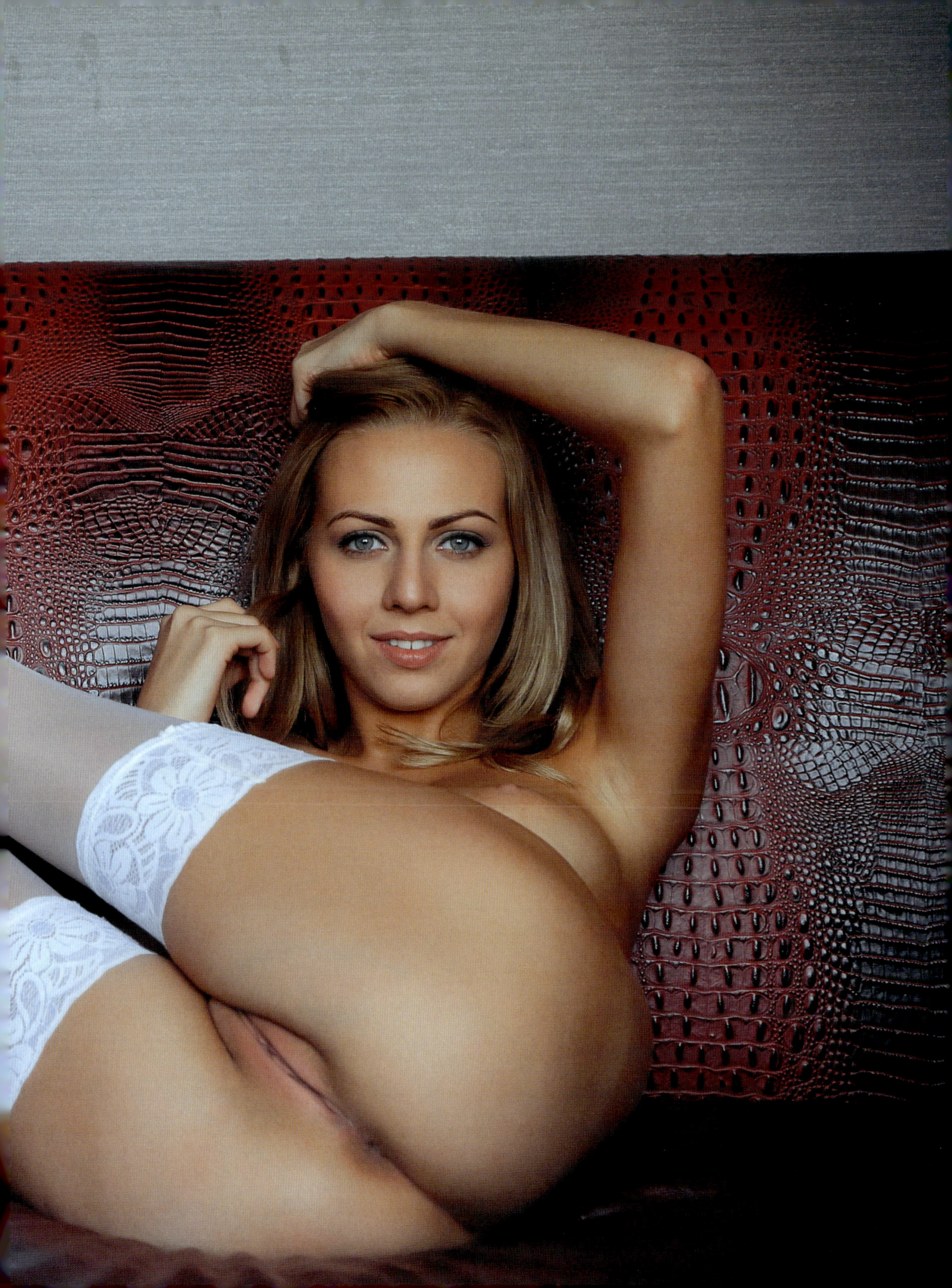

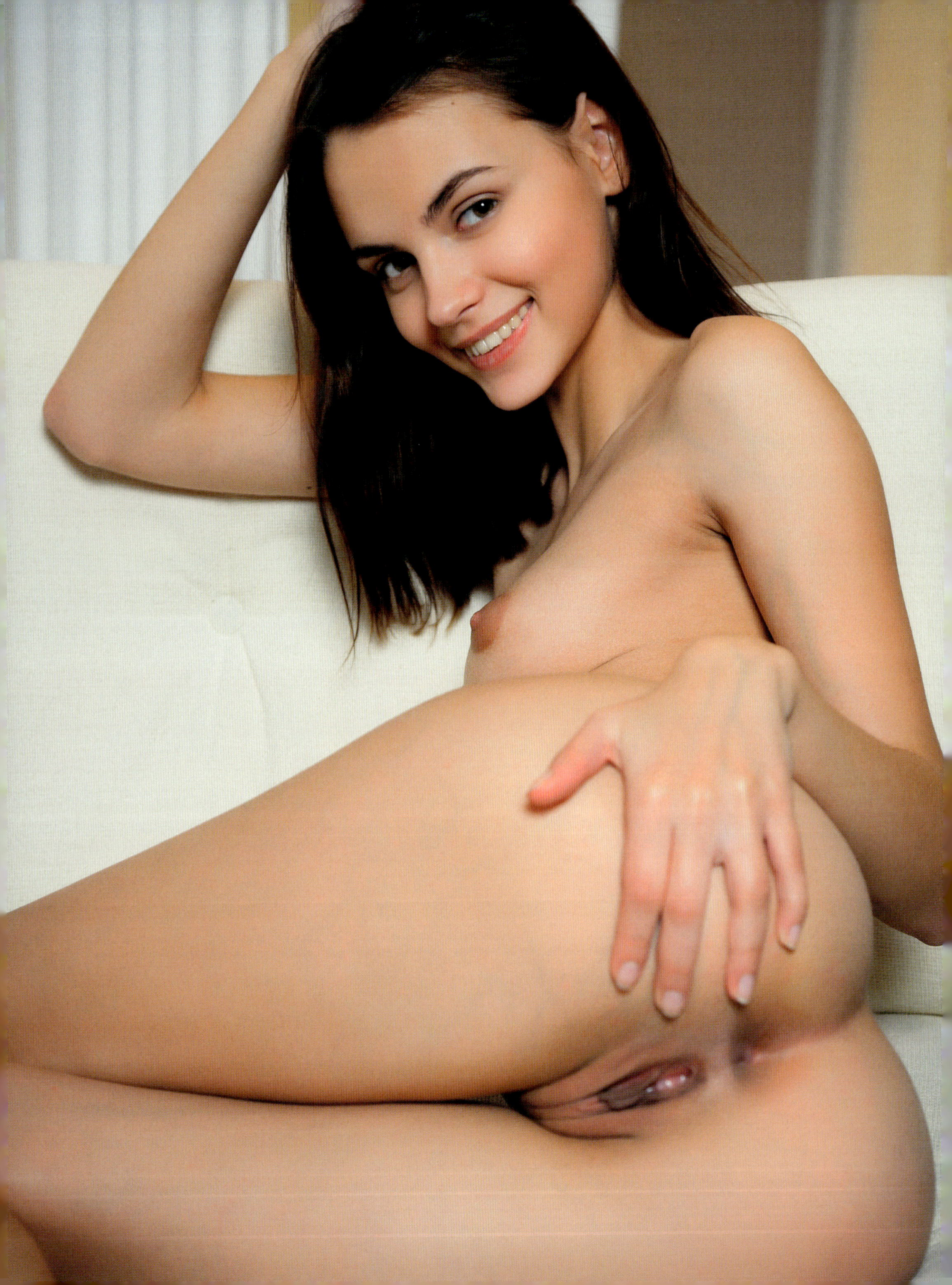

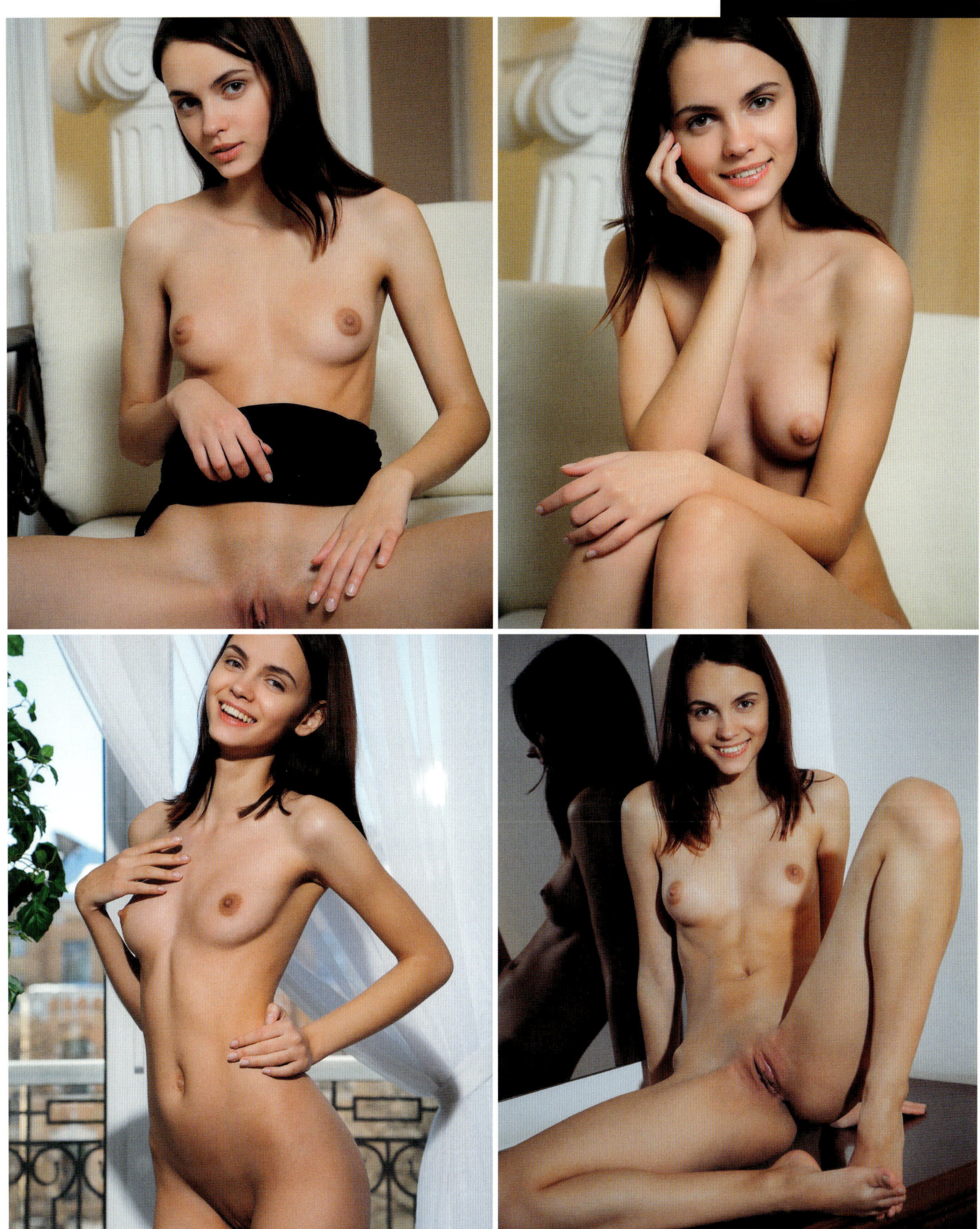

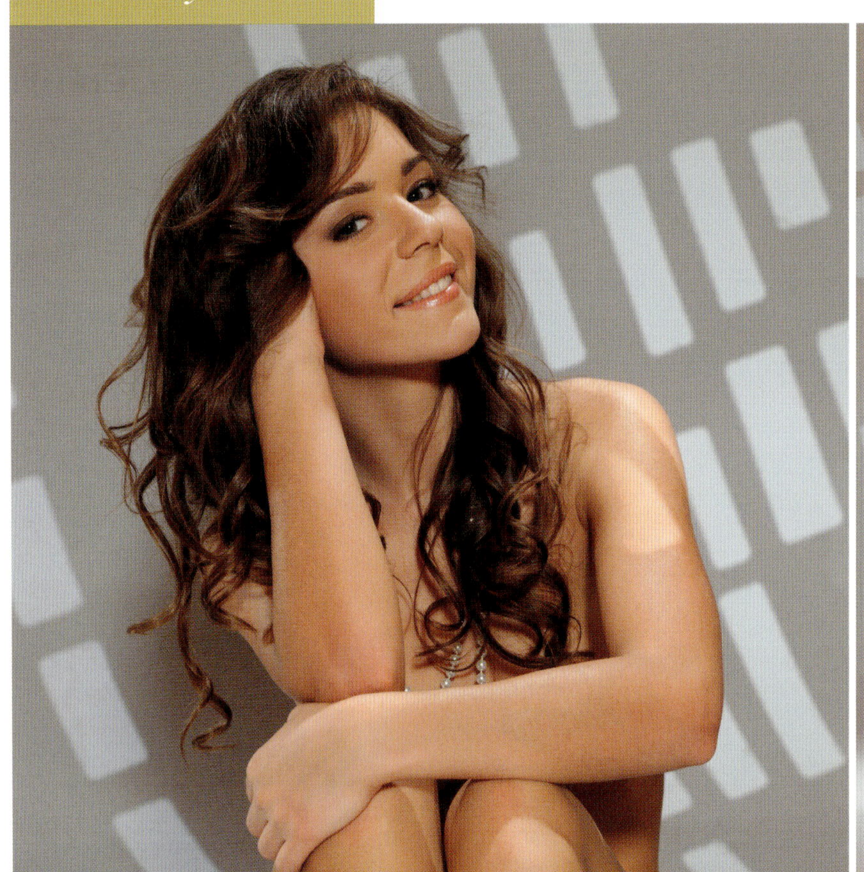

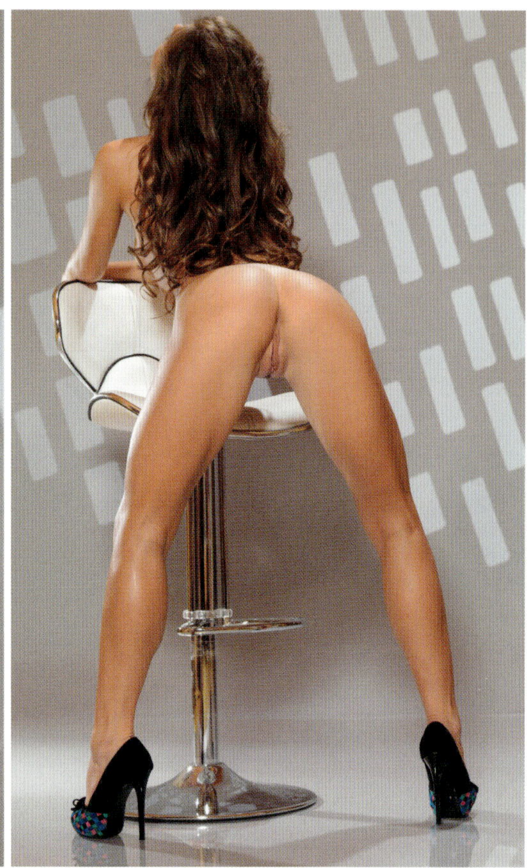

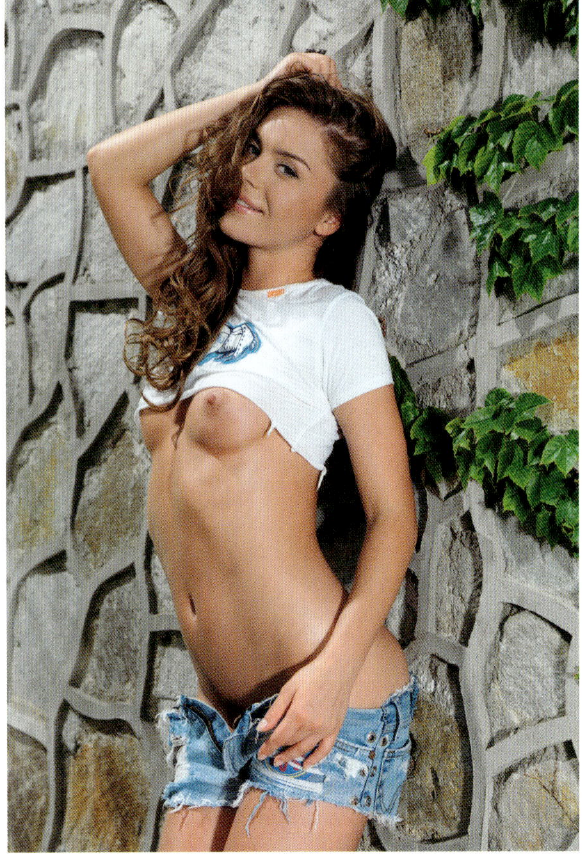

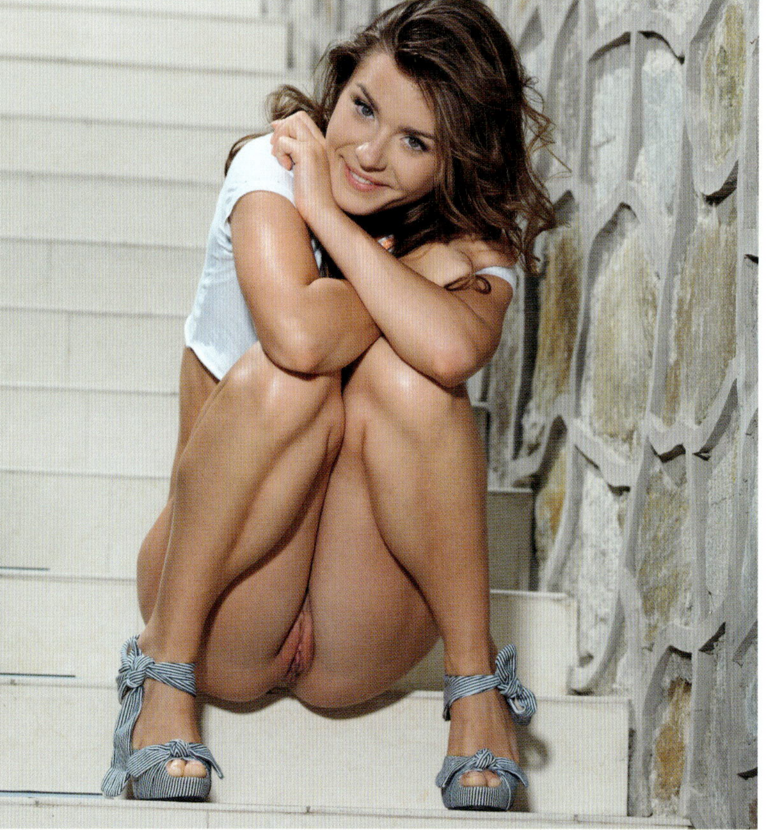

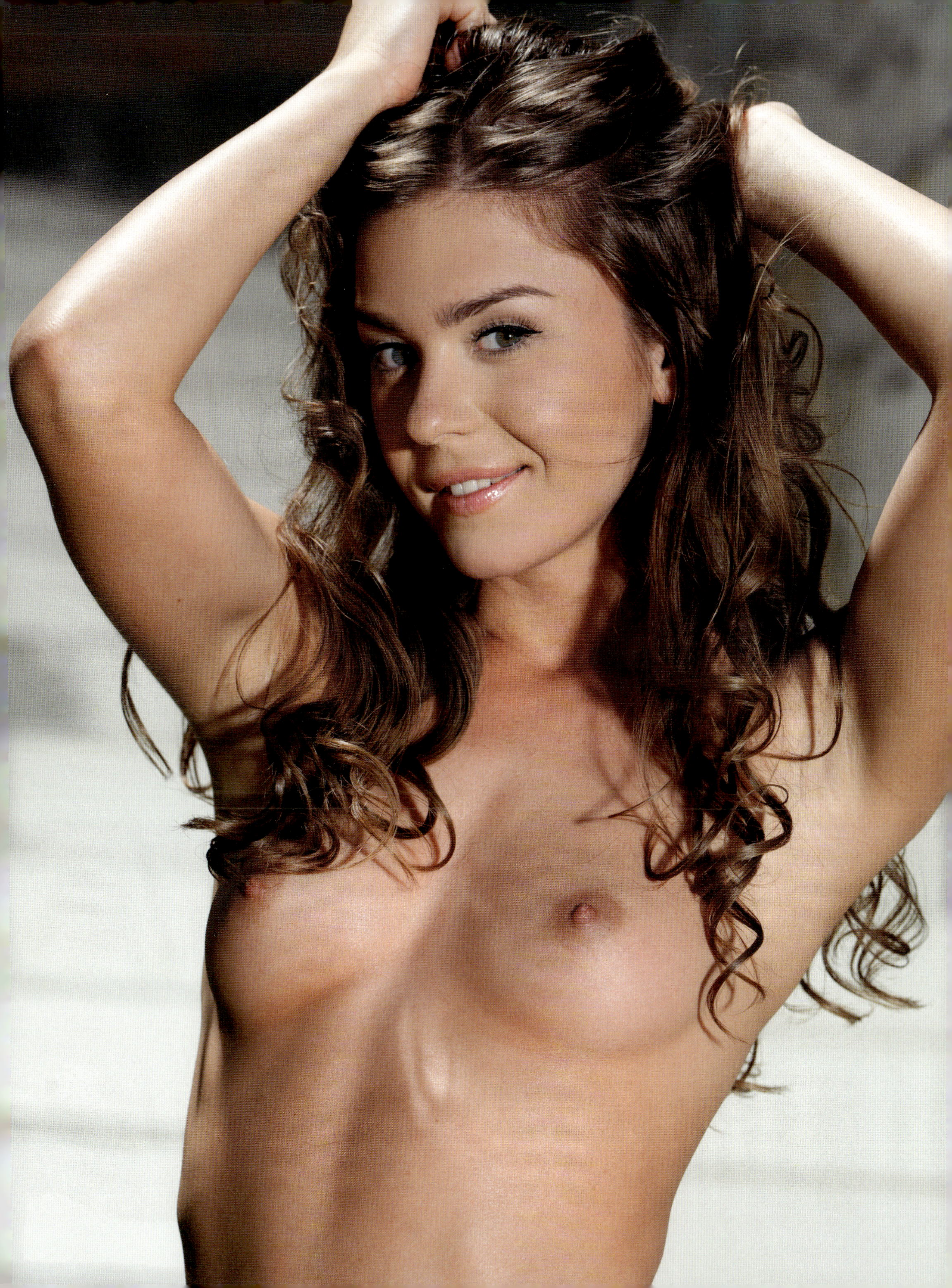

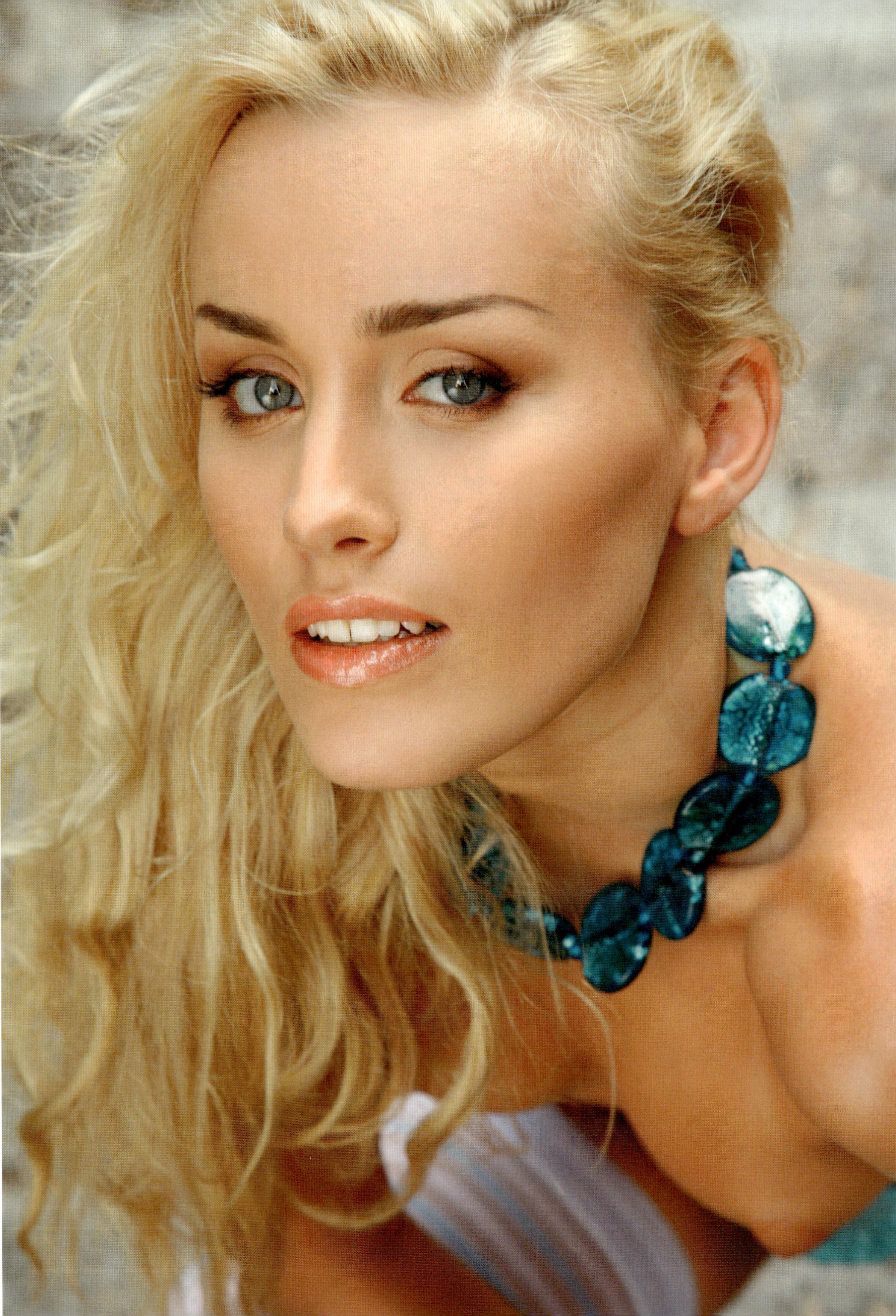

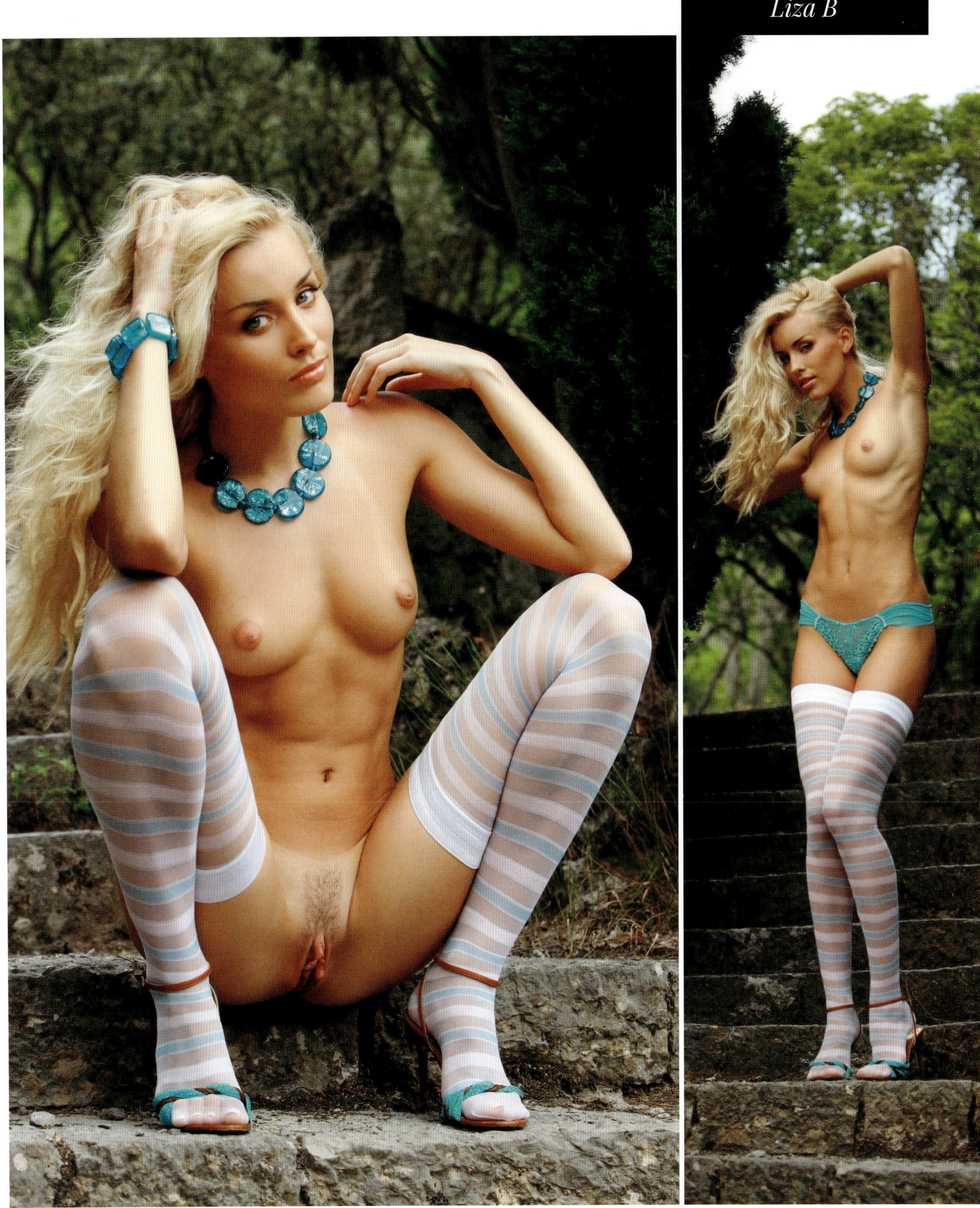

## Loreen A

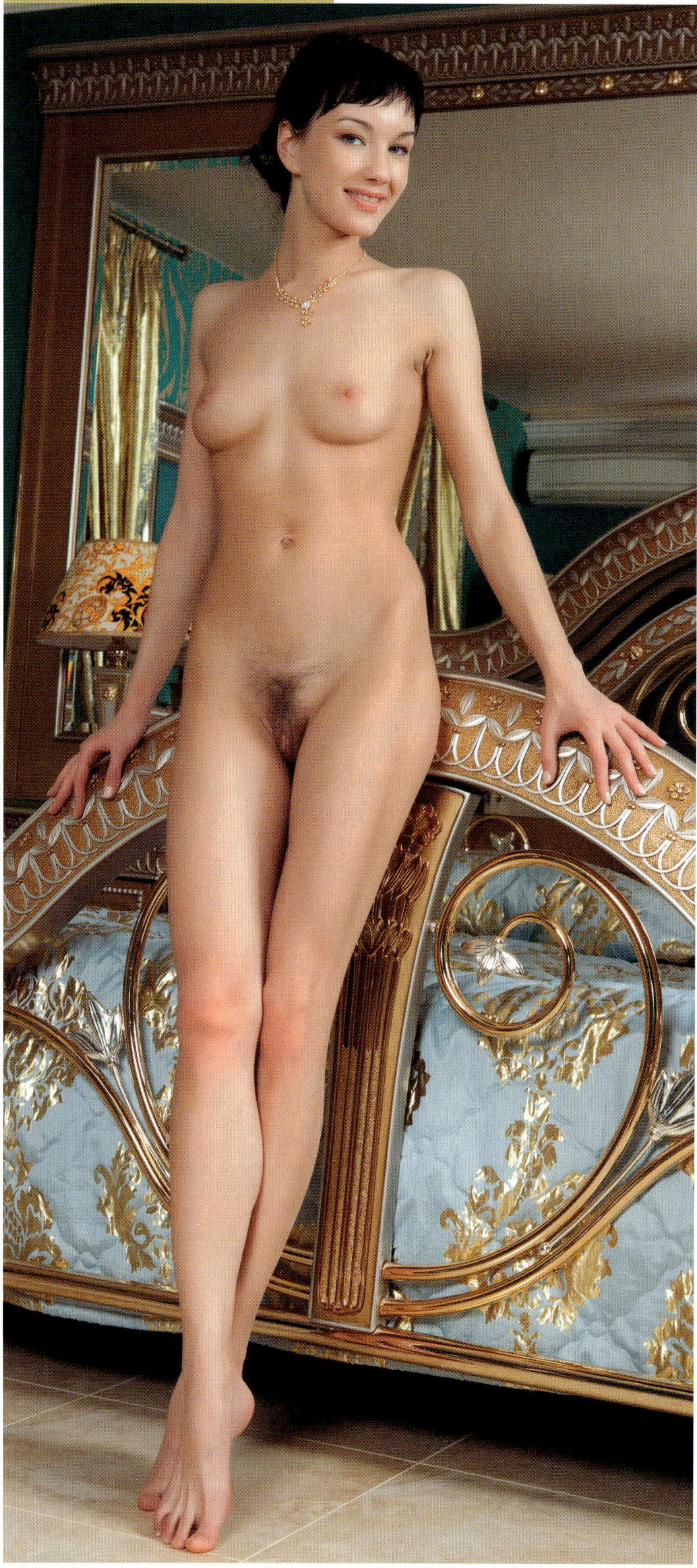

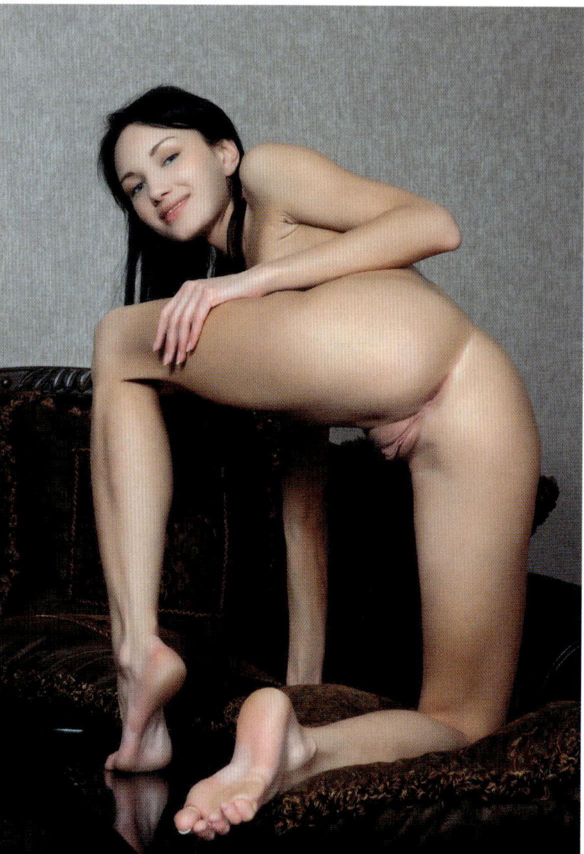

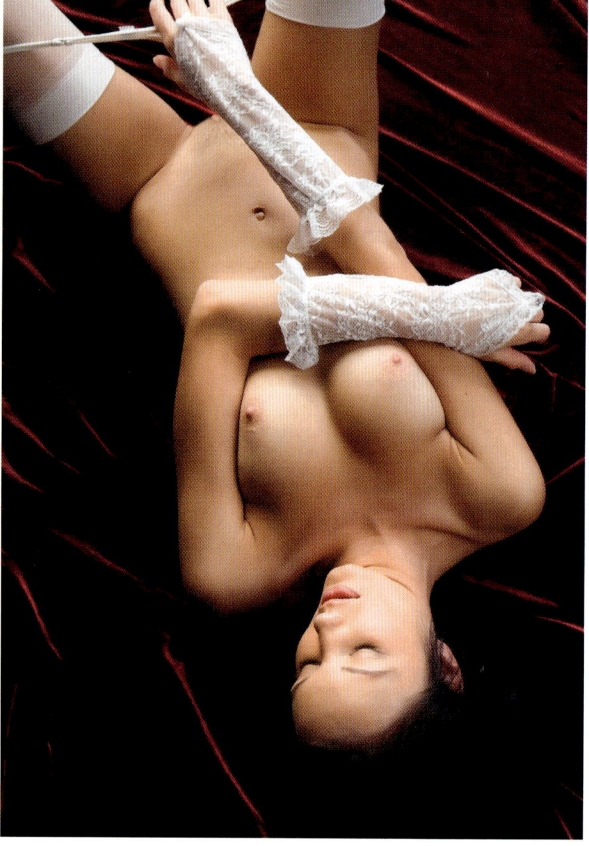

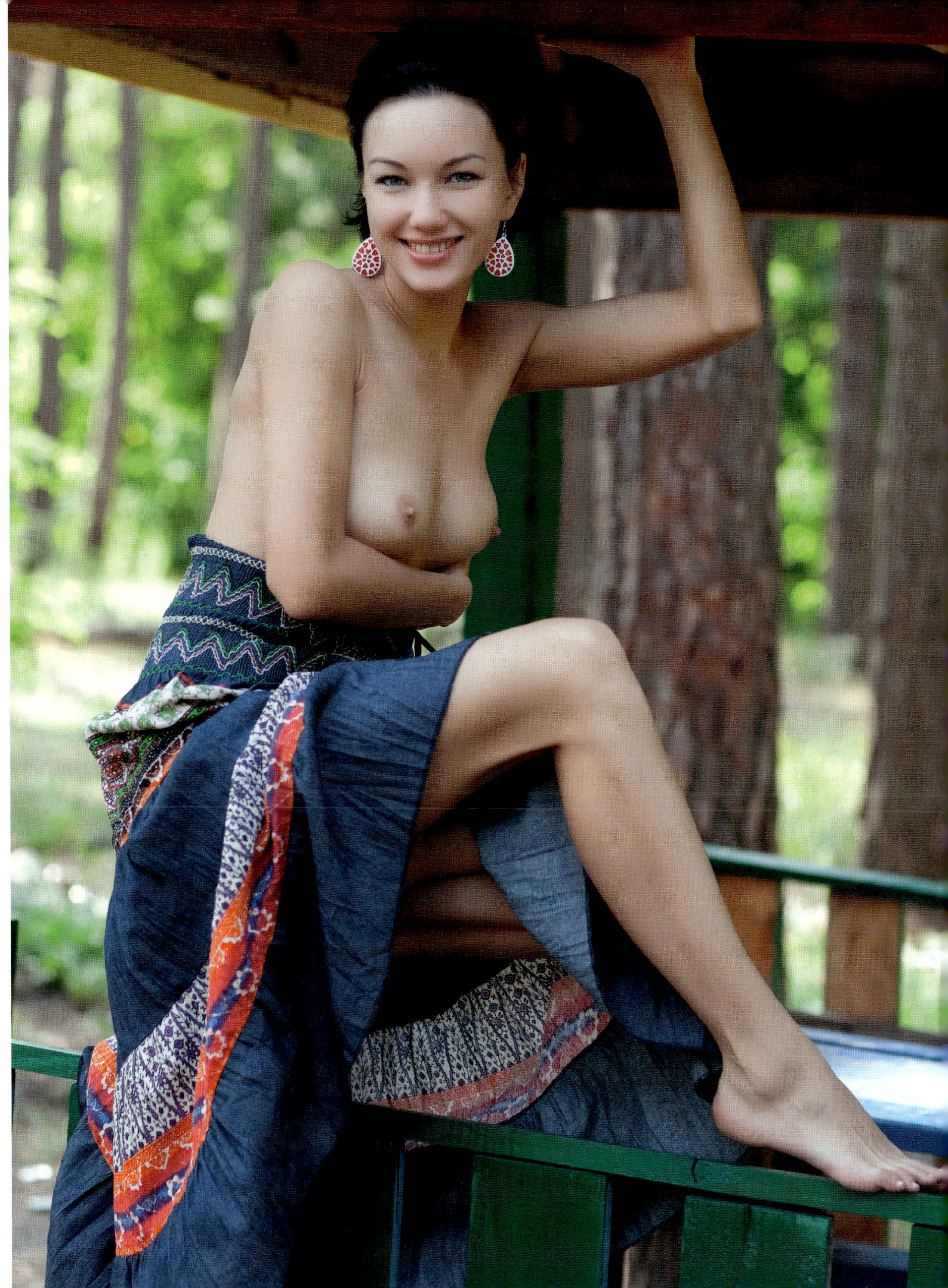

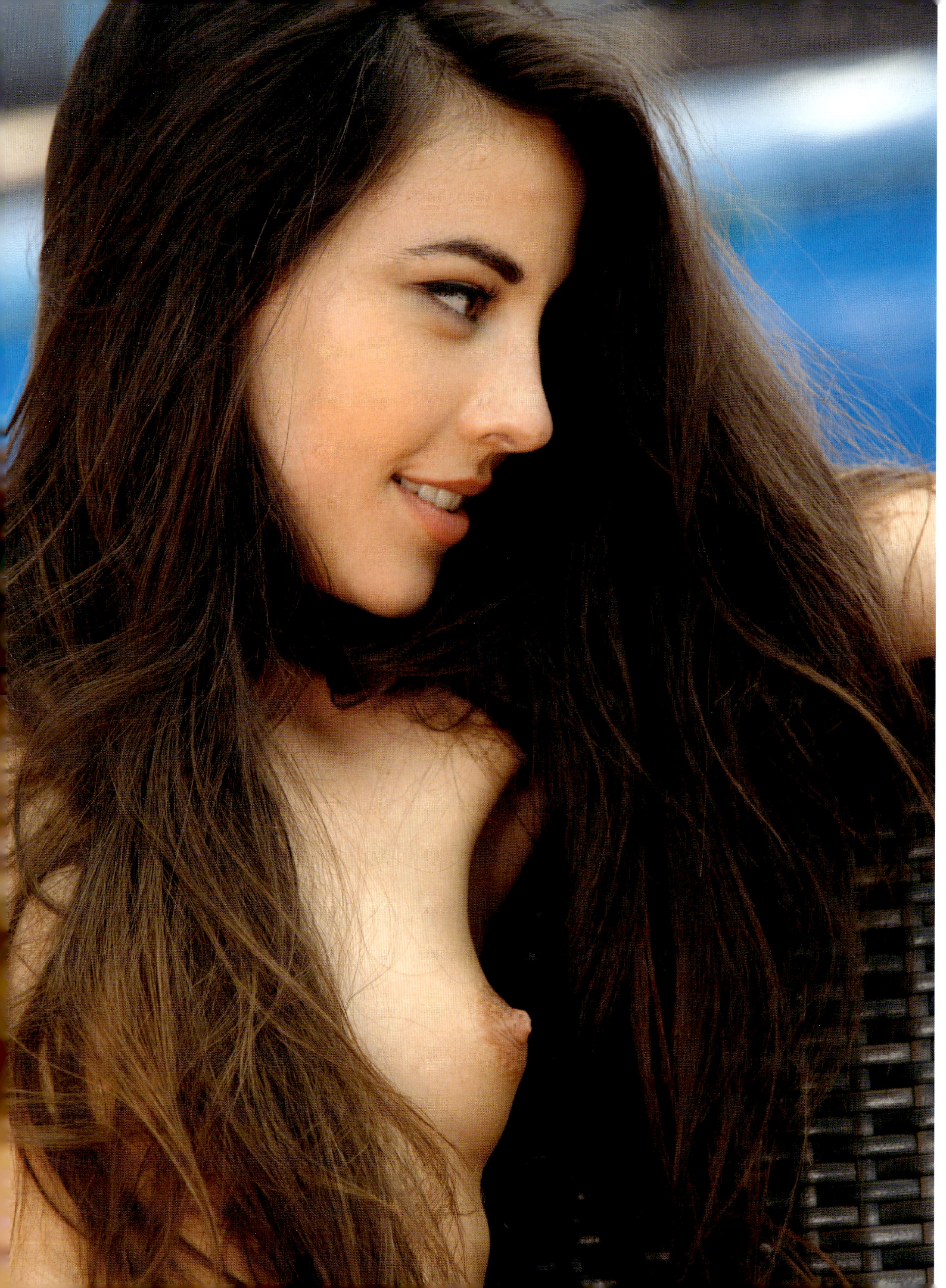

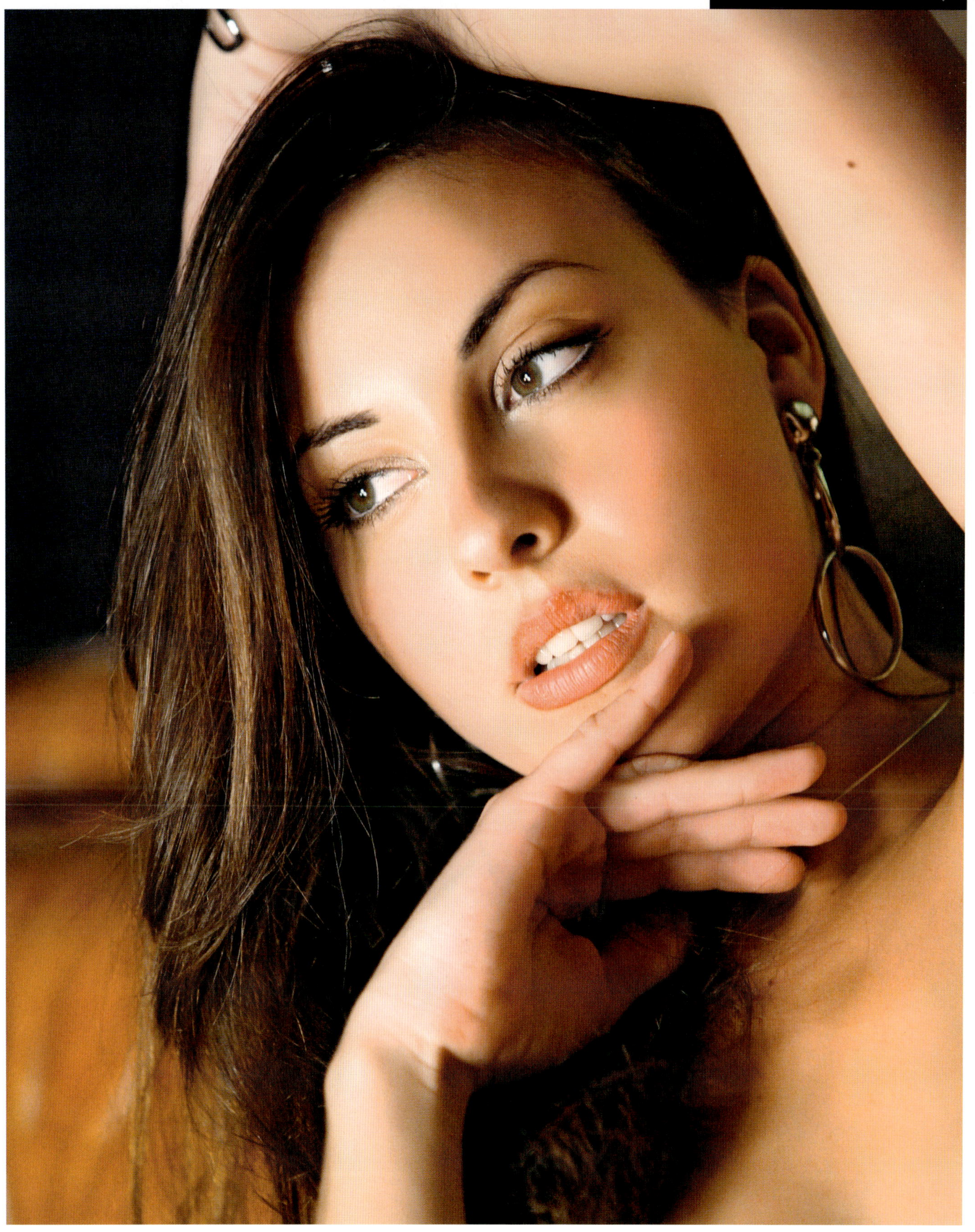

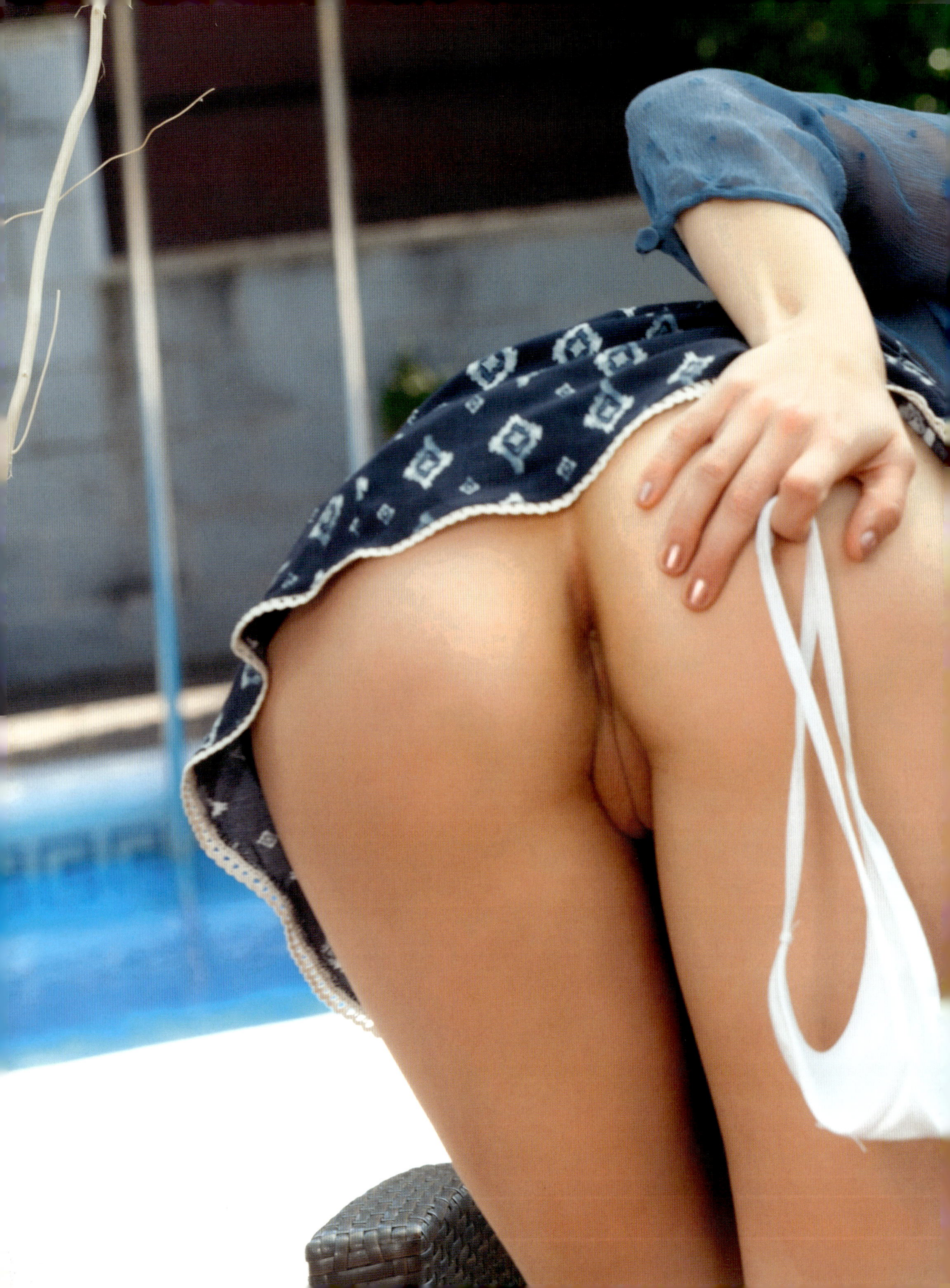

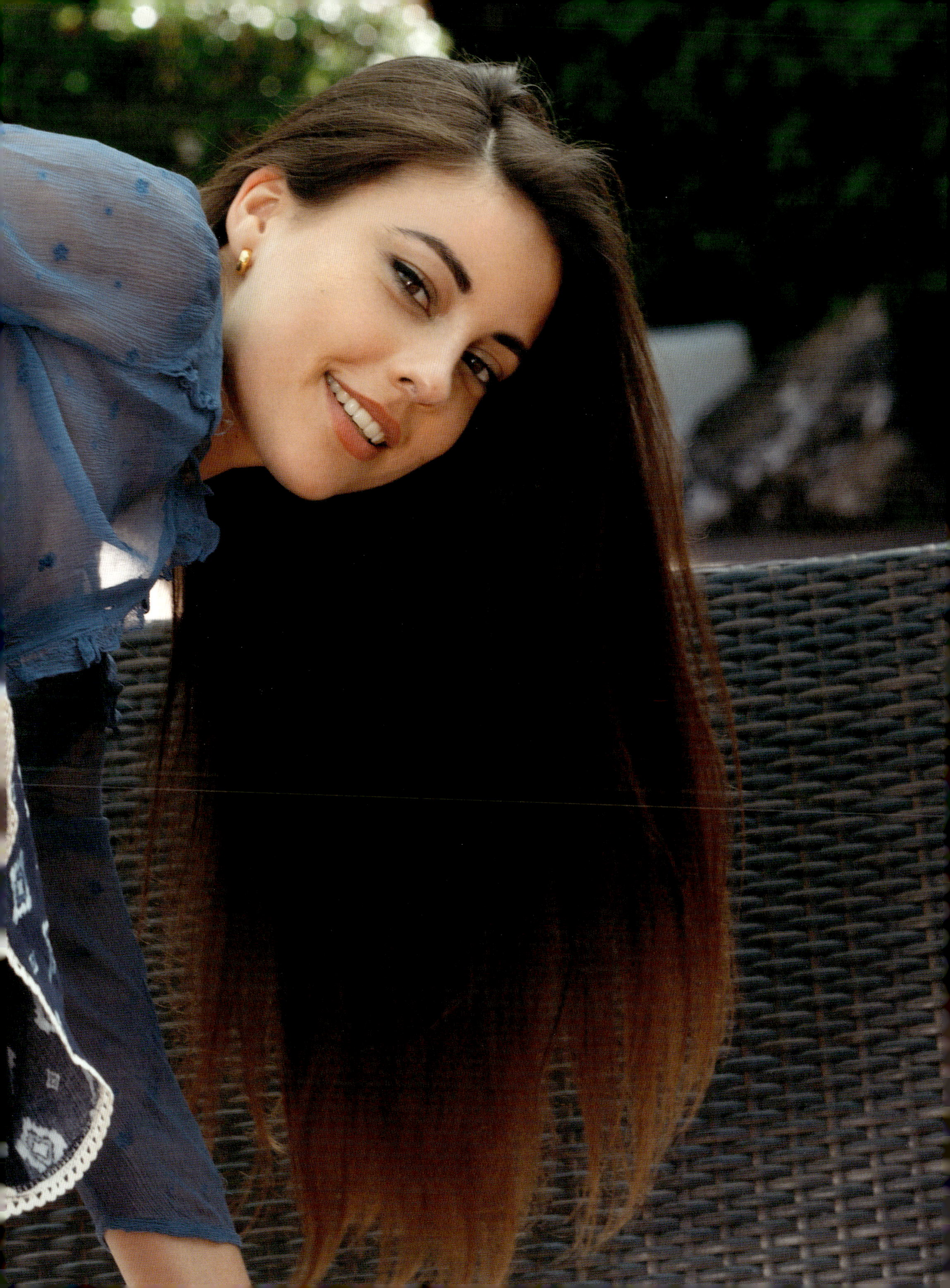

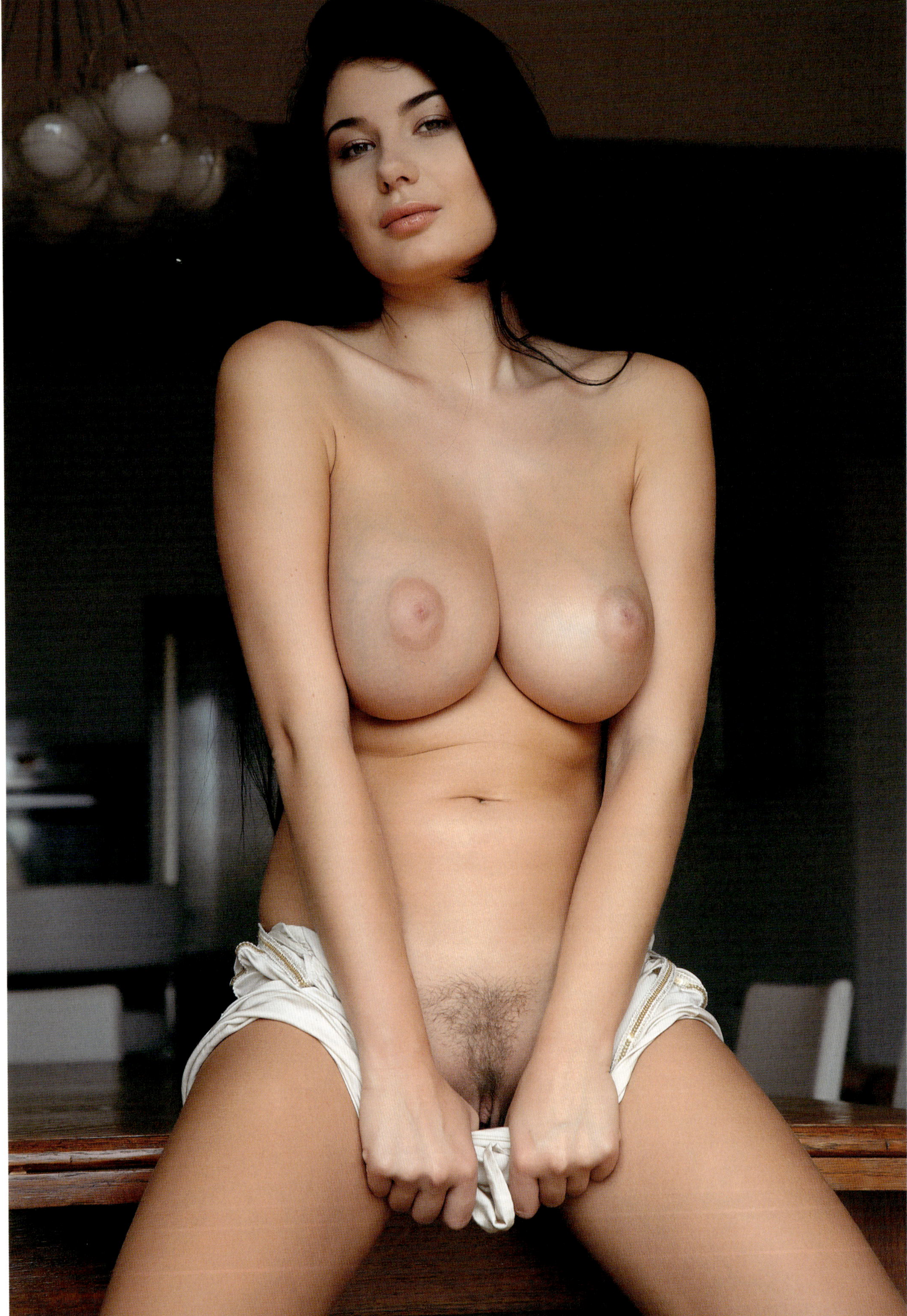

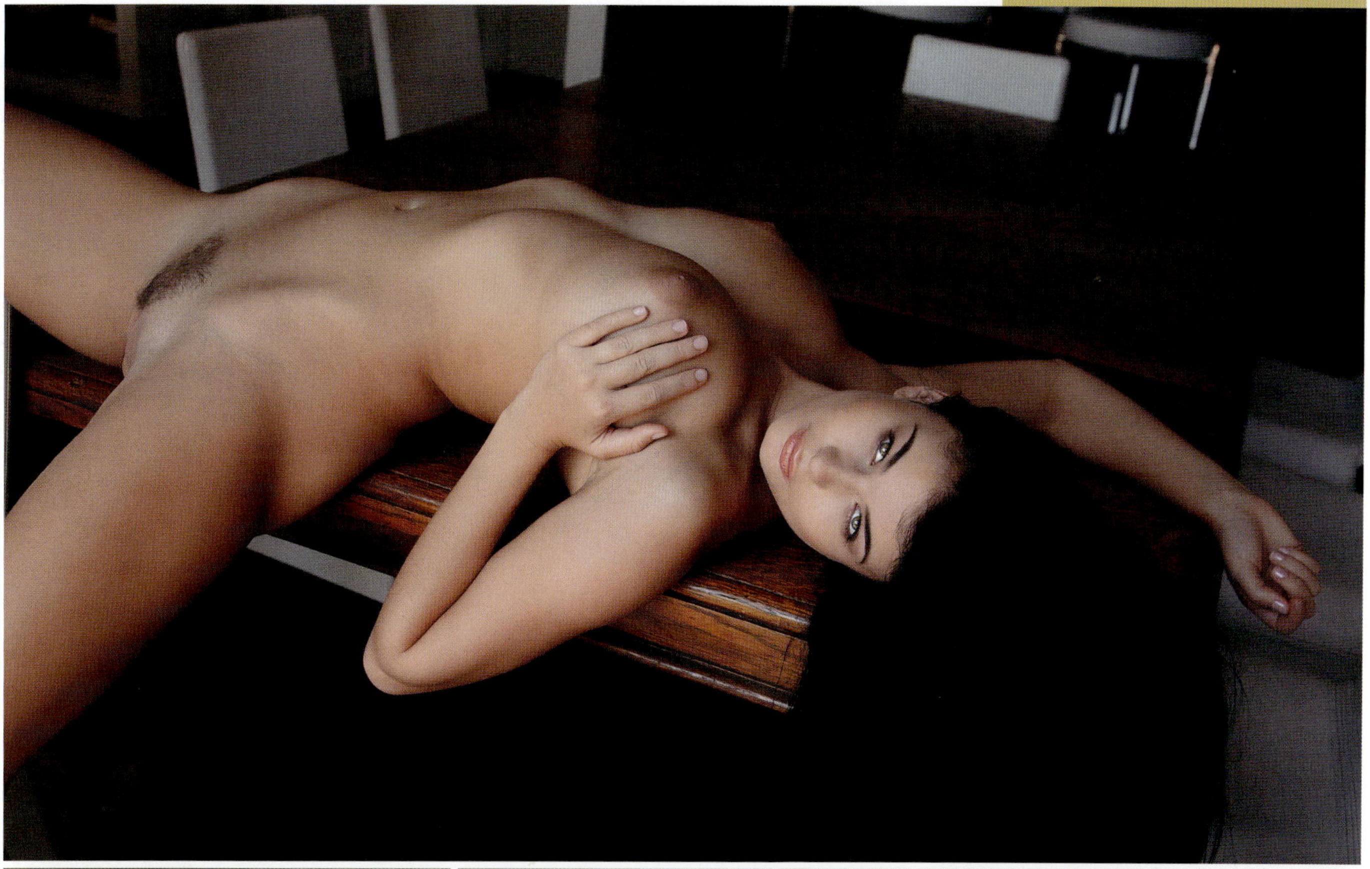

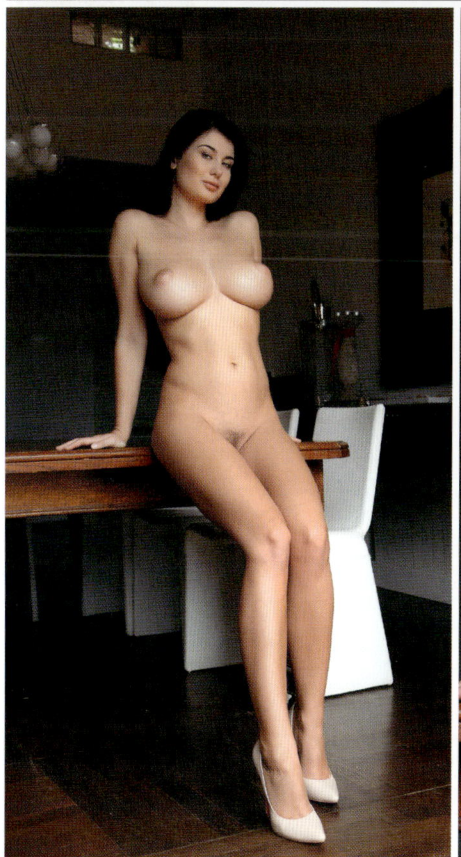

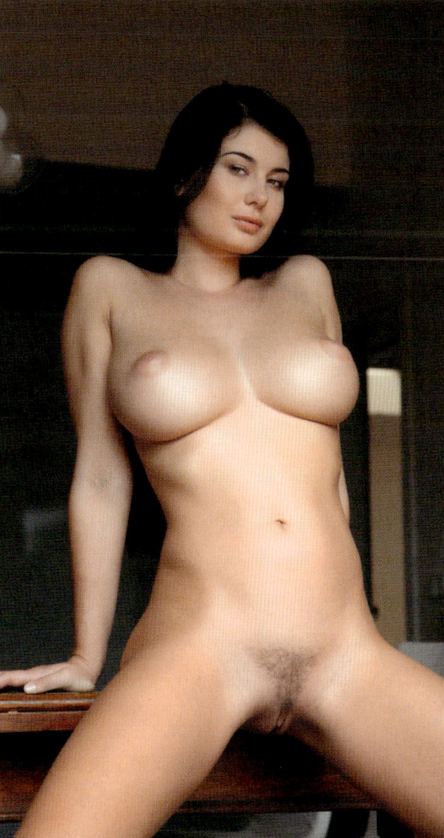

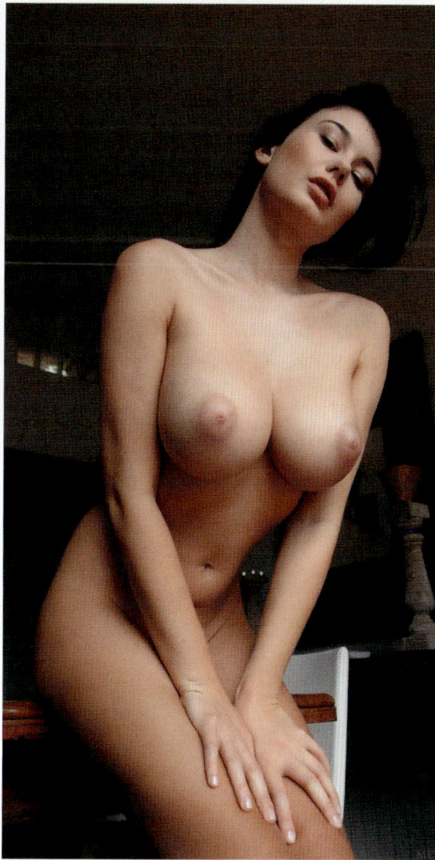

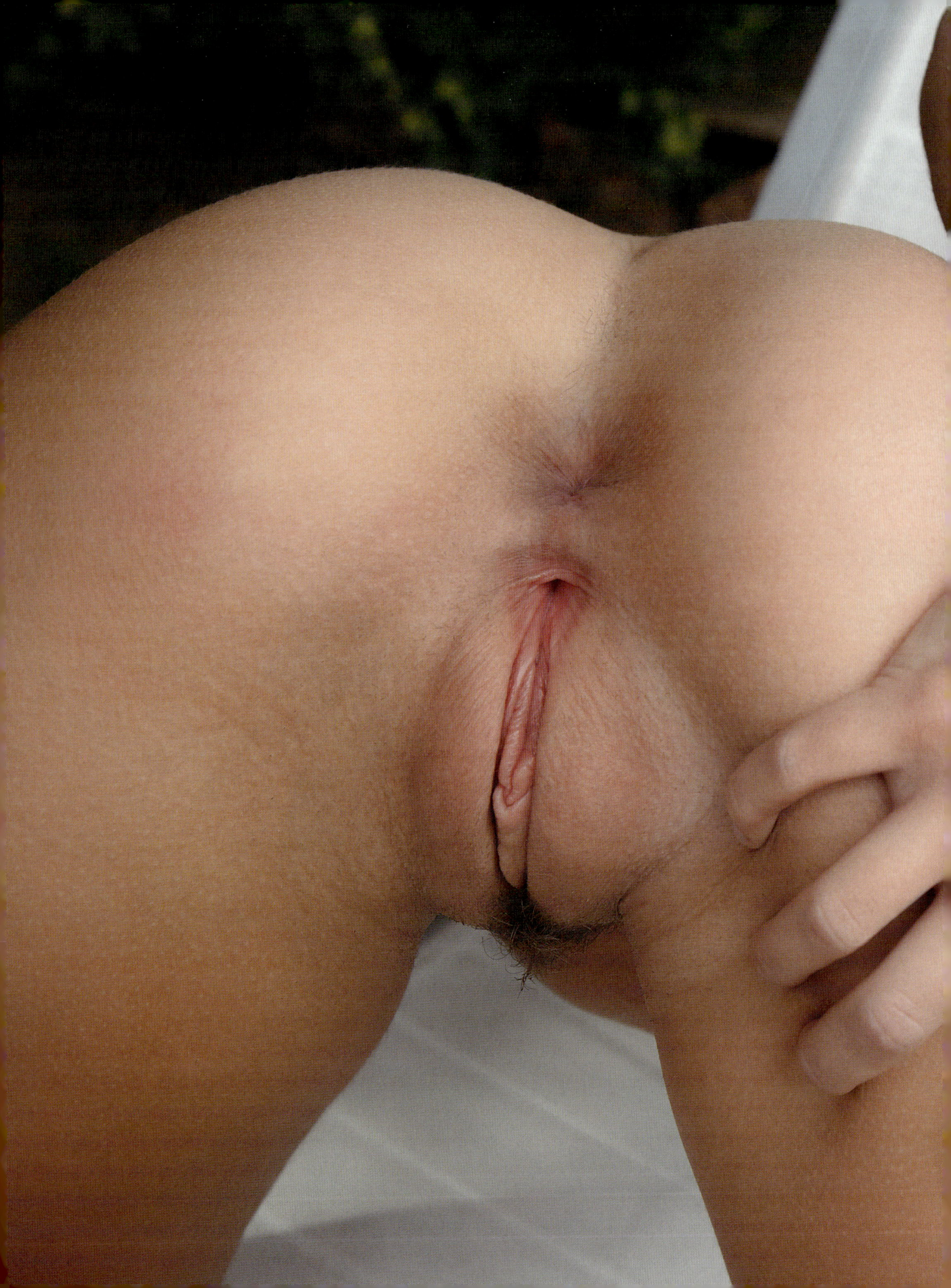

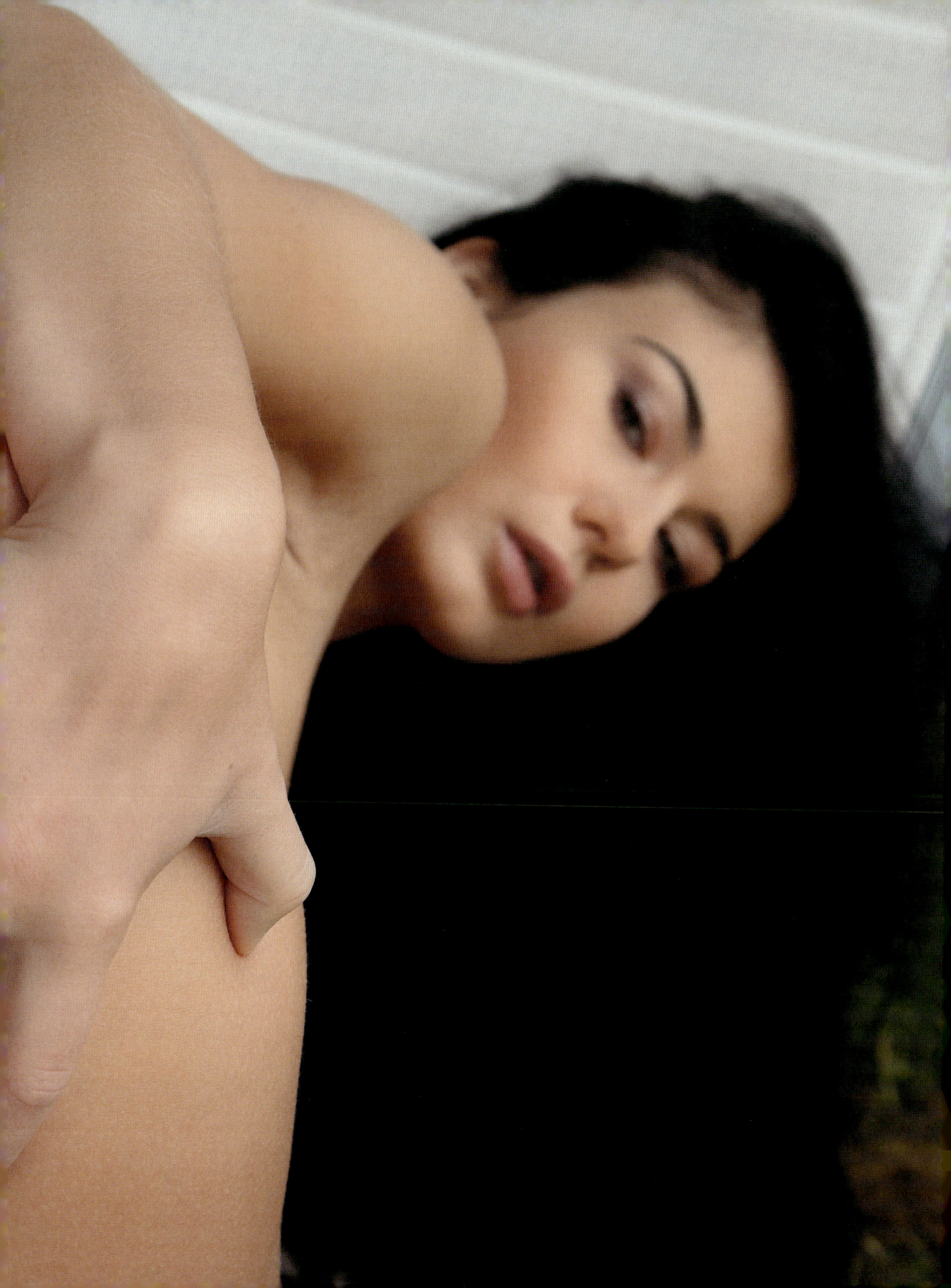

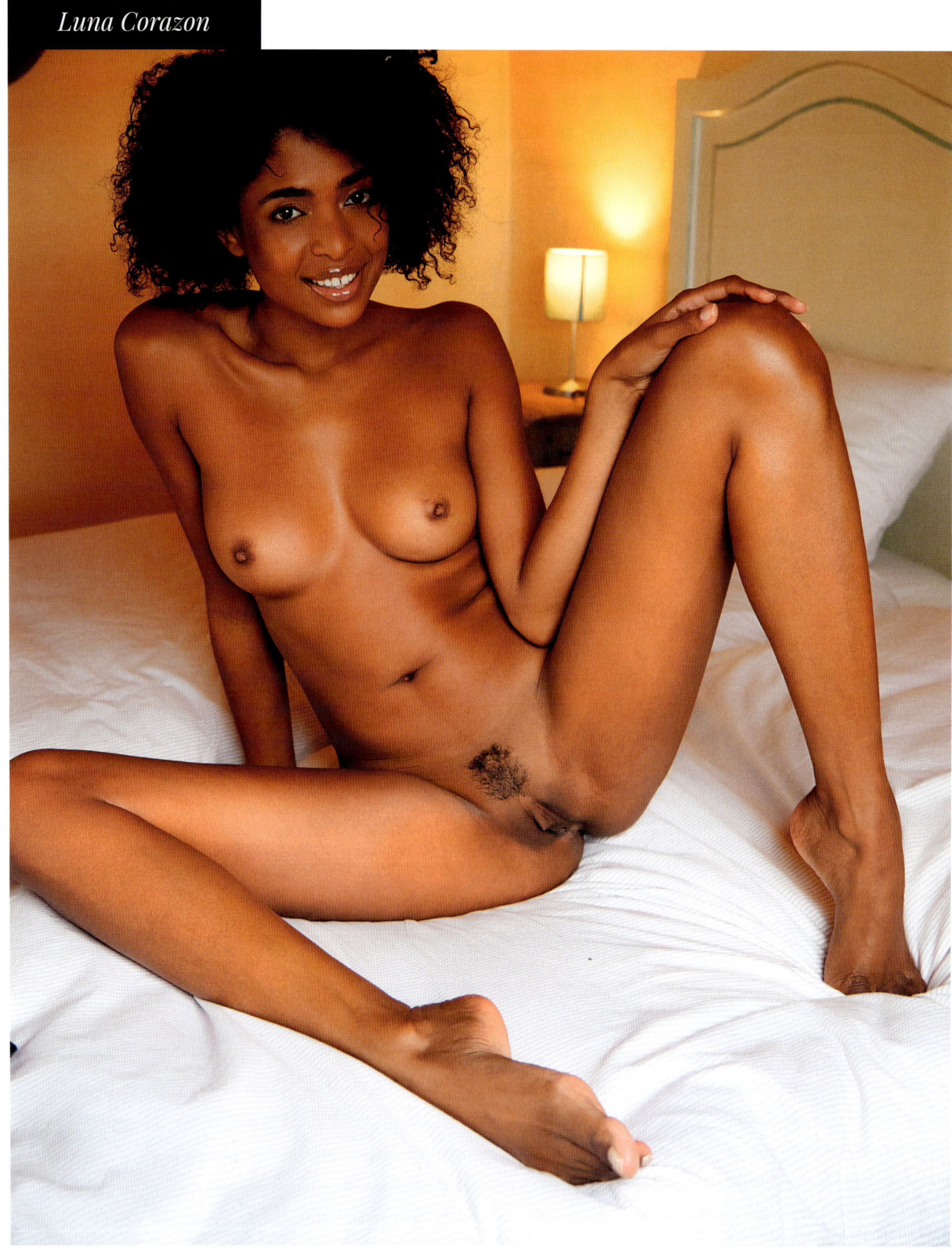

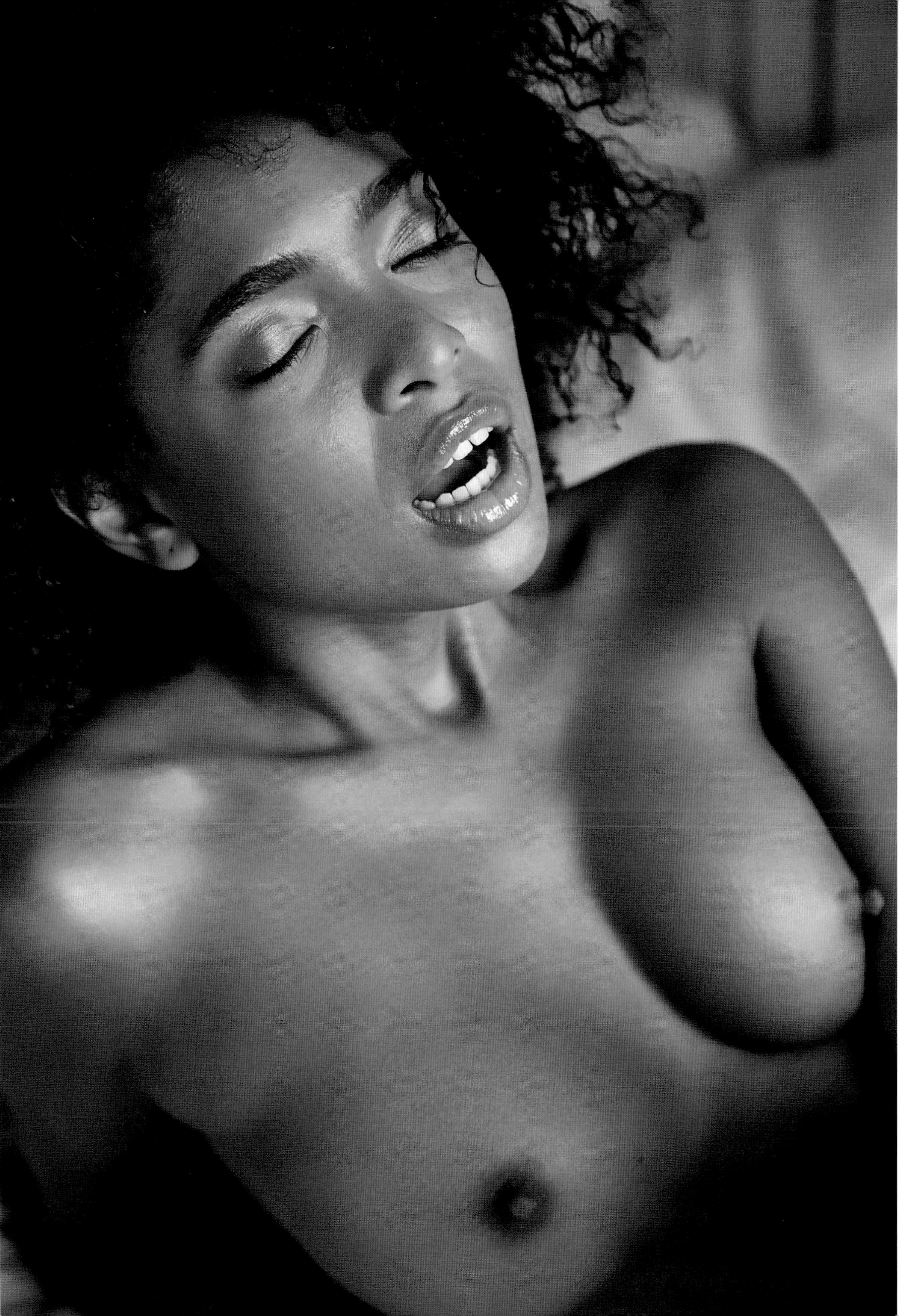

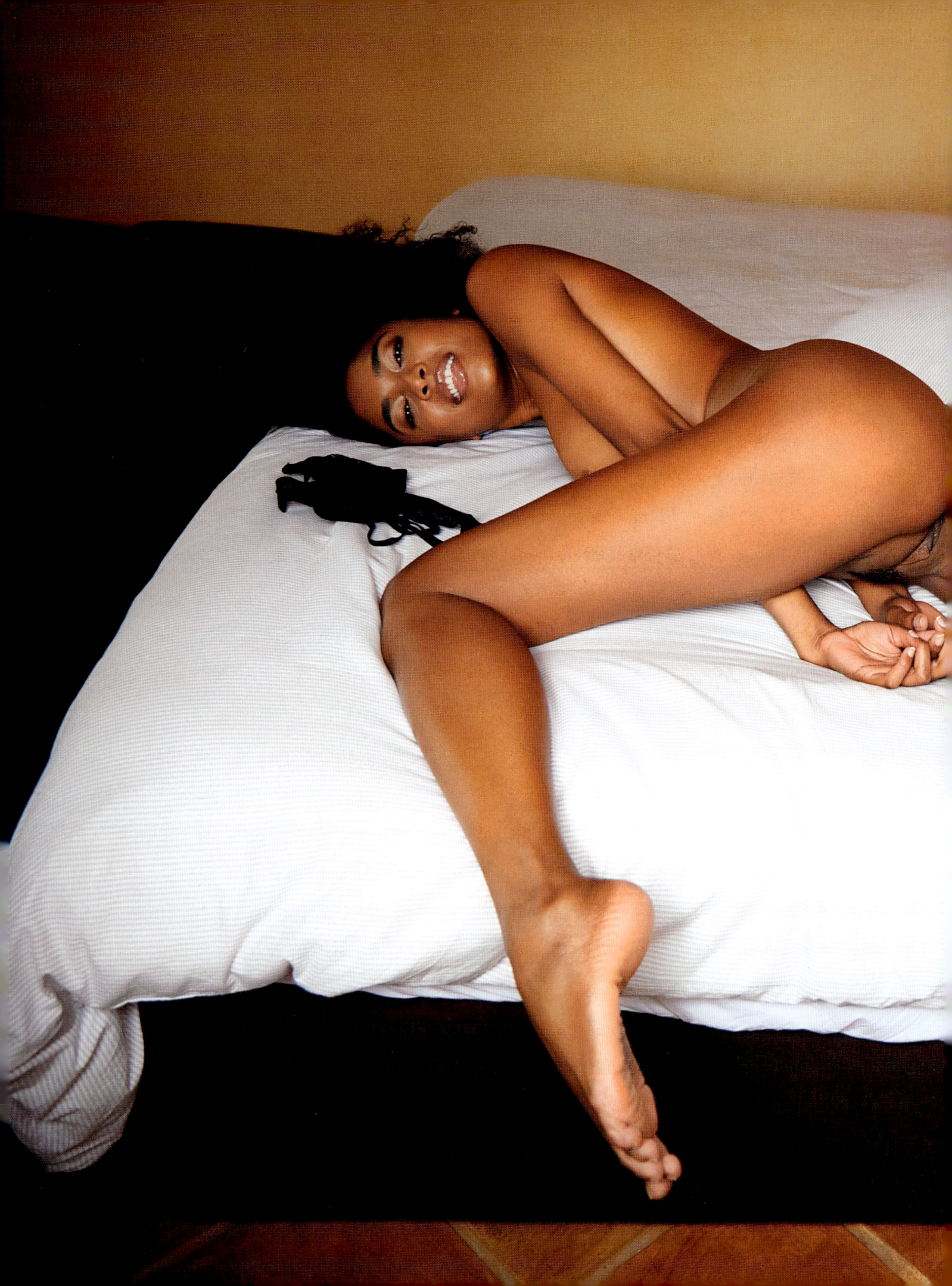

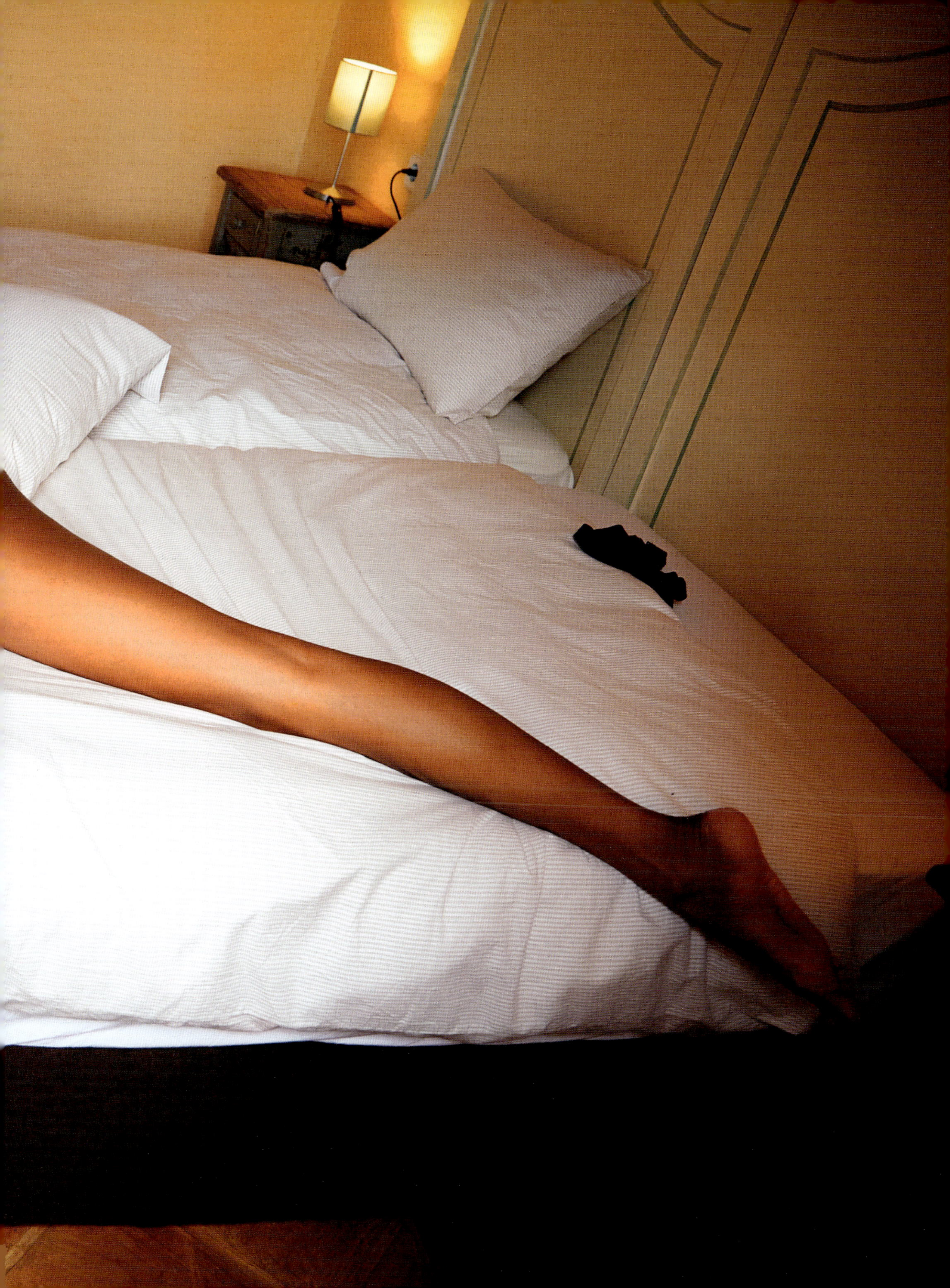

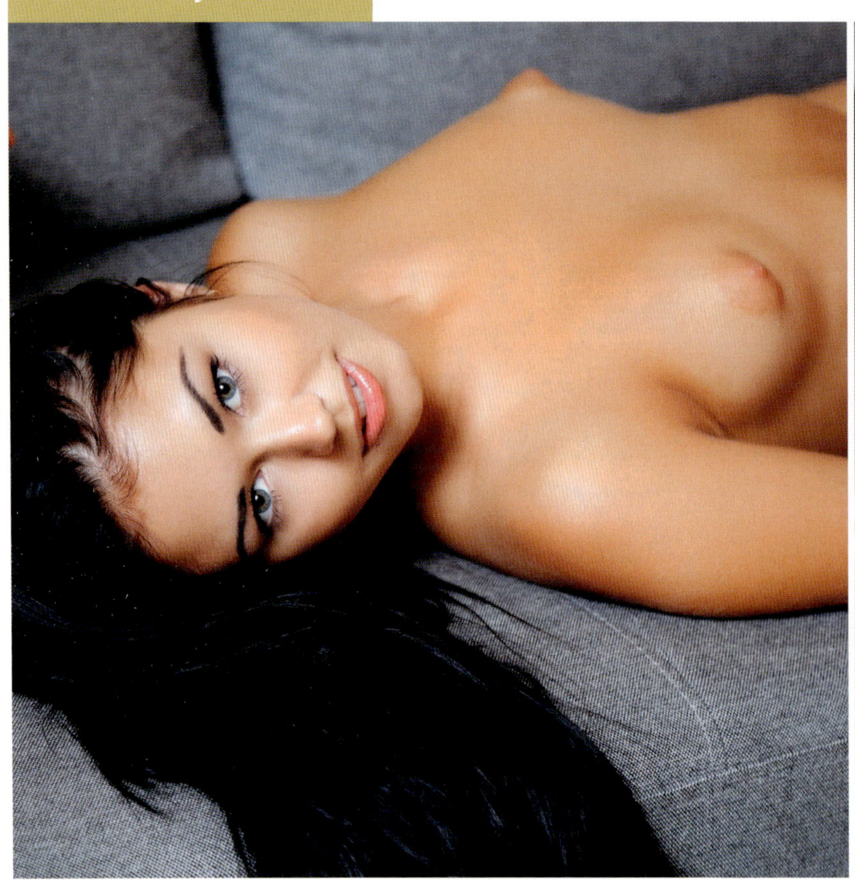

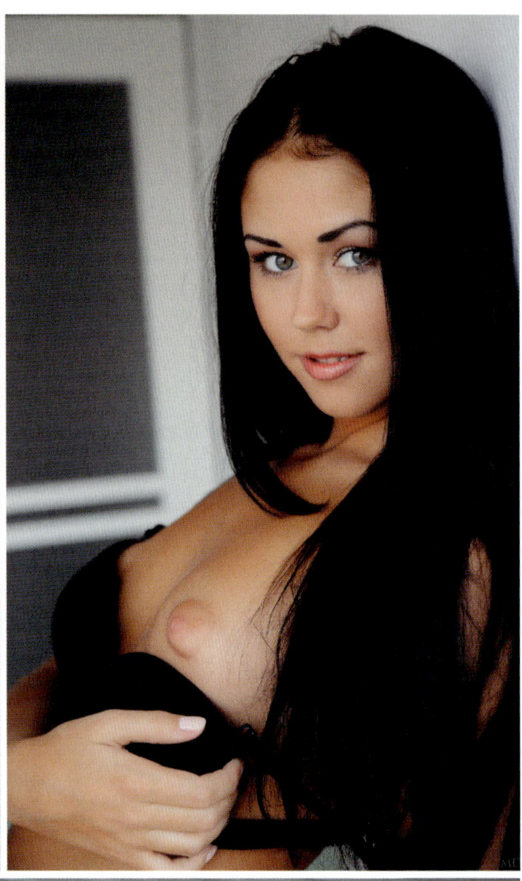

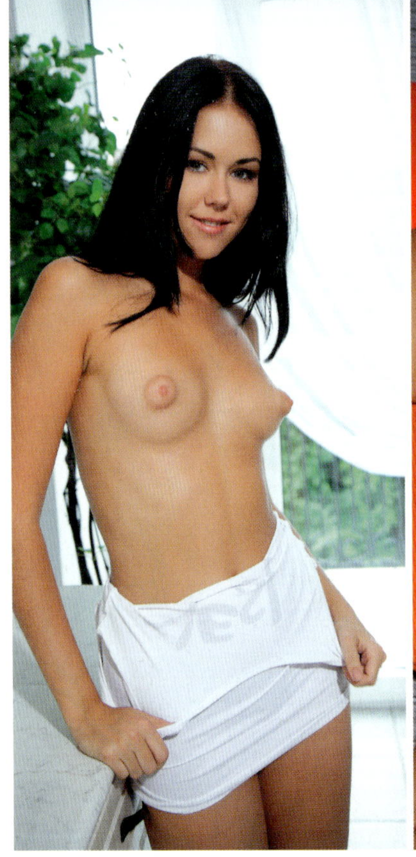

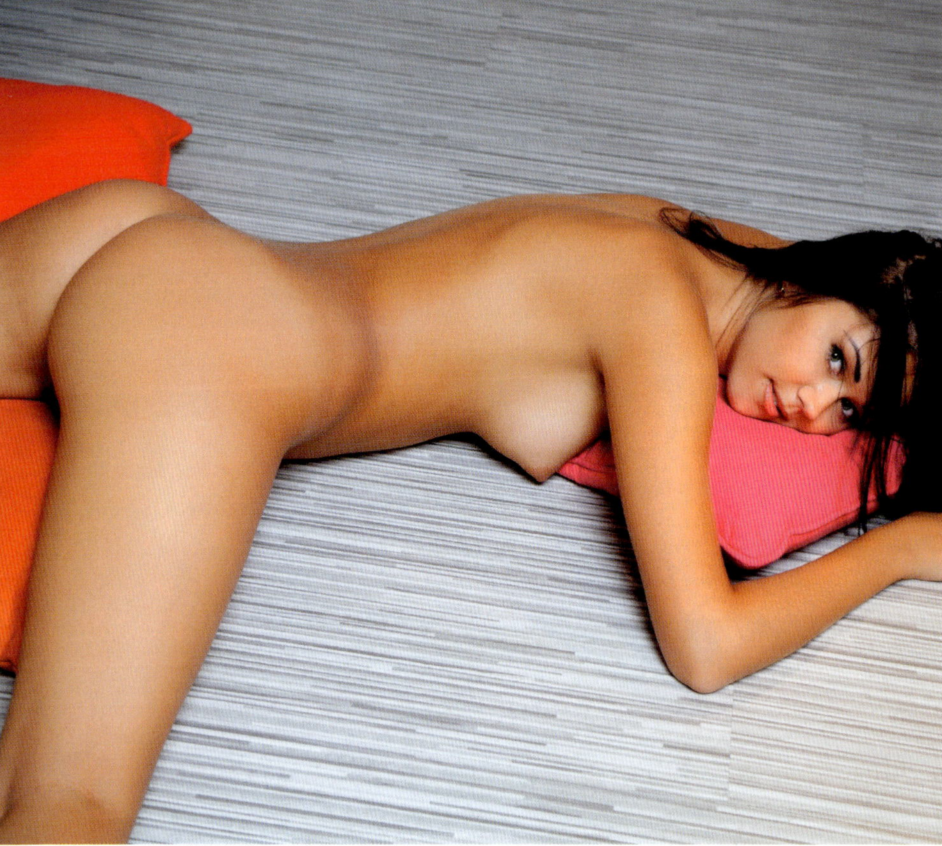

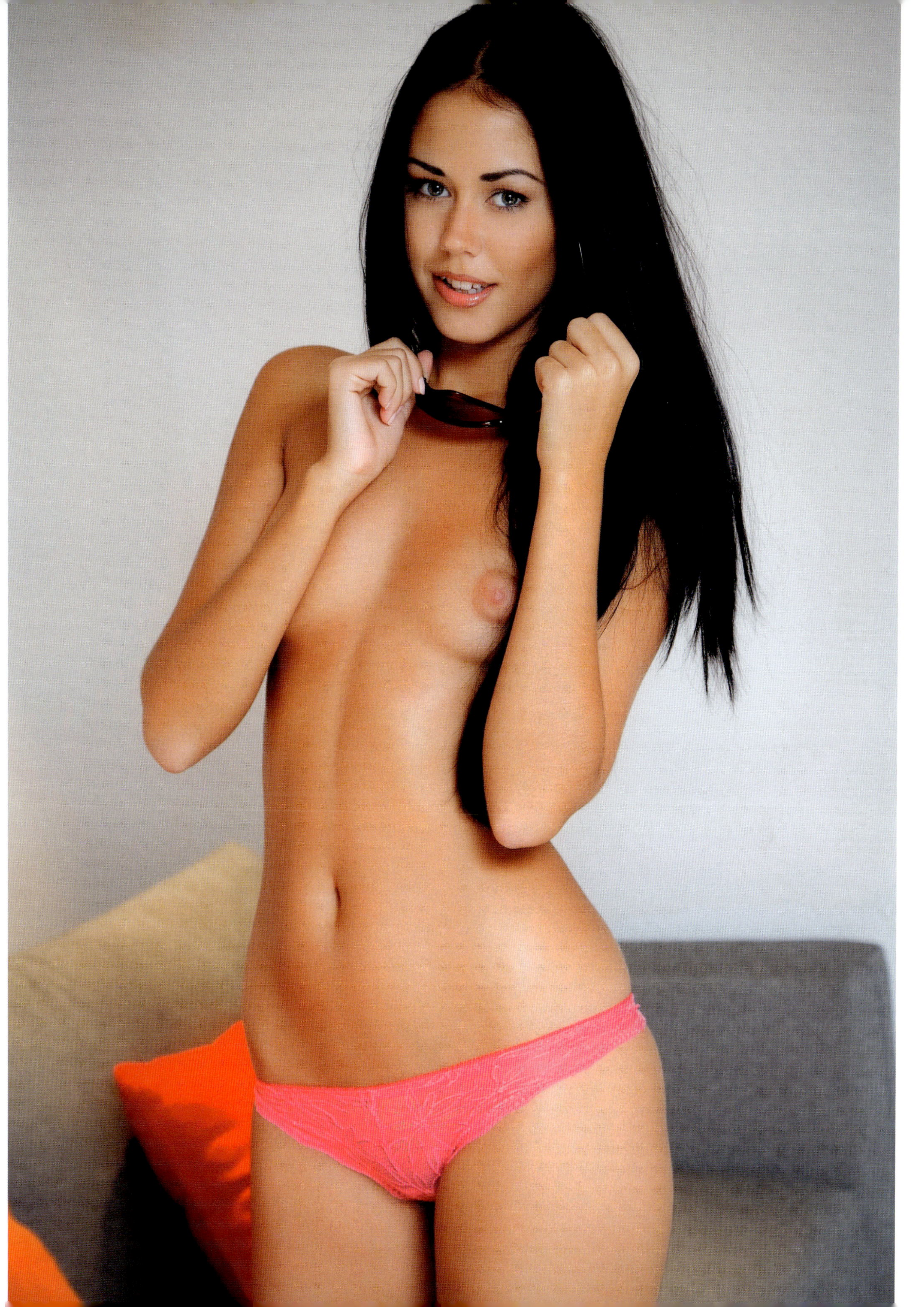

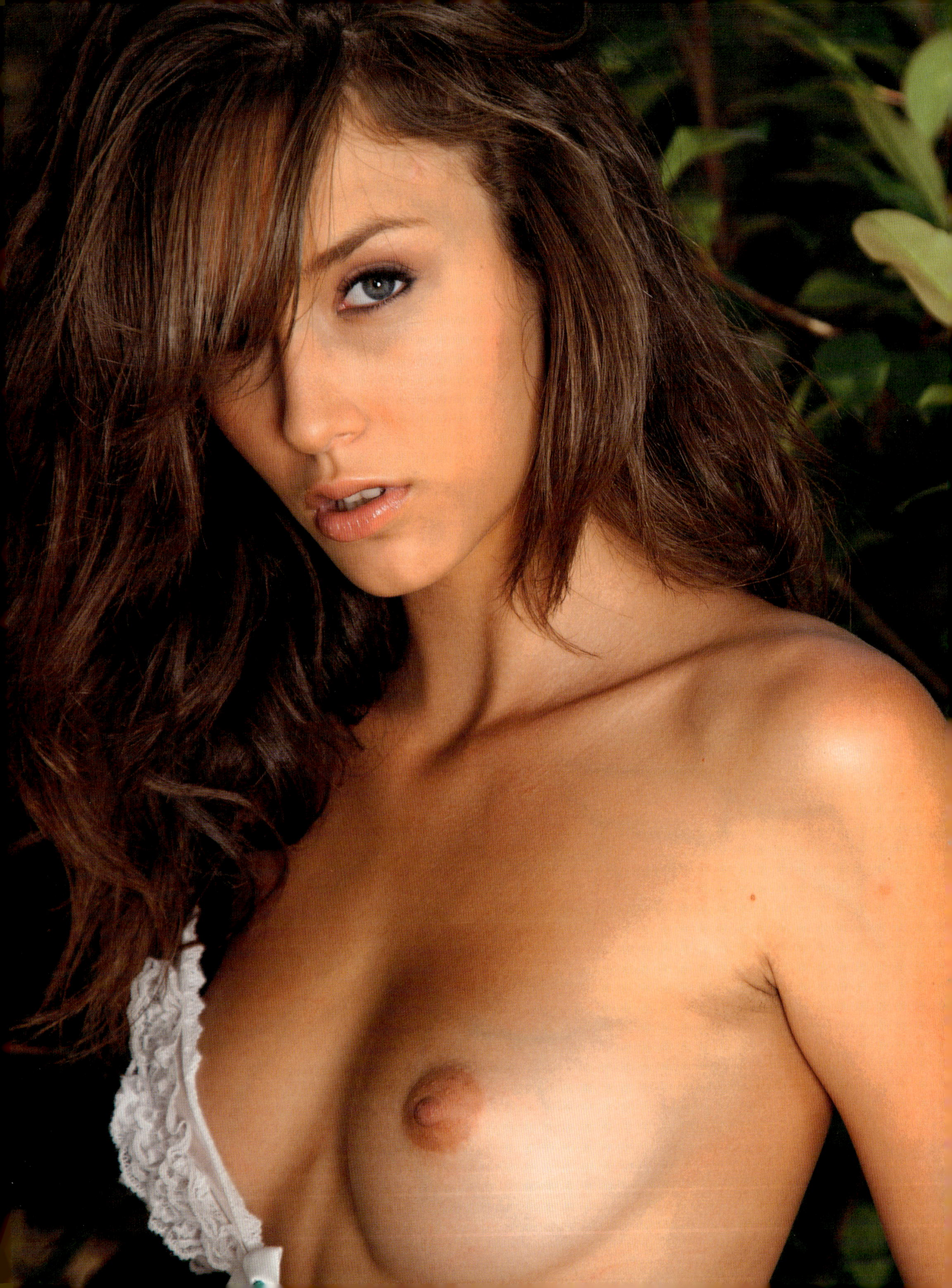

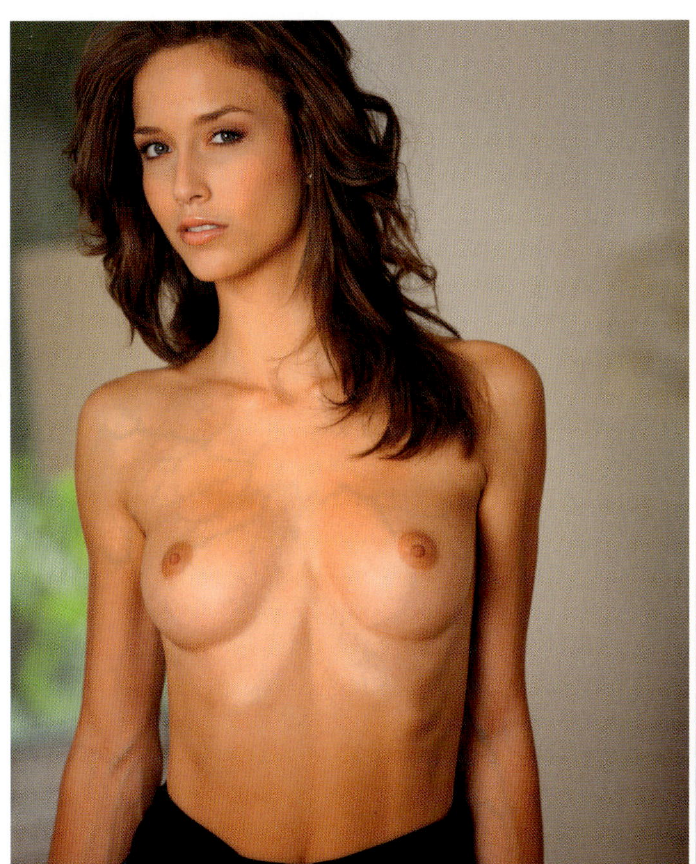

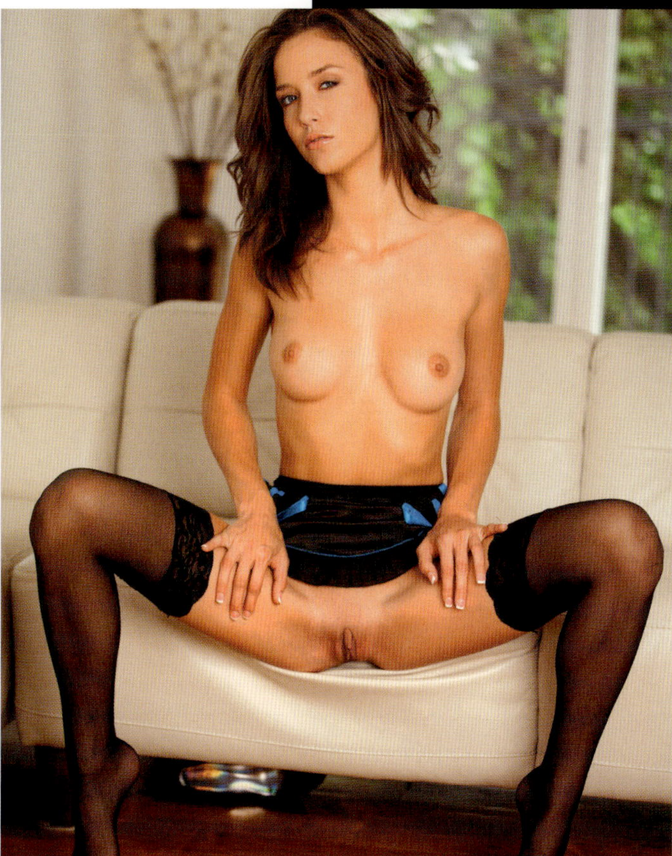

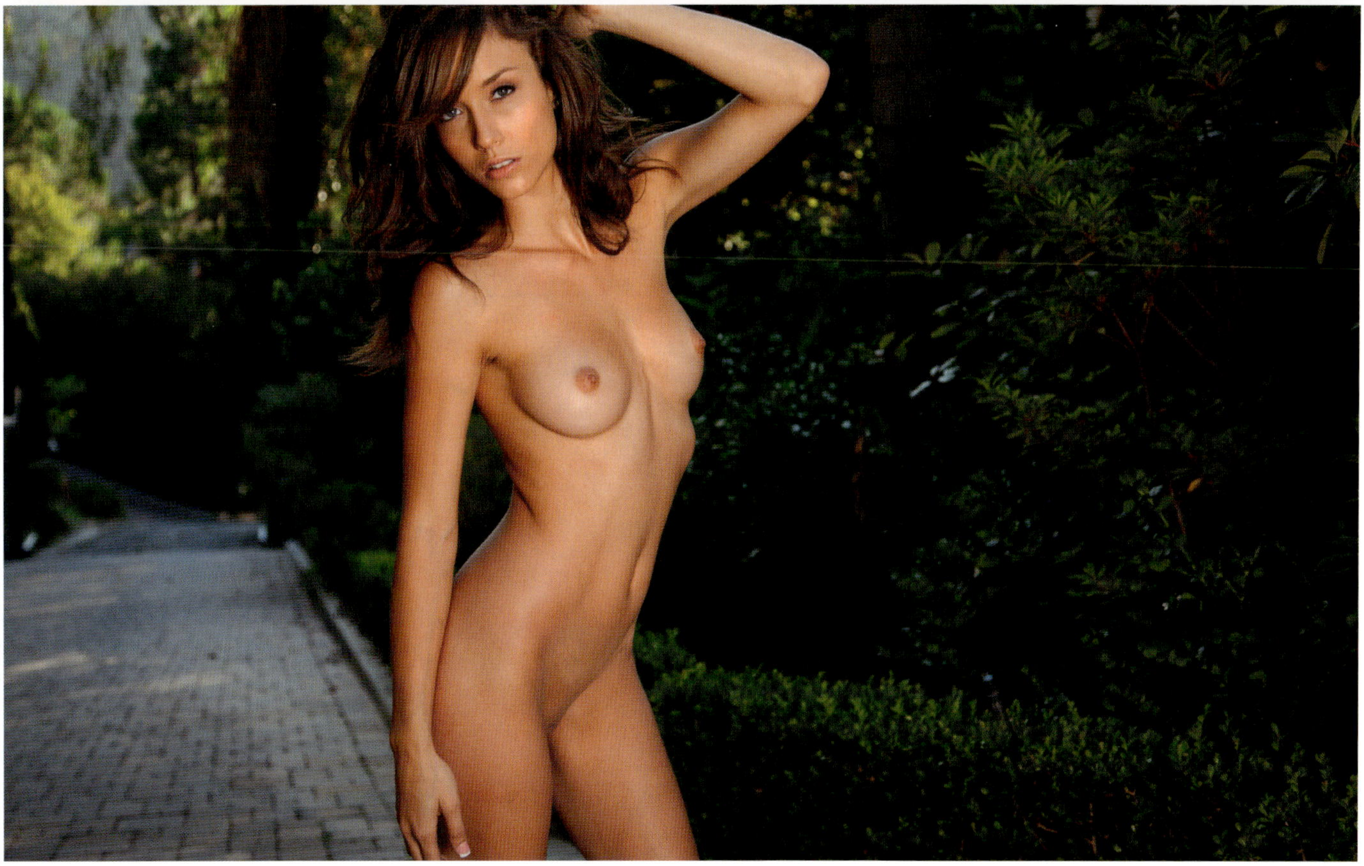

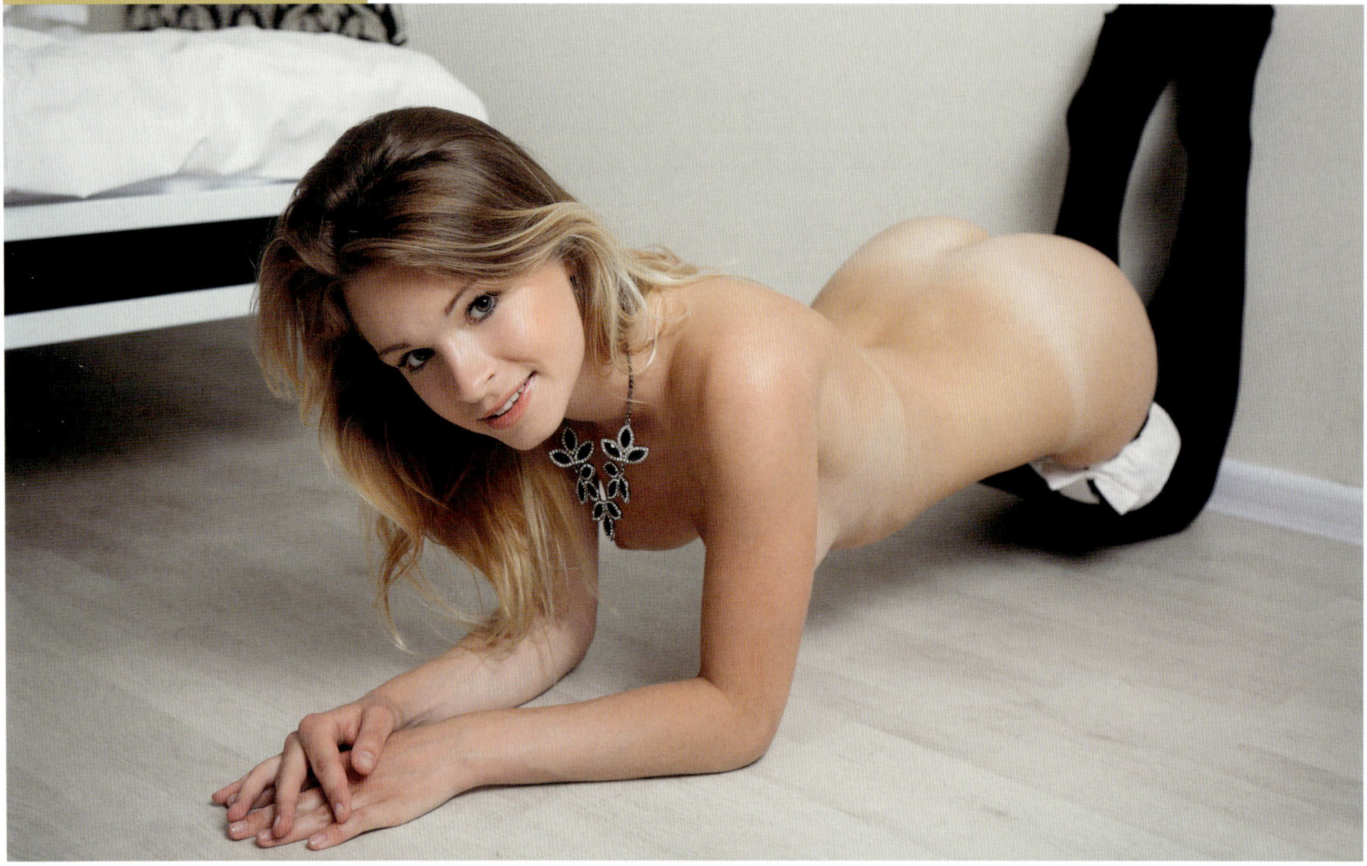

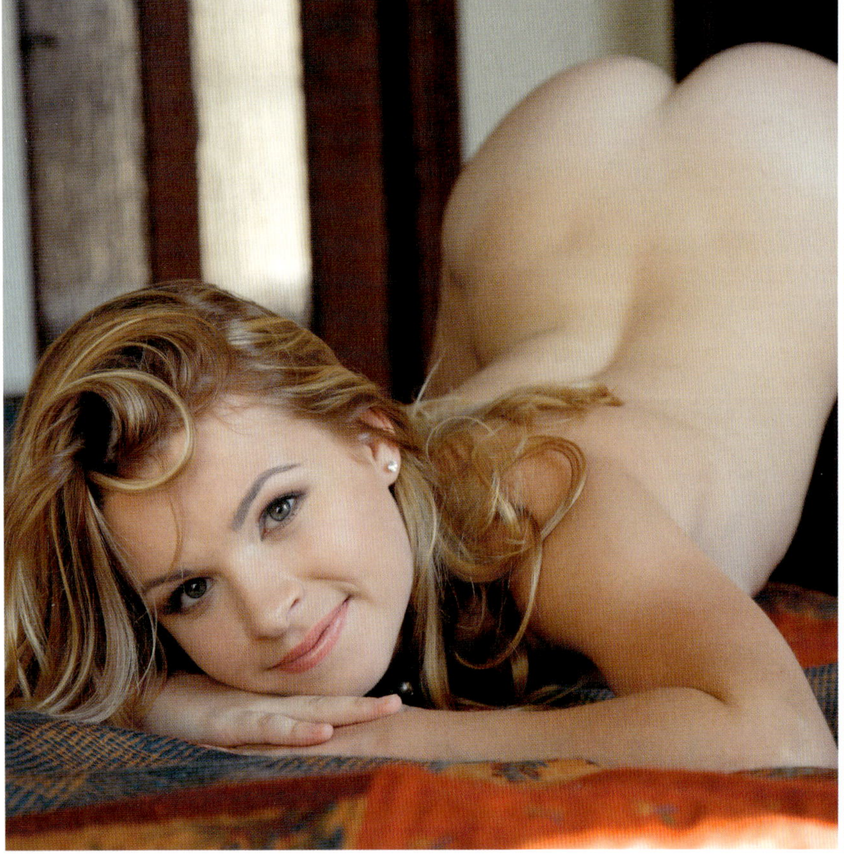

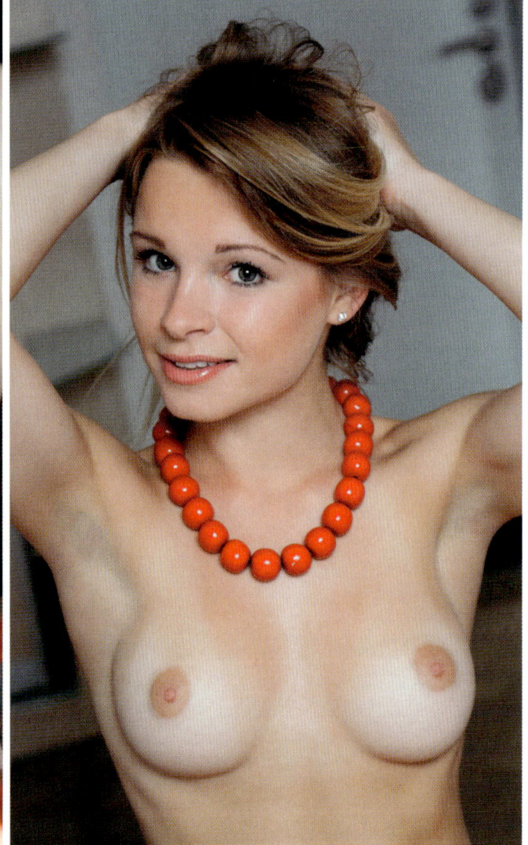

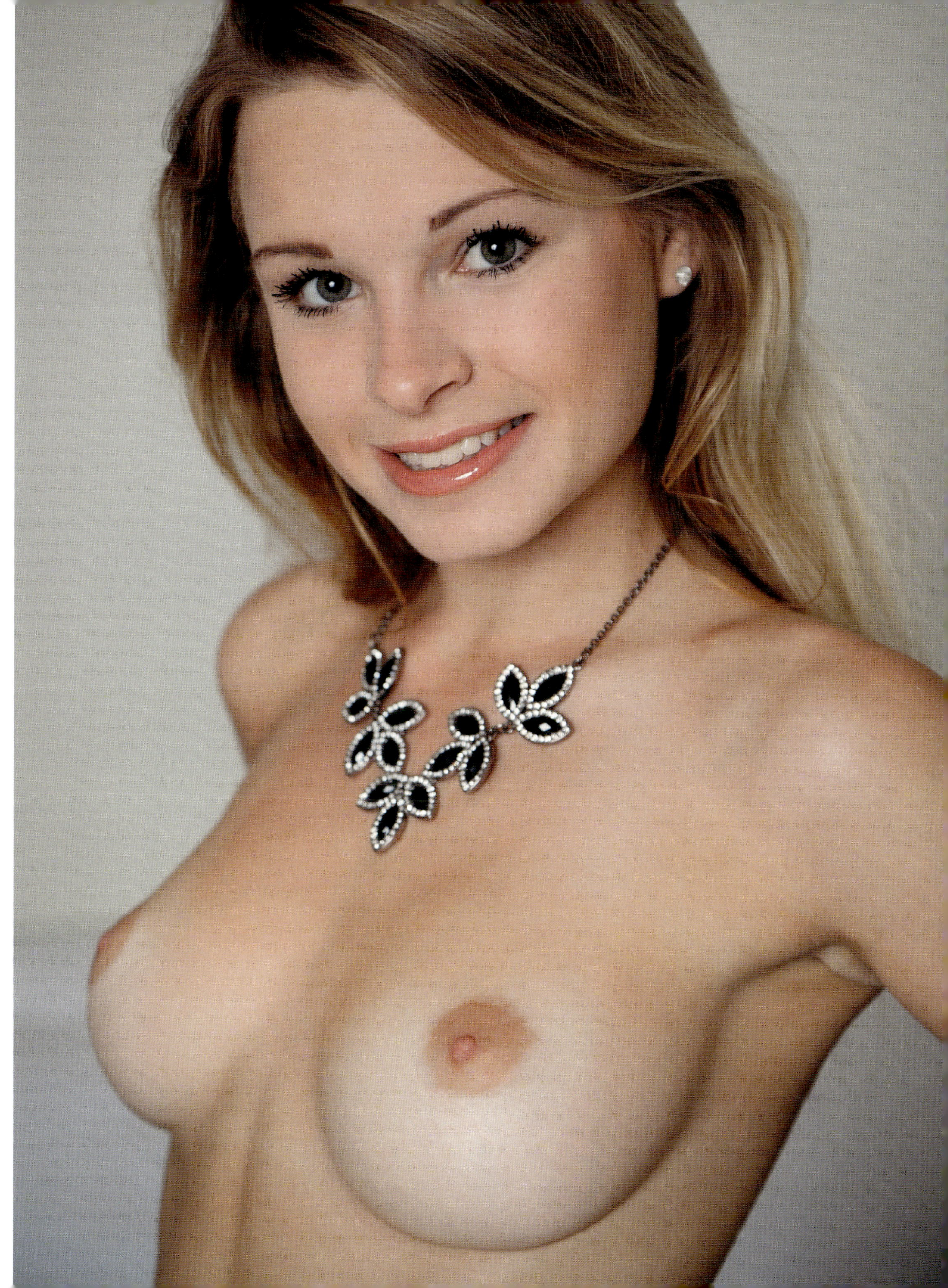

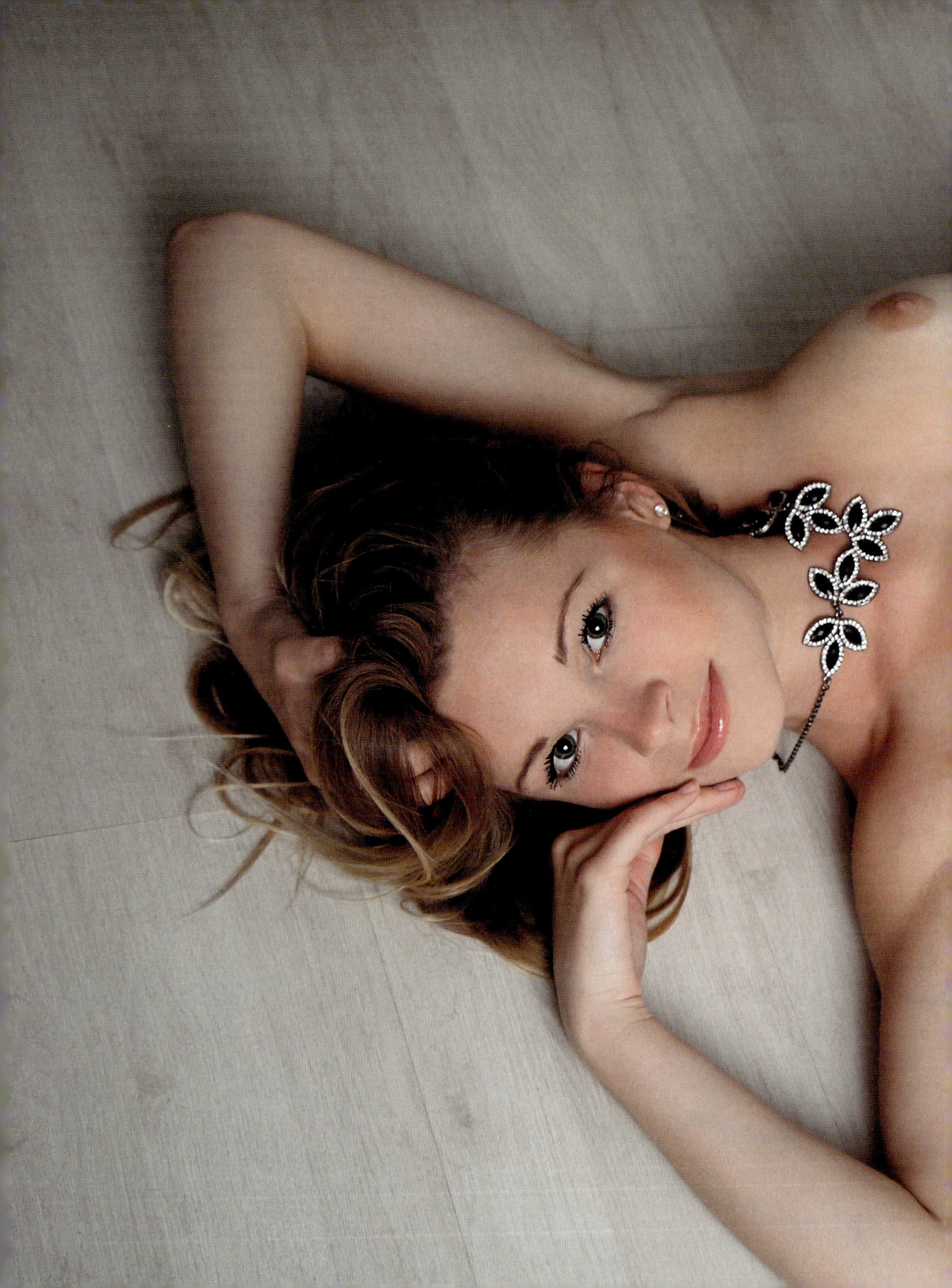

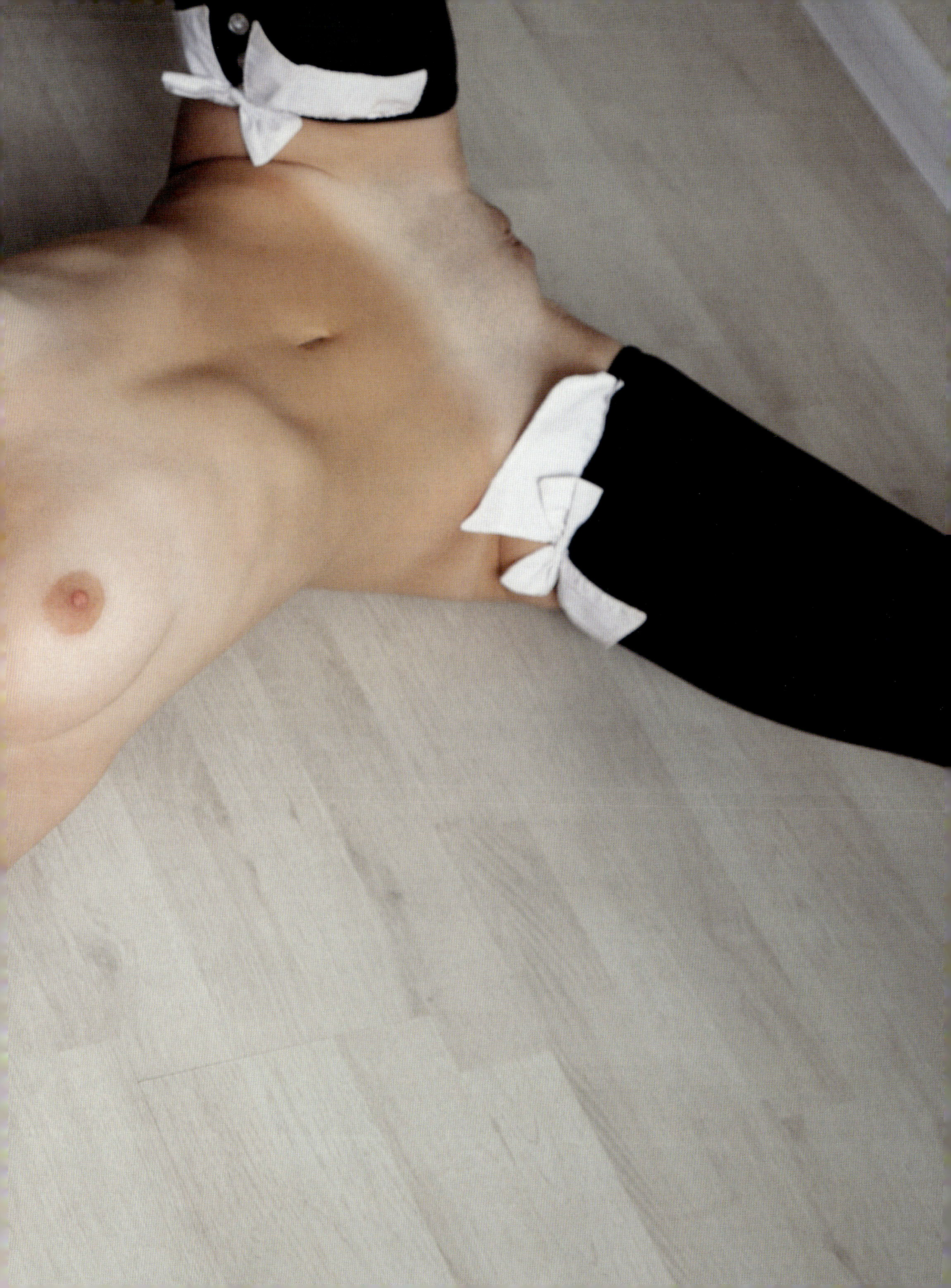

# Mango A

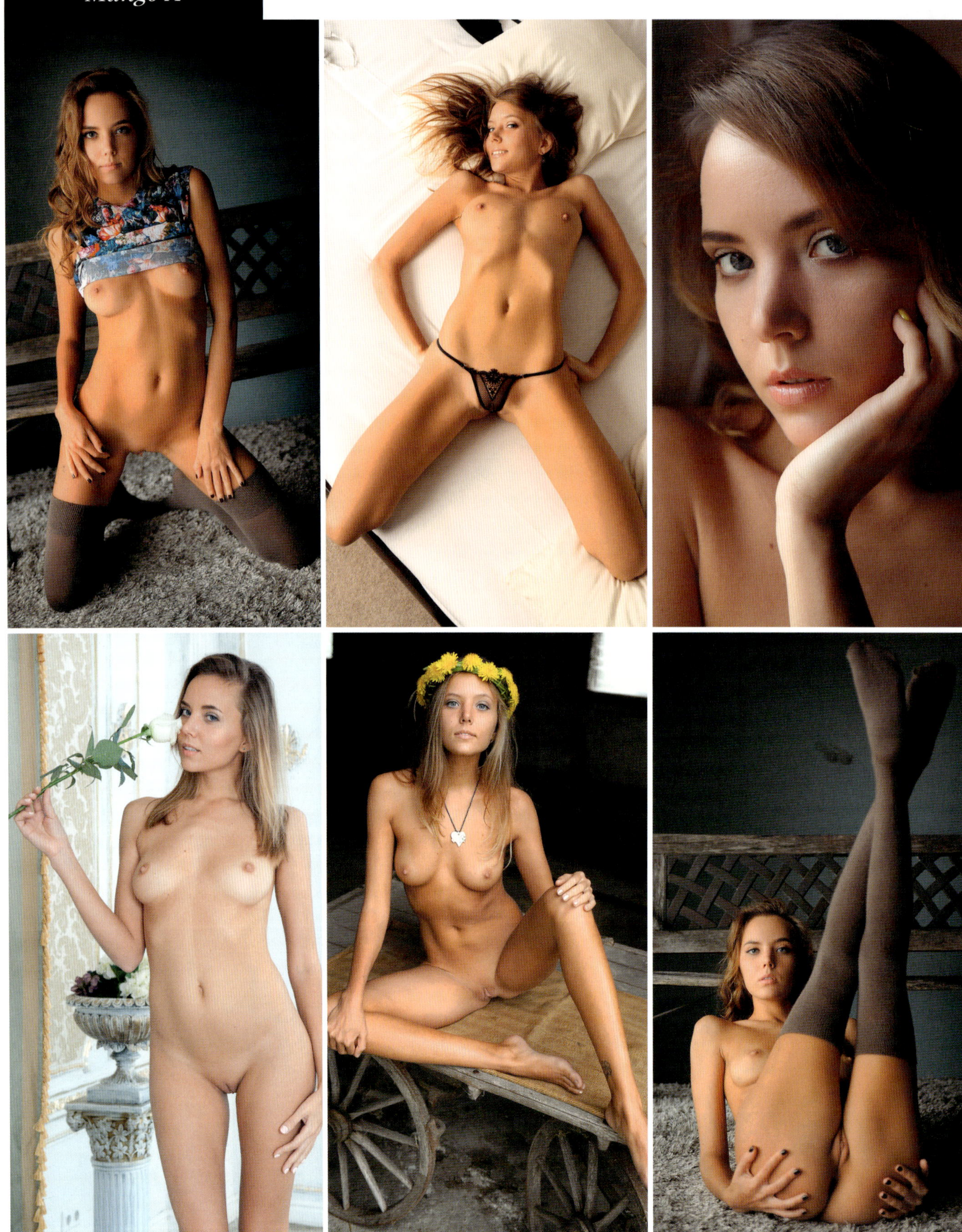

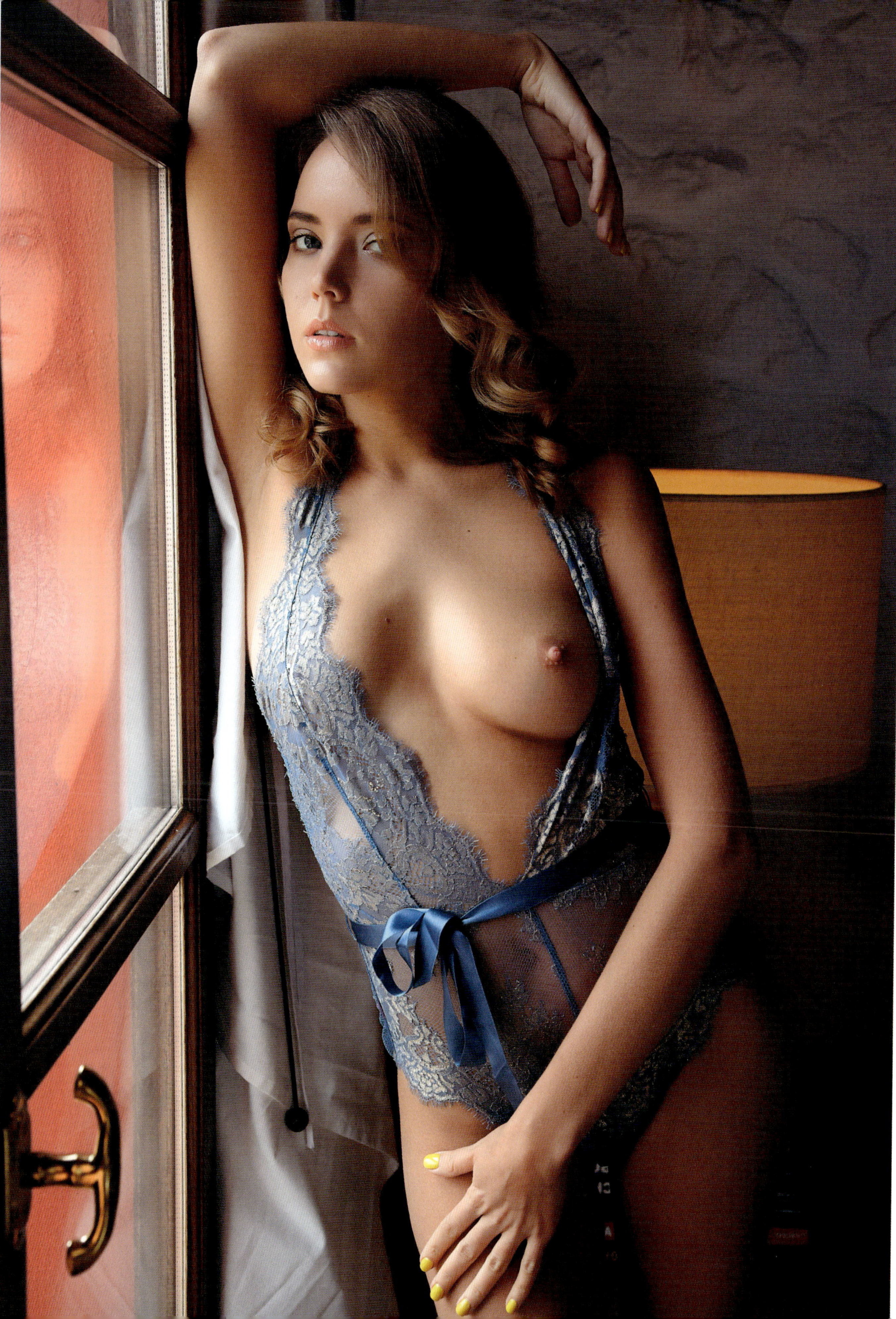

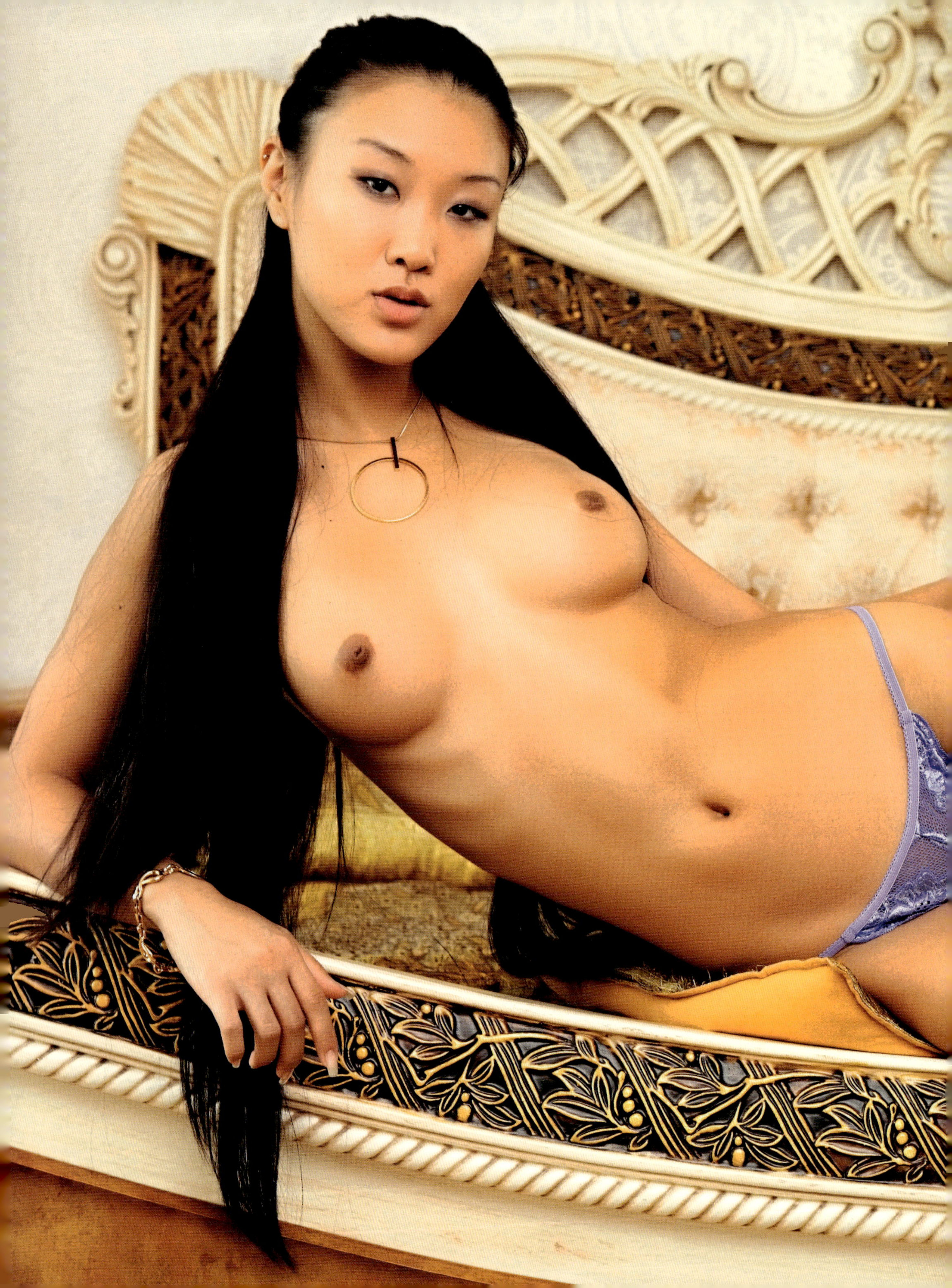

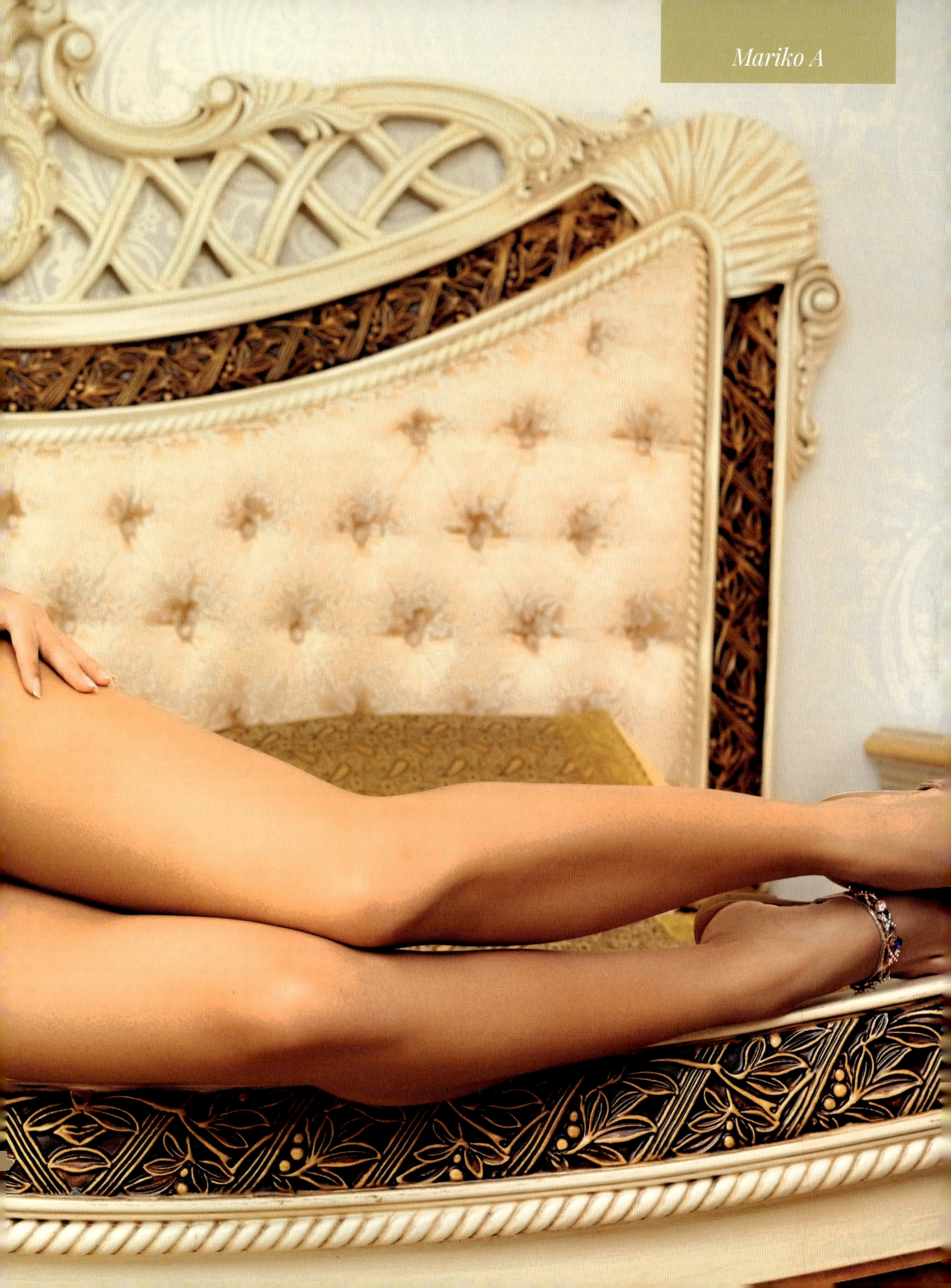

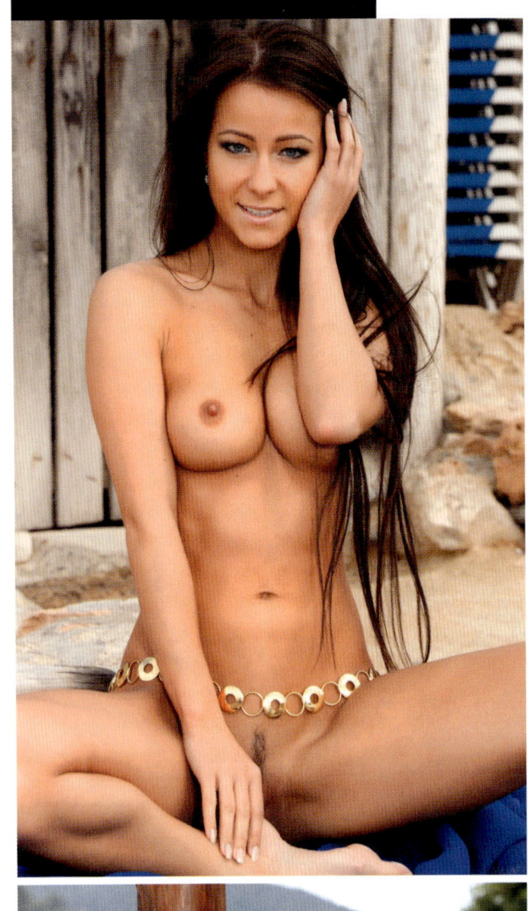

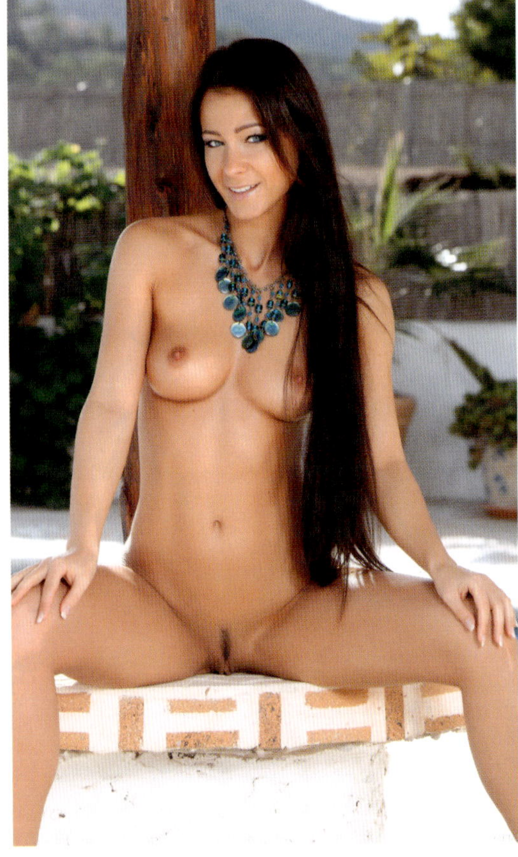

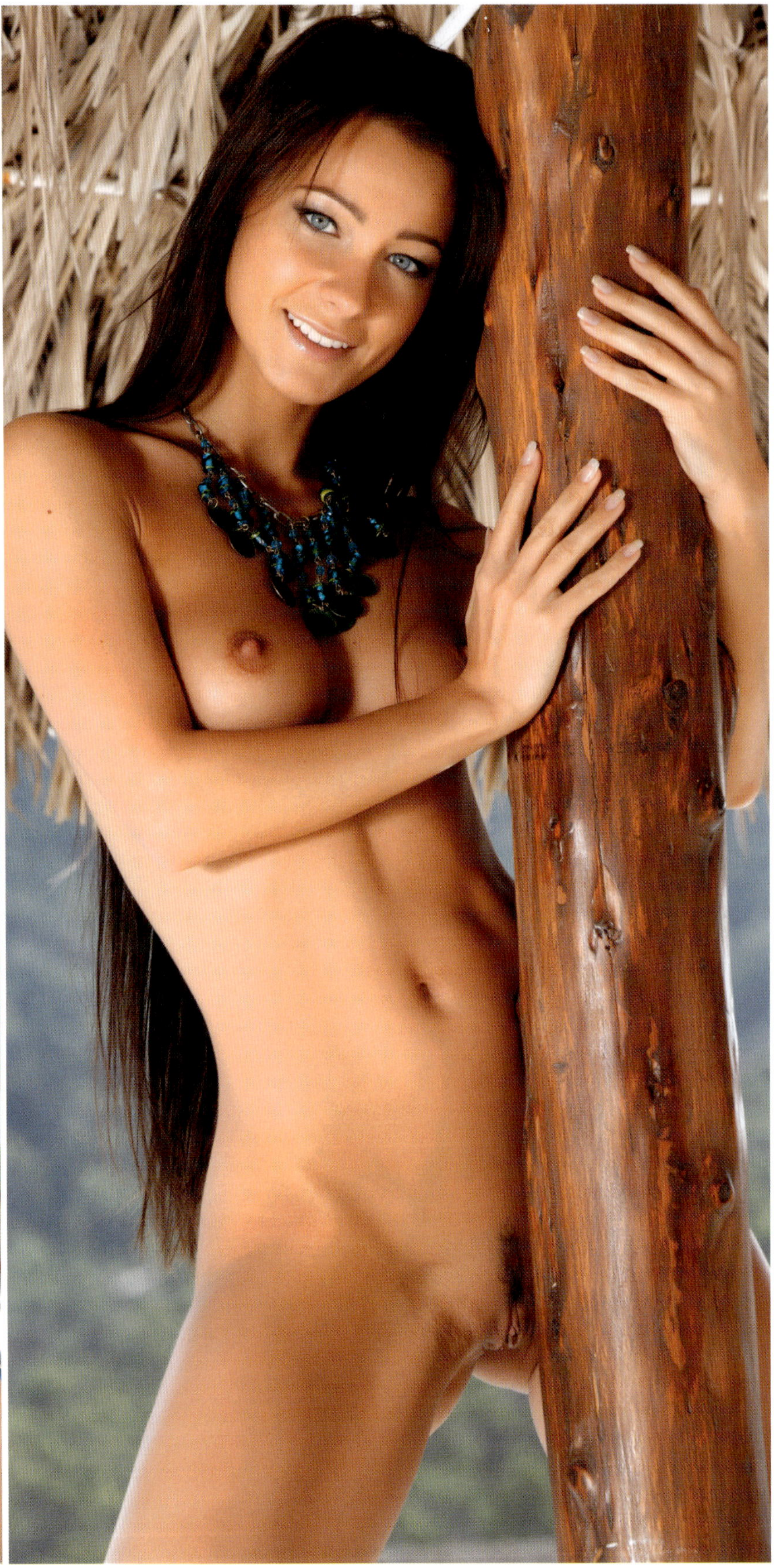

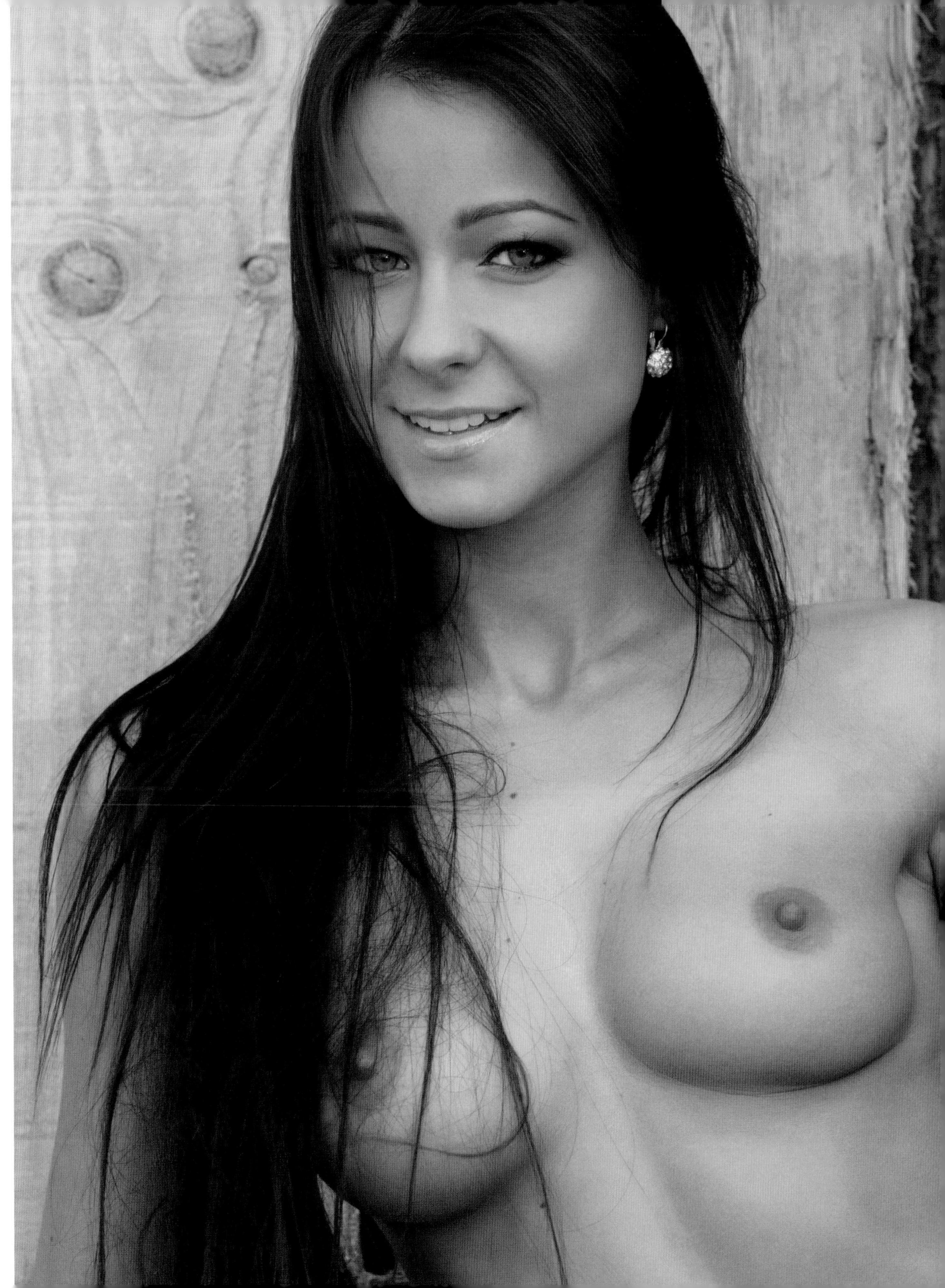

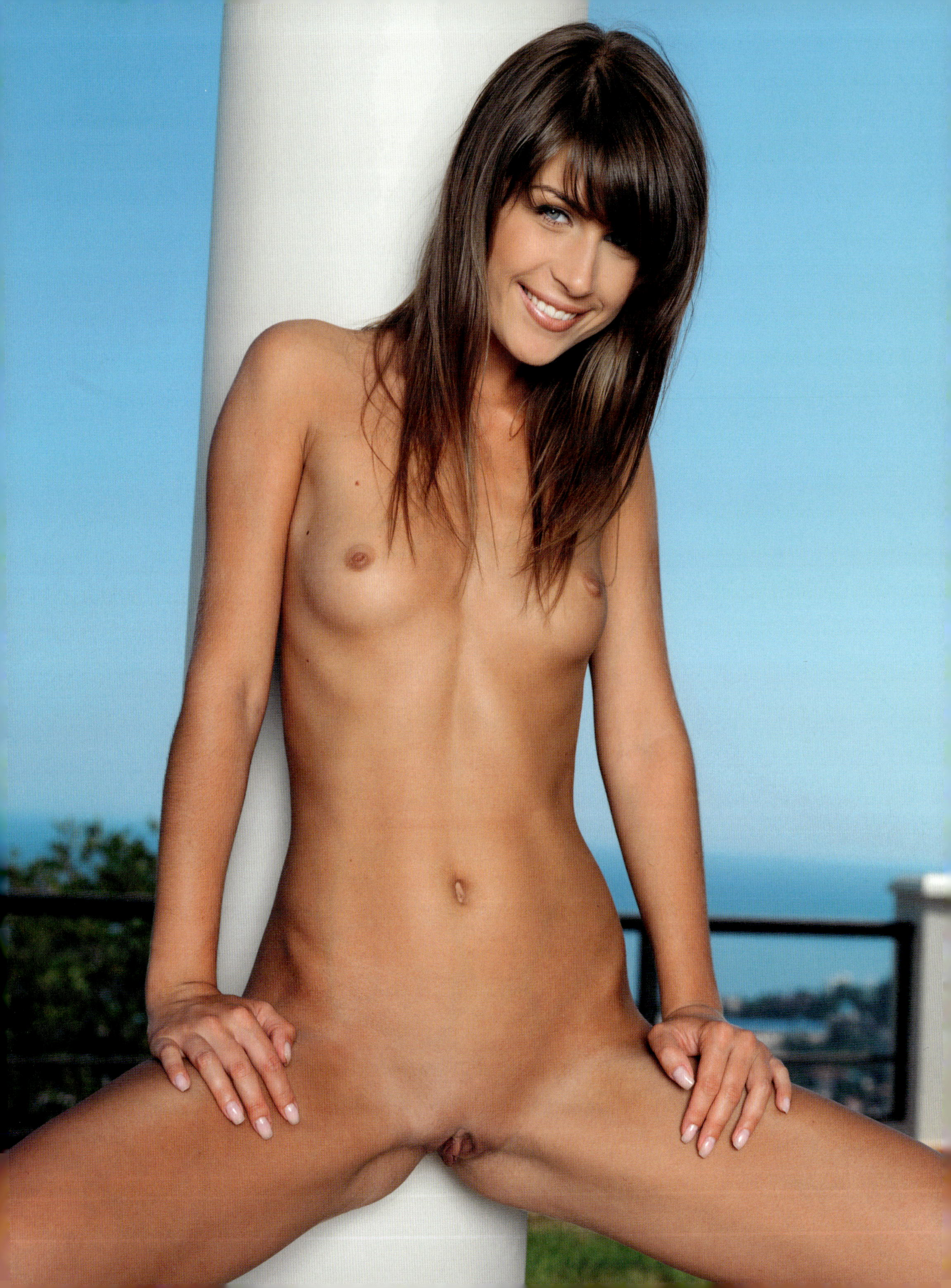

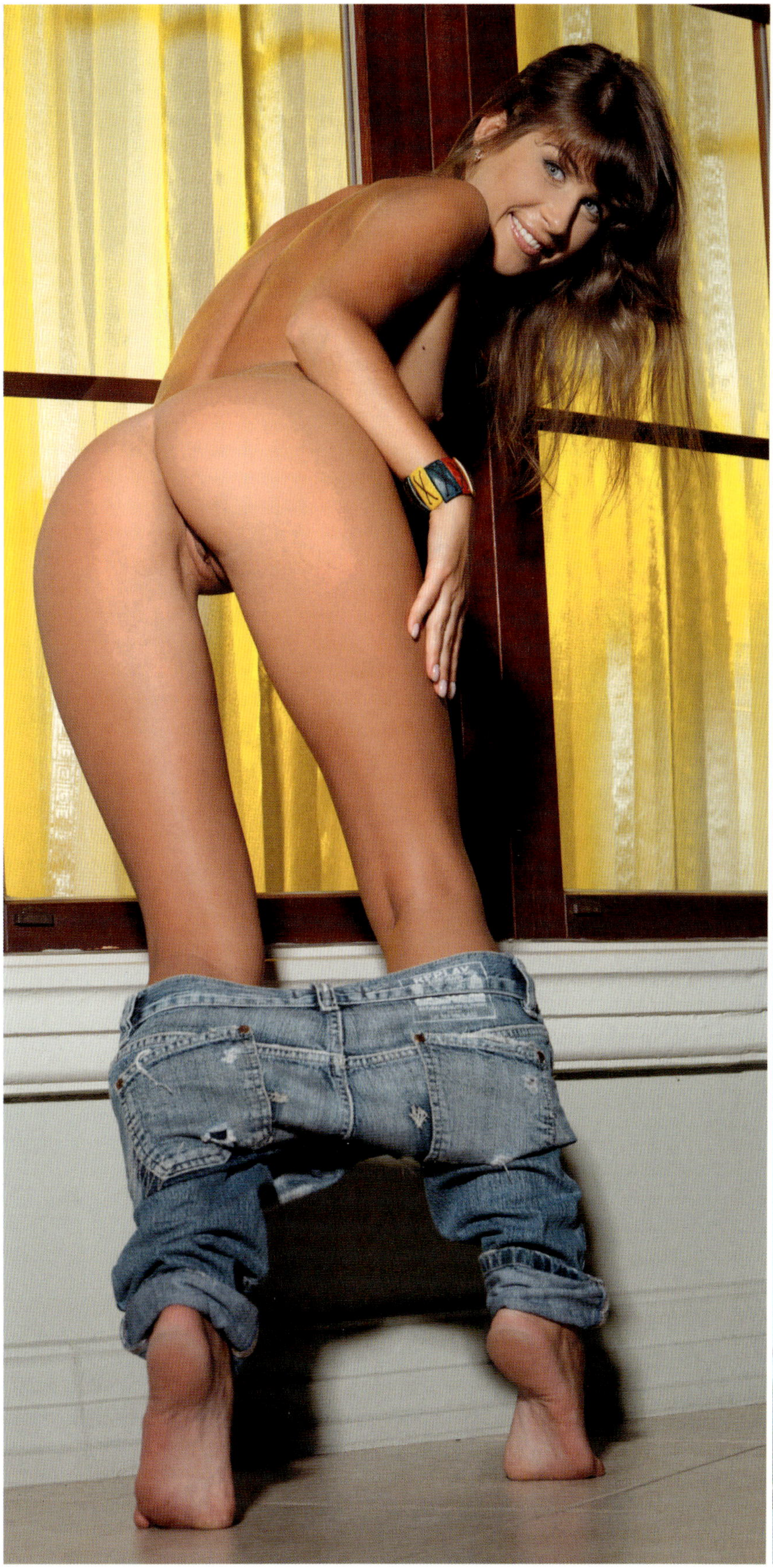

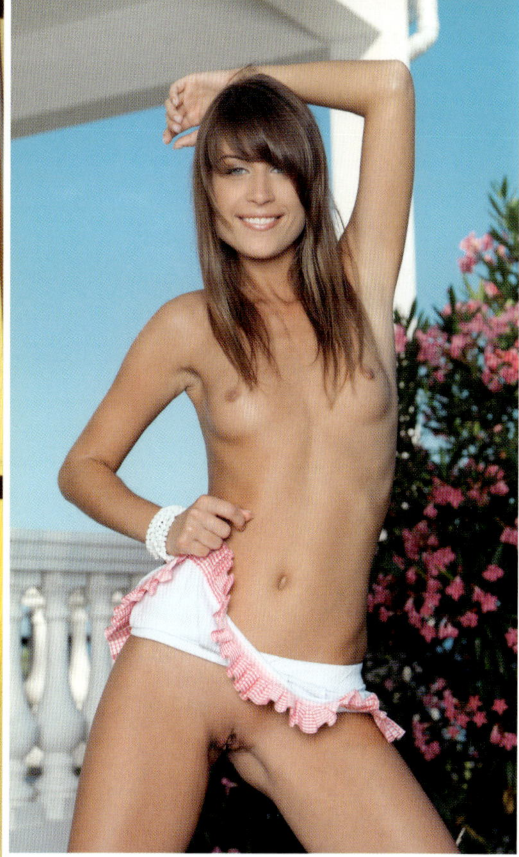

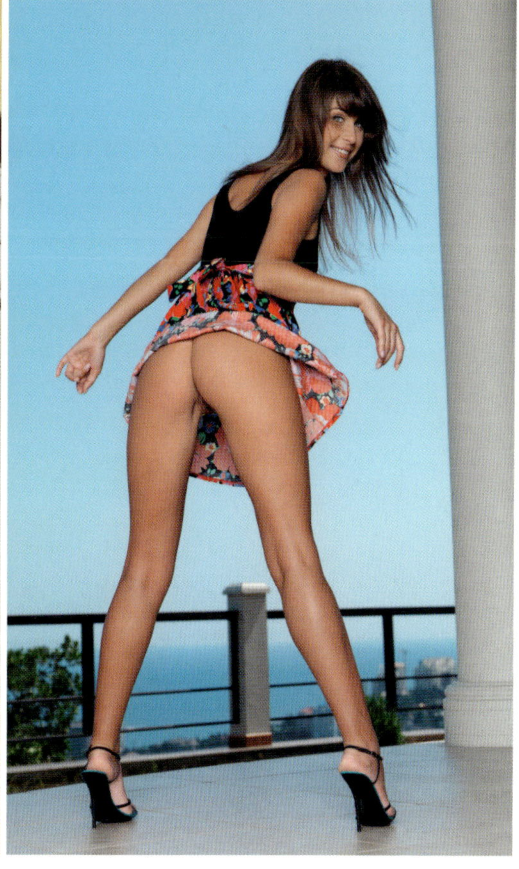

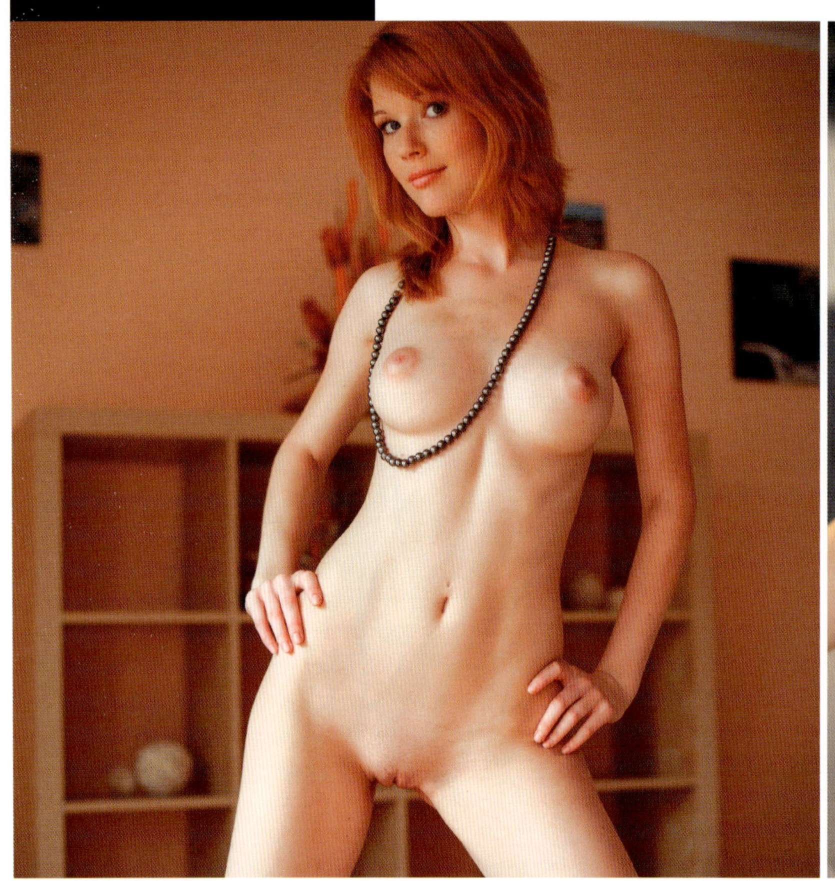

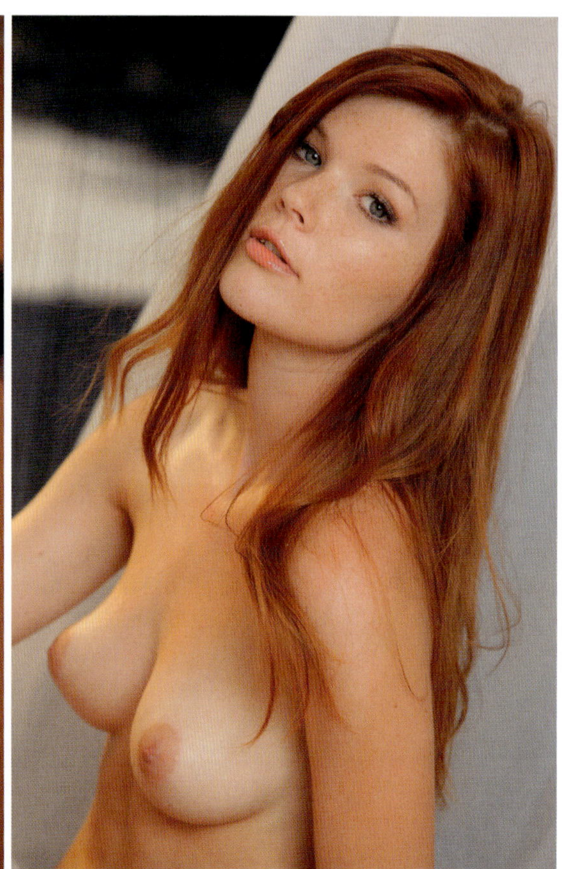

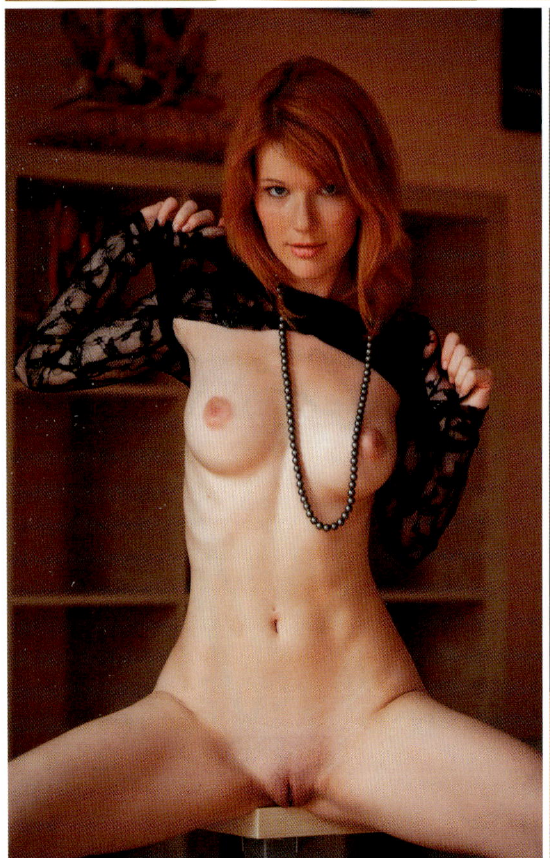

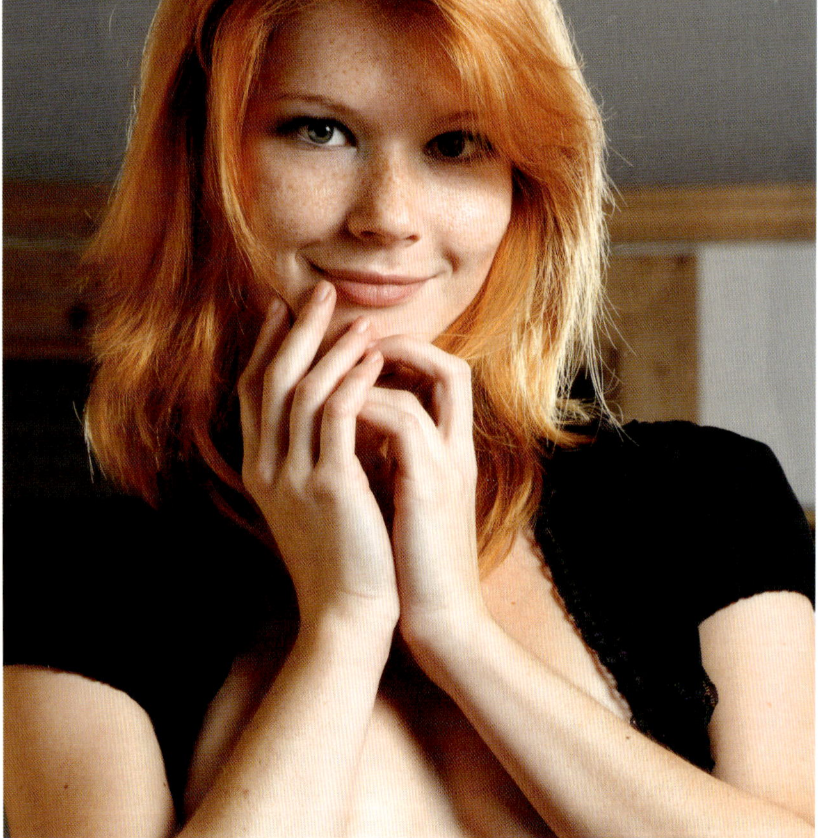

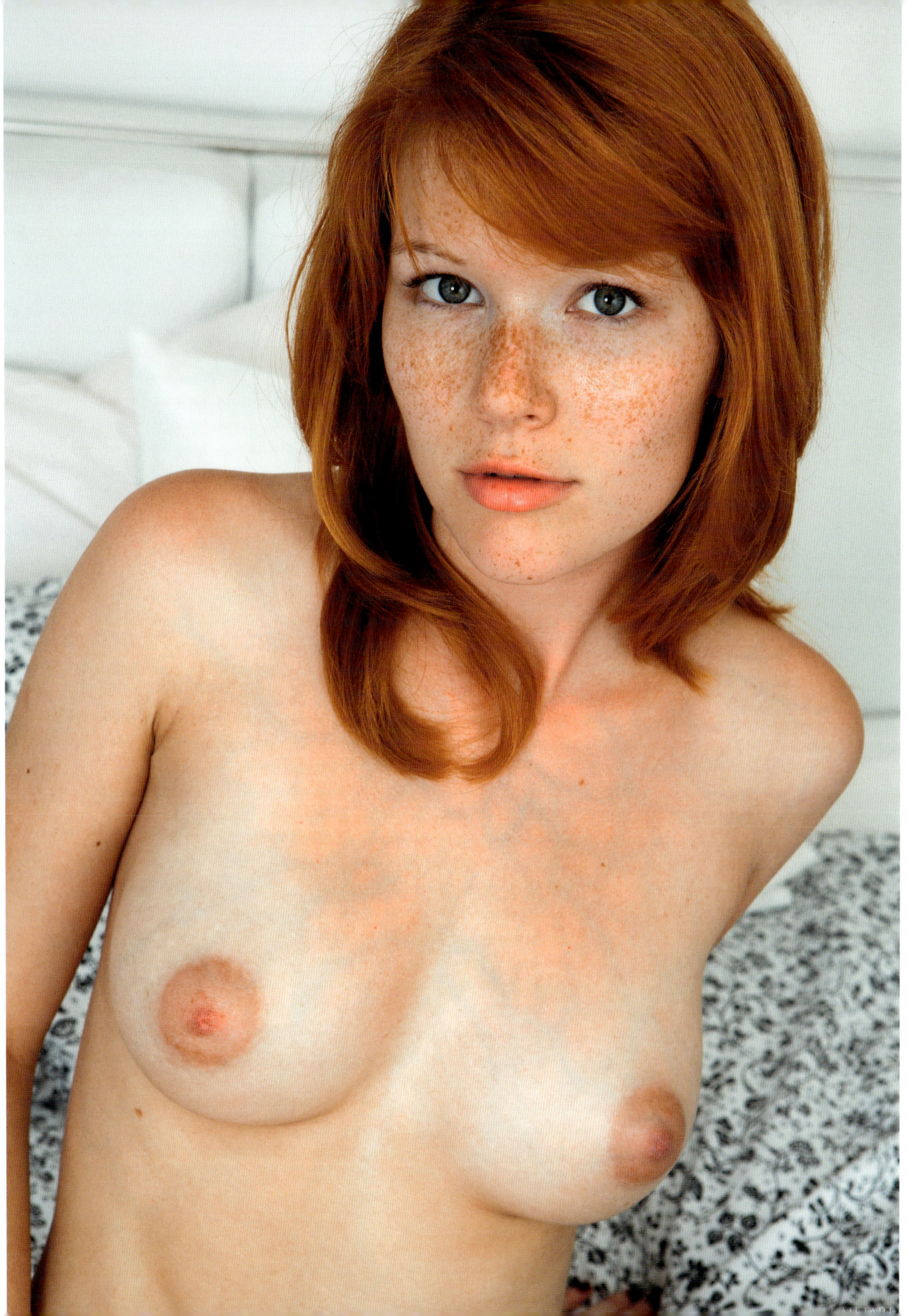

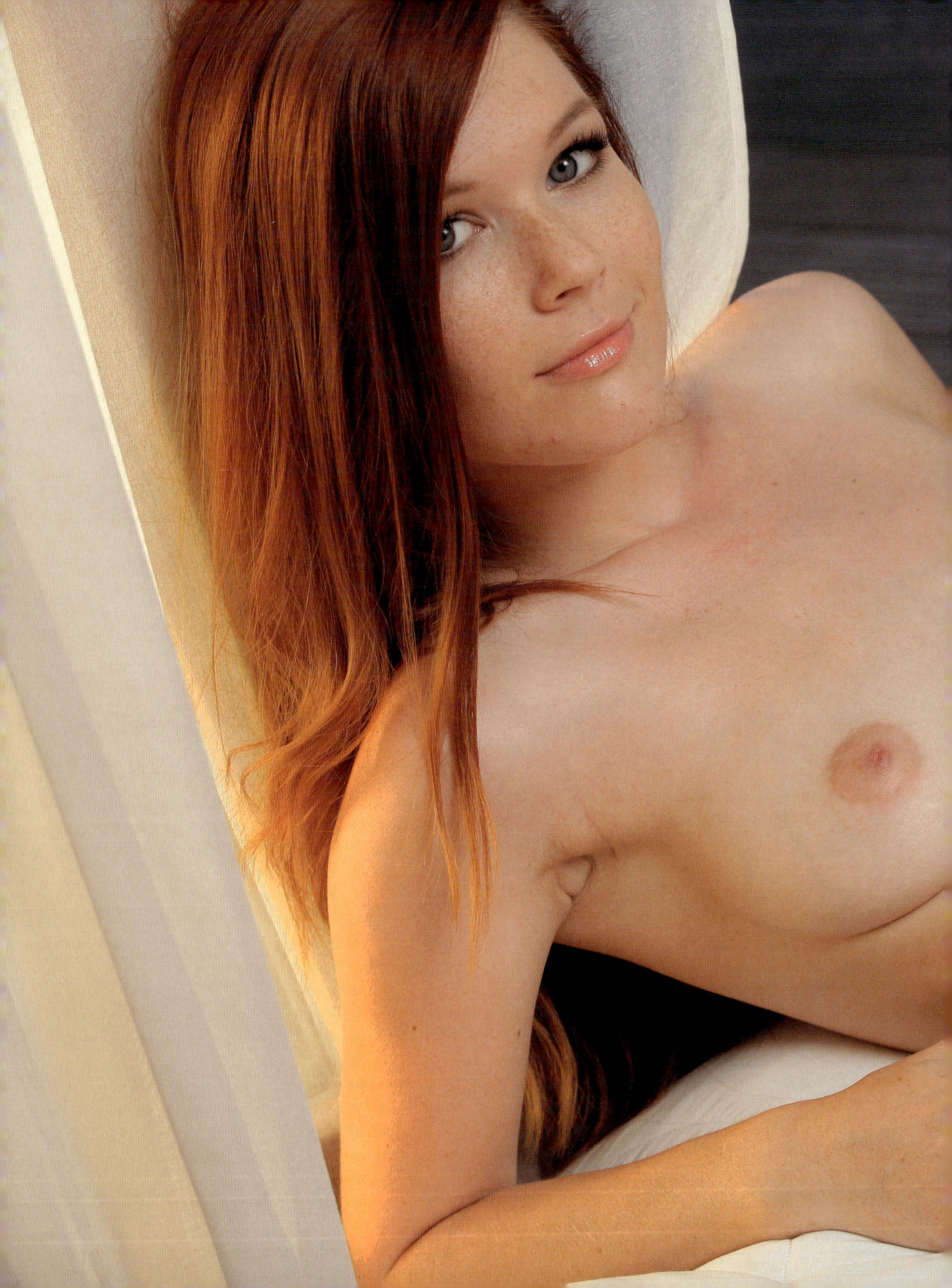

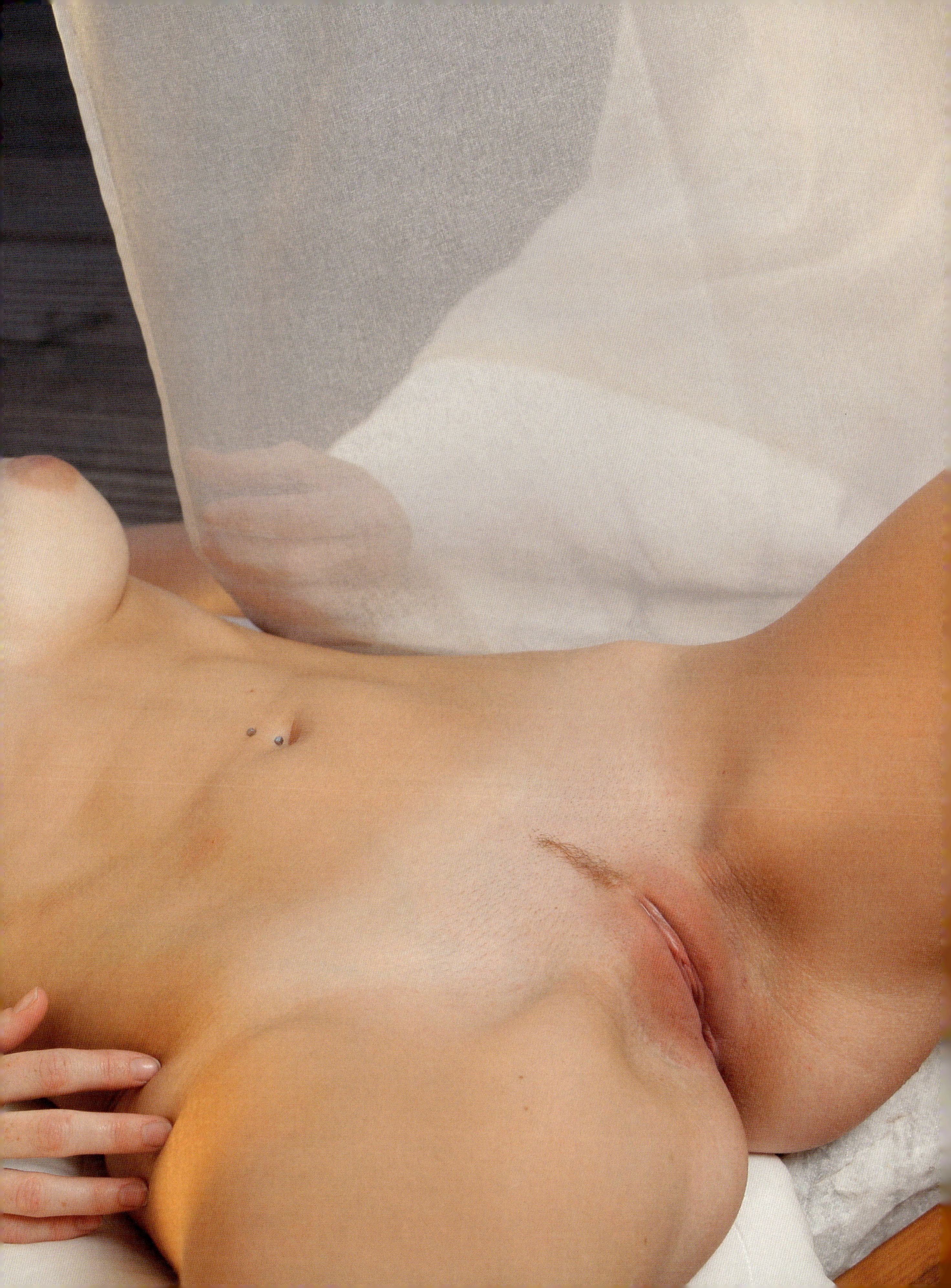

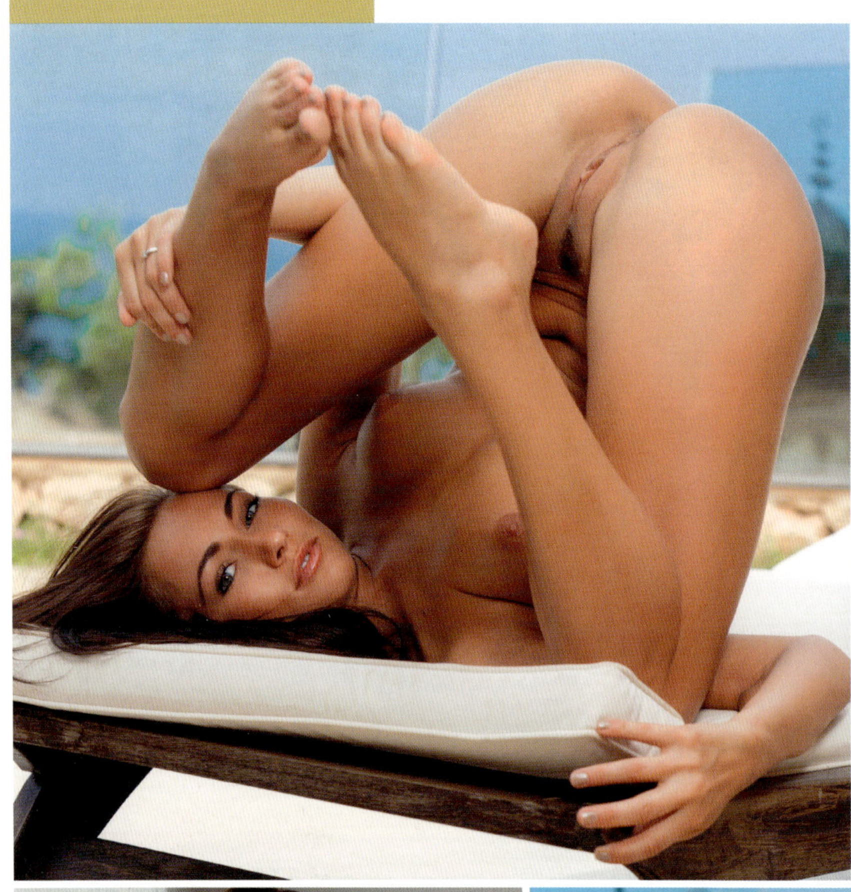

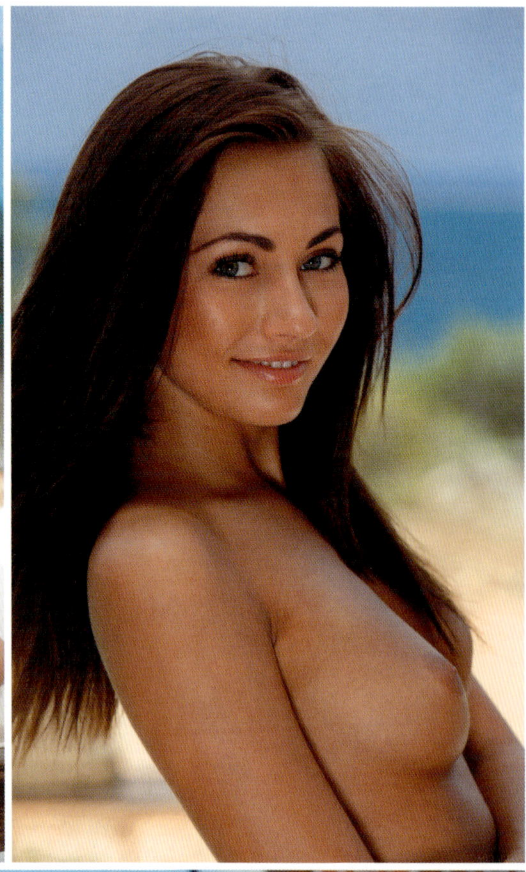

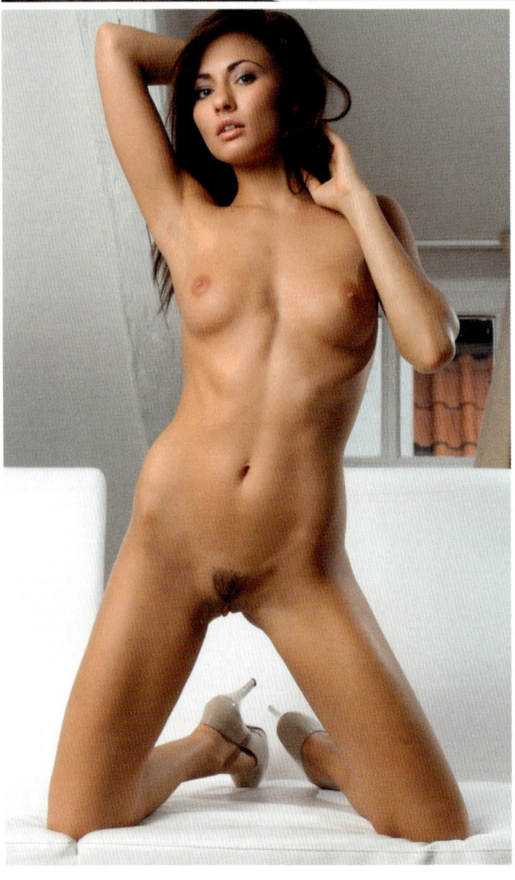

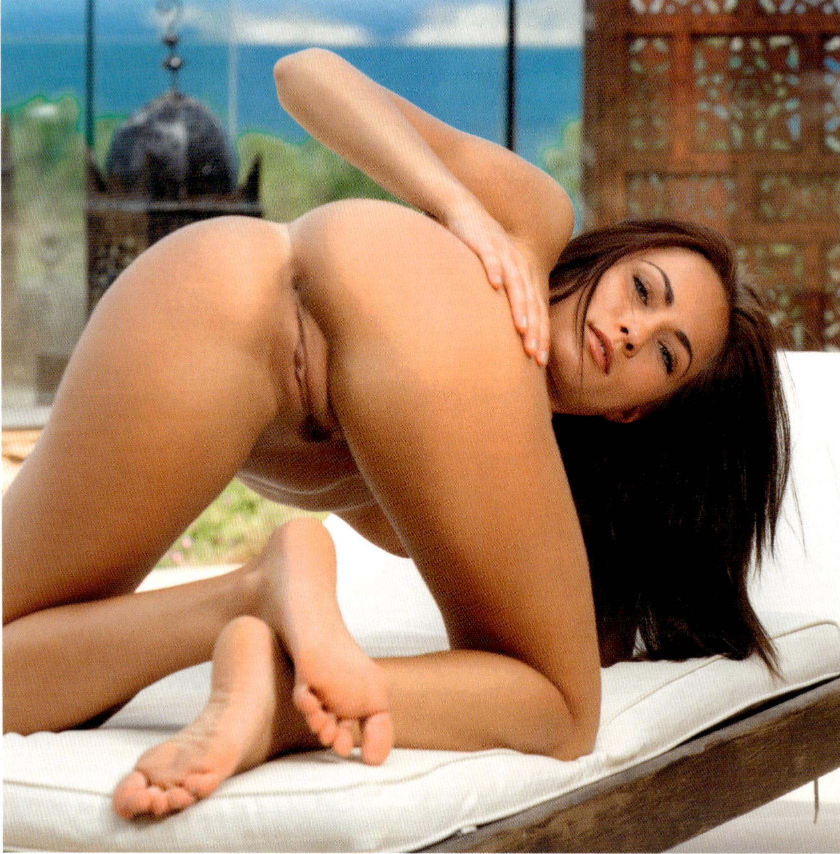

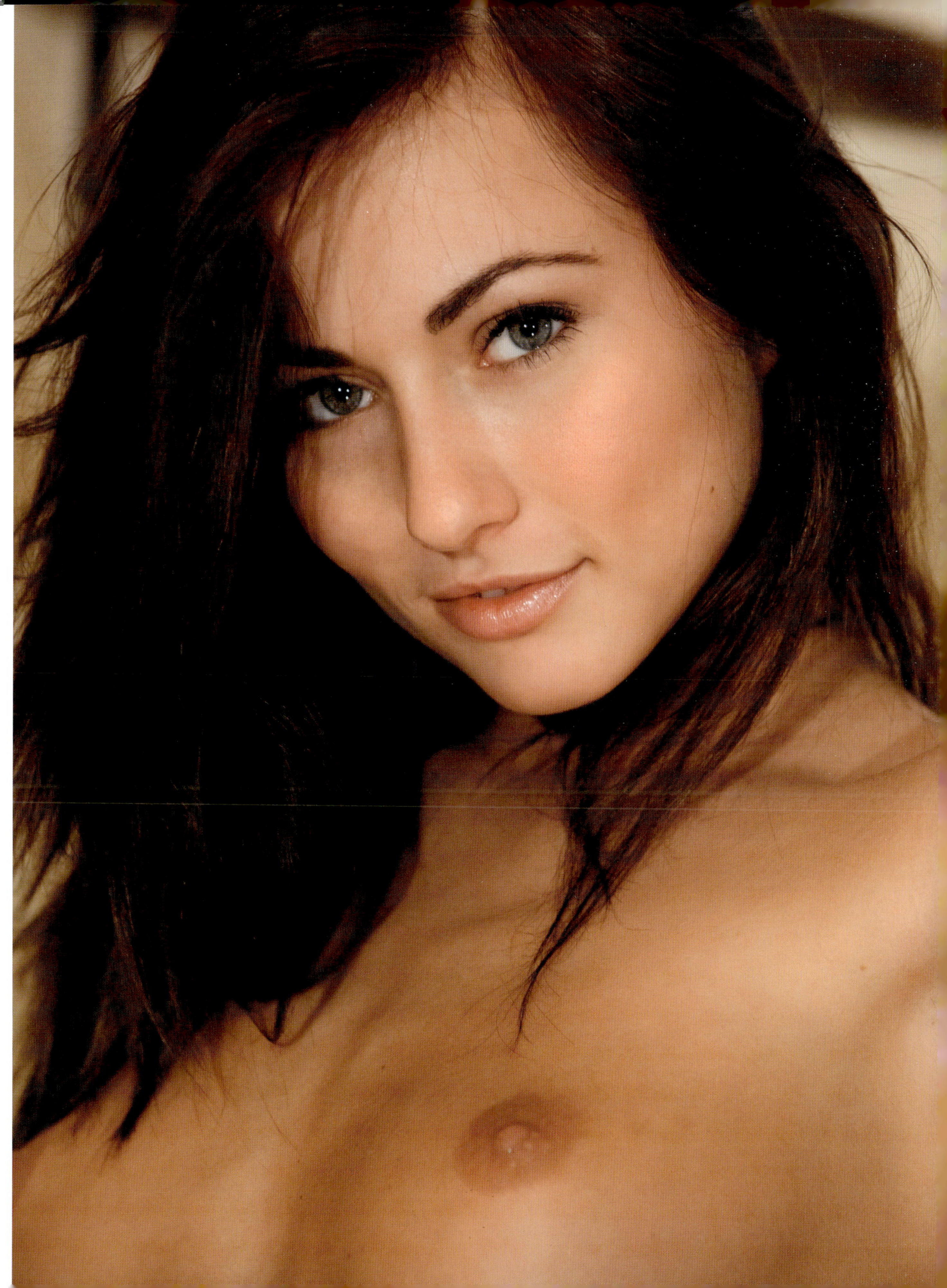

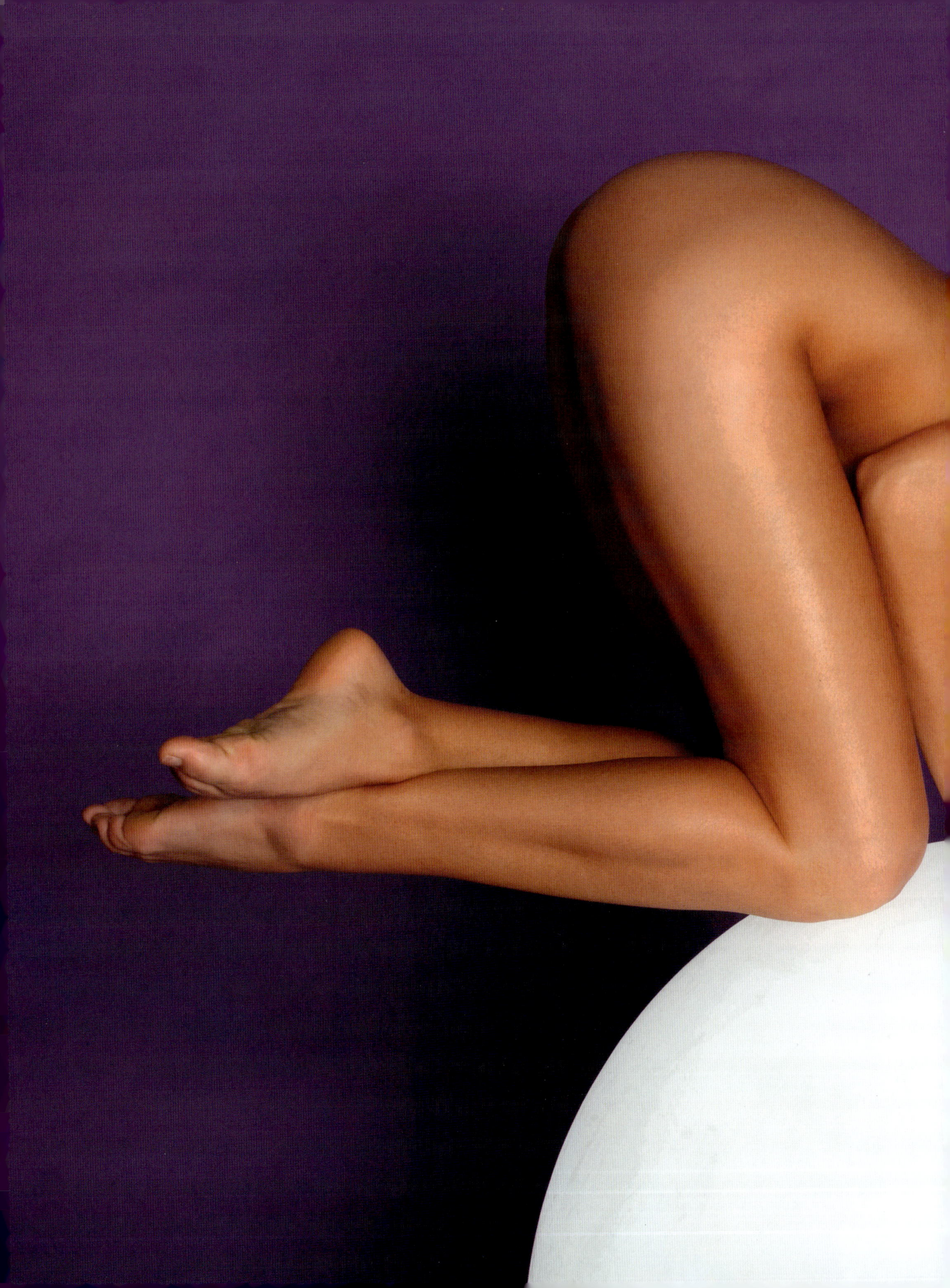

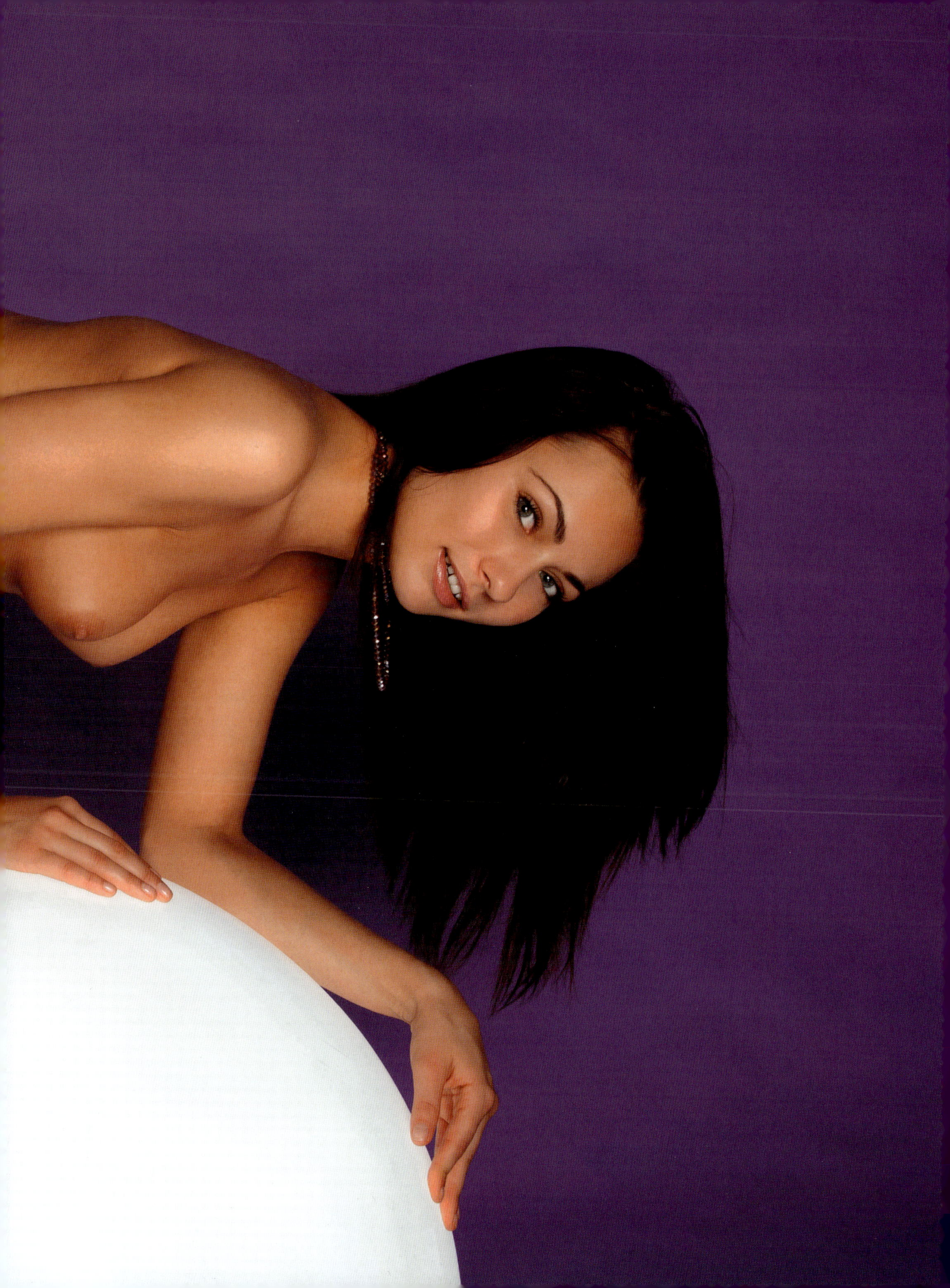

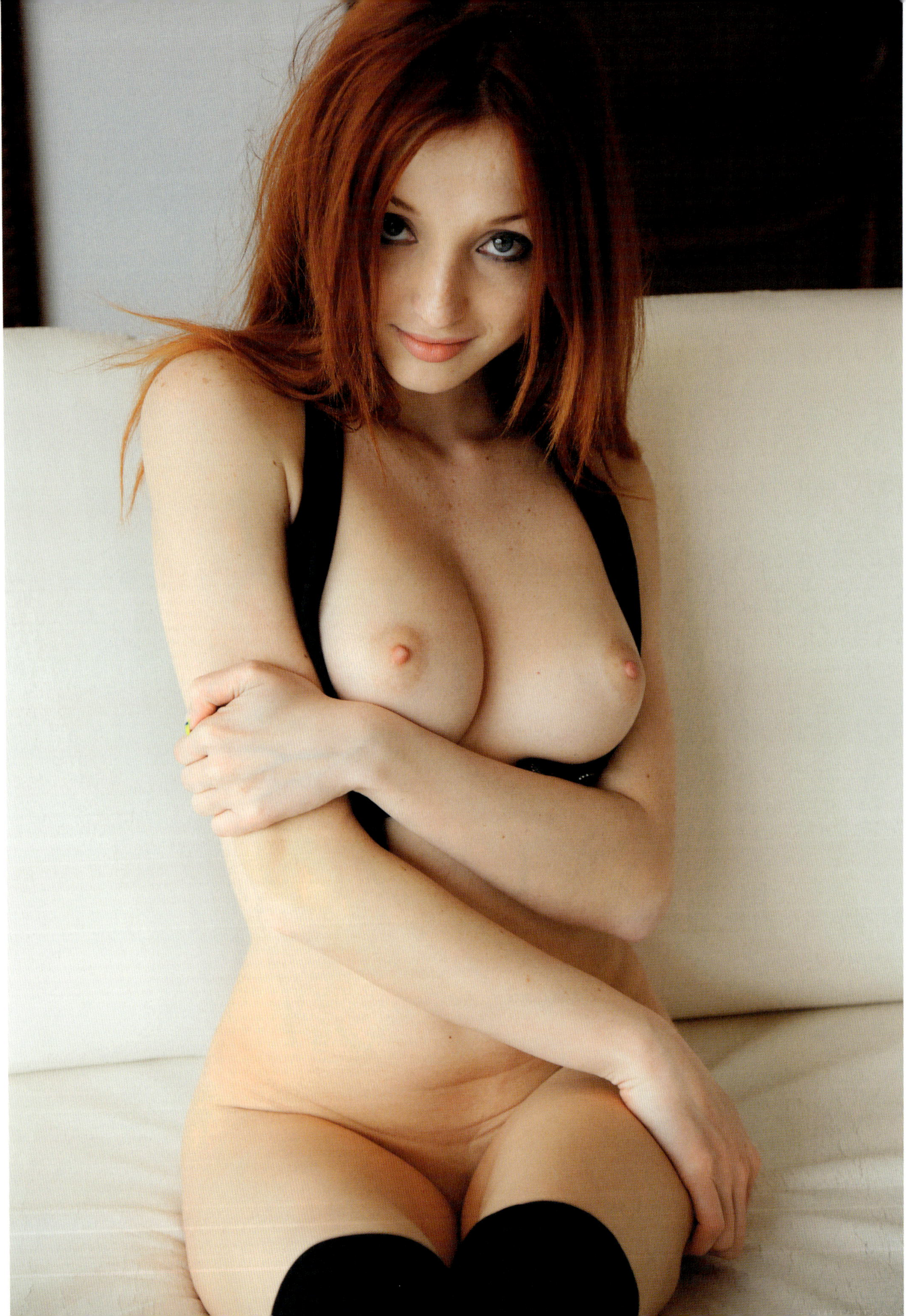

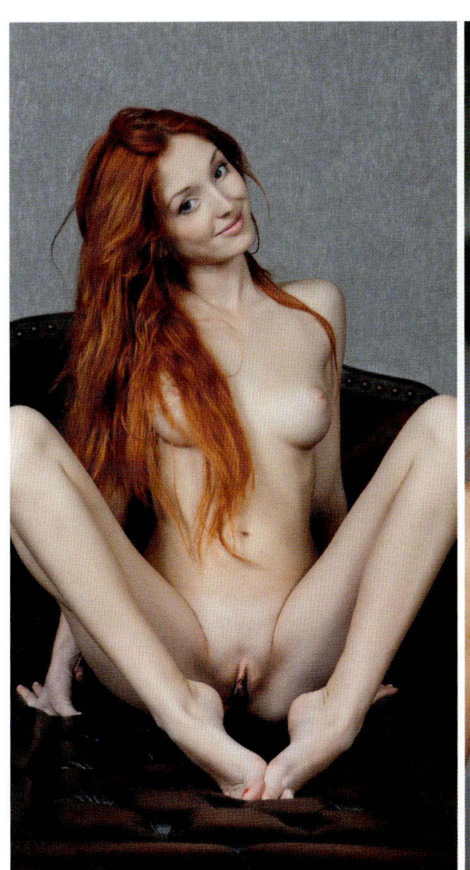
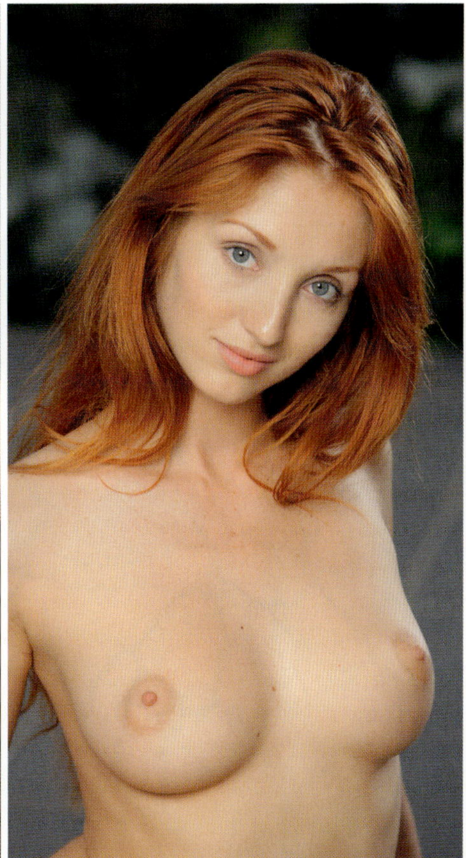
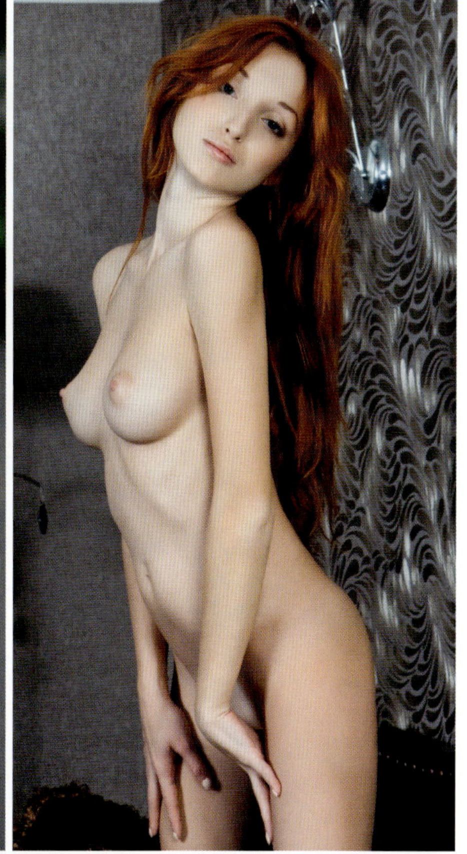
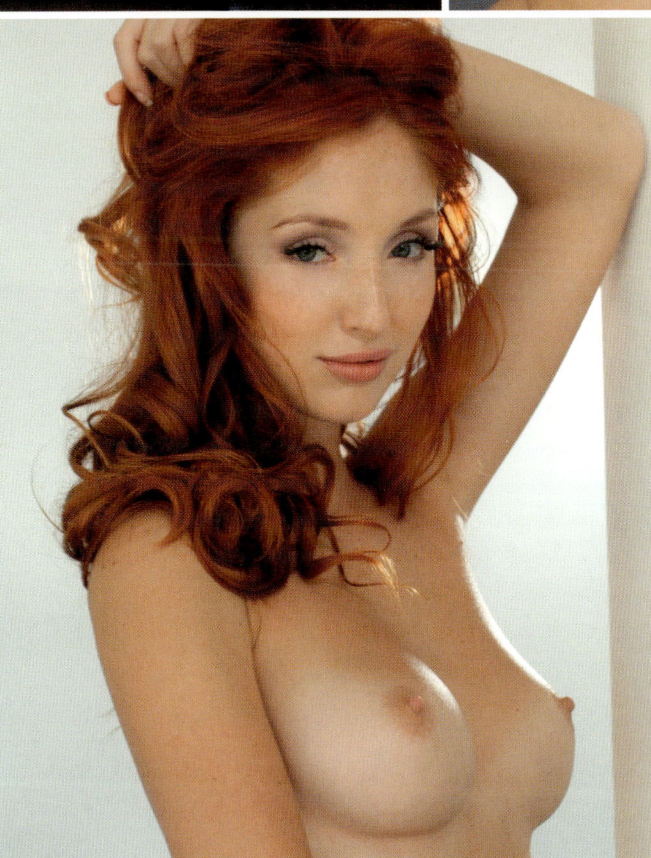
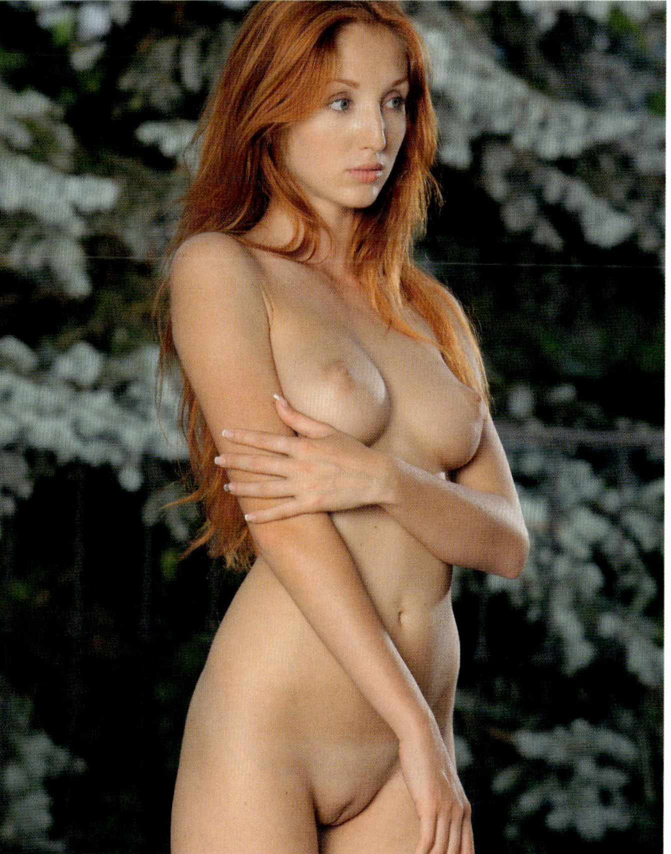

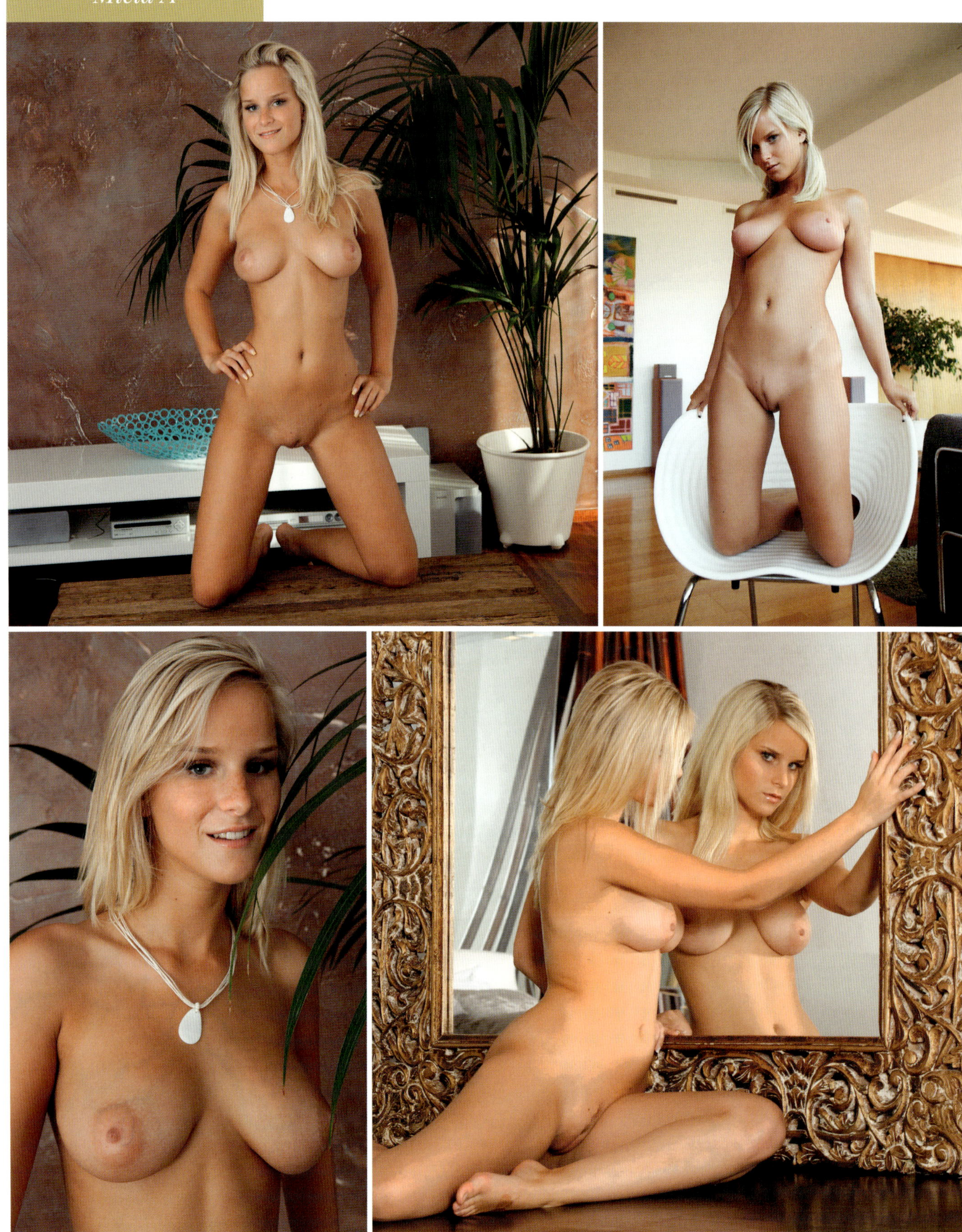

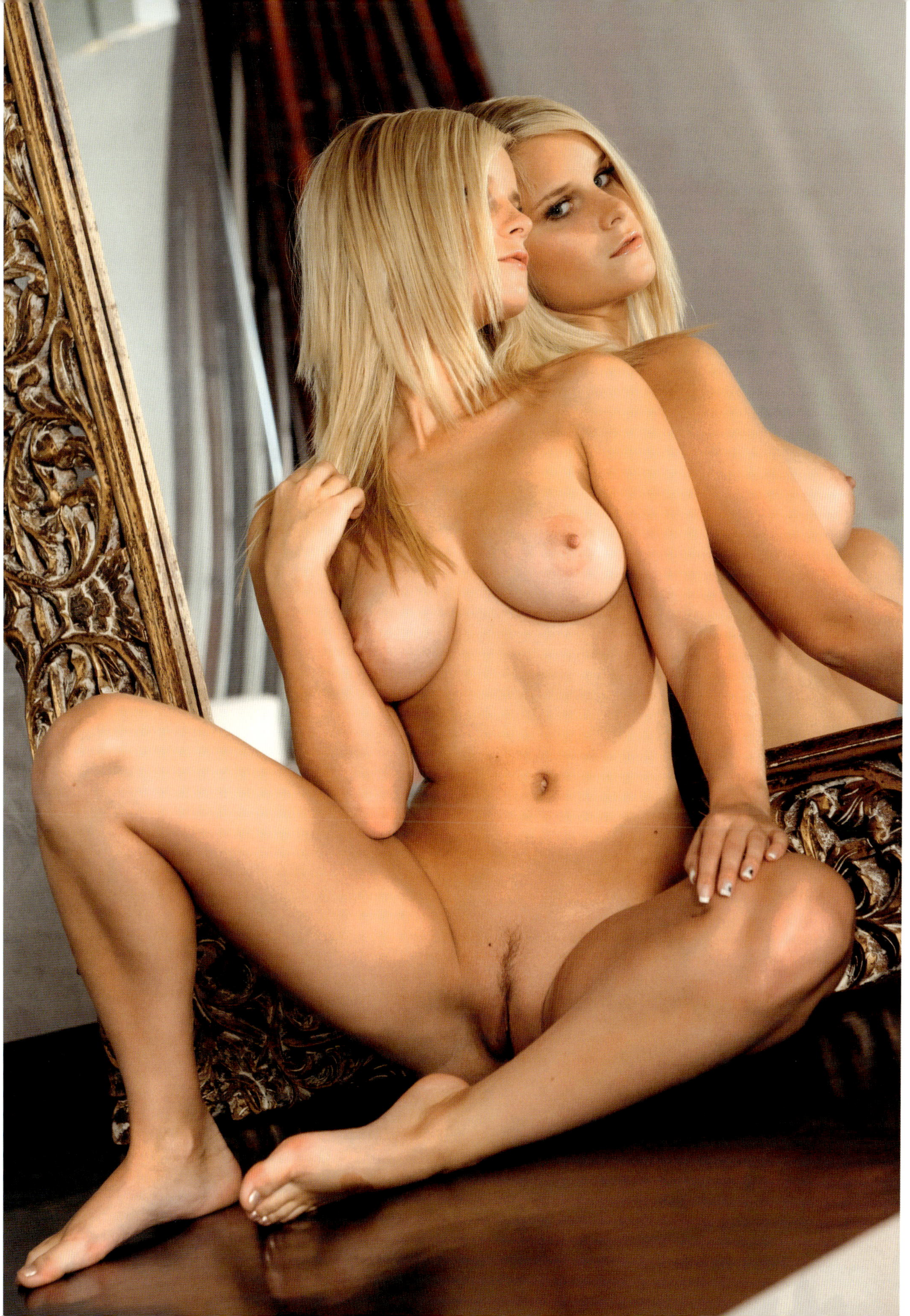

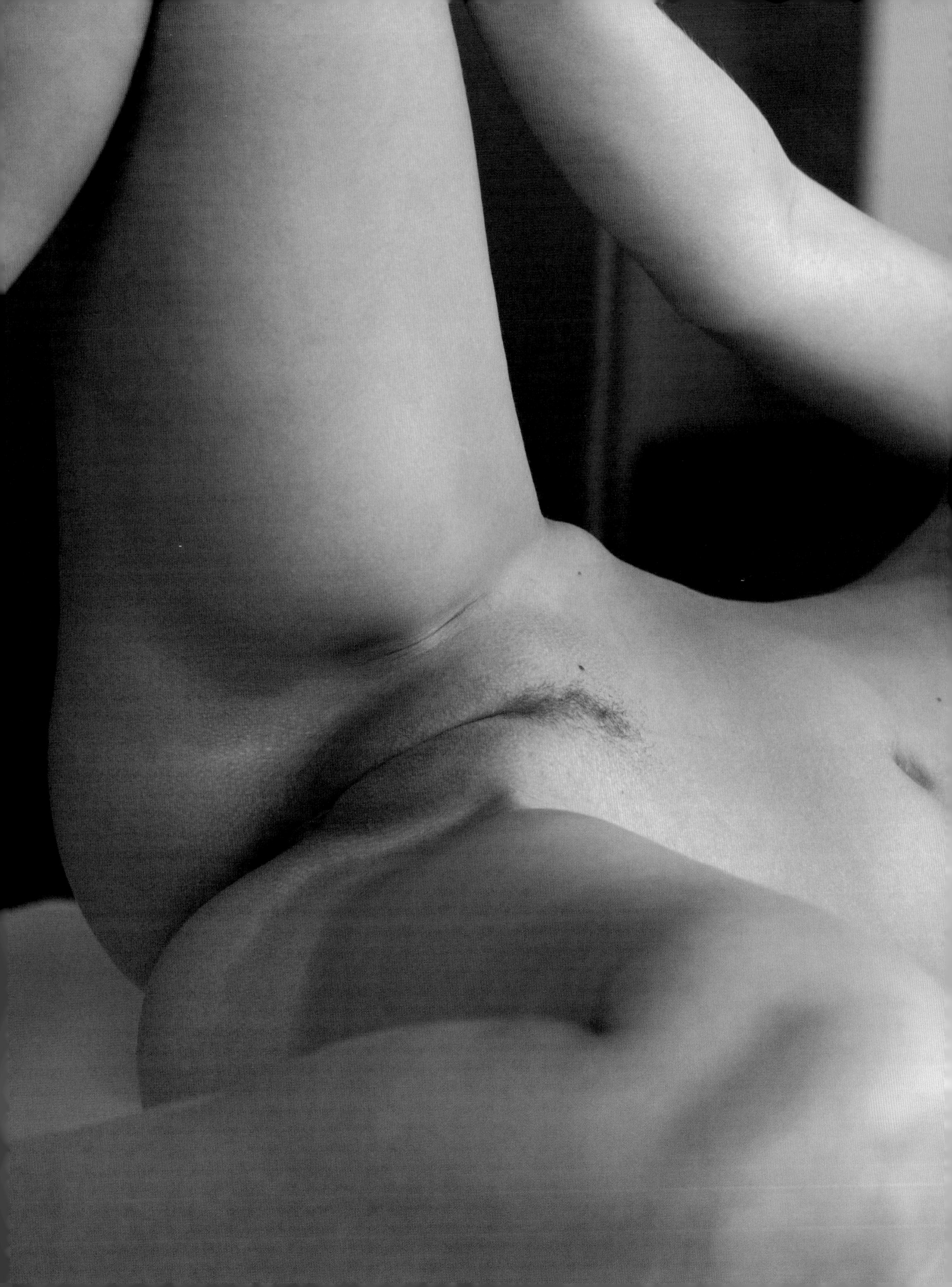

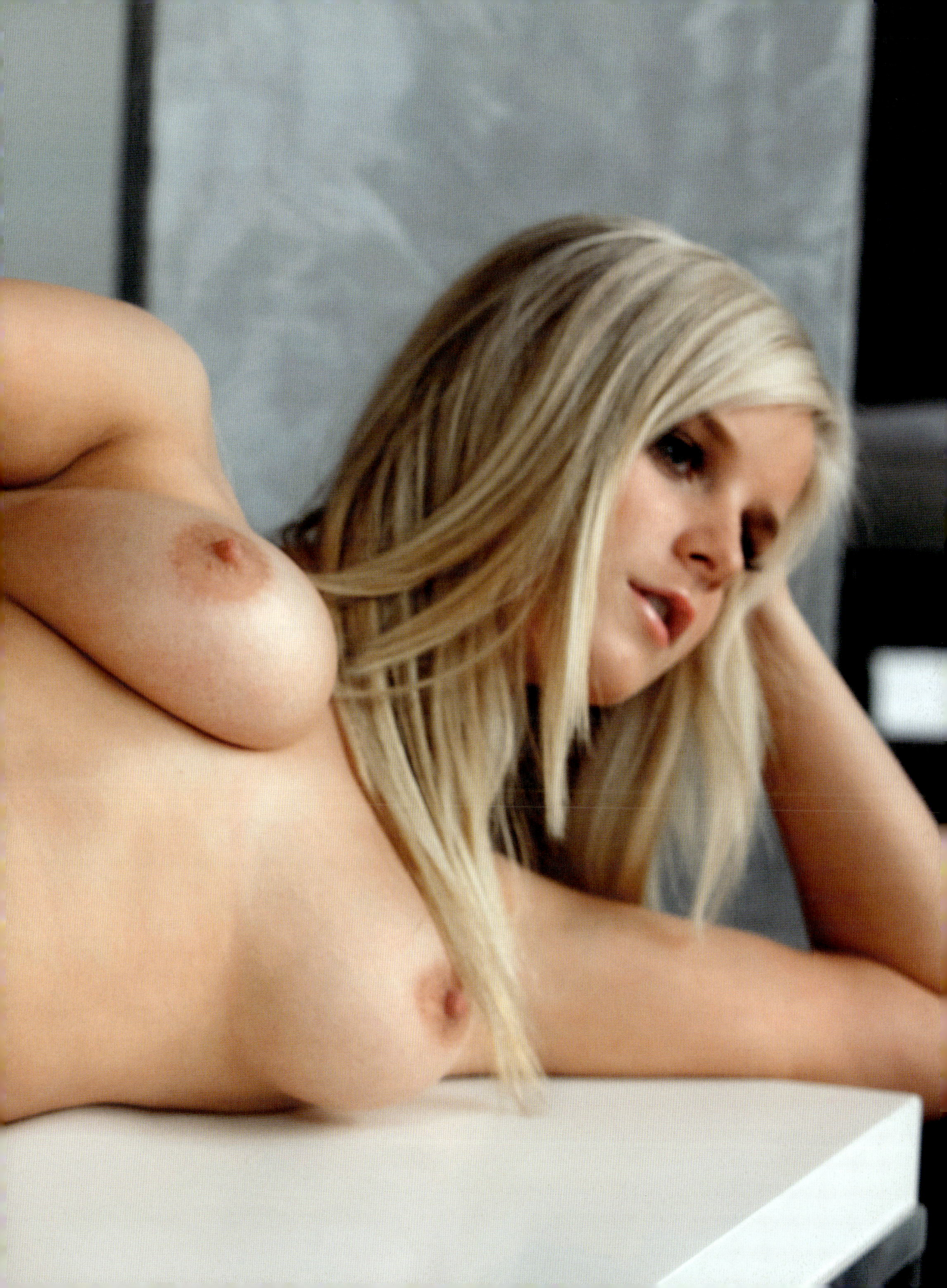

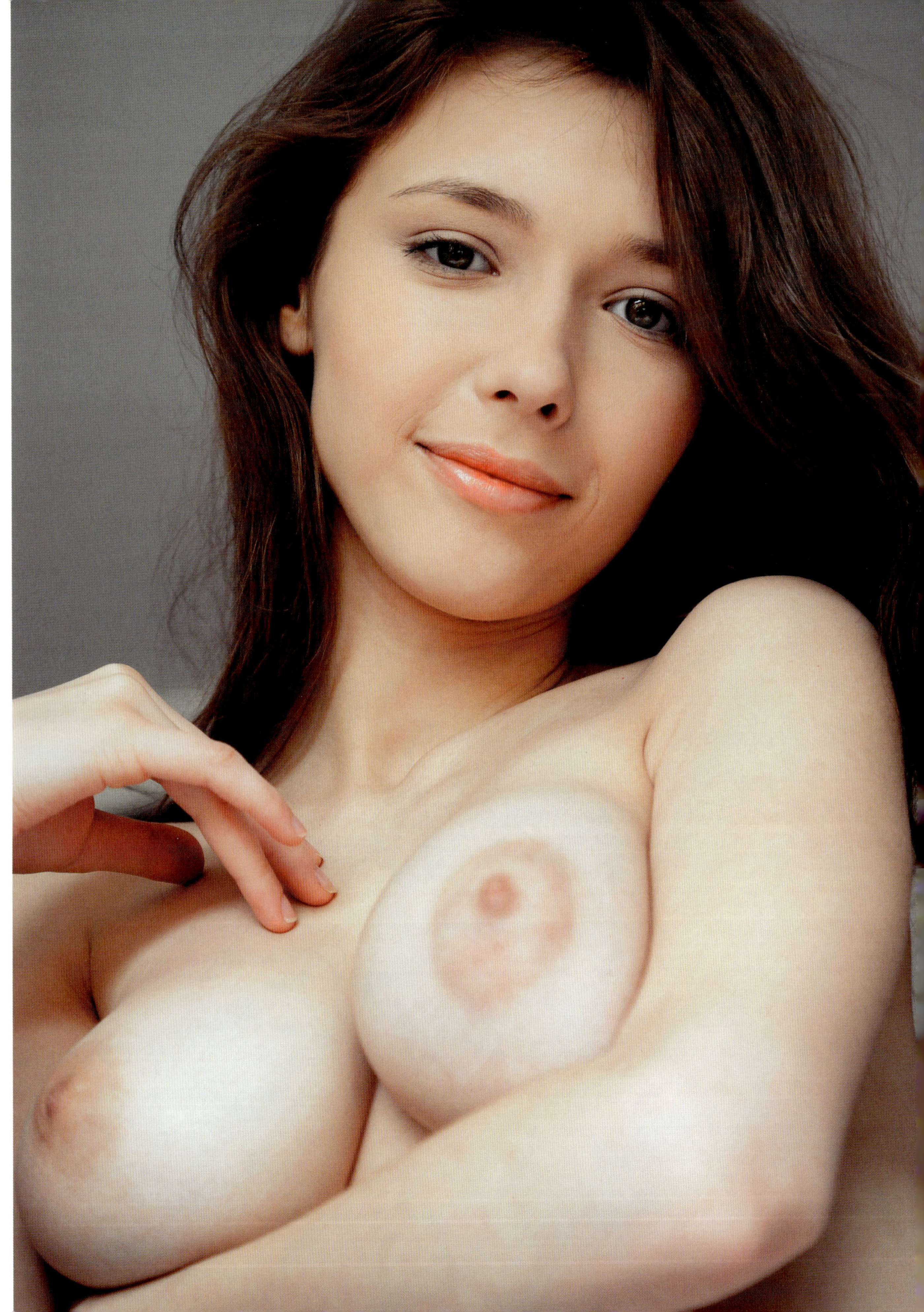

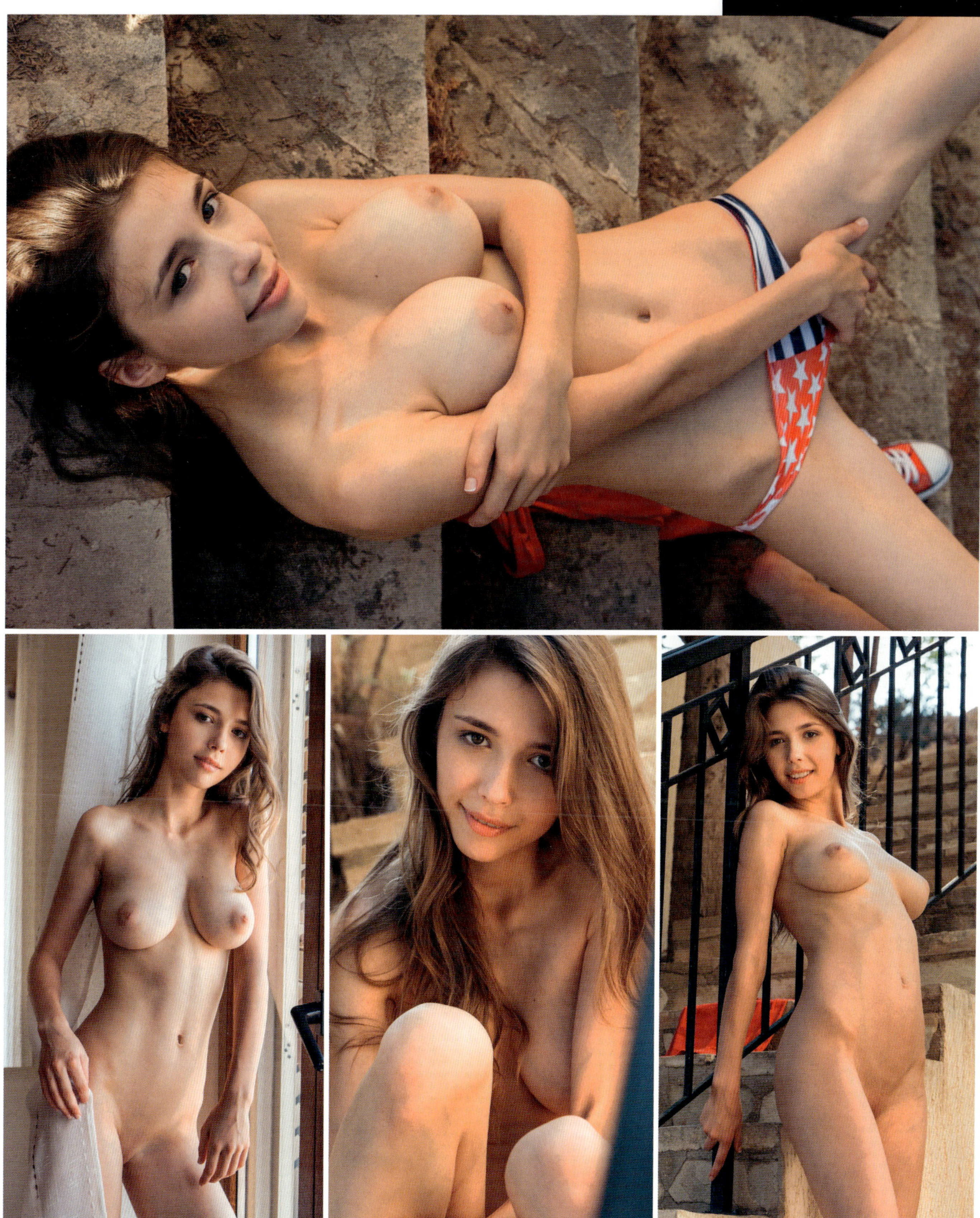

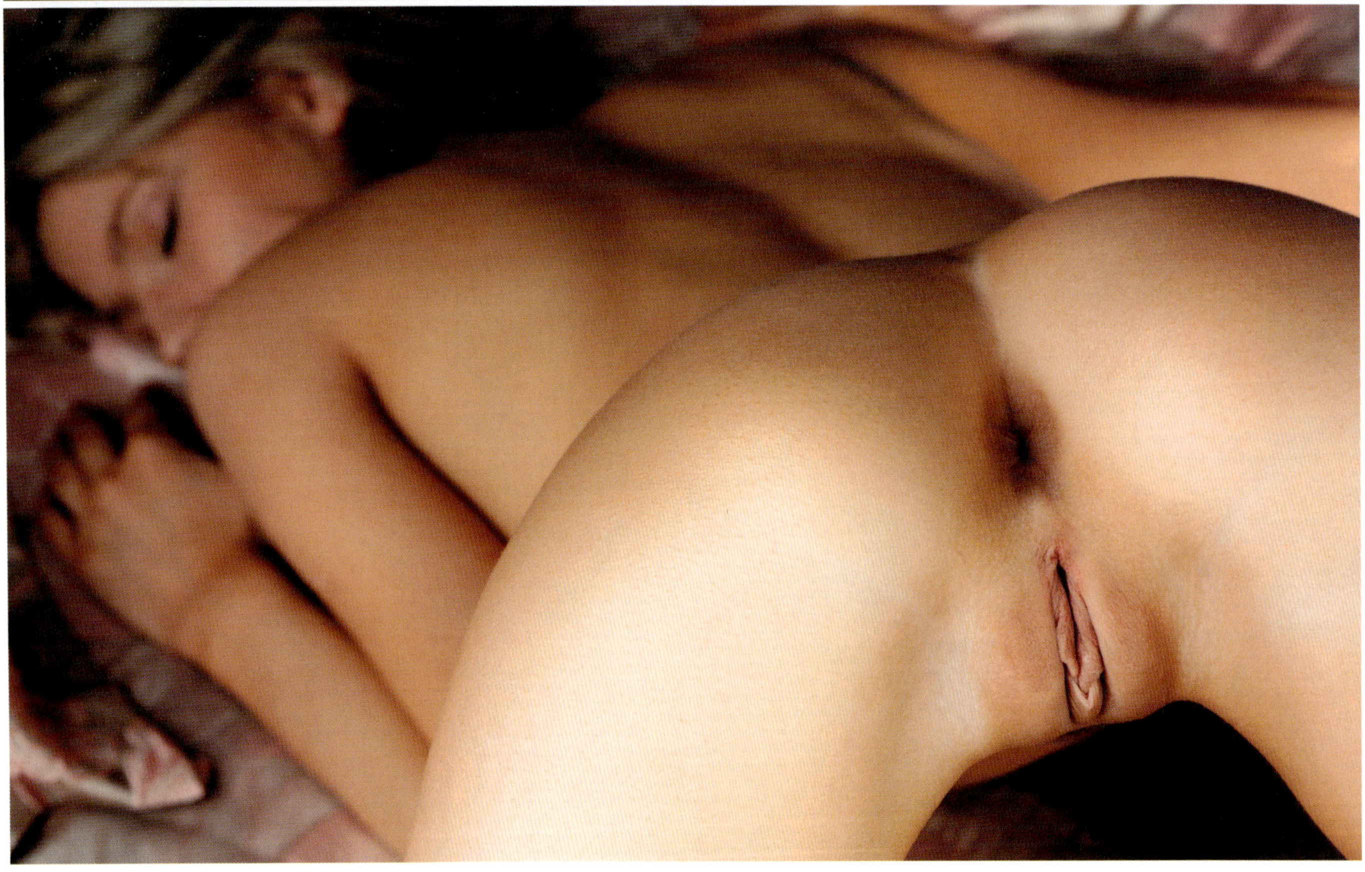

Mila I

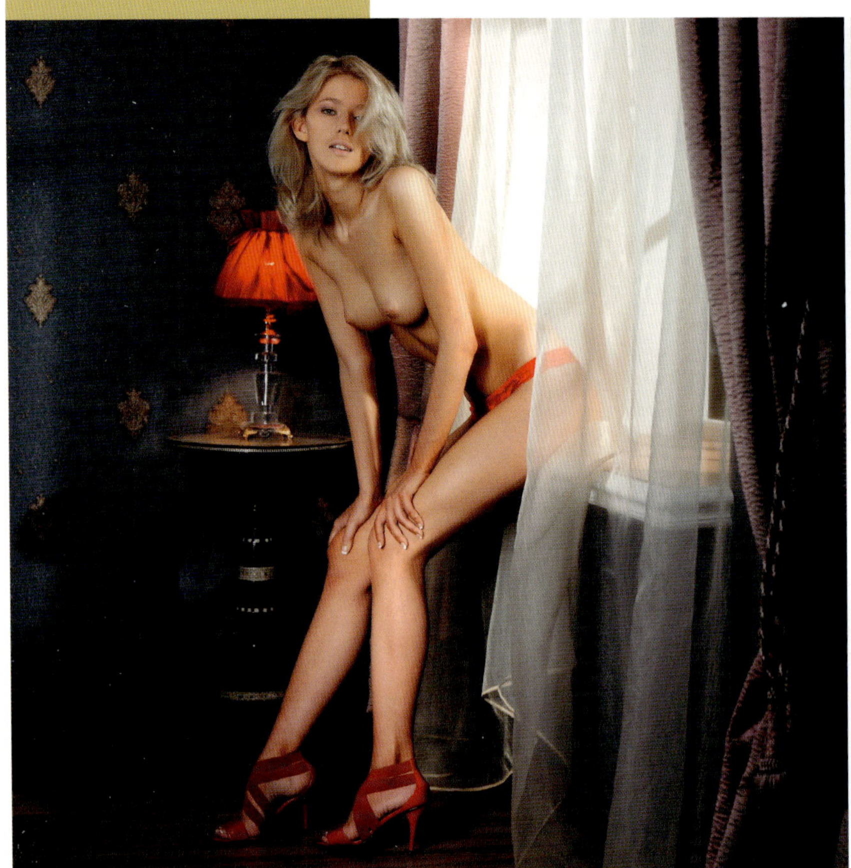

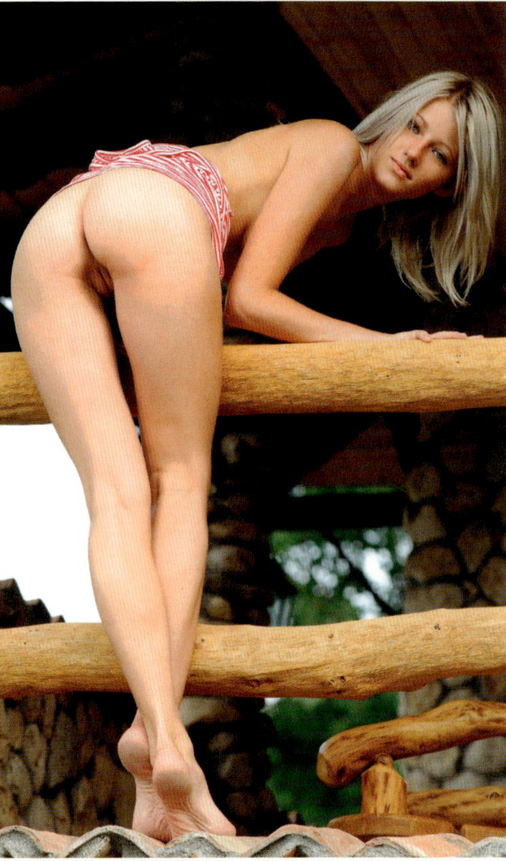

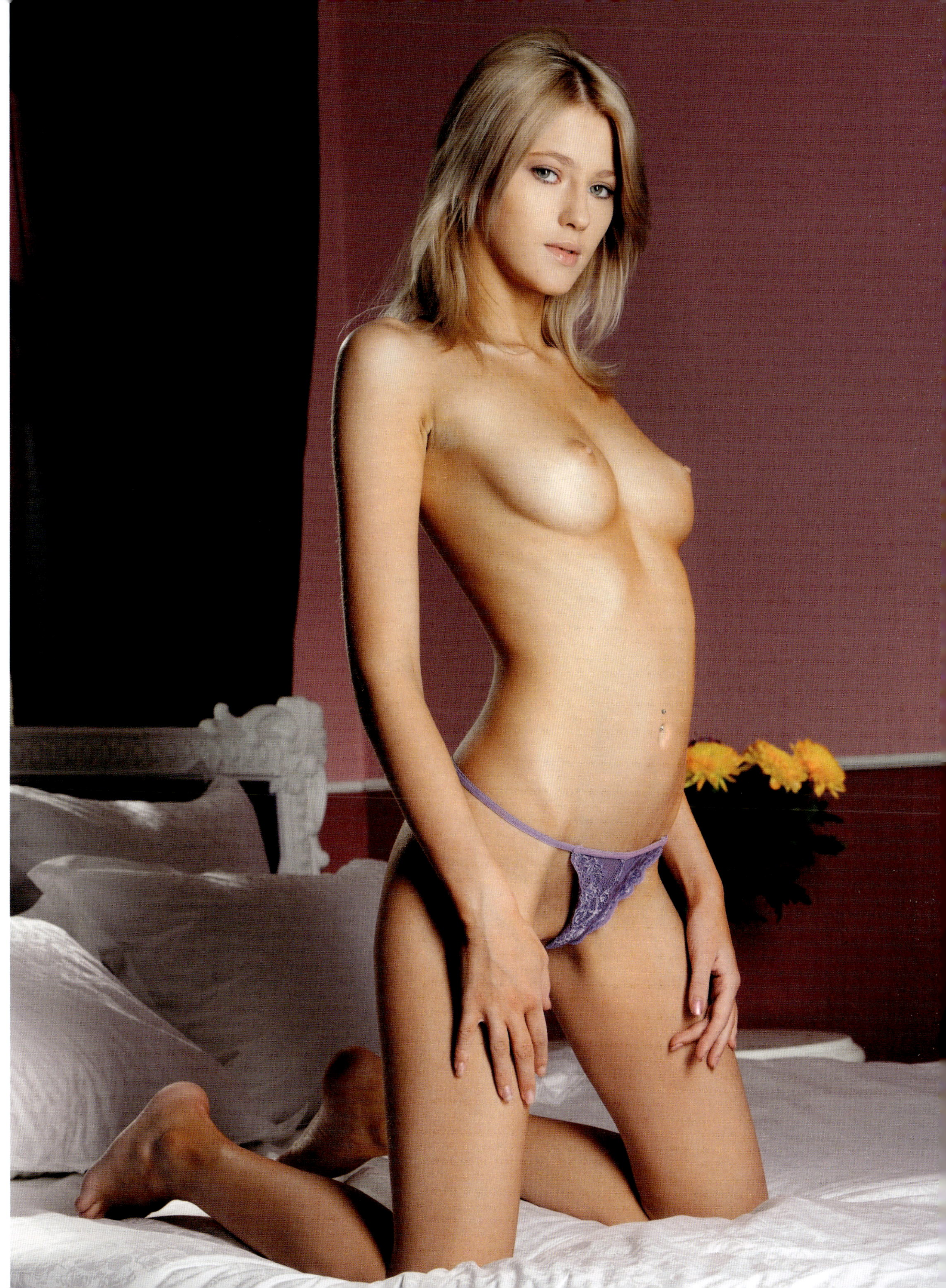

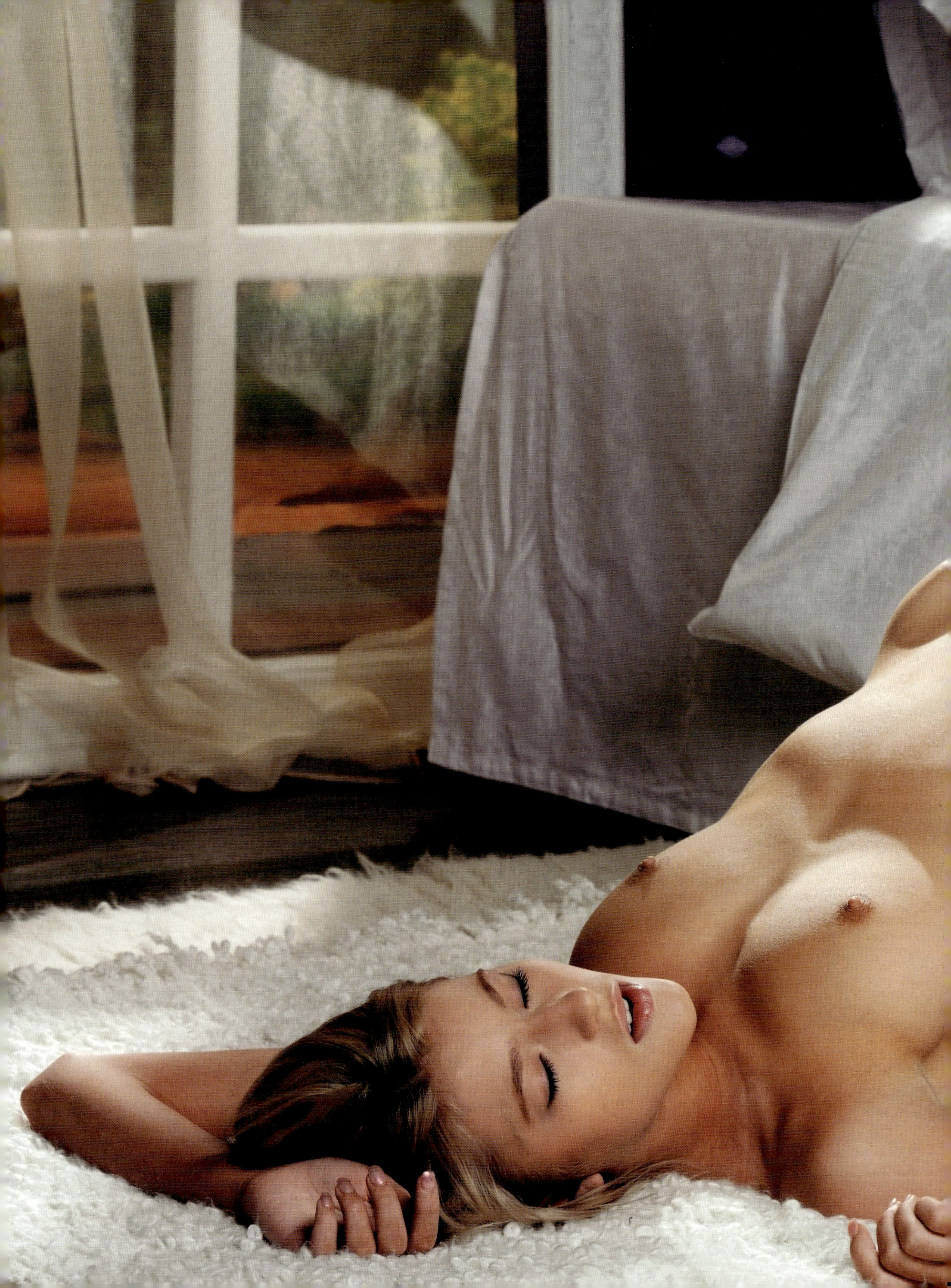

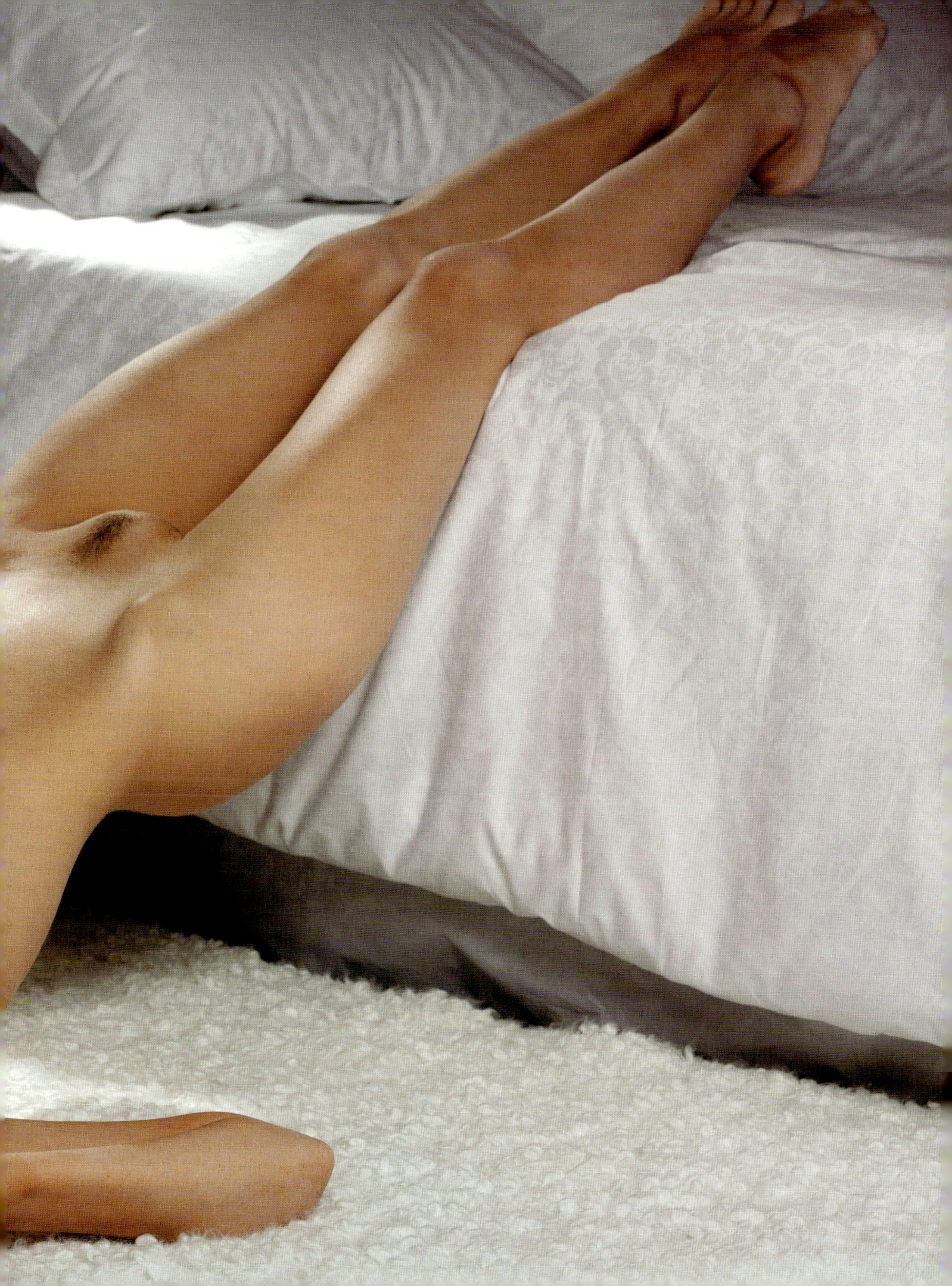

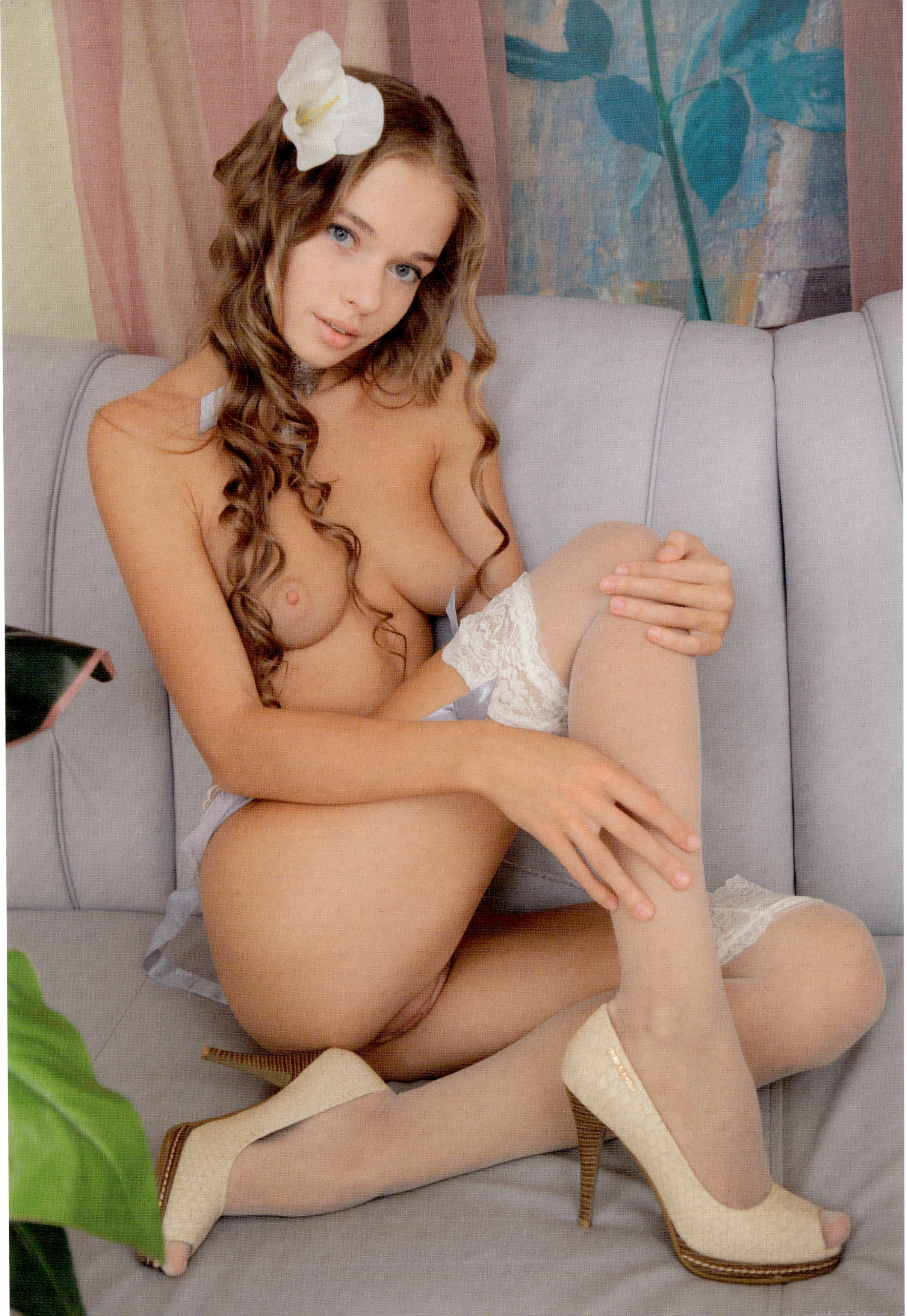

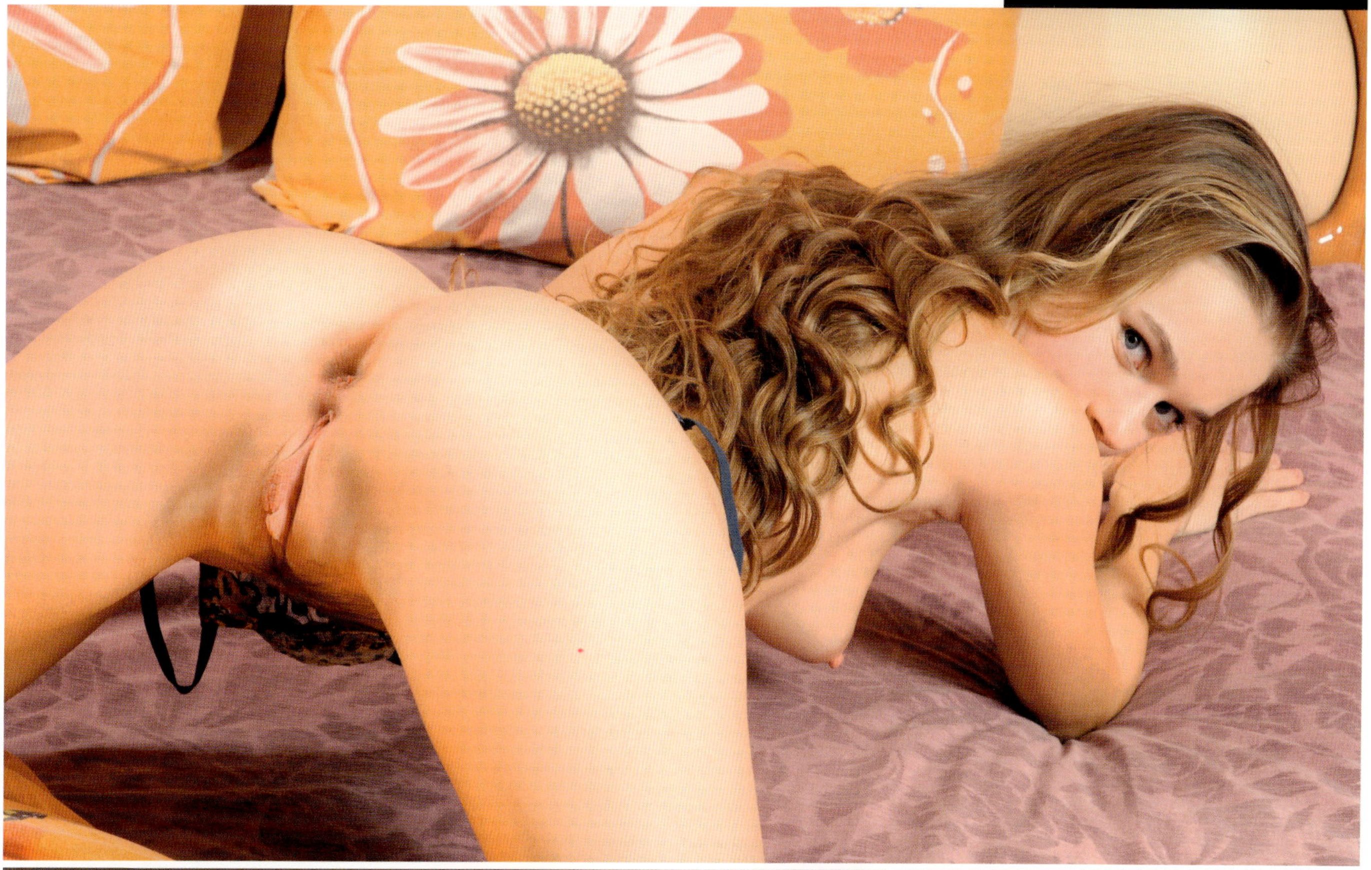

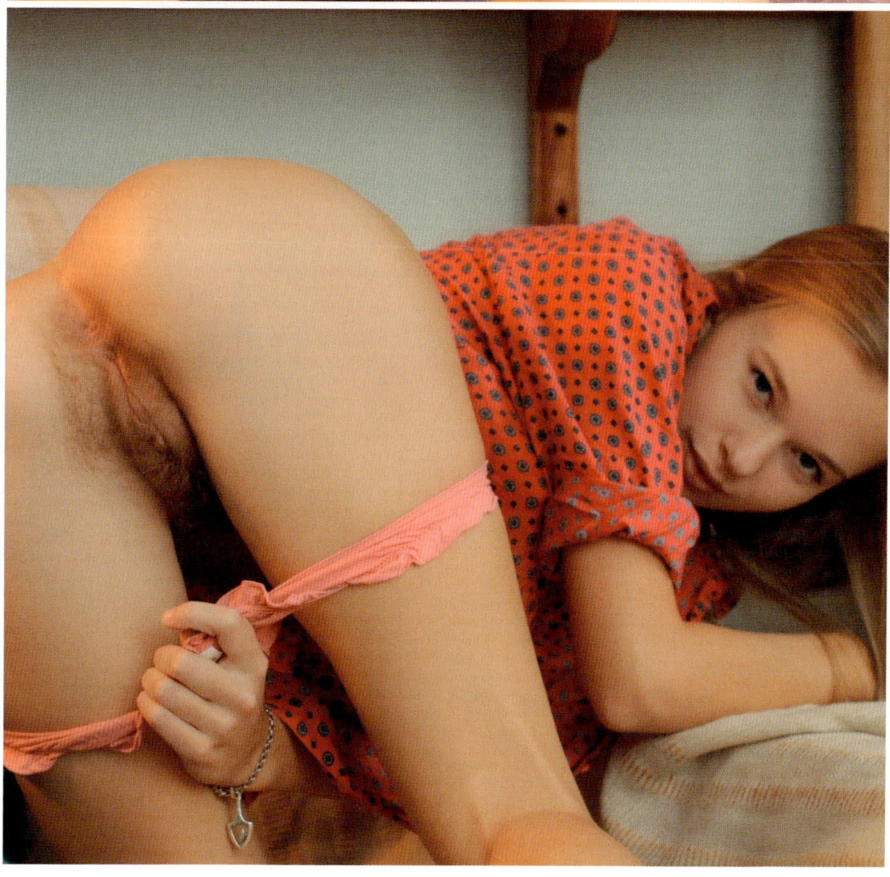

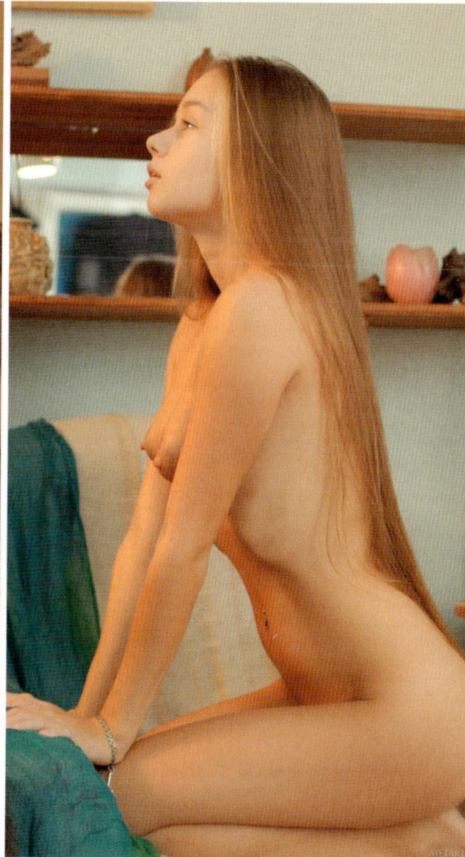

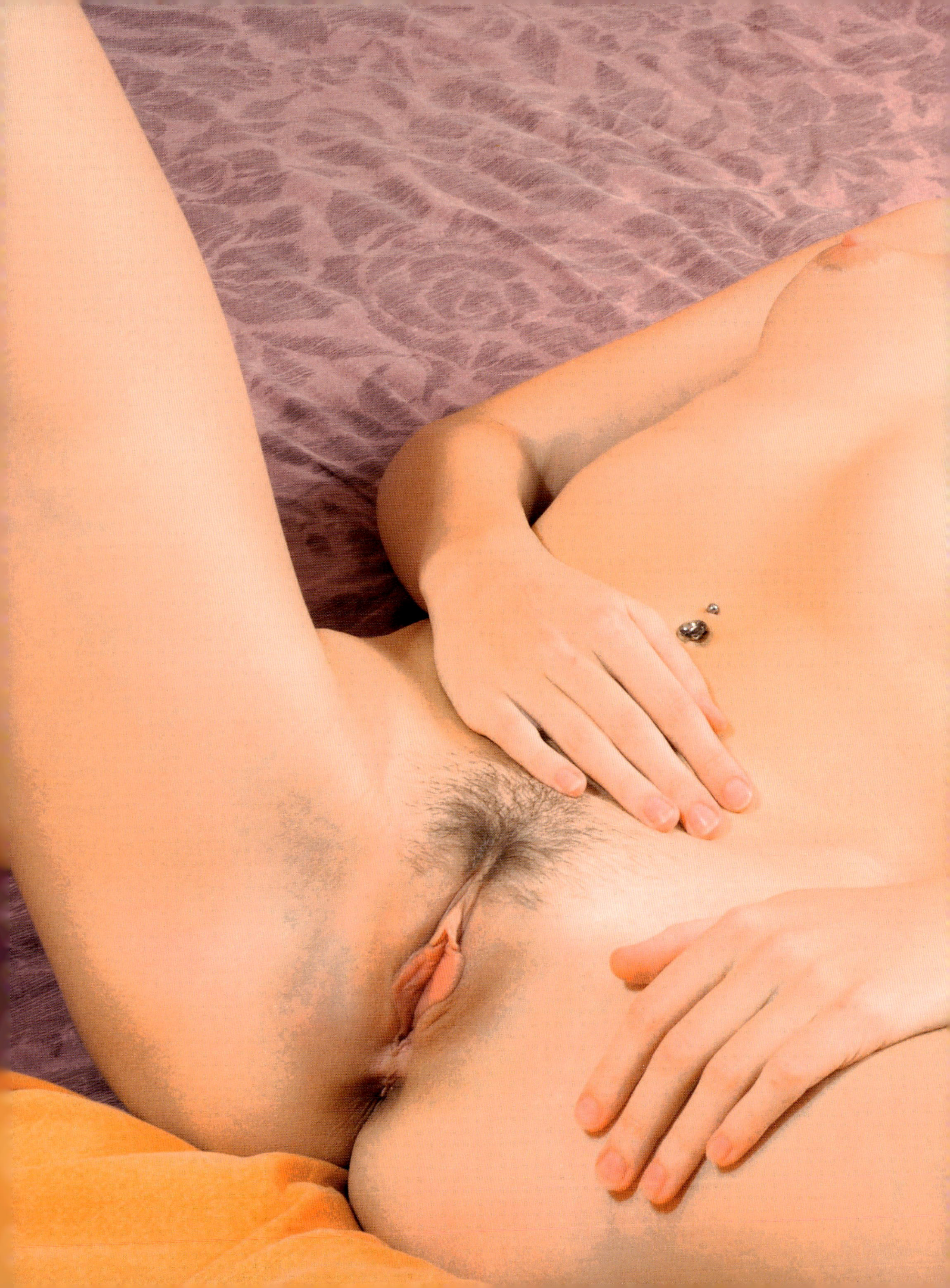

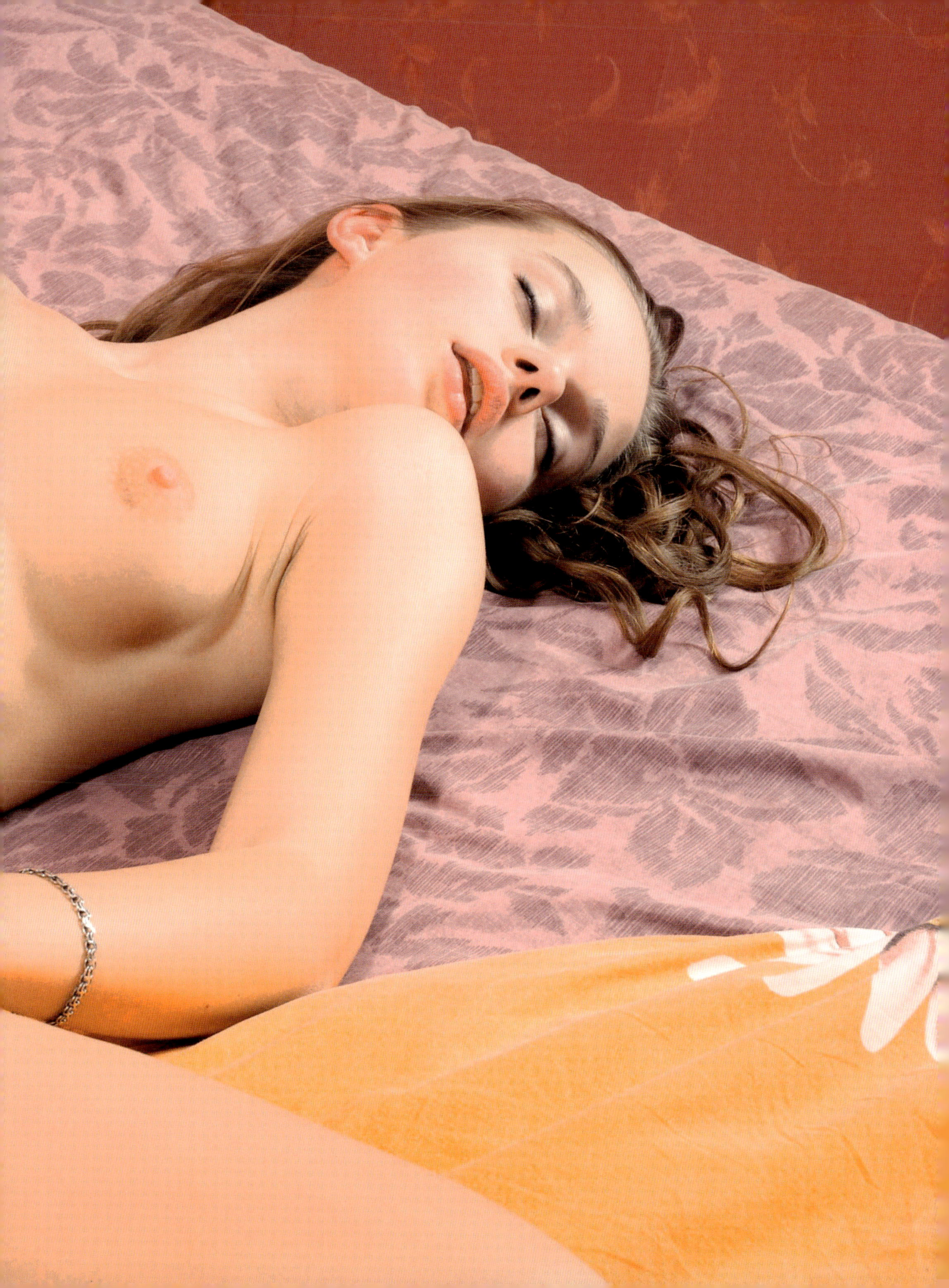

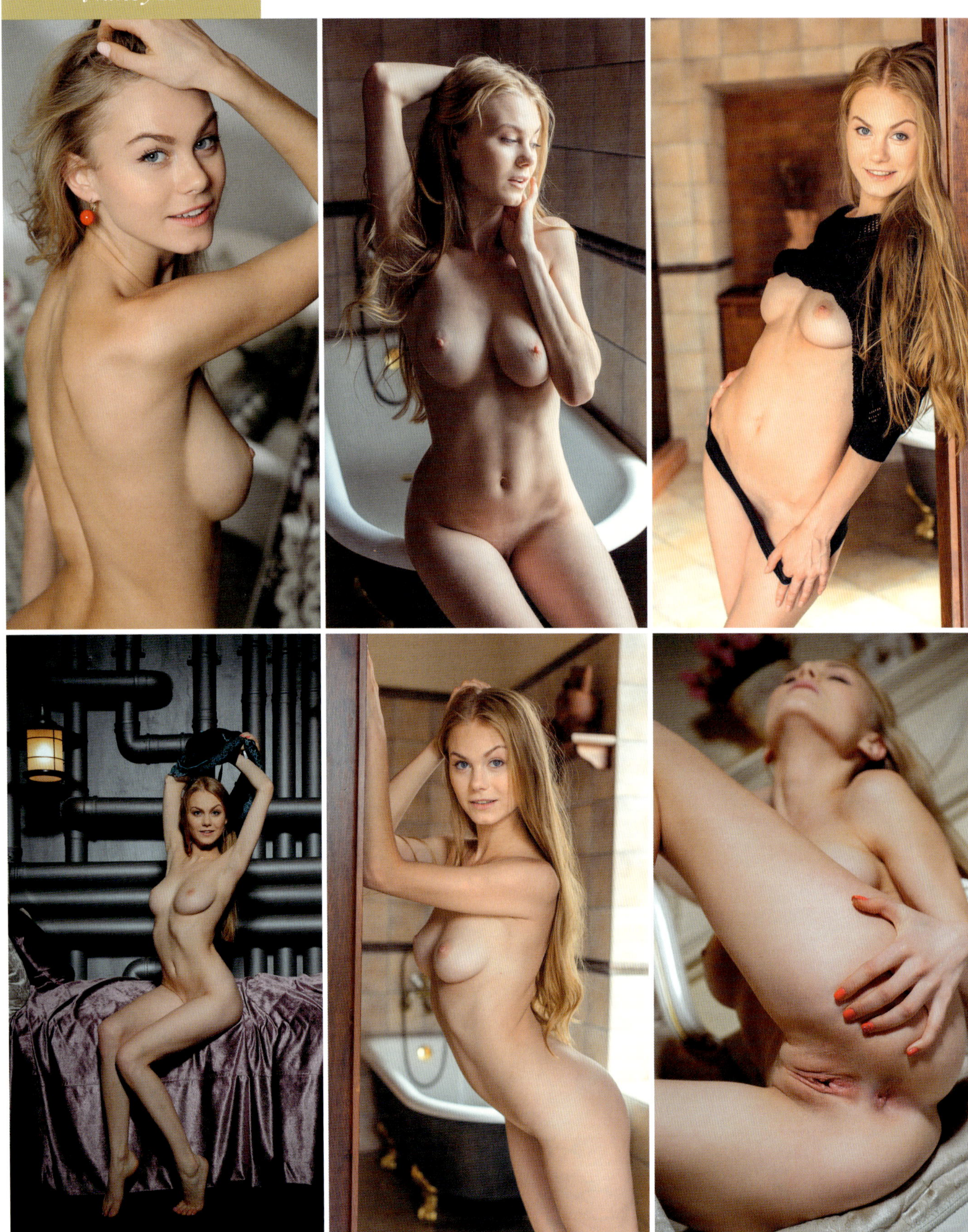

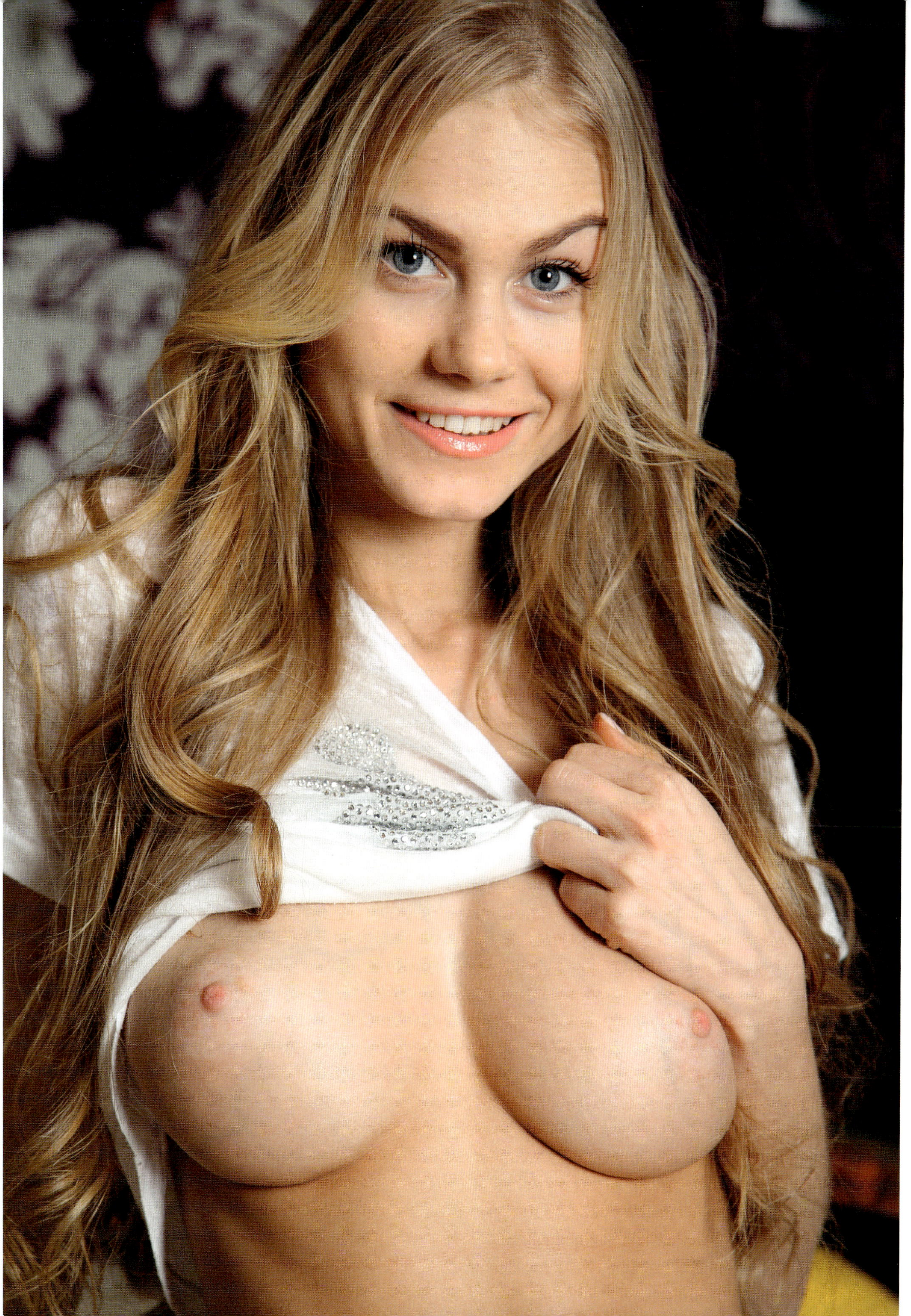

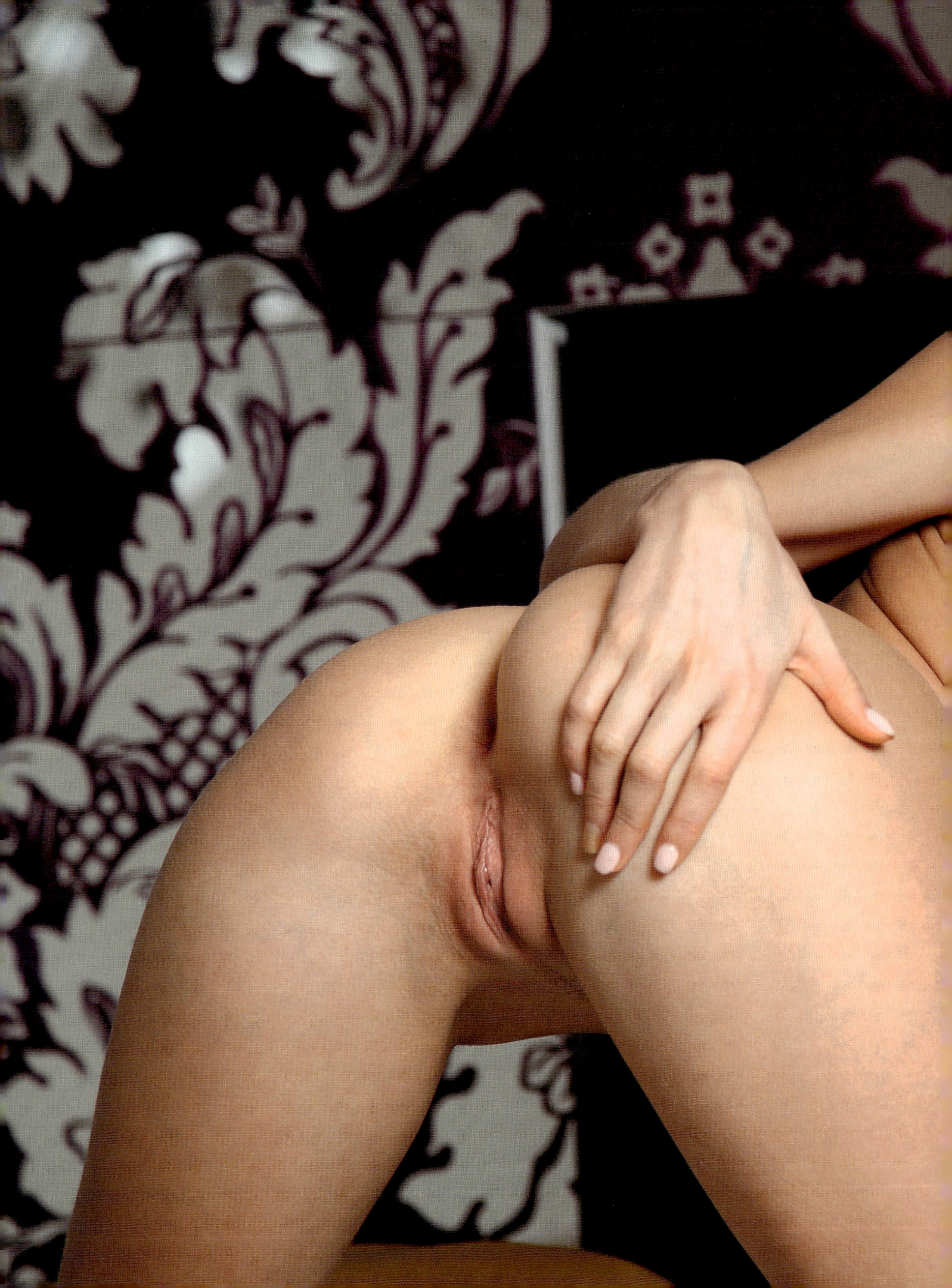

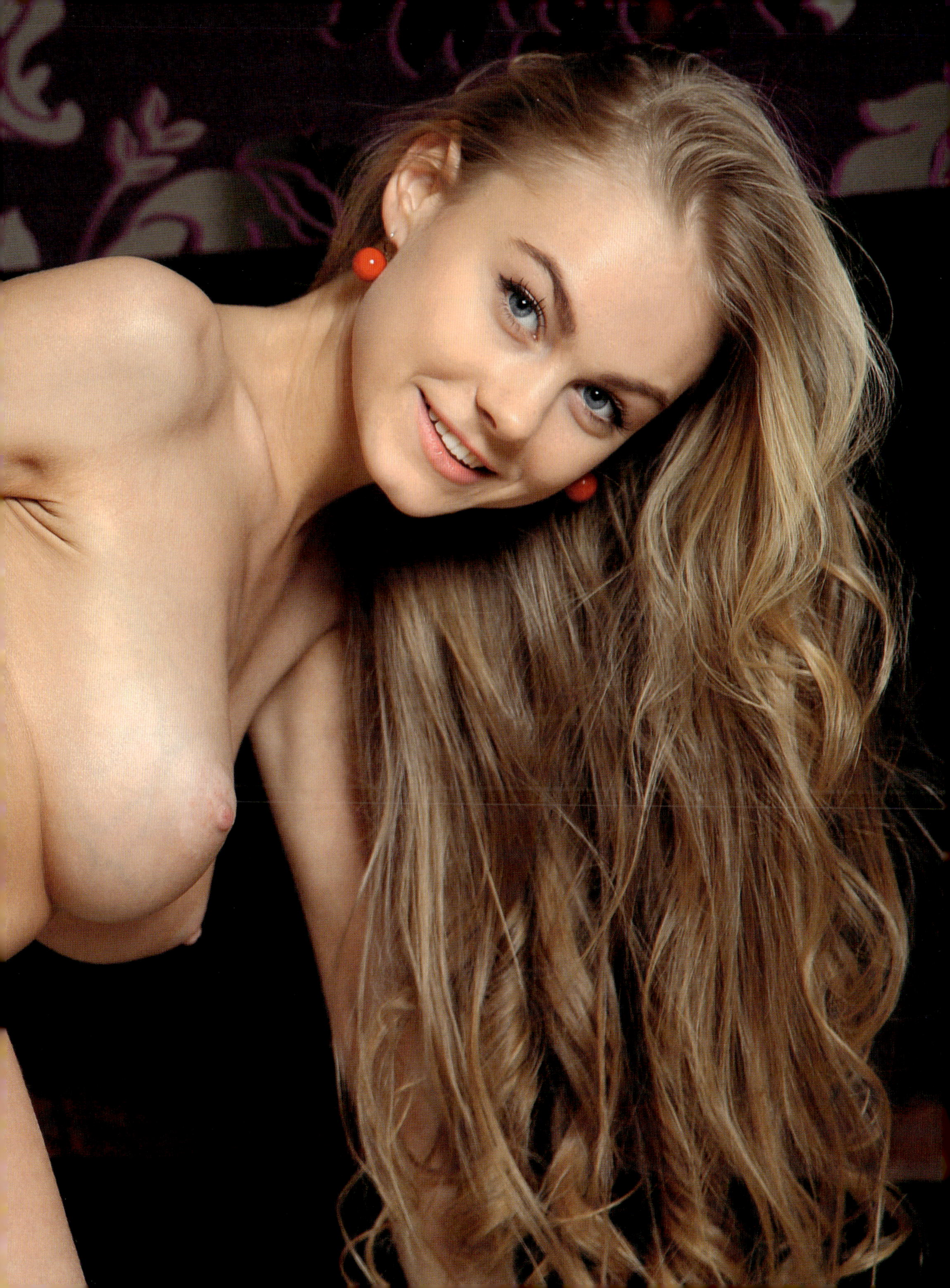

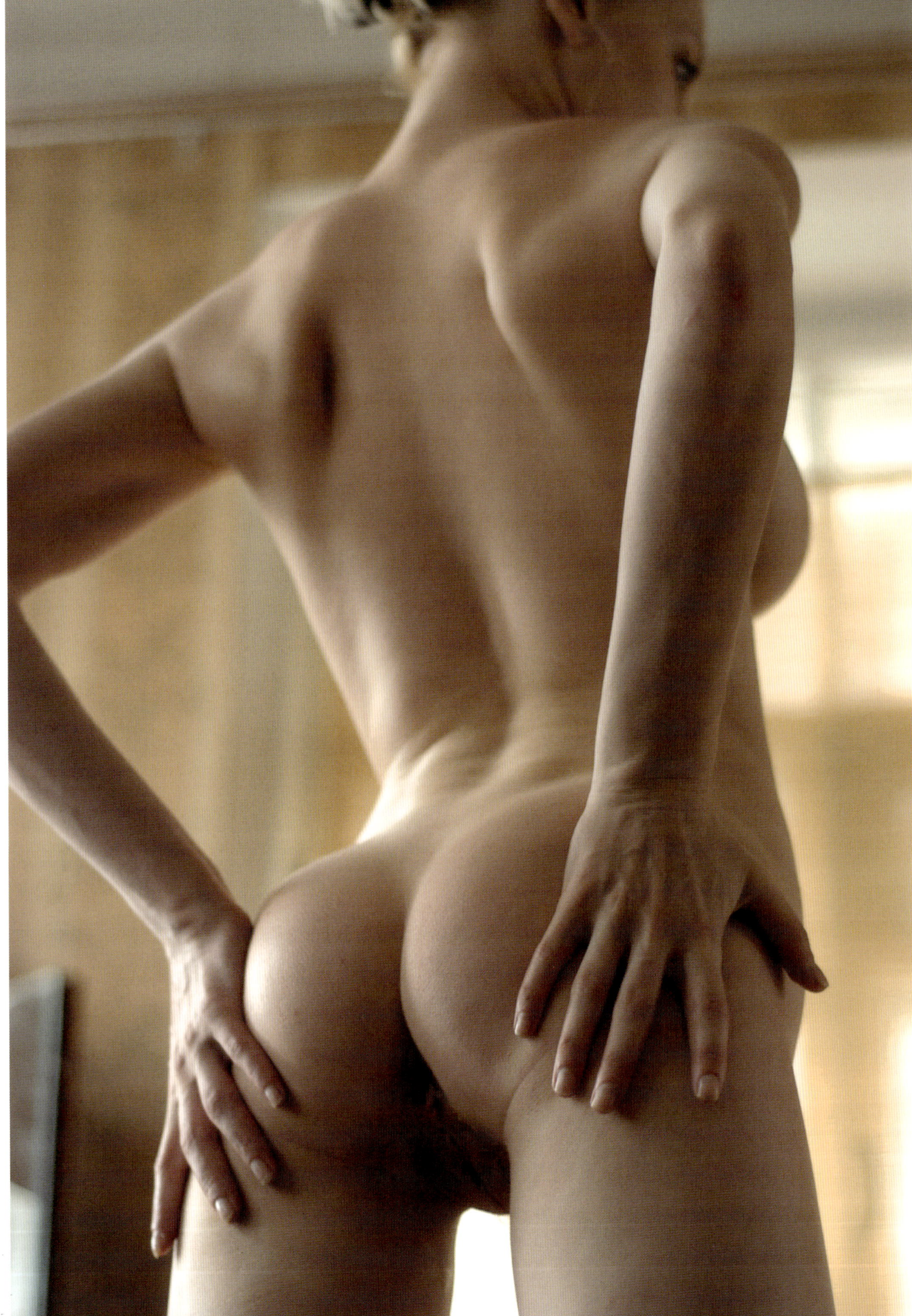

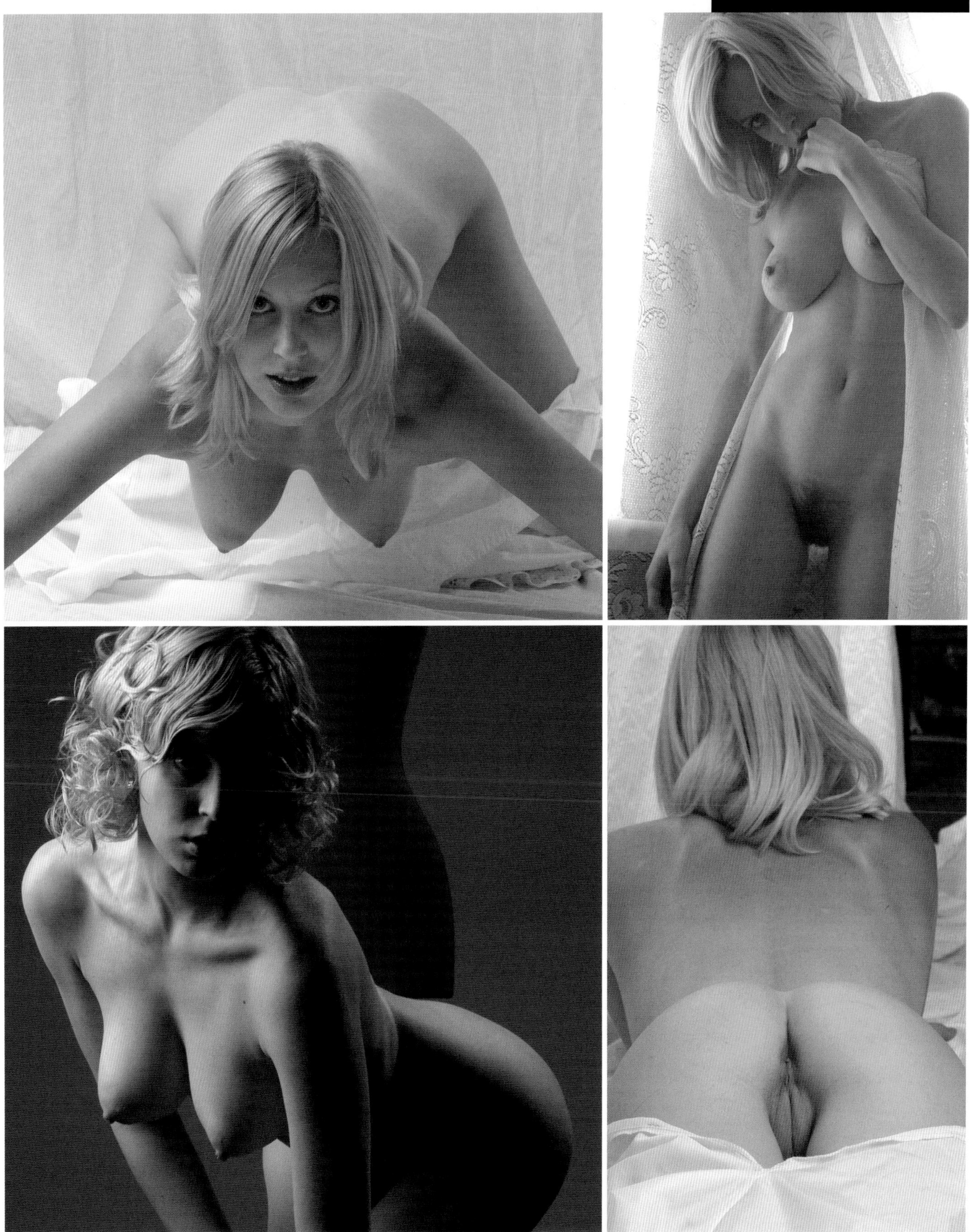

## *Nici Dee*

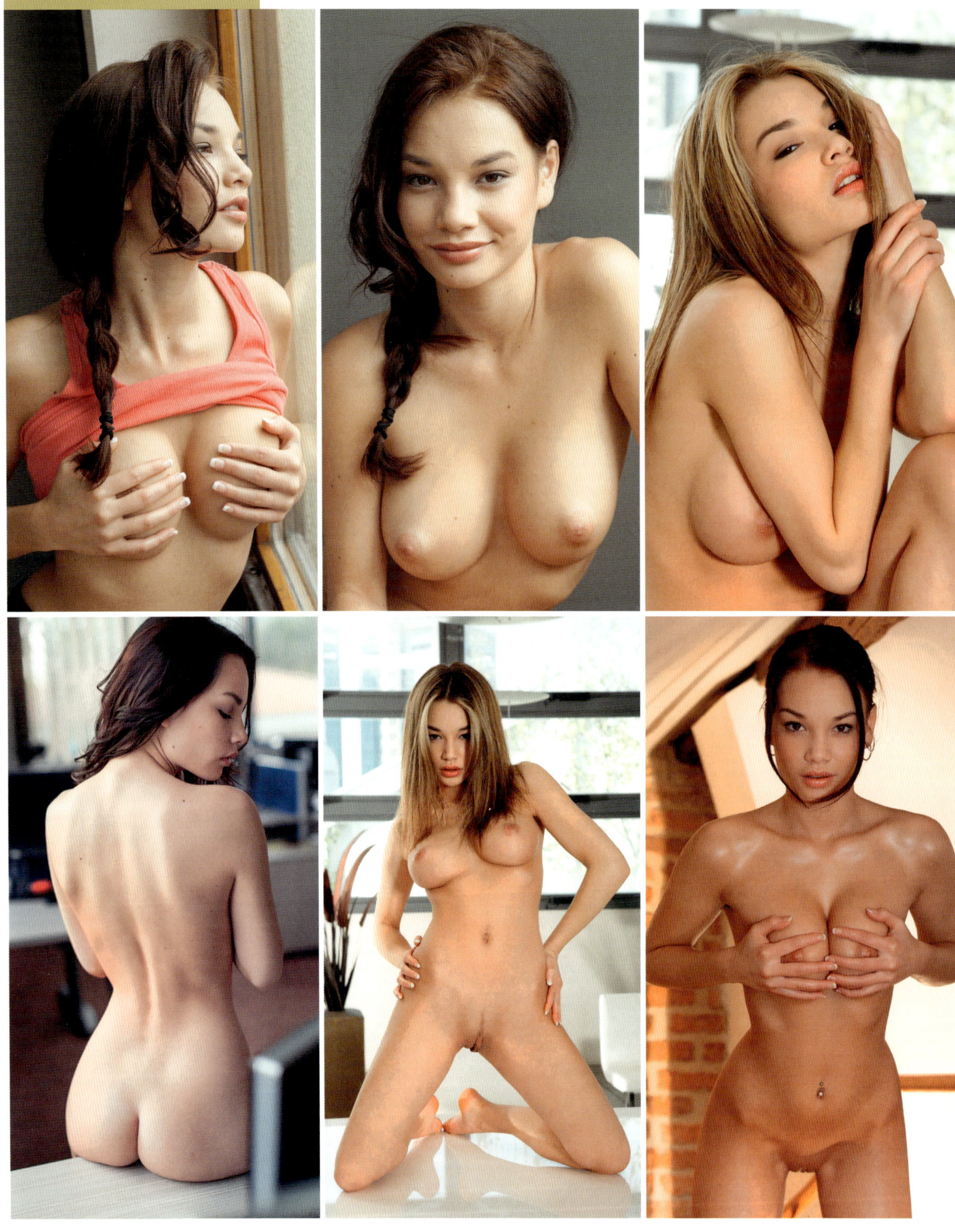

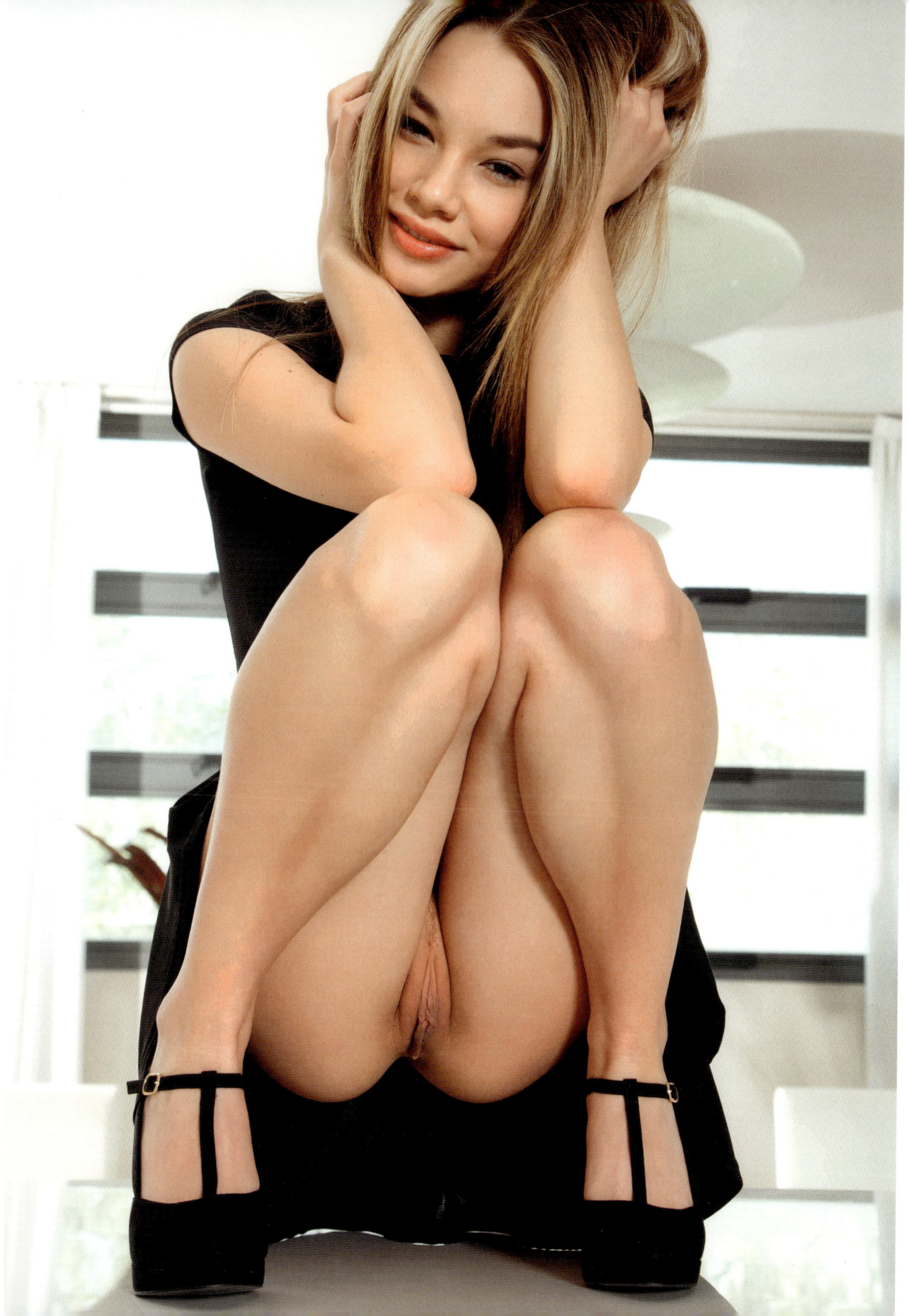

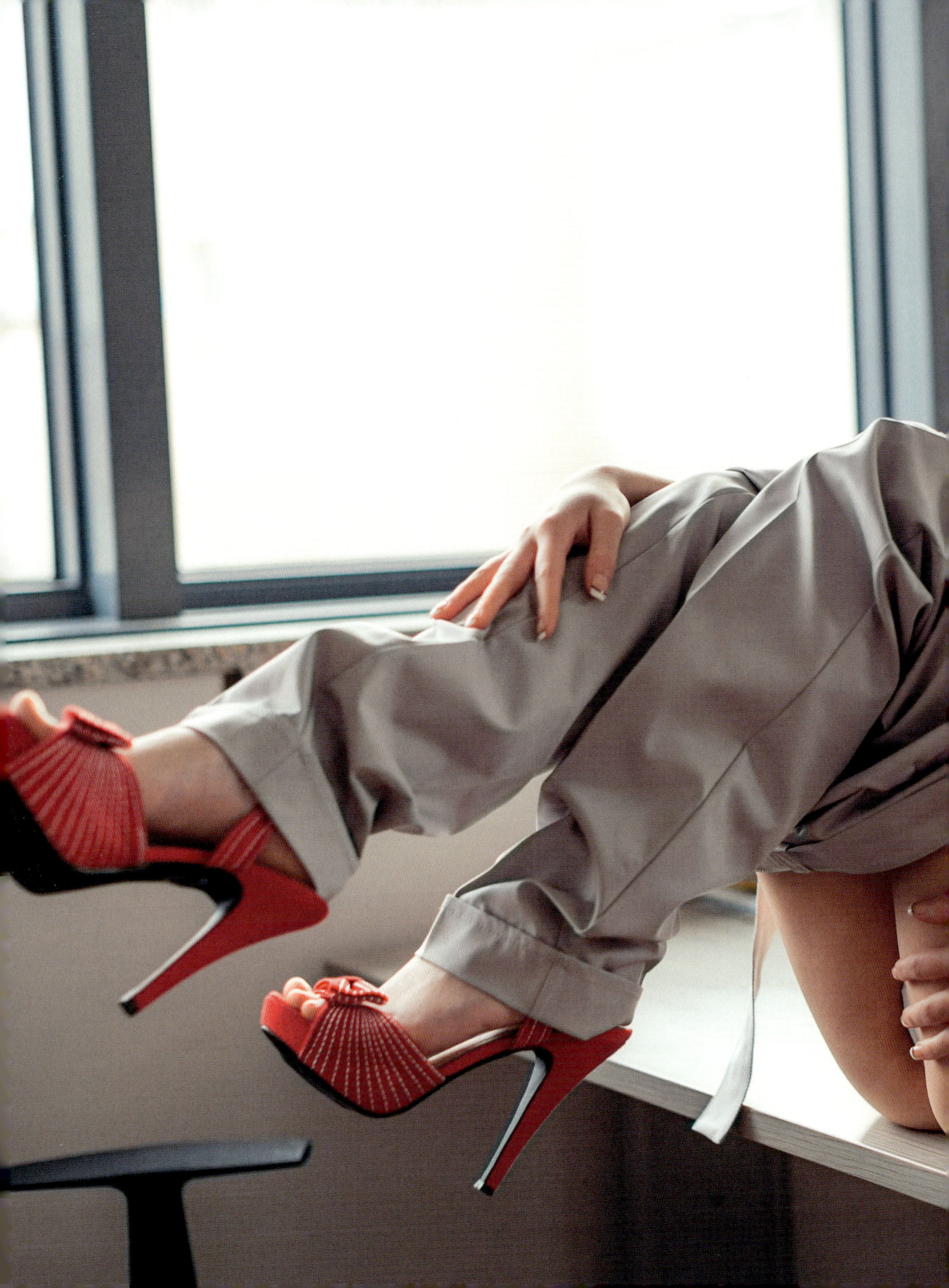

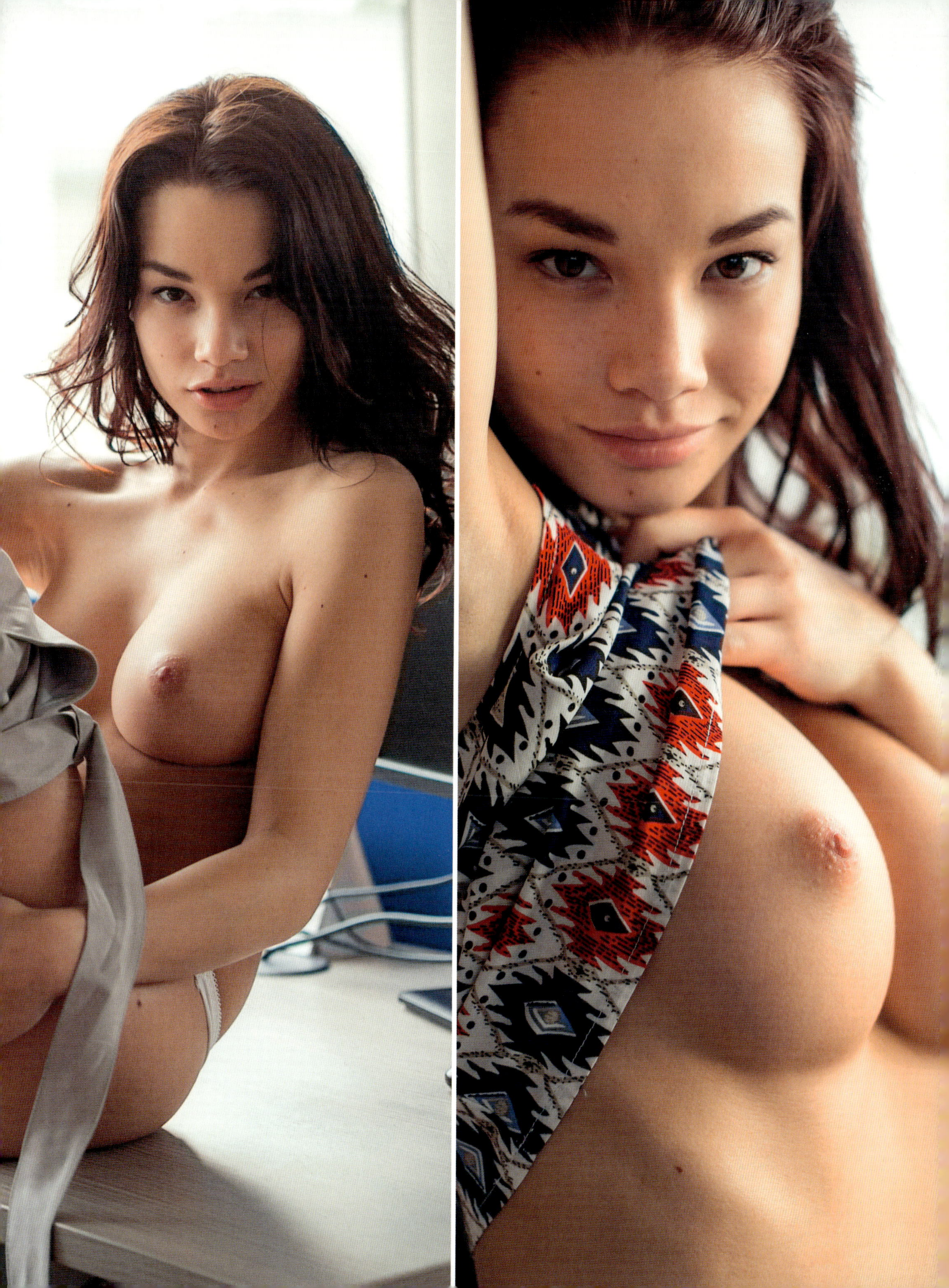

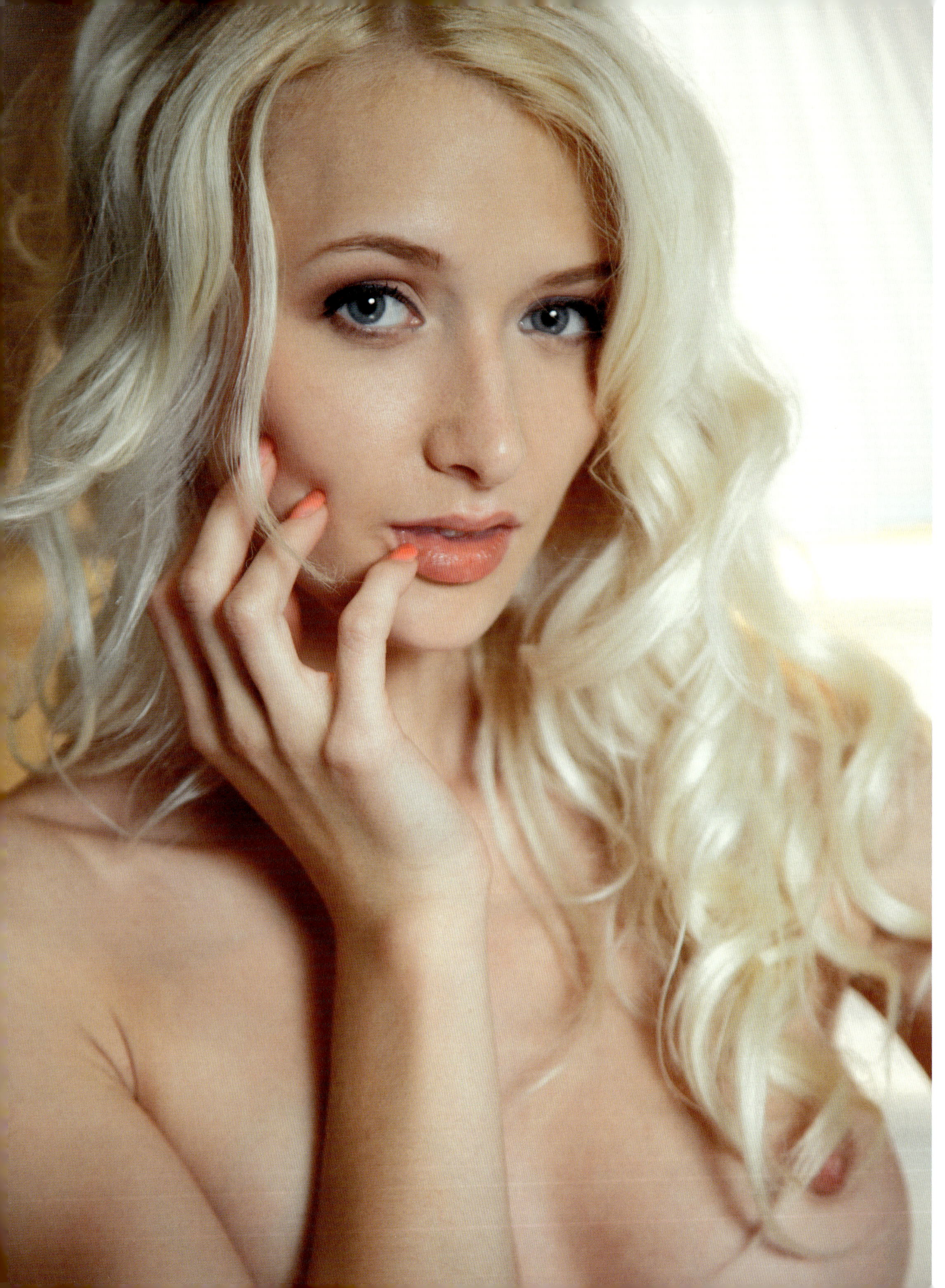

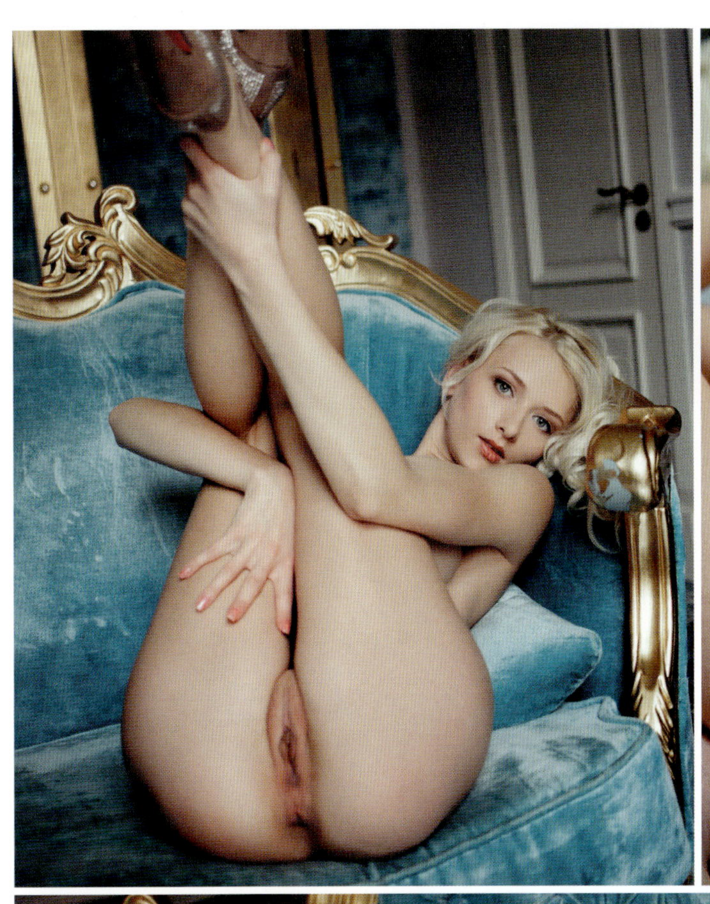

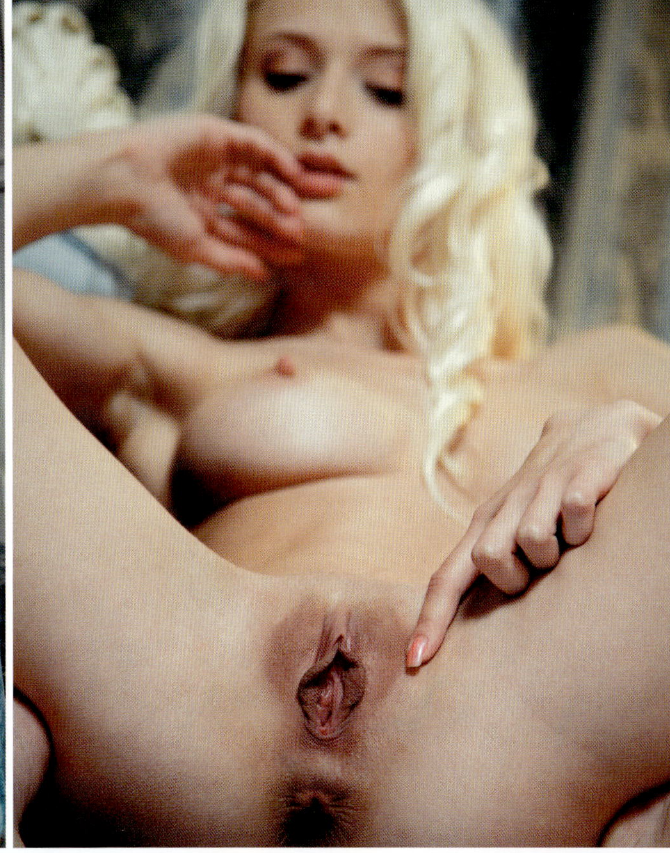

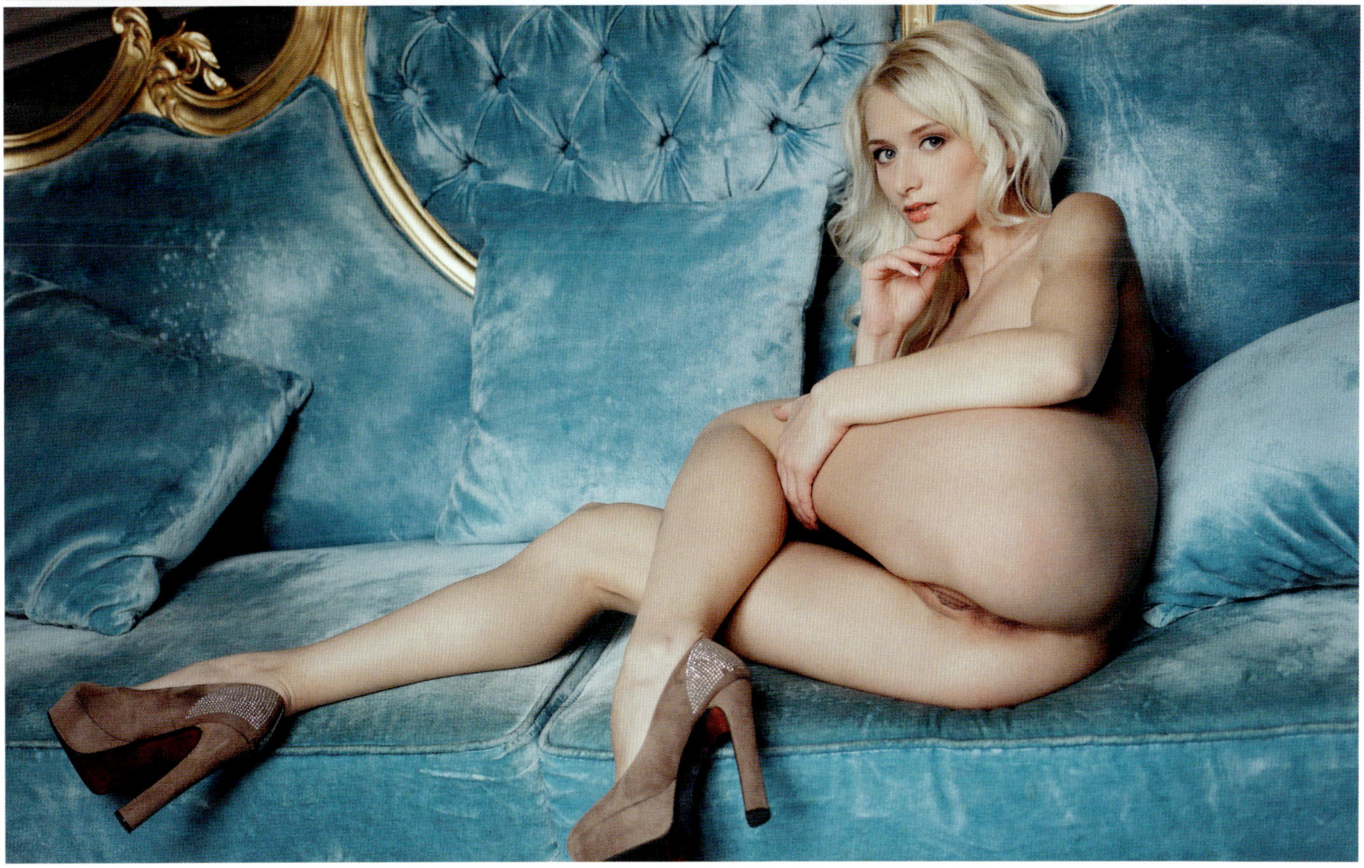

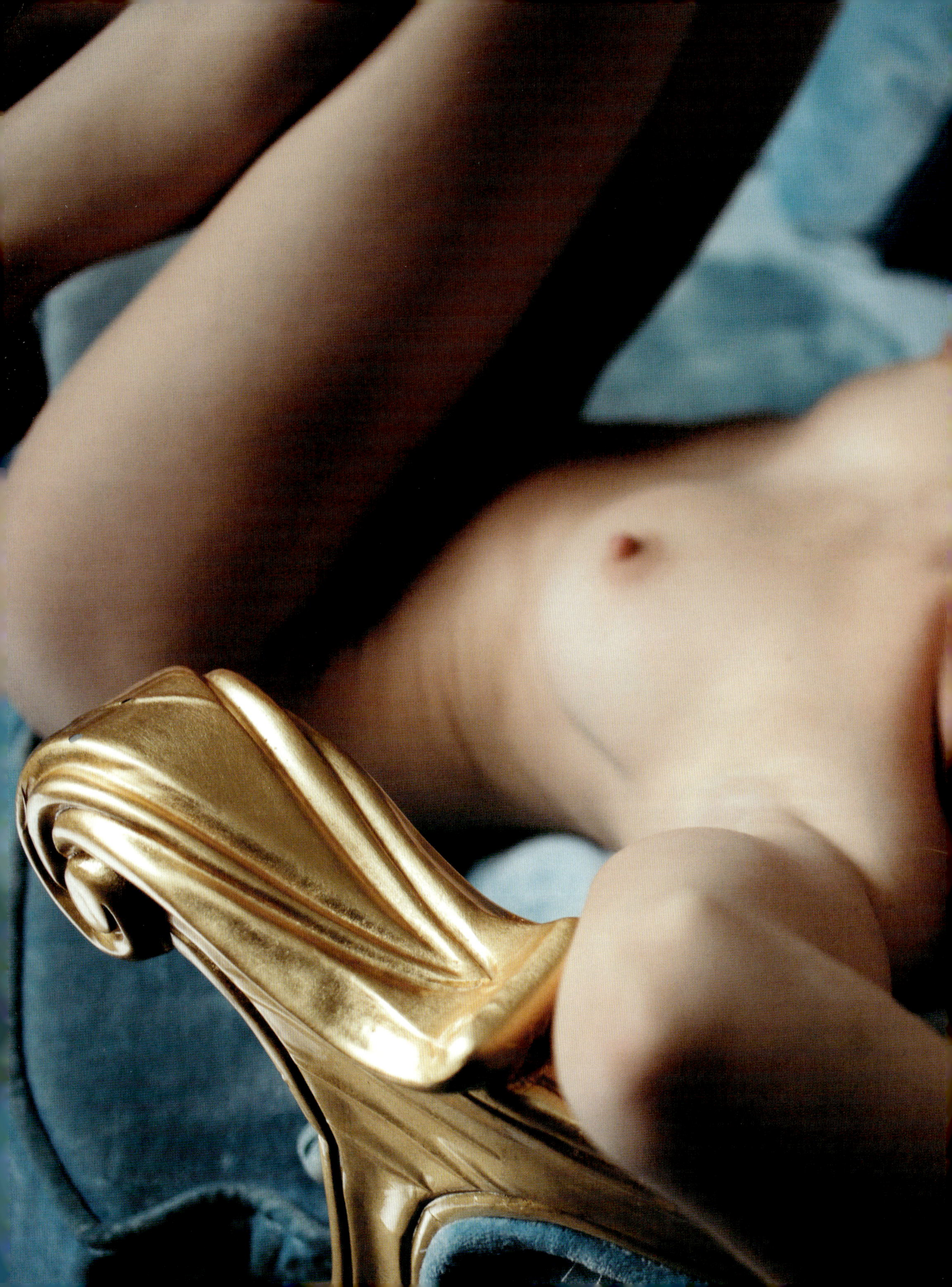

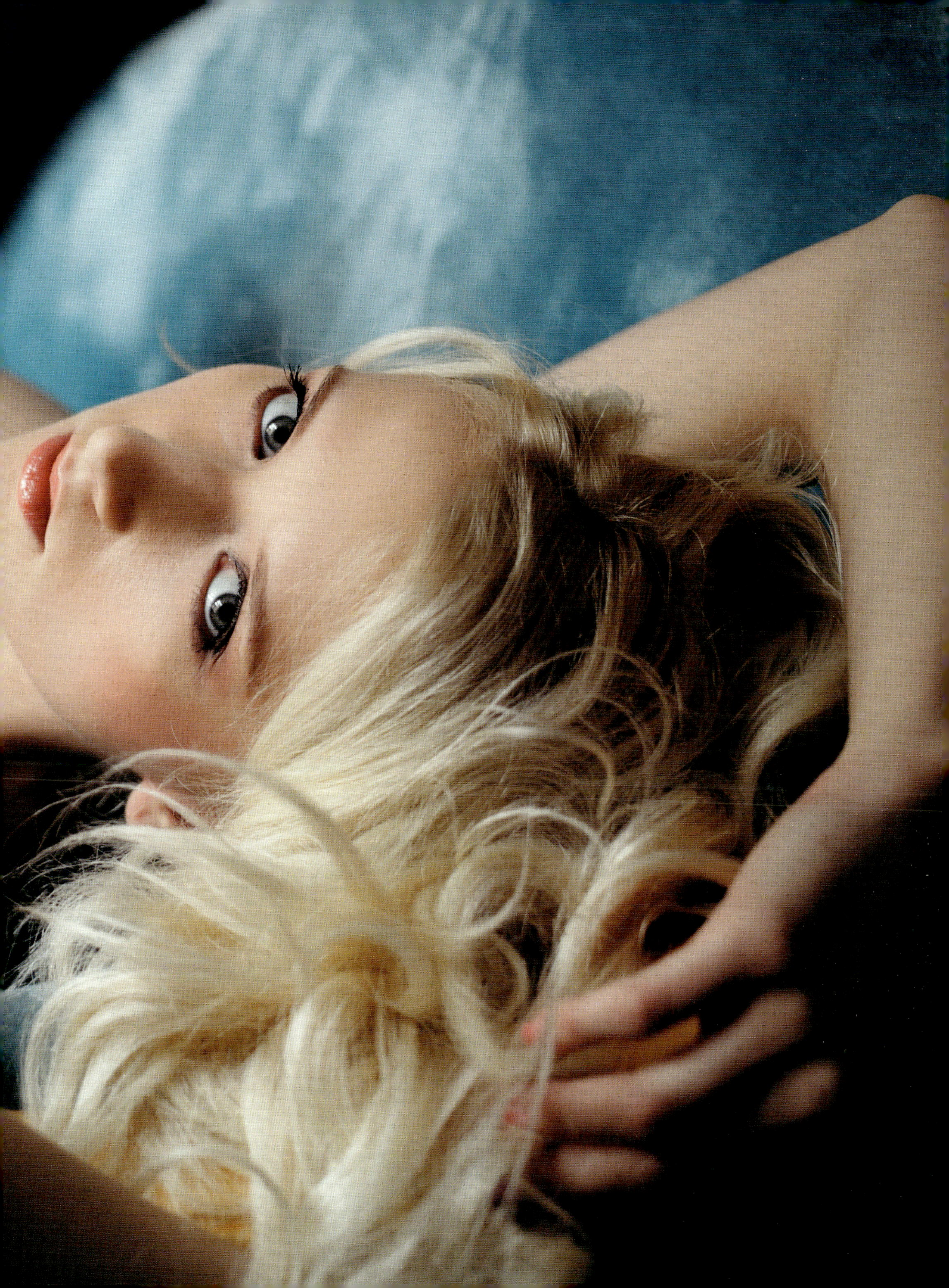

# Nikia A

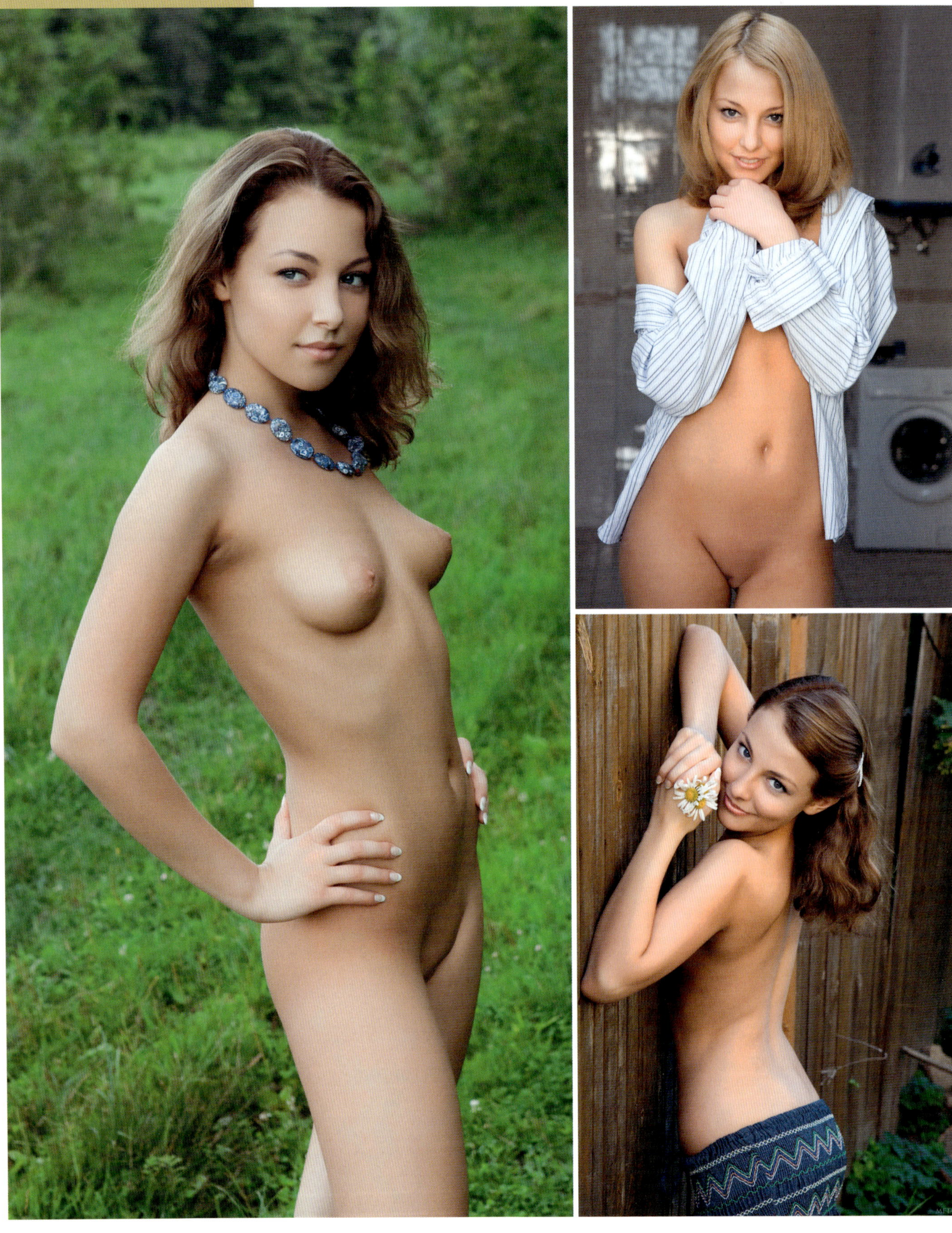

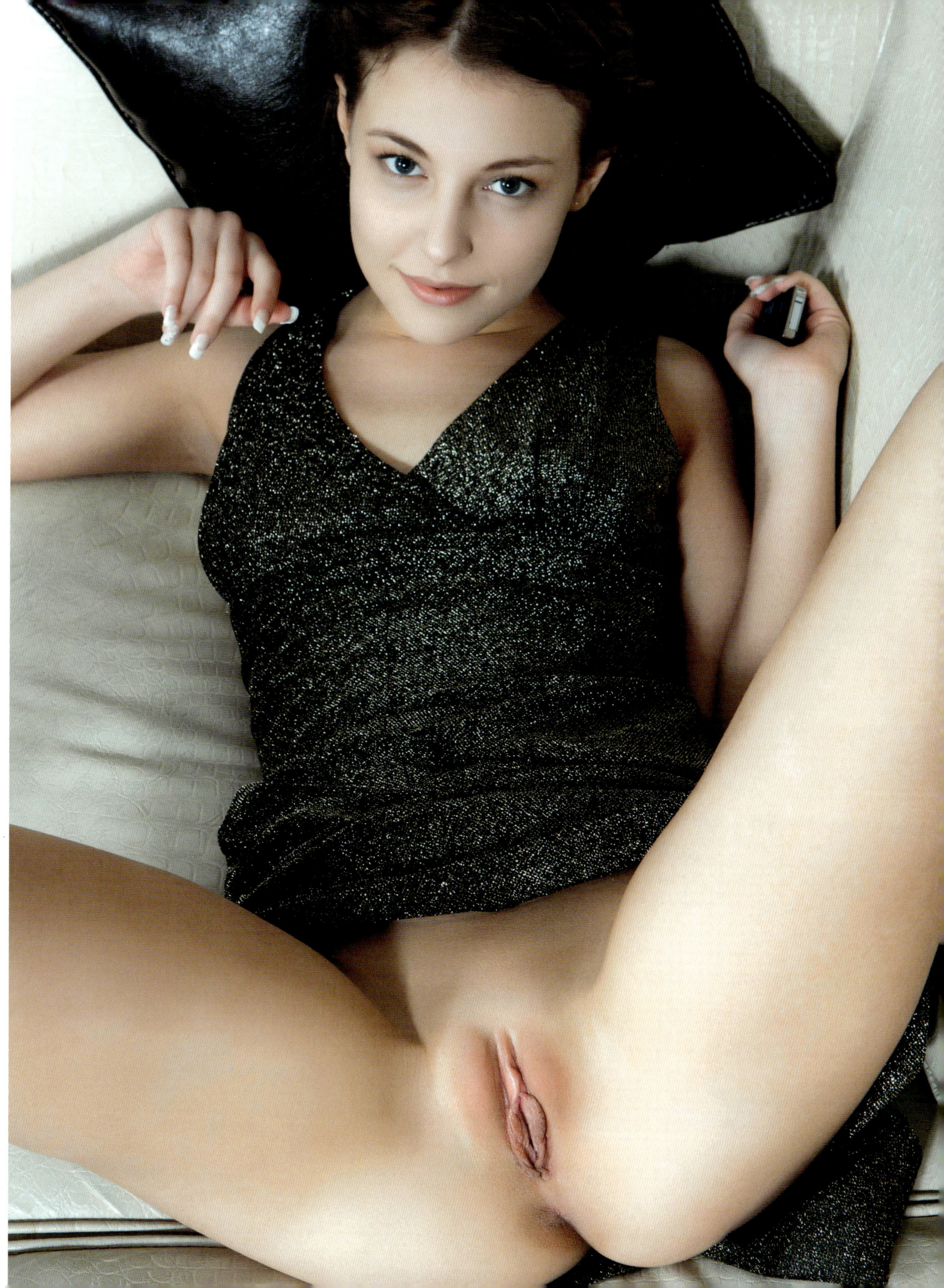

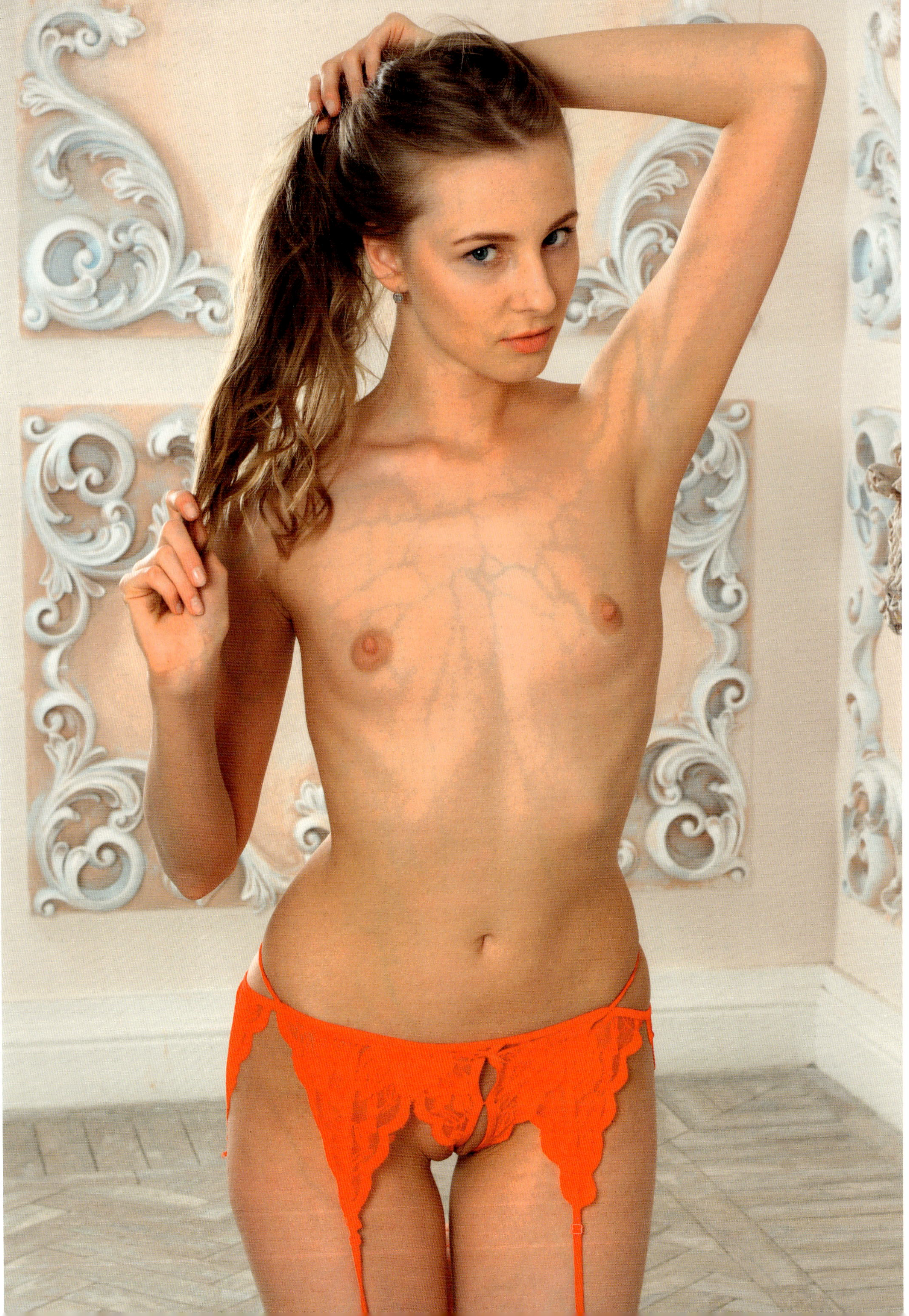

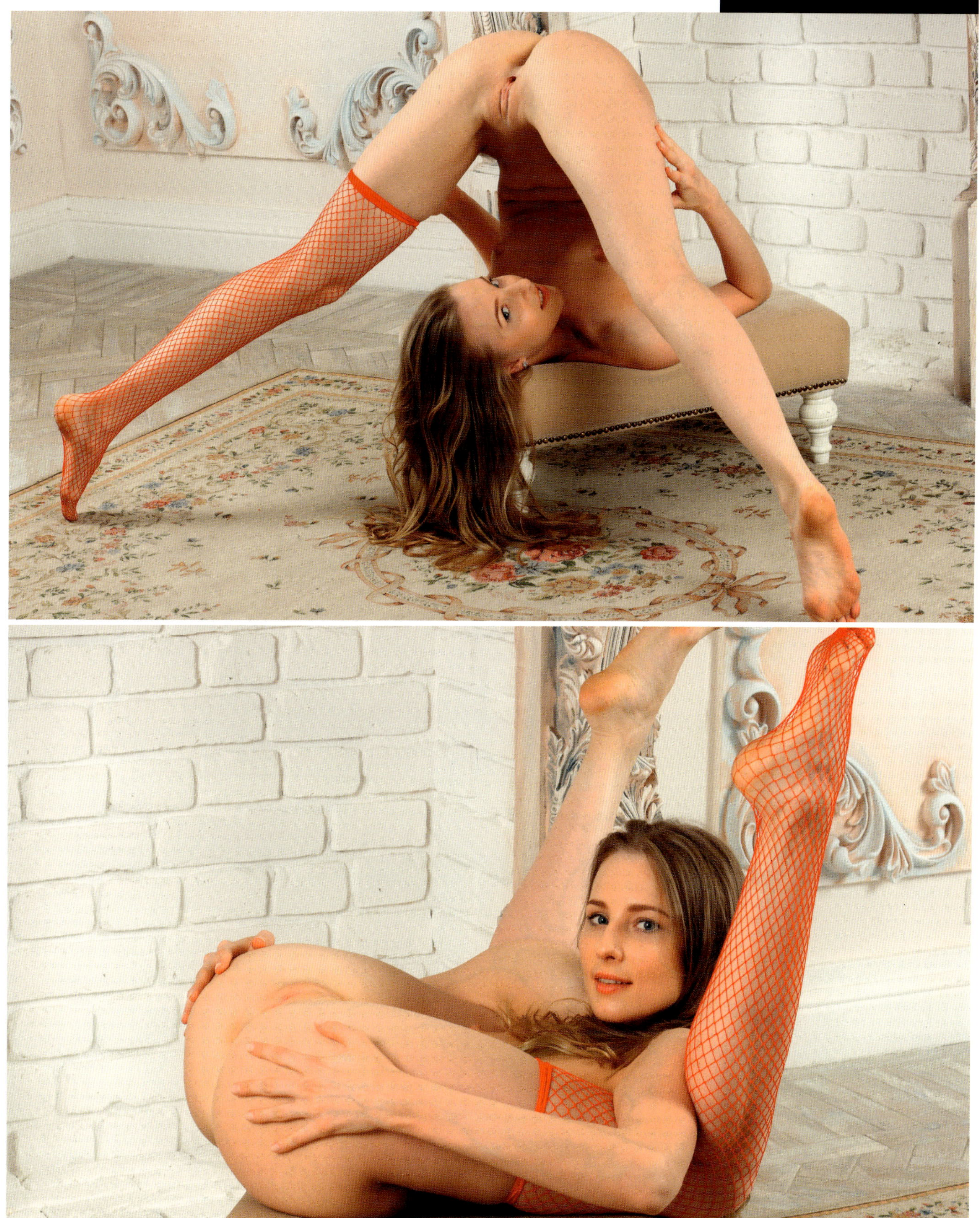

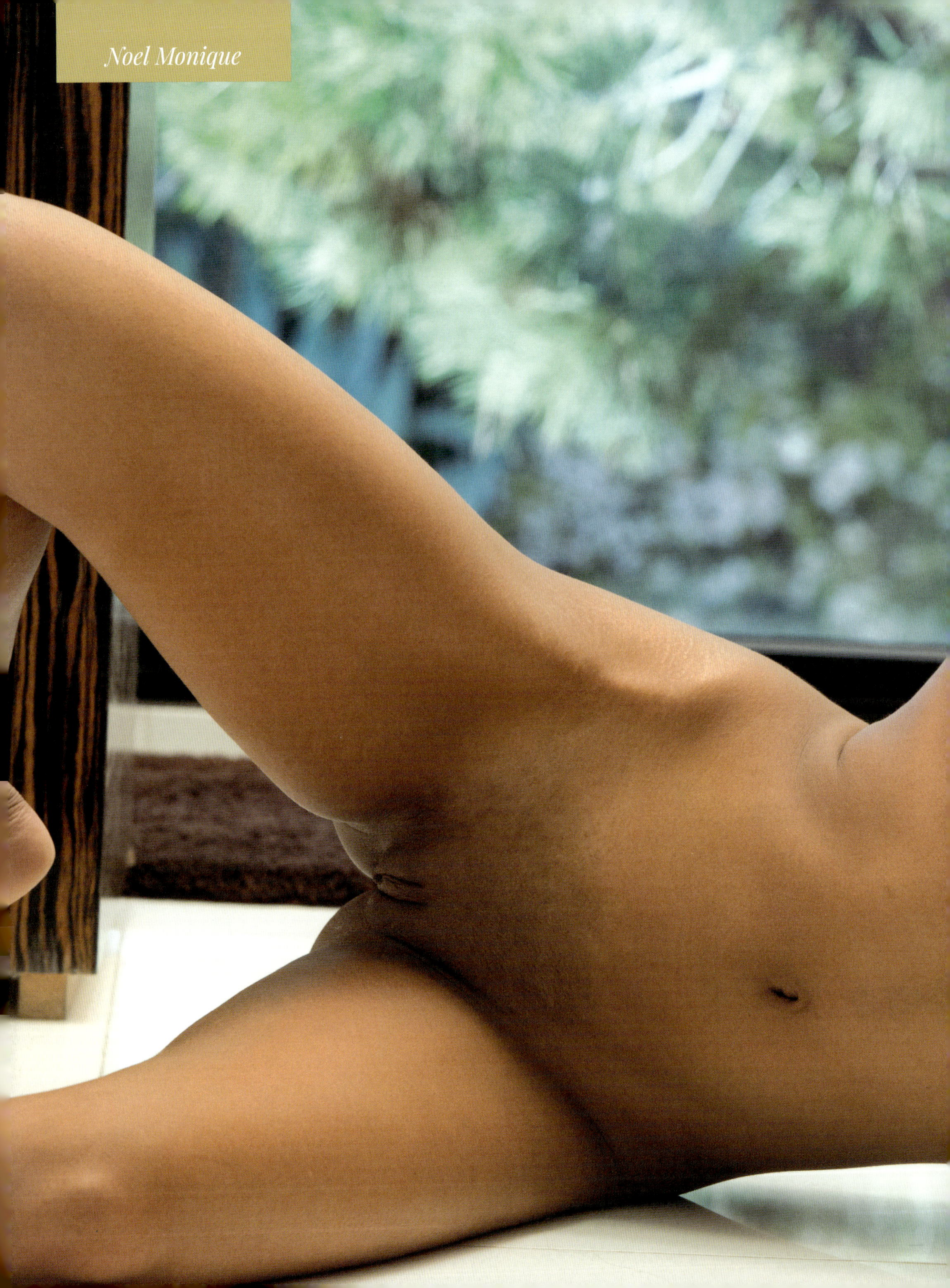

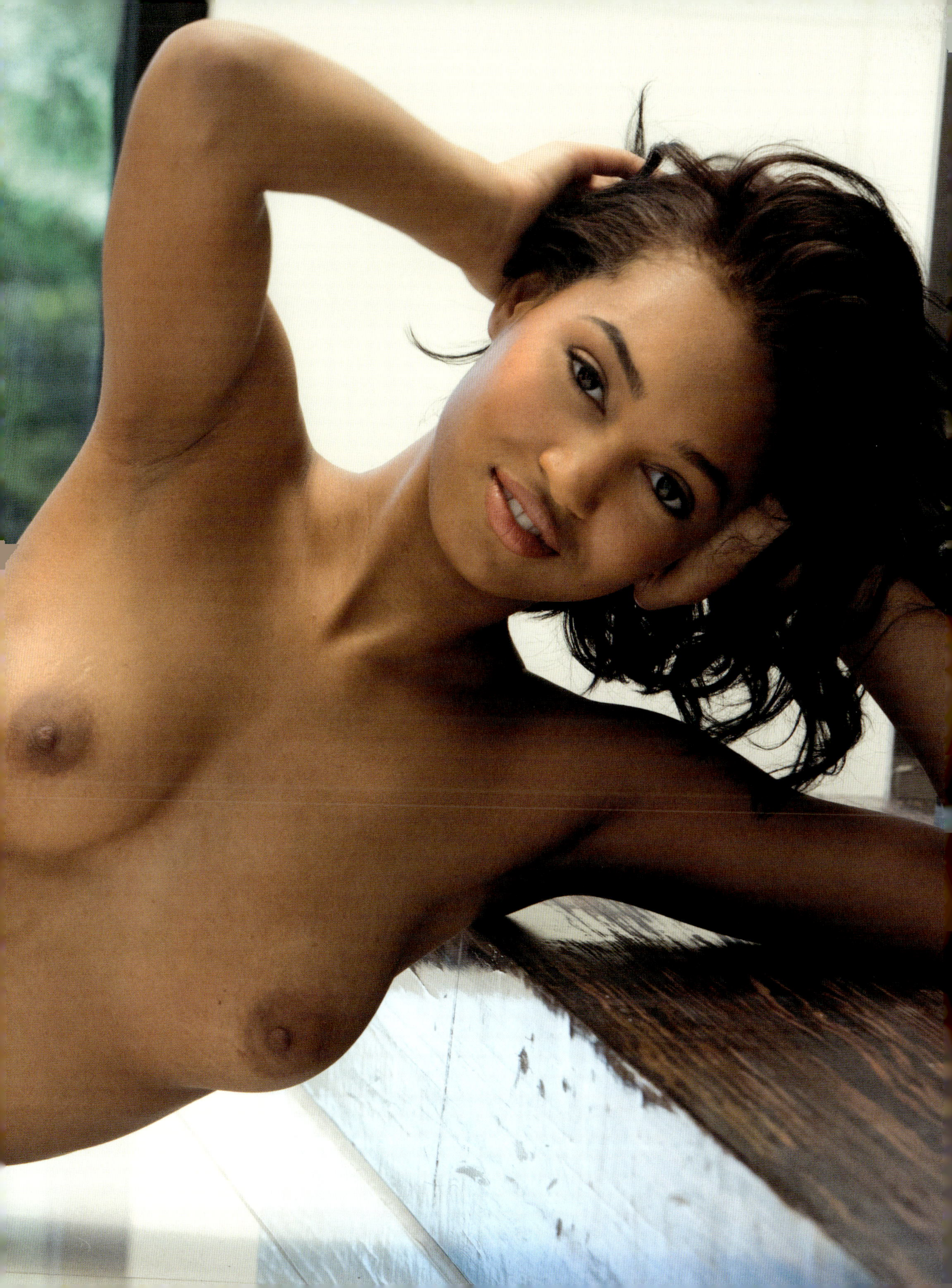

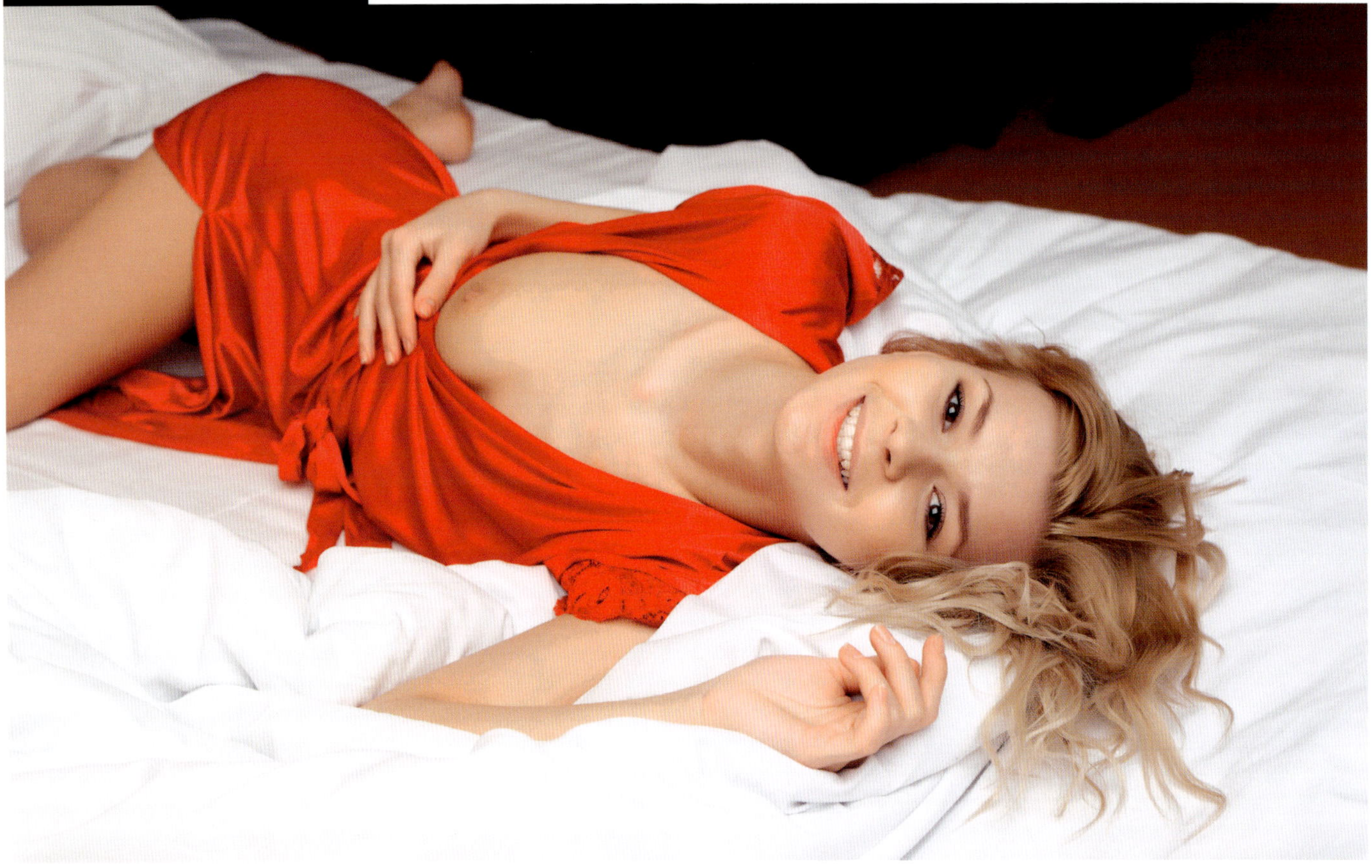

## Paloma B

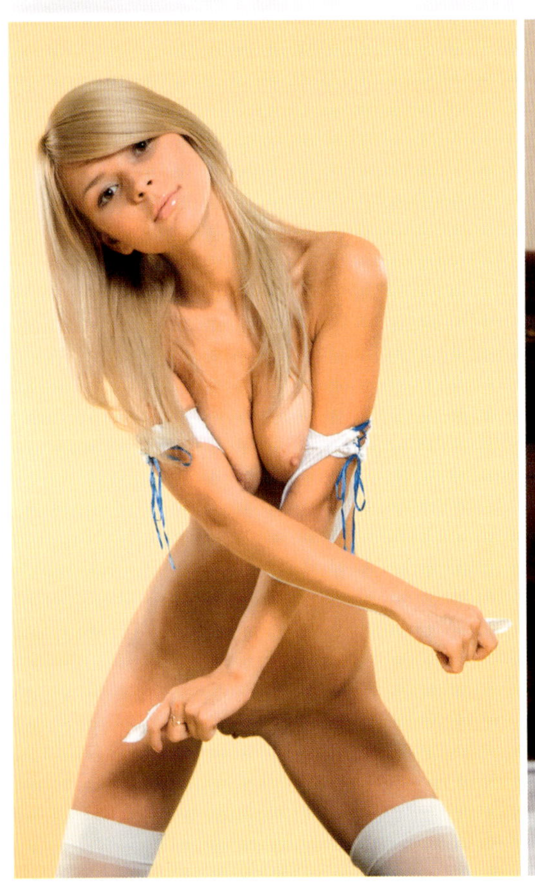

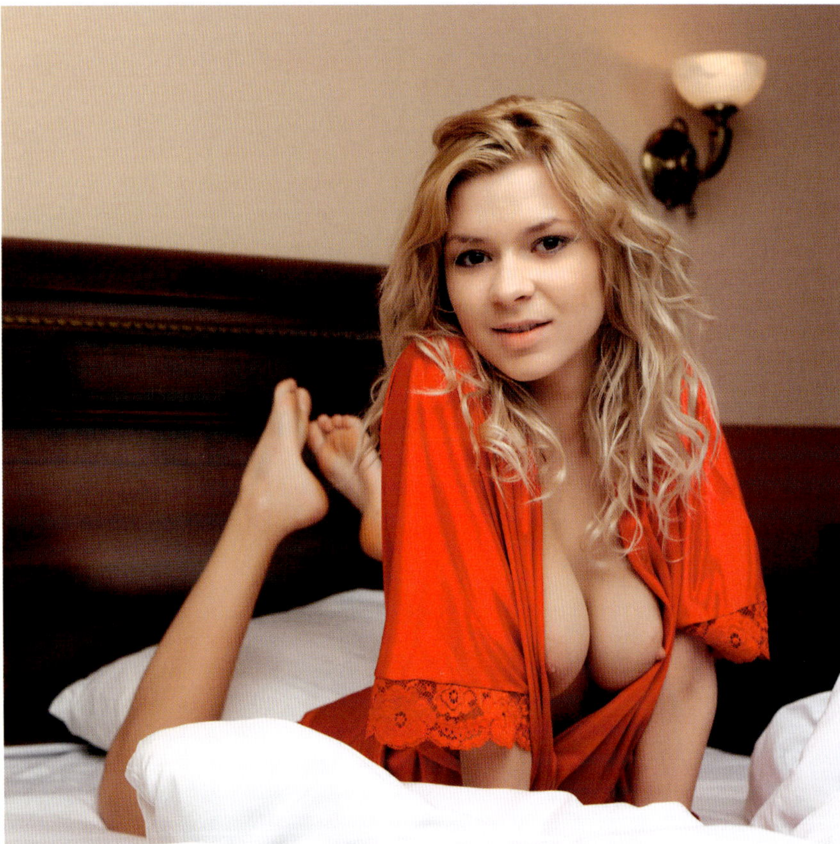

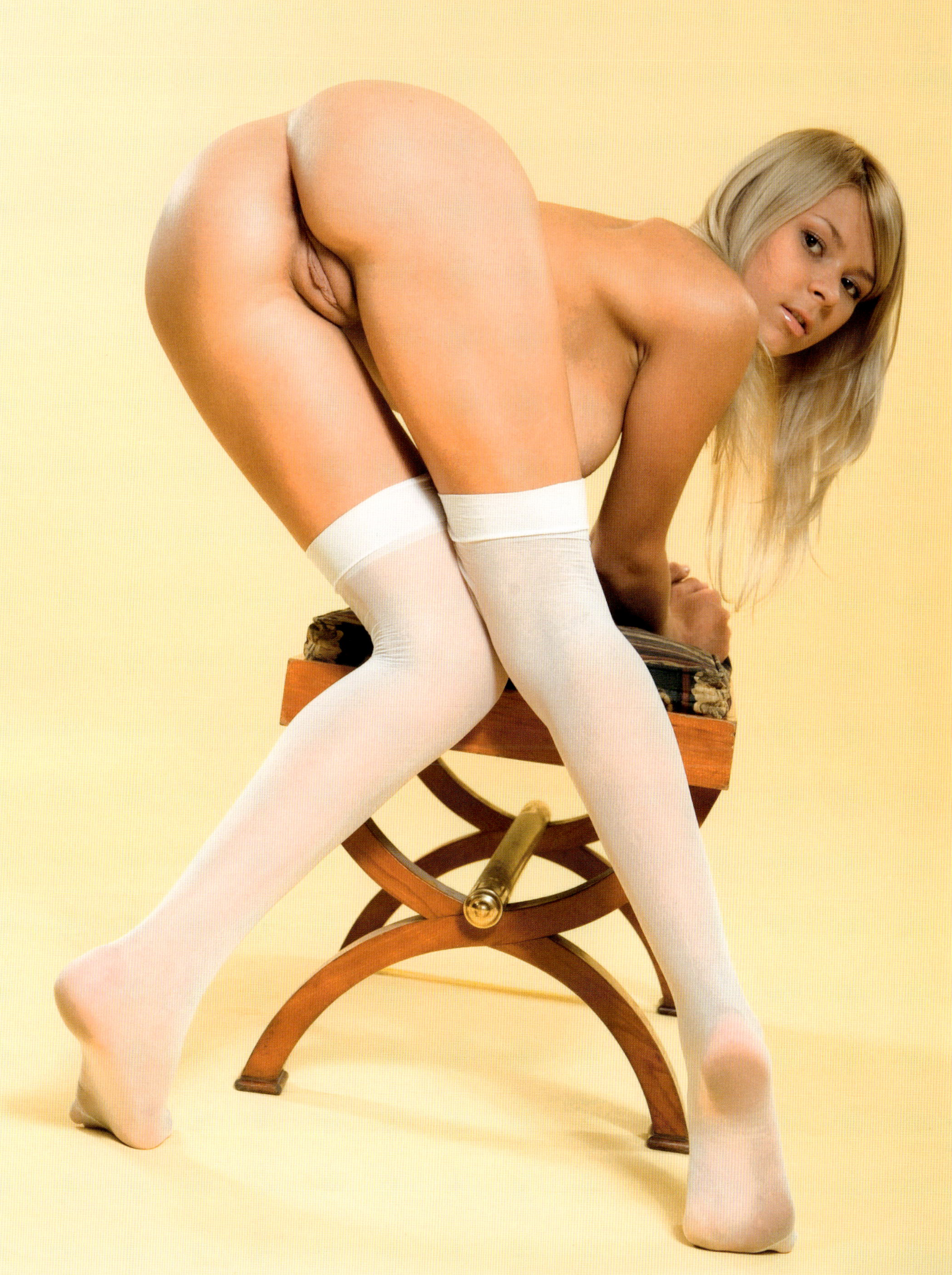

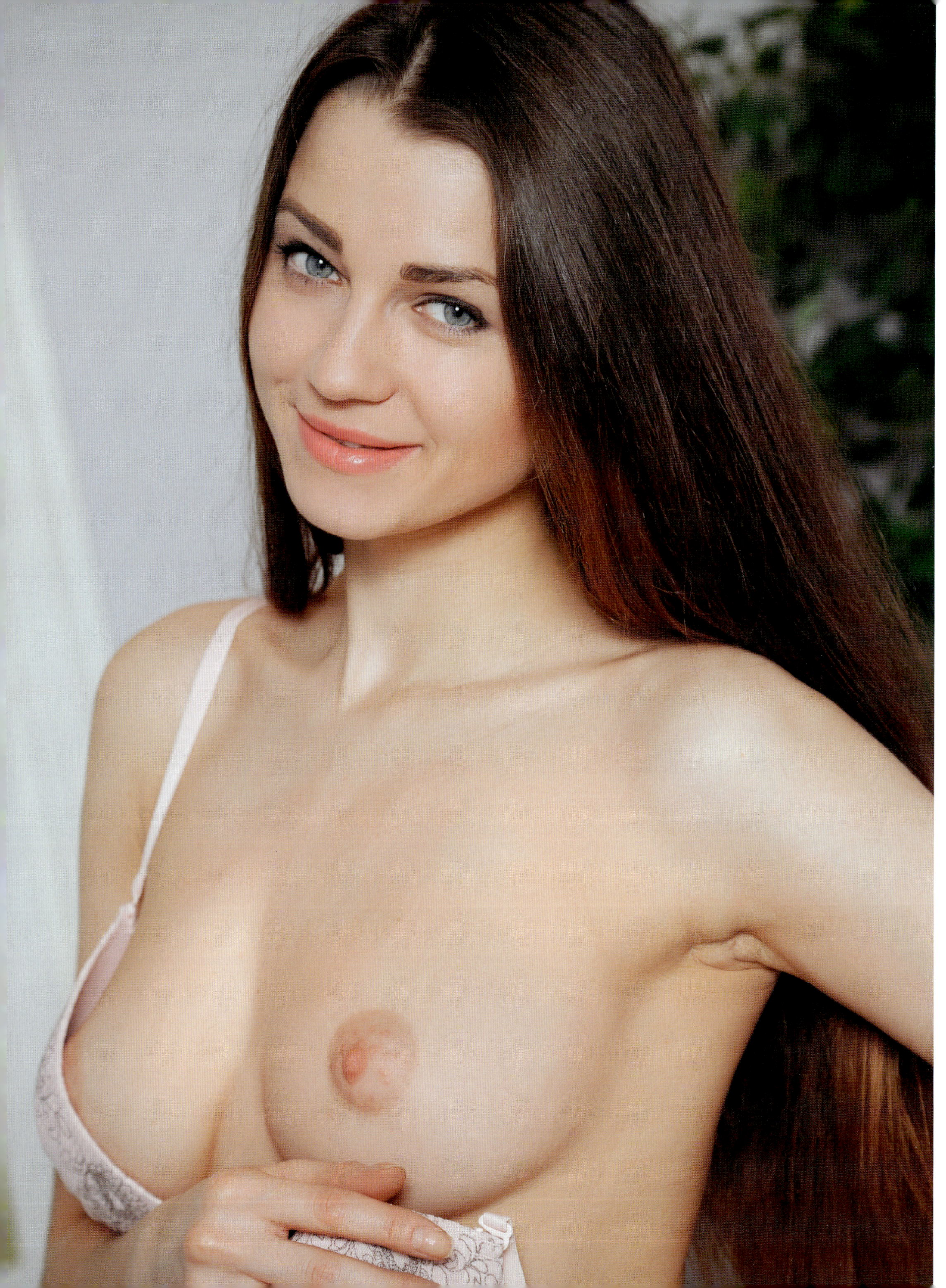

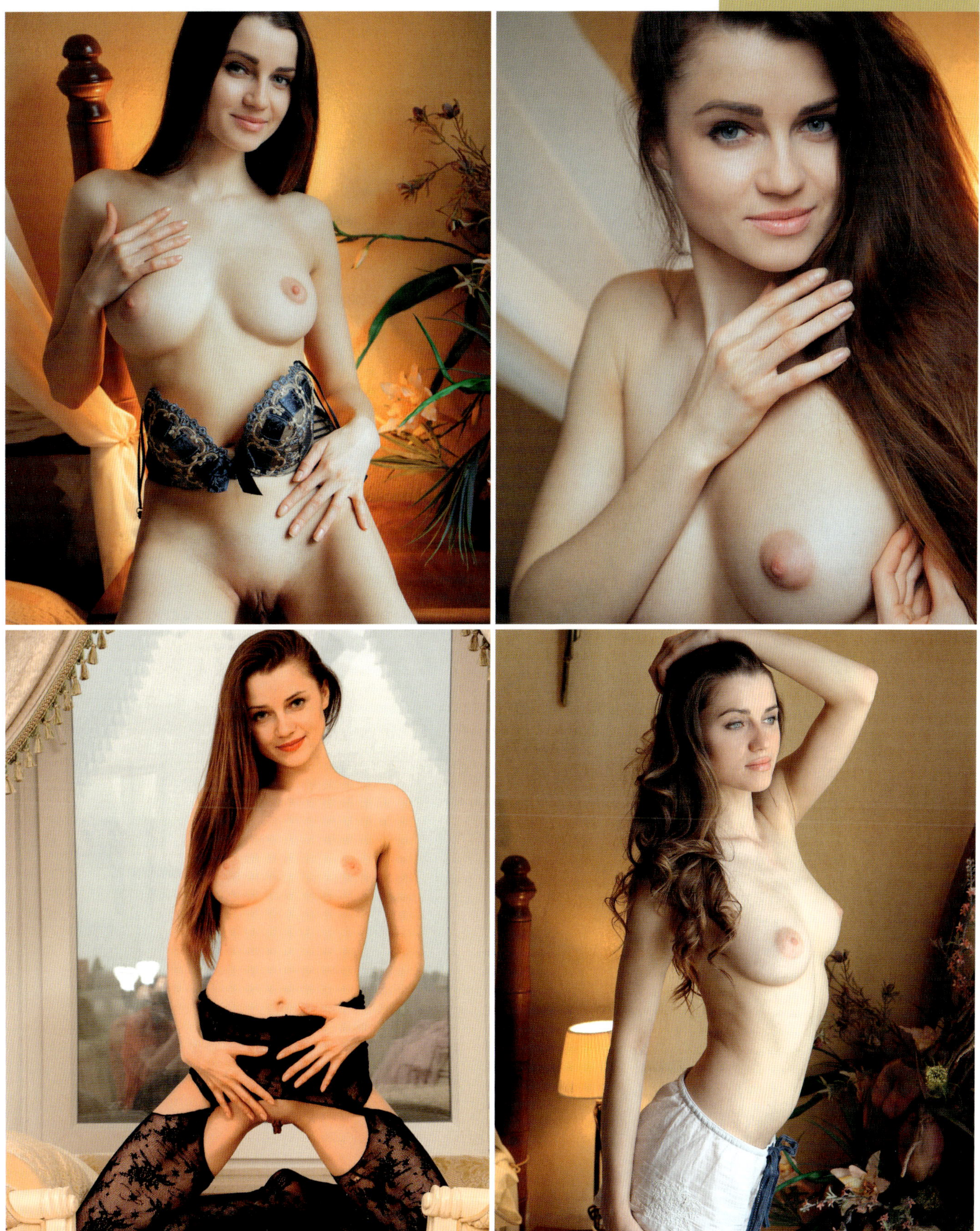

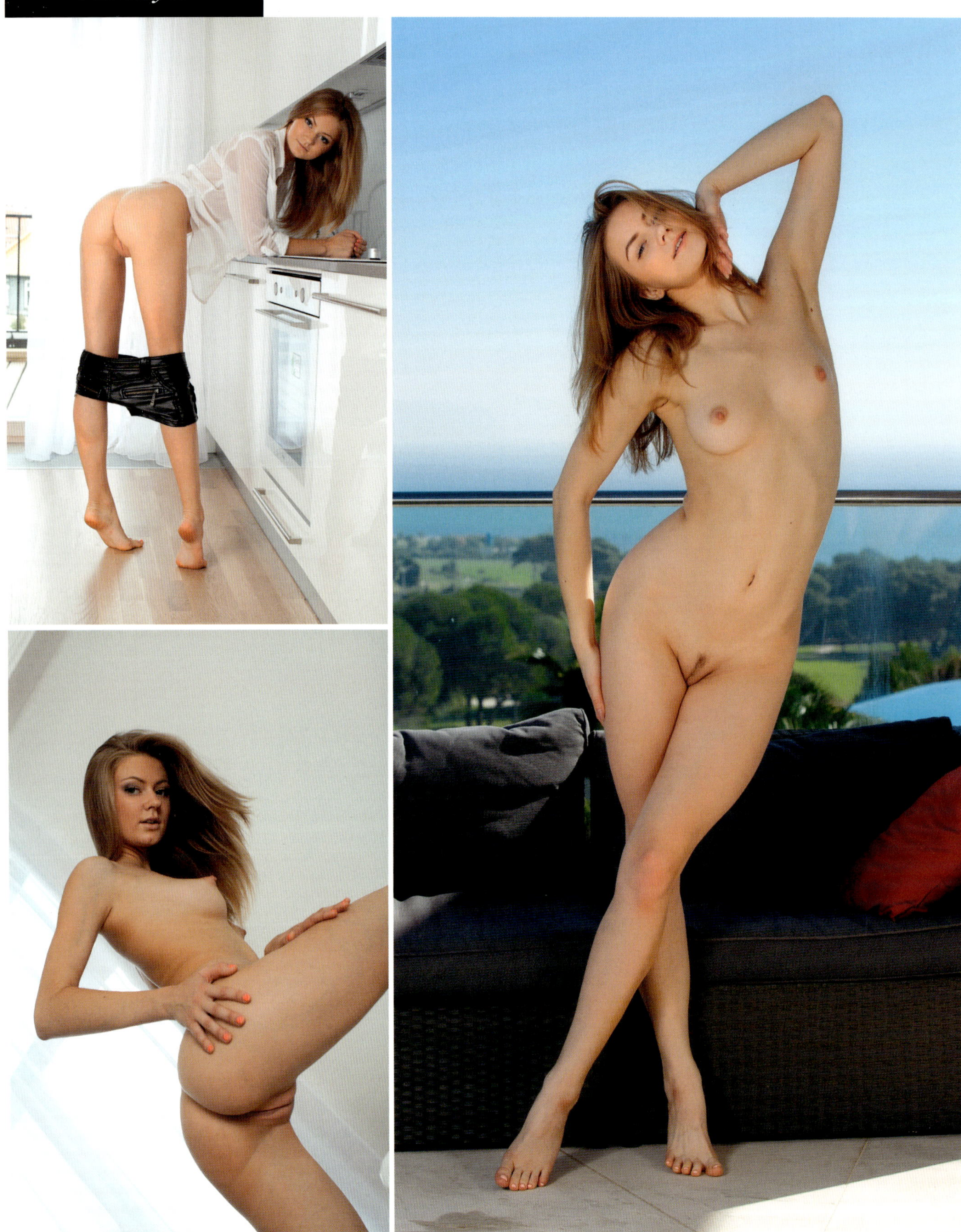

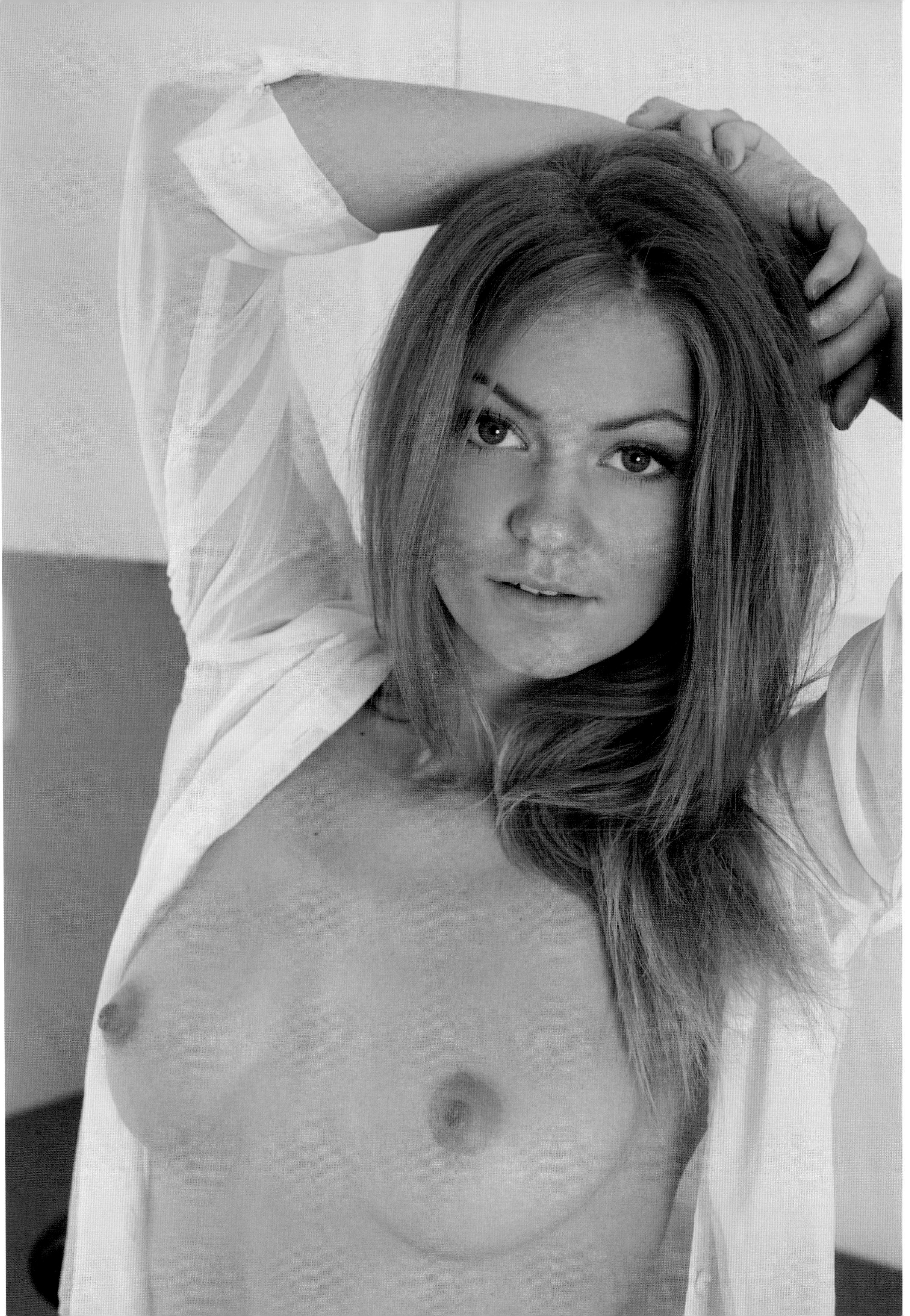

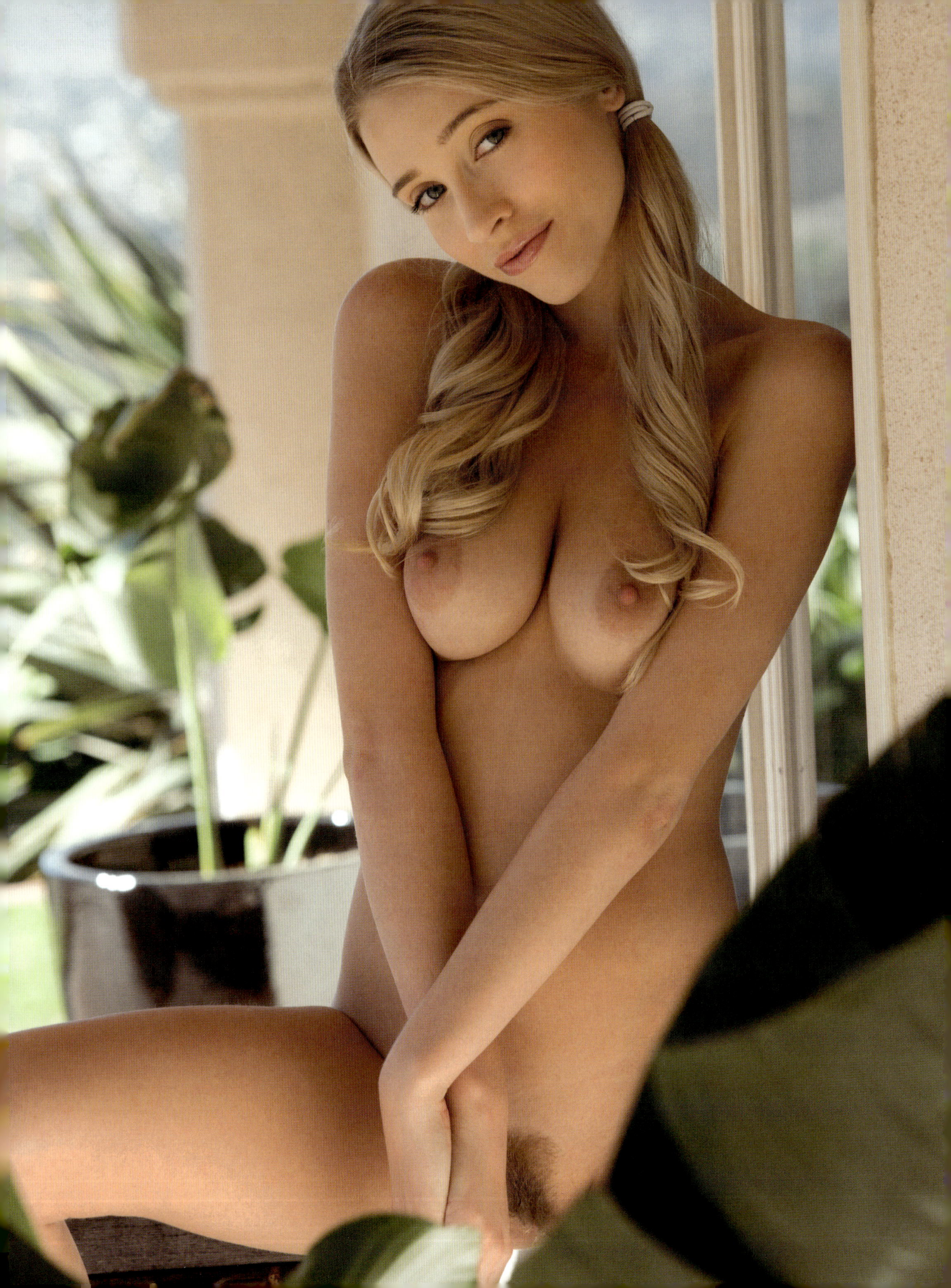

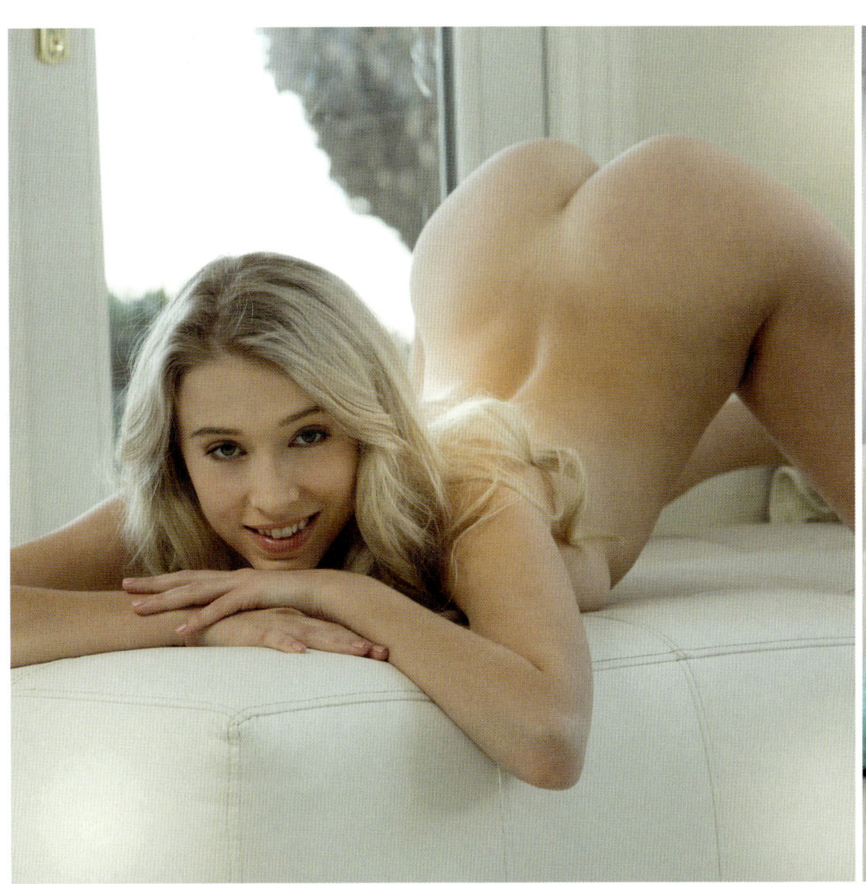

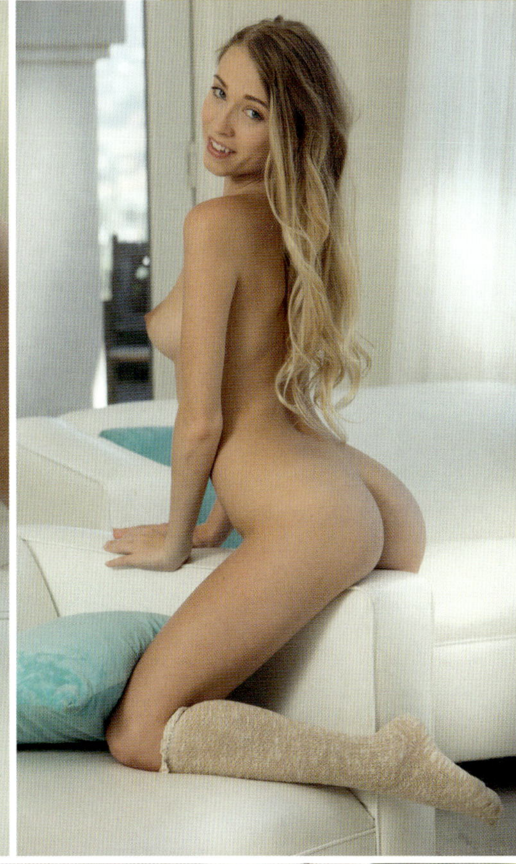

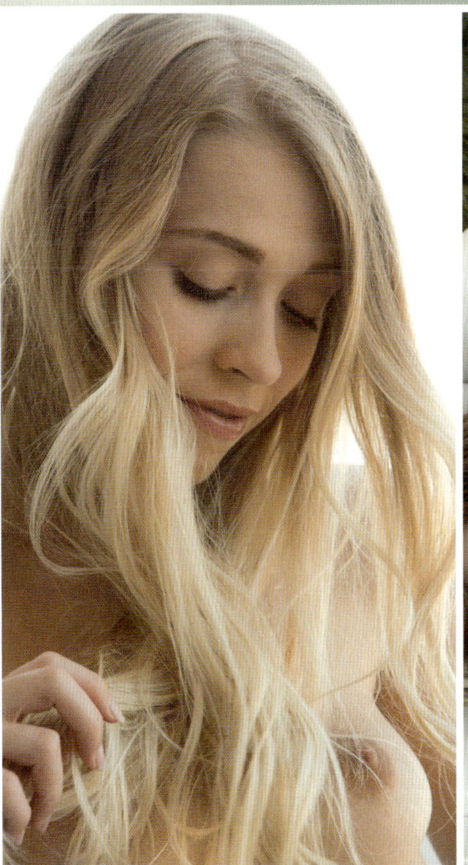

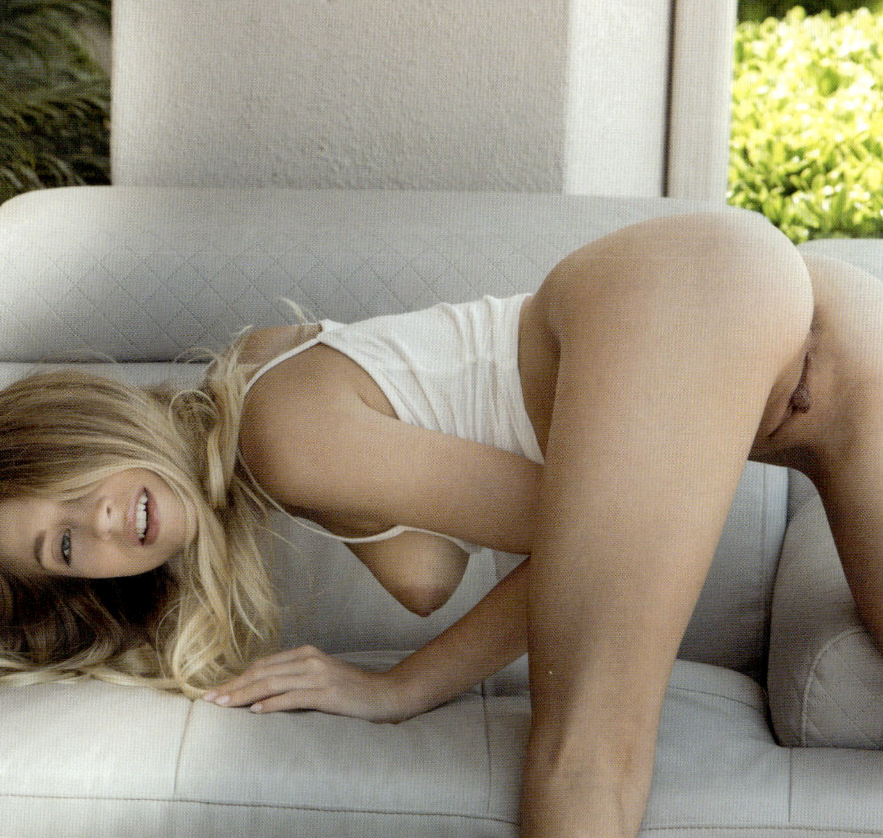

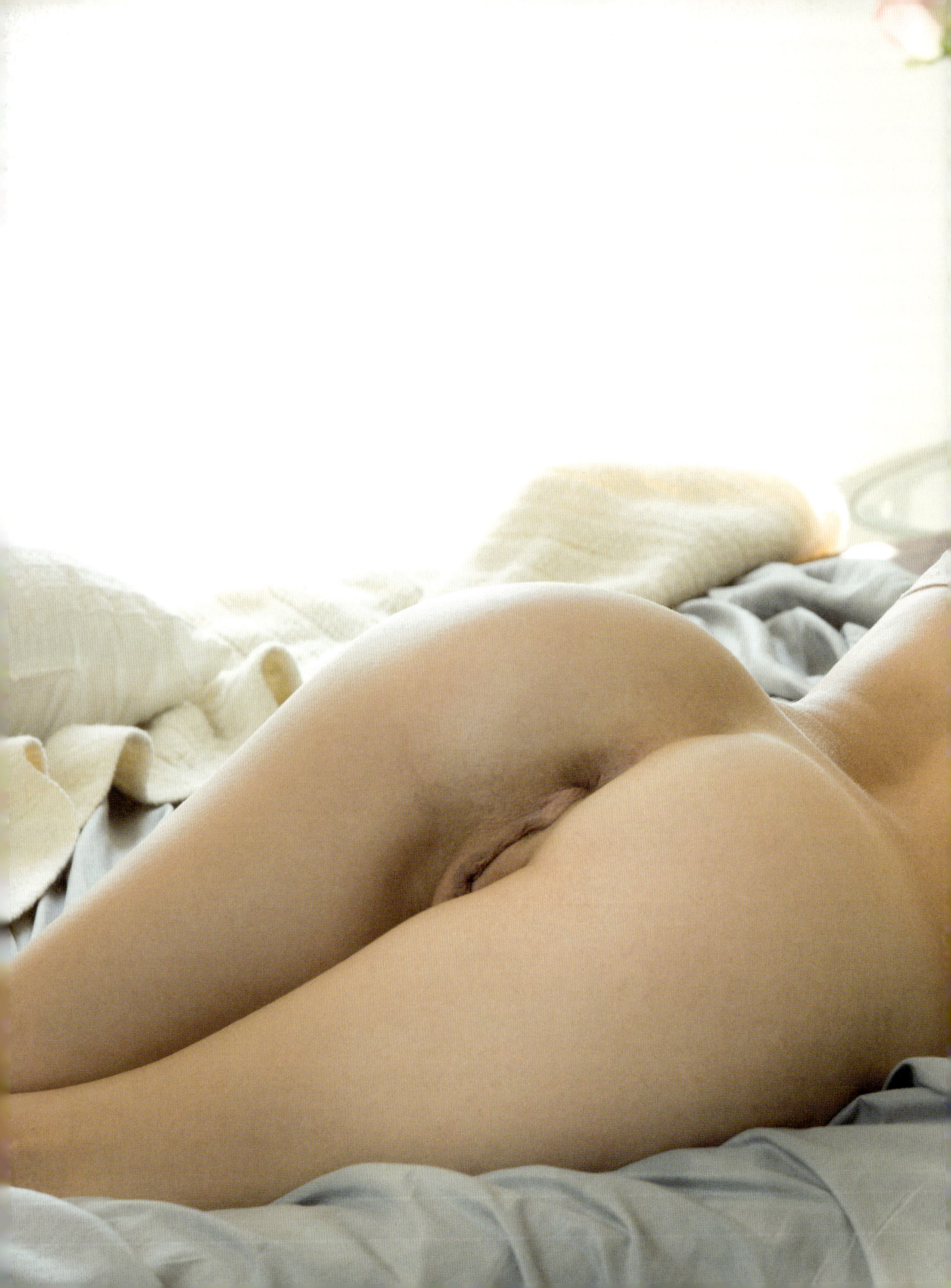

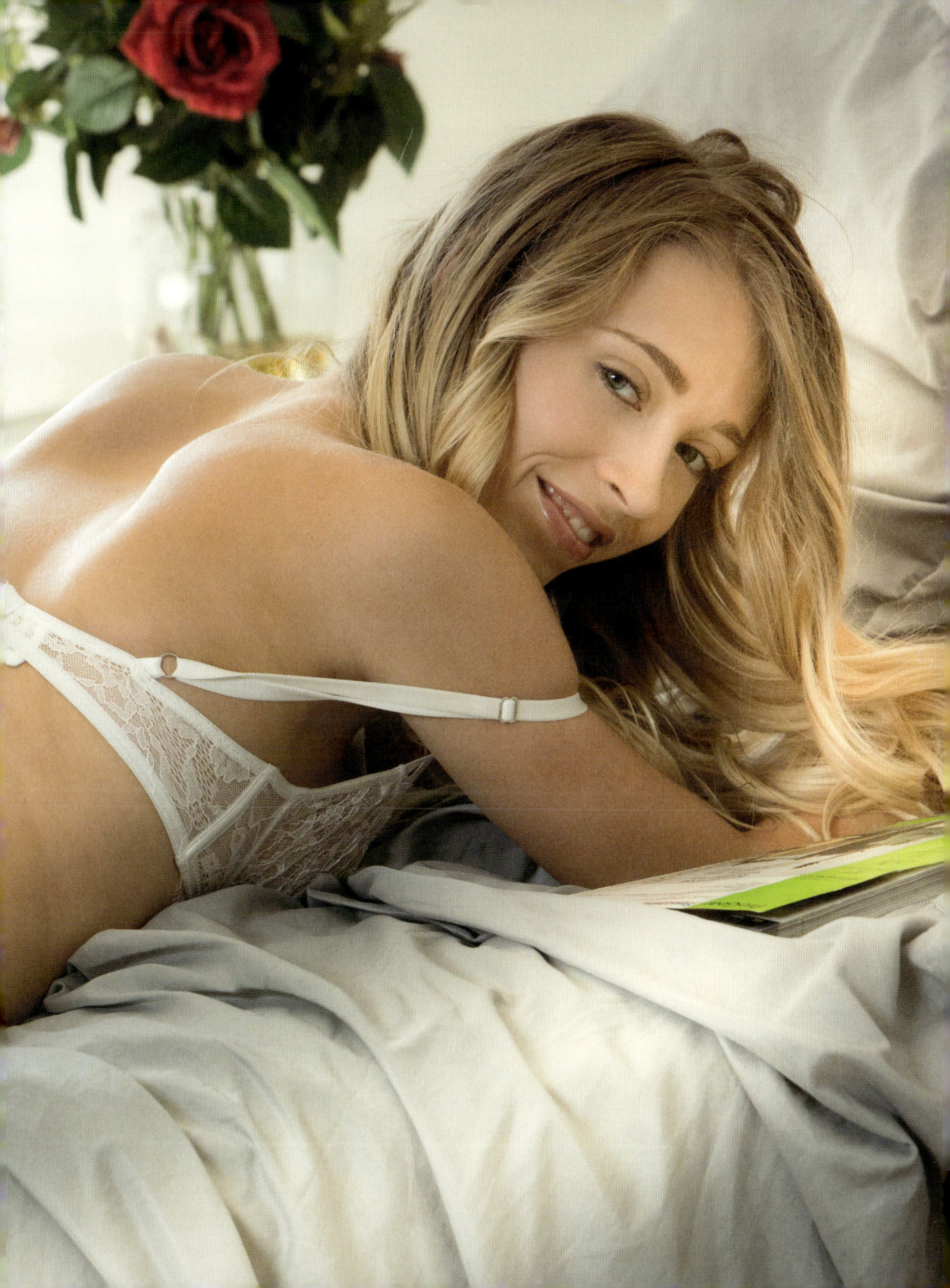

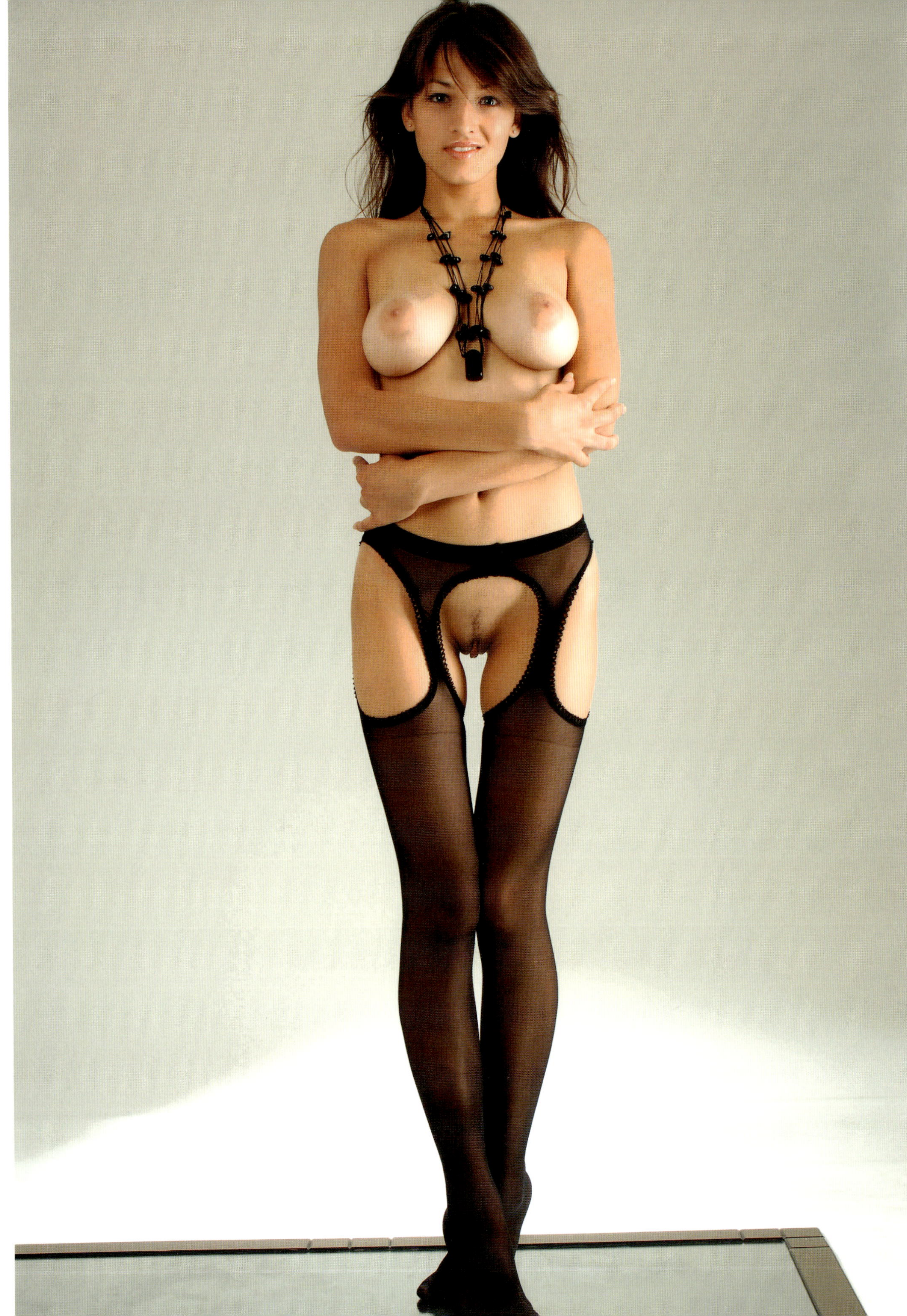

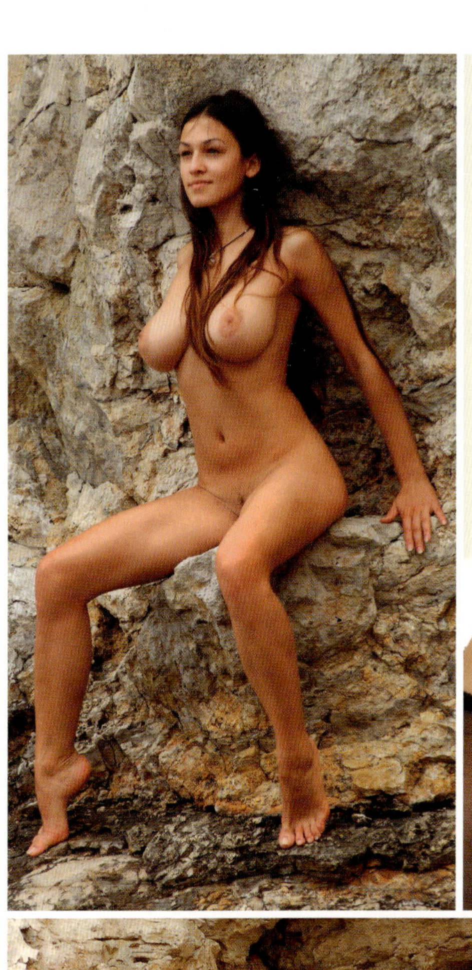

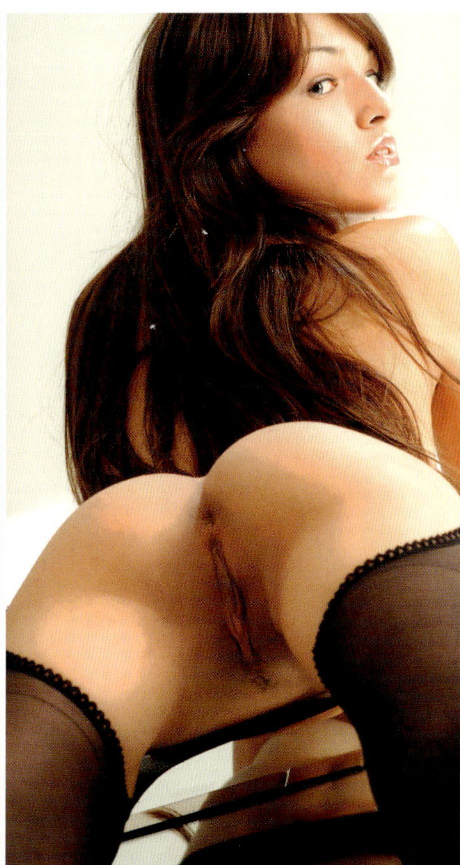

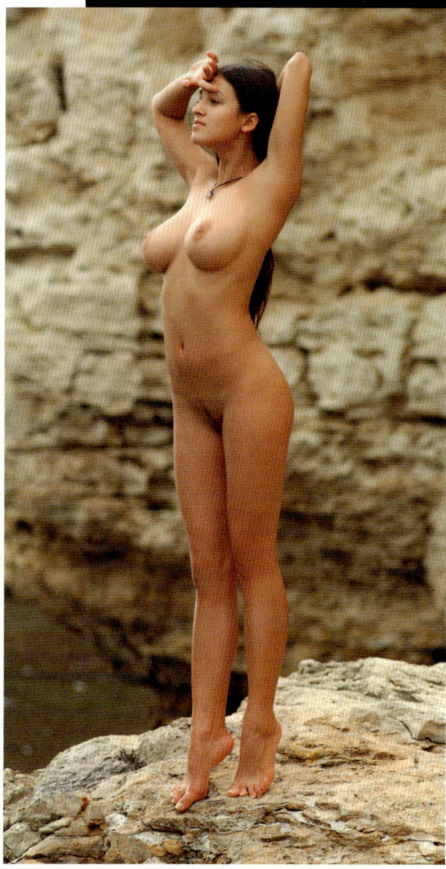

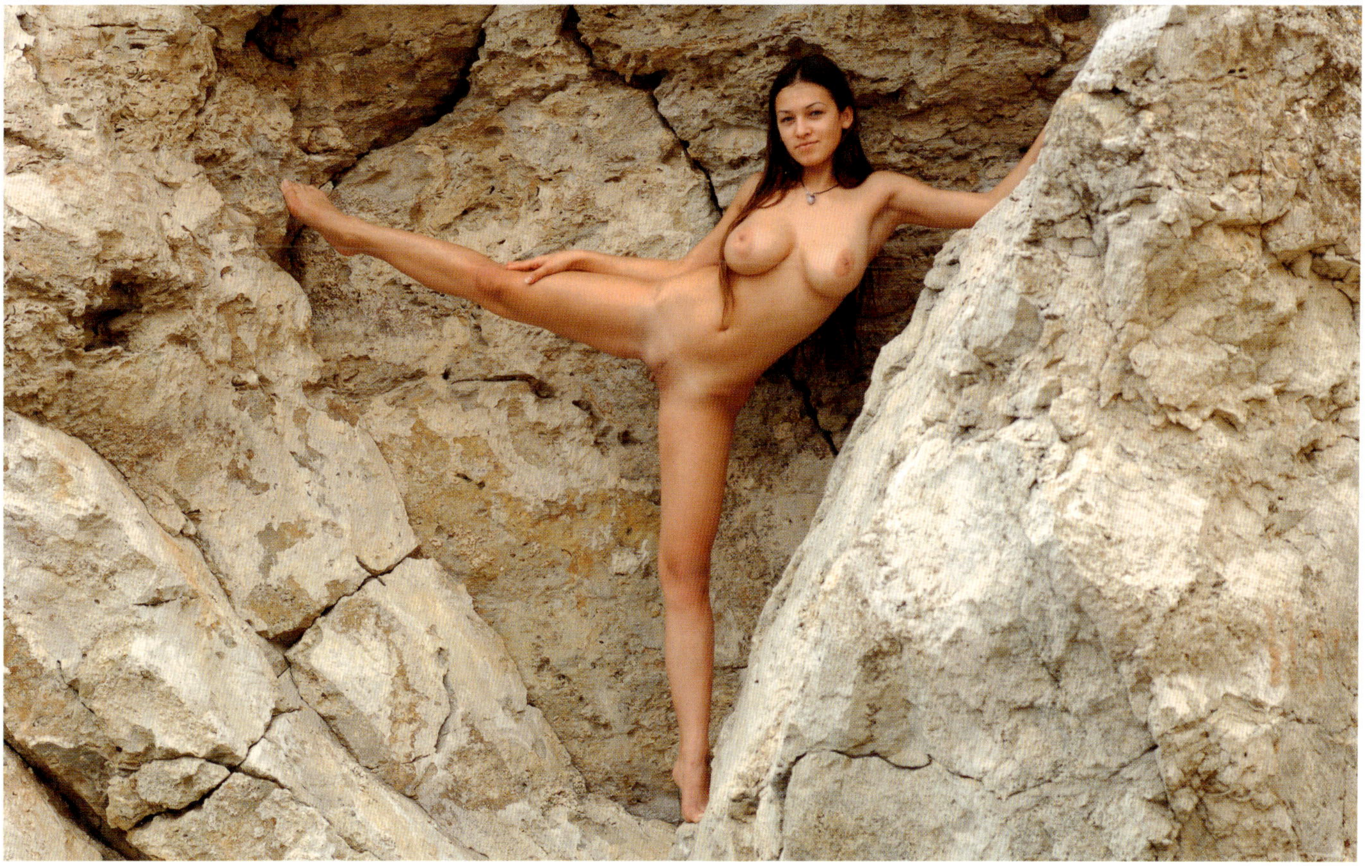

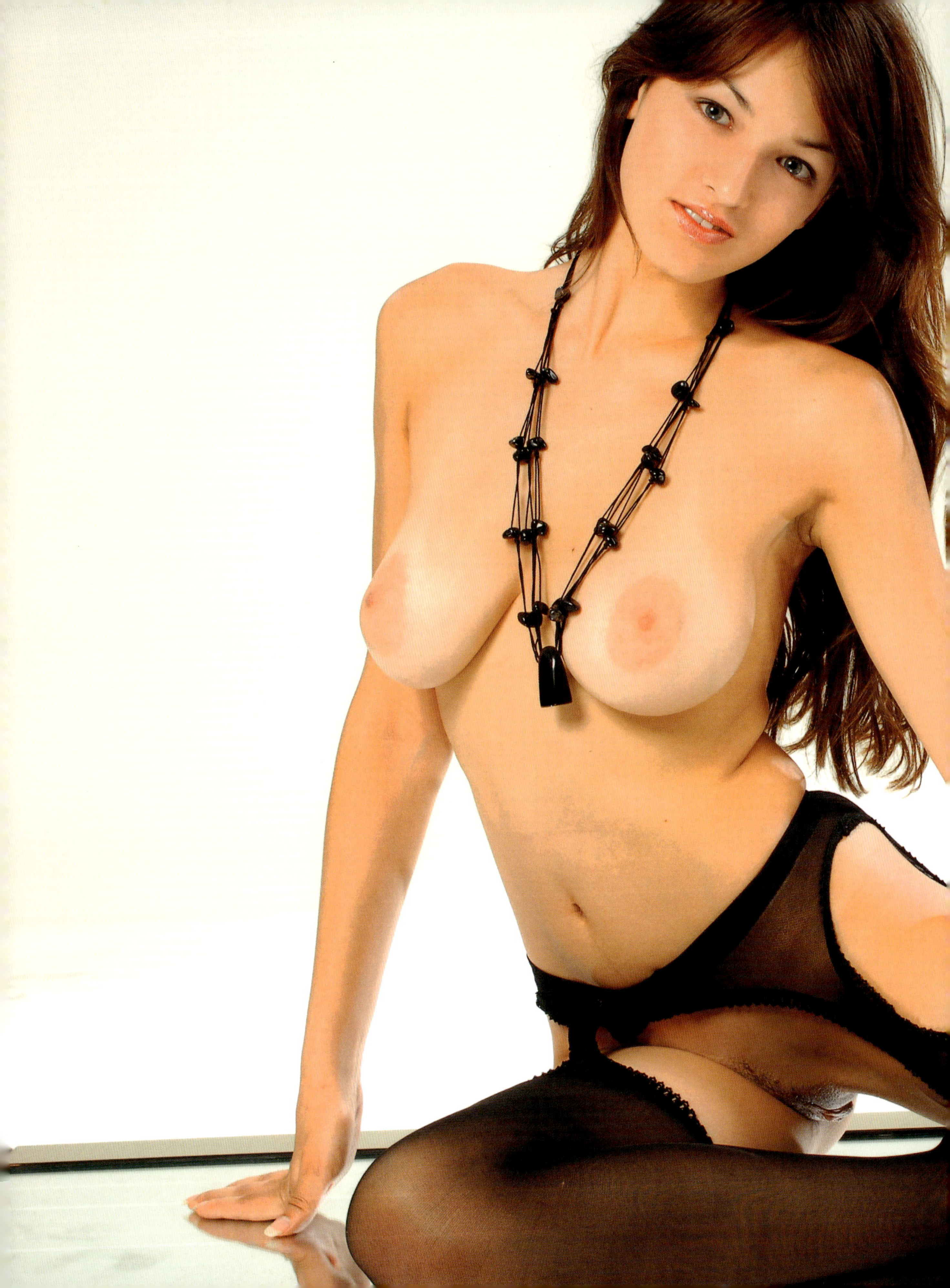

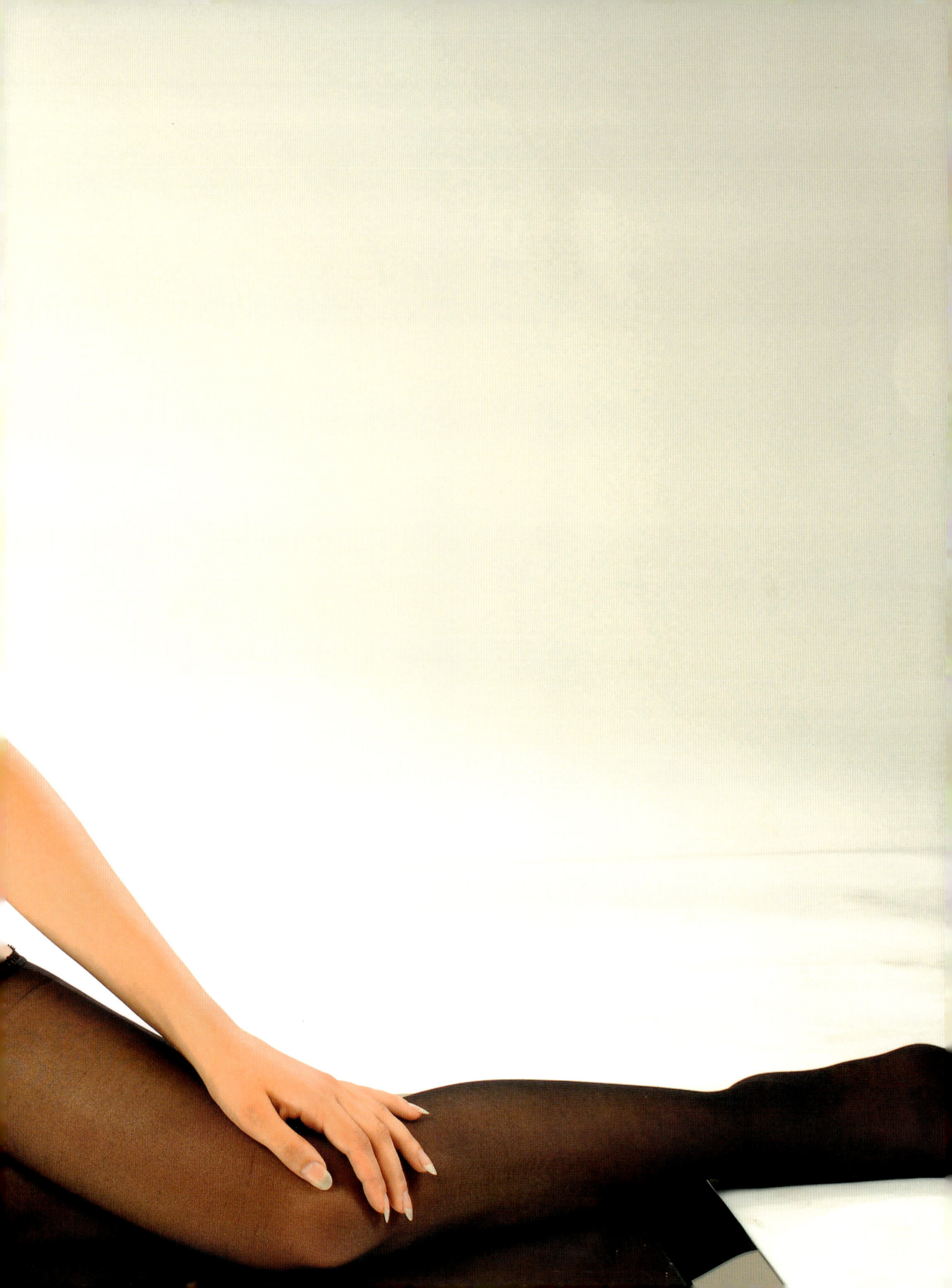

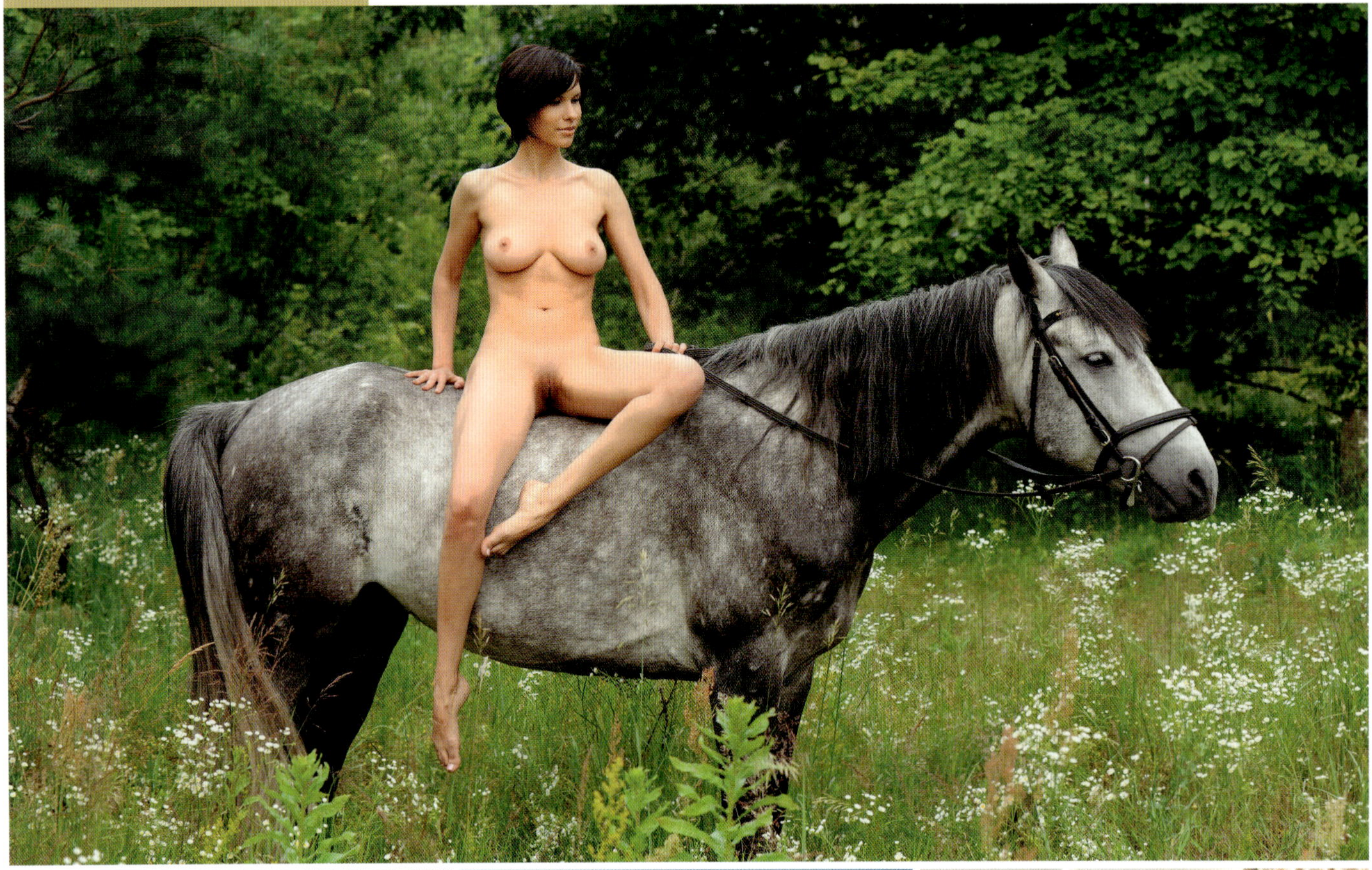

## Suzanna A

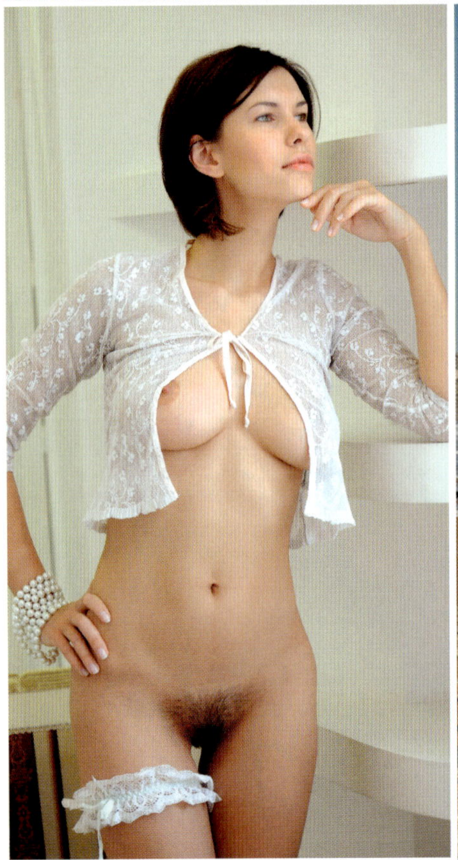

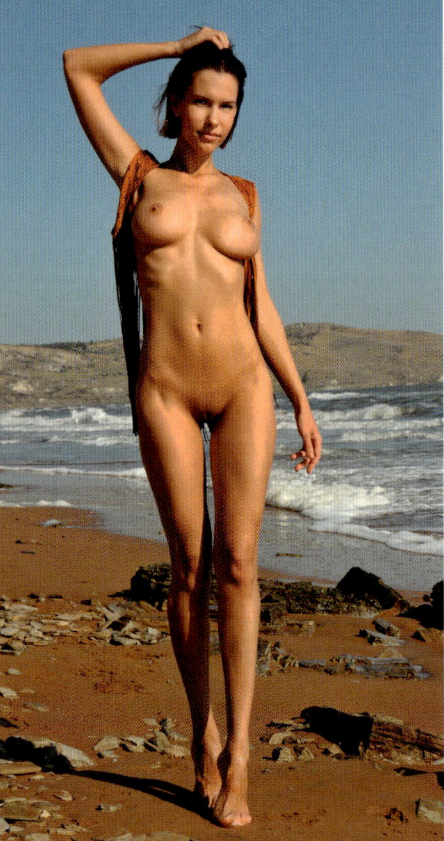

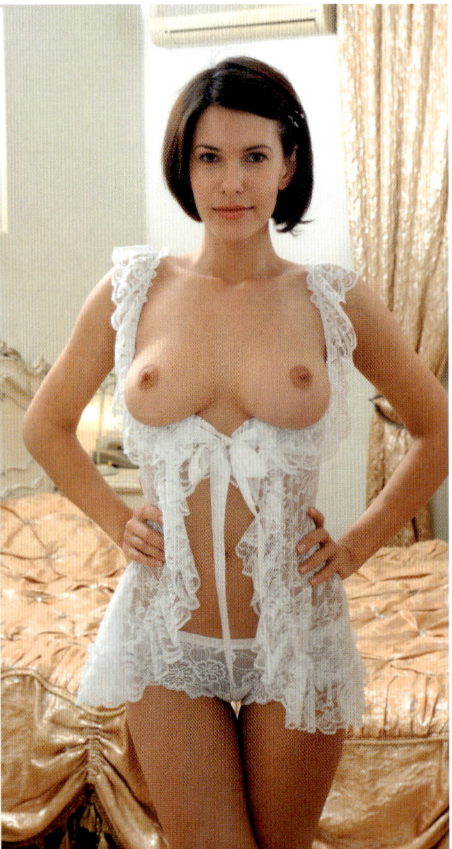

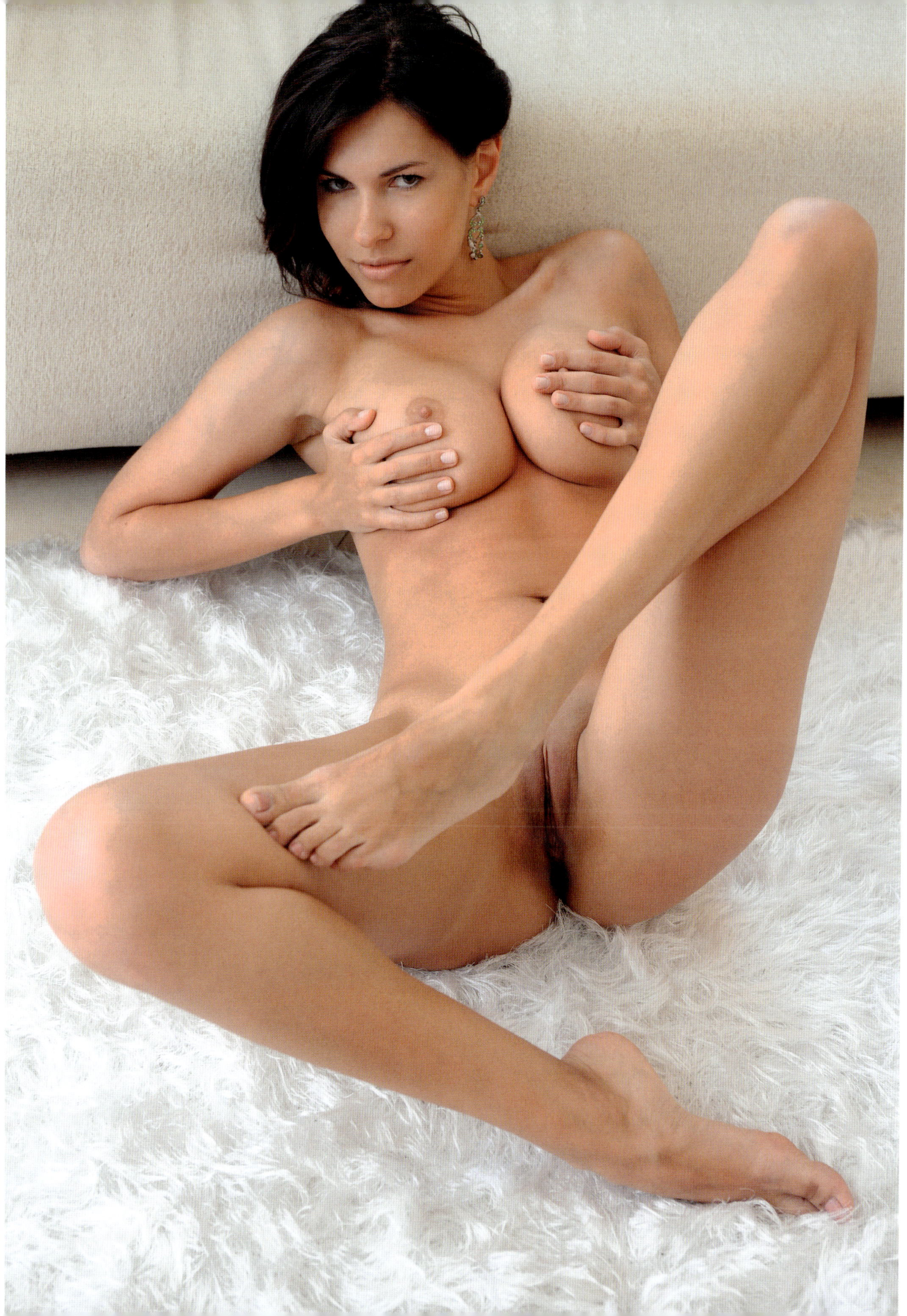

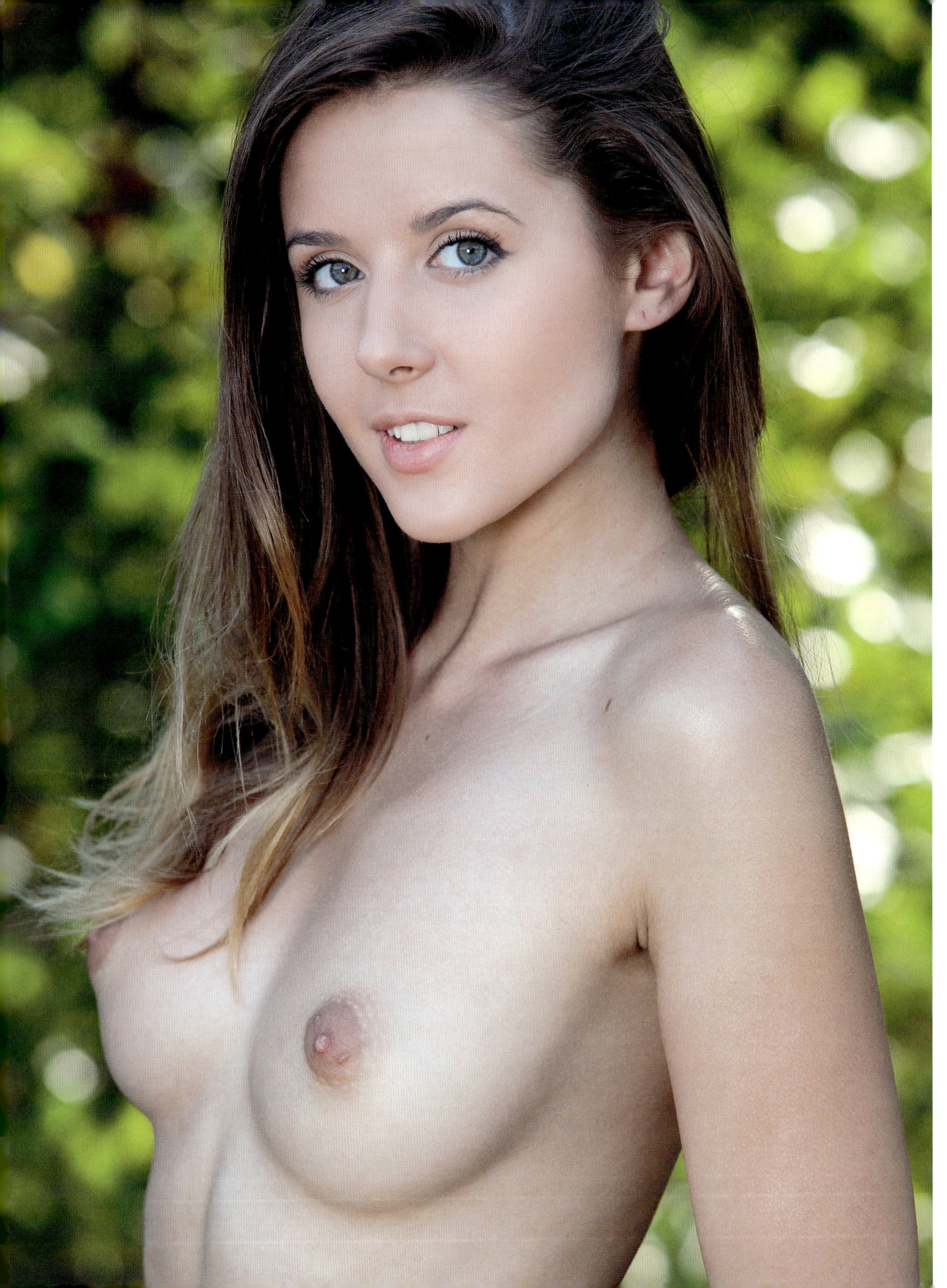

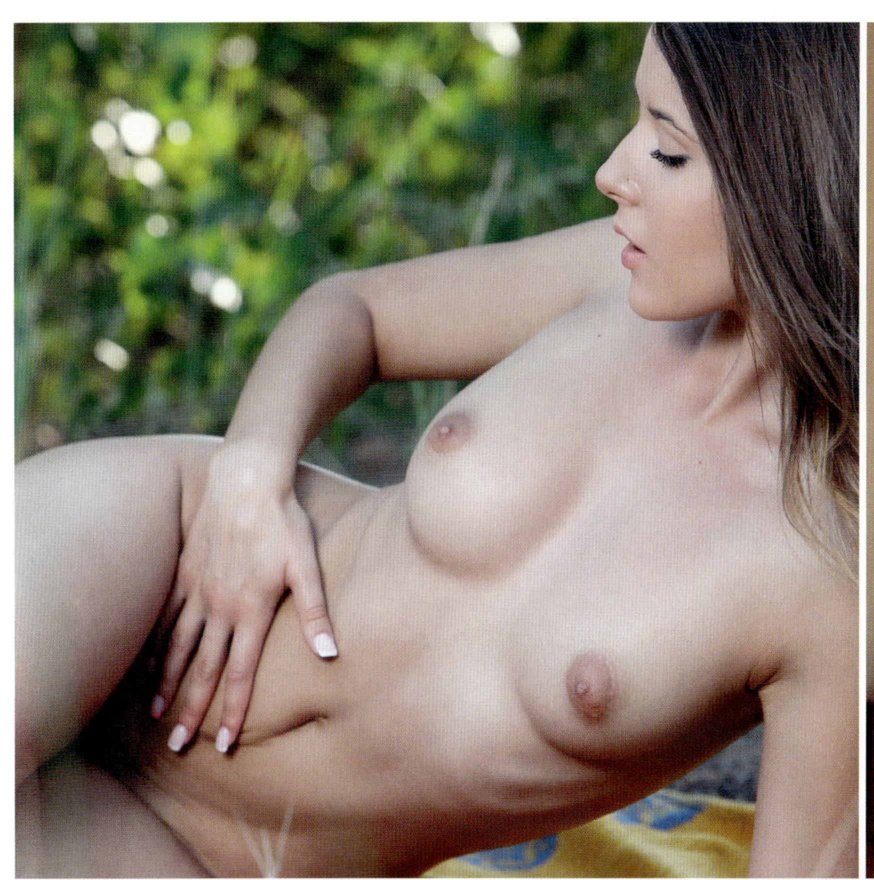

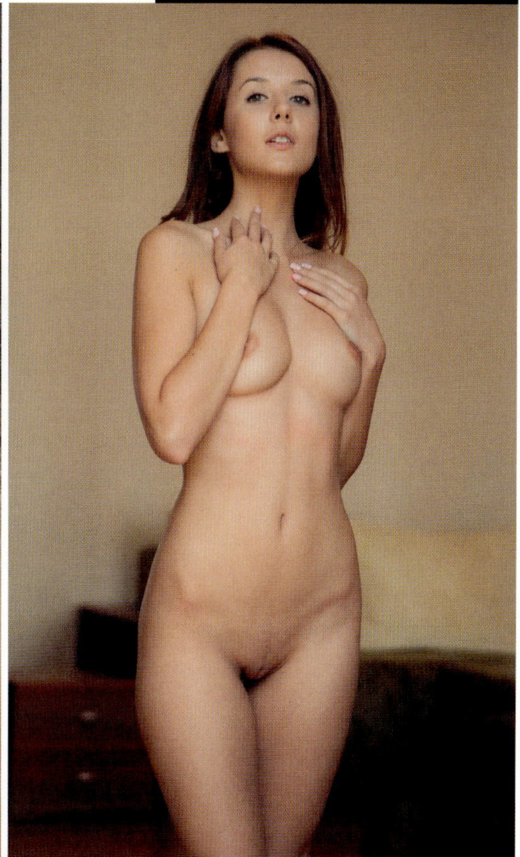

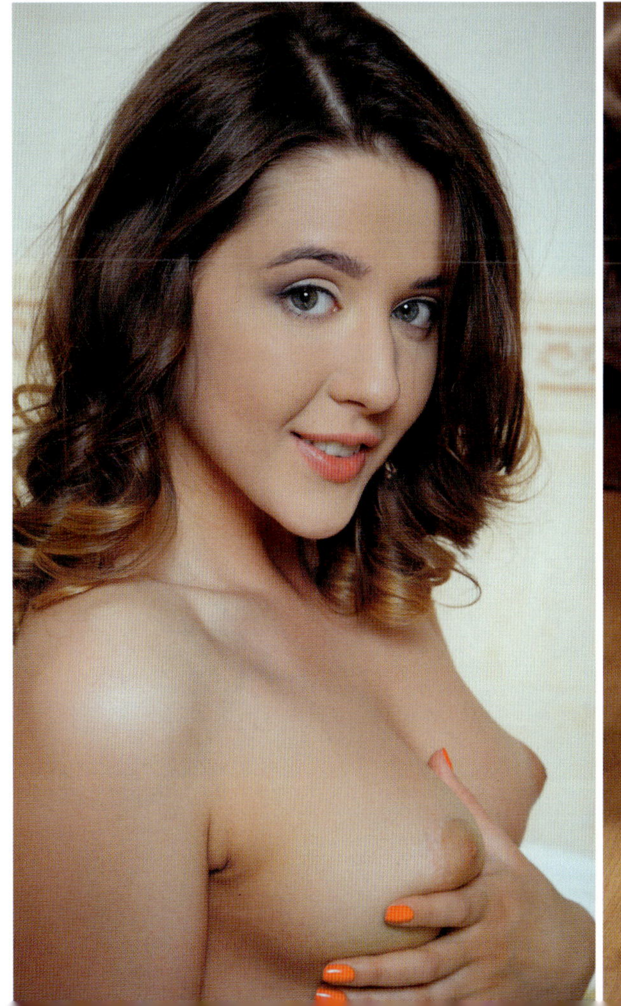

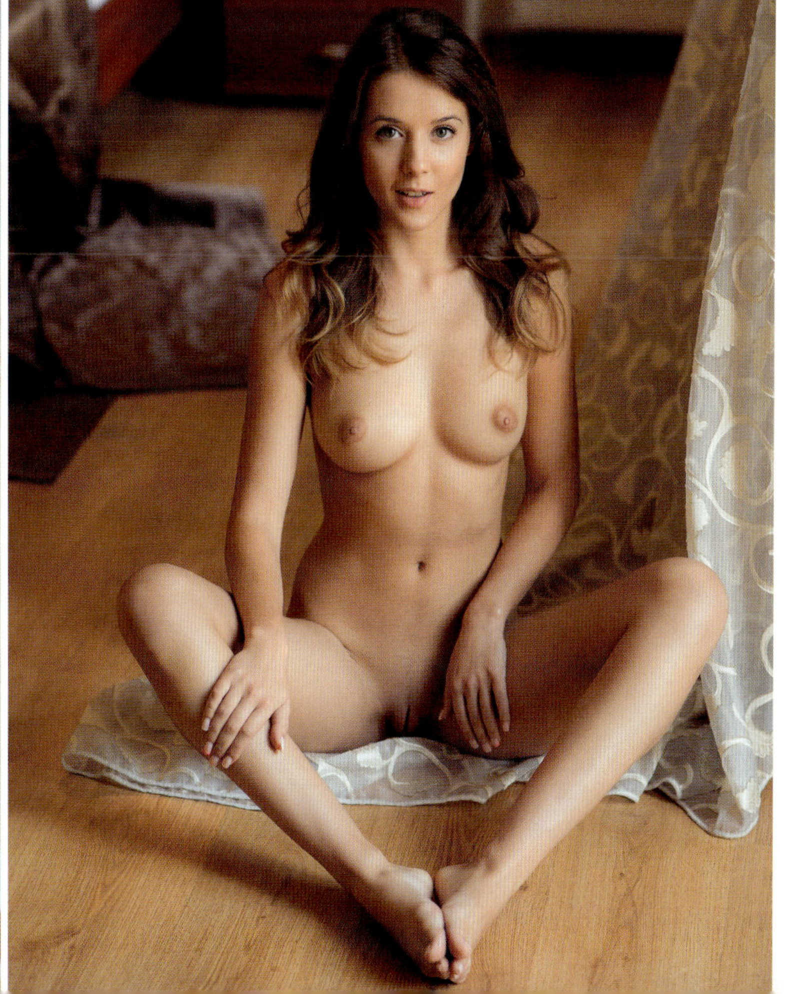

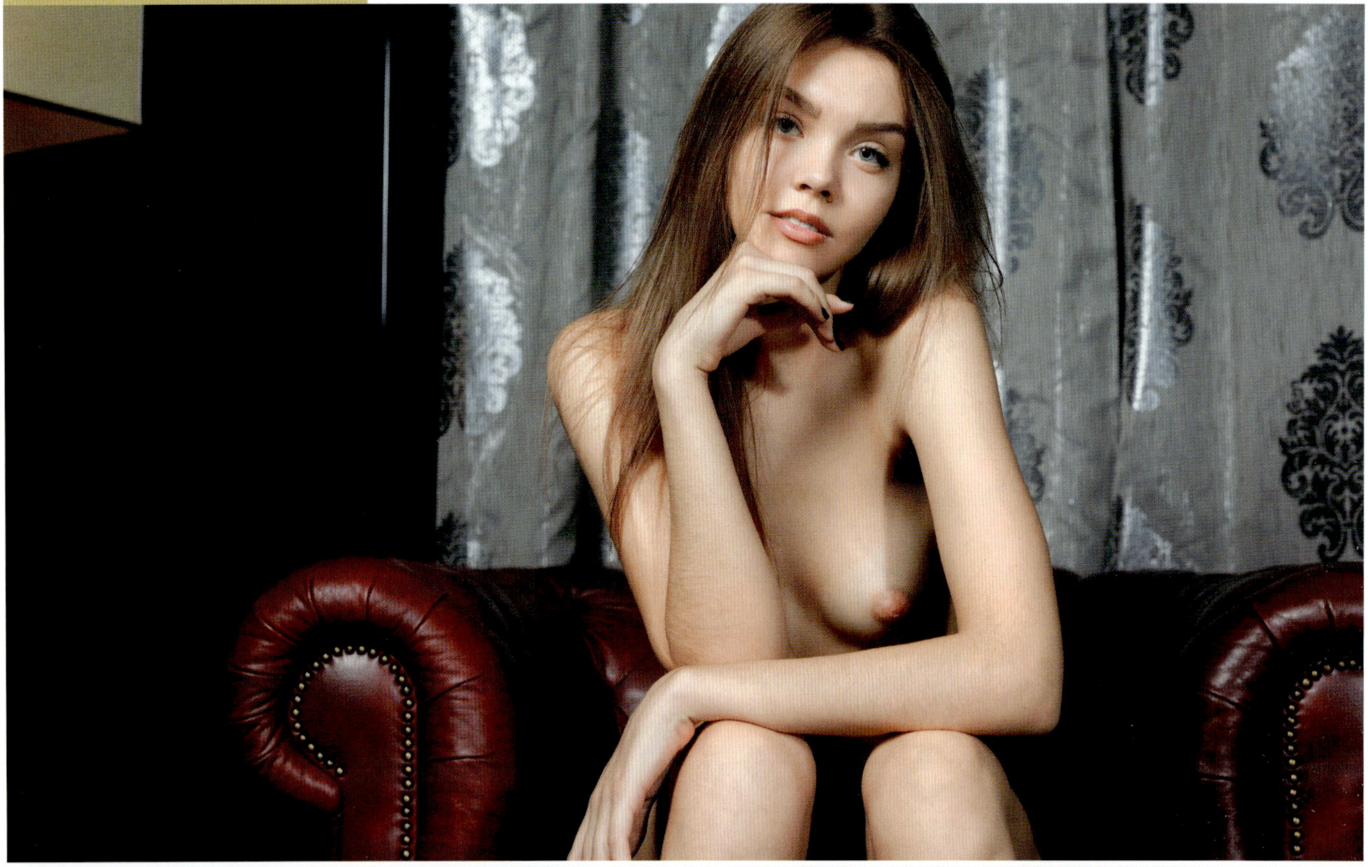

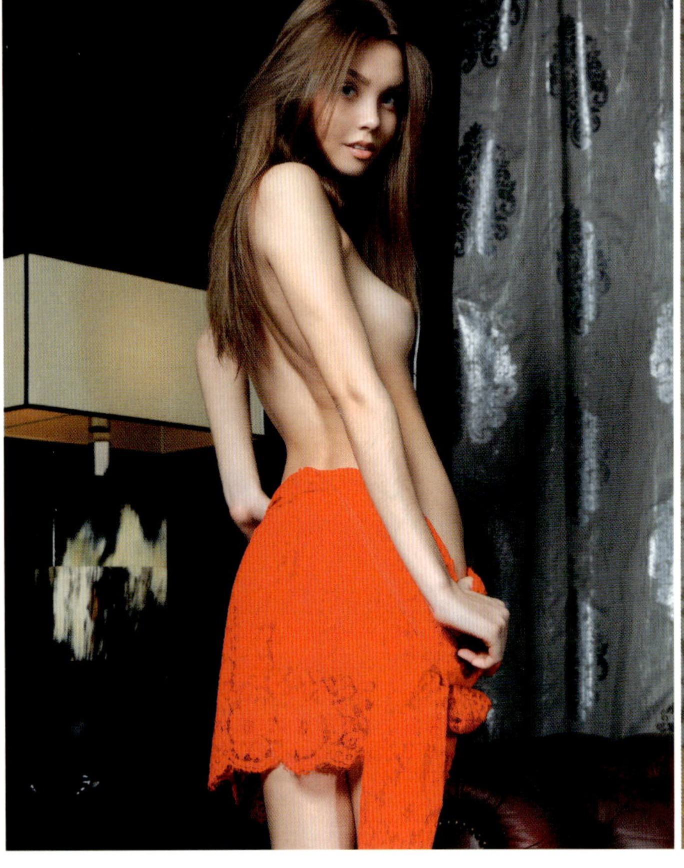

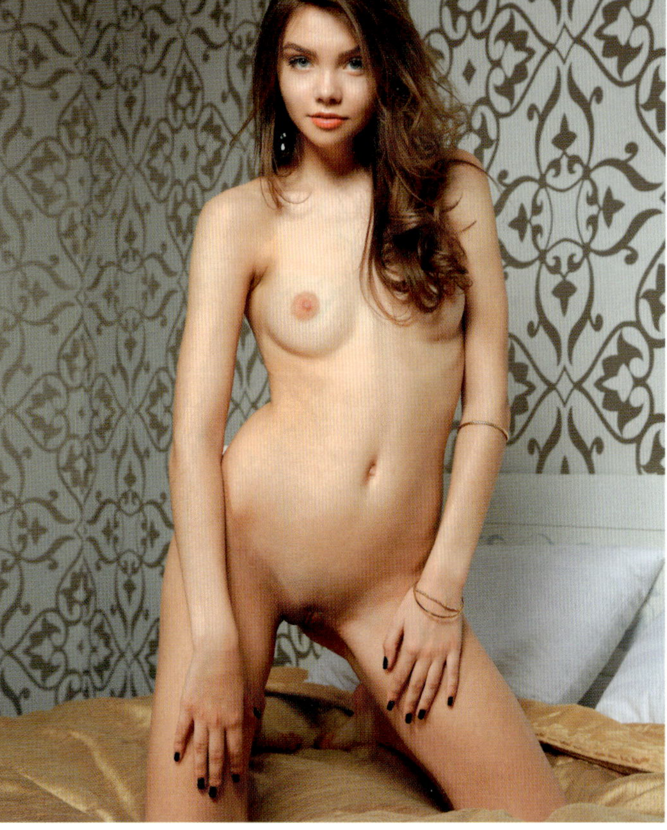

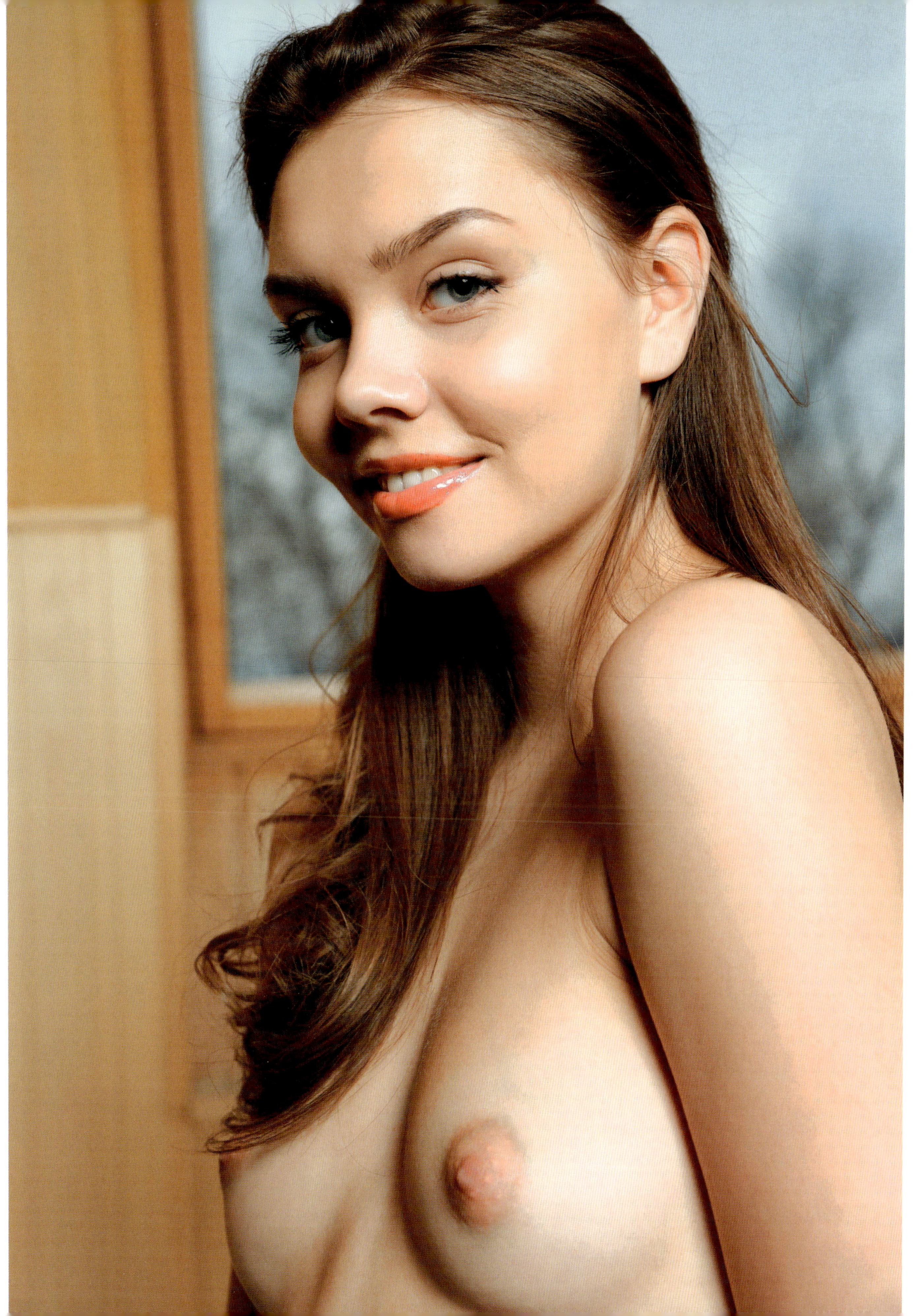

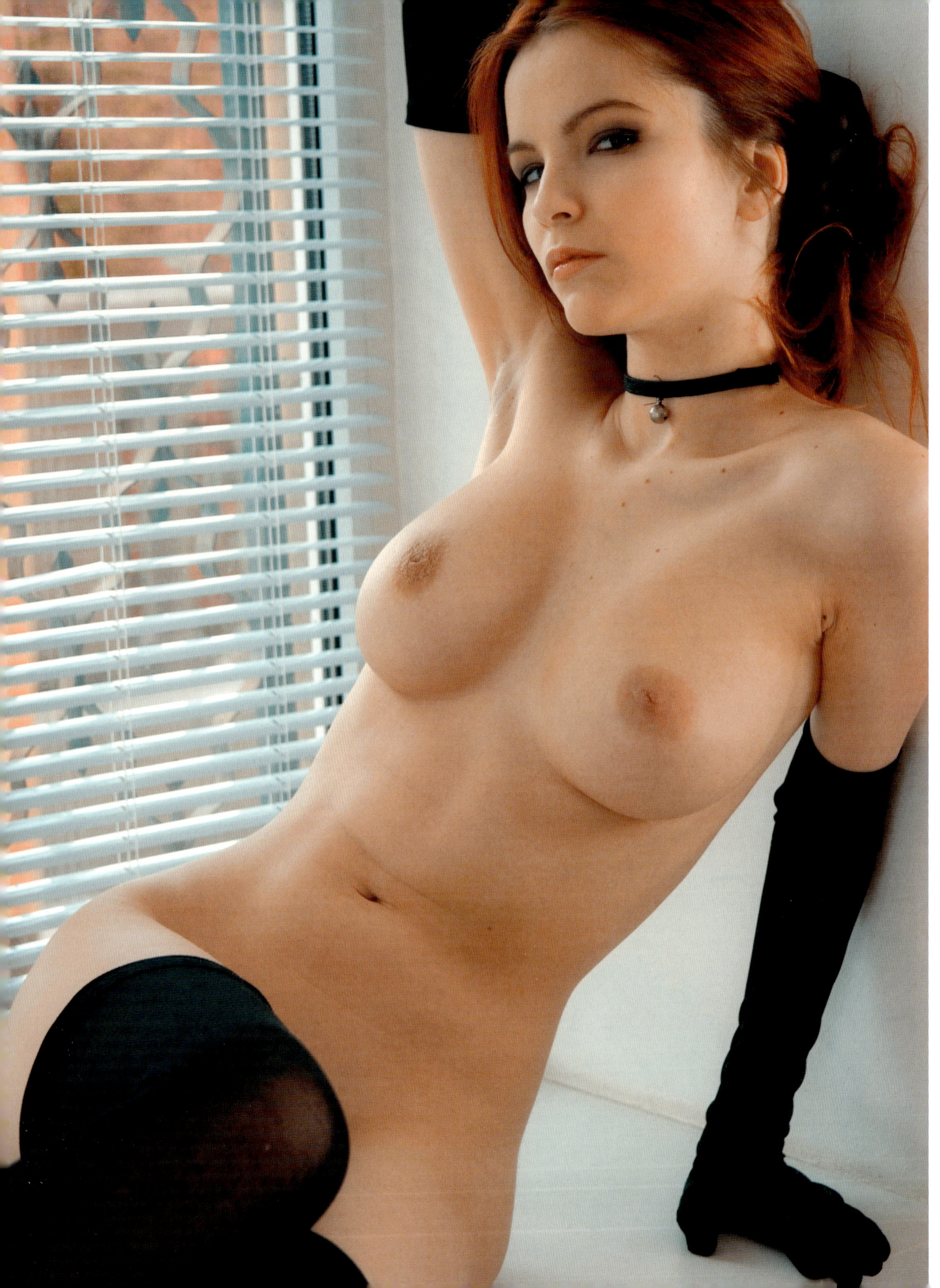

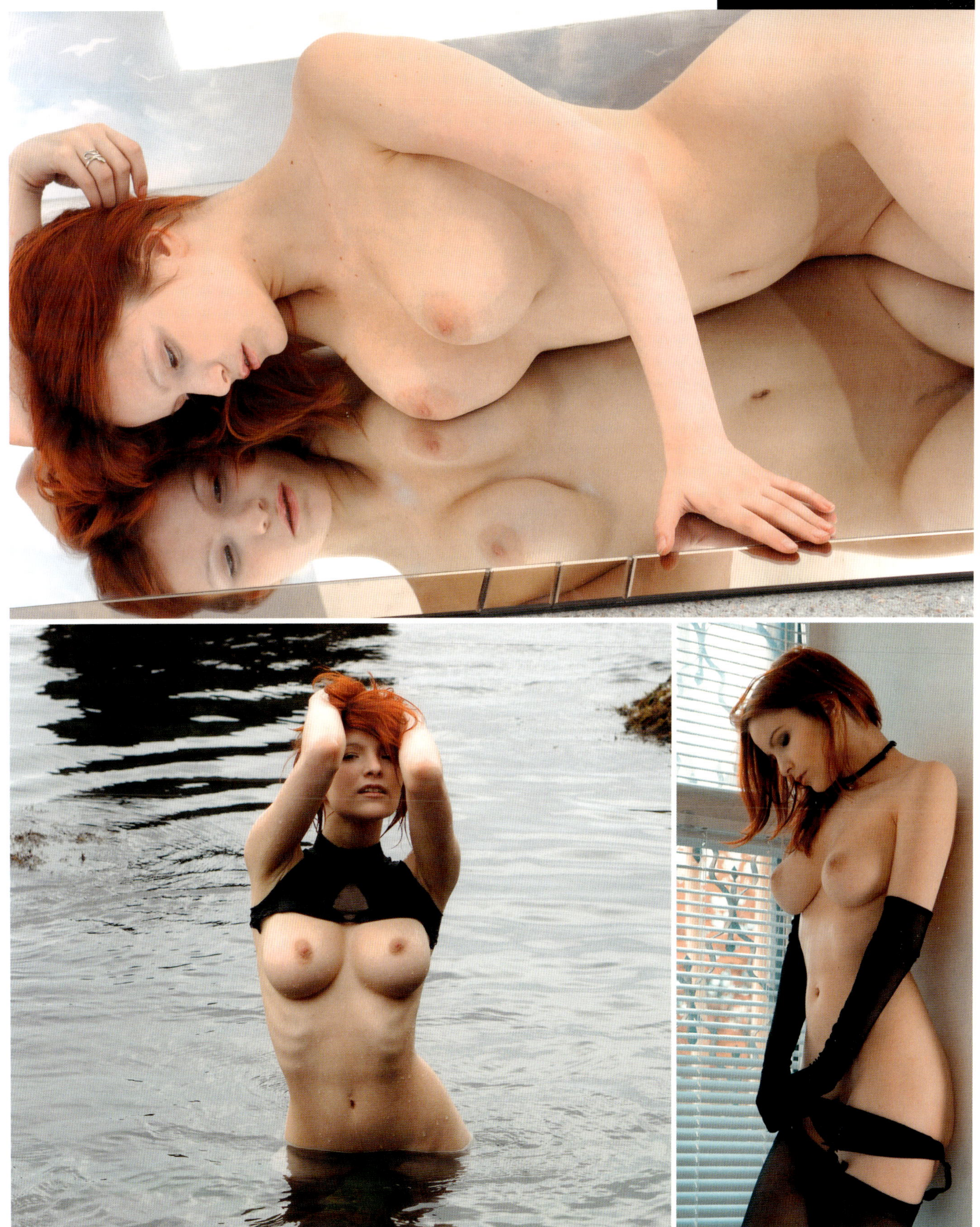

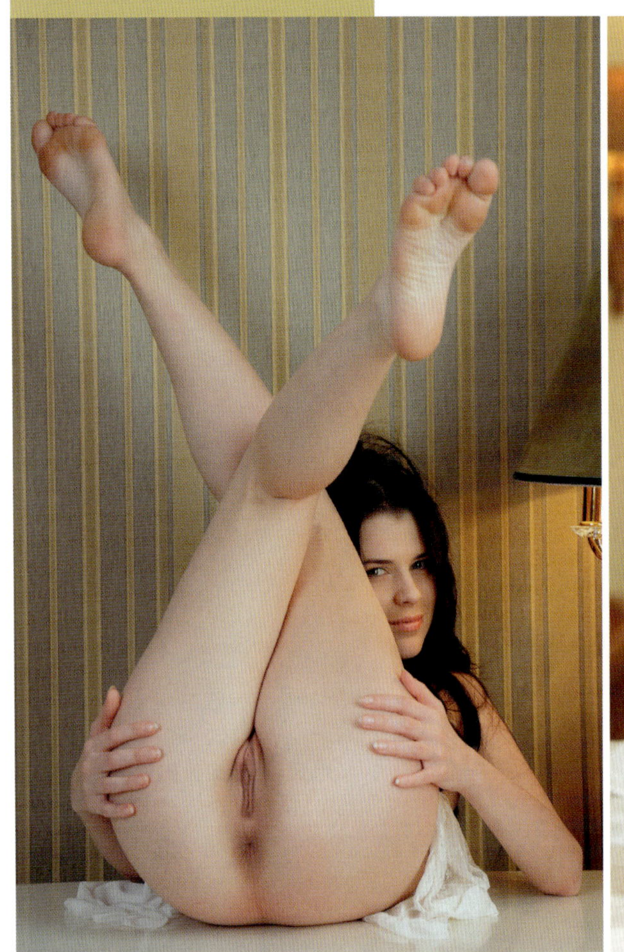

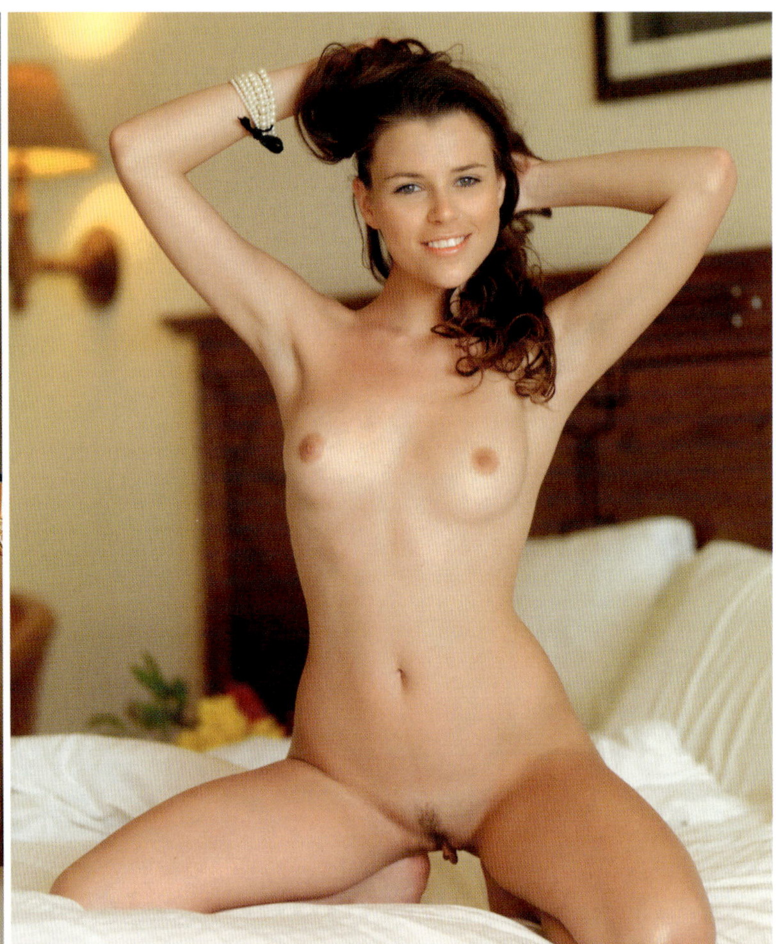

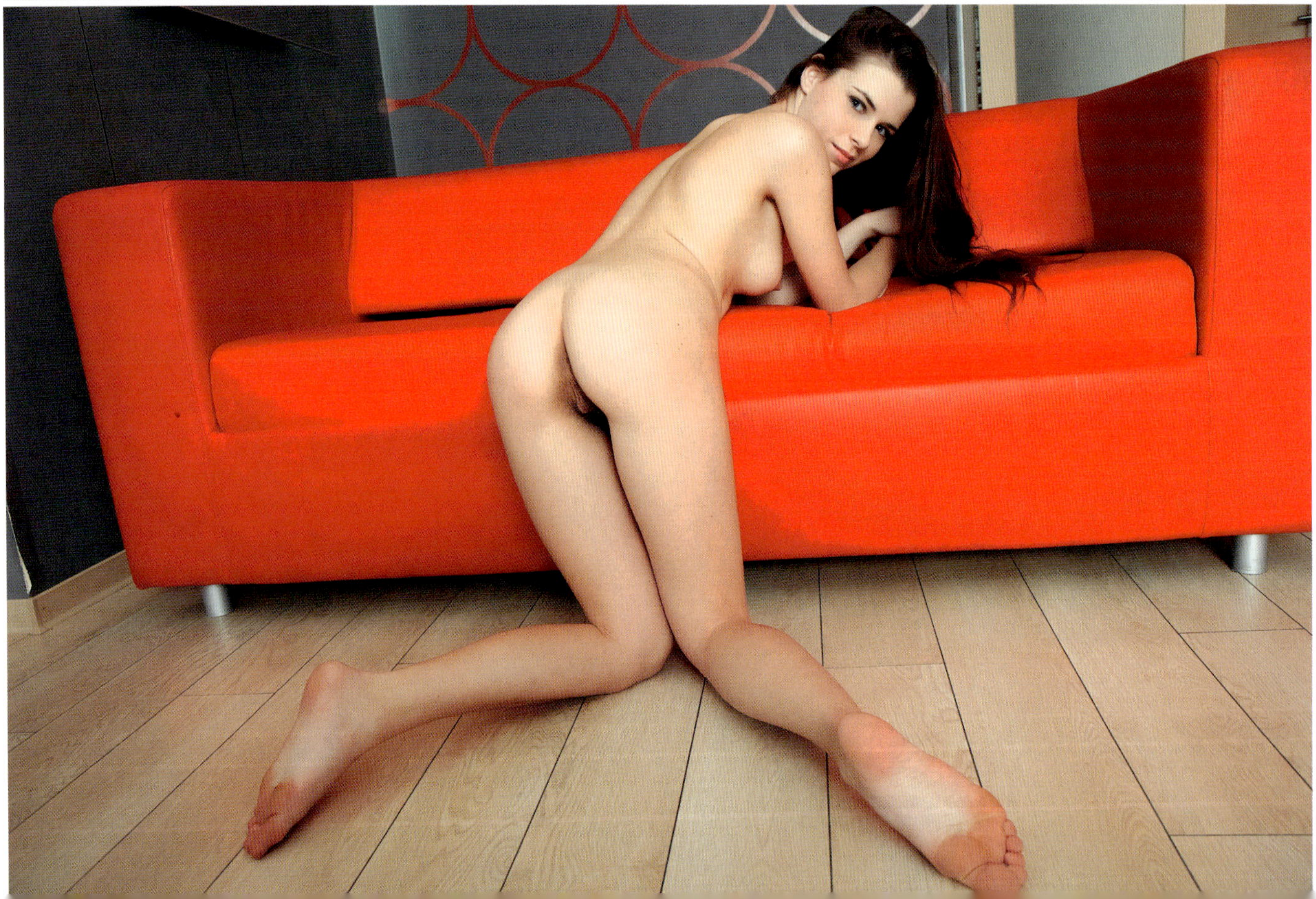

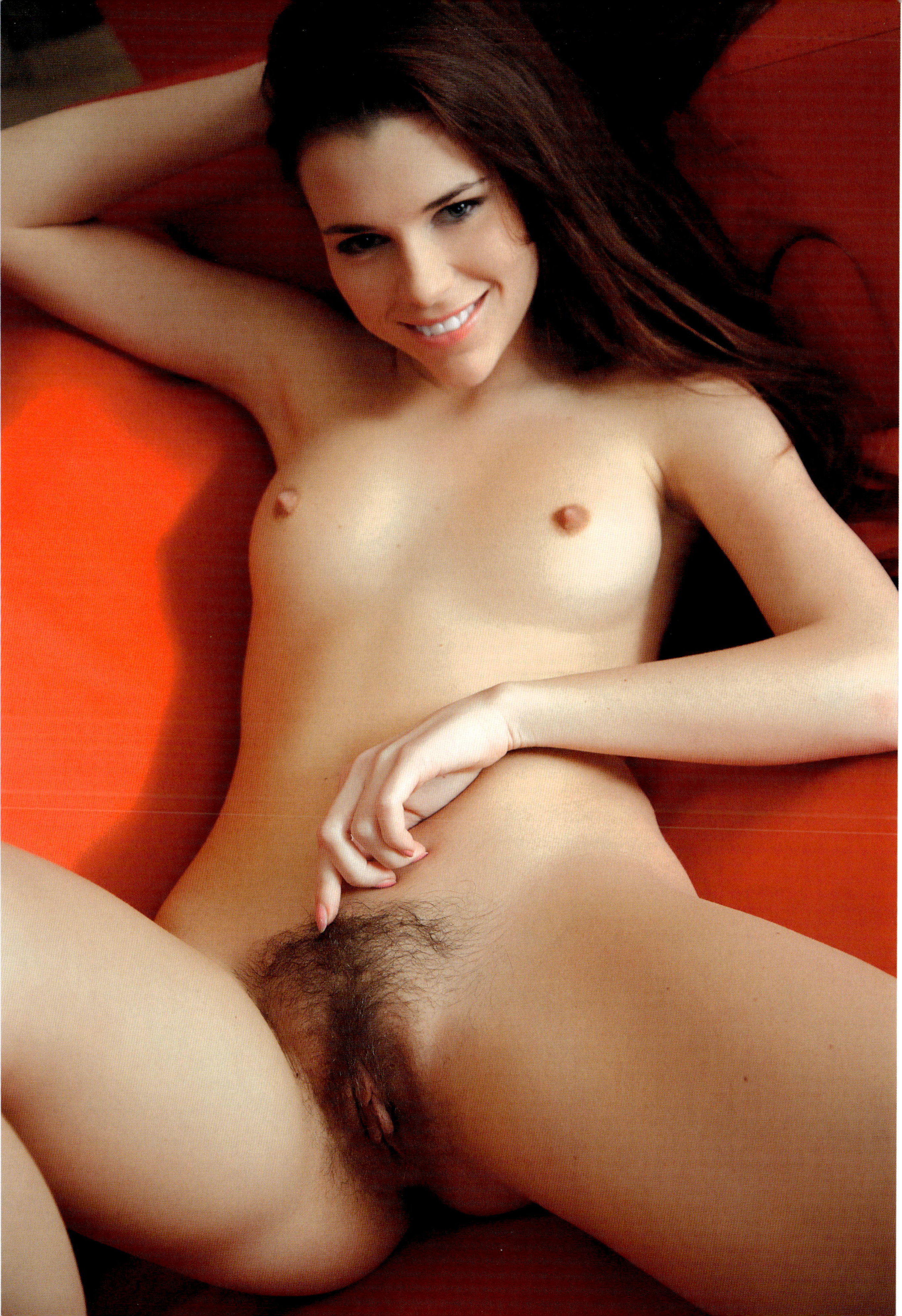

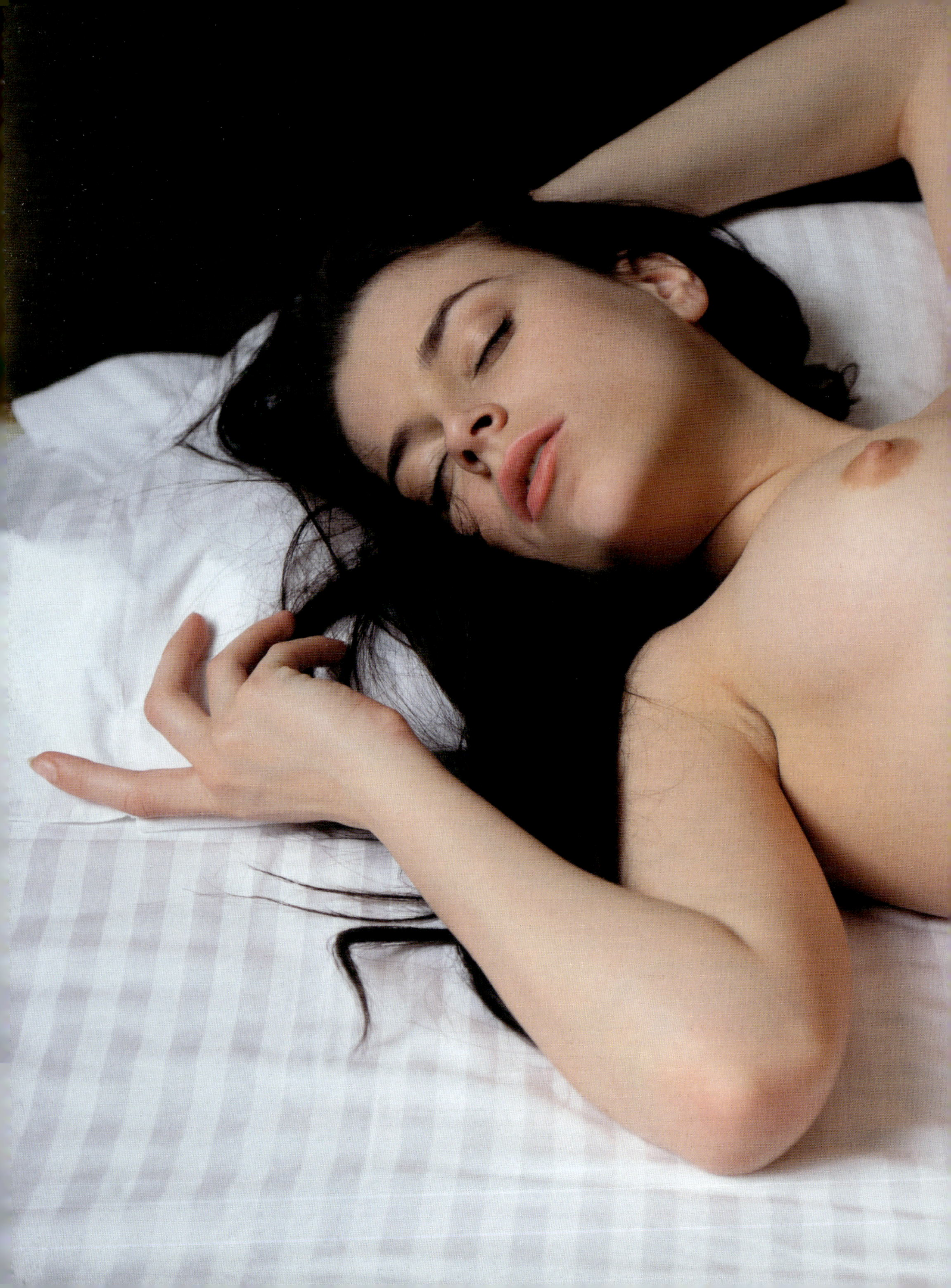

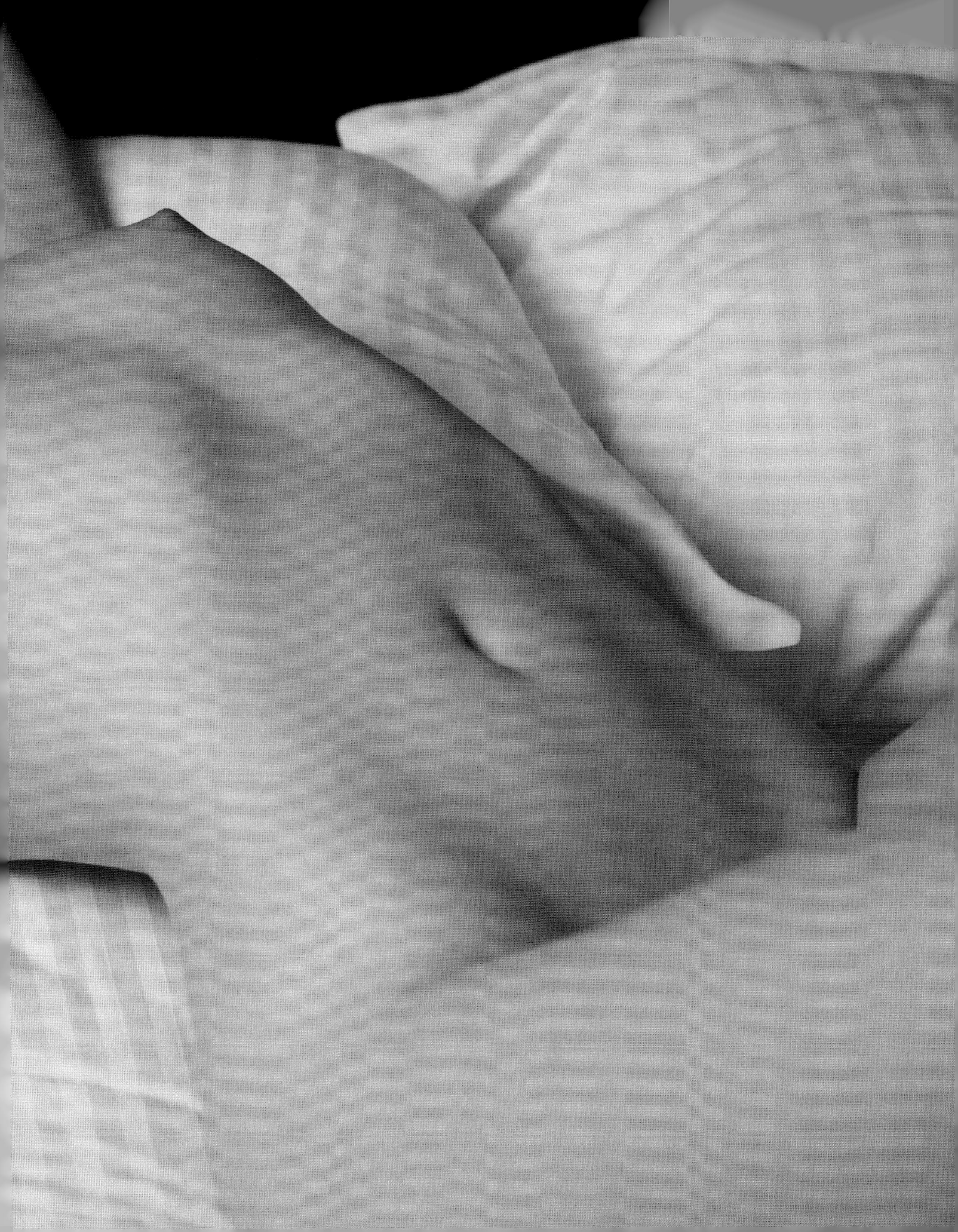

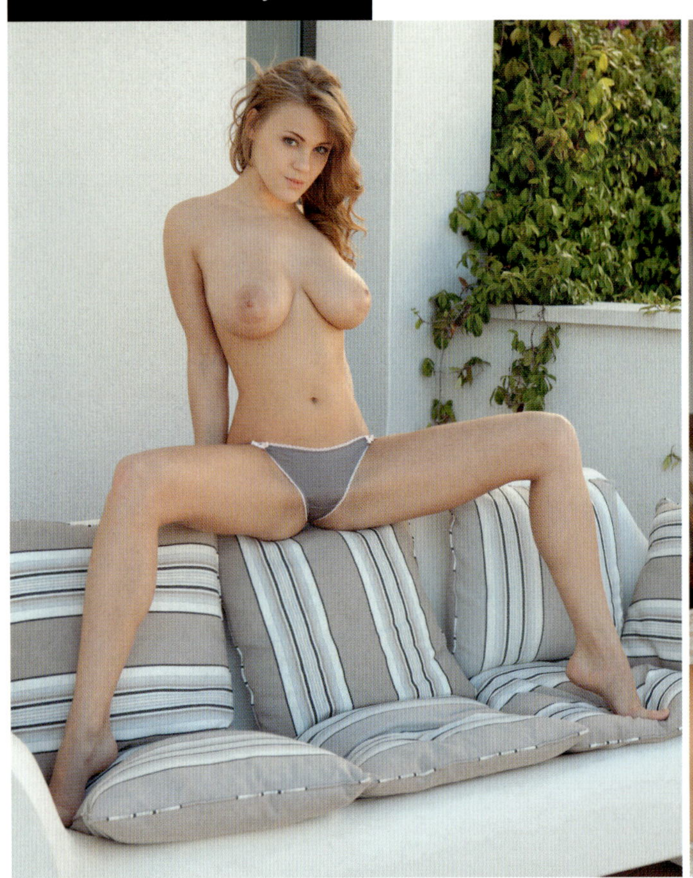

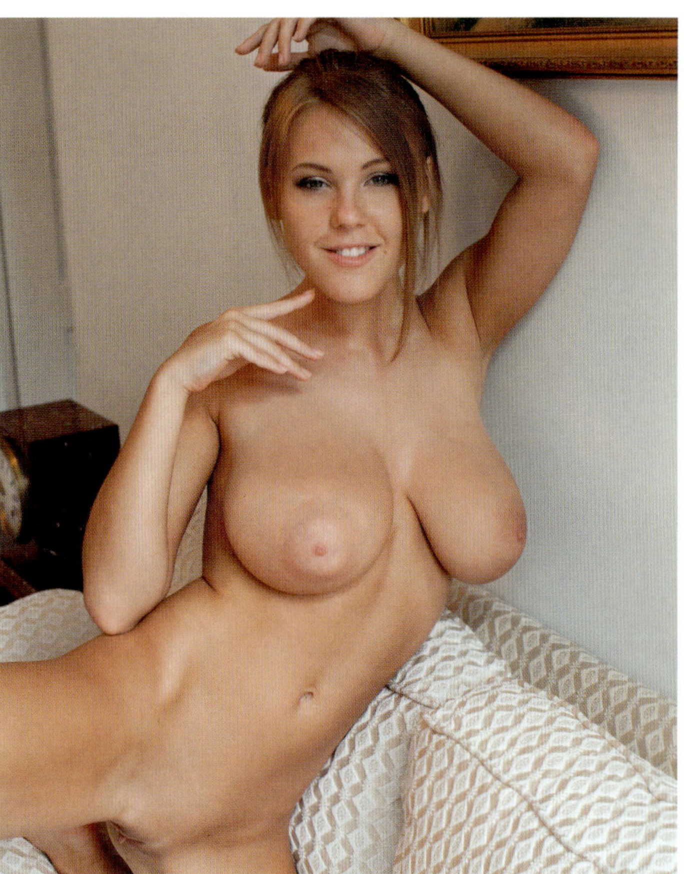

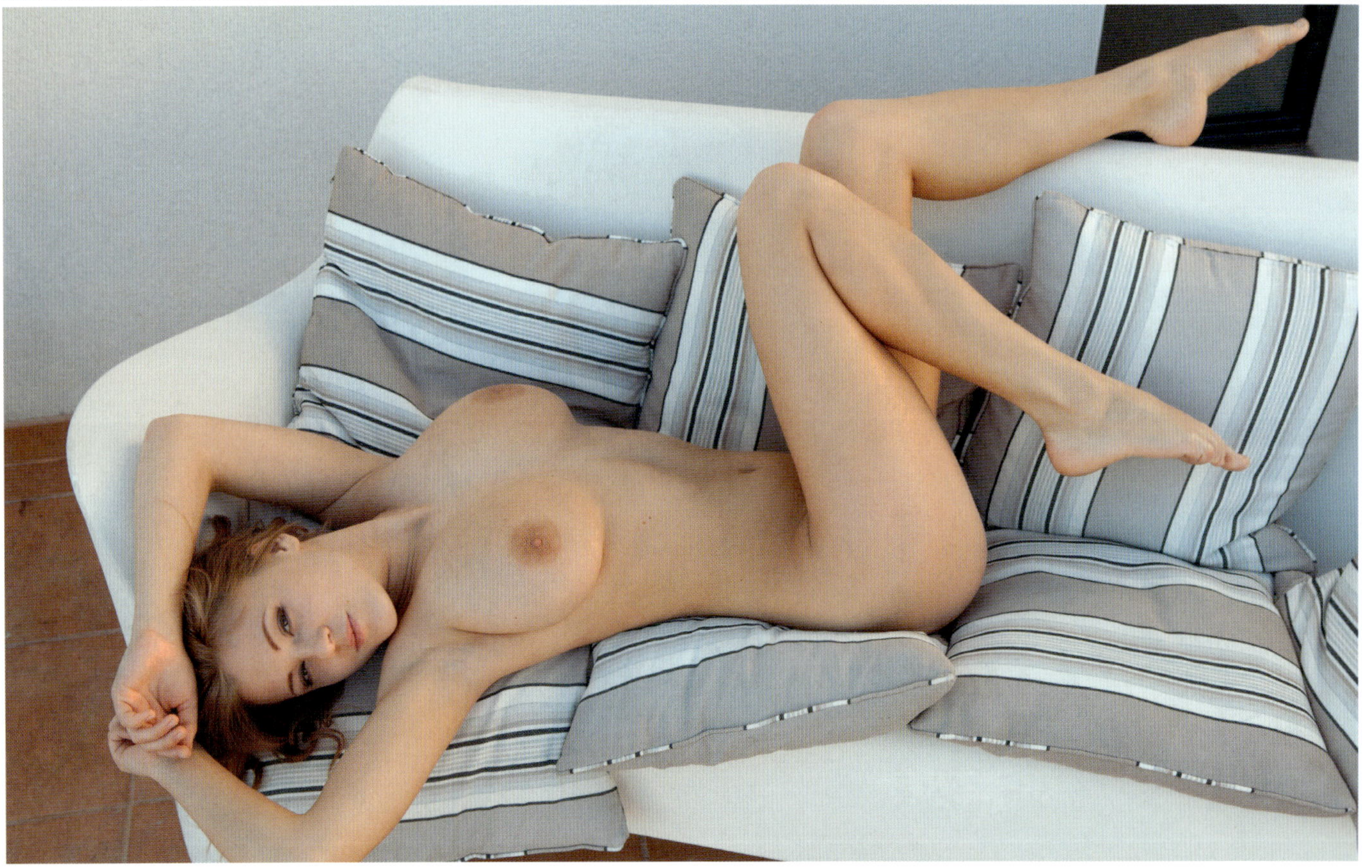

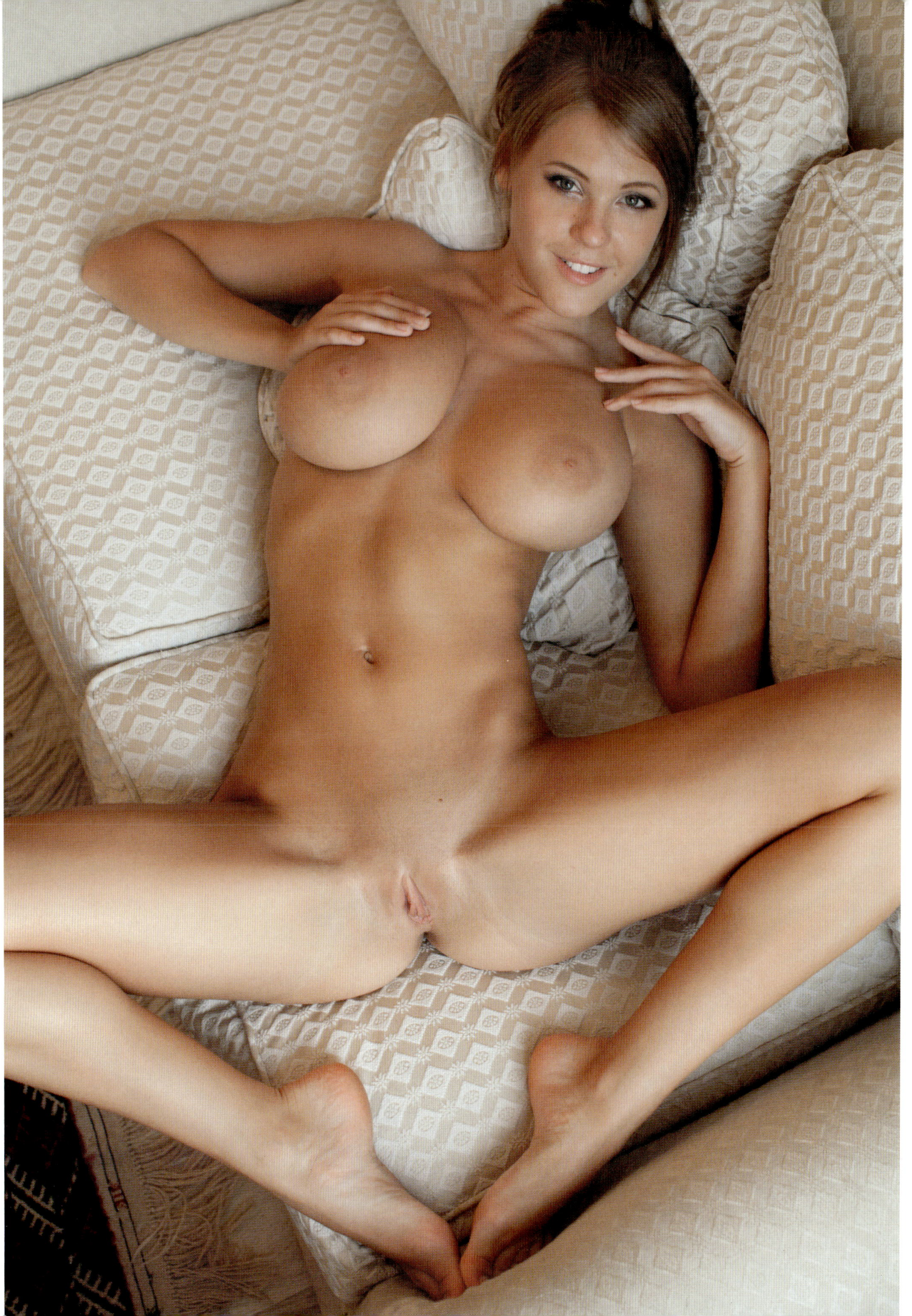

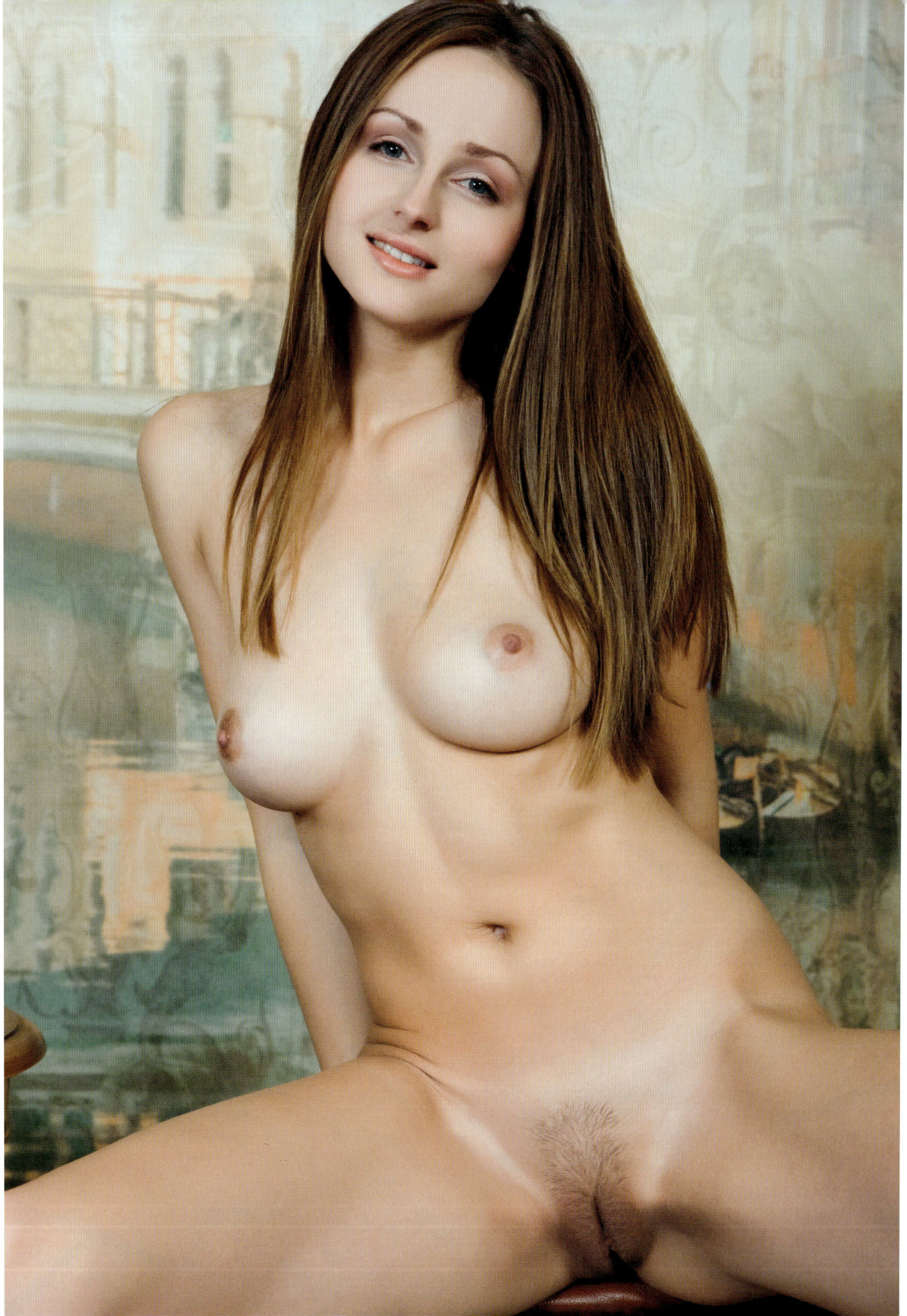

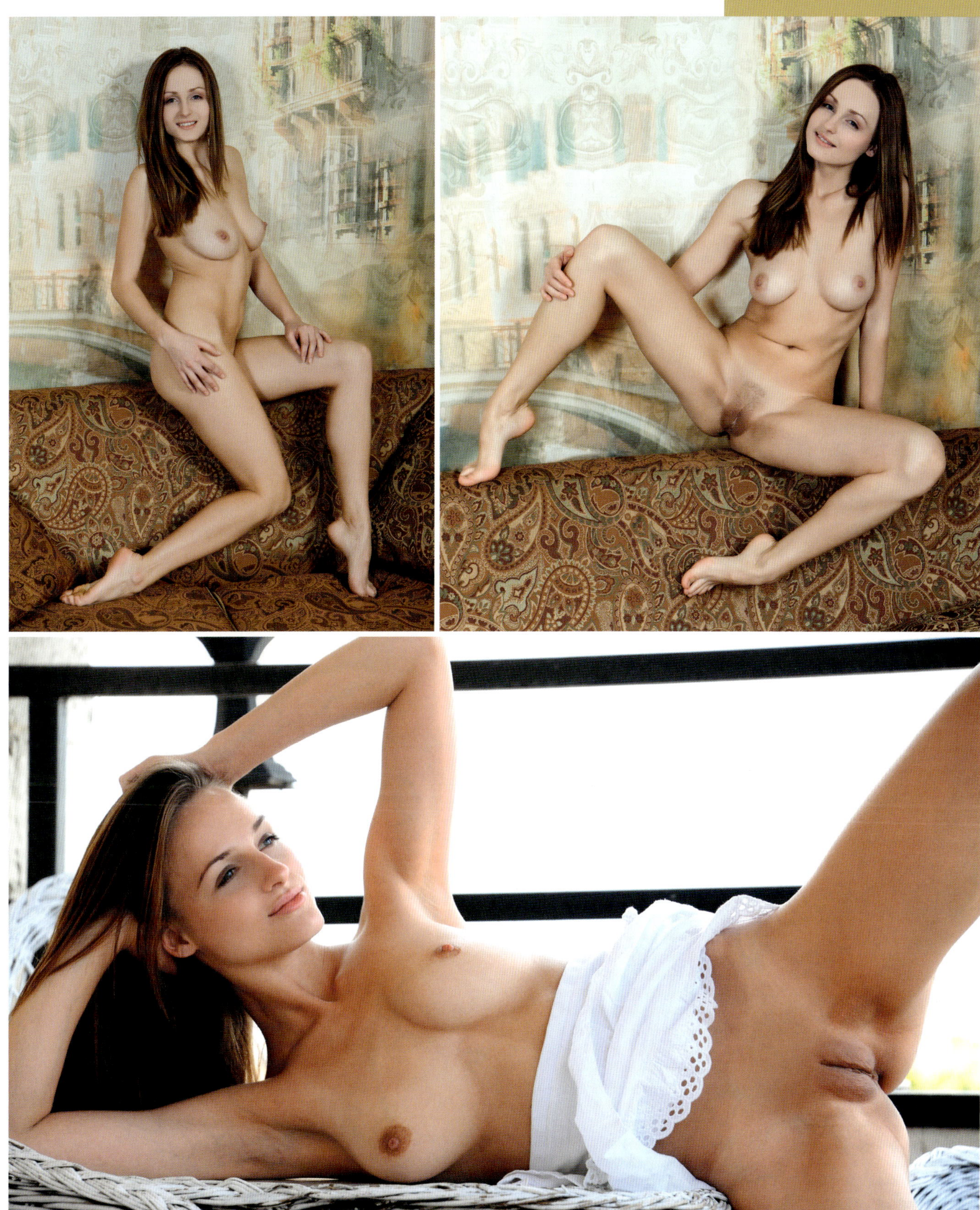

*Yarina A*

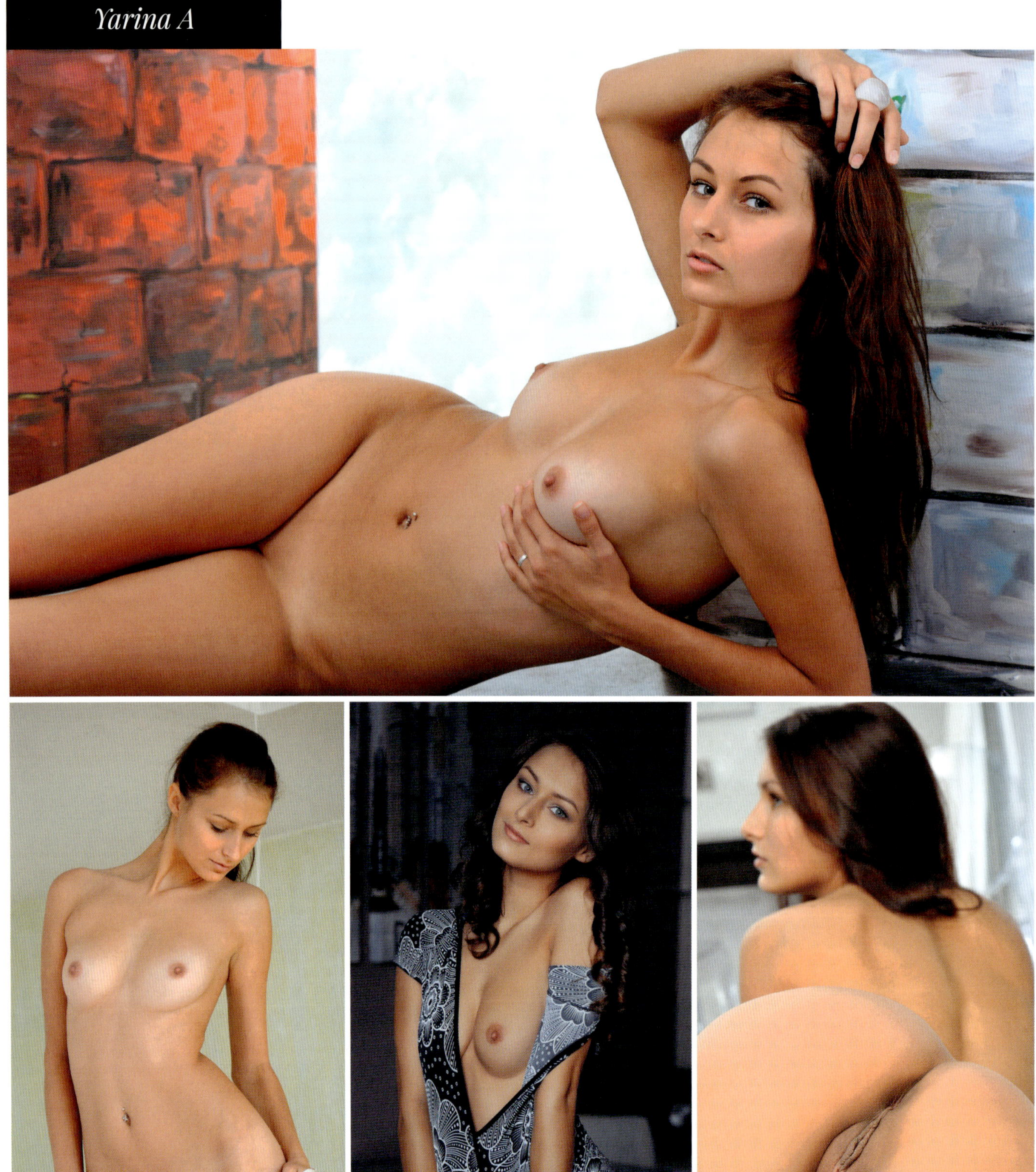

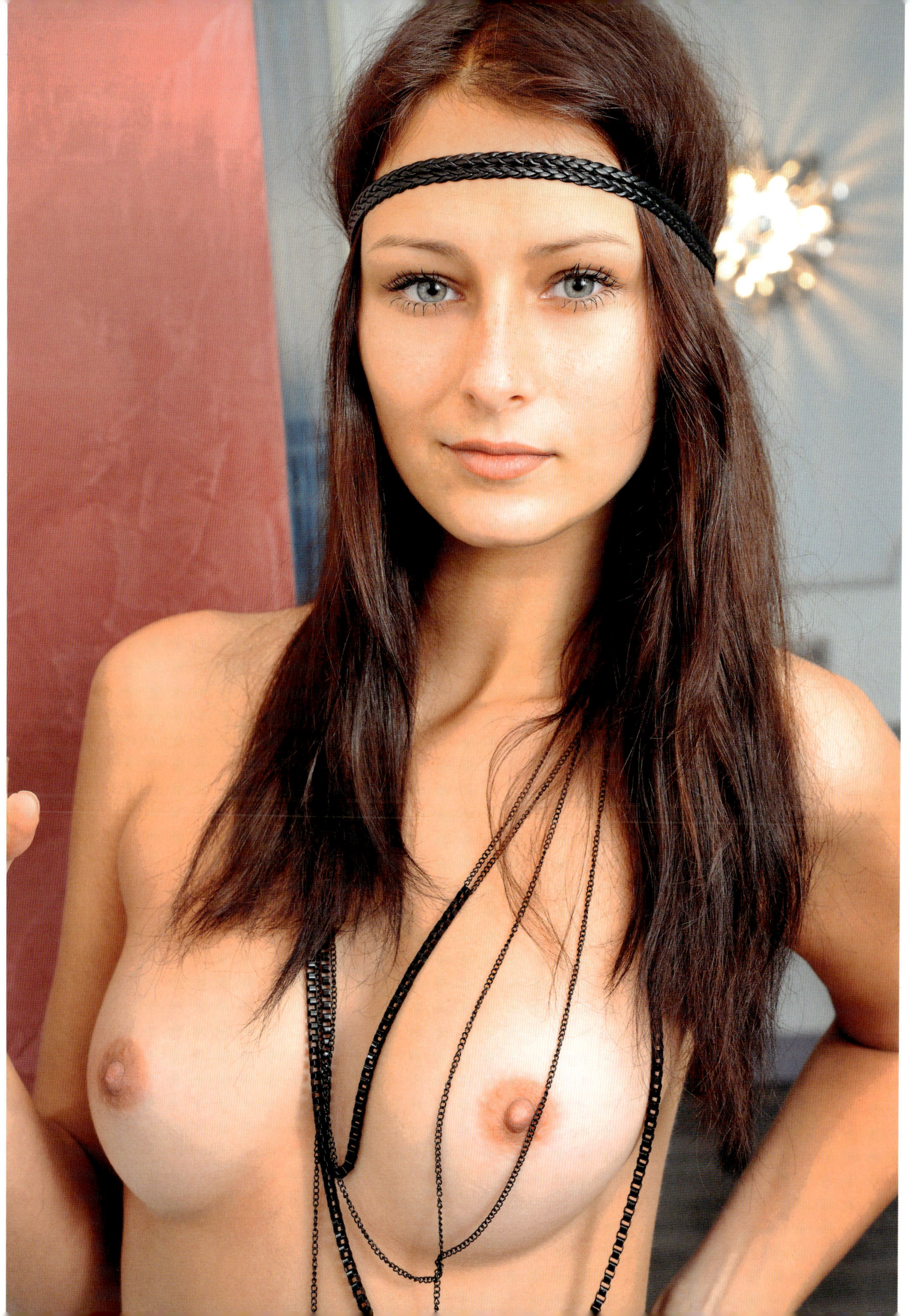

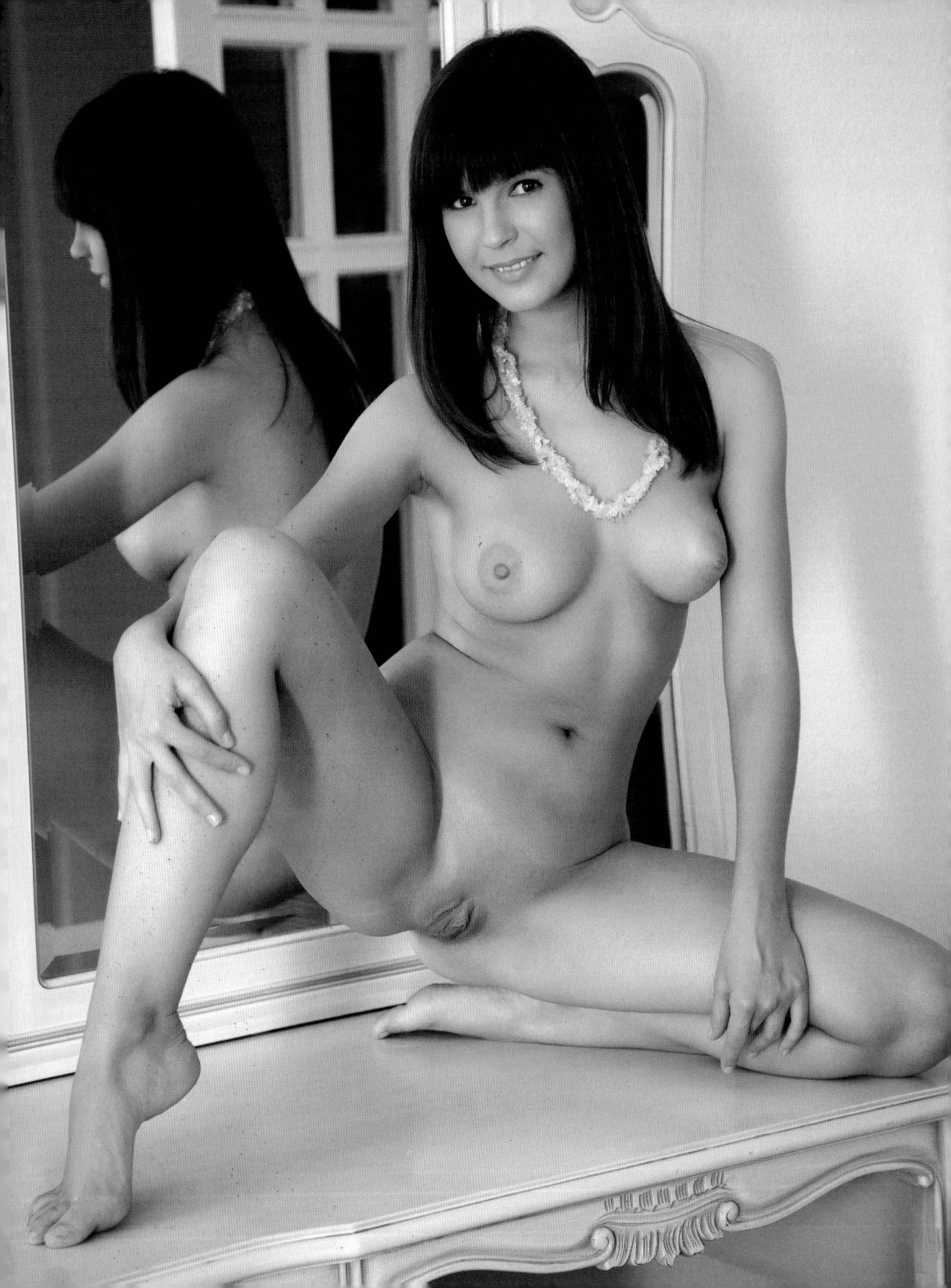

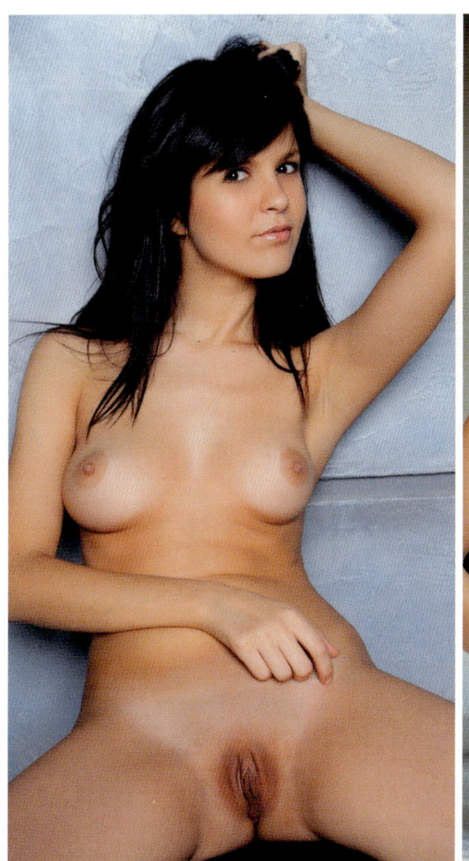

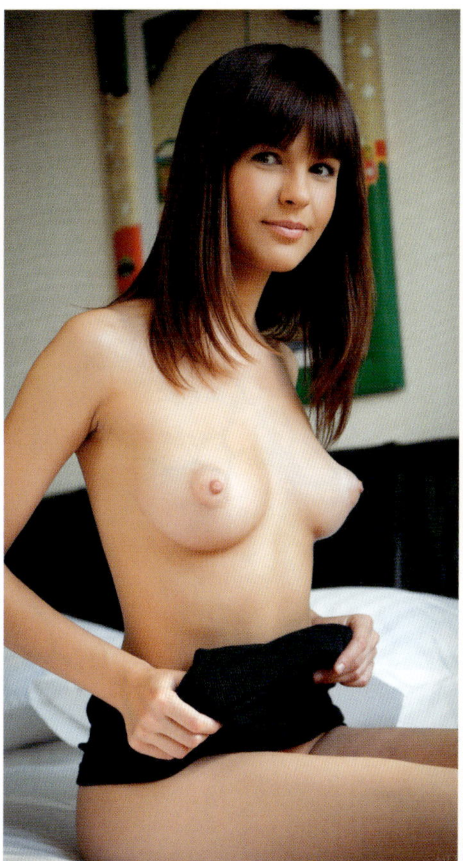

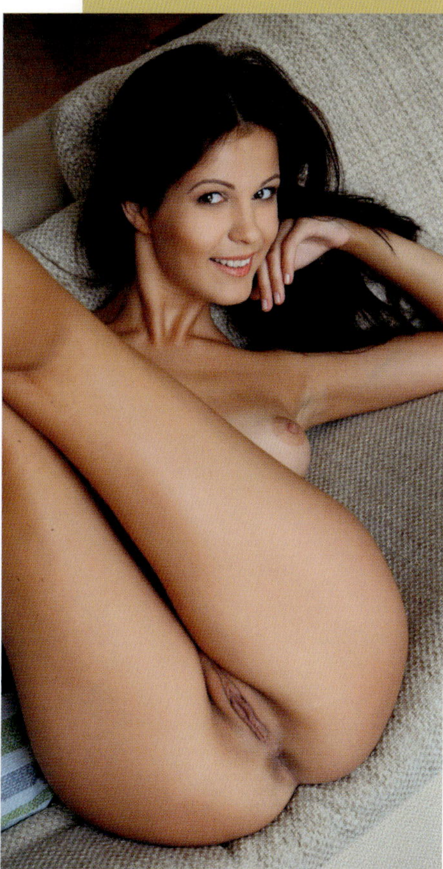

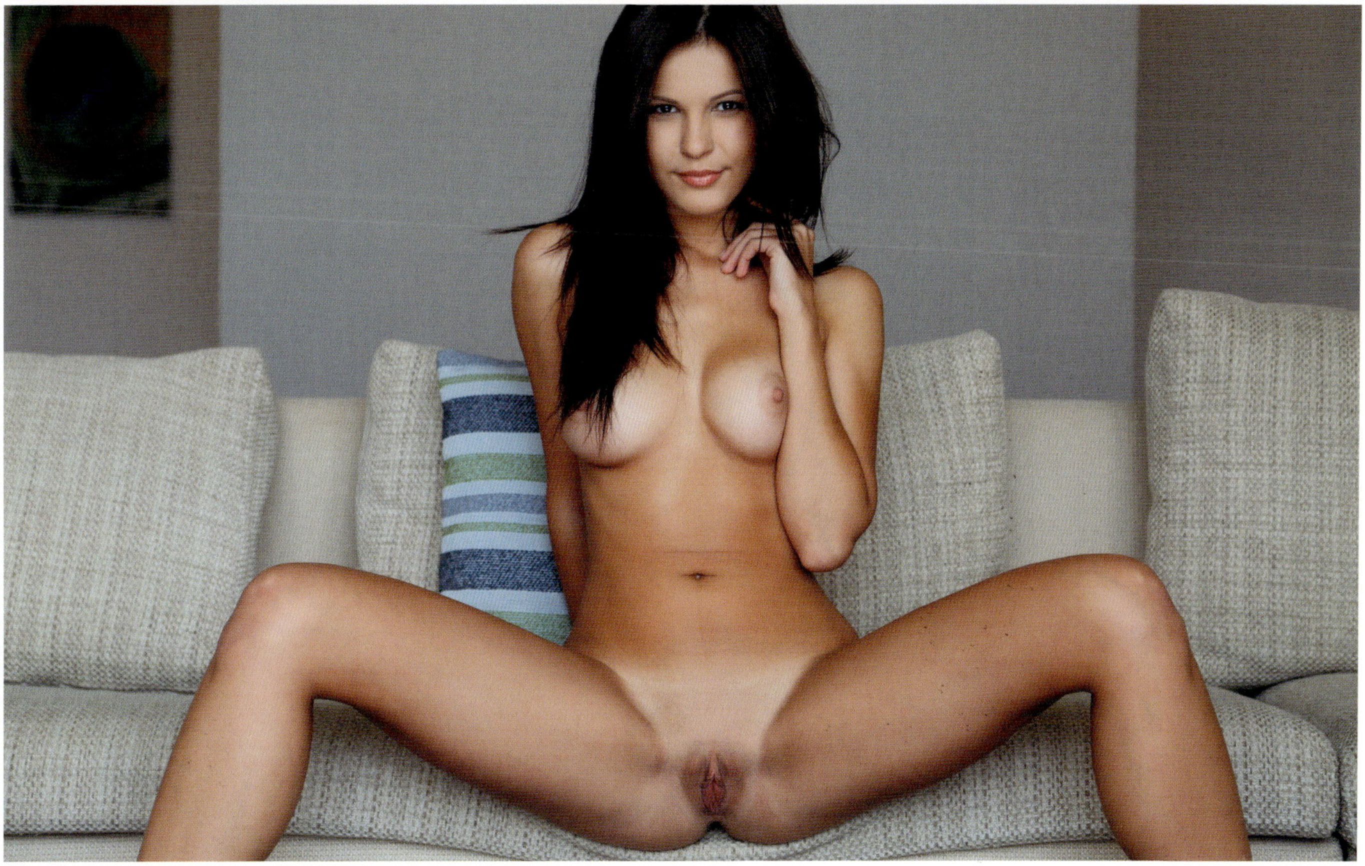

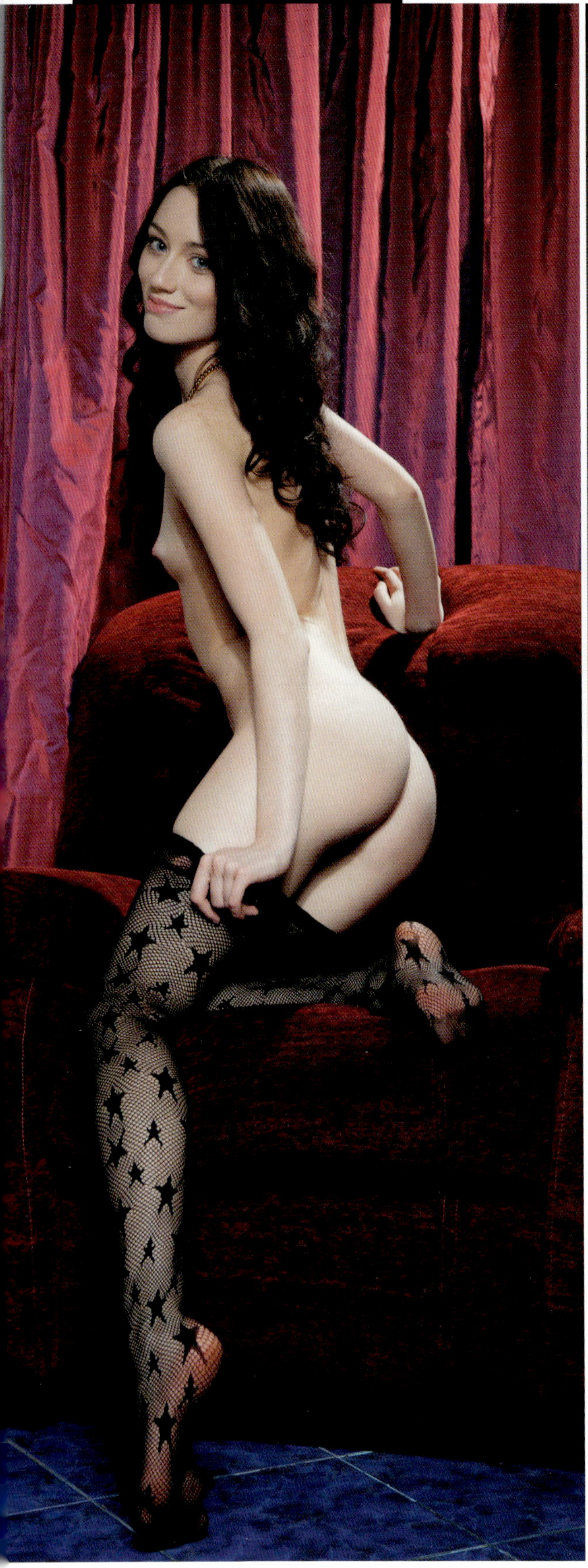

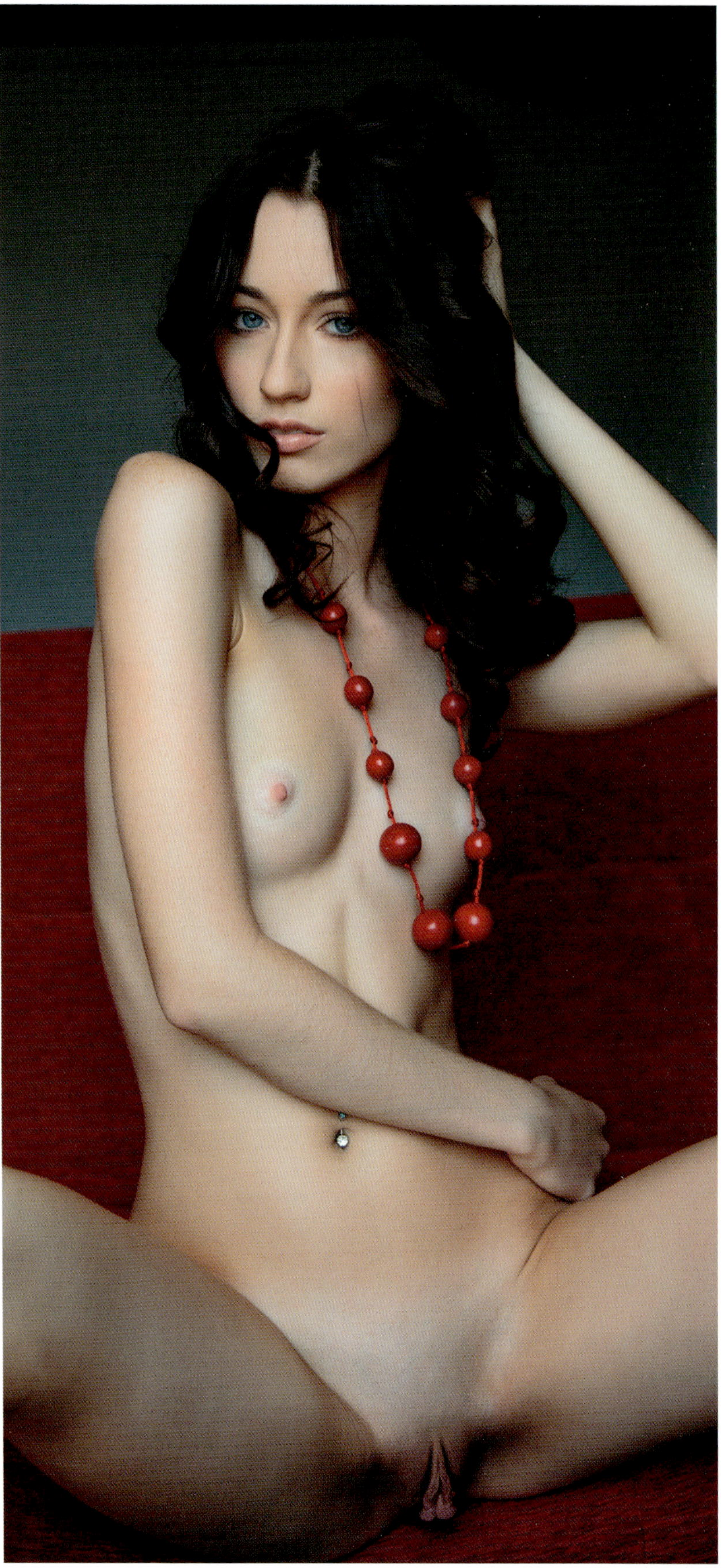

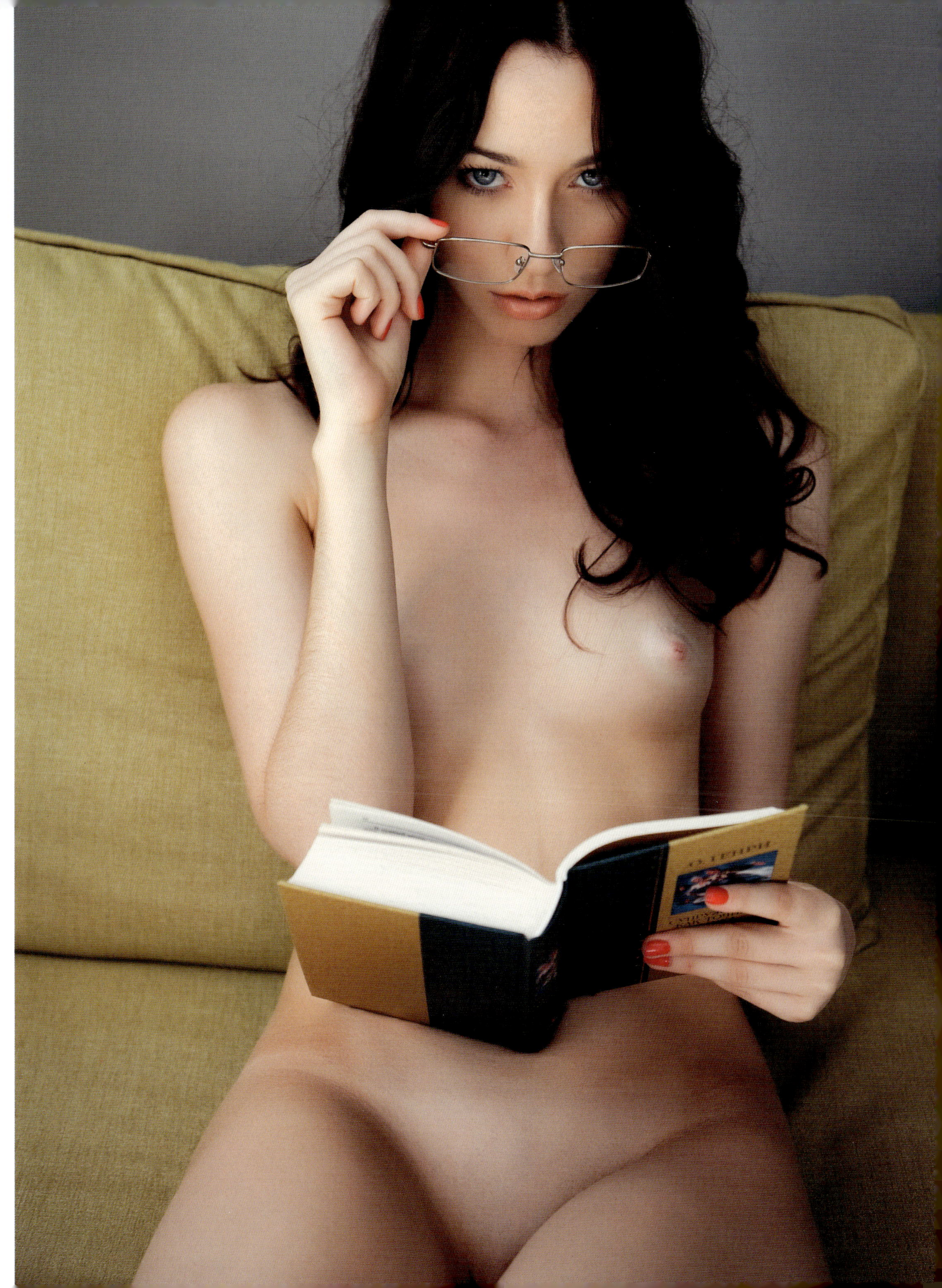

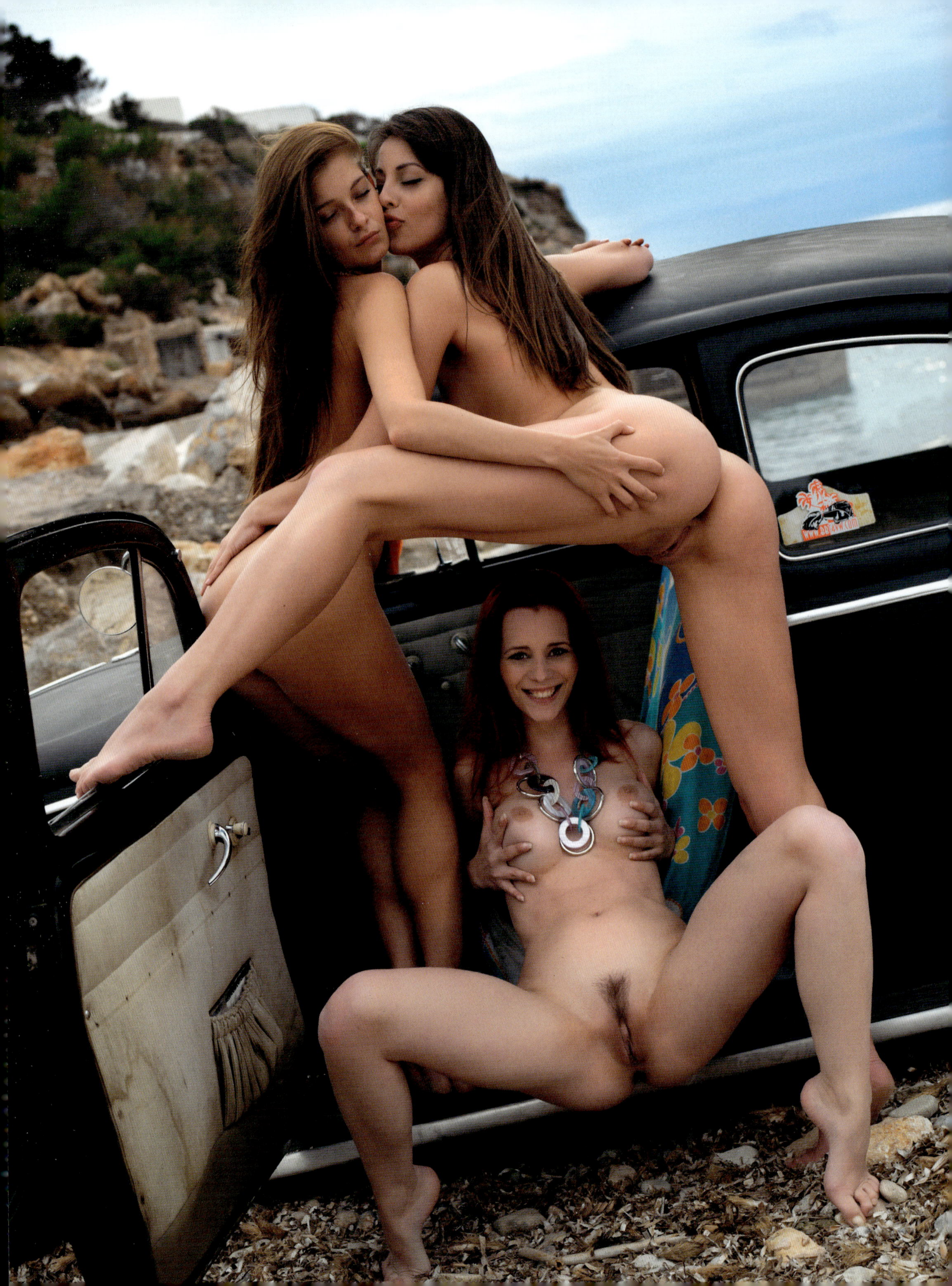

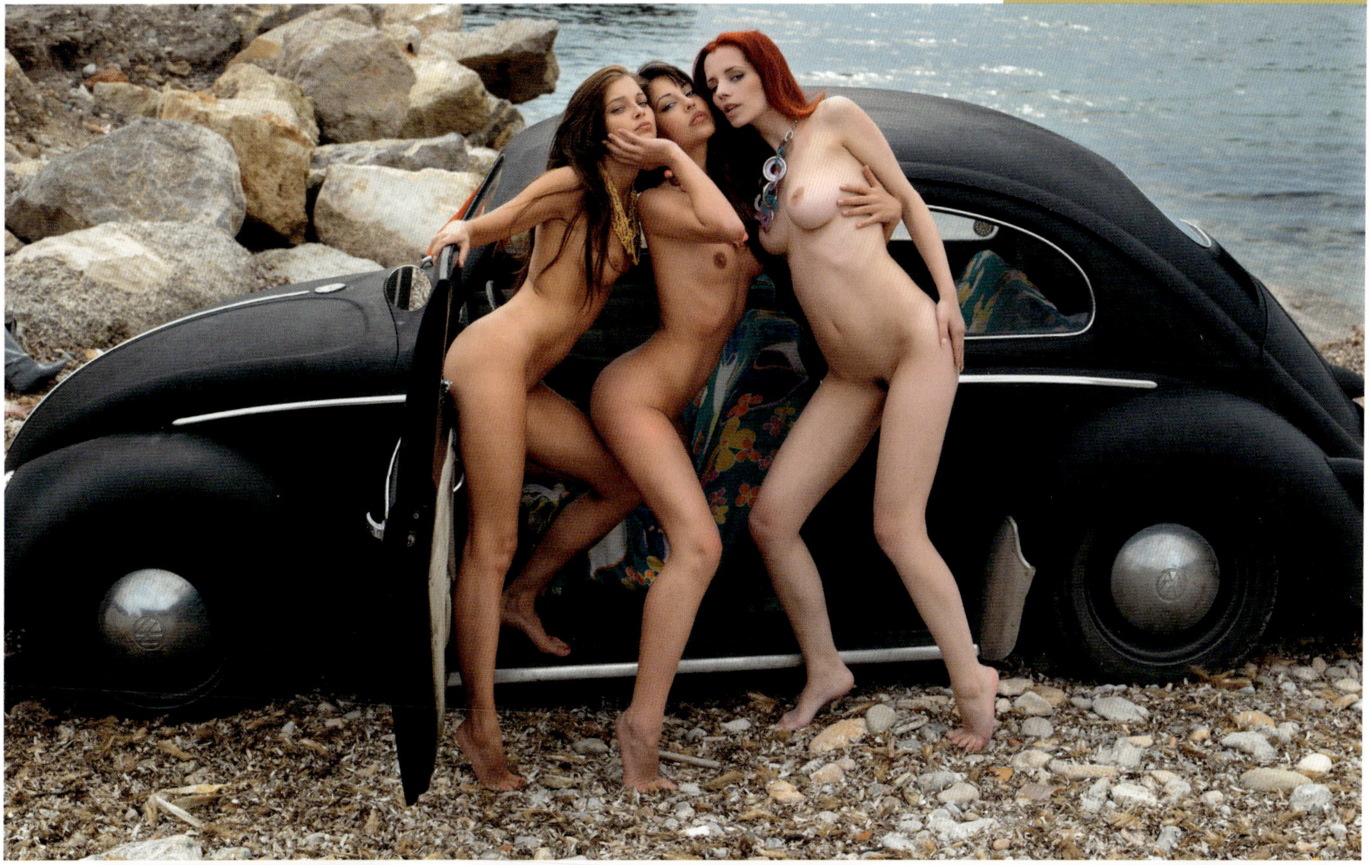

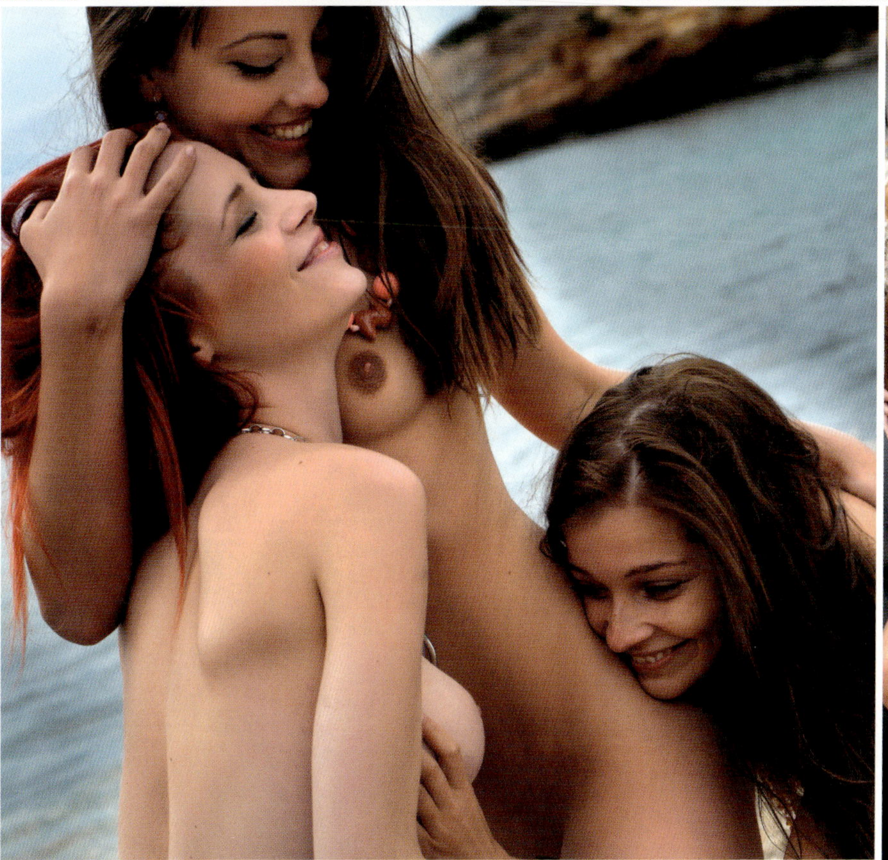

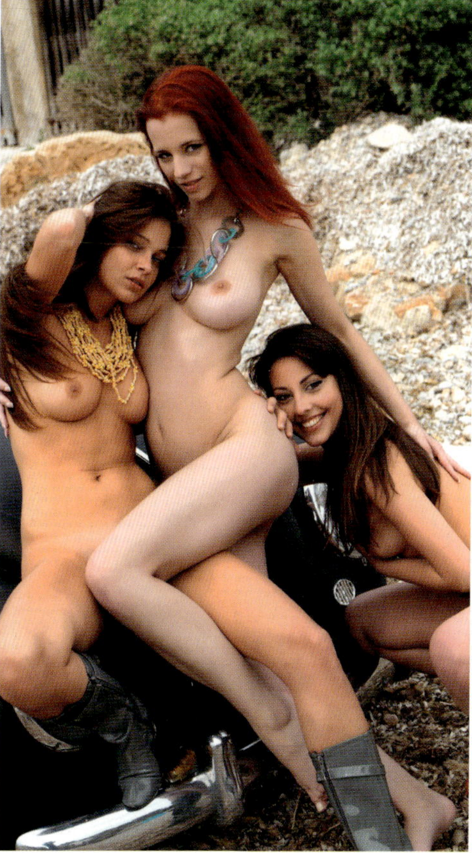

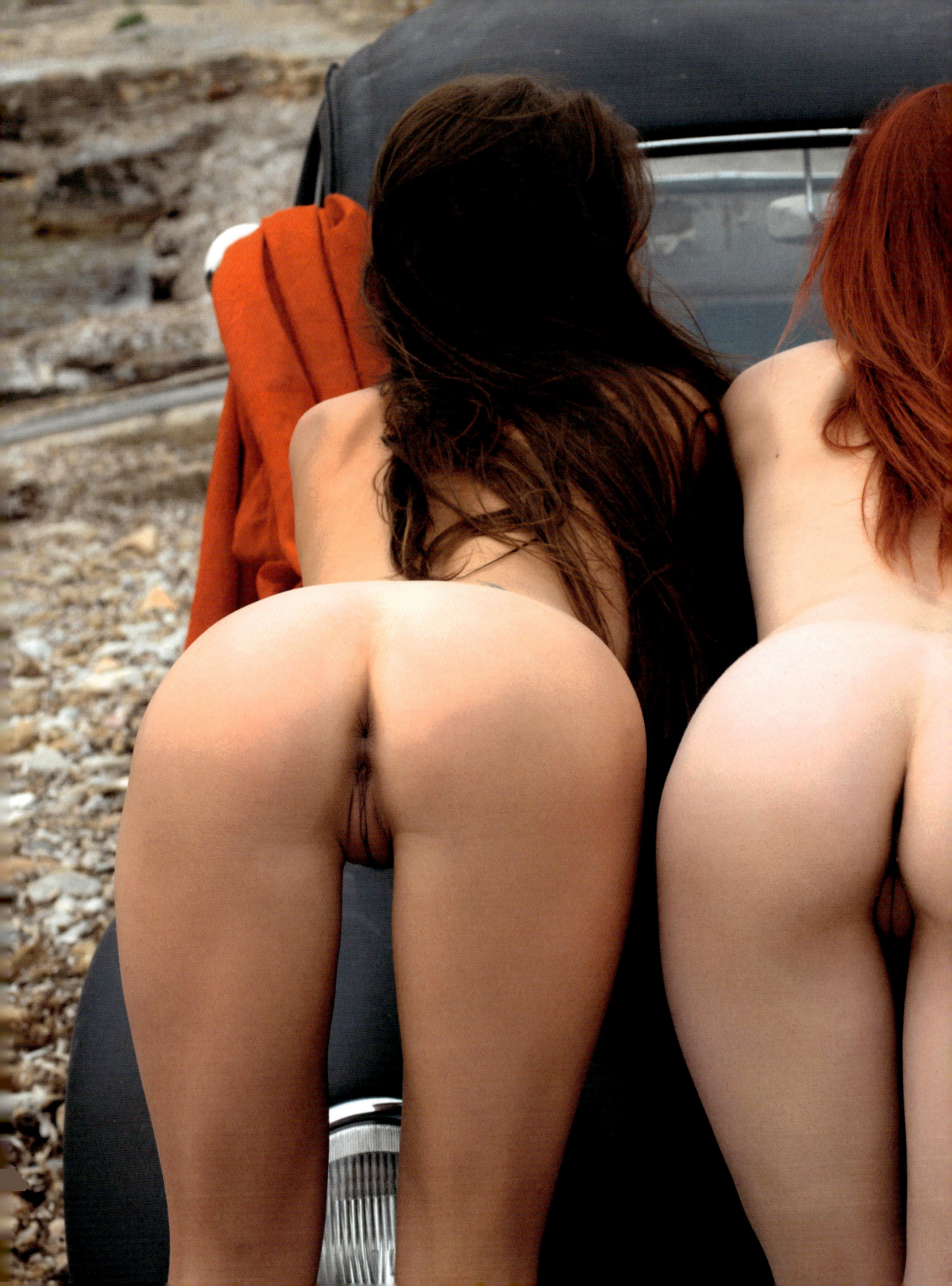

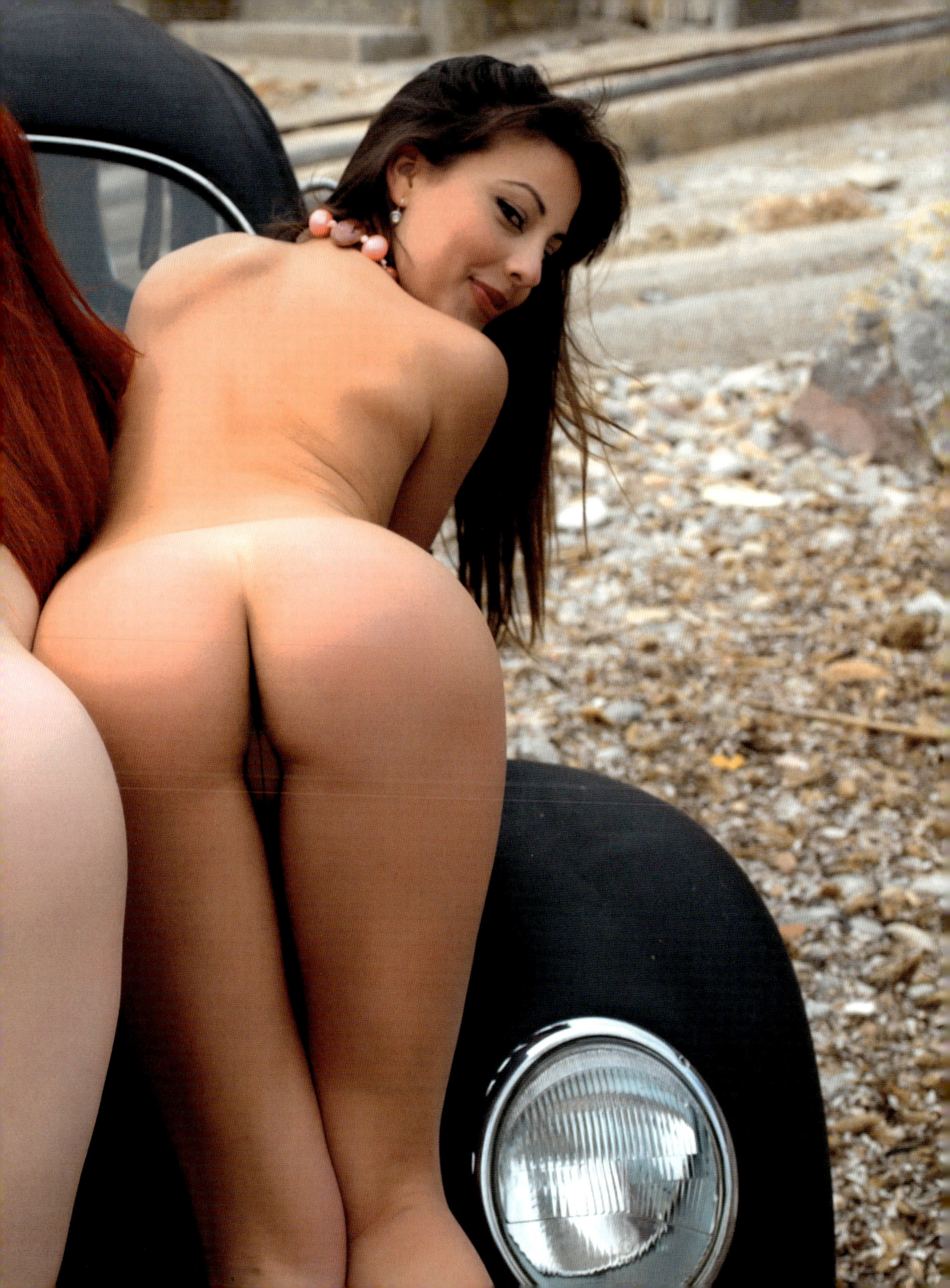

| MODEL | AGE DEBUT | EYE COLOR | HEIGHT | WEIGHT | MEASUREMENTS | COUNTRY |
|---|---|---|---|---|---|---|
| Adriana F | 20 | hazel | 165 cm | 52 kg | 86 / 61 / 91 | Latvia |
| Aislin | 19 | brown | 173 cm | 55 kg | 89 / 61 / 91 | Latvia |
| Alisa Amore | 21 | brown | 170 cm | 49 kg | 84 / 64 / 89 | Hungary |
| Altea B | 18 | brown | 170 cm | 49 kg | 89 / 58 / 89 | Slovakia |
| Alysha A | 21 | blue | 175 cm | 48 kg | 84 / 61 / 89 | Estonia |
| Anie Darling | 19 | hazel | 168 cm | 53 kg | 89 / 58 / 89 | Czech Republic |
| Anita C | 21 | blue | 170 cm | 51 kg | 94 / 61 / 94 | Russian Federation |
| Anita E | 26 | blue | 175 cm | 53 kg | 94 / 61 / 94 | Ukraine |
| Anna A | 22 | brown | 170 cm | 48 kg | 89 / 58 / 89 | Ukraine |
| Ardelia A | 20 | blue | 160 cm | 45 kg | 79 / 56 / 84 | Ukraine |
| Ariel Piper Fawn | 21 | green | 170 cm | 49 kg | 89 / 61 / 89 | Czech Republic |
| Ashanti A | 25 | brown | 173 cm | 50 kg | 84 / 61 / 89 | Russian Federation |
| Ashley Doll | 21 | brown | 163 cm | 45 kg | 81 / 61 / 86 | United States |
| Astrud A | 24 | brown | 168 cm | 48 kg | 86 / 61 / 89 | Brazil |
| Barbara D | 19 | blue | 170 cm | 59 kg | 94 / 66 / 91 | Russian Federation |
| Blake Bartelli | 19 | green | 170 cm | 50 kg | 81 / 64 / 84 | United States |
| Caesaria A | 19 | brown | 165 cm | 48 kg | 84 / 61 / 89 | Russian Federation |
| Candice B | 19 | brown | 157 cm | 45 kg | 89 / 61 / 89 | Ukraine |
| Candice Lauren | 20 | brown | 173 cm | 51 kg | 91 / 61 / 94 | Russian Federation |
| Caprice A | 21 | brown | 155 cm | 52 kg | 86 / 61 / 89 | Czech Republic |
| Carina A | 23 | brown | 168 cm | 58 kg | 89 / 61 / 89 | Czech Republic |
| Carolina Sampaio | 20 | blue | 175 cm | 55 kg | 89 / 61 / 89 | Russian Federation |
| Carolina Sweets | 21 | blue | 157 cm | 44 kg | 86 / 66 / 86 | United States |
| Chantelle A | 24 | blue | 178 cm | 52 kg | 89 / 61 / 89 | Russian Federation |
| Chiara A | 19 | brown | 175 cm | 56 kg | 89 / 69 / 97 | Czech Republic |
| Chloe D | 20 | brown | 175 cm | 52 kg | 89 / 58 / 86 | Hungary |
| Danae | 20 | brown | 170 cm | 52 kg | 94 / 61 / 91 | Czech Republic |
| Danica-Jewels | 29 | blue | 165 cm | 48 kg | 86 / 61 / 89 | Russian Federation |
| Daniel Sea | 19 | blue | 160 cm | 50 kg | 94 / 61 / 94 | Belarus |
| Divina A | 24 | brown | 163 cm | 50 kg | 79 / 56 / 84 | Ukraine |
| Dominika A | 23 | brown | 165 cm | 48 kg | 84 / 61 / 89 | Czech Republic |
| Edwige A | 21 | brown | 165 cm | 48 kg | 89 / 61 / 91 | Czech Republic |
| Elle D | 24 | green | 168 cm | 48 kg | 86 / 58 / 91 | Ukraine |
| Emily Bloom | 20 | blue | 168 cm | 49 kg | 71 / 66 / 76 | Ukraine |
| Estelle | 23 | brown | 170 cm | 50 kg | 89 / 58 / 89 | Slovenia |
| Eufrat A | 19 | green | 175 cm | 60 kg | 89 / 64 / 91 | Czech Republic |
| Evita Lima | 19 | hazel | 170 cm | 59 kg | 91 / 66 / 94 | Russian Federation |
| Genevieve Gandi | 20 | blue | 175 cm | 53 kg | 94 / 61 / 94 | Russian Federation |
| Georgia | 21 | blue | 173 cm | 54 kg | 89 / 61 / 91 | Russian Federation |
| Gloria Sol | 21 | green | 170 cm | 48 kg | 86 / 61 / 86 | Ukraine |
| Grace C | 21 | green | 165 cm | 46 kg | 81 / 61 / 86 | Czech Republic |
| Indiana A | 21 | blue | 170 cm | 48 kg | 86 / 61 / 89 | Russian Federation |
| Inga C | 20 | blue | 165 cm | 42 kg | 89 / 61 / 89 | Latvia |
| Irina J | 19 | brown | 173 cm | 50 kg | 79 / 61 / 89 | Russian Federation |
| Isabella D | 23 | brown | 165 cm | 55 kg | 91 / 69 / 91 | Ukraine |
| Iveta B | 21 | blue | 173 cm | 52 kg | 86 / 61 / 89 | Czech Republic |
| Janice A | 18 | blue | 165 cm | 47 kg | 84 / 61 / 89 | Russian Federation |
| Jeff Milton | 18 | hazel | 165 cm | 44 kg | 84 / 61 / 86 | Russian Federation |
| Jenni A | 25 | blue | 170 cm | 54 kg | 89 / 66 / 94 | Czech Republic |
| Jennifer Mackay | 19 | blue | 170 cm | 51 kg | 86 / 58 / 89 | Ukraine |
| Jenya D | 28 | brown | 168 cm | 55 kg | 94 / 61 / 91 | Ukraine |

| MODEL | AGE DEBUT | EYE COLOR | HEIGHT | WEIGHT | MEASUREMENTS | COUNTRY |
|---|---|---|---|---|---|---|
| Jia Lissa | 21 | green | 165 cm | 44 kg | 81 / 61 / 89 | Russian Federation |
| Kaleesy | 21 | brown | 160 cm | 46 kg | 86 / 58 / 89 | Ukraine |
| Katherine A | 19 | blue | 173 cm | 49 kg | 89 / 61 / 89 | Russian Federation |
| Katie A | 20 | blue | 165 cm | 47 kg | 86 / 56 / 89 | Ukraine |
| Lena Anderson | 18 | hazel | 180 cm | 61 kg | 86 / 64 / 91 | United States |
| Lija | 21 | blue | 173 cm | 50 kg | 89 / 61 / 89 | Sweden |
| Lilit A | 21 | hazel | 175 cm | 48 kg | 89 / 58 / 89 | Ukraine |
| Lily C | 21 | green | 163 cm | 47 kg | 94 / 61 / 89 | Ukraine |
| Liza B | 19 | green | 175 cm | 53 kg | 89 / 61 / 89 | Ukraine |
| Loreen A | 26 | blue | 175 cm | 54 kg | 91 / 61 / 89 | Russian Federation |
| Lorena B | 23 | brown | 170 cm | 55 kg | 84 / 61 / 89 | Spain |
| Lucy Li | 22 | green | 170 cm | 50 kg | 91 / 64 / 84 | Czech Republic |
| Luna Corazon | 26 | brown | 173 cm | 50 kg | 86 / 61 / 86 | Brazil |
| Macy B | 19 | brown | 168 cm | 50 kg | 86 / 64 / 94 | Ukraine |
| Malena Morgan | 20 | blue | 175 cm | 52 kg | 81 / 61 / 89 | United States |
| Malinda A | 18 | blue | 165 cm | 48 kg | 86 / 66 / 84 | Ukraine |
| Mango A | 22 | blue | 165 cm | 46 kg | 86 / 61 / 91 | Russian Federation |
| Mariko A | 20 | brown | 163 cm | 50 kg | 91 / 64 / 89 | Japan |
| Melisa A | 23 | blue | 157 cm | 44 kg | 89 / 61 / 91 | Czech Republic |
| Mia D | 21 | blue | 165 cm | 49 kg | 76 / 64 / 81 | Ukraine |
| Mia Sollis | 21 | hazel | 168 cm | 50 kg | 89 / 61 / 91 | Czech Republic |
| Michaela Isizzu | 22 | blue | 163 cm | 49 kg | 86 / 61 / 81 | Czech Republic |
| Michelle H | 20 | blue | 173 cm | 50 kg | 89 / 61 / 89 | Ukraine |
| Miela A | 19 | blue | 168 cm | 56 kg | 94 / 61 / 91 | Czech Republic |
| Mila Azul | 19 | green | 170 cm | 46 kg | 89 / 56 / 86 | Ukraine |
| Mila I | 18 | blue | 170 cm | 52 kg | 89 / 58 / 89 | Ukraine |
| Milena D | 19 | blue | 168 cm | 48 kg | 89 / 58 / 89 | Ukraine |
| Nancy A | 19 | blue | 170 cm | 48 kg | 89 / 58 / 86 | Ukraine |
| Narkiss | 19 | blue | 170 cm | 55 kg | 89 / 64 / 89 | Russian Federation |
| Nici Dee | 20 | brown | 155 cm | 48 kg | 99 / 58 / 89 | Czech Republic |
| Nika N | 21 | blue | 165 cm | 48 kg | 71 / 66 / 76 | Ukraine |
| Nikia A | 18 | blue | 165 cm | 51 kg | 81 / 61 / 84 | Russian Federation |
| Nimfa | 21 | blue | 173 cm | 55 kg | 86 / 64 / 94 | Russian Federation |
| Noel Monique | 19 | brown | 165 cm | 47 kg | 86 / 64 / 74 | United States |
| Paloma B | 19 | brown | 165 cm | 48 kg | 79 / 61 / 89 | Russian Federation |
| Pandora B | 22 | blue | 170 cm | 60 kg | 89 / 61 / 91 | Macedonia |
| Patritcy A | 19 | blue | 173 cm | 50 kg | 89 / 61 / 89 | Latvia |
| Riley Anne | 22 | blue | 165 cm | 48 kg | 76 / 61 / 81 | United States |
| Sabrisse A | 24 | hazel | 168 cm | 48 kg | 86 / 71 / 89 | Czech Republic |
| Sofi A | 19 | blue | 168 cm | 50 kg | 94 / 58 / 89 | Ukraine |
| Suzanna A | 22 | green | 170 cm | 51 kg | 94 / 58 / 89 | Ukraine |
| Sybil A | 20 | green | 163 cm | 49 kg | 89 / 61 / 86 | Slovenia |
| Tammi Lee | 18 | green | 173 cm | 55 kg | 89 / 61 / 91 | Russian Federation |
| Ulya I | 19 | brown | 170 cm | 56 kg | 84 / 58 / 89 | Russian Federation |
| Valeria A | 18 | hazel | 165 cm | 46 kg | 86 / 61 / 86 | Ukraine |
| Viola Bailey | 20 | brown | 165 cm | 49 kg | 91 / 66 / 89 | Ukraine |
| Vittoria A | 20 | blue | 168 cm | 49 kg | 89 / 61 / 86 | Russian Federation |
| Yarina A | 19 | brown | 170 cm | 50 kg | 86 / 61 / 89 | Ukraine |
| Zelda B | 22 | brown | 165 cm | 48 kg | 89 / 61 / 91 | Russian Federation |
| Zsanett Tormay | 20 | blue | 165 cm | 45 kg | 81 / 56 / 84 | Hungary |

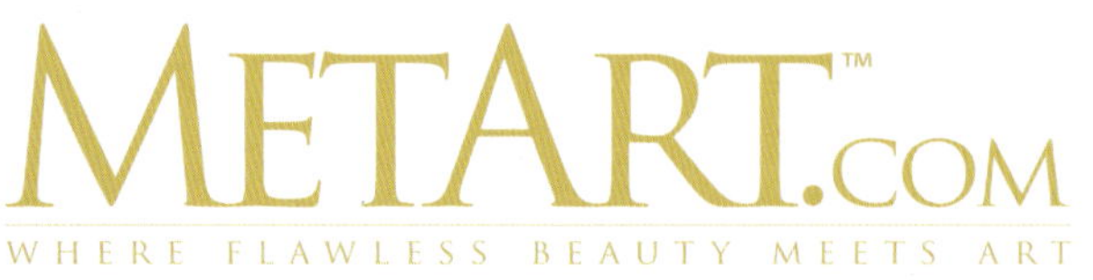
MetArt.com
WHERE FLAWLESS BEAUTY MEETS ART

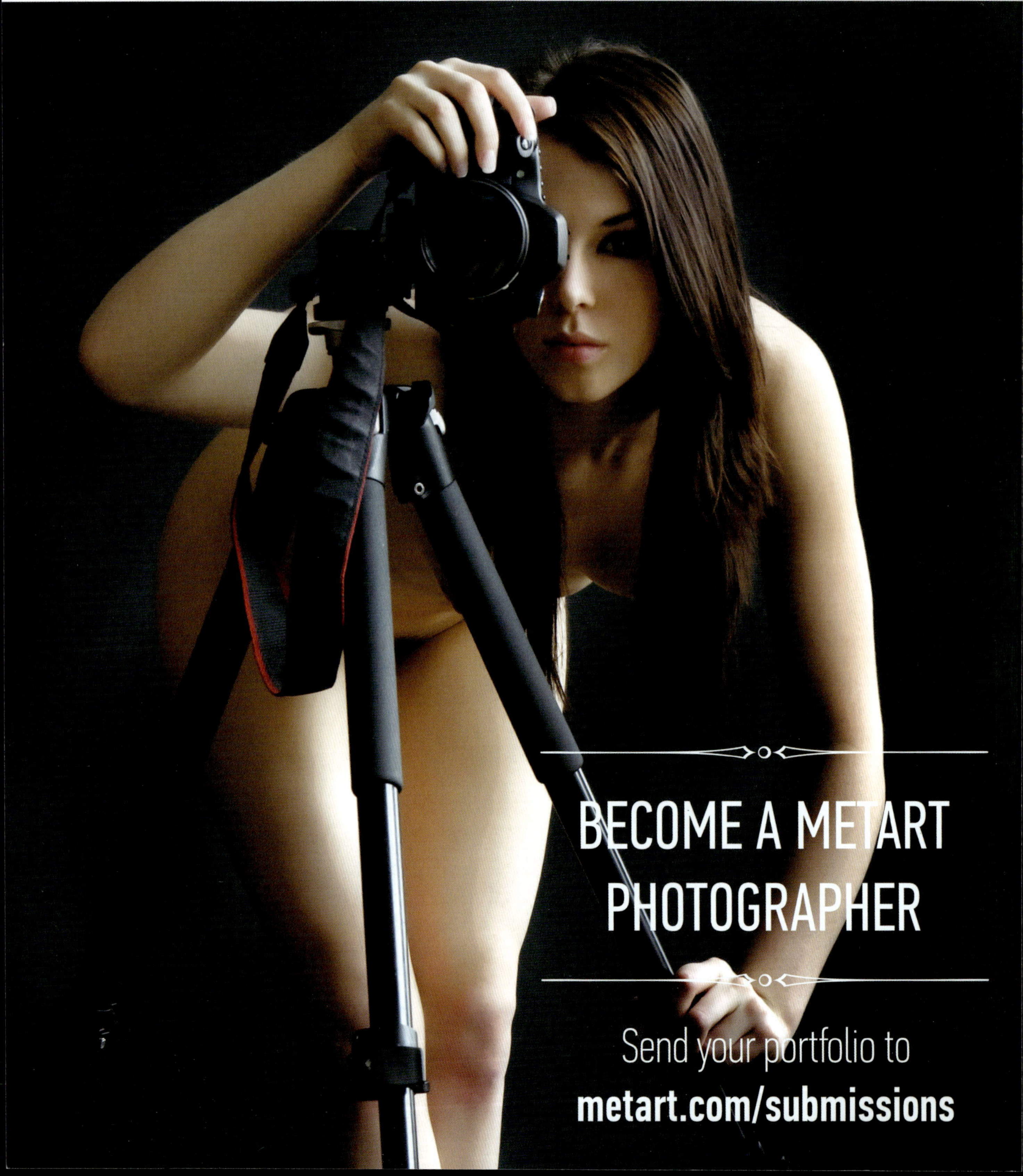